NATIONAL
GEOGRAPHIC

TRAVELER

the
caribbean

NATIONAL GEOGRAPHIC
TRAVELER

the caribbean

Emma Stanford & Nick Hanna
Photography by Matt Propert

National Geographic
Washington, D.C.

CONTENTS

Pages 2–3: Searching for stingrays off Grand Cayman Island
Opposite: Revelers dress in tobacco leaves during Carnival in Gosier, Guadeloupe.

TRAVELING WITH EYES OPEN

Alert travelers go with a purpose and leave with a benefit. If you travel responsibly, you can help support wildlife conservation, historic preservation, and cultural enrichment in the places you visit. You can enrich your own travel experience as well.

To be a geo-savvy traveler:

- Recognize that your presence has an impact on the places you visit.

- Spend your time and money in ways that sustain local character. (Besides, it's more interesting that way.)

- Value the destination's natural and cultural heritage.

- Respect the local customs and traditions.

- Express appreciation to local people about things you find interesting and unique to the place: its nature and scenery, music and food, historic villages and buildings.

- Vote with your wallet: Support the people who support the place, patronizing businesses that make an effort to celebrate and protect what's special there. Seek out shops, local restaurants, inns, and tour operators who love their home—who love taking care of it and showing it off. Avoid businesses that detract from the character of the place.

- Enrich yourself, taking home memories and stories to tell, knowing that you have contributed to the preservation and enhancement of the destination.

That is the type of travel now called geotourism, defined as "tourism that sustains or enhances the geographical character of a place—its environment, culture, aesthetics, heritage, and the well-being of its residents." To learn more, visit National Geographic's Center for Sustainable Destinations at *www.nationalgeographic.com/travel/sustainable.*

the caribbean

ABOUT THE AUTHORS & THE PHOTOGRAPHER

Emma Stanford has lived in Australia, France, and the U.K. and has been traveling and writing for 30 years. She has penned more than three dozen guidebooks to destinations throughout Europe and North America, compiled cruise guides to the Caribbean islands, and edited an adventure motorcycle handbook. Her globe-trotting newspaper articles have encompassed exploits as challenging and varied as rallying kit cars in the Sahara, scaling the Hindu Kush aboard a Badakshani stallion, and mountain biking through France and Spain to the pilgrim city of Santiago de Compostela. Stanford updated and wrote the new features and sidebars for the 2102 edition of this guidebook.

Nick Hanna has been a professional travel writer and photographer for nearly 30 years. He has worked as a freelance writer for numerous national and international newspapers and magazines and has written nine guidebooks, including one that covered more than 200 tropical beaches around the world. He has also co-authored a book on the conservation of coral reefs and written extensively on the marine environment and scuba diving.

Photographer **Matt Propert** is based in Washington, D.C. His work has appeared in many national and international publications, and it has been shown in major solo exhibitions. In addition to the Caribbean, Propert has photographed Miami and the Florida Keys and much of Italy for the National Geographic Society.

Charting Your Trip

A tropical paradise of sugar sand beaches, turquoise sea, coral reefs, and rain forest, the Caribbean is the quintessential winter escape. The region's 50-plus islands, which do not include the Bahamas or far-flung Bermuda, and several thousand uninhabited cays, rocks, and reefs, form a 2,500-mile (4,000 km) arc from Cuba, 90 miles (145 km) south of Key West on the tip of Florida, to Trinidad, just 7 miles (11 km) off the coast of Venezuela.

Encircling the million-square-mile (2.6 million sq. km) Caribbean Sea and buffeted on their windward sides by the Atlantic Ocean, the islands of the Caribbean region are divided into two major groups: the Greater Antilles, or Western Caribbean, and the Lesser Antilles, or Eastern Caribbean. The Western Caribbean islands range from Cuba (not included in this guide), through the Cayman Islands, Turks & Caicos Islands, Jamaica, Hispaniola (the Dominican Republic/Haiti; Haiti is not included in this guide), and Puerto Rico, to the Virgin Islands (both U.S. and British). The curving Eastern Caribbean chain is further divided into the Leeward and Windward Islands, interspersed with the French Antilles, the Dutch Caribbean, Barbados, and Trinidad & Tobago.

Choosing Your Destination

Choosing the right combination of ingredients for the perfect Caribbean vacation needs a little planning. There is no such thing as a typical Caribbean island. Each one has its own particular style shaped by a unique combination of geology, historical influences, and attitudes that can vary dramatically between neighbors separated by a few nautical miles. If your ideal holiday involves succumbing body and soul to the languor of the tropics, relaxing on a crescent of manicured, palm-fringed sand, nearly all of the islands of the Caribbean can deliver, no problem. To get a real feel for the islands, however, make time to explore historic colonial cities and fortresses, venture into the rain forest, dive, snorkel, and sail dazzling archipelagos. The chart on page 12 highlights your best options. Accommodations are a good place to begin planning

The heliconia, a tropical flower found throughout the Caribbean, is pollenated most frequently by hummingbirds.

NOT TO BE MISSED

For historic cities: the cobbled streets of Santo Domingo (Dominican Republic) or San Juan (Puerto Rico)   **100, 128**

For sailing: the Sir Francis Drake Channel (British Virgin Islands) or Tobago Cays (St. Vincent & the Grenadines)   **169, 287**

For hiking: Morne Trois Pitons National Park (Dominica) or parrot-spotting in the rain forest of St. Lucia   **266, 275**

For scuba diving: Saba Marine Park or the North Wall off Bonaire   **184, 191**

For beaches: Salt Cay's deserted North Beach (Turks and Caicos Islands)

or Shoal Bay's sugar-soft sands (Anguilla)   **88, 213**

For local color: Carnival in Trinidad (Feb.) or Crop Over in Barbados (July–Aug.)   **317, 301**

For music: Reggae Sunfest in Jamaica (July) or Santo Domingo's Merengue Festival (Dominican Republic, July–Aug.)   **52, 101**

For wildlife and birding: whale-watching in Dominica or birding in Trinidad & Tobago   **268, 325**

For food: coffee in Jamaica or Creole cuisine in Guadeloupe   **25, 39**

your vacation (see Travelwise pp. 352–383). Should it be a romantic plantation hotel in St. Kitts and Nevis or a family-friendly beach resort offering water sports? As a rule of thumb, the better the beaches, the more developed the island, so expect a greater choice of accommodations at top beach destinations. The Western Caribbean islands all have fabulous beaches and are among the most developed destinations in the region. Here, **Jamaica,** the **Dominican Republic,** and **Puerto Rico** also score highly on magnificent mountain scenery and a wide range of sporting activities. In the Eastern Caribbean, consider **Aruba, Anguilla, Antigua,** and the **Grenadine Islands** for beautiful beaches.

Active Vacations

Where once a Caribbean vacation was a strictly horizontal affair, activity holidays now represent a significant slice of the market. Diving is a major attraction for many visitors. The **Cayman Islands** are famously positioned on the brink of the Cayman Trench, offering dramatic wall diving. In the Dutch Caribbean, **Bonaire, Saba,** and **Sint Eustatius** forgo beaches for spectacular dive sites; or head to the Windward Islands to up-and-coming **Dominica** (whale-watching is another specialty here) and farther south to **Tobago.**

The Windward Islands, including **St. Lucia** and **Grenada,** are celebrated for their lush rain forest highlands, which offer terrific hiking, while **Trinidad** at the tail end of the island chain is an ornithologist's paradise

Tourist Information

For research in advance of your trip, all the main Caribbean islands covered in this guide have a tourist board and a website; many also maintain overseas representatives with offices in the U.S. and Europe. (For contact details, see the individual island listings in Travelwise pp. 332–351.) On arrival at your destination, tourist information offices at airports and cruise ship facilities are the places to find the most up-to-date information about sightseeing, as well as maps, transportation schedules, and taxi rates. Free magazines with details of tours and activities are also widely available.

When to Visit

The Caribbean region lies in the tropics, so temperatures are fairly consistent year-round, averaging 78–86°F (26–30°C) during the day and 59–64°F (15–18°C) at night on the coast. High season in the Caribbean is the generally cooler and drier period between December and April, when hotels charge their top rates, and reservations should be made well in advance for the popular Christmas and New Year's period. Humidity increases in the run-up to the rainy season (June–Nov.), though showers occur throughout the year and on a daily basis in the rain forest highlands. Prices drop considerably during the summer, when there are some great bargains to be had.

and one of the world's most important sea turtle nesting sites. The neighboring French Caribbean islands of **Guadeloupe** and **Martinique** share many of the same physical characteristics, and they are the crucible for the eastern Caribbean's vibrant Creole culture. True Francophiles, on the other hand, may find themselves gravitating toward tiny **St.-Barthélemy,** a distinctly European-style jet set haunt reminiscent of the French Riviera.

If you want to go sportfishing for marlin in **St. Thomas,** snorkel Stingray City in the **Cayman Islands,** or stay on a working coffee plantation in **Jamaica**'s Blue Mountains, plan ahead. Most local adventure tour, dive, and hiking operators have websites where you can check out what's on offer and make reservations.

Perfect Caribbean vacations come in all shapes and sizes, and this brief overview can only hint at the wealth of options available. For more ideas, check out the Caribbean Tourism Organization website *(www.onecaribbean.org).*

If You Have Only a Week

The first consideration when time is limited is: How quickly can I get there? Maximize your vacation time with a destination that can be reached on a direct flight, rather than waiting for connecting services to less accessible islands. Destinations combining frequent direct international flights and a raft of sightseeing and activity opportunities include **Puerto Rico, Jamaica,** the **Cayman Islands,** and the **Dominican Republic** in the Western Caribbean, and the Eastern Caribbean regional transport hubs of **St. Thomas** (USVI), **Antigua** (Leeward Islands), and **Aruba** (Dutch Caribbean).

The classic Caribbean island-hopping experience is a little more difficult to achieve in a week, unless you take a cruise (see pp. 136–137), which will whisk you from

Language

English, Spanish, French, and Dutch are all spoken in the Caribbean, a legacy from colonial days. English is spoken in the lion's share of the Caribbean islands from Jamaica, the Cayman Islands, and Turks & Caicos Islands in the north, through the Virgin, Leeward, and Windward Islands (where a form of French patois is also commonly spoken on Dominica and St. Lucia), to Trinidad & Tobago. Most Spanish-speaking Puerto Ricans also speak English, but a Spanish phrase book is essential in nontourist areas of the Dominican Republic. Dutch Caribbean islanders are generally bilingual in Dutch and English. Visitors to the French Antilles should be aware that little English is spoken outside of the upscale hotels.

Flanked by two green peaks, the capital of the island of Saba is called "The Bottom."

island to island as you sleep. The Caribbean's main cruise hubs are Puerto Rico and Barbados, and there are frequent departures from Miami and Fort Lauderdale. Chartering a yacht to explore the Virgin Islands is doable in a week (see p. 169), and there are dozens of day-trip island hops from most main destinations. Visitors to Puerto Rico can pop across to stunning **Vieques Island** (1 hr. 15 min. by ferry from Fajardo/10 min. by plane from Ceiba); the United States Virgin Islands (USVI) and laidback British Virgin Islands (BVI) are linked by frequent, inexpensive ferry services; and the 40-minute small plane shuttles between touristy **Grand Cayman** and tranquil **Cayman Brac** encourage one- or two-day excursions. **Antigua** is another excellent base, providing fast ferries (1 hr. 30 min.) to the bird sanctuaries of **Barbuda** and short hop inter-island flights (under an hour) to volcanic **Montserrat** and historic **St. Kitts &** **Nevis.** See Travelwise pages 332–350 for information on flights and ferries to/from each island.

If You Have More Time

For a Caribbean vacation lasting more than a week, the larger islands in the Western Caribbean make for a perfect two-center break. Dividing time between **Jamaica's** beach resorts

What to Wear

The dress code on most Caribbean islands is pretty relaxed. Shorts, T-shirts, and sandals should sort out everyday wear, though wearing swimsuits off the beach is frowned upon. Fine restaurants may not permit jeans or open sandals for men. If you're planning on playing a sport (golf, tennis, horseback riding) or taking part in activities such as hiking, sailing, and diving, bring appropriate gear and footwear. Hikers will find it gets cool and wet in the mountains. Adequate supplies of strong sunblock and mosquito repellent are essential.

Where the activities are among the islands

	BEACHES	BIRDING	COLONIAL ARCHITECTURE	DIVING	FOOD SPECIALTIES	GOLF	HIKING	RAIN FOREST	MUSIC FESTIVALS	SAILING	SPORTFISHING	TURTLE-WATCHING	WHALE-WATCHING
Anguilla	✔			✔		✔					✔	✔	
Antigua & Barbuda	✔	✔	✔	✔		✔				✔	✔		
Aruba	✔			✔		✔	✔				✔		
Barbados	✔		✔	✔	✔	✔				✔	✔		
Bonaire				✔			✔					✔	
British Virgin Islands	✔			✔						✔			
Cayman Islands	✔	✔		✔	✔		✔				✔		
Curaçao	✔		✔	✔		✔	✔				✔		
Dominica		✔		✔			✔	✔			✔	✔	✔
Dominican Republic	✔		✔	✔		✔	✔		✔		✔	✔	✔
Grenada	✔			✔	✔		✔	✔			✔	✔	✔
Guadeloupe	✔			✔	✔		✔	✔	✔	✔	✔		✔
Jamaica	✔	✔	✔	✔	✔	✔	✔				✔		
Martinique	✔		✔	✔	✔	✔	✔	✔			✔		
Montserrat		✔		✔			✔	✔					
Puerto Rico	✔	✔	✔	✔	✔	✔	✔	✔			✔	✔	✔
Saba				✔			✔						
St.–Barthélemy	✔			✔	✔						✔	✔	
Sint Eustatius				✔			✔						
St. Kitts & Nevis	✔	✔	✔	✔		✔	✔	✔					
St. Lucia	✔	✔	✔	✔		✔	✔	✔	✔	✔		✔	✔
St.–Martin/ Sint Maarten	✔			✔	✔						✔	✔	
St. Vincent & the Grenadines	✔	✔		✔		✔	✔	✔			✔	✔	✔
Trinidad & Tobago	✔	✔		✔		✔	✔	✔	✔		✔	✔	
Turks & Caicos	✔	✔		✔		✔					✔		✔
U.S. Virgin Islands	✔		✔	✔		✔	✔	✔			✔	✔	

and the Blue Mountains is a great way to explore the island's varied landscapes, dive, play a round of golf, and still have time to relax. A longer vacation opens up possibilities in the **Dominican Republic** too. The colonial city of **Santo Domingo** is a must-see, and there's whale-watching off **Samaná,** birding on **Lago Enriquillo,** and golf on the **Coconut Coast.**

With time to spare in the Eastern Caribbean, it is almost mandatory to make at least one island hop. **St. Vincent** is in a class of its own for combining volcano hikes with magnificent sailing through the **Grenadines.** The twin-island nation of **Trinidad & Tobago** is a tailor-made duo for nature lovers with superb birding and rain forest hikes. Challenging upcountry hikes in **Guadeloupe**'s national park can be combined with a charmingly Gallic break on **Marie-Galante** in the Guadeloupean archipelago; while adventurous trekkers can spend a whole week tackling **Dominica**'s trans-island Wai'tukubuli Trail, followed by diving and whale-watching. Or head for some less accessible spots, such as **Saba** and **St. Eustatius,** rocky islets that are a magnet for divers and accessible only by ferry or puddle-jumper flights from Sint Maarten (see Travelwise p. 341). ■

Safety

The main crime concern for travelers in the Caribbean region is theft (most violent crime is a local affair), and the best safeguard is common sense. It pays to be vigilant in crowds and at the airport, and thefts from rental cars are not uncommon, so leave nothing behind. When you are carrying documents or significant amounts of cash, keep them close, preferably in a money belt. Credit cards are widely accepted and easy to cancel if they go missing. Women traveling alone will encounter plenty of chat-up banter, but a firm "No thanks" or "I'm married" tends to disarm predators. It is very unwise to visit a deserted beach alone.

Yachting, whether for sport or leisure, is popular throughout the Caribbean.

History & Culture

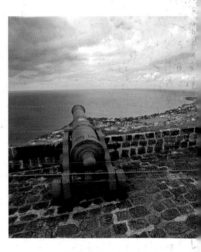

A cannon stands guard at Brimstone
Hill Fortress in St. Kitts.
Opposite: Grenada's Annandale Falls
cools visitors island style.

The Caribbean Today

"A Caribbean vacation" is one of the most evocative phrases in the English language. The merest suggestion can unleash a stream of dreamy images featuring golden beaches, coconut palms, and azure seas. But however satisfying this daydream may be, it cannot beat the reality, the feel of powder-soft coral sand between your toes, the squawk and colorful flash of a parrot in the rain forest, the taste of a fresh mango plucked straight from the tree.

Caribbean Culture

Our idea of the Caribbean typically starts with the region's obvious physical attractions: the sunshine, beaches, rain forested highlands, and coral-encrusted depths. Scratch the surface, however, and you'll soon discover that the Caribbean islands are far more multilayered and interesting. Beneath the broad brushstrokes of climate and geography, there is a cornucopia of rich and varied historical and cultural influences, which add greatly to the atmosphere and attitudes of the islands and their people.

> Language, architecture, religion, festivals, and, more significantly, the Caribbean people themselves, can trace their origins back to the days of the region's colonial rulers.

Even today, we can't interpret island culture and traditions without understanding the colonial legacy. Language, architecture, religion, festivals, and, more significantly, the Caribbean people themselves, most of whom are descended from African slaves brought here to work the plantations, can trace their origins back to the days of the region's colonial rulers. Certain attitudes remain firmly ingrained centuries later, such as the courteous greetings commonly exchanged in the French islands, and the slightly formal, British influence in Barbados, where taking afternoon tea and dressing for dinner is still something of a ritual in certain circles. For all the flamboyant spectacle of Carnival and rum-fueled reggae jump-ups, Caribbean islanders are essentially conservative at heart. For the most part, they are friendly, helpful, and delighted to share their local knowledge. In return they appreciate being treated with courtesy and respect.

Sustainable Tourism

The Caribbean region has around 30 separate political entities, and a stable, albeit deeply fragmented political scene (see Modern Era, p. 23). Tourism is the economic mainstay, though sugar, bananas, and oil production all contribute significantly to individual national economies. Sustainable tourism has become the buzz phrase in the Caribbean lexicon these days, and considerable efforts are being made to protect natural habitats both on land and at sea. Unfortunately, coral reefs, coastal mangrove areas, and native wildlife species have already suffered significant damage from the region's rapacious development, but the growing demand for ecotourism opportunities has alerted island authorities to the importance of preserving natural resources.

The growth of ecotourism has had a notably positive effect in engaging visitors with local culture. Hiking expeditions, mountain biking tours, and other activities, as well as community tourism programs, are coaxing increasing numbers of visitors out of the hotel compound to discover the charm of the islands and their people for themselves. Such forays provide a welcome bridge between residents and incomers, and generate useful income for the local community, which in the past has seen the tourist dollar flow directly into the coffers of cruise lines and foreign hotel groups.

Taking the plunge in a small Martinique beach village

Flora & Fauna

The Caribbean's mountain ranges are cloaked in dense rain forest, which grows with explosive rapidity in the fertile volcanic soil. True rain forest is the richest natural habitat on the planet and requires an annual rainfall in excess of 70 inches (178 cm), which the Caribbean islands receive courtesy of the Atlantic trade winds. In the hothouse atmosphere beneath the rain forest canopy, dozens of ferns, creepers, and bamboo flourish at the feet of giant buttress-trunked santinay trees, mahogany, gommier, and mahoe.

At higher elevations, in the montane or cloud forest, tree branches play host to a variety of bromeliads (which gain nutrients from the air) and orchids, while higher still the lichen-encrusted elfin forest opens onto grasslands frequently visited by cool, hazy drizzle and wisps of cloud.

Few mammals live in the rain forest, and indigenous species such as armadillos, opossums, and agoutis are rarely spotted. Reptiles, including tree frogs, iguanas, and dozens of species of small lizards, are a constant presence, as are winged insects such as butterflies and predatory mosquitoes. Though there are occasional sightings of non-venomous tree snakes, the sole poisonous snake is the fer de lance, found only on Martinique and St. Lucia.

Bird lovers are in for a treat in the Caribbean. Several species of rare indigenous parrot live in the Windward Islands, and the woodlands are also home to numerous varieties of hummingbirds, honeycreepers, tanagers, and cheeky bananaquits, which frequently leave the rain forest to feed on the brilliant tropical blooms in gardens.

Many species of herons, waders, ducks, and other wetland birds gather in the coastal mangrove swamps of Jamaica and Trinidad, while flamingo colonies can be found in Bonaire and Lago Enriquillo in the Dominican Republic. Seabirds, including boobies, magnificent frigatebirds, pelicans, and elegant scissor-tailed tropic birds, colonize rocky outcrops visible from the shore.

Volcanic History

The Caribbean islands are poised on the brink of the Caribbean and Atlantic tectonic plates. The majority are volcanic in origin, though there are a few low-lying coral atolls such as the Cayman Islands and Anguilla, and the arid, desertlike Dutch Leewards. The oldest islands in the region lie to the north, where Jamaica, Hispaniola, and Puerto Rico were formed approximately 70 million years ago.

In the eastern Caribbean, Montserrat, Guadeloupe, Martinique, Dominica, St. Lucia, St. Vincent, and Grenada remain volcanically active with bubbling mud pools and oozing, foul-smelling sulfur pits. Off the coast of Grenada, the active submarine volcano Kick 'Em Jenny has risen to around 590 feet (180 m) below the surface.

One of the Seven Sisters waterfalls in Grenada's Grand Étang National Park

Just as the rain forest flourishes, so does the myriad variety of other plants and trees. While many islanders cultivate colorful flower gardens, botanical gardens are the best place to see a whole range of eye-catching heliconias and gingers, spice trees such as nutmeg and cinnamon, and flowering trees such as the yellow- or pink-blossomed poui, scarlet poinciana, and spreading immortelle, which flowers in January and February.

Hurricanes

Though the Caribbean experiences few climactic extremes, the region is in the hurricane zone. In recent years, hurricanes have wreaked widespread destruction across the north of the region, while 2004's Hurricane Ivan reached as far south as Grenada. The official hurricane season runs from June to November, though a traditional rhyme advises "June, too soon; July, stand by; September, remember; October, all over." Statistically, mid-September is the most likely time for a hurricane to pass through the Caribbean. ■

History & Culture

Christopher Columbus first sighted the island of San Salvador in the Bahamas on October 12, 1492, and sailed into the Caribbean Sea intent on discovering a westward passage to the East Indian spice islands. The arrival of European explorers opened the book on the recorded history of the region, and the islands were named the Antilles after the legendary island of Antillia.

Pre-Columbian Caribbean

The Caribbean's first settlers, Amerindian tribes who paddled their canoes to the islands from Central America or possibly Florida, arrived thousands of years before Columbus. The Stone Age Ciboney people (or Archaic Indians) were the earliest inhabitants of the Greater Antilles islands. Archaeological digs in Cuba have uncovered Ciboney sites about 6,000 years old, while relics in Hispaniola are reckoned to be about 4,000 years old. These nomadic hunter-gatherers lived off a nourishing and varied diet of fish and shellfish, birds, iguanas, and snakes, supplemented by roots and wild fruits, and they crafted tools and utensils from stone, wood, bone, and shell.

About 300 b.c. the first Arawak migrated to the islands. They are thought to have originated in the Amazon Basin, and then they pushed north to make the sea crossing from northeastern South America (present-day Venezuela and Guyana) to the southernmost of the Lesser Antilles. Gradually they moved up the island chain, and by the time Columbus appeared on the scene, the three major Arawak groups were populating the Greater Antilles islands and Bahamas: the Taíno (Cuba, Jamaica, and Hispaniola), the Borequio or Borinquen (Puerto Rico), and the Lucayan (Bahamas).

> **The arrival of European explorers [in 1492] opened the book on the recorded history of the region.**

The Arawak were more sophisticated than the Ciboney. They were farmers, cultivating cassava (for flour), yams, corn, beans, cocoa, peanuts, tobacco, and cotton. Skilled hunters and fishermen, they were also potters capable of producing earthenware for domestic and religious purposes.

Arawak society was well organized. Villages were generally built close to the shore, and each community was presided over by a *cacique*, or village chieftain, who was responsible for both the temporal and religious life of the villagers. At the center of the village was a large open-sided *carbet* (thatched shelter) where the cacique and men held council: It was out-of-bounds to women and children except by invitation to attend special ceremonies. Unmarried men could sleep here or in a separate carbet, stringing maybe a hundred hammocks from the roof. Religion played an important part in Arawak daily life. There were gods associated with food crops, fertility, and weather, and benevolent spirits that inhabited plants and animals. Religious ceremonies included snorting trance-inducing narcotics and dancing, as well as the worship of *zemi*, simple shapes or human and animal figures made of wood, bone, or stone. Arawak believed in the afterlife and took great care with burial rituals. The dead were placed in a squatting position and were equipped with personal belongings (the wives of important chieftains were buried alive), as well as food for the journey to Coyaba, a plentiful land of nonstop dancing and feasting.

Arrival of the Carib

After a thousand years, the Arawak's peaceful existence came to an abrupt end with the arrival of the Carib. Also from South America, the warlike Carib progressed northward through the Lesser Antilles, slaughtering Arawak men and assimilating women and children into their tribes. Though the proof is somewhat sketchy, the Carib had a reputation for cannibalism and were said to barbecue (a Carib word) their male victims, which included Europeans as they began to explore the region. The Carib were excellent marksmen with bows and arrows and fearlessly attacked Spanish sailing ships from their wooden war canoes, or *piraguas* (from which the simple pirogue fishing

A 1562 Spanish map of the Americas

boats still used in the Windward Islands take their name). The Europeans pushed the Carib back into the rugged terrain of the Windward Islands, where they managed to hold out for more than 200 years. A few mixed-blood survivors still live on Dominica and St. Vincent.

European Invasion

Columbus made four voyages to the Caribbean in his attempt to discover a western route to the East Indies, stubbornly naming his finds the West Indies despite all the evidence to the contrary. On his fourth voyage, in 1502, he located the South American mainland and secured its vast mineral wealth for the Roman Catholic kings of Spain. However, he failed to make it back through the Caribbean islands; beaching his aging ships in Jamaica, he was forced to rely upon the hostile governor of Hispaniola for eventual rescue.

During the early 16th century, Spanish settlements sprang up in the Greater Antilles, first in Hispaniola, then Cuba, Jamaica, and Puerto Rico. The Arawak were enslaved, and within 50 years the indigenous population of these northern islands had been eradicated through warfare, disease, and transportation to work the mainland gold mines.

The Spanish treasure fleets making their way home to Europe acted as a magnet for pirates and privateers. Throughout the 16th and 17th centuries, French, English, and Dutch vessels preyed mercilessly on heavily laden armadas, lurking in the isolated cays of the Virgin Islands. The next logical step for the interlopers was to claim colonies of their own in the region, which became easier as Spanish influence declined in Europe during the 17th century. The English and French moved in on the Lesser Antilles, commencing a 250-year struggle for dominance in the eastern Caribbean, and the Dutch cannily selected islands with a view to their strategic importance on the trading routes used by their rivals.

The *Quedagh Merchant*

Centuries after Columbus sailed the ocean blue, hired pirates, genteelly known as "privateers," made a booming business out of raiding treasure-laden merchant and pirate ships. In 1698, privateer Captain Kidd captured the *Quedagh Merchant,* with its bounty of gold, silver, silk, and opium, in the Indian Ocean. Kidd made off with the loot, scuttling the ship just off tiny Catalina Island in the Dominican Republic. The *Quedagh Merchant's* remains still lie where Kidd left them, in just 10 feet (3 m) of water, and are slated to become an underwater museum in the future.

Colonial Era

Sugarcane was introduced to the Caribbean by Dutch planters from Brazil in the 1630s (see pp. 304–305). From small-scale beginnings in Barbados, the enormously profitable trade in "white gold" triggered the rapid expansion of European colonialism in the region, and its labor-intensive cultivation brought an immediate demand for a cheap and inexhaustible workforce. Spanish settlers had imported small numbers of West African slaves to work their Caribbean plantations since the early days, but the sugar trade boosted numbers to unprecedented levels. Untold millions of Africans were sold into slavery and shipped across the Atlantic to work the sugar plantations; many thousands died en route (see pp. 250–251).

You won't have to search far for friendly faces in the Caribbean.

By the start of the 19th century, the importance of the Caribbean sugar trade dwindled as sugar beet production in Europe rose to satisfy local demand. The planters' profits decreased, and in 1808, the antislavery movement in Britain succeeded in banning the slave trade to the colonies. This was followed in 1834 by the Emancipation Act, which outlawed the ownership of slaves. The other European nations followed suit, and the former sugar colonies fell into a decline.

As the freed slaves abandoned the plantations, major producers such as Jamaica and Trinidad imported East Indian indentured laborers, but most islands slipped quietly into the doldrums, largely forgotten by their erstwhile colonial masters.

The U.S. claimed its first territory with the capture of Puerto Rico from Spain [in 1898]. It followed up ... with the purchase of the U.S. Virgin Islands from Denmark in 1917.

Modern Era

The Spanish-American War of 1898 introduced U.S. influence to the region. The U.S. claimed its first territory with the capture of Puerto Rico from Spain. It followed up this belated foray into Caribbean empire-building with the purchase of the U.S. Virgin Islands from Denmark in 1917. The Caribbean islands experienced the unwanted trickle-down effect of the 1930s Great Depression, which deepened the region's economic problems and heralded the rise of grassroots labor movements. These in turn spearheaded the islands' transition toward greater independence from Europe.

In 1962, Jamaica was the first British colony to achieve full independence, and Britain divested most of its colonies during the 1970s and 1980s. Several smaller islands opted

(continued on p. 26)

Food & Drink

Caribbean cuisine, like other aspects of Caribbean culture, reflects the region's varied heritage, blending African, Spanish, French, English, Indian, Chinese, and other influences. On a warm evening, a mellow rum or a chilled local beer can be the perfect accompaniment to a satisfying meal.

A jerk shack near Ocho Rios, Jamaica

Traditional Caribbean cooking is simple, nutritious, and filling, using plentiful local ingredients from fresh fish and seafood to a wide variety of tropical fruits and vegetables, supplemented with chicken and a little red meat. Staple foods such as rice 'n' peas (the "peas" are red kidney beans), fried plantains (a variety of banana that is inedible raw), spinachlike callaloo, starchy breadfruit, and root vegetables (yam, eddoe, cassava) known as "ground provision" are found throughout the islands. Adventurous visitors should sample soursop, sugar and golden apples, tart tamarinds, and tiny plums. Markets are the best

place to find and taste what is in season.

Guadeloupe and Martinique are renowned for Creole cuisine (see sidebar opposite), while Puerto Rican specialties such as *lechón asao* (roast suckling pig), and *locrio* (a variation on paella), served in the Dominican Republic, show a distinctive Spanish influence. The Indian influence is unmistakable in Trinidad's curries and *rotis* (chapati envelopes filled with curried meat, seafood, or vegetables) that have now become a popular snack food in neighboring islands. Jamaican jerk is said to have been invented by runaway slaves who cooked in earth pits covered with branches.

INSIDER TIP:
More Caribbean restaurants are cropping up that offer locally grown, organic cuisine. You can find a listing of "locavore" establishments at *www.happycow.net.*

—LARRY PORGES
Editor, National Geographic Books

Fresh tropical fruit at a market in Fort-de-France, Martinique

Rum & Beer

Rum has been produced in the Caribbean since the 17th century, when sugar planters first distilled a spirit from molasses. Still made throughout the region, the best quality rums traditionally come from Barbados, Jamaica, Guadeloupe, and Martinique. While most islanders prefer their rum neat, visitors are more attracted to the long list of rum cocktails available, including piña coladas (flavored with pineapple and coconut), Cuba libre (with cola), fruit daiquiris, and planters punch (the original only has lime and cane juice, but added fruit juices are popular today). There are also delicious nonalcoholic fruit punches.

Wine is not produced in the Caribbean, so it is expensive. Local breweries, on the other hand, turn out some good lager-type beers. Particularly good are Banks from Barbados, Carib from Trinidad and franchises on several islands, Presidente from the Dominican Republic, and Red Stripe from Jamaica.

Creole Cuisine & Dining Out

The Creole cuisine of Guadeloupe and Martinique is an inspired fusion of French culinary élan, traditional African cooking, and local Caribbean ingredients. Seafood is a mainstay of Creole menus and comes in a wide variety of guises, from simple *accras* (shredded salt-cod fritters) to *blaff* (a fish or shellfish stew cooked in a wine and herb court bouillon).

Other specialties include *cirique* or *étrille* (little sea crabs), *chatrou* (octopus), *lambi* (conch tenderized with lime for salads), *langouste* (lobster), *ouassous* (crayfish), and *soudrons* (clams). *Crabes farcis* are stuffed land crabs, more meaty than sea crabs, and the locals are known to feed them with dried coconut and hot peppers to improve their flavor. Try *colombo*, a curried stew of chicken or goat *(cabri)* flavored with coriander, cumin, mustard, ginger, and pepper.

Traditional accompaniments are *fruit à pain*, the rather tasteless fruit of the breadfruit tree, and *christophene*, a tropical squash served cooked or grated raw in salads.

Dining out can be expensive, but Creole food is generally cheaper than French. Limited-choice menus at a fixed price *(menu touristique)* are usually good value, and service is included *(compris)*. It is de rigueur to round off a meal with a *digestif* from among the dozens of locally produced aged or fruit-flavored rums.

The Catholic cathedral in Roseau, Dominica. The island's diocese was established in 1850.

to remain Crown Colonies (now known as British Overseas Territories), while others have joined the British Commonwealth as independent states. The Dutch and French retain closer ties with their colonies.

Colonial Legacy

As European colonists staked their claims to the Caribbean islands, each nation attempted in some degree to re-create a miniature home away from home in the sun. Thus, the Spanish Catholic heritage is readily apparent in the historic cities and churches of the Dominican Republic and Puerto Rico; the ex-British colonies in the Leeward and Windward Islands are rich in four-square stone Georgian architecture; the French islands retain an inimitable savoir faire combined with gastronomic flair; and in the Dutch Leewards, Curaçao's elegantly gabled buildings have been designated a World Heritage site.

Language is another longstanding legacy of the former colonial powers—English, French, Dutch, and Spanish are the dominant languages you'll hear in the region (see sidebar p. 10).

The majority of Caribbean people are of African origin, and although African culture was subjugated by European customs during the colonial era, it did not disappear altogether. Freed from Old World dominance, the African heritage is now the strongest element of pan-Caribbean cultural trends. Its influence is unmistakable in music, traditional cooking, and the common animist beliefs that operate alongside traditional European religions in a very typically Caribbean compromise.

Music

Music is, so they say, the heartbeat of the Caribbean, and it is certainly hard to ignore. The strains of calypso, reggae, soca (soul-calypso), and steel pan throbbing bass dub music booming out from dollar buses and the dance rhythms of Puerto Rican salsa, merengue from the Dominican Republic, and zouk from the French Antilles, provide a catchy backdrop to the Caribbean experience.

Calypso is the grandfather of the music scene, with its origins buried way back in West African slave traditions. Forbidden to speak their native languages, slaves were, however, permitted to sing; the planters believed it helped them work faster. Yet unbeknownst to their employers, the slaves used song to keep alive the West African storytelling tradition and to pass along information and messages of protest concealed in allegorical terms. Today's calypsonians (calypso singers) are still judged not only on the music but also on the message they put across.

Calypso is the grandfather of the music scene, with its origins buried way back in West African slave traditions.

Trinidad is the home of calypso and steel-pan music, which originated in the dockyards of Port of Spain during World War II when oil drums were recycled for makeshift drums. Reggae emerged from the Kingston ghetto of Trenchtown, Jamaica, with its most famous exponent, Bob Marley, in the 1970s.

Live music performances in clubs and bars are easy to find throughout the islands. Music festivals are also well worth tracking down. The most famous events include Jamaica's Reggae Sumfest (July–Aug.), the St. Lucia International Jazz Festival (May), and the St. Kitts Music Festival (June).

Carnival

Carnival is a magnificent explosion of elaborate costumes, music, singing, and dance that captures the creativity and natural exuberance of the Caribbean people. The date varies from island to island, but most carnivals take place before Lent (Feb.–March), while others celebrate the end of the sugar harvest (July–Aug.) or the anniversary of emancipation.

Europeans introduced Carnival to the Caribbean, marking the approach of Lent, a traditional period of Christian abstinence, with a hectic round of feasting and parties ("carnival" is derived from the Italian *carnevale*, meaning the removal of meat). After emancipation, former slaves hijacked the party season by introducing their own processions featuring folkloric characters, dancing, and African drumming, which, once banned by the authorities, became the core of the new Caribbean-style Carnival.

> **Europeans introduced Carnival to the Caribbean, marking the approach of Lent with a hectic round of feasting and parties.**

The buildup to Lenten Carnivals, such as the famous one in Trinidad (see sidebar p. 317), begins soon after Christmas, when musicians take part in the hotly contested qualifying heats, and band members and dancers participating in the main Carnival processions put the final touches on their eye-catching costumes.

Carnival begins in earnest on the Friday before Lent, and competitions held over the weekend decide the winners of the various calypso, steel-pan, and costume prizes. The main processions begin before dawn on Monday with a wild jump-up known as Jouvert (*jour ouvert* or daybreak in French Creole), followed by Tuesday's dazzling Mardi Gras parade. ■

A small Carnival celebration erupts in the seaside town of Grand Anse, Martinique.

Magnificent waterfalls, mountains, and fascinating historic sites matched by a vibrant cultural life

Jamaica

Barrels of coffee at the Craighton Estate in Jamaica's Blue Mountains

Jamaica

The Taíno Indians who settled Jamaica named it Xaymaca (Land of Wood and Water), a description that still rings true if you venture off the tourist trail today. The island's mountainous heartland remains largely untouched, despite centuries of colonial rule beginning with the Spanish occupation of 1510. Most Jamaicans trace their ancestry to slaves brought to plantations during the 17th and 18th centuries, and lively, opinionated Jamaican culture is a vibrant fusion of African and European influences.

Under British rule the slave trade boomed, providing a labor force for the sugar plantations. Jamaica also served as a haven for pirates and buccaneers, encouraged by the British to make Kingston's Port Royal their base for harassing the Spanish fleets. Slave rebellions were a prominent feature of Jamaica's history until emancipation in 1834.

The island became a British Crown Colony in 1866, and during the 1890s the first tourists arrived on banana boats from North America. The Depression of the 1930s led to bloodshed and riots as the economy faltered,

giving birth to the country's first labor union and the socialist People's National Party (P.N.P.) led by Norman Manley (1893–1969). Universal suffrage was granted in 1944, and in 1962 Jamaica won full independence.

Jamaica's culture is a potent brew of fierce national pride, reggae and Rastafarians, sassy attitudes, and the local dialect (known as Jamaican patois). The poverty and lack of opportunity that led to political unrest and occasional riots of the past still affect much of the island.

With over one million visitors a year, Jamaica

has one of the largest tourism industries in the Caribbean—and that means it has one of the widest selections of accommodations, from luxury villas or budget cottages on the beach to private mountain retreats. The main resorts areas (Montego Bay, Ocho Rios, and Negril) are found in the north and west of the island, but it is well worth exploring further.

Jamaica's 4,244 square miles (10,992 sq km) embrace an enormous variety of landscapes. Like many of its neighbors, the island evolved from a broad arc of volcanoes rising from the seabed to form the Blue Mountains, which traverse the eastern third of the island, reaching their summit at the 7,402-foot (2,256 m) Blue Mountain Peak. The land surrounding the Blue Mountains is capped by limestone plateaus. Over the centuries, rivers have carved sinkholes, caves, and deeply rutted gullies in the limestone—most visible in the central western Cockpit Country region.

An offshore coral reef shields the white, sandy beaches of Jamaica's north shore, the island's tourist heartland. The eastern coastline,

---

NOT TO BE MISSED:

Hiking the Blue Mountains   38–39

Eating jerk pork from the stalls at Boston Bay   43

The view from Noël Coward's Firefly   45

Climbing Dunn's River Falls   47–48

The Bob Marley Centre & Mausoleum, Nine Mile   51

Listening to music at Greenwood Great House   54

Negril's hedonistic beaches   55–56

Rum-sampling at the Appleton Estate   66–67

---

unprotected from ocean swells, is far more rugged and dramatic. With a few exceptions, the south and west coasts are typified by volcanic black-sand beaches.

Almost half of Jamaica is under cultivation. Though agriculture accounts for less than 10 percent of G.D.P., huge plantations cloak the landscape with sugarcane, bananas, cocoa, coffee, rice, tobacco, and citrus fruits.

Jamaica has a population of about 2.7 million, almost one-third of whom live in the capital, Kingston. ■

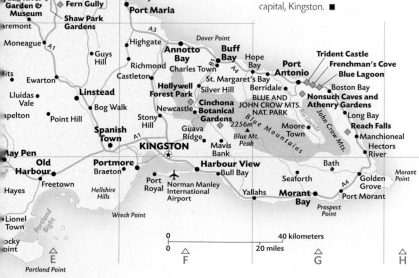

Kingston

Throbbing with energy and spirit, the dynamic capital of Jamaica is home to a population of around 800,000. The largest English-speaking city in the Caribbean, it is also one of the most important cultural and political hubs in the region.

Most visitors to Jamaica's capital stay in the New Kingston neighborhood.

Kingston

⚑ 31 F2

Visitor Information

✉ 64 Knutsford Blvd.

☎ 876 929 9200

🕐 Closed Sun. & Mon.

www.visitjamaica .com

Kingston owes its growth to its magnificent natural harbor, the seventh largest in the world. The English recognized its strategic importance, building no fewer than five forts on the sandspit of Port Royal (see pp. 36–37) in the 17th century. When an earthquake destroyed Port Royal on June 7, 1692, its inhabitants fled to Kingston, and the concentration of economic and political power in the city eventually led to the capital being transferred here from Spanish Town in 1872. The city kept on growing, and today it spreads into the foothills of the Blue Mountains.

The heart of Kingston is the downtown area, which embraces the waterfront, historic sites, and to the west some of the city's most notorious slums. In the center is the **Parade,** once the British army's parade ground. Today it reverberates with the sound of reggae as vendors of cane juice, CDs, bus tickets, and baubles ply their wares. The green heart of the Parade is **Sir William Grant Park,** a leafy square with a fountain and statues of Queen Victoria, Norman Manley (see p. 30), and Alexander Bustamante (1884–1977), founder of the country's first trade union. On the north side of the Parade is the

Ward Theatre *(tel 876 922 3213),* an elegant building completed in 1911, which hosts performances by amateur dramatic groups as well as the National Dance Theatre Company. To the west of the Parade is the colorful **Jubilee Market,** a good place to sample some of the country's exotic fruits and vegetables.

A few minutes' stroll east from here on Duke Street is Headquarters House, which was built in 1755 by a wealthy local merchant, Thomas Hibbert. Headquarters House, with its handsome white facade and graceful fan window, has served as both a military headquarters and as home to Jamaica's legislative assembly,

which met here between 1872 and 1960. Today it houses the offices of the **National Heritage Trust,** and you can visit the rest of the building, which includes the debating chamber and a lookout on the roof with splendid views of Kingston, the mountains, and the harbor. Next door stands **Gordon House** *(corner of Beeston & Duke Sts., tel 876 922 0200),* where the House of Representatives and the Senate meet. *(Entrance to the public gallery is free during debates.)*

Fronting Kingston Harbour, the waterfront area was redeveloped in the 1960s and a new shipping port was created farther west. **Ocean Boulevard** along the waterfront is lined with high-rise

Jubilee Market
- 33 A2
- Spanish Town Rd.
- Closed Sun. & Mon.

National Heritage Trust
- 33 B2
- 79 Duke St.
- 876 922 1287
- Closed Sun. & Mon.

National Gallery

- ⚑ 33 A2
- ✉ 12 Ocean Blvd.
- ☎ 876 922 1561
- ⏱ Closed Sun. &
  Mon.
- 💲 $

Institute of Jamaica

- ⚑ 33 B2
- ✉ 12 East St.
- ☎ 876 922 0620
- ⏱ Closed Sun. &
  Mon.

National Heroes Park

- ⚑ 33 B2
- ✉ Duke St.

office buildings, shops, hotels, and apartments. About midway you'll find the bronze sculpture "Negro Aroused," a famous work by Edna Manley (1900–1987), wife of Jamaican statesman Norman Manley. It captures the spirit of the 1930s labor movement in its depiction of a bowed worker uncoiling from the chains of bondage. The original bronze is in the **National Gallery,** the highlight of the waterfront area. Its impressive permanent collection includes numerous wood carvings (particularly noteworthy are those by Edna Manley), African-style and

INSIDER TIP:

While you're free to take pictures all around the grounds, photos aren't allowed inside Kingston's Bob Marley Museum.

—MATT PROPERT
National Geographic photographer

Rastafarian paintings, landscapes, and photography covering a variety of Jamaican themes.

Walk two blocks west to the **Crafts Market** *(Ocean Blvd., closed Sun.),* a good place to hunt for carvings, souvenirs, T-shirts, and jewelry. In the other direction on East Street is the **Institute of Jamaica,** which was founded in 1879 for "the encouragement of literature, science and art." The institute houses the **National Library,** which holds one of the largest collections of historical

documents in the Caribbean, as well as the **Museum of Natural History,** which chronicles the arrival on the island of coconuts, bananas, sugarcane, and other plants that now form the backbone of Jamaica's agriculture.

National Heroes Park

Poised midway between downtown and the city's uptown area, New Kingston, is the National Heroes Park, a 75-acre (30 ha) open space that was once the city's race track. It now honors the country's national heroes, including Norman Manley and Alexander Bustamante; Sam Sharpe (1801–1832) and Paul Bogle (died 1865), both Baptist preachers involved in slave rebellions; Marcus Garvey (1887–1940), father of the Black Power movement; and Nanny, a legendary 18th-century leader of the Maroons. Norman Manley, Alexander Bustamante, and Marcus Garvey are buried here.

New Kingston

New Kingston extends from the busy crossroads of Half Way Tree Road up to Vale Royal. Wealthy merchants settled this district in the 18th century, when they fled the noise and squalor of downtown to build large residences surrounded by grazing land for their horses and cattle. Today this relatively gentrified zone has both businesses and residences, and most visitors to the capital choose to stay in hotels around here.

Many people make a pilgrimage to this part of Kingston to visit the **Bob Marley Museum,** the most popular attraction in the city. The house was a recording studio for Marley's Tuff Gong record label, as well as his home from 1975 until his death from cancer in 1981. A statue of Marley with his favorite guitar and soccer ball stands at the entrance. (This is the only thing that may be photographed; cameras are prohibited elsewhere in the house.) The one-hour guided tour leads you through the grounds and house, which contains memorabilia of Marley's life, including his gold and platinum records, his favorite denim stage shirt, and several unusual guitars. There's also a re-creation of Wail'n'Soul—the shack in the poor Trenchtown area that was Marley's first house in Kingston. The tour ends with a film about his life, screened in the room that once housed the Tuff Gong studio. The complex also houses a photo gallery, restaurant, and souvenir shops.

The other main draw in New Kingston is **Devon House.** The house was built in 1881 by Jamaica's first black millionaire, George Stiebel (1820–1896), who made his fortune in gold mining in South America. This fine Georgian-style mansion has been refurbished with four-poster beds, chandeliers, Chippendale cabinets, and other original antiques. The courtyard, which was formerly slaves' quarters, houses an upscale craft souvenir shop, and an excellent bakery and ice cream shop. A restaurant occupies the former stables.

A statue of Bob Marley and his favorite guitar at his namesake museum

Also along Hope Road you can take a look through the gates of **Jamaica House**—the prime minister's office—which stands amid expansive lawns, manicured shrubbery, and graceful palms.

The **Hope Botanical Gardens,** said to be the largest botanical gardens in the Caribbean, stretch along the outskirts of New Kingston. Located on the former estate of Maj. Richard Hope, who arrived in Jamaica with Oliver Cromwell's army in 1655, the 200-acre (81 ha) gardens feature pathways meandering between pond and lakes, greenhouses, and flowering trees and shrubs. The grounds also contain diversions to keep children amused (an aquarium, small zoo, and playground) as well as a coconut museum, orchid house, maze, and palm avenue. The gardens are popular with Kingstonians escaping the heat of the city on weekends. ∎

Bob Marley Museum

- 🅰 33 B3
- ✉ 56 Hope Rd.
- ☎ 876 927 9152
- 🕐 Closed Sun.
- 💲 $$$

Devon House

- 🅰 33 B3
- ✉ 26 Hope Rd.
- ☎ 876 929 6602
- 🕐 Closed Sun. & Mon.
- 💲 Guided tours: $$

Hope Botanical Gardens

- 🅰 33 C3
- ✉ Old Hope Rd.
- ☎ 876 927 1736
- 💲 $

Port Royal

In the 17th century Port Royal was among the wealthiest ports in the Caribbean. Built on a small island in Kingston Harbour and connected to the mainland by a causeway (the Palisadoes), it was first used by the Spanish to repair their ships. When the English captured Jamaica in 1655, they strengthened its defenses by building five forts. The combined nautical and military legacies create a powerful atmosphere in the present-day fishing village.

The inner courtyard at Fort Charles, the first fort built to protect Port Royal

Port Royal

🏛 31 F1

Traders took advantage of this safe haven, and Port Royal grew to a settlement of some 6,000 people. The wealth from trade and pirate booty turned it into one of the richest ports in the Caribbean, with fine brick houses, piped water—and innumerable brothels, gambling dens, and taverns.

The Roman Catholic Church condemned Port Royal as "the wickedest city in Christendom," and for many people it must have seemed like judgment day when a massive earthquake on June 7, 1692, sent most of the city to the watery depths, killing 2,000 people and sinking all the ships in the harbor. Most of the survivors fled to Kingston. Port Royal suffered further from a major fire in 1702 and another earthquake in 1907.

Today Port Royal is a quiet fishing village and the home base of the Jamaican Coast Guard. You can reach Port Royal by car or ferry from the Kingston waterfront (*several services daily*), and it is easily navigable on foot (*allow 2–3 hours*). Of the buildings that survive, one of the most impressive is **Fort Charles,** the first of

INSIDER TIP:

Arrange a shuttle with a local fisherman at the Y-Knot Bar to Lime Cay, a spit of sand with fine snorkeling, 2 miles (3 km) offshore from Port Royal.

—CHARLES KULANDER
National Geographic Traveler
magazine writer

the five forts built around the port and constructed from ballast bricks that arrived in the holds of British ships. Although it is now landlocked, due to the 1692 earthquake, the fort's embrasures still feature cannon pointing out to sea.

Within the fort is the **Maritime Museum,** which depicts the history of Port Royal with artifacts dredged up from the sunken city. To one side of the fort's parade ground stands a raised wooden platform known as Nelson's Quarterdeck. The young British commander kept watch here against the threat of a French invasion fleet in 1779–1780. Between the fort and the water is Giddy House, a former ammunition store that now tilts at an alarming angle. Next to it is a massive gun emplacement, the Victoria and Albert Battery, which was also pitched earthward by the severe earthquake of 1907.

Other places of interest in Port Royal include the **Old Naval Hospital,** a stone-and-cast-iron building dating from 1819 and now in disrepair. **St. Peter's Church**

is noteworthy for the tombstone in its graveyard inscribed with the remarkable tale of Frenchman Lewis Galdy, who was swallowed up by the earthquake but was then spat out by an aftershock into the sea.

The submerged portion of Port Royal, covering 33 acres (13 ha), now lies in depths of up to 40 feet (12 m). Excavations by Texas A&M University's Institute of Nautical Archaeology have turned up a watch whose hands stopped at 11:43 a.m. on June 7, 1692, thus giving a precise time for the earthquake.

Fort Charles
- Off Elizabeth Ave.
- 876 967 8438
- $$

Y-Knot Bar
- Next to Morgan's Harbour Hotel

Pirates of the Caribbean

The original pirates of the Caribbean were an unsavory collection of ruthless maritime thugs. Their prime objective was Spanish galleons heavy with New World gold, but in peacetime anything sailing the high seas was a potential target regardless of nationality. In wartime British pirates were officially sanctioned as privateers fighting for the British navy. One of the most notorious, Henry Morgan (1635–1688), was eventually installed as Lord-Lieutenant of Jamaica, and in a classic poacher-turned-gamekeeper maneuver captured his former rival "Calico Jack" Rackham (so called for his preference for calico undergarments), and the female pirates Anne Bonney and Mary Read.

Port Royal belongs to an elite group of archaeological sites that have stayed undisturbed over the centuries: Everyday items such as furniture, tableware, pots and pans, tools, and shoes remain more or less in place as they were left—except, of course, that they are now underwater. ∎

Blue Mountains

One of the longest continuous mountain ranges in the Caribbean, the majestic Blue Mountains dominate the eastern third of Jamaica, rising to a height of 7,402 feet (2,256 m) at Blue Mountain Peak. On these slopes some of the world's finest coffee is grown—sharing space with a profusion of verdant forest.

Coffee farming on the hillsides of Craighton Estate in Jamaica's Blue Mountains

Blue & John Crow Mountains National Park

Ⓐ 31 G2

☎ 876 920 8278

Behind Kingston, the 28-mile-long (45 km) Blue Mountain range forms a cooling contrast with the sprawling metropolis below. High rainfall feeds the lush vegetation, towering trees shrouded in a green veil of epiphytic lichens, mosses and bromeliads, prolific bamboo and ferns, and more than 500 species of flowering plants. The mountains are also home to the largest butterfly in the Americas (the giant swallowtail with a wingspan of 6 inches/15 cm), coneys (a type of rabbit), several nonpoisonous snakes, tree frogs, and glorious native birdlife including orioles, tanagers, and the rare streamer-tailed hummingbird (or doctor bird, whose tailfeathers are thought to resemble the tailcoats once worn by doctors).

The **Blue & John Crow Mountains National Park** was

established in 1993 to protect 193,000 acres (78,100 ha) of this area. The most accessible parts are toward the park's western end, reached via Rte. B1, which runs from Kingston to Buff Bay in the north. The **Cinchona Botanical Gardens** *(tel 876 927 1257)* were established in 1886 to provide quinine from cinchona trees. The project failed, but the gardens then became a botanical research center. The 10-acre (4 ha) grounds, clinging to the ridge at an elevation of 5,000 feet (1,524 m), contain a wide range of imported and endemic trees, shrubs, and flowering plants. The road is tortuous, and it isn't an easy drive.

More easily accessible is the **Hollywell National Recreational Park** *(tel 876 920 8278)* 2 miles (3 km) north of Newcastle, which covers 300 acres (121 ha) of magical montane forest with pines, eucalyptus, soapwood, and dogwood trees, often shrouded in mist and alive with birdsong.

The area is also famed for its

EXPERIENCE:
Hiking & Biking in the Blue Mountains

Dozens of hiking trails meander across the Blue Mountains, many of which follow old mule tracks. The most spectacular is the 7-mile (11 km) **Blue Mountain Trail** from Mavis Bank to Blue Mountain Peak. Guides are recommended *(Jamaican Tourist Board, tel 876 929 9200, or local hotels);* the **Forestry Department** *(tel 876 924 2667)* maintains several basic cabins and campsites if you want to make an early start to reach the peak by dawn. Bring all your own food and supplies; it can be cool and wet, even in the dry season *(Dec.–April).* Popular downhill biking tours are run by **Blue Mountain Bicycle Tours** *(tel 876 974 7075, www.bmtoursja.com, $$$$$)* with regular pickups from main resort areas.

coffee, introduced to the Blue Mountains in the 18th century. The high-quality beans grown here soon commanded top prices in Europe, but the industry suffered a setback with the abolition of slavery in 1834. In the following century, a series of destructive hurricanes took their toll on the crops. In the 1950s the government stepped in to save the plantations; it established guidelines ensuring that only coffee grown between 2,000 and 5,000 feet (610 and 1,525 m) could use the Blue Mountain label.

At the **Mavis Bank Coffee Factory** an hour-long tour of the government-owned plant is rounded off with a cup of the country's finest brew. In operation for over a century, Mavis Bank is the biggest processor of Blue Mountain coffee. ■

Mavis Bank Coffee Factory

🅰 31 F2

✉ Mavis Bank, St. Andrew

☎ 876 977 8528

🕐 Closed Sun. & Mon.; guided tours

💲 $$$

www.jablumonline.com

Port Antonio

Port Antonio's glory days, both as a banana port and an upscale resort, appear to be well behind it, and this quiet backwater is now mostly frequented by independent travelers who use it as a base for exploring the natural attractions in the area. Behind the twin harbors, Portland Parish rises into the foothills of the eastern Blue Mountains and a verdant tropical landscape fed by cascading waterfalls and lazy rivers.

Port Antonio

🗺 31 G2

Visitor Information

✉ City Center Plaza

☎ 876 993 3051

Port Antonio was once Jamaica's chief banana port, immortalized in the "Banana Boat Song" (perhaps better known as "Day-O"). Its fortunes were already on the wane when Errol Flynn ran aground here in his yacht during a hurricane in 1946. He promptly purchased Navy Island out in the bay and introduced a touch of Hollywood glamour to this remote corner of the island. Today, it is still possible to spot the odd celebrity, particularly musicians, enjoying a break from the paparazzi while recording at the Geejam Studio at San San Beach.

Waterfront & Downtown

Down on the waterfront, the Errol Flynn Marina is the latest plan to put Port Antonio back on the map. The swish 32-slip mega-yacht facility stands alongside a small cruise ship pier with a handful of shops, a restaurant, and a wooden promenade along the beach.

The downtown area is easy to navigate, centering as it does on a central square and clock tower; alongside the square you'll find the busy **Musgrave Market,** piled high with local produce. From here it is a short stroll up to **Titchfield Peninsula,** which bisects the two harbors. At the end of this you'll find the crumbling remains of **Fort George** (Fort George St.), dating back to 1791 and now part of Titchfield High School. The fort was once one of the most powerful in the region, but little remains except for a few cannon

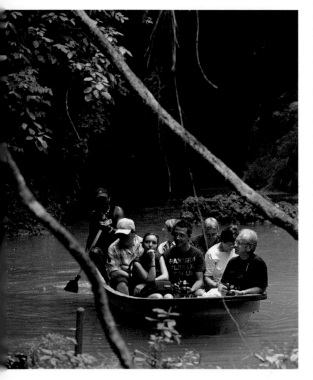

A tour boat cruises near Somerset Falls in Port Antonio.

and parts of its 10-foot-thick (3 m) walls. This historic Georgian and Victorian residential area is scheduled for restoration. While here, you might like to look in at the venerable **DeMontevin Lodge** (19 Fort George St., tel 876 993 2604), an ornate colonial relic dating from 1881 that has seen better days but retains its elegant Victorian gingerbread architecture and wood-paneled interior.

INSIDER TIP:

No visit to Port Antonio would be complete without trying "da' jelly" (frozen coconut juice). You can buy some at Musgrave Market.

—CHARLES KULANDER
National Geographic Traveler
magazine writer

Port Mall & Offshore

Back in the town center you can turn your attention toward an unusual building on the waterfront housing the Port Mall (Gideon Ave.). Conceived and built by local architect Ziggy Fahmi, this striking structure resembles a complex of town houses from different eras, ranging from Gothic to Art Deco via Tudor. Its interior conceals two levels of shops.

Across from Port Mall is the redbrick **Christ Church** (Gideon Ave.), a neo-Romanesque structure built on the site of an earlier church in the mid-19th century. It has some impressive memorials dating back to the 17th century.

Just offshore from Port Antonio is **Navy Island,** which was a ship repair yard and barracks for the British navy in the 18th century. Errol Flynn bought the 60-acre (24 ha) property when he arrived in Port Antonio and allegedly used it as a hideaway to court Hollywood starlets. Currently owned by the Port Authority, the island's lovely beaches are not open to visitors.

Nonsuch Caves & Athenry Gardens

Long before the arrival of Columbus, Arawaks inhabited caves hollowed out of the soft limestone foothills. Some 6 miles (9.5 km) northeast of Port Antonio, archaeological relics have been discovered at the site of the **Nonsuch Caves & Athenry Gardens** (tel 876 993 3740, currently closed—call before visiting). The caves feature impressive formations (including shapes resembling various figures and animals that have been given names) and caverns, as well as a bat colony hanging from the ceiling in the lofty Cathedral Cavern.

The caves are set in 3-acre (1 ha) gardens of well-tended tropical plants and flowers. They lead out onto a promontory, 600 feet (183 m) above sea level, which commands a breathtaking view of the coastline and Port Antonio. ∎

Nonsuch Caves & Athenry Gardens

🅰 31 G2

✉ Nonsuch, Portland

☎ 876 993 3740

🕐 Currently closed. Call before visiting.

💲 $$$

Around Port Antonio

The coastline east of Port Antonio embraces some of the prettiest coastal scenery in the country, its rugged headlands interspersed with golden beaches and some fine hotels on private beaches. (Day visitors generally must pay a small charge, which also includes use of the hotel facilities.)

Young Jamaicans hang out and surf at Boston Bay.

Frenchman's Cove

🏔 31 G2

✉ Rte. A4 (5 miles/3 km E of San Antonio)

💲 $$ for visitors not staying at Frenchman's Cove Hotel

Heading east from town on Rte. A4, the first major landmark is extraordinary **Trident Castle,** a fantasy creation that is part of the neighboring Trident Hotel (*P.O. Box 119, Port Antonio, tel 876 993 2602*). About a mile (1.5 km) from here you come to **Frenchman's Cove,** a gorgeous little beach framed by rocky headlands and skirted by a cool mountain stream. Another 0.75 mile (1 km) along, **San San Beach** (*$$*) is a narrow strip fronting a broad bay with reasonable snorkeling on the reef, and it is an easy swim across to a small beach on jewel-like Pelew Island, on the east side of the bay.

Just past San San Beach is the **Blue Lagoon** (*tel 876 993 7791*).

INSIDER TIP:

In Charles Town, 15 miles (24 km) east of Port Antonio, head to Safu Yard to catch a jam session of the Charles Town Drummers, a drum and dance group intent on preserving their Maroon culture.

—JENNIFER ALLARD
National Geographic contributor

jerk chicken, pork, or seafood. It is 2 miles (3 km) to the next major stopping point at **Long Bay,** a broad expanse of sand that is considered to be Jamaica's top surfing spot. A few beach bars, guesthouses, and discos have sprung up along the road to cater to independent travelers, creating a laid-back atmosphere. The beach, however, is not in the same league as the surf. Unless you're a surfer, there is little reason to linger.

Reach Falls

🏔 31 G2

✉ 9 miles/14 km E of San Antonio

🕐 Closed Mon. & Tues.

💲 $

Surrounded by forest foliage, the lagoon is a limestone sinkhole fed by underground streams. This scenic spot was indeed the setting for the Brooke Shields movie *Blue Lagoon* (1980), as well as *Club Paradise* (1986), which was filmed in the restaurant/bar hanging over the water's edge. It is a lovely spot for a swim and lunch.

Two miles (3 km) east is **Dragon Bay** *(P.O. Box 176, Port Antonio, tel 876 993 8751).* At the hotel you can have a drink at the beach bar where Tom Cruise displayed his bartending talents in the film *Cocktail* (1988).

Along the Coast

Continuing on, you then reach **Boston Bay,** a big public beach famous for its jerk cooking (see sidebar this page). This is primarily a fishing beach, but in rough weather the incoming swells can create good conditions for surfing. The main road and the beach are lined with stands selling authentic, sizzling

Jerk Cooking

Jerk cooking may have originated in the 17th century with the Maroons (see sidebar p. 54), who hunted boar in the mountains and marinated the meat in a spicy sauce. Today jerk cuisine is found all over the island and is one of Jamaica's most distinctive cooking styles. The meat (usually chicken or pork) is marinated in a special blend of spices (including peppers, cinnamon, and ginger) and then slowly grilled over a pimento wood fire. Boston Beach is the jerk aficionado mecca, although there are jerk stalls all around the island. Ten of the best are identified on the **Jamaica Jerk Trail** *(www.visitjamaica.com/jerk).*

One of the highlights of this part of the coast is lovely **Reach Falls,** accessible via a well-paved road from Manchioneal on the coast. The falls are part of the Driver River, which tumbles down from the John Crow Mountains into a series of cascades and crystal-clear pools where you can swim. The entrance fee includes a guided

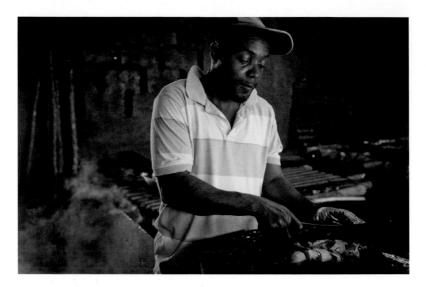

A jerk cooking shack near Boston Bay

walk up to the falls. Although not as spectacular as Dunn's River Falls (see pp. 47–48), there are far fewer people here, and it is a lovely spot to while away an hour or two.

Rio Grande

Extending deep into Portland behind Port Antonio is the Rio Grande Valley, a lush wilderness overlooked by the splendor of the Blue Mountains. The main attraction is a Rio Grande rafting trip along one of Jamaica's largest rivers. Originally the bamboo rafts were used by local farmers to carry their bananas to Port Antonio, but when Errol Flynn arrived here, he started organizing raft races for his friends; the ride has now become one of the area's most popular attractions.

The two-hour trip from Berrydale to the coast passes through some delightfully unspoiled scenery—riverside villages, gorges, and shoals. The 30-foot-long (9 m) rafts are built from lengths of bamboo lashed together, with a seat for two at the back, and are poled along by a raft captain standing at the front. There are stops along the way for swimming and to buy snacks or drinks from vendors. ∎

Rafting Logistics

If you are staying around Port Antonio, you can book the 8-mile-long (13 km) Rio Grande rafting trip through your hotel. Independent travelers will need to give some thought to the logistics of moving their car from the put-in point at Berrydale to the finishing point at Rafter's Rest. The best option is to drive to Rafter's Rest and pick up a cheap taxi ride to Berrydale. Leaving a car at Berrydale means finding an insured driver to deliver it safely to the finishing point.

Oracabessa

As you pass through this tranquil village, 15 miles (24 km) east of Ocho Rios, it is hard to imagine anything much happening. Oracabessa was once a busy port, but since the late 1960s it has slumbered peacefully, with life revolving around its daily market. In its heyday Oracabessa attracted royalty, literati, and politicians from Winston Churchill to Audrey Hepburn.

More recently, resident impresario Chris Blackwell has revived celebrity interest with the exclusive GoldenEye hotel (see Travelwise p. 353).

Oracabessa has an interesting literary heritage, and it can thank two famous writers for this. The first is the English playwright Sir Noël Coward (1899–1973), who built a modest house in the hills midway between Oracabessa and neighboring Port Maria in the 1950s. His home until his death, **Firefly** has now been restored to look as it did when Coward lived here, with his paintings on easels in the studio, two grand pianos back to back in the music room, and the table set for lunch as it was on the day the Queen Mother visited on February 28, 1965. Coward's simple grave on the hillside overlooks one of the most stupendous views on the island, taking in the Blue Mountains to the south and the coastline to the north, which stretches into the Caribbean Sea.

The Bond Connection

The second writer is Ian Fleming (1908–1964), who wrote most of the James Bond novels in **Goldeneye,** the house he built on the outskirts of Oracabessa. Fleming

wintered here every year from 1946 to 1964, and his guests included such notables as Graham Greene (1904–1991) and Truman Capote (1924–1984). The house now belongs to the Island Outpost hotel group, and has been transformed into GoldenEye, a fabulous private hotel (*www.goldeneyehotel.com*).

In Oracabessa Bay itself, the 007 connection continues with

James Bond Beach, a seafront development with changing facilities, food outlets, watersports, and outdoor performance areas. Film buffs might recognize the headland as a backdrop to scenes from *Dr. No.* ■

Oracabessa
 31 E3

Firefly
 31 F3
✉ Grants Pen St. Mary
☎ 876 725 0920
🕐 Closed Fri. & Sun.
💲 $$$
www.islandoutpost .com

The view from Firefly, Noël Coward's former residence

Ocho Rios

Situated midway along Jamaica's north shore, Ocho Rios is the country's second-largest resort after Montego Bay. The town, which lies at the intersection of the main north coast route and Rte. A3 to Kingston, is a popular getaway spot for residents of the capital. But far more visitors disembark from the massive cruise ships that moor at the western end of the bay. For visitors with more time, Ocho Rios has some superb hotels in quiet coves on either side of town.

For many Ocho Rios visitors, a dip in the water at Dunn's River Falls is a must.

Ocho Rios

🅰 31 E3

Visitor Information

✉ Ocean Village Shopping Centre

☎ 876 974 2582

The Spanish who settled here christened the area Las Chorreras, referring to the "gushing water" of Dunn's River Falls (see pp. 47–48). The British mistook the name as Ocho Rios, or "eight rivers," even though no such rivers existed. Today its name is usually shortened to Ochi.

Despite the wide sweep of the bay and the mountain backdrop, Ocho Rios is not the most attractive of resorts. Nor are there many relics of its past, save two rather

forlorn cannon pointing out to sea from the surviving stone ramparts of an 18th-century British fort.

In the 19th century, Ocho Rios was surrounded by plantations, principally for sugarcane and pimentos. In the 1920s an old plantation house at Shaw Park became the country's first upscale hotel, and it was soon followed by several others—but development was held back by the absence of an accessible beach. By the 1960s a cruise

INSIDER TIP:

Stop along the north shore roadside for a fresh jelly coconut or a Jamaican patty, a flaky pastry filled with meat, fish, or vegetables.

—CHRIS BLACKWELL
Hotelier & entrepreneur

ship terminal was in place, the swamps behind the town had been drained, and thousands of tons of white sand imported to create a beach.

Today **Turtle Beach** buzzes with activity and water sports. Around and behind the beach, you'll find plenty of opportunities for eating out and enjoying the varied nightlife, and you can easily stroll around Ocho Rios in an hour or two. The main daytime activity is shopping, with several malls and dozens of stalls providing an outlet for all manner of handmade crafts as well as duty-free items for cruise ship passengers. Strategically positioned almost at the foot of the cruise ship pier, **Island Village** is a 5-acre (2 ha) themed shopping-dining-entertainment complex developed by Island Records impresario Chris Blackwell. Street hagglers are forbidden within this gingerbread evocation of a Jamaican village, but probably the best reason to visit is **Reggae Xplosion,** a museum of Jamaican music with interactive exhibits and the obligatory Bob Marley homage. Music fans will enjoy the journey from the early days of ska through to present-day dancehall.

The rest of Ocho Rios's attractions lie a short distance outside the town center. They are ideally placed for cruise ship visitors on limited shore leave, so you may want to time your visits to the sites at quieter times when the cruise berths are empty or early in the morning.

Foremost among these attractions is **Dunn's River Falls.** The

Turtle Beach
§ $

Reggae Xplosion
☒ Main Street, Island Village
☎ 876 675 8995
🕐 Closed Sun.
§ $$

EXPERIENCE: Meet the People

All too often tourism in the Caribbean creates a gulf between local people and visitors, particularly when the latter are isolated in all-exclusive properties offering little contact with the real life of the island. If you are interested in exploring Jamaica in more depth, there are two grassroots programs that can help. The first is the Jamaica Tourist Board's **Meet the People,** which can muster 700 local volunteer hosts from doctors and teachers to musicians and farmers prepared to welcome you into their lives. You can sign up online (*www.visitjamaica.com/about-jamaica/meet-people.aspx, no fee*) or ask at a local JTB office, give a few details about yourself (job, hobbies, interests), and they will line you up with a suitable local host for the day. In Mandeville, **Countrystyle Community Tourism** (*tel 876 488 7207, www.countrystylecommunitytourism.com, $$$$$*) opens the doors to a number of local sites, including Cecil C. Charlton Mansion (see p. 61). They can also arrange birding tours, a day with a Rastafarian family, and three- to seven-day community experience packages with accommodations.

One of many vendor stalls in an Ocho Rios market

Dunn's River Falls

 31 E3

✉ Rte. 1A bet. St. Ann's & Ocho Rios

☎ 876 974 2857

💲 $$$$

Dolphin Cove

🔼 31 E3

☎ 876 974 5335

🕐 Reservations recommended

💲 $$$$$

www.dolphincove jamaica.com

Mystic Mountain

🔼 31 E3

✉ Balmoral Rd., Ocho Rios

☎ 876 974 3990

💲 $$$$$

www.rainforest adventure.com

spectacular falls cascade down 600 feet (183 m) of slippery rocks and ledges before spilling out onto the beach below. All day, long daisy chains of tourists wend their way up the falls, getting thoroughly drenched (a bathing suit is essential) in the process. The surefooted guides carry dozens of cameras as they lead the climbers upward. The whole process is as entertaining to watch from the wooden steps running alongside the falls as it is to do.

Adjacent to Dunn's River Falls is **Dolphin Cove,** where you can swim with dolphins, sharks, and stingrays. There are several interactive dolphin programs daily, a jungle trail, where you will be introduced to native birds and reptiles, and a beach grill and bar. There's a sister facility—**Dolphin Cove Negril**—in Lucea, 45 minutes west

of MoBay and northeast of Negril (see map 31 B3).

The latest visitor attraction is **Mystic Mountain,** a 100-acre (40 ha) swath of sensitively developed rain forest featuring four family-friendly "soft adventure" rides. Visitors can soar up the mountainside aboard the SkyExplorer, a state-of-the-art chairlift ride ascending 700 feet (213 m) above sea level, then return to earth via the Cool Runnings–style Bobsled Ride roller coaster. The rain forest canopy can also be admired on the Canopy Zip Line, swooping between seven high-level platforms, while the 252-foot-long (77 m) Mystic Waterslide swooshes down into an infinity pool. Various ride packages are available, and there's a panoramic restaurant at the top of the chairlift, plus a butterfly garden and all the usual craft and souvenir sellers. ∎

Around Ocho Rios

The area around Ocho Rios offers a number of gardens, trails, and working farms that allow the visitor to enjoy tropical plantlife.

Coyaba River Garden & Museum

Near Shaw Park Gardens, the wooden walkways of these landscaped gardens traverse well-tended beds, miniature waterfalls, and ponds. The site was once an Arawak settlement (*coyaba* means "heaven" in Arawak), and the small museum concentrates on pre-Columbian Jamaica as well as its more recent history. There is also a café-bar and craft shop, as well as a lookout point adjoining the falls that offers a panoramic view of Ocho Rios Bay.

Cranbrook Flower Forest

A green and glorious retreat from downtown Ochi, Cranbrook showcases the extraordinary beauty and diversity of tropical plant life. Imaginatively landscaped flower gardens and emerald lawns have been carved from the woodland surrounds. There's a beautiful forest trail for walking or horseback riding along the banks of the Little River, and low-key attractions such as bird-watching, fishing, swimming, and paddling provide a relaxing way for visitors to interact with the forest. Picnickers are welcome.

Prospect Plantation

A working plantation 2 miles (3 km) east of Ocho Rios, Prospect cultivates cocoa, soursop, ackee, pimentos, and limes. This popular tour takes you around the farm in a tractor-drawn jitney (open trailer) and provides a commentary on the crops. You are given the chance to stop occasionally and sample them.

Camel safaris and horseback rides along the White River provide more active ways to tour the plantation. A walk through the Butterfly Aviary is also offered, and guests can climb the nearby Dunn's River Falls. ■

Coyaba River Garden & Museum
- 31 E3
- Shaw Park Ridge Rd.
- 876 974 6235
- $$$

www.coyabagardens.com

Prospect Plantation
- 31 E3
- Prospect
- 876 994 1058
- $$$$

www.prospectplantationtours.com

Cranbrook Flower Forest
- 18 miles (29 km) W of Ocho Rios, signed off North Coast Hwy.
- 876 770 8071
- $$$

www.cranbrookff.com

Shaw Park Gardens

Within a few minutes' drive of Ocho Rios, in the hills high above the town, lies Shaw Park Gardens *(Shaw Park Rd., tel 876 974 2723, www.shawgardens.com, $$$)*. Once the grounds of the original Shaw Park Hotel, which burned down in 1937, the 25-acre (10 ha) gardens overflow with frangipani, bougainvillea, crotons, bamboo, and many other glorious tropical plants. A lovely cascade drops almost vertically from the rock face and a magnificent 80-year-old banyan tree arches its massive branches over a large pond. The lawns command superb views of the coast from 550 feet (168 m) above sea level. The site has a bar and gift shop.

Falmouth & Around

The town of Falmouth, 23 miles (37 km) east of Montego Bay, was once one of the busiest ports in Jamaica, exporting sugar from nearby plantations and importing slaves and goods. Today Falmouth wears a down-at-the-heels air, but the riches accumulated in the past are reflected in the many elegant, Georgian-style town houses erected here. Providing a contrast is the town of Nine Mile, where Jamaican legend Bob Marley grew up. Sugar, slavery, and reggae provide a shorthand view of Jamaican history.

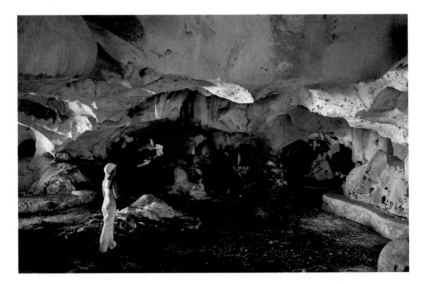

The entrance to Green Grotto Caves near Falmouth seems almost otherworldly.

Falmouth
 30 C3

**Good Hope
Great House**
🅰 30 C3
✉ Trelawny
☎ 876 469 3444

**www.goodhope
jamaica.com**

The town centers on **Water Square** (so named because Falmouth was Jamaica's first town to provide piped water) and nearby **Market Street.** Here you'll find the old courthouse, the Baptist Manse, Barrett House, Tharp House, the William Knibb Memorial Baptist Church (named after an antislavery campaigner), and other reminders of the glory days. The buildings include St. Peter's Anglican Church (1791), which is said to be an almost exact copy of the local

church in Falmouth, England.

East of Falmouth on Rte. A1 is **Oyster Bay,** also known as the Luminous Lagoon. The shallow inlet, where fresh and salt waters meet, is believed to contain one of the world's largest concentrations of bioluminescent microorganisms (dinoflagellates). After dark, the inlet's water lights up with bright green phosphorescence when disturbed. You can rent a boat and a local guide for a mini-cruise—or indeed for a dip—through Glistening Waters *(tel 876 954 3229)*, a restaurant and marina on the lagoon's shoreline.

South of Falmouth is the **Good Hope Great House,** one of the most impressive of Jamaica's remaining plantation houses. Built in 1755, it commanded a sugar estate of 10,000 acres (4,050 ha) and 3,000 slaves. Today the Georgian-style house is a deluxe guesthouse offering bird-watching, river swimming, and horse riding on a 2,000-acre (810 ha) estate.

Running through the estate is the **Martha Brae River,** which rises in Cockpit Country and reaches the sea east of Falmouth. Rafting trips start at the **Rafter's Village,** signposted from Martha Brae *(tel 876 952 0889).* Two-man rafts made of giant bamboo poles lashed together and manned by a local guide glide 3 miles (2 km) downstream for around 90 minutes through dense tropical vegetation and limpid pools.

Discovery & Runaway Bays

Midway between Falmouth and Ocho Rios, these two bayfront towns are essentially resort strips lined with shoulder-to-shoulder all-inclusive hotels on their own beaches and surrounded by beautifully manicured grounds and golf courses.

Just west of Discovery Bay, **Columbus Park** is an open-air museum with historical artifacts as well as a mural depicting Columbus's landing nearby in 1494.

A short distance inland *(Rte. B3),* you can visit the **Green Grotto Caves,** an impressive and extensive cave system once inhabited by Taíno Indians. During the turbulent 17th century, Spanish troops fleeing the English hid here. The 45-minute tour includes a boat ride on an underground lake.

Rte. B3 heading inland to Alexandria is the best road to take to reach the **Bob Marley Centre & Mausoleum** in his hometown of Nine Mile. Surrounded by high fences topped with characteristic flags of red, gold, and green, the compound is revered by Rastafarians and visited by fans from all over the world. At its center is the hut where Marley was brought up, complete with the small bed he sang of in "Is This Love." Behind the hut is the meditation stone

INSIDER TIP:

To ensure safety standards are met, be sure to hire only authorized and licensed guides for rafting trips down the Martha Brae River.

—MATT PROPERT
National Geographic photographer

where he rested his head to sleep or contemplate.

The mausoleum itself is housed in a small chapel of Ethiopian design, which also contains his guitars, favorite soccer ball, a Bible, and other items. There is a vegetarian restaurant on site and a gift shop. *(Transport and tours from nearby resorts can be arranged through Chukka Caribbean Adventures, tel 876 953 6699.)* ∎

Columbus Park
- Rte. A1
- $

Green Grotto Caves
- 30 D3
- 876 973 2841
- $$$$$
- www.greengrotto cavesja.com

Bob Marley Centre & Mausoleum
- 30 D2
- Nine Mile
- 876 995 1763
- $$$

Montego Bay

Montego Bay is the country's second largest city and its biggest resort, offering a wider range of accommodations and amenities than anywhere else on the island. Although its beaches cannot compare with Negril, it has an undeniably attractive setting in a sweeping natural harbor backed up by a fringe of gently sloping hills. Generally referred to as Mo'Bay, Jamaica's tourism capital is a good base for visiting a brace of historic great houses, golfing, and summer's Reggae Sumfest (July), which draws crowds for a week-long celebration of Jamaican music.

The Montego Bay area is filled with inviting beaches.

Montego Bay

🅰 30 C3

Visitor Information

✉ Cornwall Beach

☎ 876 952 4425

🕐 Closed Sun.

When Columbus anchored here in 1494, he christened it El Golfo de Buen Tempo (The Bay of Good Weather), but its modern name derives from the days when the Spanish hunted the wild boars that lived in the surrounding hills. They called it Manteca Bahia, the Bay of Lard. The English interpreted this as Montego Bay.

A sugar and banana town during the 19th century, Montego Bay gained international recognition as a spa in the late 19th century when a local physician, Alexander McCatty, began to extol the virtues of swimming in salt water at his Sanatorium Caribee. The discovery of mineral springs at what had become known as Doctor's Cave Beach marked the beginning of tourism at the resort.

Today **Doctor's Cave Beach** forms part of touristy Gloucester Avenue, known as the Hip Strip. The beach club has good swimming and all the necessary facilities (changing rooms, lifeguards, etc.). Nearby, **Walter Fletcher Beach** combines activities such as tennis and go-karting with watersports and a beachfront restaurant. Both beaches are open 9 a.m.–sunset daily and charge a nominal usage fee. Most of the other beaches along here belong to individual hotels.

Away from the Beaches

Encircling these beaches is an extensive fringing reef that forms part of the **Montego Bay Marine Park,** covering some 9 square miles (23 sq km) of coral reef, sea-grass beds, and mangroves. Snorkeling, diving, and glass-bottom boat tours are readily available if you want to experience the reef at closer quarters.

Around 1 mile (1.5 km) south of the Gloucester Avenue hotel zone is the downtown, a lively, typically Caribbean area. Its focal point is **Sam Sharpe Square,** named after a slave who led the Christmas Slave Rebellion in 1831 (see sidebar this page) and died on the gibbet in this square. There is a small local history museum in the Old Courthouse, and in the northwest corner you can also see the **Cage,** a lockup that was once used to house drunken sailors or

slaves who were out past the Sunday curfew of 3 p.m. Nearby is a tableau of five bronze statues, the **Sam Sharpe Memorial,** which depicts him alongside fellow martyrs who shared the credit for hastening the abolition of slavery. A short walk away is the **Crafts Market** with about 200 artisan stalls *(Harbour St., 7 a.m.–7 p.m.)*.

Also worth a look is the 18th-century parish church of **St. James,** a handsome white limestone building in the shape of a Greek cross. Considered

Christmas Slave Rebellion

Jamaica's infamous ten-day slave rebellion began around Christmas in 1831. Samuel Sharpe, a slave and Baptist preacher, originally designed the revolt as a peaceful general strike. Because the Caribbean was attuned to the abolitionist movement happening at the same time in London, the idea was to show solidarity with the cause. The strike turned violent but was quickly suppressed, and the Jamaican government responded harshly to those involved. Hundreds of slaves were killed, and Sharpe was hanged in a town square in Montego Bay as punishment for his leadership.

to be one of Jamaica's finest churches, the building was extensively restored after an earthquake in 1957 caused considerable damage.

Great Houses

Eight miles (13 km) east of Mo'Bay is one of Jamaica's most famous plantation houses, **Rose Hall Great House.** Occupying a

Reggae Sumfest
☎ 876 953 2933
www.reggaesumfest .com

Rose Hall Great House
🅰 30 C3
✉ Rose Hall
☎ 876 953 2323
$ $$$$$
www.rosehall.com

Scotchies Jerk Centre

✉ Falmouth Rd.,
    Rose Hall

☎ 876 953 8041

⑤ $

Greenwood Great House

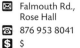 30 C3

✉ Greenwood (14
    miles/23 km
    E of Montego
    Bay)

☎ 876 953 1077

⑤ $$$$$

www.greenwood
greathouse.com

commanding position on the hillside with lawns sweeping downward toward the sea, it was built between 1770 and 1780 at the heyday of the sugar plantation era.

Local legend says that this splendid Georgian house is haunted by the ghost of a wicked mistress, Annie Palmer, who ruled over it for 13 years and murdered several husbands. Supposedly a voodoo practitioner, she is said to have been strangled in her bed by one of her slave lovers: The story was fictionalized in Herbert Lisser's 1958 book, *The White Witch of Rose Hall.* The house was abandoned in the 19th century and sympathetically restored in the 1960s; it contains beautiful original antiques and is well worth a visit.

Farther off the beaten track, less visited and consequently rather more evocative, **Greenwood Great House** was built for the Barrett family between 1780 and 1800. Cousins of British poet Elizabeth Barrett Browning, the

cultured Barretts lived in some considerable style, furnishing their house with beautiful antiques and family portraits, setting the dining table with Wedgwood china, and amassing a library containing rare volumes dating back to 1697.

Another highlight of Greenwood is an extraordinary collection of antique musical instruments, some of which are played by the knowledgeable guides. There's a small bar, and the spectacular view from the veranda, where you can see the horizon curve, more than repays the effort of getting here. ∎

EXPERIENCE: Cockpit Country

South of Montego Bay is an area known as Cockpit Country, a 500-square-mile (1,300 sq km) region of strange limestone formations riddled with caves and sinkholes. This jungle-covered landscape was one of the main refuges for runaway slaves known as Maroons (from the Spanish *cimarrón*, wild or unbroken). The Maroons' intimate knowledge of the terrain and guerrilla tactics meant that few missions to track them down succeeded. Also known as the District of Look Behind (which the pursuing British soldiers were

obliged to do frequently), the region is peppered with evocative place-names such as Me No Sen You No Come, Rest and Be Thankful District, and Quick Step. Learn more about Maroon history and culture while supporting the local community with a **Cockpit Country Adventure Tour** (tel 876 610 0818, www.stea.net, $$$$$). This little ecotourism outfit based in Albert Town is managed by the Southern Trelawny Environmental Agency, who train local guides to lead nature walks and cave explorations in the backcountry.

Negril

At Jamaica's western tip, Negril is often regarded as the island's most permissive and hedonistic resort. The truth is perhaps somewhat more prosaic, but nonetheless Negril has traded on its laid-back, indulgent image since the genuinely decadent 1970s.

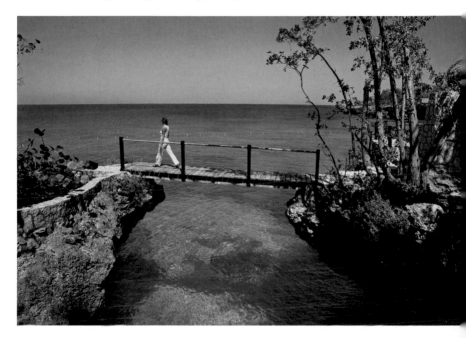

The cliffs and clear blue water at the Rockhouse Resort in Negril

Like so many others, the resort started out as a simple fishing village. Cut off from the rest of the country by swampland, it received its first trickle of visitors when the road to Montego Bay (52 miles/84 km to the east) was completed in 1965. Soon afterward its glorious 7-mile-long (11 km) beach was discovered by hippies, who descended en masse to live in simple huts beneath the coconut palms and while away their days smoking marijuana (ganja) and experiencing sunsets enhanced by readily available hallucinogenics. ("Mushroom tea" is still a specialty you can find on the beach.)

In the late 1970s one of Jamaica's first all-inclusive resorts, Hedonism II (there was no Hedonism I), opened at the eastern end of Long Bay, Negril's main beach. Tales of unlimited alcohol, nudity, and sex soon cemented Negril's reputation as a center for uninhibited bacchanalia. A building boom that began in the 1980s marked the beginning of mass tourism, inevitably quashing the

Negril
🅰 30 B2
Visitor Information
✉ Coral Seas Plaza
☎ 876 957 9314
www.negril.com

Picnic With a View

Negril's lighthouse stands on the western-most point of Jamaica, affording visitors a beautiful view of the cliffs and sea. It's accessible via a short walk from central Negril, and vendors sell fruit, cheese, and drinks along the road leading up to it. The open area around the lighthouse provides a perfect spot for a picnic. The keeper will give a history of the lighthouse and take visitors to the top for a few dollars.

freewheeling spirit it tried so hard to emulate. Today Negril offers a full range of upscale hotels, simple guesthouses, and frat-party-style all-inclusives.

The bay is a nonstop parade of Jet Skis, parasail boats, day-trip catamarans, glass-bottom boats, and dive boats, and you have to be careful now where you plunge into its once pristine waters. There is even a water and theme park for family-fun seekers.

For all the new elements, Negril retains a certain insouci-ant attitude, and the traditional ingredients—beach bars where reggae plays nonstop, ganja and Red Stripe beer circulating freely—are still there. It has a great reputation for live music too, and big-name bands visit the resort regularly.

Long Bay

Most of the action takes place along the sandy swath of **Long Bay,** which fronts the main strip of hotels, beach bars, discos, and vendors offering everything from aloe massages to hair braiding. To the north of Long Bay is **Bloody Bay,** a perfect crescent-shaped beach that

takes its name from the days when whales were once butch-ered in its waters. Offshore lies a small island, **Booby Cay,** named for the booby birds (sooty terns) that nest here.

Right on the main drag, the **Kool Runnings Water Park** *(Norman Manley Blvd., tel 876 957 5418, www.koolrunnings.com, $$$$)* has added an adventure park element to the usual array of water slides, lazy river tube rides, and the little kids' splash zone. You can now get all hot and bothered paintballing, take a spin in a go-kart, try bungee trampolining, or head off-site for a Great Morass (see below) kayaking expedition, and rafting on the Martha Brae River.

The Great Morass

Behind the beach, Norman Manley Boulevard separates the hotels from an area of swampland known as the Great Morass. Jamaica's second largest wetland, this 6,000-acre (2,300 ha) refuge protects croc-odiles, land crabs, and numer-ous species of birds, including egrets, parakeets, jacanas, and Jamaican euphonias.

Within the Great Morass is the **Royal Palm Reserve** *(Shef-field, tel 876 364 7407, $$$)*, named for the rare and stately palms that flourish here. The 300-acre (120 ha) site boasts a further 113 plant species and over 300 species of birds, butterflies, and reptiles. This beautiful spot can be visited for guided and independent walks, nature tours, bird-watching, and fishing.

Norman Manley Boulevard continues on into Negril town; there are a couple of shopping malls and a craft market in the small town center but little else to detain you.

West End

Beyond Negril is **West End,** a quieter 3-mile (5 km) stretch of coastal road along the cliffs peppered with guesthouses and hotels. This area is now undergoing a resurgence in popularity as an alternative to the mass tourism that has taken hold on the beaches, and some of Negril's most imaginatively designed resorts (such as the Rockhouse and The Caves; see Travelwise p. 353) can be found here. There are no beaches, but you can reach the waters below the cliffs via stone steps, iron ladders, and diving boards.

Cliff diving is one of West End's hallmarks, particularly at Rick's Café. Every evening, busloads of tourists watch the sun sink beneath the horizon from this spot. West End terminates at **Negril Point,** where there is a historic lighthouse, built in 1894.

A popular inland excursion from Negril is to **Mayfield Falls** (*Glenbrook, Westmoreland, tel 876 610 8612, www.mayfieldfalls.com, $$*), a 5-acre (2 ha) rain forest property in the Dolphin Head Mountains. There are 21 natural pools and two waterfall cascades to negotiate on the guided hike upriver. It's quite a scramble (bring sensible footwear and a change of clothes; you will get wet), but the sure-footed guides provide plenty of assistance and a knowledge-able commentary on local plant and wildlife along the way. Bring swimwear too for a rewarding and cooling dip in one of the bathing holes. ■

A keeper still staffs Negril Point's lighthouse, which was built in 1894.

Rastafarianism

The characteristic colors of Rastafarianism—red, black, green, and gold—are highly visible in Jamaica, adorning everything from bar fronts to bus stops and braided belts. The Rastas themselves, with their dreadlocks piled high under tall hats or knitted tams, have come to symbolize the face of Jamaica—even though for mainstream society they are still cultural rebels.

A sugarcane harvester sports Rastafarian colors: red, yellow, and green.

Looking to Africa

The Rastafarian movement has its roots in the teachings of the black activist Marcus Garvey (1887–1940), a national hero who prophetically advised his followers to "look to Africa, where a Black King shall be crowned." In 1930 Ras Tafari Makonnen (Ras is an honorific given to royalty, Tafari his family name) was crowned Negus of Ethiopia, taking the title Emperor Haile Selassie, King of Kings, Lord of Lords, Conquering Lion of the Tribe of Judah. The Scriptures seemed to support his claims to divinity, and Selassie was elevated to the role of the messiah who would redeem black people from suffering and white oppression.

In its early days Rastafarianism provoked considerable antagonism as it developed support in the poorer parts of Kingston, and police consistently harassed Rasta communities, which they believed were drug-crazed and planning to undermine white society. In the 1970s Rastafarianism gained a degree of respectability when the politician Norman Manley visited Haile Selassie in Ethiopia and was presented with a sacred rod, which he employed with great effect in political rallies back home. Casting himself as the people's savior, he swept to power in the 1972 elections with the support of Rastas and their allies.

Musical Breakthrough

But the real turning point for Rastafarianism came in the 1970s with the huge success of Bob Marley and the Wailers, whose music spread the word about Rasta beliefs worldwide. Reggae and Rastas became Jamaica's trendiest cultural export, but inevitably a certain commercialization set in, affecting the credibility of the movement.

The Rastafarian faith is based on the belief that Rastas are one of the lost tribes of Israel, and that eventually they will be delivered from Babylon (the corrupt white world) and returned to the promised land in Ethiopia, or Zion. Rastas let their hair grow until it mats together into dreadlocks, following the directive in Leviticus (21:5): "They shall not make baldness upon their heads, neither shall they shave off the corner of their beard, nor make cuttings in the flesh." Following the injunction not to make "cuttings in the flesh," Rastas believe in herbal bush medicine, and many are also strict vegetarians following a regime of natural and unprocessed foods, known as Ital. Salt, meat, dairy products, and alcohol are eschewed in favor of pulses and vegetables.

INSIDER TIP:

Jamaican roadside restaurants marked by red, yellow, and green signs are devoted to Ital—Rastafarian cuisine—which is delicious, healthy, and cheap.

—CHARLES KULANDER
National Geographic Traveler *magazine writer*

Rastas are renowned for their copious consumption of marijuana (ganja or herb), which was introduced to Jamaica by Indian plantation workers in the late 19th century. Smoking it is a religious sacrament, as outlined in Psalms 104:14: "He causeth the grass to grow for the cattle, and the herb for the service of man." Smoking the sacred herb is believed to provide

Reggae musician Crucial Bankie performs at the St. Kitts Music Festival.

access to a higher level of spirituality and is often accompanied by recitations of prayers or poems at "reasonings," when the communal pipe or chalice is passed around the group counterclockwise.

Many latter-day Rastas don't follow all these precepts and smoke ganja whenever they wish, eat meat, drink, and allow their dreadlocks to hang loose. The 100,000 Rastas in Jamaica today are split into different sects, and many have gravitated toward the more Christian-based Ethiopian Orthodox Church. The more traditional still remain in rural communes (called camps), venturing out only to secure supplies they cannot produce themselves.

Finally, what do those vibrant Rasta colors represent? Red stands for the blood spilled in Jamaica's history, black represents the skin color of the majority of the population, gold stands for the victory over oppression, and green symbolizes the fertility of both Jamaica and Ethiopia.

Mandeville

Jamaica's fifth largest town, Mandeville (located 2,000 feet/600 m above sea level), was established in the early 19th century and once served as a hill station for British soldiers recuperating from the heat of the coastal areas. The landscape around Mandeville has been shaped—and in places, marred—by large-scale bauxite mining. Yet the surrounding hills are scented with a heady aroma of coffee, chocolate, and spices.

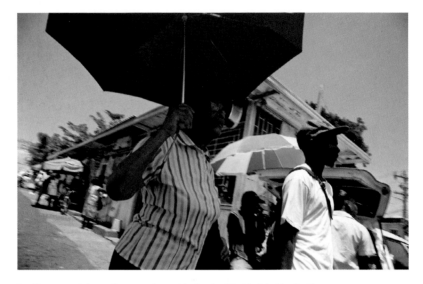

Strolling around the market near the parish church of St. Mark in Mandeville

Mandeville
🏛 30 D2

Marshall's Pen Great House
🏛 30 D2
✉ Winston Jones Hwy.
☎ 876 877 7335
🕐 House tours (min. 6 people) and bird-watching by appt. only
💲 $$$$

Mandeville, the capital of the parish of Manchester, was once the center of Jamaica's bauxite industry. As you approach, you cannot fail to notice the massive, red-stained bauxite factories and the huge scars on the landscape caused by the extraction of Jamaica's "red gold." Global recession has called the future of the sprawling alumina plants into question, but in their heyday, the bauxite companies built housing for their employees on the undulating hillsides outside the town center. Mandeville's

air of prosperous tranquility has turned it into one of the main centers for expatriate Jamaicans returning to their homeland.

The oldest buildings in the town cluster around Mandeville Square, recently renamed **Cecil Charlton Park** after a former mayor. On the south side of the square is the parish church of **St. Mark,** built in 1819. Opposite the church is the Georgian-style **courthouse,** constructed a year later next to the market, one of the biggest and busiest in the region. The venerable **Mandeville Hotel,** just to the east, was established as an officers' quarters and mess in 1875. It claims to be the oldest hotel in Jamaica; the entrance is shaded by three equally old sandbox trees. To the east is the Manchester Golf Club, one of the oldest in the Caribbean, founded in 1868. Overlooking the town center from the leafy heights of the Bloomfield district is **Bloomfield Great House & Art Gallery** (tel 876 962 7130). Built on the site of an 18th-century coffee plantation, this restored Georgian great house makes a great lunch stop (see Travelwise p. 352), and the walls are hung with local artwork.

A short distance northwest of Mandeville is **Marshall's Pen Great House.** Built in 1795, the house was once used as a "factory" for preparing coffee beans. It has since become a home furnished with antiques and artifacts, including shell and stamp collections, and antiques belonging to renowned local ornithologist Anne Hayes-Sutton. There are tours of the house and bird-watching visits of the grounds, which serve as a bird sanctuary and nature reserve.

To the south of town at Huntingdon Summit, **Cecil C. Charlton Mansion** is a monument to a local self-made millionaire who was also mayor of Mandeville for more than 20 years. The pagoda-like house is renowned for its ostentatious interior, esoteric furnishings, and trophy-filled library. An indoor swimming pool is connected to another one outdoors by an underground tunnel.

If you want to see what made Mandeville so wealthy in the 20th century, arrangements can be made through Countrystyle Community Tourism (see sidebar p. 47) to visit the **Kirkvine Works,** if it is in operation. To the northeast of town, this is the largest alumina plant in Jamaica.

Countrystyle also visits the **High Mountain Coffee Factory,** Williamsfield, where producers JSP roast, grind, and package some of the finest coffee in Jamaica. There is another olfactory treat next door and one chocoholics won't want to miss: a tour of the delectably scented **Pioneer Chocolate Factory.** This miniature gourmet excursion can be rounded off at the **Pickapeppa Factory,** Shooter's Hill, which produces spicy Pickapeppa sauce (see sidebar this page). ∎

Cecil C. Charlton Mansion

- ✉ George's Valley Rd., Huntingdon Summit
- ☎ 876 962 0585

High Mountain Coffee Factory

- ✉ Williamsfield
- ☎ 876 963 4211
- 🕒 By appt. only. Closed Sat. & Sun.

Pickapeppa Factory

- ✉ Shooter's Hill
- ☎ 876 603 3439
- 🕒 By appt. only. Closed Sat. & Sun.

Pickapeppa Sauce

The Pickapeppa Factory produces a world-renowned, sinus-searing spicy sauce that is found in most Jamaican households. Visitors can take a 30-minute tour of the factory and learn more about the creation of the sauce. It still tastes just like it did almost a century ago when the business was founded by Norman Nash, who made the sauce in his kitchen as a hobby. The condiment is made from natural ingredients only, including tomatoes, onions, sugar, mangoes, raisins, tamarinds, peppers, and spices, with vinegar as a preservative, and is aged in oak barrels before being shipped worldwide. It was named the official sauce of the Olympic Summer Games twice—in 1984 and 1996.

Mandeville Drive

This drive from Mandeville into the neighboring parish of St. Elizabeth passes through lovely stretches of countryside. The road is in reasonably good repair, and driving conditions are relatively easy.

North from Mandeville, follow signs out of town toward Christiana, and then turn left at a sign marked Kendall. After 2 miles (3 km) you'll see the massive **Kirkvine Works** ❶. When it is operating, scouring the "red gold" from vast pits in the surrounding area, this huge alumina plant leaves a fine red film of bauxite powder over the countryside. Some of the unused pits on either side of the road are being rehabilitated as farmland.

Follow the road for about a mile (1.6 km), and turn left toward Christiana. At Shooter's Hill, home of the Pickapeppa Sauce factory, turn left onto Rte. B6.

The stretch of road between here and **Balaclava** ❷ is an idyllic farming region reminiscent of the English countryside. Sheep and cattle graze in well-tended pastures surrounded by low stone walls, presided over by towering tropical trees like the silk cotton. Occasionally these majestic specimens are found on their own in the middle of a field—shrouded sentinels with a green mantle of luxuriant bromeliads and hanging lichens.

About 21 miles (34 km) from the start, the road opens out to reveal a panorama of hills stretching into the distance to the south. To the north rise the higher peaks of Cockpit Country (see sidebar p. 54), forest-clad and almost impenetrable.

From Balaclava, Rte. B6 gently drops to the valley floor, where a good, wide road bisects the massive sugarcane fields on either side, the crops rolling off into the distance like a vast green carpet.

Two miles (3 km) beyond the ramshackle little town of Siloah is the **Appleton Estate** ❸ (see p. 67). After visiting the estate, drive to the town of **Maggotty** and then head south to the junction with Rte. A2 (8 miles/13 km).

NOT TO BE MISSED:

Kirkvine Works factory • Balaclava • Appleton Estate • Bamboo Avenue • YS Falls

---

Turn right and soon you find yourself driving along **Bamboo Avenue** ❹, a 2-mile (3 km) stretch completely overshadowed by giant bamboo, which arches over it to create a photogenic tunnel of foliage.

See also area map p. 30
► Mandeville
🕐 Allow 3–4 hours
↔ 74 miles (118 km)
► Mandeville

The aptly named Bamboo Avenue takes motorists through an arch of giant bamboo plants.

One mile (1.6 km) farther west, take a right signposted to reach **YS Falls** ❺ (see p. 65) on an upcountry cattle ranch. There's a shortcut from Maggotty to YS Falls, on Rte. B6, but the poor road conditions means that the route is recommended only for experienced drivers.

From YS Falls return to Rte. A2 and turn left to head back to Mandeville. This is a big busy road, but the driving conditions are good.

South Coast

Though Jamaica's south coast is off the main tourist trail, it repays more adventurous travelers with handsome mountain scenery, busy coastal fishing villages, hidden beauty spots, and discreet resorts tucked away in tranquil coves.

Laidback Calabash Bay is Treasure Beach's hub.

Black River
⬛ 30 C2
Visitor Information
✉ 2 High St.
☎ 876 965 2074

The landscapes of the southern parishes range from arid, cactus-strewn savannas to lush cattle pastures and vast swamplands. In the easternmost parish, St. Elizabeth, the main town is **Black River,** a peaceful port facing Black River Bay. Its main street has several colonnaded wooden houses harking back to Black River's heyday in the mid-19th century, when the town was a thriving depot for the export of logwood, used to produce textile dyes. Black River claims to have been the first town in Jamaica to introduce electricity, telephones, and the automobile.

The invention of synthetic dyes killed off the logwood industry, and the town reverted to its existence as a quiet backwater.

Main Street

Most of the activity in Black River centers on the wharfside and the main street, where you'll find such faded gems as the Waterloo Guesthouse, the Invercauld Great House and Hotel with its ornate Victorian fretwork, bay windows and gabled roofs, and the yellow-brick parish church of St. John's. Alongside the town's bridge, where the river cruise boats depart, is the **Hendrick's Building,** dating from 1813.

River Safaris

The majority of visitors come here for a 90-minute **boat safari** *(regular daily departures)* on the Black River itself, one of the few easily accessible waterways in Jamaica for spotting wildlife. The 44-mile (71 km) river, Jamaica's longest, is named for the inky black color of its waters (due to the peat moss lining the riverbed). The river is the main source for a vast swampland known as the Great Morass (see p. 56), which covers about 125 square miles (324 sq km) on either side of the lower reaches of the river as it descends from its source in Cockpit Country (see sidebar p. 54) south of Montego Bay. Over its relatively short route, the Black River travels through an astonishing variety of landscapes.

The river boats navigate about 6 miles (10 km) upriver through swaths of water hyacinths and beneath the boughs of venerable mangrove trees. You're likely to see flocks of roosting cattle egrets and possibly whistling ducks, herons, ospreys, and jacanas—just some of the hundred or so species of birds that live here. The main attractions, however, are the crocodiles. Once abundant around Jamaica's coastline, their numbers are now severely depleted due to loss of habitat. Of the 300 or so survivors, around a dozen crocodiles are regularly spotted on the boat safaris. They all have names (albeit a different name depending on which boat you take!) and are used to being approached by the boats and fed scraps. Don't, however, be lulled into complacency.

YS Falls is 10 miles (16 km) to the north of Black River, signposted off Rte. A2. This scenic cascade lies at the heart of the 2,500-acre (1,000 ha) **YS Estate,** where the owners raise pedigree Red Poll cattle and Thorough-bred racehorses. The origin of the name YS has been debated for decades. One version is that it derives from the Gaelic word

INSIDER TIP:

For a unique Black River safari, try a guided canoe. Ask at the iron bridge in town for guide suggestions.

—JENNIFER ALLARD
National Geographic contributor

wyess, meaning "winding" or "twisting," to describe the river; another is that it comes from the original 17th-century owners, John Yates and Richard Scott.

The tour starts at the visitor center, where a tractor-drawn jitney takes you on the ten-minute ride across farmland to the falls. This is a well-maintained area, with grassy spots for picnics and shaded gazebos. A wooden stairway leads up the highest and most spectacular waterfall, and there are caves behind some of the cascades to explore and cool pools where you can swim. ■

YS Estate & Falls

🅰 30 C2

✉ Off Rte. A2

☎ 876 997 6360

🕐 Closed Mon.

💲 $$$$

www.ysfalls.com

More Places to Visit in the South

Jamaica's varied south offers many beaches, rivers, ponds, and savannas. Visitors can spy manatees, watch rum being produced in a centuries-old factory, or simply relax in riverine pools and laid-back fishing villages.

Grinding sugarcane the old-fashioned way at the Appleton Estate

Alligator Hole

 30 D1

Appleton Estate Rum Tour

🗺 30 C2
☎ 876 963 9215
🕒 Closed Sun.
💲 $$$$ or $$$$$ for tour with lunch

www.appletonrum tour.com

Alligator Hole

Just beyond Gut River Pool, near Milk River Spa, is a small nature park, Alligator Hole, which is home to rare and endangered manatees. The manatees live in a maze of reeds in the river delta and come in close to the jetty to be fed. You can rent a boat at the jetty with a guide to take you out to look for them, but don't expect too much. Manatees are reclusive creatures, and the most you might see is a shadowy form gliding past underwater near the riverbank or telltale bubbles rising from the reeds as you drift by. You can also rent kayaks here.

Along the South Coast

Rearing up at the far end of Great Pedro Bay is hulking **Great Pedro Bluff,** one of the few places in the Caribbean where a dry savanna exists in the coastal zone. Beyond here (signposted from Southfield) are the sheer cliffs and lighthouse at **Lover's Leap,** where, legend has it, two slaves who were forbidden to meet each other leaped to their deaths. Entrance to the clifftop is through a café-restaurant complex. The view is spectacular, with the sheer bluff of the Santa Cruz Mountains dropping 1,700 feet (518 m) almost straight down to the ocean; the panorama extends down the coastline to Rocky Point and Clarendon in one direction, and back toward Great Pedro Bluff and Treasure Beach in the other.

Ten miles (16 km) east of Treasure Beach is the fishing village of Alligator Pond. From here a scenic drive winds 18 miles (29 km) along the south coast toward Alligator Hole and Milk River Spa. This wild, unspoiled part of the country embraces dry savanna as well as the extensive swamplands of the Long Bay Morass.

Midway along is an exquisite little spot known as the **Gut River Pool.** The river flows under the road and emerges in an oasis of palm trees, bulrushes, and water lilies, with crystal-clear pools that you can jump into from the surrounding rocks. It's very popular with local lads cooling off on weekends.

Appleton Estate

Three miles (5 km) east of YS Falls, beyond the small junction town of Maggotty, lies the Appleton Estate. Set amid the rolling sugarcane fields of the Black River Valley, this venerable institution is the oldest rum-producing factory in the English-speaking Caribbean, founded in 1749, and its products are among the most popular on the island. Most of the process is now mechanized, although some of the copper distillation pots are over a century old. An aging donkey demonstrates the old fashioned method of squeezing the juice out of the cane by turning a grinder. You can peek into the warehouse where more than 8,400 barrels of maturing rum rise up in tiers to the ceiling. The tour ends in the visitor center, where you can sample some of the assorted rums and other liquors produced here.

INSIDER TIP:

Don't miss Floyd's Pelican Bar, located on stilts in the middle of the Caribbean about a quarter mile (0.5 km) off the Jamaican coast between Black River and Treasure Beach.

—MELINA BELLOWS
Chief creative officer, National Geographic Books, Kids, and Family

Treasure Beach

Some 19 miles (30 km) east of Black River by back roads, Treasure Beach is the collective name for a string of little fishing villages, beaches, coves, and rocky strands running along the seashore to the Great Pedro Bluff headland. This laid-back beach community is as close as you can get to Negril in the 1970s, albeit with slightly better communications, including a new private aerodrome attached to funky Jake's hotel (see Travelwise p. 354) on Calabash Bay. Calabash is Treasure Beach Central, with the greatest choice of restaurants, bars, and accommodations. ■

Floyd's Pelican Bar

 30 C1

✉ Offshore bet. Black River and Treasure Beach

Spanish Town

Jamaica's capital for more than 300 years, Spanish Town is today a large industrial city with few traces of its past prominence. Called St. Jago de la Vega by the Spanish who founded the first capital here in 1523, the city was later razed by British soldiers during the invasions in 1596 and 1643, and rebuilt. It remained the capital under the British until 1872, when Kingston took over the role. Nestled within the modern cityscape are fascinating reminders of Spanish Town's past—and of the European powers that shaped Jamaica.

An ornate cannon at the Rodney Memorial

Spanish Town
- 🅰 31 E2
- ✉ 12 miles (19 km) W of Kingston

People's Museum of Craft & Technology
- ✉ Old King's House, Emancipation Sq.
- ☎ 876 907 0322
- 🕐 Closed Sat. & Sun.
- 💲 $

At the heart of the city is **Emancipation Square,** a park surrounded by the faded grandeur of Georgian buildings. On the north side is the **Rodney Memorial,** built to commemorate Admiral Rodney's defeat of the French fleet off Guadeloupe in 1782. Sculpted by John Bacon, the marble statue depicts Rodney in classical attire and is flanked by two rare cannon captured from the French flagship. The cupola housing the statue is adorned with friezes depicting the battle itself. The buildings that flank the memorial, linked by a porticoed walkway, house the **National Archives** *(closed weekends).*

The redbrick Georgian facade on the west side of the square is all that remains of the **Old King's House,** built in 1762 as the governor's residence but largely destroyed by fire in 1925. The residence's former stables now house the **People's Museum of Craft & Technology,** which features industrial and agricultural equipment (including an ancient sugar press, coffee huskers, and corn grinders) and other items relating to the country's industrial heritage. The equipment provides a snapshot of Jamaican history. Opposite the Old King's House is the former House of Assembly, now occupied by local government offices.

To the south of Parade Square stands the **Cathedral of St. Jago de la Vega** *(White Church St.).* The oldest Anglican cathedral outside England, it was built in 1714 on the site of a 16th-century Spanish church. The black-and-white checkered floor tiles in the aisle belonged to the original Spanish Catholic church. The elaborate interior contains many important monuments from the colonial era and elaborately carved pews and choir stalls. ■

One of the most prosperous enclaves in the region, poised above the deepest point in the Caribbean Sea

Cayman Islands

A sea turtle glides off the Cayman coast.

Cayman Islands

The low-lying Cayman Islands group is situated in the western Caribbean, 480 miles (772 km) southwest of Miami. There are three islands in this British Overseas Territory, each different in character. The biggest, Grand Cayman, is the home of the capital, George Town. About 90 miles (145 km) to the northeast lie the two sister islands of Cayman Brac and Little Cayman, both comparatively undeveloped.

The tips of submarine mountains, the three islands share a similar appearance—surprisingly flat, mostly covered with dry scrub and mangrove forest. They sit on the edge of the Cayman Trench, a massive trough that drops some 25,000 feet (7,620 m) into the deepest part of the Caribbean Sea. The reef walls that surround the islands descend into the depths and attract scuba divers from all over the world. The Cayman Islands have become one of the Caribbean's top diving destinations thanks largely to vigorously implemented conservation measures.

Stingray City, Grand Cayman's most popular underwater attraction, is home to more than 100 friendly stingrays, which can be handled and stroked in open water. Glass-bottom boat trips and mini-submarine rides that reach depths of 100 feet (30 m) allow even non-divers to experience the thrills of the underwater world.

The first European sighting of the islands was by Columbus on May 10, 1503, when he was blown off course on his way to Hispaniola. The explorer spotted the two smaller islands, Cayman Brac and Little Cayman. Although he didn't stop to explore, Columbus noted the enormous numbers of turtles in the surrounding waters and named the islands Las Tortugas. Over the next hundred years or so they came to be known as Las Caymanas, from the Carib name for the saltwater crocodiles that were also abundant around the islands.

In the 16th century, Dutch, French, English, and Spanish sailors used the islands to replenish their freshwater supplies and capture sea turtles, a plentiful source of fresh meat for the long sea

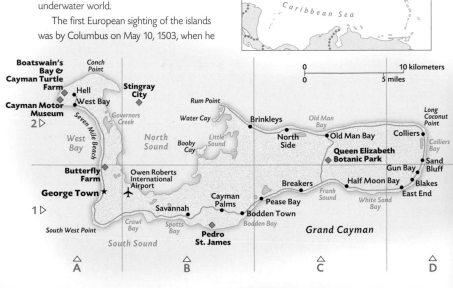

voyage back to Europe. Even though Sir Francis Drake visited Grand Cayman in 1586 and reported that the caimans were edible, the islands remained unclaimed and uninhabited.

The Cayman Islands came under English jurisdiction in 1655, when England wrested Jamaica and neighboring islands from the Spanish; they were formally recognized as English territory in 1670. In the mid-1660s the first settlers arrived from Jamaica, setting up semipermanent habitations on Little Cayman and Cayman Brac to trade turtles, vegetables, water, wood, and coconuts with passing ships. Grand Cayman, which offered better protection from pirate attacks, was settled from 1700.

The Cayman Islands developed a maritime economy. By the late 1800s up to one-third of the population was employed as merchant sailors, fishermen, or turtle catchers. The islanders rescued numerous mariners shipwrecked on the

NOT TO BE MISSED:

Visiting Boatswain's Beach & Cayman Island Turtle Farm, Grand Cayman 73

Touring Grand Cayman's Pedro St. James 74

A blue iguana safari on Grand Cayman 75

Diving Bloody Bay Marine Park, Little Cayman 76–77

The seabird nesting sites on Little Cayman's Booby Pond Nature Reserve 77

Checking out Brac Parrot Reserve, Cayman Brac 82

offshore reefs and salvaged lumber and cargo to build their houses and supply other needs. Over the course of time, however, a growing sense of self-sufficiency began to take hold among the islanders. They turned from salvage to construction. By the 1780s the Caymanians were building their own schooners and becoming renowned throughout the Caribbean as master boatbuilders. Shipbuilding prospered for more than 150 years, until the launching of the last traditional Caymanian ship in January 1967.

Although the first legislative assembly was formed in 1832, the islands remained a

dependency of Jamaica until 1959. Following Jamaica's independence from Britain in 1962, the Cayman Islands chose to remain a British Overseas Territory. In 1966 they introduced landmark legislation to encourage growth of the offshore banking industry, recognized today as one of the largest in the world.

The first tourists arrived on board the cruise ship *Atlantis* in 1937, and they have kept on coming in droves. Damage caused by Hurricanes Omar and Paloma in 2008 is all but invisible today, and several new visitor attractions have recently opened to add to the fun. ■

Grand Cayman

The largest of the three Cayman islands, Grand Cayman is 22 miles (35 km) long and 4 to 8 miles (6 to 13 km) wide. The most prosperous of the islands, it is home to 96 percent of the country's population. A busy coastal fringe gives way to an interior of mangroves, lakes, and native woodlands.

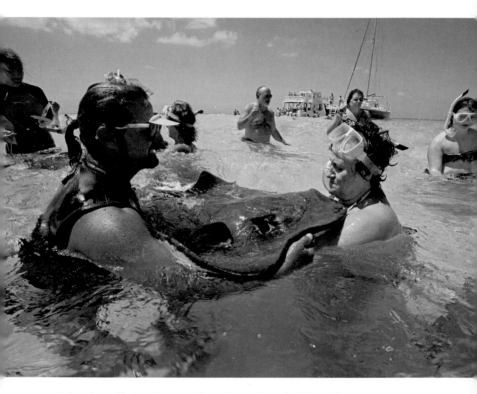

Get up close with giant stingrays at Grand Cayman's popular Stingray City.

George Town
🅰 70 A1

Visitor Information

✉ Regatta Office Park, Windward 3, West Bay Rd.

☎ 345 949 0623

www.caymanislands.ky

Most of the development on Grand Cayman is concentrated along **Seven Mile Beach** (which is actually just 5.5 miles/8.8 km long), a glorious stretch of powdery sand on the west side of the island sloping into the shallow waters of West Bay. A ribbon of hotels and condominiums lines the beach, while behind it lies a strip of shopping malls, fast-food outlets, restaurants, and bars. The big excitement offshore, at least for divers, is the arrival of the **ex-U.S.S. *Kittiwake,*** a 251-foot (77 m) submarine research vessel that was scuttled in 2011 to form an artificial reef dive site *(www .kittiwakecayman.com).*

George Town

Grand Cayman's capital, George Town, is primarily a business center clustered around a protected harbor. The harbor is a popular stop for cruise ships, which disgorge their passengers by the thousands into the duty-free souvenir and jewelry shops on the surrounding streets. One of the few remaining 19th-century structures has been converted into the commendable **National Museum**. Displays here chronicle the natural and seafaring history of the islands.

INSIDER TIP:

Calypso Grill, located in West Bay about 5 miles (8 km) north of George Town, is considered the best restaurant by locals and expats. Combine the view and colorful decor with the lobster bisque, and you're in heaven.

—ALAINA APPLEMAN
National Geographic Channels

West Coast

To the north of Seven Mile Beach, **Boatswain's Beach** is a 23-acre marine park incorporating the **Cayman Island Turtle Farm**. Attractions include a saltwater snorkel lagoon with tropical fish, a 300,000 gallon freshwater lagoon with views of the predator tank, an aviary, and an iguana sanctuary, and a research facility. However, it's the farm's famous green sea turtles, many thousands of them, ranging in size from hatchlings to 600-pound adults, that draw the biggest crowds.

Just down the road, the **Cayman Motor Museum** showcases an extraordinary collection of antique and luxury automobiles and motorbikes belonging to Norwegian millionaire Andreas Ugland. Among the treasures displayed in the state-of-the-art building are an 1886 Benz, the original 1960s Batmobile, and Queen Elizabeth II's Daimler.

A short distance inland, you can go to **Hell**. In the 1930s, so the story goes, a British

---

EXPERIENCE: Cooking Caymanian Food

The **Cayman Islands National Trust** *(Dart Park, 558 S. Church St., George Town, www.nationaltrust.org.ky)* is a great source of information about the islands. In the shop you can pick up excellent maps and information sheets, and also sign up for activities, including cooking classes run by local chefs. The Caymanians are passionate foodies (the **Taste of Cayman** festival takes place in January; see *www.tasteofcayman.org*) and, on the second Wednesday of each month, the Trust offers visiting cooks the opportunity to join local experts for a lesson in preparing old Caymanian food. *(Information and booking: tel 345 749-1123, e-mail: dbodden@nationaltrust.org.ky.)*

National Museum
- ✉ Harbour Dr., George Town
- ☎ 345 949 8368
- 🕐 Closed Sun.
- 💲 $$
- www.museum.ky

Boatswain's Beach & Cayman Island Turtle Farm
- 🗺 70 A2
- ✉ North West Point
- ☎ 345 949 3894
- 💲 $$$$$
- www.boatswainsbeach.ky

Calypso Grill
- ✉ Morgan's Harbour, West Bay
- ☎ 345 949 3948
- www.calypsogrillcayman.com

Cayman Motor Museum

 70 A2

✉ 86 North West Point Rd., West Bay

☎ 345 947 7741

🕐 Closed Sun.

💲 $$$$$

www.caymanmotor museum.com

Pedro St. James

 70 B1

✉ Savannah, off coast road

☎ 345 947 3329

💲 $$$

www.pedrostjames .ky

Queen Elizabeth II Botanic Park

 70 C2

✉ North Side

☎ 345 947 9462

💲 $$$

www.botanic-park.ky

commissioner shot at a bird and missed. His exclamation, "Oh, hell," was adopted as a place-name. The small area of phytokarst rocks is supported by the **Hell post office** and souvenir shop.

South Coast

An excursion along the south coast promises several attractions. The first of these is **Pedro St. James,** just outside the township of Savannah. Built around 1780, this historic building is the oldest surviving structure in the Cayman Islands. The solid stone house was built using slave labor and was originally referred to as St. James Castle. It was in the dining room

INSIDER TIP:

After the Botanic Park closes, I circle northwest to Rum Point and sit on the jetty in the late afternoon sunshine to watch stingrays glide in and the moon rise over the water. It is pure magic.

—JOHN LAWRUS
Manager, Queen Elizabeth II Botanic Park

here that judges held court and Caymanians decided to form an elected legislature. The Proclamation of Emancipation abolishing slavery was read from the Palladian staircase in 1835.

Immaculately restored and furnished with period antiques,

Caymanite

Caymanite is a rare, semiprecious rock that is found only in Cayman Brac and on the eastern end of Grand Cayman. A hard dolomite, it has a composition similar to manganese nodules found on the ocean floor. The stone's colored layers are formed by its various metallic contents, with manganese dominating in the black layers, iron in the red layers, and nickel, titanium, and copper among the others. Polished caymanite jewelry is a popular local souvenir, widely available in Grand Cayman's numerous jewelry stores.

Pedro St. James has a visitor center and audiovisual theater showing a 20-minute multimedia presentation. A stroll in the landscaped gardens is recommended and there are marvelous views from Great Pedro Bluff.

The south coast road then continues east to **Bodden Town,** the original island capital, where the former Mission House has been restored to depict the lifestyles of the families who once lived here.

Queen Elizabeth II Botanic Park

Farther on again, just outside the township of Breakers on Frank Sound, is the Queen Elizabeth II Botanic Park. This 65-acre (26 ha) park is a treasury of colorful

The Caymans' National Museum is housed in a 19th-century George Town building.

and exotic plant life, native woodlands, and a lakeside nature reserve. Halfway around the woodland trail is an iguana enclosure with several specimens of Grand Cayman's endangered blue iguana (see sidebar this page).

Highlights of the park include the new **Orchid Garden** and the dazzling **Floral Colour Garden,** one of Grand Cayman's hidden gems, where flora are laid out by color and open, grassy spaces are interspersed with native trees.

The park's evocative **Heritage Garden** focuses on plants with important roles in Cayman's history, such as medicinal plants and plants of economic importance. The island's heritage is also displayed in a native Caymanian home that was donated to the park.

EXPERIENCE:
Meet Blue Iguanas

The Cayman blue iguana *(Cyclura lewisi)* is the most endangered rock iguana in the West Indies. These gentle blue giants can grow up to 5 feet (1.8 m) in length and are primarily herbivorous. Destruction of their natural habitat has brought the species to the brink of extinction. Fortunately, help is at hand in the form of the Blue Iguana Recovery Program, which offers behind-the-scenes "safari" tours of its captive breeding facility in the **Queen Elizabeth II Botanic Park** *(tel 345 925 7599 for advance reservations, www.blueiguana .ky, closed Sun., $$$$$).*

The house, circa 1900, is now fully restored and a sand garden surrounds it, showing visitors the traditional ornamental plants that once flourished here. ∎

Little Cayman

The smallest and least developed of the Cayman islands, Little Cayman is a far cry from the commercial frenzy of Grand Cayman's Seven Mile Beach. Nine miles (15 km) long and just 1 mile (1.5 km) across at its widest point, the island is predominantly flat scrub in the interior and fringed with palm trees and sea grapes along its shoreline.

Silverside fish make way for a tarpon. Each year the silversides briefly swarm the Cayman waters.

Little Cayman
 71 A1

**Booby Pond
Nature Reserve**
 71 A1
✉ Outside
    Blossom Village
🕐 Closed Sun.

Carib and Arawak peoples may have visited the island from Cuba and Jamaica, drawn by supplies of fresh turtle, but the first permanent settlers were a ragged band of escaped slaves and shipwrecked sailors who set up a turtling station here in the 1660s. By 1900 there were still only 200 people on the island, making a living from phosphate mining, shipbuilding, and turtle catching. A hurricane destroyed most of the houses in 1932,

and the inhabitants migrated to Cayman Brac or Grand Cayman in search of work.

Isolated for decades, Little Cayman (population 150) has remained comparatively undeveloped, and it is the peace, quiet, and wilderness that now attract visitors. Diving, bird-watching, and fishing are the main activities.

The diving is superb (see Travelwise p. 390). Extending along the north shore of the island is **Bloody Bay Marine Park,** one of the Caribbean's most spectacular dive locations. The reef wall here starts in just 20 feet (6 m) of water and plunges some 6,000 feet (1,830 m) to the ocean floor. These pristine walls feature an abundance of marine life, including giant barrel and elephant ear sponges, massive elkhorn corals, lush forests of sea fans, and reef fish of all sizes and descriptions. Eagle rays and turtles flip lazily past in the deep blue, and the coral canyons and crevices harbor a mass of gobies, blennies, basslets, wrasses, and other brilliantly colored fish. Marine scientists monitor conditions from the Little Cayman Research Center at Jackson Point, which can be visited by appointment (see sidebar p. 79).

Around the Island

Life ashore on Little Cayman, where lumbering iguanas enjoy right of way on the roads, can seem a little pedestrian by contrast. The island's hub is Blossom Village, sandwiched between the south coast and **Booby Pond Nature Reserve,** home to the largest colony of red-footed boobies in the Western Hemisphere. Some 20,000 of these pelagic seabirds nest on the RAMSA-designated wetlands preserve, wandering the oceans in search of food by day and returning to roost at night. The Cayman Islands' only breeding colony of magnificent frigatebirds also nests here, and you'll often see them engaged in aerial battles with the boobies as they return at sundown, trying to get them to disgorge

their catch. Drop in at the **Little Cayman National Trust House** (tel 345 749 1121, www .nationaltrust.org.ky) for a peek through the telescopes on their viewing platform. You will also find a selection of local crafts, including caymanite jewelry, and a friendly café. Nearby, the **Little Cayman Museum** (tel 345 948 1033) opens a couple of times a week tracing the island's potted history with exhibits and marine memorabilia.

How Bloody Bay Got Its Name

Legend has it that Little Cayman was once settled by pirates and buccaneers who anchored their ships on the north shore and made forays out to attack passing ships. The British finally dispatched a squadron to deal with this problem by using the element of surprise. As the British vessels sailed into view, the pirates raced for their ships but were cut off and attacked as they attempted to board. The subsequent massacre gave Bloody Bay its sanguinary name.

Beyond **Tarpon Lake,** a large, brackish pond inhabited by a subspecies of tarpon deposited there by Hurricane Gilbert in 1988, the round-island road continues to East End Point Lighthouse and delectable **Point of Sand** beach with terrific views across to sister island Cayman Brac.

For fishing fanatics the main attractions are spectacular bonefishing on the flats of **South Hole Sound** and deep-sea fishing for marlin, tuna, and wahoo. ■

Coral Reefs of the Caribbean

Beneath Caribbean waters lies the complex and colorful environment of coral reefs. This mysterious, enchantingly beautiful world more than matches the terrestrial flora and fauna of the islands. It is second only to the rain forests in terms of biological diversity.

A Cayman Island reef. About a thousand species of fish live in the Caribbean.

The Coral Reef

Coral reefs have existed for 450 million years, making them among the oldest ecosystems on the planet. These remarkable structures have been built up over the centuries by tiny coral animals, or polyps, which convert sunlight and the carbon dioxide from seawater into calcium carbonate with the help of captive partners known as zooxanthellae plants that live within their tissues. The polyps use this calcium carbonate (or limestone) to build the stony structure in which they live. This symbiotic relationship only functions in warm, clear tropical waters where there is enough sunlight for the zooxanthellae to perform.

Like reefs all over the world, Caribbean reefs are subject to numerous stresses including anchor damage, pollution, sedimentation, and coral bleaching caused by ocean warming. Marine tourism can help to preserve coral reefs, but snorkelers and divers must play their part by not touching the corals while underwater and not buying marine souvenirs.

The Caribbean is home to around 50 species of hard corals; each builds its own unique structure. Among the more familiar are the brain corals, which can grow up to 6 feet (1.8 m) across and resemble a human brain; staghorn corals, which branch out like deer antlers; elkhorn corals, which form dense patches in the surf zone; star corals, which are important reef builders; pillar corals, whose distinctive pillars can grow up to 10 feet (3 m) high; and boulder corals, which are found almost everywhere.

There are also about 20 species of soft corals, the most prominent of which are large sea fans, or gorgonians. Others include black corals, sea whips, sea plumes, and sea rods. Colorful sponges of all descriptions—delicate azure vase sponges, bloodred barrel sponges, and bright yellow tube sponges—are another important component in the dynamic reef environment, playing host to tiny invertebrates or providing hiding places for fish.

Reef Fish

The Caribbean is home to about a thousand species of fish belonging to more than 140 families. Many of them display a dazzling array of colors as they school around the reef. Among the most common are butterfly fish, particularly the four-eyed and banded butterfly fish, and angelfish, such as the magnificent queen angelfish, the yellow-and-gray French angelfish, and the black-and-yellow rock beauty. Damselfish are at home on the shallow reefs, darting out from their hiding places in the coral to graze on algae; one species, the striped sergeant major, lays its eggs in round patches and defends them aggressively against all comers.

The wrasse family are prime scavengers on the reef, and their behavior is full of surprises. The males rule a harem of females, but should the dominant male get eaten,

Coral and sponges on a reef in Bonaire in the Dutch Caribbean

then one of the females changes sex to take his place. Closely related to the wrasses are the brightly colored parrot fish, 14 species of which live in the Caribbean. Parrot fish feed off algae on the coral rock, grinding up surprisingly large quantities of coral with their powerful jaws and then expelling it as coral sand.

EXPERIENCE:
Research the Reef

An adjunct of the nonprofit Central Caribbean Marine Institute, the **Little Cayman Research Center**'s dual remit is to promote conservation awareness through education and carry out a year-round program of ocean field research monitoring the health of the local marine environment and its residents. Experienced divers interested in extending or enhancing their knowledge of the reef can join the **Dive With a Researcher** (DWAR) program, assisting the center's own reef experts in collecting and collating underwater data on a variety of projects (*information and reservations, www.reefresearch.org, $$$$$*).

Food-catching tentacles

Mouth

Stomach

Polyp skeletons

Coral polyp

Young coral

Volcanic cone continually erodes as its base sinks into the sea.

The volcanic cone vanishes beneath the sea, and coral grows over it.

Volcanic cone: layers of ash and lava

Tropical vegetation

Sandy lagoon

Channels in the coral let nutrient-bearing water flow into the lagoon.

Limestone formed by skeletons of polyps

Predator species often seen hovering near the reef include jacks, pompano, and scads, as well as the ubiquitous snappers, of which there are 19 species. Snappers usually school facing into the current, maintaining the same position in the water column and grabbing anything that comes their way. Groupers, like snappers, are prime food fish and are therefore not as common as they once were. Groupers are impressively large and can grow up to 8 feet (2.5 m) in length and weigh more than 650 pounds (295 kg). The great barracuda usually hunts on its own, often around a chosen reef or wreck site; the three smaller species of reef barracuda are more often seen in schools.

Vegetation grows on the sandy islands that ring the lagoon.

Manta

Eagle ray

Staghorn coral

Green turtle

Nurse shark

Elkhorn coral

Redtail parrot

Sergeant major fish

Four-eyed butterfly

Banded butterfly

Damsels

Barracuda

Grouper (yellow mouth)

Rainbow parrot

Snapper

Blue sponge

Scads

Tiger shark

Electric ray

Jack

Queen angel

Sand and fine material are deposited at low tide until sandy islands are formed.

Black coral

French angel

Brain coral

Rock beauty

Yellow tube sponge

Sharks, Rays, & Turtles

The Caribbean has 44 recorded species of sharks, although most of these stay away from areas with people. The most common is the harmless nurse shark, often found resting on the seabed. There are 22 species of rays, among them the southern stingray (which inhabits Grand Cayman's famous Stingray City), the majestic eagle ray, and the electric ray. Probably the most awe-inspiring ray is the Atlantic manta, also known as the devilfish or giant devil ray, but it is rare to encounter these graceful creatures. Other Caribbean residents include hawksbill and green turtles, although their numbers are now much reduced because of human predation for their meat and shells.

Cayman Brac

Although it's just 90 miles (145 km) to the northeast of Grand Cayman, Cayman Brac seems a world away from the frenetic atmosphere of the main island. Quiet, easygoing, and laid-back are some of the adjectives used to describe this little island, which is usually referred to as "the Brac."

Cayman Brac

🅰 71 C2

Visitor Information

✉ Department of Tourism, West End Community Park

☎ 345 948 1649

www.itsyours toexplore.com

The island supports a thriving community of about 1,800 people. Residents (known as Brackers) are renowned for their hospitality and friendliness, and there's a warm welcome at the island tourist office too, which offers every visitor a free nature tour accompanied by a local guide.

The Brac is 12 miles (19 km) long and just a mile (1.5 km) wide. Its western portion is flat, whereas the eastern half is dominated by a central bluff, which rises to dramatic cliffs some 140 feet high (42 m) at the shoreline. This landmark bluff gives the island its name (*brac* is Gaelic for "bluff").

The bluff supports a wide variety of plant life, most notably saguaro cactuses and century plants, and bird species including boobies, frigatebirds, white tropic birds, herons, egrets, and bananaquits.

Other island inhabitants include a small population of endangered Cayman Brac parrots. The best place to look for them is in the **Brac Parrot Reserve,** which covers 180 acres (73 ha) of rocky woodland on the bluff. The reserve is reached by taking the main cross-island route, and turning down Major Donald Drive (also known as Lighthouse Road), toward the lighthouse at North East Point.

The island is crisscrossed with hiking trails, and you can explore limestone caves around the bluff, such as **Peter's Cave** at Spot Bay, famous as a hurricane shelter.

Offshore, the main attraction on Brac is scuba diving. The Brac is surrounded by pristine reefs teeming with fish and has around 60 registered dive sites. Of particular note is the spectacular wreck of a former Soviet warship sunk off the West End in September 1996 to become an artificial reef. Renamed the **M.V. *Captain Keith Tibbets*** in honor of a local personality, it now lies in 55 to 110 feet (17–33 m) of water, a swimmable distance from the shore. ■

Brac Boatbuilding

The Brac's first settlers were a random assortment of pirates and refugees, including Jamaican planters, shipwrecked mariners, and adventurers. In 1833 slaves from Africa arrived on Cayman Brac and quickly established the island's reputation for boatbuilding, which remained one of its principal activities until the 1960s, when sail was superseded by motor yachts. Small, simple sailboats used for turtle catching, known as "catboats," were also built here, originally with local wood shaped by hand. The story of the Brac's early days is related in the quaint **Cayman Brac Museum** *(Stake Bay, tel 345 948 2622, closed Sat.& Sun., donations).*

An unspoiled natural gem, some 40 low-lying islands and cays
scattered across nearly 250 square miles (650 sq km) of ocean

Turks & Caicos Islands

A Turks & Caicos beach

Turks & Caicos Islands

The Turks & Caicos Islands lie about 575 miles (926 km) southeast of Miami and consist of two island groups separated by the 22-mile-wide (35 km) Columbus Passage. To the west is the Caicos group: West Caicos, Providenciales, North Caicos, Middle Caicos, East Caicos, and South Caicos. To the east is the Turks group: Grand Turk and Salt Cay. The country's eight main islands and assorted small cays translate to just 193 square miles (500 sq km) of dry land, 80 percent of which is uninhabited.

The Turks & Caicos Islands (TCI) are more sea than land. They are located on two huge, shallow, sand-covered limestone banks, larger than the land above sea level, that provide important habitats for marine life. Many are covered with sea-grass meadows harboring burrowing sea urchins, sea cucumbers, and mollusks. The banks are a rich fishing ground, and the 8,000-foot-deep (2,400 m) passage that divides them is popular with migrating humpback whales, rays, turtles, and dolphins. The breathtaking underwater scenery has propelled the islands into the top five rankings of the world's best dive destinations.

The first inhabitants of these islands were Lucayan migrating from Haiti; they arrived in the Bahamas chain around 1,200 years ago. After making landfall on Sand Cay or the Seal Cays, the Lucayan established themselves on the northwest corner of Grand Turk. This site, which has been extensively excavated, is the oldest known settlement in the Bahamas chain and was occupied from around A.D. 705 to

1170. Analysis of bones at the site reveals that the inhabitants ate mostly sea turtles. Artifacts recovered include shell beads, a mother-of-pearl pendant, a nearly complete greenstone ax, and conch-shell tools. The most important find from pre-Columbian times on Grand Turk has been a wooden paddle, dating from A.D. 1100. It is now on display in the Turks & Caicos National Museum.

No one lived on the islands when the first

NOT TO BE MISSED:

Europeans arrived. Controversy surrounds the issue of whether Columbus made his landfall here or on San Salvador in the Bahamas; the evidence points to the latter. In the 17th century, Bermudians settled Grand Turk, Salt Cay, and South Caicos, using slave labor to rake the *salinas* (salt pans) for the salt trade. They also deforested the islands in order to speed up the evaporation process.

During the American Revolution, Loyalists fleeing the conflict set up plantations here for sisal and cotton, again using slave labor. With the abolition of slavery in 1834 the plantation system collapsed, and the Loyalists left the islands. The slaves remained and relied on subsistence farming and fishing. The old plantations eventually returned to wilderness.

Despite their connections with the Bermudian salt rakers, the islands were under the jurisdiction of the Bahamas from the 18th century until annexed to Jamaica in 1873. After Jamaican independence in 1962, the salt industry foundered and TCI became a British Crown Colony.

Tourism on the islands has exploded in recent years, and the islands have garnered a reputation for a distinctive brand of laid-back luxury teamed with a strong element of eco-awareness as the local industry strives to avoid the pitfalls of overdevelopment. Opinion is still divided over the merits of certain hotel developments on Providenciales, but TCI can still boast dozens of stunning untouched beaches and dive sites, and a choice of boutique boltholes on quiet cays, so nobody needs to worry quite yet. ■

Grand Turk

Grand Turk covers only 7 square miles (18 sq km), but it is the second most populous island in the group and home to Cockburn Town, an attractive old colonial port and the seat of government. As with other islands in the Turks & Caicos, the vegetation is chiefly scrub and cactus, interspersed with flat expanses of unused salt pans. Wild donkeys and horses wander freely, descended from ancestors who once played a vital role in the salt industry.

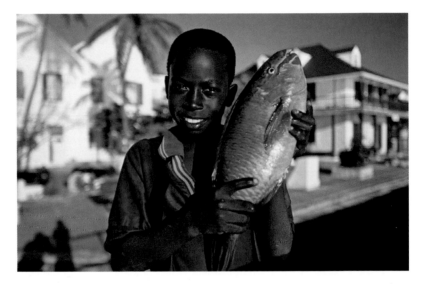

A boy shows off a parrot fish, which are able to change their gender and coloration.

Grand Turk
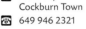 85 E2

Visitor Information

✉ Front St.,
Cockburn Town

☎ 649 946 2321

**www.turksand
caicostourism
.com**

What Grand Turk lacks in natural beauty on land is more than made up for by the glorious, exuberant world of its coral reefs. Just a stone's throw offshore on the west side of the island, a sheer wall drops away from about 40 to 7,000 feet (12–2,134 m) in one fell swoop, providing some of the most thrilling reef diving in the Caribbean. All diving off Grand Turk is within 10 to 15 minutes of the shoreline, so operators simply pick up clients from the beach outside their hotels and whisk them straight to the

dive sites. All the operators use small boats, carrying around six people, and offer a personal service.

One of the best excursions is Sea Eye's half-day barbecue trip to **Gibb's Cay,** an uninhabited island where you can hand-feed and snorkel with stingrays and free dive to the seabed for conch, which the crew will then use in a conch salad.

Don't come to Grand Turk if you're looking for shopping or sophisticated nightlife. Who needs them when you can watch Atlantic humpback whales migrating from an observation point up by the old lighthouse? The island is perfect for those who appreciate quirky, out-of-the-way places, friendly "belongers," and a relaxed pace. You can cycle the entire length of the island in a couple of hours.

Cockburn Town

Grand Turk's hub is Cockburn Town. Its pretty, historic heart around Duke Street and Front Street is ideal for a gentle stroll and a cool drink in one of the old inns. The government offices reside in a series of brightly painted buildings surrounding a small square where old cannon still face out to sea. Slightly to the north, you'll see the blue-trimmed **Odd Fellows Lodge,** one of the oldest buildings on the island. Folklore has it that the emancipation of the slaves was announced here in 1832.

INSIDER TIP:

I always recommend that visitors try parasailing or taking a helicopter ride—each provides a bird's eye view of the islands' pristine beauty.

—KIMO TYNES
Turks & Caicos Tourist Board

Grand Turk's unexpected jewel is the superb **Turks & Caicos National Museum.** It is housed in the pre-1825 stone Guinep House, which is thought to have been built by a former

---

Conked Out

One of the most popular visitor attractions on Providenciales (see p. 94) has established a sister facility on Grand Turk. ConchWorld *(Matheson's Point, tel 646 242 5797, www.conchworld.com, $$$$)* **lifts the lid on marine mollusk farming in the islands, but it opens only if there's a cruise ship in the harbor.**

---

shipwright, who named it after the magnificent guinep tree outside its door.

The museum's centerpiece is its extensive display on the Molasses Reef Wreck, the oldest European shipwreck so far discovered in the Caribbean. The early 16th-century Spanish caravel foundered on the rim of the Caicos Bank, and numerous items from the ship are on display. Remains of the hull and rigging, as well as cannon, crossbows, tools, and the crew's personal possessions, provide a fascinating time capsule of the daily life of early explorers. The upper floor of the museum is devoted to natural history, the salt trade, the Lucayan, and other aspects of the islands' history.

If you continue on down Front Street, passing the governor's office, **Waterloo** *(Front St., tel 649 946 2308),* built as a private residence in 1815, you'll reach South Base, a former U.S. Air Force missile tracking base that had its moment of fame in 1962 when the first U.S. astronaut to go into orbit around the Earth, John Glenn, was brought ashore here after his Mercury capsule splashed down just offshore. ∎

Turks & Caicos National Museum

✉ Guinep House, Front St.

☎ 649 946 2160

🕐 Closed Sun.

💲 $$

www.tcmuseum .org

Islands Around Grand Turk

With few inhabitants but a wealth of history, East Caicos, Salt Cay, and South Caicos once held plantations and salt pans. Now they offer birds, whales, beautiful beaches, and spectacular diving in pristine locations.

The salt ponds on Salt Cay are reminders of the industry that once supported the island.

East Caicos
🅰 85 D3
☎ 649 946 2321

Salt Cay
🅰 85 E2
☎ 649 946 2321

South Caicos
🅰 85 D2
☎ 649 946 2321

East Caicos

Covering some 18 square miles (47 sq km), East Caicos is one of the largest islands in the archipelago and the largest uninhabited island in the Caribbean. **Flamingo Hill,** on its north side, is the highest point (156 feet/48 m) in the Turks & Caicos, but most of the island consists of swamps, mangroves, and tidal mudflats.

At the beginning of the 20th century, the settlement of Jacksonville, now empty, administered a 50,000-acre (20,000 ha) sisal plantation and cattle farm. Near Jacksonville are several caves with evidence of Lucayan occupation, including petroglyphs carved on the walls.

Salt Cay

The only other inhabited island in the Turks group, Salt Cay lies 7 miles (11 km) to the south of Grand Turk. Bermudians first landed here in 1645, and salt production began in 1673, lasting until the collapse of the industry in the 1960s.

Declared a UNESCO World Heritage site, Salt Cay has a landscape dominated by reminders of its age-old industry. Miles of intricate low stone walls and canals (used to speed up evaporation) are still visible, as are numerous derelict windmills. The old salt ponds have renewed purpose as an important habitat for wading birds and ospreys. Bermudian architecture predominates in the sleepy settlement of **Balfour Town,** where Salt Cay's residents (there are fewer than 100 of them) will welcome you with open arms. There are a couple of small hotels and bars, shops, and the **White House,** which was built in the 1830s from stone ballast carried in ships' holds.

In the 19th century, Salt Cay was also a major center for whaling. Nowadays the whales are more valuable alive than dead. Visitors may be lucky enough to spot migrating humpbacks from January through March.

Like Grand Turk, Salt Cay was deforested long ago, but the lack of terrestrial flora is more than compensated for by a flourishing underwater environment. The island has many buoyed dive sites and offers virgin diving on its reef walls with their tunnels, undercuts, and caverns. A diving highlight is the wreck of the **H.M.S. Endymion,** a British warship dating from 1790; it lies in about 25 feet (8 m) of water.

South Caicos

Tourists very seldom visit South Caicos, once a major commercial center for the islands, but this was not always the case. In fact, the island had the first hotel in the Turks & Caicos Islands, the Admiral's Arms Inn; it opened in the 19th century to serve the Brazilian pilots who stopped here en route between Miami and South America.

During the 19th century, South Caicos was a major player in the salt trade when the salinas of Grand Turk and Salt Cay could not meet the demand for salt from the North American market. The salinas here were fed by a unique boiling hole, a subterranean passage that allowed salt water to naturally flow into the pans, where windmills pumped it into a series of reservoirs. The island exported more salt than any of the other islands and even to set up three steam-driven salt mills.

Island Donkeys

Grand Turk was once famous for its donkeys, which were found all over the island, roaming the scrub, foraging in gardens, standing quietly in the shade, or even holding up traffic on the roads. They were introduced by settlers in the 17th century to haul cartloads of salt to waiting ships. By the 1800s more than 800 of the long-eared beasts resided on the island, but after the salt trade collapsed in 1964, the donkeys came to be viewed as a nuisance rather than an asset. Some were exported to Islands that needed them, such as Jamaica. Many now live in a donkey sanctuary on the north shore. About 50 animals, however, still roam free.

Today South Caicos is a fishing center still recovering from damage caused by Hurricane Ike in 2008. **Cockburn Harbour** has one of the best anchorages in the archipelago, superb beaches (particularly Long Beach), excellent diving on the breathtaking coral walls near its eastern shoreline, and beautiful, uninhabited cays nearby (Long Cay, Ambergris Cays, Fish Cays, and Bush Cay) that can be visited on day trips. Accessible only by boat, none of the cays have any accommodations. ■

Middle Caicos

With an area of 48 square miles (124 sq km), this is the largest island in the Turks & Caicos archipelago, linked by a divable causeway to North Caicos (see p. 92). The 275 inhabitants of Conch Bar, Lorimers, and Bambarra depend on fishing and small-scale tourism.

Dolphins can often be found frolicking off the Turks & Caicos Islands.

Middle Caicos

🅰 85 C3

Visitor Information

✉ Front St., Cockburn Town, Grand Turk

☎ 649 946 2321

www.turksand caicostourism .com

Since the arrival of the causeway, twin-island day-trip tours to both Middle and North Caicos have become a popular option from Providenciales and Grand Turk (see sidebar opposite). Independent travelers can rent bikes or cars to get around, but guided tours can pack more in with easy access to sites such as the caves of Conch Bar and old plantation ruins.

Middle, or Grand, Caicos was occupied by the Taíno between A.D. 750 and 1500; these early settlers called it Aniyana. **Armstrong Pond,** south of Bambarra, was an important Taíno settlement (one of 38 on the island). It features the only ceremonial ball court in the region and an arrangement of stones that may have had astrological significance for the Taíno.

Wild About Wildlife

Middle Caicos is one of the main nesting sites in the archipelago for the impressive ocean-going frigatebird, which also nests on Penniston Cay and other uninhabited islands. The pristine cays are important nesting areas for the sooty and roseate terns, Audubon's shearwater, and brown noddies as well. Four species of turtles (hawksbill, green, loggerhead, and leatherback) live in the surrounding waters, although local consumption of these endangered species is still common. The islands have a flourishing population of playful bottlenose dolphins, and in the winter months (January to March), majestic Atlantic humpback whales pass by on their way from cold northern seas to their breeding grounds southeast of Grand Turk. Divers often hear their haunting songs underwater.

INSIDER TIP:

The beaches of Middle Caicos are secluded and simply spectacular. To explore, arrange to have a rental car meet your ferry at the dock.

—CLARE JARDINE
Owner, Dive Provo

In the town of **Conch Bar,** on the north coast, you can explore a series of imposing limestone caves decorated with stalagmites and stalactites and home to bats and saltwater lagoons (included on island tours). Lucayan artifacts have been found here.

The island's northwest coast is characterized by dramatic limestone cliffs (unique in the archipelago) interspersed with beautiful, deserted beaches. A trail along the coastline, known as the **Crossing Place Trail,** was the main highway on the island for centuries. It runs for 12 glorious miles (19 km) through some of the most memorable scenery in the TCI, ending up at the causeway crossing to North Caicos.

Another unusual feature is **Ocean Hole,** on the southwest coast of the island, which is 1,200 feet (366 m) wide and about 200 feet (60 m) deep. This "blue hole" is thought to have been a land cave before being flooded many thousands of years ago and losing its roof. This marine sinkhole is home to bonefish, sharks, and other pelagic fish, and visitors can reach it only by boat. ■

EXPERIENCE:
Heart of the Islands

Island tour specialists **Big Blue Unlimited** (tel 649 946 5034, www.bigblue.tc, $$$$$) offers an excellent guided day trip to Middle and North Caicos that combines sightseeing with activities. The full-day excursion departs from Providenciales, and the fun begins with snorkeling around the Caicos Bank reefs. On North Caicos, there's a tour of Wade's Green and home-cooked lunch with a local host, followed by flamingo spotting. Across the causeway on Middle Caicos, a caving experience and shopping for local crafts is followed by a swim. Big Blue also leads kayaking, birding, biking, and hiking trips.

North Caicos

In contrast to the aridity of most islands in the group, North Caicos is comparatively lush and is considered the garden center of the country. It has a higher rainfall (for reasons not fully understood) and its fertile soil produces abundant crops of tomatoes, corn, papaya, yam, pumpkin, lime, and avocado on farms tucked away in the interior.

North Caicos

🅰 85 C4

Visitor Information

✉ Front St.,
Cockburn Town,
Grand Turk

☎ 649 946 2321

**www.turksand
caicostourism.com**

Like its sister islands Middle and East Caicos, its southern reaches consist mostly of mangrove lagoons and swamps. On the north coast, powdery sand beaches slope into a shimmering lagoon that leads out to a line of breakers crashing onto the offshore reef. Most of the 1,400-strong population lives in a handful of modest settlements. **Bottle Creek** is the commercial center, while hotels

Caicos idiosyncratic history: Hungry Hole (a hidden lagoon); Ready Money (a plot of land that changed hands swiftly because the buyer had just that); Pumpkin Bluff Pond; and Laughland. **Wade's Green Plantation** is the legacy of a Loyalist refugee from Florida who was granted 860 acres (340 ha) for a cotton plantation near Belleville. By the time of his death in 1821 Wade Stubbs had nearly 400 slaves working on his plantation, now one of the best preserved ruins in the Caicos Islands from the Loyalist period.

Bird-watching is a major attraction. North Caicos has the second largest population of flamingos in the Caribbean, but depending on where they are in the extensive **Flamingo Pond Nature Reserve,** you may see them only as pink dots in the distance, so take binoculars. Flamingos can also be spotted at **Three Mary Cays Sanctuary,** where ospreys nest. Indigenous rock iguanas inhabit **East Bay Island National Park.**

Protected under the international RAMSAR convention, the **Caicos Nature Reserve** (see sidebar this page) supports West Indian flamingos and other waterbirds, including West Indian whistling ducks and breeding colonies of magnificent frigatebirds. ∎

Caicos Nature Reserve

Stretching over 210 square miles (544 sq km), the North, Grand, and East Caicos Nature Reserve is one of the Caribbean's largest protected areas. A wilderness of tidal sloughs, mangroves, mudflats, and saline ponds, this important wetland zone links the dry uplands of the islands with the turquoise coastal shallows. Submerged banks, creeks, and lagoons provide critical nursery habitat for flamingos, lobsters, conchs, turtles, and other marine species.

**Wade's Green
Plantation**

☎ 649 941 5710

🕐 Tours by appt.

💲 $

**www.tcinational
trust.org**

and guesthouses are found on the north coast at **Whitby.**

A popular day-trip destination, North Caicos is just a 10-minute flight from Providenciales; ferries take 30 minutes. Bicycles are a good way to get around and some rental cars are available.

Place-names echo the North

Providenciales (Provo)

On a cloudy day you can sometimes see a green sheen on the underside of the cloud banks over Providenciales. This unique phenomenon is caused by reflections from the shallow, dazzlingly blue inland lagoons that stretch across Chalk Sound National Park.

About 25 miles (40 km) long and 3 miles (5 km) wide, Providenciales is the most developed of the islands in terms of tourism and commerce, and is the main airport gateway to the TCI. Commonly called Provo, the island has wide sandy beaches and dramatic offshore diving sites. It makes an excellent jumping-off point for exploring further afield.

Along the north shore, **Grace Bay's** superb 12-mile (19 km) sweep of fine, powdery white sand ranks among the top beaches in the Caribbean and has attracted most of Provo's hotel and condominium development. Bordering the bay is the **Princess Alexandra Marine Park,** a vast area of offshore patch reefs, walls, and lagoons. There is excellent diving here and along the coast at Northwest Point.

Parks & Plantations

Behind the south coast, the **Chalk Sound National Park** encompasses a huge expanse of shallow turquoise water dotted with green rocky cays, popular with a variety of bird species. In the eastern corner, Sapodilla Bay has a lovely secluded beach; on the cliffs behind the bay, shipwrecked sailors once carved their names in the rock.

Snorkelers ply the crystal-clear waters off Provo.

EXPERIENCE: Go Fish

The TCI are a Mecca for keen anglers. Deep-sea fishing expeditions set out from the islands in search of marlin, tuna, wahoo, and more. Closer to the shore, grouper, snapper, and jacks are commonly caught, and the shallows are bonefish territory. Also known as "phantoms," bonefish bottom-feed on shrimp and crab and can grow up to 10 to 14 pounds (4.5–6 kg). They're notorious fighters, and once hooked can take off at speeds of up to 25 mph (40 kph).

If you want to pit your wits against local gamefish, let experienced fishing guides **Silver Deep** (Grace Bay, tel 649 946 5612, www.silverdeep.com, $$$$$) or **Beyond the Blue** (tel 649 231 1703 or U.S. 321/795-3136, www.beyondtheblue.com, $$$$$) guide you to your quarry.

Providenciales

🅰 84 B3

Visitor Information

✉ Stubbs Diamond Plaza, Le Deck Rd., The Bight

☎ 649 946 4970

www.turksand caicostourism .com

ConchWorld

🅰 84 B3

✉ Heaving Dock Rd.

☎ 649 946 5330

🕐 Closed Sun.

💲 $$$

www.conchworld .com

Heading back toward the north coast, the ruins of **Cheshire Hall** can be seen just off the Leeward Highway. This was one of three large cotton and sisal plantations started by Loyalists fleeing the American revolution.

Blue Hills

Of Provo's three original settlements—Five Cays, Blue Hills, and The Bight (meaning "the Bay")—the most scenic is Blue Hills, a small fishing port on the north coast. Government offices and other businesses are located in the downtown, near the airport, but in general the island lacks a focal point. Shopping malls and other facilities have sprung up haphazardly along the main road, the Leeward Highway. The closest the island has to a central focus

is **Turtle Cove,** where you'll find hotels, a few restaurants, and a tourist office clustered around the yacht basin. At the eastern end of the island, the 6,560-yard (6,000 m), par-72 championship golf course designed by Karl Litton is one of the best in the Caribbean.

Continue on until the road runs out and you will reach the deep channel that separates Provo from adjacent Mangrove Cay. Sheltered in this natural harbor is the busy **Leeward Marina,**

INSIDER TIP:

There are several excellent restaurants in Providenciales, but prepare for sticker shock—expect to pay double mainland U.S. prices.

—ROBERT GIROUX
Programmer, National Geographic Global Media

where ferries and boat trips depart for the out islands.

Alongside the marina is **ConchWorld.** The only one of its kind in the world, this mollusk farm was set up in 1984 to develop techniques for conch harvesting (the creature is becoming endangered in the wild). The educational tour of the farm embraces the various stages the conchs move through, from the hatchery to the subsea pasture, where they grow to maturity. The conch farm exports live conchs to Florida and also sells them to local restaurants. ∎

Islands Around Providenciales

Easily reached by boat from Provo, these islands and cays are a nature lover's delight. Little Water Cay features endangered iguanas, West Caicos flamingoes, and Parrot Cay a sybaritic getaway complete with diving, sailing, excursions, and a spa.

Little Water Cay

This uninhabited cay close to Provo, now a protected area under the Turks & Caicos National Trust, is popular with day-trippers who come to see its endangered rock iguanas (see sidebar p. 96). Several tour companies, including Sail Provo *(tel 649 946 4783, www.sailprovo .com)* run boat excursions to the island.

Parrot Cay

Originally known as Pirate Cay, this 1,300-acre (526 ha) luxury resort island was once run as a plantation. Between 1718 and 1720 it was home to the notorious pirate Anne Bonney and her lover, pirate captain "Calico Jack" Rackham. Today, you are more likely to encounter A list celebrities enjoying a little

An isolated beach's conch shack

secluded down time *(Parrot Cay Resort, tel 649 946 7788, www.parrotcay.com)*.

West Caicos

Isolated and uninhabited, West Caicos is renowned for its excellent diving *(visited by day boats*

Little Water Cay
🅰 84 B3

Parrot Cay
🅰 84 B4

West Caicos
🅰 84 A3

Island Conchs

The beautiful, pink-lipped shellfish known as the queen conch *(Strombus gigas)* has been a staple of the Caribbean diet since long before Columbus arrived in the New World. Millions of conchs (pronounced "conks") are harvested annually in the shallow waters surrounding the Bahamas, Bermuda, Florida, and the Turks & Caicos. Conch shells are often sold to tourists as souvenirs or jewelry, placed on Caribbean graves, and even used as building materials in place of bricks.

The high demand for conch and subsequent overfishing in the waters surrounding the Caicos Bank has resulted in a noticeable decline in the conch harvest, to the point that conchs are now listed as an endangered species. Some countries in the Caribbean have banned the export of queen conch shells, and tourists returning home will often find their conch shells confiscated while clearing customs. It's better to admire the living animals in their habitat and leave the shells behind.

This rock iguana may look fierce, but the species is actually gentle and shy—and endangered.

from Providenciales). During the mid-18th century the island was used as a base by the French corsair Jean Thomas Dulaien. Later, when known as Yankee Town, it was cleared for salinas (salt ponds) and sisal plantations in the 1890s. Today, ruins of the sisal plant, railroad tracks, and steam engines can still be seen. At the island's center is **Lake Catherine,** a nature reserve that is home to ospreys, herons, and pink flamingos.

Diving West Caicos

West Caicos has 6 miles (10 km) of reefs along its leeward shoreline, with a reef wall that starts around 35 to 45 feet (11–14 m) dropping away to depths of 6,000 feet (18,000 m). The dive sites here are renowned for their enormous, colorful sponges, beautiful coral formations, black corals, and gorgonia.

Fish life includes jacks, Nassau groupers, moray eels, and French angelfish, while out in the blue there is always the chance of spotting big pelagics such as sharks, eagle and manta rays, turtles, and possibly even hammerheads or enormous whale sharks. ■

Rock Iguanas

The rock iguana species *(Cyclura carinata)* seen on Little Water Cay is unique to these islands. This long-lived, territorial reptile mates but once a year, producing 7 to 12 eggs per clutch. Rock iguanas have disappeared from many inhabited islands due to predation by humans, cats, and dogs. About 50,000 rock iguanas remain in the Turks & Caicos, the largest population in the world, with about 2,000 on Little Water Cay and the rest on Ambergris Cay, at Fort George, and in other island reserves.

Site of the first Spanish colony in the Americas, with everything from colonial architecture to superb beaches

Dominican Republic

A stained-glass window in Santo Domingo's Catedral Basilica Santa María la Menor

Dominican Republic

Occupying the eastern two-thirds of the island of Hispaniola (the remaining third is Haiti), the Dominican Republic was home to the first European colony in the New World. It has the Caribbean's highest peak, largest lake, and biggest city. But above all it is known for its extensive white-sand beaches, around 1,000 miles (1,500 km) of them. Beyond the beach resorts, if you're adventurous, you will discover an enormously diverse country.

This fertile island was heavily populated by Taíno Indians when Columbus first arrived on its shores in 1492. He named it Isla Española (or Hispaniola) and decided it would be ideal for a colony, especially since gold deposits were also discovered.

The present-day capital, Santo Domingo, was established at the mouth of the Ozama River in 1496. During the early years of Spanish rule, the economy was fueled by gold, but by 1515 the gold had run out and the Spanish began to ignore Hispaniola in favor of the more lucrative mines of South America and the prospect of wealth in Mexico.

By the 17th century the northwestern part of the island was occupied by pirates and French buccaneers, who managed to resist attempts by the Spanish to drive them out. France took advantage of this to claim the

western third of the island in 1697. Over the next century Saint Domingue, as the French portion was known, became one of the richest colonies in the Caribbean thanks to sugarcane

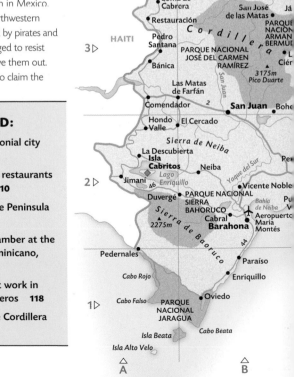

plantations. The eastern part of the island languished under the Spanish, whose attentions had moved elsewhere.

In the 1790s Toussaint L'Ouverture (1743–1803) led a slave uprising in Saint Domingue. This began several decades of unrest, in which independence forces fought both the French and Spanish. On January 1, 1804, the Republic of Haiti was declared on the western part of the island, and in 1821 independence was declared in the east. But it was not to last. The Haitians invaded in 1822 and controlled the whole island for the next 22 years. An underground opposition movement, La Trinitaria, seized control in 1844 and declared the independence of the new country, known as the Dominican Republic.

Since independence and the dark years under Gen. Rafael Leonidas Trujillo (1891–1961), from 1930 until 1961, the Dominican Republic has gradually established itself as a stable Latin-Caribbean democracy. The economy is based on tourism, agriculture, and mineral exports. Concentrated on the north and east coast beaches, tourism is the big breadwinner, far outweighing the contribution of the agricultural sector. However, farmers have been encouraged to diversify, and traditional crops, such as sugarcane, coffee, cocoa, and tobacco, have been augmented by fruits and vegetables, live plants, and cut flowers. The Dominican Republic is also the world's leading exporter of hand-rolled cigars, producing 500 million stogies annually. ■

Santo Domingo

The capital and chief port of the Dominican Republic, Santo Domingo is the oldest city in the New World. The city was founded by Christopher Columbus's brother Bartoloméo in 1498, after the Spanish abandoned their attempts to found a colony on the north coast. Today, it is the commercial heart of the Dominican Republic and home to some 2.5 million people.

Students from nearby schools often meet in verdant Parque Colón, in Santo Domingo's colonial city.

Built on the east bank of the Río Ozama, the city was christened Nueva Isabel. The name changed to Santo Domingo when the city was moved to the west bank after a hurricane in 1502. It flourished as a port, and from here the Spanish launched major expeditions to Mexico, Puerto Rico, Cuba, and the Pacific. As the riches of the Spanish Main were revealed, Santo Domingo lost its preeminent position in the Caribbean. It suffered a further blow in 1562, when an earthquake destroyed much of the city. English privateer Sir Francis Drake (circa 1540–1596) also caused considerable damage when he attacked the port in 1586.

Despite its decline, Santo Domingo remained the political and commercial center of the country. During the regime of Rafael Trujillo, Santo Domingo was known as Ciudad Trujillo, but with the death of the dictator it reverted to its previous name.

These days, Santo Domingo is the hub of life in the Dominican Republic, a magnet for commerce from neighboring islands, and a must-see for its beautifully restored colonial heart. The Ciudad Colonial (Colonial City), a 12-block UNESCO World Heritage site, is the most attractive

Dominican Merengue

Throughout the Dominican Republic you'll hear the sound of merengue, the national passion and the music at the heart of Carnival, local fiestas, and dances. Traditionally this fast music has been played by a *perico ripiao* (three-man combo) performing on either a *tres* or *cuatro* (both are similar to a guitar), a *tambora* (double drum), and a *güira*. Once fashioned from a calabash gourd, the hollow güira cylinder makes a distinctive rhythmic buzzing sound when scraped.

The country's exuberant annual Merengue Festival is held between late July and early August. Most of the action takes place on Santo Domingo's Malecón, transformed into a vast open-air disco. Several days of music, hosted by popular DJs, keep your body moving in the D.R.'s most sultry dance; a "best artist" is chosen and awarded a large cash prize.

part of the metropolis, with pleasant squares, outdoor cafés, and a wealth of historic buildings.

The Colonial City

The historic colonial city lies on the western banks of the Río Ozama, overlooking the cruise ship terminal and Puerto Ozama. You should certainly allow at least a day to visit its sights; come equipped with a map and comfortable shoes (see also pp. 106–107).

Among the key historic buildings in this area is the **Fortaleza Ozama.** Built by Governor Nicolás de Ovando in 1503 on a steep bank overlooking the mouth of the Río Ozama, the fortress was Santo Domingo's principal defense from the 16th century on and was occupied by the military until the 1970s. The last fort to be built by the Spanish as they moved from north to south across the island, it guarded the harbor throughout the colonial period. You enter via a neoclassical gateway added in 1787.

Directly ahead is the impressive **Torre del Homenaje** (Tower of Homage), a solid structure with 7-foot-thick (2 m) walls whose clean lines and battlements give it the semblance of a medieval castle. Its design is unique in the New World. You can climb to the top of the turret to gain some idea of the strategic importance of the fort, which guarded every major Spanish flotilla as it left the harbor for the conquest of the Americas—although the historical illusion is hard to conjure up in the face of the giant cement factory looming on the opposite side of the river.

To one side of the tower is an 18th-century armory, beyond which can be seen the remnants of a temporary fort built before the tower was erected. The statue on the grounds is of Gonzalo Fernandez de Oviedo, the fort's governor from 1533 to 1557.

For a fascinating insight into colonial domestic life, don't miss the **Museo Alcázar de Colón.** Built between 1511 and 1516 by Diego de Colón (Columbus's son, who became the first viceroy of the New World), this impressive building has a beautiful Renaissance facade with graceful arcades and is

Santo Domingo

🅰 99 D2

Visitor Information

✉ Calle Isabel La Catolica 103, Ciudad Colonial

☎ 809 686 3858

Fortaleza Ozama

✉ Calle Las Damas

☎ 809 686 0222

💲 $

Museo Alcázar de Colón

✉ Plaza de España

☎ 809 682 4750

🕒 Closed Mon.

💲 $

Museo de las Casas Reales

✉ Calle Las Damas
☎ 809 682 4202
🕐 Closed Mon.
💲 $

Panteón Nacional

✉ Calle Las Damas
☎ 809 689 6010
🕐 Closed Mon.

Plaza de la Cultura

✉ Ave. Cesar Nicolas Penson, Gazcue
☎ 809 686 2472

Museo del Hombre Dominicano

✉ Plaza de la Cultura
☎ 809 687 3622
🕐 Closed Mon.
💲 $

a copy (on a slightly smaller scale) of a castle in Toledo, Spain. Most of the superb furnishings and artworks date from the 16th century, and were a gift from the Spanish government when the palace was restored in the 1950s. Take time to admire the wooden ceilings,

INSIDER TIP:

For great pictures in the colonial city, head out to the Plaza de España, just north of the Panteón Nacional, at twilight.

—RAUL TOUZON
National Geographic Traveler
magazine photographer

particularly the one in the entrance hall decorated with 42 sculptured animal heads—a Spanish custom to ward off evil spirits.

For an overview of the history of the Dominican Republic, you can look into the **Museo de las Casas Reales.** The collection covers the country's history from displays on the Taíno through Columbus's arrival, colonization, the plantations, and slavery. Local archaeological finds and artifacts salvaged from shipwrecked Spanish galleons are displayed alongside a highly credible reconstruction of an 18th-century pharmacy (the brightly colored ceramics are, however, reproductions). The highlight is an extraordinary collection of ancient armaments, including elaborately decorated Turkish and Moroccan muskets, Japanese

samurai swords, and English crossbows. Between the court rooms you'll see a carved elephant's tusk dating from 1552.

The **Panteón Nacional** lies at the northern end of the Calle Las Damas. Originally built in the mid-18th century as a Jesuit convent, the pantheon was used as a tobacco warehouse and, later, as a theater after the Jesuits left the island. In the 1950s Trujillo converted it into a memorial to the heroes of Dominican history; the huge chandelier suspended from the dome was a gift from the Spanish dictator General Franco. Every two hours you can see the changing of the guard.

The Modern City

The modern center of Santo Domingo extends north and west of the colonial city, down to the seafront and Avenida George Washington, usually referred to simply as **El Malecón.** This seafront avenue is at its liveliest in the evenings, when Dominicans stroll or even dance to the sounds of merengue (see sidebar p. 101) blasting out from portable stereos.

In the heart of downtown is the **Plaza de la Cultura,** a large park that includes four major museums *(all closed Mon.),* the **Teatro Nacional** *(tel 809 687 3191),* and **Biblioteca Nacional** *(tel 809 688 4086).* The best of the museums is the excellent **Museo del Hombre Dominicano,** the largest archaeological and anthropological museum in the Caribbean. It contains a wealth of material relating to pre-Columbian civilizations. The museum occupies the third and fourth floors of a large building, and the best exhibits are found on the third floor. Here you'll see the fossil remains of an extinct bear, *Megatorio,* once hunted by the prehistoric Taíno, as well as ceremonial axes dating from 2000 B.C. Comparative displays of South American indigenous cultures place Taíno history in context. Hundreds of prehistoric pieces include necklaces and jewelry, shaped stones used to grate the staple food, yucca, dozens of examples of the three-headed god of agriculture (Trigonolito), heart-shaped pots with phallic necks (fertility symbols), artistically decorated conch shells that were used as trumpets for communicating across a distance, and elaborately carved stone rings whose purpose is unknown. A burial display shows skeletons in a fetal position (the

Taíno believed in reincarnation, and therefore buried corpses in the fetal position so that they were ready for rebirth); one skeleton's jaws are open in a grimace of suffocation (Taíno chiefs were polygamous, and when they died their wives were buried with them—alive). The fourth floor, which documents the influences that have shaped today's culture in the Dominican Republic, will take less of your time.

Next door, and less diverting by comparison, is the **Museo Nacional de Historia y Geografía.** Alongside a selection of Arawak artifacts, it contains a mountain of memorabilia from the Trujillo era (including the briefcase, wallet, comb, photos, and other items that belonged to the former dictator), and model ships relating to the Haitian-Dominican conflicts in the 19th century. The neighboring **Museo de Historia Natural**

Modern sculptures rise from the floor of the Museo de Arte Moderno.

The serene Jardín Botánico lies in northwestern Santo Domingo.

Museo de Arte Moderno
☎ 809 682 2153
🕐 Closed Mon.
💲 $

Palacio Nacional
✉ Calle Dr. Delgado
☎ 809 686 4771
🕐 By appt. only

Jardín Botánico
✉ Ave. República de Colombia
☎ 809 385 2611
💲 $$
www.jbn.gob.do

Parque Zoológico
✉ Ave. Nacional, Los Arroyos
☎ 809 378 2149
🕐 Closed Mon.
💲 $$
www.zoodom.gov.do

contains a few mounted birds and is equally missable.

On the other hand, the **Museo de Arte Moderno** is well worth a visit, displaying a broad range of contemporary works by both Dominican and foreign artists in the permanent collection.

Go east from the Plaza de Cultura to see the **Palacio Nacional,** an imposing neoclassical building constructed in 1947 for Rafael Trujillo. The ostentatious interior houses government offices and is open for tours.

A welcome retreat from the heat and bustle of Santo Domingo can be found on the city's northwest outskirts at the **Jardín Botánico.** Established in 1976, the gardens cover 0.75 square mile (2 sq km). You could easily pass half a day here. A "road train" takes visitors around the broad perimeter track, but a leisurely walk will give you more chance to appreciate the tropical plants and trees. There are separate areas for orchids, water plants, bromeliads, palms, cacti

and other succulents, medicinal plants, and a wide variety of endemic Caribbean species. The Japanese garden, with its bamboo groves and ornamental ponds, is a particular highlight. Although labeling is haphazard, these lovely gardens are a delight.

East from the botanic gardens is the **Parque Zoológico.** Located in an unused limestone quarry landscaped with native plants and trees, the zoo covers 24 acres (9.5 ha). Most animals are in open enclosures, such as zebras, elands, and rhinos in the Great Plains area; there are aviaries displaying parrots and macaws; and a reptile house inhabited by boas and pythons, among others. The zoo's symbol is the rare Antillean solenodon, a small, insectivorous mammal that looks a bit like a large rat.

Eastern Quarters

Across the Río Ozama, Santo Domingo's eastern quarters are the home of one of the city's most extravagant showcases, the **Faro a Colón** (Columbus

Lighthouse; *tel 809 591 1492),* which was built as part of the 500th anniversary of Columbus's landfall in 1492. A dramatic series of caves nearby offer a natural counterpoint to the controversial monument.

Without doubt, the hulking Faro a Colón provokes strongly divided opinions. While its drab and unprepossessing exterior resembles a shoddy, concrete apartment complex (appropriately enough, since many slum houses were bulldozed to clear the site), the interior is surprising, and well worth a visit. The idea of a monument to Columbus was first proposed over a century ago, and a lighthouse seemed an appropriately symbolic memorial to the great seafarer. In 1929, a design competition was won by a British architectural student, J. Cleave. The structure, in the shape of a recumbent cross, was eventually completed in 1992.

The building covers an area of 107,500 square feet (10,000 sq m), its outer walls featuring plaques bearing the names of every Latin American state. At the center of the cross is the marble **tomb of Columbus,** guarded by uniformed sentries. A sarcophagus said to hold his remains was moved here from the city's cathedral on the opening day—October 6, 1992. The corridors on either side of the tail of the cross contain some rather uninspiring cultural displays contributed by 50 countries around the world. One highlight, however, is an original **Mayan almanac** (one of only four known) dating back to the

14th century. Another precious artifact is the original anchor of the *Santa María,* Columbus's flagship, salvaged from the north coast of Haiti, where the ship sank in 1492. Near the Faro a Colón, the **Acuario Nacional** (National Aquarium) is a popular stop with families. The shark tunnel and turtle exhibits are visitor favorites.

The Mysterious Journey of Columbus's Ashes

The Faro a Colón claims to hold the remains of Christopher Columbus, but is this true? When the explorer died in 1506, he was buried in Valladolid, Spain. Three years later his body was moved to Seville and in the 1540s sent back to Santo Domingo. His remains were then said to be shipped to Cuba when France gained control of Santo Domingo in 1795, and from there back to Seville in 1898. However, in 1877 renovations in the cathedral revealed a casket beneath the altar bearing the inscription "Almirante Cristobal Colón," and it is these ashes that now lie in state in the Faro a Colón. Whether the ashes are those of Columbus can probably never be proven.

A few minutes' drive down the Avenida de las Américas, toward Boca Chica, are a series of caves known as **Los Tres Ojos** (The Three Eyes). This spectacular series of collapsed caves contains dramatic formations and underground lakes, the last of which is reached via a rope-winched raft. Luxuriant tropical vegetation adds a lost-world atmosphere to this unusual location—all the more striking because it's so close to a major city center. ■

Acuario Nacional
- ✉ Avenida España
- ☎ 809 592 1509
- 🕐 Closed Mon.
- 💲 $

Los Tres Ojos
- ✉ Parque Los Tres Ojos, Ave. de las Américas
- ☎ 809 472 4204
- 💲 $

Colonial City Walk

The walk starts and ends in the Parque Colón (Columbus Square), a busy meeting place surrounded by old stone buildings and arched walkways, with a statue of the explorer at its center. On the way you have a chance to savor the pride of Santo Domingo's colonial legacy, an ensemble of handsome buildings and monuments that mirror the country's sometimes turbulent history.

The Catedral Basilica Santa María la Menor, the Americas' oldest cathedral

On the south side of the square is the **Catedral Basilica Santa María la Menor** ❶ (no shorts or short skirts allowed). Built between 1514 and 1540, it was the first cathedral in the New World—as well as the oldest church of any description in the Caribbean—and the remains of Columbus were supposedly uncovered here during restoration work in 1877 (see sidebar p. 105). The tranquil interior features a 17th-century mahogany throne as well as stained-glass windows. The cathedral was fully restored in 1992.

Palacio de Borgella ❷ flanks the east side

NOT TO BE MISSED:

Catedral Basilica Santa María la Menor • Museo de las Casas Reales • Monasterio de San Francisco

of the square. Built during the Haitian occupation in the mid-19th century, the building has a graceful, porticoed facade on two levels. It served as the seat of congress until 1947 and now houses administrative offices and a post office.

From here make your way to El Conde, a lively pedestrian street lined with shops and cafés that bisects the heart of the colonial zone. El Conde leads down toward the seafront and the Calle Las Damas, a pleasant, tree-lined street where the ladies of the court would take their evening stroll in colonial days. Most of the oldest and loveliest buildings in the colonial city are located on this street.

The Heart of the Old City

Turn right onto Calle Las Damas to visit the **Fortaleza Ozama** (see p. 101), then double back toward the north: On your right is the **Hostal Palacio Nicolás de Ovando ❸**, built in 1502 as the residence of the governor after whom it is named. This beautiful building has been restored as the five-star Sofitel Nicolás de Ovando (53 Calle Las Damas). Opposite is the **Panteón Nacional** (see p. 102).

Continue on to the end of Calle Las Damas, where you'll find the imposing palace of the **Casas Reales ❹** (corner of Calle Las Mercedes and Calle Las Damas), which once housed the governor's office, the royal court of justice (Real Audiencia), treasury, and military administration. Built in the early 16th century, it now houses the excellent **Museo de las Casas Reales** (see p. 102). Opposite is a sundial, dating from 1753, on a site with fine views over the port.

Beyond here the street opens out into a large plaza. On the east side is the imposing **Museo Alcázar de Colón** (see pp. 101–102). Opposite the Alcázar, **Las Reales Atarazanas ❺** (the royal shipyards) once housed the royal armory, customs house, and warehouses; today the buildings are shops, restaurants, and bars.

From the plaza turn left onto Calle Isabel la Católica to see the **Casa del Cordón ❻** (corner of Calle Emiliano Tejera). Built in 1509, it was one of the first stone buildings on the island; it is named after the cord monks of the Franciscan order wore around their robes and which is carved in stone above the doorway. Today it is a branch of the Banco Popular.

Follow Calle Emiliano Tejera across Calle Arzobispo Merino and then onto Calle Hostos: Here you will find the ruins of the **Monasterio de San Francisco ❼**, the first monastery in the New World. Built in the early 16th century, it was sacked by Sir Francis Drake and then further damaged by earthquakes in 1673 and 1751. Take Calle Arzobispo Merino back to the Parque Colón.

🅰	See also area map p. 99
▶	Parque Colón
↻	Allow 2–3 hours
⏱	3 miles (5 km)
▶	Parque Colón

Southeast Coast

The southeast coast has some of the country's most spectacular white sand beaches, lapped by the azure waters of the Caribbean and backed up by swaying palms. In recent years large, luxurious all-inclusive hotels have sprung up on many of the better beaches. Wealthy Dominicans have also built luxury villas here, an easy two- to three-hour drive from Santo Domingo.

Close to the capital city, Boca Chica's beaches draw families on weekend outings.

Boca Chica

🔺 99 D2

Visitor Information

✉ Calle Duarte, esquina Caracol, 2da, Plaza Boca Chica

☎ 809 523 5106

The countryside of this part of the country is mostly flat plains in the center and south, carpeted by extensive sugarcane plantations, with a low range of mountains—the Cordillera Oriental—to the north. Much of the wealth of the major towns in the region, such as San Pedro de Macorís and La Romana, comes from the sugar industry.

The region also has its natural attractions, in the form of dazzling offshore islands and the Parque Nacional del Este (see p. 111), and man-made ones, such as the mock Italianate village, Altos de Chavón.

Heading east from Santo Domingo along the Autopista de las Américas, you pass some fine stretches of coastline before arriving at the main international gateway to the island, Las Américas airport. A short distance beyond is **Boca Chica,** a beach resort on a shallow, palm-fringed bay not more than 5 feet (1.5 m) deep. It was one of the first areas to be developed for tourism on the island and fills up rapidly with residents from the capital on weekends and holidays. A short distance west of town, divers flock to Parque Nacional Submarino La Caleta, an underwater preserve where several shipwrecks feature among the 28 dive sites on offer.

The beaches at **Juan Dolio,** 25 miles (40 km) east of Santo Domingo on Rte. 3, are a better choice, although they can also be noisy and crowded on weekends. The main beaches along here are **Embassy Beach** (a small cove popular with body surfers), **Playa Guayacanes** (calmer and more extensive), and **Playa de Juan Dolio** (also a reasonable beach).

INSIDER TIP:

La Romana's Tabacalera de García will satisfy any aficionado's curiosity with an in-depth tour of the largest handmade cigar factory in the world.

—JENNIFER ALLARD
National Geographic contributor

One of the biggest towns on the south coast, **San Pedro de Macorís,** lies at the mouth of the Río Higuama, 9 miles (14.5 km) east of Juan Dolio. This town was the center of the Dominican sugar industry at the turn of the 20th century, and remnants of its glory days can be seen in its houses, fire station, and the neoclassical church of **San Pedro Apostol**

on the banks of the river.

San Pedro de Macorís is unusual in that it shows a marked cultural influence from the Leeward and Windward Islands. In the 19th century, skilled craftsmen and builders were brought in from the smaller British islands to help build the Victorian-style wooden houses that can still be seen on Avenida Independencia. They brought with them their own dances (called *guyolas*) and music *(cainanés).* You can see both performed during the annual **Fiestas Patronales** (June).

La Romana

The provincial capital, La Romana, is also a sugar town, and the noise of diesel engines pulling carloads of cane to the Central Romana Corporation factory, which forms much of the skyline, is a familiar sound during the cutting season (Nov.–July). The factory's name comes from *la balanza romana,* the Roman scales once used to weigh the sugar exports. The privately owned sugar company is one of the largest cane sugar producers in the world. La Romana features a bustling market, **Mercado Municipal** *(Calle Frey Juan de Utrera & Calle Dr. Teófilo Ferry),* featuring religious tokens.

Casa de Campo

A drop in sugar prices in the 1970s led to the development of the deserted area of scrub, east of La Romana, into a tourist complex that has since grown into the gigantic **Casa**

San Pedro de Macorís
🗺 99 D2

La Romana
🗺 99 E2
Visitor Information
✉ Avenida Libertad 7
☎ 809 550 6922

Tabacalera de García
✉ Zona Franca, Casa de Campo, La Romana
☎ 809 552 2127
💲 $–$$$

Casa de Campo, Altos de Chavón & Museo Arqueológico Regional

🅐 99 E2

☎ 809 523 3333

www.casadecampo.com.do

de Campo (Country House). The biggest resort in the region, it boasts its own international airport, with direct flights from the United States. Its 11 square miles (28 sq km) of grounds include three golf courses (the Pete Dye–designed Teeth of the Dog is ranked as one of the finest in the Caribbean), a 245-acre (100 ha) shooting center, an equestrian center offering lessons, trail rides, and polo, 19

EXPERIENCE: Showtime

You can take in a range of local and international music and dance performances under the stars in the scenic Altos de Chavón amphitheater. Inaugurated by Frank Sinatra in 1982, the venue has hosted world-class performers from Julio Iglesias to Sting.

Between these visiting performers, the local Caribbean culture meets Las Vegas in the colorful and exuberant Kandela music and dance spectaculars (tel 809 523 2424, www.kandela.com.do, $$$$$). The artists onstage encourage audience participation. It's a unique chance for visitors to get involved in and connect with a show that rivals any Las Vegas production for flash and glamour.

---

swimming pools, a private beach and marina, 13 tennis courts, 20 restaurants, and much more. The resort is so big that people get around it on golf carts.

Altos de Chavón

Under the same ownership and on the same site as Casa de Campo is the **Altos de Chavón.** Anyone may visit this pretty Italianate village built in the 1970s and 1980s. It is a re-creation of a 16th-century medieval village and constructed entirely from coral rock and stone, with attractive cobbled alleyways festooned with hibiscus and bougainvillea and a huge amphitheater, which seats 5,000 people. The village overlooks the deep cleft that the Río Chavón has carved through the landscape and features several art galleries, a school of design, craft shops, a church, cafés and restaurants. A surprising highlight is the **Museo Arqueológico Regional,** which contains an excellent collection of Taíno art and ceremonial objects. Only the capital's Museo del Hombre Dominicano can rival it. The centerpiece is a rare, carved wooden idol, but the museum is also strong on finely crafted amulets, jewelry, ceremonial objects and axes, and household items (closed Mon.).

East of La Romana

Offshore from La Romana is the uninhabited Isla Catalina, which has beautiful white-sand beaches and reef diving. The **Museo Vivos del Mar** (Living Museum of the Sea) showcases the underwater remains of Captain Kidd's pirate ship, the Cara Merchant, shipwrecked in 1699. For information on dive trips, contact Casa de Campo. Excursions are also run from dive operations at Punta Cana.

The fishing village of **Bayahibe,** popular with independent

Carnival

In the Dominican Republic, the Carnival tradition has become associated with the historic dates of February 27, 1844, when national leader Juan Pablo Duarte retook Santo Domingo from the Spanish, and August 16, 1865, when the Dominican Republic became a fully independent country. Carnival is celebrated on these days irrespective of when Lent is. The days preceding these dates are animated by street dancing, parades, and parties.

The highlight of these spectacles, however, is the Carnival costumes of the *diablos cojuelos*, or lame devils, which chase people around the streets. They're known as *lechones* in Santiago, *cachuas* (horned devils) in Cabral, *toros* (bulls) in Montecristi, *papeluses* (paper devils) in Cotuí, *diablos de hojas de platano* (plantain leaf devils) in Barahona, and *mascaros* (masked devils) in Bonao. Each of these different forms is represented by suitably decorated masks. Some of the best examples of the craft can be seen in the Santiago Museo Folklórico de Tomás Morel (see p. 119).

travelers and divers, is about 15 miles (25 km) southeast of La Romana on Rte. 3. A couple of new resorts have sprung up here, and several budget hotels are dotted among the small wooden houses and cafés in the village. Bayahibe's mile-long (1.6 km) sandy beach is fringed with coconut palms and is a popular spot for catamaran tours hopping off to Isla Saona offshore.

Isla Saona forms part of the **Parque Nacional del Este,** which includes the island itself as well as a stretch of coastline from Bayahibe to the Bahía de Yuma. The 53-square-mile (137 sq km) Isla Saona has only two small fishing villages—Adamanay on

Parque Nacional del Este
⚐ 99 E2

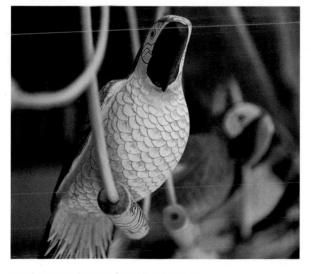

Wood carvings of macaws from Altos de Chavón

Higüey

◭ 99 E2

Visitor Information

✉ Calle de la
Altagracia

☎ 809 554 2672

Manatí Park Bávaro

◭ 99 E2

✉ Plaza Bávaro

☎ 809 552 6100

$ $$$$$

**www.manatipark
.com**

the southwest coast and Punta Gorda on the west coast—but hundreds of people visit the area each day, drawn to its fantastic white sand beaches, where Columbus is said to have put ashore.

About 20 miles (32 km) inland from La Romana is the town of **Higüey,** one of the oldest on the island, founded in 1502. It holds little of interest to the visitor apart from being a major center of pilgrimage; in the heart of the town is the **Basilica de Nuestra Señora**

Dolphins in Captivity

Dolphins are sensitive mammals that suffer in captivity. On average a dolphin lives 45 years In the wild, yet half of all captives die within their first two years. For a dolphin used to roaming free for up to 40 miles (64 km) a day, any enclosure is like a concrete prison.

---

de la Merced, a 16th-century Spanish church. Just 550 yards (500 m) to the north of this is the massive, modern **Basilica de Nuestra Señora de Altagracia,** which is dedicated to the country's patron saint. This huge concrete structure was built in the 1950s and is intended to resemble a 200-foot-high (60 m) pair of hands praying. An annual pilgrimage is made to the site each year on January 21.

Coastal Attractions

Due east from Higüey is the **Coconut Coast,** an uninterrupted stretch of some of the most gorgeous beaches on the island, stretching from **Punta Espada** through **Punta Cana** and **Bávaro** almost all the way to **Punta Sabaneta.** Fine white sand, backed by coconut plantations, slopes off into a reef-protected lagoon that offers excellent swimming and water sports. There are scuba diving and snorkeling opportunities offshore. This area has become one of the most intensively developed in the country, with a string of all-inclusive hotels, many with first-class facilities, spread out along different stretches of the beach.

Behind the beach hotels is the **Manatí Park Bávaro.** The park has enclosures with iguanas, parrots, vultures, butterflies, storks, an aquarium with sharks and rays, plus regular performances by parrots, dancing horses, sea lions, and dolphins. (There are concerns about the welfare of the dolphins in captivity; see sidebar this page.)

A reconstruction of a lost Taíno village is included in the park, allowing visitors to explore the island's culture and folklore. Dance rituals are brought to life by some of the park's artistic players. There is also a museum where Dominican statues, paintings, and traditional clothing give insight into native life. The gift shop offers reproductions of the museum items produced by local craftsmen. ■

Peninsula de Samaná

One of the most beautiful regions of the Dominican Republic, the Peninsula de Samaná juts out from the northeastern corner of the island. The peninsula is bisected by the Cordillera de Samaná (Samaná Highlands). The cordillera's slopes, luxuriant with coconut palms and pines, plunge into the azure waters of the Bahía de Samaná on one side and the Caribbean on the other. Fine beaches and whale-watching provide sea-level attractions.

Colorful paintings brighten the street scene in Las Terrenas.

Settlers from the Canary Islands founded the town of Santa Bárbara de Samaná in 1756. Quiet and unhurried, **Samaná** is belatedly awakening to tourism, prompted by the arrival of a new expressway from Santo Domingo and a couple of beach resorts. It is the departure point for boat trips to view humpback whales: Up to 3,000 arrive in the bay to mate and give birth between January and March (*tel 809 538 2494, www.whalesamana .com*). Samaná is also a jumping-off point for trips to the off-shore island of **Cayo Levantado,** with its superb beaches.

You can make day trips from Sánchez over to the **Parque Nacional Los Haitises** on the south side of the bay, a protected area of coastal mangroves and small cays that is a haven for birdlife. Its inland section preserves several caves with petroglyphs and shards of pottery. Trips to the park can be arranged by tour operators from resorts in Puerto Plata, Sosúa, and Cabarete.

On the north coast is the resort of **Las Terrenas.** It boasts some of the country's best beaches, which run for around 7.5 miles (12 km) eastward and westward. ■

Samaná
- 99 D3

Visitor Information
- ✉ Calle Santa Bárbara, Edificio Gubernamental
- ☎ 809 538 2332

Parque Nacional Los Haitises
- 99 D3
- ☎ 809 472 4204

Las Terrenas
- 99 D3

North Coast: Around Puerto Plata

The Atlantic coast of the Dominican Republic extends for some 150 miles (241 km) from Monte Cristi on the Haitian border in the west to the Peninsula de Samaná in the east. In the scenic hinterland a patchwork of canefields lies beneath the rugged Cordillera Septentrional. The coast has some excellent beaches, but because they border the Atlantic the sea can be rougher here, and some of these beaches are more suited to bodysurfing than snorkeling.

Smaller bonefish, tarpon, and permit await anglers off the Domincan north coast.

Puerto Plata

🏔 99 C4

Visitor Information

✉ Calle Harmanas, Mirabel 8

☎ 809 586 3676

Fortaleza de San Felipe

✉ End of the Malecón

💲 $

The coast's main town is **Puerto Plata** (Silver Port), founded in the early 16th century beneath the dramatic outline of **Pico Isabel de Torres** (2,554 feet/779 m). Part of the mountain forms a nature reserve, the Reserva Cientifica Isabel de Torres, and there is a spectacular cable-car ride up to the botanical gardens at the top. Go early in the morning for clear skies and the best views.

Puerto Plata is in the midst of a major regeneration program that has included the restoration of several historic Victorian homes and the attractive and very long seafront promenade, the Malecón. At its western end the **Fortaleza de San Felipe** is one of the oldest fortresses in the Caribbean, built between 1564 and 1577 to deter pirate attacks. Partially destroycd in 1659, it was rebuilt on the orders of King Philip II of Spain, after whom it is now named.

Restored in the 1970s, the fortress has neat lookout

towers facing the sea and a massive keep at its center, where you'll find the small museum. The exhibits, mostly remnants of 16th-century armaments, are not as compelling as the interior of the keep itself.

Puerto Plata's town square, the **Parque Central,** has several turn-of-the-20th-century wooden houses with characteristic gingerbread-style fretwork on the balconies and windows. At the center of the square is a Victorian pavilion, known as **La Glorieta,** and on its southern side is the modern **Catedral de San Felipe,** built in imitation Art Deco style.

Apart from the fort, the town's star attraction is the excellent but highly commercialized **Museo del Ambar Dominicano** (Dominican Amber Museum), just a short stroll from the Parque Central. You'll find some fascinating exhibits in this well-presented museum, mostly of insects and other small creatures frozen in time since they got stuck on a resinous tree some 50 million years ago.

Toward Haiti

Westward from Puerto Plata, the arid, cactus-strewn landscape stretches toward the Haitian border. At Cofresí, **Ocean World Adventure Park** *(tel 809 291 1000, www.oceanworld adventurepark.com, $$$$$)* is a popular family attraction. Set in a sprawling waterfront entertainment complex that includes a casino and marina, the adventure park offers the full gamut of marine shows,

animal encounters, walk-through aviaries, and a rain forest exhibit.

East of **Luperón** is the site of the first European town in the New World, **La Isabela.** Founded by Columbus on his second trip to the New World in 1493, and named in honor of the Spanish queen, this remote and beautiful spot is now the **Parque Nacional Histórico La Isabela.** Excavations have revealed the stone foundations of the church and Columbus's house.

The last town before the border is **Monte Cristi.** Faded Victorian buildings hark back to its heyday in the 19th century when it flourished as a major port for the export of timber and agricultural produce.

The Amber Coast

The northern coastline is sometimes called the Amber Coast, thanks to the amazing discoveries in amber deposits that form the basis of Puerto Plata's amber museum. The title is something of a misnomer, though, because the amber actually comes from 15 or so mines in the shale and sandstone sediments between Puerto Plata and Santiago in the interior.

Of more scenic interest is the nearby **Parque Nacional Monte Cristi,** which covers 204 square miles (528 sq km) of coastline and offshore islands, known collectively as the Cayos Siete Hermanos. This important sanctuary is home to alligators and several rare species of birds, such as the wood stork and the American oystercatcher. ∎

Museo del Ambar Dominicano

✉ Calle Duarte 61

☎ 809 586 2848,

🕐 Closed Sun.

💲 $

www.ambermuseum .com

Puerto Plata to Playa Grande

Some 3 miles (5 km) to the east of Puerto Plata is the resort complex of Playa Dorada, with a fringe of hotels along its sandy bay. The complex also has a first-class golf course and a commercial center with a good selection of shops, restaurants, cafés, and other facilities. Continuing east, you encounter a less built-up coastline, and the lovely lagoon by Río San Juan is a highlight for many visitors.

Cabarete's lively bars and restaurants spill onto the beach.

Sosúa
🅰 99 C4
Visitor Information
✉ Calle Duarte 1
☎ 809/ 571 3433

Cabarete
🅰 99 C4
Visitor Information
✉ Calle Principal
☎ 809 571 0962

Sosúa (17 miles/27 km east of Puerto Plata) has a big, lively beach and an extensive beach market. Most water sports, including scuba diving and snorkeling excursions, are available from operators at the beach. The town is divided into two sections. To the west of the beach is **Los Charamicos,** a fishing community. The district known as **El Batey,** where most of the hotels, restaurants, shops, and tourist facilities are located, flanks the eastern side. El Batey was settled by about 600 Jewish refugees fleeing from Nazi Germany in 1941. The settlers developed a thriving dairy industry, and although many moved away after the war, their legacy is preserved in the small museum attached to the synagogue, by several memorial plaques, and by the specialty breads sold in local bakeries.

Cabarete

Cabarete, which is 7 miles (11 km) east of Sosúa, is one of the top windsurfing resorts in the Caribbean and frequently hosts world championship events. It's a very safe destination, thanks to the sideshore winds that bring tired windsurfers back to the beach. From December through September, the trade winds generally blow at 15 to 25 knots in the afternoon, with the strongest winds from late spring through summer.

The constant play of the trade winds has also brought kiteboarding to Cabarete. But, even if you're not a windsurfer, you can enjoy an excellent beach that stretches around the bay. Not surprisingly, the resort boasts the highest concentration of budget guesthouses and small hotels on the island.

Cabarete is also a major center for mountain biking, horseback riding, 4x4 trails, and hiking tours of the surrounding countryside, thanks to the presence of leading adventure tour operator **Iguana Mama** (tel 809 571 0908 or U.S. 800 849 4720, www.iguanamama.com). Founded in 1993, this company offers well-organized, fully guided adventure tours that include everything from mountain biking and ziplining to kayaking. These tours can be tailor-made to fit the needs of visitors, and the company also plows a percentage of its profits back into local environmental and educational programs.

Along the Coast

Some 39 miles (63 km) east of Sosúa is the small fishing village of **Río San Juan,** a picturesque jumping-off point for trips on the nearby Laguna Grí Grí. Boats set off from the

jetty at the end of the main street, Calle Duarte, for a two-hour trip through a mangrove-lined canal that eventually opens out to the sea. The excursion continues along the coastline and enters one or two sea caves before stopping for a swim in a natural pool (piscina natural).

Continuing on some 7 miles (11 km) past Río San Juan, you'll come to **Playa Grande,** an impressive ribbon of sand that curves more than 0.5 mile (1 km) around a lovely bay. It's a great spot for beach walks, but swimming can be dangerous due to strong riptides.

Just past here is the **Parque Nacional Cabo Francés Viejo,** a protected coastal rain forest with dirt tracks leading off the road to deserted beaches and bays. Finally, there is the provincial capital of **Nagau** on the Bahía Escocesa, but it has very little to offer tourists. ■

EXPERIENCE: Catching the Breeze

The Professional Windsurfers Association and the Professional Kiteboard Riders Association rank Cabarete among the world's premier destinations. **Cabarete Race Week** (June) is the high point of the year here, when the resort is engulfed by a tidal wave of young, lively, international windsurfers and kiteboarders gathered for world-class competitions and equally competitive after-dark partying. Accommodations get booked up well in advance, so make reservations early (tel 809 571 0882, www.cabareteevents.com, $$$$$).

Río San Juan
🅼 99 C4
Visitor Information
✉ Calle Duarte
☎ 809 598 2831

Playa Grande
🅼 99 D4

Parque Nacional Cabo Francés Viejo
🅼 99 D4

Santiago de Los Caballeros

The second largest city in the Dominican Republic (population 750,000), Santiago de Los Caballeros is the major industrial and agricultural center in the fertile Valle de Cibao. Any industrial smoke, however, can probably be linked to the main crop, tobacco; Santiago is a major producer of hand-rolled cigars and mass-produced cigarettes. The city's name derives from the 30 Spanish nobles *(caballeros)* who founded the town on Columbus's orders in 1495.

A mural in Fortaleza San Luís, just southeast of Parque Duarte, honors the women of the nation.

Santiago de Los Caballeros

🗺 99 C3

Visitor Information

✉ Ayuntamiento Municipal

☎ 809 582 5885

A sprawling, prosperous metropolis, Santiago has built its fortunes on tobacco and rum. The huge Martinez factory alone still turns out tens of thousands of cigars a day—all made by hand—and millions of machine-rolled cigarettes in the same period. The cigarmaking process is fascinating to watch, as the skilled workers roll the leaves and bind them into the familiar tubular shape. More than 20 such factories are still in operation, and the local tourist office can provide details about tours. A popular choice for visitors is **E. León Jimenes Tabacalera,** founded in 1903 and still owned by one of the city's leading families. Next to the factory is the **Centro Cultural León,** opened in 2003 to commemorate the tobacco

INSIDER TIP:

For a great souvenir of your trip, look for reproductions of indigenous Indian pottery for sale at many local Dominican shops and markets.

—ALICE SAMSON
*National Geographic field
researcher*

group's centenary. Exhibits there showcase Dominican arts and anthropology in a stunning postmodern building.

On the northeast corner of Santiago's central square is the **Parque Duarte,** whose shady confines are alive with shoe-shine boys, vendors of shaved ice, and picnicking office workers, though it is remarkably small for a city of this size. On the west side you'll find the **Centro de Recreo,** built in 1894. Inside it houses a private billiards club. The splendid facade has been painstakingly restored.

Next door to the club is the privately owned **Palacio Consistorial,** a more sober edifice from the same period. Santiago has a plethora of fine Victorian architecture, much of it built by local merchants who profited handsomely from the agricultural wealth of the Cibao Valley in the late 19th century. The style is predominantly Spanish Colonial, and many of the city's buildings are attractively decorated with painted tiles, ornate wrought iron, and lacy gingerbread work.

Museo Folklórico de Tomás Morel

A few minutes' walk from the Parque Duarte is the Museo Folklórico de Tomás Morel. This quaint museum is a treasure trove of curiosities, from Taíno pottery to early calculators and cameras, but the main draw is a priceless collection of hundreds of carnival masks (see sidebar p. 111). Santiago is famous for carnival masks, and those presented here range from the grotesque and surreal to the humorous. Worth noting are the masks from the Hoya district of Santiago, characterized by forests of spiky protuberances on the horns.

Heroes Monument

One monument you can't miss— even if only by virtue of its

Bachata

The twangy guitar notes of *bachata* are a ubiquitous accompaniment to any journey around the country. This immensely popular musical genre evolved about five decades ago in the Dominican countryside. A Dominican equivalent of blues, it derives from traditional romantic bolero: *Bachateros* (singers) croon about broken hearts and betrayal (bachata was originally called *amargue,* "bitterness"). The ever evolving genre also features a more fast-paced merengue style.

E. León Jimenes Tabacalera & Centro Cultural León

- ✉ Ave. 27 de Febrero 146, Villa Progresso
- ☎ 809 535 5555; Centro León, 809 582 2315
- 🕐 Centro León closed Sun.
- 💲 $

www.centroleon .org.do

Museo Folklórico de Tomás Morel

- ✉ 174 Calle Restauración
- ☎ 809 582 6787
- 🕐 Closed Sat. & Sun.
- 💲 Donation

Rolling handmade cigars at a factory in Santiago de Los Caballeros

commanding position above the city—is the **Monumento a Los Héroes de la Restauración** on Avenida Monumental, which rises some 220 feet (67 m) from a hilltop in the center of Santiago. Made of white marble, this huge monument was constructed during the Trujillo era and honors the heroes of 1844 who helped expel the Haitians and restore self-government to the Dominican Republic (in fact, Trujillo intended it as a monument to himself).

The interior of the monument houses displays about the creation of the republic. An elevator (often not working) and steps take you to a platform with panoramic views over Santiago, the Valle de Cibao, and the mountains. Note the frescoes at the top of the stairs, which are by the well-known contemporary Spanish painter Vela Zanetti.

The city's main thoroughfare, **Calle del Sol,** runs from the monument down to Parque Duarte, where most of the better shops in the city are found. ■

Cigarmaking

Cigarmaking has a long tradition in the Dominican Republic and plays an important role in the culture and economy of the country.

The prime tobacco-growing area is along the Yaque Valley, which borders the Río Yaque del Norte for some 15 miles (25 km) from the outskirts of Santiago northwest to the town of Esperanza. Despite a period of decline in the 1960s, the recent upsurge in demand for premium cigars around the world has generated a welcome boom in this area.

The Dominican Republic currently produces two-thirds of the premium hand-rolled cigars sold on the world market, making it the top exporter in the region, ahead of Honduras and Cuba. Internationally known brands such as Dunhill, Partaga's, and H. Upmann are produced here.

Cordillera Central

The remote mountains of the Cordillera Central (Central Highlands) run diagonally across the western half of the Dominican Republic, culminating in the island's highest point—Pico Duarte (10,417 ft/3,087 m). There is no easy access to this wilderness area, which includes two major national parks (the Parque Nacional Armando Bermúdez and the Parque Nacional José del Carmen Ramírez) and the sources of some of the country's major rivers.

One of the most easily accessible of the hill stations is **Jarabacoa.** You can reach it on Rte. 28, winding up from the central highway (Rte. 1) through pine forests that have earned this region the title of the Dominican Alps. The alpine-style chalets set in the woodlands are popular with vacationers.

Nestled in a broad valley and surrounded by the foothills of the Cordillera Central, Jarabacoa is a cool retreat with equable year-round temperatures. Many wealthy Santiago residents have weekend homes here, scattered around the outskirts of town amid fields of cultivated flowers, strawberries, pimentos, and manioc.

There is little to see in the town of Jarabacoa itself, although the charming park at its center, shaded by a magnificent tree whose branches arch over the entire square, is typical of small Dominican towns. A church, which adjoins the park, contains modern frescoes by a well-known local artist, Roberto Flores.

Jarabacoa's appeal lies mostly in its proximity to mountainous terrain, rushing rivers, and unspoiled countryside. One of

Jarabacoa
🅰 99 C3
Visitor Information
✉ Playa Ramírez
☎ 809 574 7287

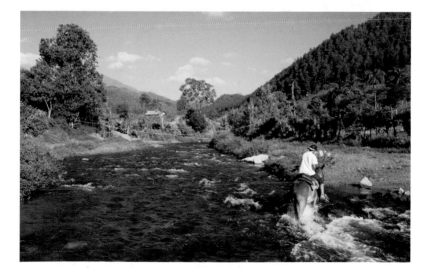

Crossing the Río Yaque del Norte, near the village of La Ciénega, en route to Pico Duarte

Salto de Jimenoa

⛰ 99 C3

💲 $

the most popular places to visit is the impressive **Salto de Jimenoa** waterfall; it is easily reached via a turnoff 2.5 miles (6.5 km) from the town center on La Vega road and a 4-mile (6 km) drive along a dirt track to a hydroelectric station below the falls. The falls themselves are an easy 10-to-15-minute walk from here across a series of swinging bridges. Set in a jungle-filled, natural amphitheater, the cascade tumbles down an 80-foot-high (24 m) rock face into a huge pool where you can swim.

EXPERIENCE:
Climbing Pico Duarte

Climbing Pico Duarte, the highest mountain in the Caribbean, is usually undertaken as part of an organized trip because it's a three-day round-trip from the village of La Ciénega to the peak itself. Outfitters include Rancho Baiguate (tel 809 574 6890, www.ranchobaiguate.com, $$$$) **and Iguana Mama** in Cabarete (tel 809 571 0908, or U.S. 800 849 4720, www.iguanamama.com, $$$$$).

The Río Jimenoa converges on the other side of the town with the Río Yaque del Norte at a spot 2 miles (3 km) from Jarabacoa known as the **Balneario La Confluencia.** This spot is popular with locals for weekend picnics and swimming.

The countryside around Jimenoa is perfect for exploration and adventure sports, with a network of paths and dirt tracks winding through remote hamlets and small farms. On the fringes of town (1 mile/1.6 km to the south) is

the busy outward-bound operation **Rancho Baiguate.** This multiactivity adventure center offers a wide range of things to do, including horseback riding, quad biking, mountain biking, parapente (descending from hills or mountaintops beneath a specially designed canopy), rafting, trekking, canyoning (rappelling into canyons), tubing, Jeep safaris, and expeditions to the top of the Pico Duarte. Within a short distance of Rancho Baiguate are the **Baiguate Falls,** which can be reached on quad bikes from the ranch down several dirt tracks (journey time is around 20 to 30 minutes) and then a short walk. Here you'll find another natural swimming pool. Rafting takes place on the upper section of the Río Jimenoa, an 8-mile (13 km) ride downstream with Class III rapids. The ranch also provides accommodations and can arrange visits to a local coffee factory and excursions to watch the making of Indian bread (casabe), and other local activities.

Continuing southeast of Jarabacoa, Rte. 28 brings you to the town of **Constanza,** set in a high valley surrounded by the peaks of the Cordillera Central. Like Jarabacoa, it is a prime growing area for soft fruit crops such as strawberries, raspberries, peaches, pears, and apples. The town itself is very peaceful, with just a handful of restaurants and hotels, and in December and January temperatures drop below freezing. The main activities are walking and visits to the **Aguas Blancas** waterfalls, 6 miles (10 km) to the south. At 272 feet (83 m), the two-part cascade is the highest in the Caribbean and much less visited than the falls around Jarabacoa. ∎

West of Santo Domingo

The southwestern corner of the Republic is an arid region with some unusual coastal landscapes. This is an area scarcely touched by tourism, although the opening of an international airport in Barahona and a fast highway from the capital means that access is now getting easier.

La Iglesia Nuestra Señora de la Consolación, San Cristóbal

Some 15 miles (24 km) to the west of Santo Domingo is the town of **San Cristóbal,** where the country's first constitution was signed (on November 6, 1844), but it is better known as the birthplace of the dictator Rafael Trujillo. Trujillo built an ornate church and mausoleum to house his remains (eventually buried in France), as well as several palatial residences including the **Castillo del Cerro,** a grandiose, six-story house on a nearby hilltop. Today it houses a police academy *(closed to the public).*

From San Cristóbal the main road (Rte. 2) leads to Baní, to the southwest of which is **Las Salinas** Just outside this fishing village on the Bahía Las Calderas are the largest sand dunes in the Caribbean. From Baní, Barahona is just over 60 miles (100 km) to the west.

South of Barahona

Located on the Bahía de Neiba, a three-hour drive from Santo Domingo, **Barahona** has a population of more than 80,000. Its airport, the Aeropuerto María Montés (named after a Dominican actress who starred in Hollywood movies in the 1940s and 1950s), is intended to promote tourist development in this relatively remote part of the country. One of the main attractions is the coastal scenery south of Barahona. Here the Sierra de Bahoruco peaks at over 6,500

San Cristóbal
⛰ 99 C2

Barahona
⛰ 98 B2
Visitor Information
✉ Ave. Enriquillo
☎ 809 524 3650

Visiting Parque Nacional Jaragua

The main entrance to the park is on Highway 44, north of Oviedo. A car is necessary to explore the land-based sections of the park; local guides wait by the entrance offering two- to three-hour boat rides around the lagoon (*$$$$$, by negotiation*). However, to really get to grips with the park's wildlife and extraordinarily diverse terrain, consider a guided day trip with **EcoTour Baharona** (*tel 809 243 1101, www.ecotour-repdom.com, $$$$$*). Choose from a variety of minibus excursions, hikes, bike rides, and boat trips on the lakes or off to the out-islands.

Parque Nacional Jaragua
🏞 98 A1
Visitor Information
☎ 809 472 1036
www.grupojaragua .org.do

Isla Cabritos
🏞 98 A2

feet (2,000 m) and plunges almost down to the Caribbean, where small fishing villages are interspersed with coves and inviting sandy beaches (swimming is not always possible due to surf conditions). After the fishing village of Enriquillo, the route turns inland and toward the town of Pedernales on the border with Haiti.

Natural Wonders

The **Parque Nacional Jaragua** covers 875 square miles (1,400 sq km) on the southwesterly tip of the island. The park is distinguished by its dry climate, limestone formations, lagoons, and saltwater lakes. You need to be well prepared to visit this area, with its rough terrain and lack of water and decent maps. The largest protected area in the Dominican Republic, Jaragua park is known for its flamingos, sea turtle nesting sites, and critically endangered Ricord's iguanas. It includes two uninhabited offshore islands, **Isla Beata** and **Isla Alto Velo.**

Inland 36 miles (58 km) on Rte. 46 from Barahona lies **Lago Enriquillo**, a massive saltwater lake that is said to be the biggest in the Caribbean. The lowest point in the Caribbean, lying between 100 and 130 feet (30–40 m) below sea level, the lake is fed by streams from the Sierra de Neiba and the Sierra de Bahoruco, but it has no outlet to the sea. Water loss is purely by evaporation, leading to a salt content in the lake three times higher than that of the Caribbean Sea. The lake is home to an abundance of wildlife, including crocodiles, rhinoceros iguanas, and flamingos.

Of the three islands in the lake, the biggest is the 5-mile-long (8 km) **Isla Cabritos** (Goat Island), the only one protected as a national park. Home to goats, the island also holds crocodiles and many resident and migratory birds, including flamingos, clapper rails, and roseate spoonbills. The two smaller islands are known as **La Islita** and **Barbarita.** You can drive all the way around the lake, and boat tours leave from the park entrance, some 2.5 miles (4 km) to the east of the sleepy desert outpost of **La Descubierta**. (Early morning departures are better for viewing the crocodiles.)

About 0.5 mile (800 m) to the east of La Descubierta at the western end of the lake is a series of pre-Columbian petroglyphs carved into the rock face. These are marked by signs from the Carretera Enriquillo. ■

A commonwealth territory of the United States with U.S.-style communications and highways, but a Spanish heart

Puerto Rico

The Catedral de San Juan Bautista in old San Juan, Puerto Rico

Puerto Rico

The most easterly of the Greater Antilles, Puerto Rico lies 1,000 miles (1,600 km) southeast of Miami between the Virgin Islands and the island of Hispaniola. Almost rectangular in shape, it measures 112 miles (180 km) from east to west and 40 miles (65 km) from north to south. A mountain range, the Cordillera Central, runs across the center of the island, reaching its highest point at the Cerro de Punta (4,387 feet/1,338 m).

Puerto Rico is unusual in that it is the first Overseas Commonwealth Territory of the United States, and although Spanish is the island's first language, English is widely spoken and Puerto Ricans are U.S. citizens. Puerto Rican culture is Latin American in inspiration, but commercial life is organized with American efficiency. The island has wonderful four-lane highways, but turn off into the countryside and you can find yourself on a potholed rural road.

Puerto Rico's interior is partially clad in dense tropical rain forest, although just one percent of the island's original forest now remains. The central mountains are ringed by coastal plains. In the northwest the landscape is shaped by the strange hillocks and caves of limestone karst formations, while in the drier southwest the land is dominated by cactus and other drought-resistant plants.

To the native Taíno, the island was known as Boriquen, which meant "land of the noble lord." When Columbus arrived here on his second voyage to the Americas in 1493, he named it San Juan Bautista. With Columbus was Juan

Area of map detail

ATLANTIC
OCEAN

Caribbean Sea

Ponce de Léon, who returned to settle the island in 1508; he soon renamed it Puerto Rico, or "rich port."

The Spanish enslaved the island's 30,000 Taíno and set them to work in the gold mines; the native population was decimated. Once the gold was exhausted in the late 16th century, Spain neglected the island. However, in 1765 the Spanish king Carlos III sent an envoy to develop the island's sugar plantations, and trade began to pick up; coffee and tobacco were also exported. In 1809 Puerto Ricans were given Spanish citizenship, but as the century progressed, an independence movement grew and the populace struggled against a series of military governors.

In 1897 Puerto Rico achieved a short-lived period of autonomy until the United States, then at war with Spain, invaded the island. Puerto Rico was ceded to the United States in December 1898, and U.S. citizenship granted to islanders in 1917. In 1952 the island became a commonwealth, but its status is a matter of ongoing debate. In December 1998, the Puerto Rican electorate rejected a proposal to induct Puerto Rico as the 51st state of the Union.

Nearly a third of Puerto Rico's 3.9 million residents live in and around the capital, San Juan. Over the last 50 or so years the economy has shifted from a rural to an industrial base, and the island now has a well-developed tourist infrastructure with first-rate hotels and good communications. ■

NOT TO BE MISSED:

Taking in Old San Juan and the Castillo de San Felipe del Morro   129–130, 132–133

Hiking in El Yunque National Forest   134

A nighttime boat trip on Mosquito Bay, Vieques   138

Appreciating the fine arts collection of the Museo de Arte, Ponce   141

Touring a working coffee estate at Hacienda Buena Vista   142

The spectacular views of La Ruta Panorámica (the Panoramic Route)   144–145

San Juan

Founded in 1510, Puerto Rico's capital city of San Juan has grown from a small town into one of the biggest metropolitan areas in the Caribbean, with a population of more than two million. The island's cultural, political, and economic center, it is also an important air and sea hub for the region. From its initial location at the entrance to the Bahía de San Juan, it has spread to the mainland, enveloped the Laguna San José, and sprouted industrial suburbs and canals.

Nighttime in Old San Juan

San Juan

🅰 127 E3

Visitor Information

✉ Ochoa Building, 550 Calle Tanca

☎ 787 721 2400; 787 250 6064 (public transportation information)

If the outskirts of San Juan appear unappetizing, the center, by contrast, is a real delight. Old San Juan covers just seven blocks on a long, narrow islet at the northeast entrance to the bay; four causeways connect it to the mainland.

San Juan (New City)

Unlike Old San Juan, where everything is within walking distance, in the city proper you'll need to use public transportation, taxis, or a rental car to get around. Make the effort, though, since the rewards range from lively stretches of beachfront to bustling merchant districts and a chance to see Puerto Rico's famous Bacardí rum being made.

Within 550 yards (500 m) of the confines of Old San Juan is **El Capitolio**, a white marble building built in the 1920s as the seat of the island government (Senate and House of Representatives). A guided tour will take you inside the rotunda, where friezes depicting the country's history decorate the elaborate dome.

On the Atlantic seafront, immediately beyond where Old San Juan is connected to the mainland, is **Condado,** a beach strip of high-rise resort hotels behind which are streets full of restaurants, designer stores, fast-food outlets, and souvenir shops. This hotel strip continues along the coast as far as **Isla Verde** (6 miles/10 km), another major beach resort area.

Inland from Condado is the downtown district of **Santurce** and, beyond here, the financial district of **Hato Rey,** where glass-fronted skyscrapers line the street known as the Golden Mile.

Three miles (5 km) farther south still is the suburb of Río Piedras, home to the University of Puerto Rico. The **University Museum** *(Ave. Ponce de Léon, tel 787 764 0000 ext. 2456, closed Sat. & Sun.)* features displays on Puerto Rican history and archaeology as well as contemporary art exhibitions. To the south and east of the university campus are the **Botanical Gardens** *(corner of Rtes. 1 and 847, tel 787 758 9957),* a tranquil retreat with numerous walks and waterways meandering among some 200 acres (80 ha) of lush tropical vegetation. The palm garden is particularly appealing.

Another attraction outside Old San Juan is the **Bacardí Rum Distillery** *(Rte. 165, Cataño, tel 787 788 8400),* which you can reach by a short ferry ride from Pier Two in Old San Juan. The 45-minute guided tour takes in the bottling plant, a museum, and the distillery.

Old San Juan

An area of considerable charm, much of Old San Juan has been lovingly restored to its original 18th-century character. The streets are paved with cobblestones, originally brought over as ships' ballast, and lined with pastel-painted houses with wrought-iron balconies and shuttered windows.

The entire old town is surrounded by more than 6 miles (10 km) of walls, 50 feet (15 m) high and 20 feet (6 m) thick,

INSIDER TIP:

The first Tuesday of every month in Old San Juan is known as "Noche del Galerias"—it's a night of art gallery-hopping that usually includes complimentary wine.

—KATHLEEN SQUIRES
Food and travel writer

studded with small stone sentry boxes known as *garitas.* Old San Juan has two massive and formidable forts, built to protect the city in the days when buccaneers and pirates were a constant threat.

Today the only invasion the old town faces is by cruise-ship passengers. The passenger piers lie at the very foot of the town, and when several berths are

El Capitolio

 Ave. Ponce de Léon

787 721 5200 ext. 4609

EXPERIENCE:
Savor Puerto Rico

Puerto Rico's finest chefs and a galaxy of visiting culinary stars gather in the capital every April for the annual **Saborea** food and wine festival. Stalls and demonstration kitchens are set up on Escambrón Beach over a long weekend and visitors are encouraged to *saborea* or "savor" Puerto Rico. There's a fantastic variety of different foods, wines, and spirits to sample, from traditional *comida criolla* (home-cooked Puerto Rican specialties) to gastronomic offerings from San Juan's leading restaurants, locally brewed beers, and the finest Puerto Rican coffee blends *(information and tickets: www.saboreapuertorico.com/events, $$$$$)*.

Castillo de San Felipe del Morro

✉ Calle del Morro
☎ 787 729 6754
💲 $$

Museo Casa Blanca

✉ 1 Calle San Sebastián
☎ 787 725 1454
🕐 Closed Sun.& Mon.
💲 $

Museo de las Américas

✉ Calle Norzagaray
☎ 787 724 5052
🕐 Closed Sun. & Mon.
💲 $

occupied it can seem overrun with day-trippers. Nevertheless, Old San Juan is clearly a community with a life that isn't solely defined by tourism, and locals go about their business, play dominoes in the cafés, and promenade in the evenings, much as they would anywhere else in Puerto Rico.

Old San Juan is a fascinating storehouse of the island's treasures, from colonial fortresses and civic buildings that underpinned Spanish rule to the wealth of historical artifacts in its museums.

The most prominent feature of the old town is the massive **Castillo de San Felipe del Morro,** or El Morro as it's known. Sprawling over a rocky promontory at the northwestern tip of the old town, El Morro was begun in 1540 and gradually added to over two centuries until it achieved its present form in 1783. Built on six different levels, the fort's interior

is a fascinating complex of tunnels, labyrinths, dungeons, turrets, and ramps. A small museum traces the fort's history, and a reconstruction of an 18th-century military barracks evokes the soldiers' lives. Together with Fuerte San Cristóbal (below), the Castillo forms the **San Juan National Historic Site** *(joint ticket available).*

Although not as well-known as El Morro, the **Fuerte San Cristóbal** *(Blvd. del Valle, tel 787 729 6777)* is much bigger, covering some 27 acres (11 ha). Completed in 1678, it was designed to protect the landward side of the town and has five separate bastions linked by underground tunnels.

The downtown area has many restored historic buildings of interest. The foremost is **La Fortaleza** *(Calle Recinto Oeste, tel 787 721 7000, closed Sat. & Sun.),* built between 1533 and 1540 but later considerably modified. Today it houses the governor's residence and is believed to be the oldest executive residence in continuous use in the Western Hemisphere. Various imposing ceremonial rooms and the gardens are open to visitors on free guided tours.

Another reminder of the Spanish establishment is the **Museo Casa Blanca,** originally built as a home for Ponce de Léon in 1521. The explorer died before he could move in, and the original frame house was destroyed by a fire. Ponce de León's son-in-law built the present house in 1523, making it the oldest of about 800 Spanish colonial buildings in Old San Juan, and his descendants occupied it for some 250 years. It's now a museum of domestic life, with some fine examples of colonial furniture. It also has three lovely courtyards: the Italian courtyard, with fountains and brickwork; the classical courtyard, a wild area leading down to the sea; and the Spanish courtyard, modeled on the Alhambra in Granada, Spain.

One of the most fascinating of the old town's museums is the **Museo de las Américas.** Here exhibits trace the evolution of New World cultures over the centuries, including the pre-Columbian period, and features a comprehensive collection of carnival costumes from various countries. Another interesting museum is the **Museo de San Juan,** which houses exhibitions of Puerto Rican art and offers an audiovisual presentation on the history of the city. There are intriguing exhibits at the **Museo de Nuestra Raíz Africana,** which examines the role African slaves played in the development of Puerto Rican culture. The **Casa del Libro** *(225 Calle Cristo, tel 787 723 0354, closed Sun. & Mon.)* is housed in an 18th-century building and features exhibits related to books and bookbinding. Its 5,000 volumes include many rare editions. For exhibits on a lighter note, visit the enjoyable **Museo del Niño.** It contains a wide variety of exhibits relating to childhood, such as large collections of dolls and other toys.

A popular exhibition in the central old town is that of **The Butterfly People** *(257 Calle de la Cruz),* who have created a gallery of mounted butterfly art in a restored 18th-century building. It's purely a commercial venture, with no educational value. To learn about the flora and fauna of Puerto Rico, visit the **Conservation Trust of Puerto Rico,** which has displays on the island's ecology. ■

Museo de San Juan

- ⊠ 150 Calle Norzagaray
- ☎ 787 723 4317
- 🕐 Closed Mon.

Museo de Nuestra Raíz Africana

- ⊠ Plaza de San José
- ☎ 787 724 4294
- 🕐 Closed Sun. & Mon.
- 💲 $

Museo del Niño

- ⊠ 150 Calle Cristo
- ☎ 787 722 3791
- 🕐 Closed Mon.
- 💲 $$

Conservation Trust of Puerto Rico

- ⊠ 155 Calle Tetuán
- ☎ 787 722 5834

An informal serenade in the plaza fronting Old San Juan's Cathedral de San Juan Bautista

Old San Juan Walk

This lovely walk through Old San Juan traces a roughly circular path, beginning and ending at the Plaza de Colón, one of the many elements of San Juan that play up a Columbus connection. Along the way you can appreciate the diverse components—fortresses, churches, museums, and monuments—that combine so harmoniously in this colonial district.

The Fuerte San Cristóbal is the largest fort the Spanish built in the New World.

NOT TO BE MISSED:

Convento de los Dominicos • Museo Pablo Casals • Catedral de San Juan Bautista

Start in the **Plaza de Colón** at the entrance to the old city, where a statue commemorates the explorer. The shady square is edged by restaurants where you can enjoy a meal or a drink before setting out. Follow Avenida Muñoz Rivera uphill to the **Fuerte San Cristóbal ❶** (see p. 130). After a look at the fort, take Boulevard del Valle along the seafront. On your right you'll see a sprawling collection of closely packed houses clinging to the seashore beneath the city walls. This is the **Barrio La Perla,** originally a village that sprang up to serve the military establishment; it is now home to some 10,000 people who form a tight-knit community quite distinct from other areas of the city.

As you continue toward Calle Norzagaray and the **Museo de San Juan** (see p. 131), the **Convento de los Dominicos ❷** is on your left. Built in the early 16th century, it was later

used as a headquarters for the U.S. Army. It has now been fully restored and houses the Puerto Rican Institute of Culture *(tel 787 721 6866),* which features a chapel with an ornate altar, religious manuscripts, and an art gallery *(closed Sun.).* Just past here is the **Plaza del Quinto Centenario.** One of the highest points in San Juan, it was built as part of the 500th anniversary of the discovery of the New World. Its centerpiece, Totem Telúrico, is a 40-foot-high (12 m) sculpture in black granite and ceramics, referred to locally simply as "the totem" due to its tall, cylindrical shape. It's the work of Jaimé Suarez, one of the country's foremost artists.

On the west side of the square stands the **Museo de las Américas ❸** (see p. 131). This handsome, three-story neoclassical building has porticoed galleries overlooking the courtyard, and it used to house the military barracks. It was constructed in the mid-19th century and was the largest building erected in the Americas by Spanish engineers.

Continue on toward the broad expanse of park that leads across the headland to the impressive **Castillo de San Felipe del Morro ❹** (see p. 130). Then return across the park and follow the road down to the **Museo Casa Blanca ❺** (see pp. 130–131). From the Casa Blanca take Calle San Sebastián to the Plaza de San José, in one corner of which is the **Iglesia de San José ❻** *(tel 787 725 7501),* the family church of the Ponce de Léon family. A statue of the city's founding father, Juan Ponce de León, strikes a dashing pose on the plaza. It is made from melted-down cannons. The Spanish explorer was originally laid to rest here, but his ashes were moved to the Catedral de San Juan Bautista in 1971. The simple 16th-century church has a particularly ornate altarpiece, and note the fresco (1550) on the far left.

In one corner of the Plaza San José is the **Museo Pablo Casals** *(tel 787 723 9185, closed Sun. & Mon.)*, dedicated to the memory of the famous Spanish cellist who founded the Casals Festival, held on the island every year since 1957 at the Luis A. Ferré Performing Arts Center *(tel 787 620 4444)*. The museum is a collection of memorabilia from the cellist's career, with videotapes of the festival concerts.

Follow Calle del Cristo downhill, passing

the archbishop's residence (No. 50) on your right, to reach the **Catedral de San Juan Bautista ❼** *(tel 787 722 0861)*, a grandiose structure topped with three cupolas. Inside, a tomb holds the remains of Ponce de León.

Turn right and walk down the Caleta de San Juan, one of the prettiest little streets in Old San Juan, to reach the **Puerta de San Juan ❽**, a fortified portal dating from 1520, and once the city's main entrance. Go through the gateway and turn left, following the attractive promenade running alongside the harbor and past **La Fortaleza** (see p. 130).

Turn east past the fountain, continuing on past **Presidio de la Princesa** down the Paseo de la Princesa back toward the docks. Follow Calle Recinto Sur back to the Plaza de Colón.

🅰	See also area map pp. 126–127
▶	Plaza de Colón
🕐	Allow 2–3 hours
↔	1.5–2 miles (2.5–3 km)
▶	Plaza de Colón

The East

Easily accessible from San Juan, the eastern end of the island is the area most frequently visited by day-trippers and has several important nature reserves, including El Yunque National Forest. This 28,000-acre (11,210 ha) tropical preserve is by far the most popular attraction in Puerto Rico, with around a million visitors each year.

Water plunges 85 feet (26 m) from La Coca Falls, one of many waterfalls in El Yunque.

El Yunque
🏞 127 F2

El Portal Tropical Forest Center
🏞 127 F2
☎ 787 888 1810
💲 $$

www.fs.fed.us/r8/
caribbean

The largest forested area on the island, **El Yunque** harbors many spectacular waterfalls, thousand-year-old trees, brightly colored flowering plants, and a wealth of bird species. Although much can be seen from the road, the best way to experience the forest is to set off on any of the 13 hiking trails, which cover 23 miles (37 km) of varied terrain throughout the park.

The forest is located in the Sierra de Luquillo, 25 miles (40 km) east of San Juan. Take Rte. 3 from the capital, and near Luquillo turn south into the mountains on Rte. 191. About 3 miles (5 km) along this road is the **El Portal Tropical Forest Center.** Approached via an elevated walkway through the forest canopy, this excellent visitor center has more than 10,000 square feet (930 sq m) of exhibits. These relate to fauna such as the national emblem—the *coquí* frog—and the different types of forest within the park (which include tabonuco, colorado, palm, and cloud), local geology and ecosystems, and the management of tropical forests worldwide. A film on El Yunque is shown every half hour, alternating between Spanish (9 a.m.–4 p.m.) and English (9:30 a.m.–4:30 p.m.).

The area was sacred to the Taíno Indians, who venerated the numerous waterfalls and carved petroglyphs carved on rocks along the riverbeds. It is possible that El Yunque was named for the Taíno word for a good spirit, but its more likely derivation is from the Spanish *yunque,* meaning "anvil," on account of its flat-topped mountains. In 1876 King Alfonso XII of Spain declared 12,000 acres (4,800 ha) of mountainous land in the Sierra de Luquillo as a forest reserve. After the Spanish-American War in 1898, Spanish crown lands became U.S. property, and in 1903 the area became the Luquillo Forest Reserve, making it the only tropical rain forest in the U.S. national forest system.

From El Portal the road (Rte. 191) leads up toward **La Coca Falls** (alongside the road at 5 miles/8 km), which has an 85-foot (26 m) drop. The **Yokahu Tower** (5.5 miles/9 km), one of several observation towers within the park, affords magnificent views across the mountains. About 0.5 mile (1 km) past here you'll see signs for the **Big Tree Trail.** This lovely mile-long (1.6 km) route, which leads past some of the largest trees in the forest, also passes **La**

Mina Falls, probably the most spectacular in the park. At 7 miles (11 km) is the **Sierra Palm Information Center,** which has a picnic area and ranger service, and slightly farther on is the **Palo Colorado Information Center.** Here a trail winds up to the **Mount Britton Lookout Tower** and the peak of El Yunque itself, at 3,496 feet (1,065 m). Allow two hours for the round-trip to the summit.

INSIDER TIP:

Be sure to wear non-skid footwear when you visit El Yunque. The rocks on the rainforest footpaths can be as slippery as ice.

—CAROLINE HICKEY
Editor, National Geographic Books

On the island's northeastern tip, beyond the port of Fajardo, is **Las Cabezas de San Juan Nature Reserve.** Call ahead to arrange a tour of this 316-acre (128 ha) reserve, renowned for its unusual range of different ecological communities—sandy beaches, rock escarpments, coral reefs, offshore cays, dry forest, mangroves, and lagoons. The site's most significant natural feature is the **Laguna Grande,** one of three bioluminescent lagoons on the island. At its eastern end is a lighthouse, **El Faro,** built in 1880, which houses a nature center and an observation tower. ∎

Las Cabezas de San Juan Nature Reserve & El Faro

🅰 127 G2
✉ Rte. 987
☎ 787 722 5882
🕐 By appt. only. Closed Mon. & Tues.
$ $$$

Cruising

The Caribbean is the ultimate cruising destination, an idyllic combination of sun, sea, and varied landscapes, where it is possible to wake up every morning with a new island group on the bow and a different port at the foot of the gangplank. Christopher Columbus and Sir Francis Drake may have pioneered Caribbean cruising half a millennium ago, but today's pleasure trips are a far cry from those early missions of exploration and plunder.

St. Thomas (U.S. Virgin Islands), one of the Caribbean's most popular cruise destinations

More cruise ships ply Caribbean waters than any other place on Earth. There are more than a hundred vessels to choose from, and they vary considerably in terms of size, atmosphere, facilities, and itineraries. For first-time cruise passengers, selecting the perfect cruise can be a bewildering experience, but there are ways of narrowing down the field.

Vessel Sizes

One of the first rules of cruising is that size does matter. Although no indicator of price or the vessel's position on the luxury scale, size does influence the type of cruising experience available. For instance, smaller ships catering to as many as 500 passengers can visit offbeat destinations inaccessible to larger vessels; they tend to allow their guests additional time ashore and to enjoy a more relaxed, intimate atmosphere. On the downside (although several smaller vessels offer a positively sybaritic degree of luxury), space is necessarily restricted.

The most common Caribbean cruising options are the medium (500- to 1,000-passenger) and large (1,000- to 2,000-passenger) cruise ships. They fall into three main categories: luxury-class vessels appealing to a sophisticated clientele with top-notch facilities from water sports and spa treatments to gourmet cuisine and spacious accommodations;

premium-class cruise ships offering good food, a high standard of service, and a broad spectrum of organized activities and entertainment; and standard-class vessels aimed at a more casual crowd with fewer facilities, simpler menus, and limited cabin space. In a class of their own are the megaships, giant floating resorts with 2,000-plus passengers and a lifestyle that revolves around shipboard activities and a wild night-life, which rather precludes much in the way of sightseeing.

Shipboard Activities

The onboard activities package is a major consideration when planning a week or two afloat. Most medium to large cruise ships offer a day-long program of activities, which might include exercise classes, shore excursions, quiz competitions, cocktails to the accompaniment of a steel band, and an elaborate Las Vegas–style evening show, followed by a session in the discothèque. Mainstream vessels are all equipped with movie theaters, casinos, game rooms, and exercise facilities (worth remembering because the average cruise passenger gains around 4 pounds/2.2 kg during a weeklong cruise). All these features and up to five meals a day (excluding alcoholic drinks) are included in the price of the cruise. Families

should also check that the cruise line offers adequate children's facilities. Make sure that the supervised daytime activities programs cover the right age group(s), and ask about the availability of babysitters, kids' meals, cribs, high chairs, and other vital equipment.

Itineraries & Logistics

The most popular cruise duration on the Caribbean run (excluding shorter trips to the Bahamas) is between one and two weeks. The majority of round-trip itineraries originate from the South Florida ports of Miami and Port Everglades in Fort Lauderdale, although some cruise lines operate out of San Juan, Puerto Rico. Most cruise itineraries feature a different port every day with two days at sea (sometimes three days on longer trips). High season (and high prices) is mid-December through April, but cruises are possible throughout the year and ships stay well clear of the Hurricane Belt from August through October. Cruises are rarely booked directly with the cruise line. For the best deals and expert advice consult a travel agent with membership in the Cruise Lines International Association (CLIA; www.cruising.org) or the National Association of Cruise-Oriented Agencies (NACOA). A wealth of cruising information is found on the Internet, too.

EXPERIENCE: Cruising With Kids

Cruise-ship vacations are not just for honeymooners or retirees anymore. Many cruise lines offer activities to keep children interested, as well.

When booking a cruise, families should check into stateroom sizes and options. In some cases, newer cruise vessels have the best family accommodations. Parents with kids who will need a nap might look for a stateroom with a balcony or separate living space.

The **Royal Caribbean** cruise line (www.royalcaribbean.com) offers a variety of family activities, including interaction with DreamWorks Animation characters and family activities like ice-skating and mini-golf. There's also a dining option where kids are picked up after they've finished eating dinner with their families to go to evening Adventure Ocean activities.

Norwegian Cruise Line (www.ncl.com) ships host Nickelodeon entertainment activities for kids. The whole family can also go bowling or play with the ship's Wii game system, which is hooked up to a two-story screen.

Vieques & Culebra

Located 7 miles (11 km) off the port of Fajardo, Isla de Vieques is the largest of Puerto Rico's offshore islands, covering about 55 square miles (88 sq km). Until 2003, most of the island was owned by the U.S. Navy. Its legacy is a largely undeveloped island, with dry hills fringed by spectacular beaches, beyond which excellent snorkeling and diving abound. Tourism is on the increase and a handful of boutique hotels and hip restaurants have sprung up.

Waves roll onto the west coast of Vieques.

Isla de Vieques

🅰 127 G2

Visitor Information

✉ Casa Alcaldía,
449 Carlos
Lebrón St.,
Isabel Segunda

☎ 787 741 0800

El Fortín Conde del Mirasol

☎ 787 741 1717

🕐 Closed Mon.&
Tues.

💲 $

Most of the 10,000 residents of Vieques live in the main town of **Isabel Segunda,** where the ferries arrive from the mainland. The town has an attractive central square (with a bust of South American revolutionary Simón Bolívar, who came here in 1816), where you'll find the tourist information center.

On the hill above the town is a restored fort, **El Fortín Conde del Mirasol,** which was one of the last forts to be built by the Spanish.

The other main settlement on the island is lively **Esperanza,** on the south coast, which has a string of bars and restaurants along its seafront.

To the south of Esperanza is **Sun Bay,** one of the island's biggest and most popular beaches, with picnic and camping areas.

Vieques's best known natural attraction, **Mosquito Bay** (also known as Bio[luminescent] Bay), lies just beyond Sun Bay. This large, shallow inlet is surrounded by mangroves and is full of bioluminescent organisms (dinoflagellates), which glow eerily when disturbed by a boat paddle,

INSIDER TIP:

Pick up a local treat: Island Woman's Hot Sauce, sold near Culebra's steel bridge, with offbeat flavors like habanero/mango with honey, vinegar, onion, and garlic.

—KATHLEEN SQUIRES
Food and travel writer

prop, or your hand dangling in the water.

The former Navy base of Camp Garcia is now part of the **Vieques National Wildlife Refuge.** It is the largest wildlife refuge in the Caribbean and a good place to see nesting sea turtles and maybe a manatee. Some areas of the former naval site are closed to the public, but you can visit the beaches at **Bahía Corcho** (formerly Red Beach) and **Bahía de la Chiva** (Blue Beach).

Vieques can be reached either on the frequent ferries from Fajardo *(90-min. crossing, tel 787 860 2005, arrive in plenty of time on weekends)* or by flying from either San Juan or Ceiba (see Travelwise p. 336). Once there, you can get around by *publicos* (shared public taxis), or you can rent a car from Island Car Rentals *(tel 787 741 1666)* or Vieques Car and Jeep Rental *(tel 787 435 1323).*

Isla de Culebra

Even more unspoiled than Vieques is the island of Culebra, measuring about 7 miles by 3 miles (11 by 5 km) and surrounded by a series of rocky cays and islets. The landscape is hilly, with tropical rain forest. This peaceful island is home to just 2,000 people, most of whom live in and around the main settlement, **Dewey** (known locally as Pueblo).

About 40 percent of the island forms part of the **Culebra National Wildlife Refuge** *(El Campamento, tel 787 742 0115, www.fws.gov/southeast/refuges),* which includes 23 offshore islets and four reserves on Culebra itself. The most important nesting beaches for birds such as terns and boobies are Playa Resaca and Playa Brava. Contact the refuge for information on guided nighttime walks to watch the leatherback turtles nesting.

The island's best known beach is the mile-long (1.5 km) **Playa Flamenco** on the north coast. This gorgeous stretch of white sand is best visited during the week, because on weekends it fills up with day-trippers. Other good beaches include **Playa Soni** and **Playa Resaca,** on Culebra's east coast.

You can reach Culebra from San Juan by air (see Travelwise p. 336) or by ferry from Fajardo (see above). You can get around the island by bicycle, or you can rent a car from Carlos Jeep Rental *(tel 787 742 3514)* or Jerry's Jeep Rentals *(tel 787 742 0587).* The municipal tourist office is located in the City Hall.

Diving can be arranged through Culebra Divers *(tel 787 742 0803, www.culebradivers.com).* ∎

Vieques National Wildlife Refuge

✉ Vieques Office Park, Road 200, KM 0.04, Vieques

☎ 787 741 2138

www.fws.gov/ southeast/refuges

Isla de Culebra

▲ 127 H2

Visitor Information

✉ 250 Pedro Márquez St., Dewey

☎ 787 742 1033

Ponce

Puerto Rico's second largest city, Ponce lies midway along the island's southern coastline. Established in 1692, the city flourished during the late 19th century when it was a major exporter of sugar and rum. The architectural gems from this period benefited from extensive renovations as part of the Columbus quincentennial celebrations; more than 600 of its 1,000 historic buildings have now been restored.

The Parque de Bombas served as Ponce's firehouse for more than 100 years.

Ponce

🇦 126 C1

Visitor Information

✉ Porta Caribe

☎ 787 290 2911

Parque de Bombas

✉ Plaza las Delicias

☎ 787 284 3338

🕐 Closed Tues.

At the heart of the city is the aptly named **Plaza Las Delicias** (Square of Delights), where fountains and shady trees provide a cool atmosphere in which to sit and watch the world go by. At it's center is the 17th-century Spanish Creole-style **Catedral de Nuestra Señora de Guadalupe** *(tel 787 843 4322)*, while immediately behind the church is Ponce's most famous monument, the red-and-black-striped **Parque de Bombas,** or fire station. Built for an agricultural fair in 1882,

it only later became the city's fire station. It seems a strange juxtaposition, with the gaudy building abutting the classical cathedral. The church authorities tried to have this colorful structure moved, but the people of Ponce had become so attached to it they refused to do so. Inside, a **museum** contains antique firefighting tools and a splendid old fire engine.

City History

The story of the city is well documented in the nearby

Museo de la Historia de Ponce. An exhaustive but rewarding tour of the ten exhibition halls embraces the ecology, economy, architecture, politics, and daily life of Ponce over the centuries. It ends with a 35-minute documentary about the city.

Calle Isabel

After leaving the museum, note the buildings on Calle Isabel. You can see houses built in the four different styles for which the city is famous—classical, Creole, Ponce Creole, and Art Deco. Note also the chamfered pavements on each street corner. These facilitated the easier passage of horse-drawn carriages, allowing the wheels to ride smoothly up on a turn, thus avoiding an uncomfortable jolt for passengers.

On the other side of Calle Isabel from the museum is the **Casa Wiechers Villaronga.** Now fully restored, this interesting building was constructed in 1911 and is notable for its many adaptations to the tropical climate—underfloor ventilation, louvered fretwork windows, stained-glass panels to filter the sunlight, and the pressed-tin ceilings that are a hallmark of Ponce architecture. One of its peculiarities is a *mirador,* an outdoor observatory on the roof, supported by columns. The dining room contains some outstanding examples of Art Deco furniture, ceiling lights, and glass, all of which were imported from Spain.

The city is extremely proud of its **Museo de Arte,** which was

designed by Edward Durell Stone, the architect of the Museum of Modern Art in New York. Noted for its elegant interior, the museum claims to hold the largest collection of art in the Caribbean—more than 850 paintings, 800 sculptures, and 500 prints spanning more than five centuries of Western art. It is particularly strong on the Pre-Raphaelites, the baroque period, and contemporary Latin American works. One of its most famous paintings is the sinuous, colorful "Flaming June,"

by the Pre-Raphaelite painter Frederick, Lord Leighton. The museum also stages frequent special exhibits.

Perched high above the town is the **Museo Castillo Serrallés.** Built in the 1930s in Spanish revival style, the mansion was originally the home of the Serrallés family, owners of the Don Q rum distillery. This airy, multilevel house combines Spanish and Moorish elements; the interior

Museo de la Historia de Ponce

✉ 51–53 Calle Isabel

☎ 787 844 7042

🕐 Closed Mon.

Casa Wiechers Villaronga

✉ 106 Calle Reina, cnr. Méndez Vigo

☎ 787 / 843-3363

🕐 Closed Mon.

💲 $

Museo de Arte de Ponce

✉ 2325 Ave. las Américas

☎ 787 848 0505

🕐 Closed Tues.

💲 $$

www.museoarte ponce.org

Take to the Hills

In the southwestern foothills of the cordillera, the charming hillside town of San Germán is Puerto Rico's second oldest settlement, founded in 1573. Its leafy central plazas showcase an impressive compendium of local architectural styles from handsome Spanish colonial mansions to 19th-century gingerbread villas built during the boom years of the coffee industry. The town's most popular attraction is the **Iglesia Porta Coeli**, a Dominican chapel dating from 1606, housing a museum of religious art.

Museo Castillo Serrallés
- ✉ 17 El Vigía
- ☎ 787 259 1774
- ⊕ Closed Mon.
- $ $$$

www.castillo serralles.org

Centro Ceremonial Indigena de Tibes
- ✉ Rte. 503
- ☎ 787 840 2255
- ⊕ Closed Mon.
- $ $$

Hacienda Buena Vista
- ✉ Rte. 10
- ☎ 787 722 5882 ext. 7020
- ⊕ Closed Mon.–Thurs.; reservations essential for 2 hr. tours
- $ $$$

features period furnishings and a beautiful inner courtyard.

The fascinating tour includes the history of the oldest rum-making family on the island, permanent and temporary exhibits, and a short film on the sugar and rum industries. The site also has a gift shop, lovely gardens, and an excellent café with views over Ponce.

Centro Ceremonial Indigena de Tibes

This intriguing Taíno site, located just outside of Ponce, is said to be the oldest cemetery in the Caribbean, with burials dating back to A.D. 700. Two dance grounds and nine ball courts have been unearthed on this 5-acre (2 ha) site, evidence of its importance as a major ceremonial center. It is assumed that there is a correlation between the positions of these constructions and solstices or equinoxes. The largest court, measuring about 110 yards (100 m), is the longest in the Caribbean; 187 skeletons have been unearthed here.

A re-creation of a Taíno village and a small museum display Indian ceremonial objects, pottery, and jewelry. The bilingual guides give informative tours about this particular site and about the pre-Columbian Taíno culture generally. Among other things, they shed light on similarities between Taíno culture and that of the Maya in Mexico.

Hacienda Buena Vista

Farther north of town, this wonderful old coffee plantation has been restored using 19th-century techniques and tools. Built in 1833, when the country's coffee production was at its peak, the whole estate is powered by an ingenious system of hydraulics. The original owners received permission to divert the Río Canas to provide power for their machinery if all the water was returned to its source—and this is how the system still works. Not a drop is wasted as the hydraulics power the depulping, husking, and polishing machines. The house has also been fully

INSIDER TIP:

If you're driving into Ponce, be sure to have a good map or GPS on hand. The roads can be baffling: There is no grid structure and everything is one way.

—MATT PROPERT
National Geographic photographer

restored, with the help of old photographs and family documents, to show how the hacienda was furnished and managed. The estate is set in a subtropical environment, home to the Puerto Rican screech owl, hummingbirds, and the mangrove cuckoo—among other noteworthy local birds. ∎

West of Ponce

The southwestern corner of the island is the driest part of the country, especially in the 1,618-acre (655 ha) Guánica Bosque Seco, just outside the port of Guánica. This dry coastal forest is a UN Biosphere Reserve harboring some 700 plant species, 48 of which are endangered, and 16 of which exist nowhere else.

A cactus catches the late afternoon light in Guánica Bosque Seco, Puerto Rico's dry forest.

The **Guánica Bosque Seco** (Guánica Dry Forest) is also home to snakes, lizards, and endangered birds. About ten marked trails cross the arid scrub within the park, fronted by a large double bay, **Playa de Ventenas,** popular with surfers.

Guánica itself was the beachhead for U.S. troops during the Spanish-American War. On the hill above town is an old fort, currently being restored. Between Guánica and the forest, the Copamarina Beach Resort stretches along the shore opposite **Gilligan's Island,** a popular destination for divers and day-trippers. You can also take excursions from the hotel into coastal mangroves.

Farther west is **La Parguera,** which has grown from a fishing village into a popular resort area. It's a lively spot, particularly on weekends, and is also well known for the nearby **Bio Bay.** This lagoon amid the coastal mangrove swamps is similar to the bay on Vieques (see p. 138), although not quite as dramatic *(boat tours make regular departures from La Parguera).*

At the southwestern tip of the island, **Cabo Rojo Lighthouse** *(tel 787 851 7070)* provides views back down the coast. Five miles (8 km) inland, wildfowl sanctuary **Cabo Rojo National Wildlife Refuge** has 12 miles (19 km) of hiking trails around Boquerón lagoon, near the resort of Boquerón. ■

Guánica Bosque Seco

- 126 C1
- Rte. 116 to Rte. 334 and follow signs
- Closed Mon.
- 787 821 5706

Cabo Rojo National Wildlife Refuge

- 126 B1
- Rte. 301
- 787 851 7258
- Closed Sat. & Sun.

www.fws.gov/ southeast/refuges

The Panoramic Route

Snaking its way through some of Puerto Rico's most fabulous scenery as it traverses the length of the island, the Panoramic Route is a classic drive, unlike any other in the Caribbean. It takes at least two days, but there are several mountain *paradores* (country inns) where you can stay. Many parts of the road are extremely narrow, so drive carefully.

The route starts in the coastal town of **Maunabo,** heads inland to Yabucoa, and then crosses the Río Guayane before starting to climb into the foothills. (Note that the route throughout this drive is marked at most junctions with brown signs—but not all.) Small settlements dot the ridge along which the road runs, with valleys and ravines on either side overflowing with clumps of bamboo, tree ferns, and banana plants. After about 6 miles (10 km), the road starts to climb even more steeply. At this elevation, small coffee plantations replace the cattle pastures of the lowlands.

The route then enters the **Reserva Forestal Carite ❶** *(tel 787 747 4545),* 6,000 acres (2,430 ha) of rain forest. The reserve is home to 50 species of birds and has several waterfalls and a blue pool known as the Charco Azul. Past here the views open up on both

NOT TO BE MISSED:

Reserva Forestal Carite • Cañon San Cristóbal • Cerro Doña Juana

sides, with the sea and coastal plains visible to the south. Lago Carite and Lago Patillas can be seen, too.

The road continues along the ridgebacks of the Sierra de Cayey, bypassing the town of Cayey itself and rising again to a high point at the **Mirador Piedra Degetau ❷.** An observation tower, plus picnic and other facilities, marks this summit, which is dedicated to the memory of Don Frederico Piedra Degetau y Gonzales (1862–1914), a distinguished writer and patriot who was inspired by this panorama.

Just to the north is the town of **Aibonito ❸,**

☒ See also area map pp. 126–127
► Maunabo
⊕ 1.5–2 days
↔ 150 miles (240 km)
► Mayagüez

once a cool mountain retreat for the wealthy and still retaining some of its grandiose homes. It is also the highest town in Puerto Rico. Beyond Aibonito the **Cañón San Cristóbal** (San Cristóbal Canyon) ❹, the island's deepest gorge, plunges 700 feet (210 m) to the Río Usabon. There are some rough hiking trails into the canyon, but only experienced hikers should attempt to descend its steep slopes.

The route twists and turns along the spine of the Cordillera Central, offering stunning panoramas across to the north and south coasts. Beyond the Cerro El Malo (2,957 feet/902 m), the road enters the 7,000-acre (2,830 ha) **Reserva Forestal Toro Negro** (Toro Negro Forest Reserve; *tel 787 867 3040*), with a choice of trails and a lookout tower. This is a particularly scenic area, with the road shrouded by a leafy canopy of bamboo.

Six miles (10 km) northeast of here is the **Area de Recreo Doña Juana** (Doña Juana Recreation Area). It's worth stopping and taking the path opposite, which leads to a huge natural swimming hole in the forest. The route beyond here leads upward to the **Cerro Doña Juana** ❺ at 3,538 feet (1,079 m). This is an easy path to the summit with no steep gradients. It takes around 90 minutes for a

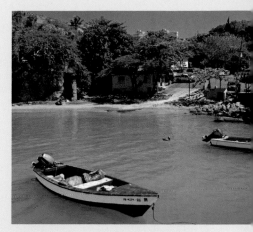

The picturesque harbor in the small coastal town of Maunabo

round trip. At the top you can climb a small tower for a panorama of the mountains and the coastline. Beyond here you pass the **Cerro de Punta** (4,387 feet/1,338 m), the island's highest point and bristling with radio masts.

The road descends momentarily to the quiet little township of Adjuntas before climbing once more through the Cordillera Central, skirting the Montanas de Uroyan and finally ending on the west coast at **Mayagüez.**

The Northwest

Northwest Puerto Rico is a limestone labyrinth laced with caves, underground rivers, and massive sinkholes. You can tour the Parque de las Cavernas del Río Camuy and admire natural wonders of the subterranean world; go stargazing at the fascinating Observatorio de Arecibo; or visit the prehistoric Parque Ceremonial Indigena Caguana.

The main entrance to Río Camuy Cave Park

Parque de las Cavernas del Río Camuy

🅜 126 C2
✉ Rte. 129, N of Lares
☎ 787 893 3100
🕐 Closed Mon.& Tues.
💲 $$$$

Parque de las Cavernas del Río Camuy

In the heart of the limestone karst country near Arecibo is the Río Camuy Cave Park. The caves have been carved out over the centuries by the Río Camuy as it carries the rainfall off the Cordillera Central down to the sea. Only two other rivers in the world (the Metali in Papua New Guinea and the Reha in Yugoslavia) are known to match this underground torrent.

Your guided exploration of this world of lofty caverns, mighty stalactites, and huge sinkholes begins at the visitor center, where there is a short audiovisual presentation on the cave system. You then board a motorized tram for the descent through a steep, winding ravine to the main cave, the **Cueva Clara de Empalme** (Clear Cave at the Crossroads). Sunlight filters through a natural entrance to the cave. The main cavern reaches some 200 feet (60 m) at its highest point, and stalactites hang from the ceiling in various strange shapes. Five different species of bats live in the caves, as well as crickets, guavas (a kind of tarantula), and microscopic shrimp that thrive in the cave's pools. On one side of the Cueva Clara is a deep cleft, at the bottom of which the Río Camuy flows.

To the east, you emerge into a vast sinkhole (a collapsed cave) more than 420 feet (128 m) deep. Lianas hang down from the uppermost cliffs, and water cascades down the sinkhole's moss-covered sides.

After the Cueva Clara, the tour continues to the **Sumidero Tres Pueblos** (Three Townships Sinkhole). Its 6-acre (2.5 ha) base could hold all of San Juan's El Morro fortress. In one cave at the side of this sinkhole, artifacts have been discovered that show it was once occupied by the Taíno.

The last sinkhole on the tour is the **Espiral,** which spirals downward toward the underground river. A series of 200 steps and walkways leads down to it.

Avoid crowds by visiting on weekdays. Tours are available in Spanish or English.

Parque Ceremonial Indigena Caguana

South of the cave park, between Utuado and Lares, this pre-Columbian site dates from around A.D. 1200. Caguana is one of the largest and most important Taíno ceremonial centers in the Caribbean. In addition to the large central court here, there are ten rectangular ball courts edged by granite dolmens decorated with petroglyphs. Although permanently inhabited by very few people, the center attracted large crowds to religious ceremonies and events.

Circled by limestone hills, the setting is impressive. The grounds contain plants such as silk cottonwood, sapodilla, palms, and cedars. A small interpretive center has displays of ceramics, carvings, and other Taíno artifacts. ■

Parque Ceremonial Indigena Caguana

 9 miles (14.5 km) W of Utuado on Rte. 111

☎ 787 894 7300

Arecibo Observatory

As you drive through the deeply cleft landscape of limestone karst to the south of Arecibo, a slender concrete tower becomes visible: the first indication of the extraordinary Observatorio de Arecibo (Arecibo Observatory), the world's largest radio telescope, operated by scientists from Cornell University.

The enormous central dish, which covers more than 20 acres (8 ha), is surmounted by a cat's cradle of wires suspended from three concrete pylons. Hanging like a giant spider in the middle is the receiver itself, weighing just under a thousand tons. It is so big that it cannot move: The planet itself has to move for it to change direction. But Arecibo has paid off handsomely. Major discoveries made here include the existence of pulsars

(most of those known were mapped here), pulsars orbited by planets, ice in Mercury's polar regions, and the rotational cycles of Venus and Mercury.

But Arecibo has also become associated with something that has more to do with *The X-Files* than radar astronomy—the search for extraterrestrial intelligence, or SETI. In 1974, the telescope transmitted a binary message into space in hopes of contacting alien civilizations.

Visitors can tour an interpretive center, the **Angel Ramos Foundation Visitor Center** (*tel 787 878 2612, www.naic.edu, closed Mon. & Tues., $$$*). Located at the foot of one of the giant towers supporting the telescope, the center has a viewing platform, some excellent interactive exhibits, and displays on science and astronomy.

Mona Island

Sometimes called "the Galápagos of the Caribbean" because of its remoteness and abundance of wildlife, Mona Island is located 46 miles (74 km) off the western coast of Puerto Rico. It is classified as a subtropical dry region, with areas of mangrove forest and superb white sand beaches fringed by coral reefs.

Mona Island
🅰 See inside
 back cover

Just under 7 miles (11 km) long and around 4.5 miles (7 km) wide, the island was once inhabited by Taíno Indians who left behind a series of petroglyphs and rock paintings in the caves that dot the 200-foot-high (60 m) cliffs along the shoreline.

In the 1880s a German entrepreneur, Anton Mobins, was granted a license to mine phosphate on Mona, and for a

time about 200 people lived on the island as a mining community. It was during this brief period of commercial activity that roads were built and the caves first explored. Since the mining company ceased trading in 1896 due to competition from Peru and the United States, Mona Island has been largely uninhabited.

Splendidly isolated, Mona is renowned for its wildlife, which includes bats, seabirds, indigenous Mona rock iguanas that can measure over 3 feet (90 cm) long, and their tiny 1-inch-long (2.5 cm) cousins, *Geco Oriundo*. The untouched coral reefs, particularly off the eastern and western coastlines, are known for their marine life. Sea turtles are regular visitors, as are humpback whales accompanied by their young in winter.

Visiting the Island

Lying in the middle of the Mona Channel between Puerto Rico and the Dominican Republic, Mona is accessed by boat. Charter boats make the six-hour round-trip from Mayagüez and Cabo Rojo, but it's a long, rough sea passage (calmer by night) for a day trip. A better option is a camping expedition with permission from the Department of Natural and Environmental Resources *(tel 787 722 1726)*, which maintains a new visitor center with quarters for a resident biologist and rangers, or travel with an adventure tour operator (see sidebar this page). There are basic campsites on three beaches in the southwest of the island, but no shops or any other facilities, so you have to bring your food and water. ∎

EXPERIENCE:
Mona Expedition

A great way to get the best out of Mona Island is an expedition with adventure tour operators Nature Adventures *(tel 787 706 0695, www.acampapr.com, $$$$$)*. You need to plan ahead and give them eight weeks' notice in order to put together a customized four-day, three-night package including transport and supplies, kit for caving, and a range of activities you've chosen for yourself.

A jewel-like scattering of tiny volcanic islands, rocks, and reefs embedded in a turquoise sea

Virgin Islands

Fishing nets in Tortola

Virgin Islands

Spreading out from the Virgin Passage, 50 miles (80 km) east of Puerto Rico, the 100-plus Virgin Islands lay a ragged trail across 1,000 square miles (2,600 sq. km) at the northeastern corner of the Caribbean Sea. Only a few of the greenest islands are inhabited; the rest are Robinson Crusoe islets and secretive cays once favored by pirates, rocky outcrops colonized by seabirds, and razor-sharp, wave-washed reefs.

Christopher Columbus first sailed into this nautical maze on his second voyage to the New World in 1493. Struck by their beauty (and profusion), he named the islands Las Once Mil Virgines, after the legend of St. Ursula and the 11,000 virgins (see sidebar p. 155). The tiny islands held little attraction for the major European powers, but their numerous secluded harbors and safe anchorages were a godsend for pirates, smugglers, and privateers such as Sir Francis Drake (1540–1596), who gave his name to the Sir Francis Drake Channel, one of the most picturesque maritime channels in the world.

The earliest European settlers were mid-17th-century Dutch *boucaniers,* who moved onto Tortola and raised cattle to supply passing ships with dried meat cured in smokehouses

called *boucans.* The British snatched control of the island in 1672 and laid claim to the 60 or so cays and crags at the eastern end of the archipelago, now the British Virgin Islands (BVI). Meanwhile, the Danes secured the western islands of St. Thomas (1665) and St. John (1684) and purchased St. Croix from the French in 1733. St. Thomas they transformed into a flourishing free port; St. John and St. Croix were carpeted with sugarcane. In 1917, the

4 ▷

UNITED STATES VIRGIN ISLANDS (U.S.)

3 ▷

Virgin Passage
Cockroach Island
Outer Brass I.
Dutchcap Cay
Inner Brass I.
Magens Bay
Big Hans Lollik I.
Salt Cay
Mountain Top 474m
Estate St. Peter Great House
Thatch Cay
Crown Mt.
Fortuna
Cyril E. King Airport
Charlotte Amalie
Cora Wor
Savana I.
St. Thomas
Water I.
Bovoni Bay
Red Hook
Saba I.
Capella Is.
Gree Toba Islar
Little Tobago Island

A   B

Danish possessions were sold to the United States for $25 million. Today, together with 70 more rocks and reefs, they comprise the United States Virgin Islands (USVI).

Only 2 miles (3 km) separate the islands of St. John (USVI) and Tortola (BVI), but the U.S. and the British islands are light-years apart in style. St. Thomas and St. Croix are indubitably

American, upbeat, and among the most developed and prosperous islands in the region. St. John is altogether quieter and boasts an unspoiled national park, which covers two-thirds of the island.

A 40-minute ferry ride away are the relaxed British Virgin Islands, laid-back to the point of horizontal. With a population of around 25,000 compared to the 125,000 on the U.S. Virgin Islands, the islands have a more traditional rural West Indian feel. Yachting is a top attraction and many visitors simply use the islands as a jumping-off point for a sailing trip. ■

U.S. Virgin Islands

With three distinct identities, the islands of St. Thomas, St. John, and St. Croix (pronounced Croy) are linked by their common history. During the colonial era, the islands were Denmark's only Caribbean possessions, and both St. Thomas and St. Croix preserve attractive Danish colonial architecture in their main waterfront towns.

The idyllic beach along St. John's Cinnamon Bay

With the emancipation of slaves on the Danish islands in 1848 and the subsequent collapse of the sugar industry, the Caribbean colonies were on the wane by the 1860s when the strategic potential of the island group first attracted U.S. interest. The need to protect the Panama Canal (opened in 1914), coupled with German naval activity in the region during World War I, finally prompted the United States to purchase the islands from Denmark and place them under the administration of the U.S. Navy. The Department of the Interior took over in 1931, and self-government was introduced in 1936, but the islanders were not permitted to elect their own governor (previously selected by the President) until 1968. Today, Charlotte Amalie on St. Thomas is the capital of the U.S. Virgin Islands, which are unincorporated territories of the United States. The islanders are U.S. citizens and taxpayers, and their 15-member legislature is represented by a non-voting delegate in the House of Representatives in Washington, D.C.

Cosmopolitan St. Thomas is the main gateway to the islands. It is a major cruise-ship destination offering excellent duty-free shopping, fine dining and accommodations, several lovely beaches, and a few sightseeing attractions, all combining to make it an ideal choice for a short break. St. John is an easy day trip away, although for visitors in search of peace and quiet this tiny island could well be a better option. St. John is a leader in the sustainable tourism field and its national park is a major attraction. St. Croix is the least known of the USVI trio but well worth a visit. The

island provides a good balance of pretty towns, shopping bargains to match St. Thomas, and more varied and interesting sightseeing opportunities. It is culturally distinct, too, celebrating a variety of musical and culinary traditions.

St. Thomas

The foundations of St. Thomas's fortunes were laid in the 1670s by the traders of the Danish West India Company The original settlement on the site of Charlotte Amalie provided a welcome watering hole for Caribbean merchants and pirates, including Edward Teach (died 1718), better known as Blackbeard. A certain raciness lingers on busy St. Thomas, as islanders offer cruise-ship passengers their first taste of the Caribbean.

St. Thomas
🗺 150 B3
Visitor Information
✉ Tolbod Gade, Charlotte Amalie, USVI 00801
☎ 800 372 8784

Island-Hopping Excursions

There are all sorts of ways to explore the Virgin Islands. Interisland public ferries are a great (and inexpensive) way to island-hop. Frequent daily ferries link St. Thomas and St. John. The crossing takes just 15 minutes from Red Hook on the east end of St. Thomas to Cruz Bay, St. John; or 45 minutes from Charlotte Amalie *(schedules and information from Transportation Services, tel 340 776 6282)*. There are also daily ferry services from St. Thomas and St. John to Tortola, the transportation hub of the British Virgin Islands (see pp. 166–172), and less frequent direct services to Virgin Gorda and Jost van Dyke. Proof of citizenship is needed for travel between the USVI and BVI.

Day sails are another delightfully hassle-free way to experience the islands.

For boat trips with lunch, swimming and snorkeling action, contact **The Charter Boat Center** *(Red Hook Plaza, tel 340 775 7990, www.charterboat.vi, $$$$$)*, **Limnos Charters** *(Compass Point Marina, tel 340 775 3203, www.limnoscharters.com, $$$$$)*, or **Treasure Isle Cruises** *(tel 340 775 9500, www.treasureislecruises.com, $$$$$)*.

Lastly, for something completely different and much more extravagant, **Air Center Helicopters** *(tel 340 775 7335, www.aircenterhelicopters.com, $$$$$)* offers short-hop aerial tours with amazing views around St. Thomas and the closer BVI; or treat yourself to a helicopter shopping trip to St. Croix or Sint Maarten, bonefishing in Anegada (BVI), or a visit to the private island resort of Peter Island *(www.peterisland.com)*.

As the town prospered, it was renamed Charlotte Amalie in honor of the Danish queen (wife of King Christian V) in 1691, and by the early 18th century its waterfront warehouses were crammed full of silks, guns, gold, and manufactured goods, which

Island Attractions: Bustling Charlotte Amalie is the hub of the 12-by-3-mile (19 x 5 km) island. Beaches, bays, and hotels dot the island's ragged central and eastern shorelines (the western end is largely undeveloped), and the interior rises

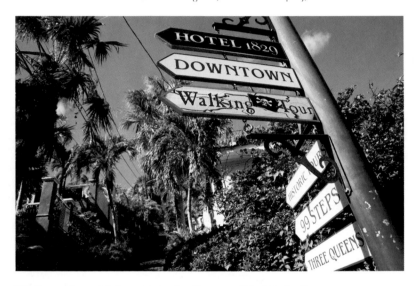

What's your pleasure? A sign points to attractions around Charlotte Amalie.

were traded for Caribbean sugar, rum, indigo, and cotton. While European conflicts were mirrored among the colonial powers of the Caribbean, St. Thomas continued to grow rich on the strength of Danish neutrality. The islanders also supplied arms to colonists fighting the American Revolution. For a time at the height of the plantation era, St. Croix eclipsed St. Thomas as the most important island in the group, and the capital was moved to Christiansted on St. Croix in 1775; it returned to Charlotte Amalie in 1871.

steeply to the 1,556-foot (474 m) peak of Crown Mountain, its ridges and crags peppered with houses and vacation homes. More than 50,000 people live here, making it one of the most populous islands in the region, and numbers are boosted daily by thousands of cruise-ship passengers who are shepherded to mountaintop observation points and spectacular Magens Bay (see p. 159). In St. Thomas you can find diving and water sports, deep-sea fishing, and the magnificent Mahogany Run golf course, but the island's chief

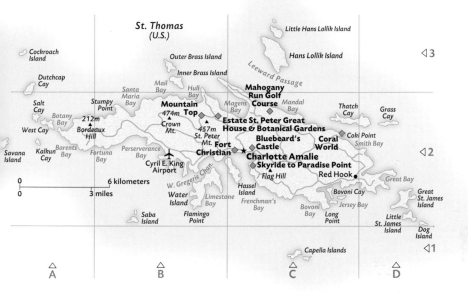

sport is undoubtedly bargain hunting in Charlotte Amalie.

Charlotte Amalie: Radiating from its charming Danish colonial origins, Charlotte Amalie skirts the outline of St. Thomas Harbor and clambers up into the amphitheater of surrounding hills. In the bay, giant cruise ships (up to ten at a time on a busy day) lie at anchor and disgorge their human cargo onto the waterfront, where the merchants of Main Street await, their mercantile instincts as finely honed as the 18th-century traders whose warehouses they now occupy.

Make an exploratory foray down **Dronningens Gade** (as Main Street is also known) and its warren of narrow alleys to discover a commercial kaleidoscope every bit as dazzling and cutthroat as it must have been 250 years ago, although the barrels and bales have been replaced with designer labels and electronic gadgets.

Main Street is at the heart of Charlotte Amalie's historic district, which stretches from Rothschild Francis Market Square in the west to Emancipation Park in the east.

The Legend of St. Ursula

The obscure and highly questionable legend of St. Ursula dates from the Dark Ages, when the Christian daughter of an English king sought to avoid marriage to a barbarian chief. Agreeing to the marriage on the condition she could undertake a visit to Rome in the company of virgins, she selected her retinue and sailed away. For three years she trained the women into a fighting force, hoping to overthrow her betrothed, but he discovered the ruse and had all 11,000 virgins massacred in the city of Cologne in Germany.

The 99 Steps

The Danes, who built stairway streets in St. Thomas in the mid-1700s, found that stair steps made the vertiginous hills of Charlotte Amalie easier to climb than steep, flat streets or switchback streets that wind and curve (like those of modern-day San Francisco). The 99 Steps make up the best known example of these stairway streets in the capital city.

The worn brick steps are located between Government House, which holds the offices of the territorial governor, and Hotel 1829, a hotel originally built as a town house for a French sea captain. Visitors who reach the top of the steps are rewarded with beautiful harbor views and the statue of the Three Queens, who represent the islands of St. Thomas, St. John, and St. Croix.

Virgin Islands Museum

✉ Waterfront Hwy., Fort Christian

☎ 340 776 8605

🕑 Closed Sat. & Sun.

The park is a good place to begin a walkabout, outside **Fort Christian** (currently undergoing major restoration). The squat bloodred fort dates from 1672, and houses the **Virgin Islands Museum** laid out in the former jail cells. Alongside detailed historical displays, small exhibits cover bush medicine and colonial furnishings, and pride of place in the central courtyard goes to an antique, animal-powered cane crusher. From the battlements, there is a view down to the 19th-century **Danish barracks building** near the waterfront, which has been spruced up with a lick of peppermint green paint to accommodate the Virgin Islands Legislature.

Above the park is the area of **Government Hill,** crisscrossed with a grid of narrow streets and flights of steps lined with attractive private homes, public buildings, and monumental churches. Near **Government House,** a white neoclassical edifice on Kongens Gade, the **99 Steps** (actually 103) strike up toward **Blackbeard's Castle,** a stone watchtower with tremendous views. The bricks used to construct the

steps and many local buildings were brought to the Caribbean as ballast carried from Denmark in the holds of ships.

Danish banker and merchant Hans Haagensen built a family home up here on the hill in the 1830s. Set in leafy terraced gardens, **Haagensen House**

INSIDER TIP:

You can find local produce, jewelry, clothing, and souvenirs at Market Square, originally the site of an 18th-century slave market.

—MARSHALL KIKER
Associate managing editor, National Geographic Books

has been carefully restored and furnished with period art and antiques as one of a pair of 19th-century town house museums, together with neighboring **Villa Notman** (*Government Hill, tel 340 7746 1234, off-season by appt. only, $$$*). The houses can be viewed on guided or self-guided tours. On

Crystal Gade near the junction with Raadets Gade is **St. Thomas Synagogue,** flanked by palms and dating from 1833. St. Thomas's first Jewish congregation consisted of refugees from Dutch Sint Eustatius, exiled for their involvement in the arms trade during the American Revolution. The beautifully maintained building is the second oldest synagogue in the Western Hemisphere (after Curaçao), and the adjacent small museum celebrates three centuries of Jewish worship on this site. Back down on the main drag, the Jewish Pissarro family once ran a trading store at **Dronningens Gade 14,** where Impressionist artist Camille Pissarro (1830–1903) was born. The art gallery, which now occupies part of the building, displays a couple of pages from the artist's sketchbook. Four blocks west, between Store Strade and Strand Gade, is the covered market at **Market Square,** which comes alive on Saturdays when farmers from the West End venture into town to sell their homegrown fruits and vegetables.

Harbor Views & Water Island: Around the harbor in the eastern suburbs, and fronted by the shops of Havensight Mall, is the West Indian Company Dock, Charlotte Amalie's main cruise-ship berth.

Across the street from Havensight is the **Skyride to Paradise Point,** which hoists a fleet of glass-enclosed cable cars to an observation deck 700 feet (210 m) above sea level (road access also). The deck provides splendid views

of the harbor, sheltered by Hassel Island in the foreground, and Water Island beyond.

On the harbor's western edge, the **Water Island** ferry *(tel 340 690 4159)* departs from Crown Bay Marina for the ten-minute crossing to Phillip's Landing. A great escape from the crowds, visitors can relax on lovely Honeymoon Beach.

Skyride to Paradise Point

✉ Long Bay Rd.

☎ 340 779 2625 or 340 775 1555

💲 $$$$

www.sttparadise point.com

The statue at the top of St. Thomas's famous 99 Steps

Coral World Ocean Park

🅰 155 C2

✉ Coki Point

☎ 340 775 1555

💲 $$$$$

www.coralworld
vi.com

Estate St. Peter Great House & Botanical Gardens

🅰 155 B2

✉ St. Peter Mountain Rd.

☎ 340 774 4999

🕐 Closed Sun.

💲 $$$

www.greathousevi
.com

Around St. Thomas

There's more to St. Thomas than the sights of Charlotte Amalie. The island's flora, fauna, beaches, and hilltops are well worth exploring and have particular appeal for families with children.

Coral World Ocean Park:

An 80,000-gallon (363,000 liter) reef tank display, aquariums showcasing rare marine plant and animal life, a predator tank, and stingray pool are among the attractions at this popular marine park on St. Thomas's northeast coast. But the real showstopper lies beneath the waves, where the picture windows of

the underwater observatory resemble a darkened marine theater in the round, opening onto a 360-degree panorama of the ocean bed. A touch pool and the rescued baby turtle exhibit are particular hits with kids, and there are daily talks by marine experts as well as feeding sessions at the baby shark pool. The park is adjacent to busy Coki Beach, which has a dive and snorkel center.

Estate St. Peter Great House & Botanical Gardens:

Draped across the hillside 1,000 feet (305 m) above Magens Bay, these 5-acre (2 ha) botanical gardens have been laid out in the grounds of a former 19th-century plantation. You can tour the gardens on wooden boardwalk trails shaded by banana plants and breadfruit trees, tall stands of lobster-claw heliconias, and brilliant tropical gingers. Along the way, enjoy bird aviaries, fish ponds, waterfalls, and more than 20 varieties of orchids.

The great house has been reconstructed and furnished in contemporary style with a gallery selling eye-catching Caribbean artwork. Viewing decks are equipped with orientation boards that point out local landmarks as well as more than 20 neighboring Virgin Islands. Slated to open in April 2012, is the **Tree Limin' Extreme Zip Line,** the first of its kind in the USVI, which will introduce zipline adventures and skywalks with dramatic views across the island.

EXPERIENCE:
Get Scuba Certified

Becoming a certified diver is a great way to become more comfortable in the water while exploring the Virgin Islands' many coral reefs and shipwrecks. The **St. Thomas Diving Club** (*7147 Bolongo Bay, tel 340 776 2381, www.stthomasdivingclub.com, $$$$$*), a five-star diving center that belongs to the Professional Association of Diving Instructors, offers visitors the chance to earn an open-water diving certification and kick a diving vacation into high gear. There's an e-learning program to complete before arriving on the island, and then the diving club instructors help visitors finish their certification dives in St. Thomas.

The diving club has classes for all levels of divers, and class sizes are small, so each student gets personal attention. They're also willing to work with cruise ships to organize shore excursions.

The view of St. Thomas and Charlotte Amalie from the ridge leading to Magens Bay

Magens Bay: Over the mountain ridge from Charlotte Amalie, St. Thomas's most famous beach lines the base of a huge rectangular bay carved out of the north coast. Magens Bay's idyllic mile-long (1.5 km) stretch of powder-soft sand fringed with palm trees is a prime contender in any list of the world's top beaches. It certainly gets busy, but on weekdays there is usually plenty of room for everyone. Several beach bars and restaurants cater to the crowds.

Mountain Top: The top of St. Peter Mountain is the setting for yet more superb views over Magens Bay and as far as St. John and the British Virgin Islands. This spot also claims to be the birthplace of the banana daiquiri; alcoholic and non-alcoholic versions are available at the viewing deck bar.

St. John

A 2-mile (3 km) ferry ride across the Pillsbury Sound from St. Thomas, St. John is the unspoiled gem of the USVI. Two-thirds of it is Virgin Islands National Park, created with the help of Laurance Rockefeller, who donated the first chunk of land in 1956 (a cunning move to prevent anybody else building near his Caneel Bay resort), and much of the remaining third is untouched. Dense woodlands carpet the rolling hills of the interior, while sandy bays punctuate the irregular coastline.

During the colonial era, St. John was planted with sugarcane

Magens Bay
🏔 155 C2
✉ Magens Rd.
💲 $

Mountain Top
🏔 155 B2
✉ Off Crown Mountain Rd.
☎ 340 774 2400
www.mountaintop
vi.com

St. John
🏔 151 C3
Visitor Information
✉ Cruz Bay St. John USVI 00831 Tourism Office
☎ 340 776 6450

and cotton. One of the Caribbean's most successful slave revolts was staged on the island in 1733, when slaves armed with cane machetes massacred settlers and managed to hold the Danish garrison for nine months. The uprising was eventually quashed

St. John at the **Cruz Bay ferry dock,** to be greeted by a coterie of taxi drivers and an engaging huddle of shops and restaurants set back from the waterfront. Over the hill south of town is **Great Cruz Bay,** the island's busiest resort area. But most set

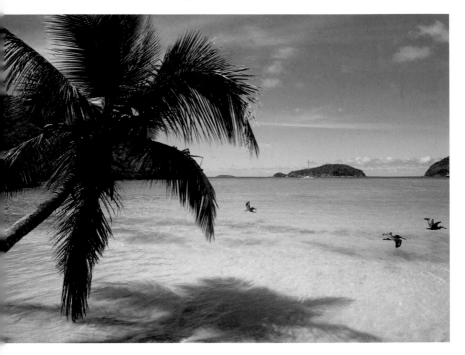

St. John's Maho Bay

with the help of French troops, and the last rebels are believed to have leaped to their deaths from Mary's Point on the north coast. Things have been very quiet since, and the population of 5,000 mainly consists of incomers from down island and American expatriates lured by the serenity.

Cruz Bay & Around the Island: Most visitors arrive in

off on their round-island tour by taking the North Shore Road out of Cruz Bay, past the attractive Mongoose Junction mall, housed in a local plantation-style stone complex, and the informative **Virgin Islands National Park Visitor Center** *(tel 340 776 6201, www.nps .gov/viis).*

St. John's best beaches rim the north coast from Honeymoon

Beach on Caneel Bay, through Hawksnest Bay, famously gorgeous **Trunk Bay,** and Cinnamon Bay (backed by a campground) to Maho Bay. Beyond Maho, a side road heads off to the **Annaberg Plantation** (*tel 340 776 6201*), where a self-guided tour leads visitors around the foundations of slave cabins, the old windmill, boiling room, and storehouse.

The North Shore Road then meets Centerline Road, which returns to Cruz Bay along a twisting mountain route with sensational views across to Drake's Passage. Its eastern arm continues to the quiet village of Coral Bay, St. John's original settlement.

Straddling the island around three 1,000-foot (300 m) peaks,

INSIDER TIP:

For a feel of the history of the island, hike to the Taíno rock carvings at Petroglyph Pool off the Reef Bay Trail.

—RAFE BOULON
Chief of Resource Management, Virgin Islands National Park

culminating in Bordeaux Mountain (1,277 feet/389 m), the land-based portion of the **Virgin Islands National Park** is a subtropical tangle of forest greenery that has swallowed up all but the merest traces of the hundred-plus plantation estates that once carpeted the landscape. The visitor center provides a helpful introduction with maps, historical

and natural history displays, and an activities program. A relief model graphically illustrates St. John's rugged terrain and details the park's 20-plus trails. These vary from short walks around Cruz Bay to more challenging hikes such as the **Reef Bay Trail,** which descends to the south coast from Centerline Road.

Accessible Nature Trails in Virgin Islands National Park

An inspired new initiative in the VI National Park has seen the introduction of accessible trails, allowing wheelchair users, stroller-pushers, and those less "sure of foot" to enjoy St. John's backcountry. A 610-foot (185 m) ramp now winds through the sugar factory ruins at Cinnamon Bay, and there is another accessible trail at Francis Bay.

A smart way to avoid the strenuous return trip on this route is to take the park service guided tour (check schedules). Walkers are bused to the trailhead for the 2.5-mile (4 km) downhill hike through wet and dry forest to the Reef Bay sugar mill ruins. The trail detours to a petroglyph site decorated with rock carvings attributed to Arawak Indians. Take time to swim and snorkel before the boat trip back to Cruz Bay.

The park's 5,650-acre (2,287 ha) **marine preserve** offers excellent snorkeling in the clear waters off the north coast beaches (see sidebar p. 162) and the less accessible south coast around Saltpond and Lemeshur Bays. Parrot fish, angelfish, tangs, grunts, rays,

St. Croix

🗺 151 E1

Visitor Information

✉ Kings St., Christiansted

☎ 340 773 1404

NOTE: The **Annaly Bay Trail,** on the north coast of western St. Croix, is approximately 2 miles (3.3 km) in length. Ask the guard at the Carambola Beach Resort & Spa *(Kings Hill, tel 340 778 3800, www .carambolabeach.com)* for directions to the trailhead. Bring plenty of water and wear sensible shoes.

snappers, jacks, and tarpon are frequent visitors to the reef areas and shallow sandy bays. One reason for the wealth of marine life is the mangrove nurseries where fish and marine species breed in the safe, nutrient-rich waters of the coastal swamp. The **Francis Bay Trail,** just around from Maho Bay, has a boardwalk section leading out into the mangroves where herons, Western Indian whistling ducks, pintails, teals, sandpipers, and other waterbirds come to feed.

St. Croix

The largest of the USVI at 84 square miles (217 sq km), St. Croix lies 40 miles (64 km) to the south of St. Thomas and the main body of the Virgin Islands. A former sugar island with mountains in the west and flat, fertile agricultural plains in the center, St. Croix takes its history seriously. The **St. Croix Heritage Trail,** a self-guided driving

INSIDER TIP:

A dip in the Annaly Bay tide pools on the north coast is worth the trek across rocky (and occasionally muddy) terrain from the Carambola Beach Resort & Spa.

—MARSHALL KIKER
Associate managing editor, National Geographic Books

tour, lists 200 sites of historic and cultural interest along its route, including the Cruzan Rum Distillery (see sidebar p. 164).

Columbus made landfall at Salt River Bay on the north shore in 1493. He beat a hasty retreat on encountering the belligerent Carib but claimed the island for Spain and named it Santa Cruz (Holy Cross). Claimed by France in 1650, the island's name was translated to St. Croix, and it stuck

EXPERIENCE: Snorkeling in St. John

Snorkeling is something of a specialty in St. John. The island's numerous protected coves and shallow coastal waters make for an abundance of snorkel sites directly accessible from the beach. **Trunk Bay** in the national park even offers a 225-yard (205 m) self-guided snorkel trail with underwater signs indicating reef features. Less crowded and more colorful corals can be found farther off the beaten track at sites like **Hawknest Bay,** and **Watermelon Cay** in Leinster Bay.

St. John's snorkeling conditions are ideal for beginners, but if you're still not sure, why not try a snuba dive with **Virgin Islands Snuba Excursions** *(Trunk Bay, tel*

888 294 1083 or 340 693 8063, www .visnuba.com, $$$$$)? Snuba is a cross between snorkeling and diving with air pumped from the surface and suitable for kids from age eight on up, so it can be a fun family experience. No special equipment is required beyond a mask and fins, and participants wear a light harness attached to a scuba tank, which floats above them on a raft. The outing takes around 90 minutes, beginning with an onshore familiarization talk. The dive starts in the shallows and can reach a maximum depth of 20 feet (6 m). The maximum group size is six people; reservations are essential.

when the Danes purchased the island in 1733.

The capital of St. Croix is Christiansted, a delightful little Danish-style town with a miniature fortress and shops tucked into a clutch of 18th- and 19th-century arcaded buildings. The island's main sightseeing attractions lie off Centerline Road, heading west, although there are lovely drives along the North Shore Road (Rte. 80) and on Mahogany Road (Rte. 76) through the rain forest.

On the west coast, Frederiksted (see p. 165) is where the cruise ships dock. It is another pretty town, splendidly renovated in 1998 to celebrate the 150th anniversary of the abolition of slavery in the Danish colonies. Denmark was the first nation to abolish the slave trade in 1803, although King Frederik VIII made no move toward emancipation until 1848, when he issued an edict stating that all slaves would be freed in 1859. The slaves on St. Croix and St. John rose up in revolt at the news, and the Danish governor, Peter von Scholten, taking the law into his own hands, declared the slaves free on July 3, 1848, at Fort Frederik.

Christiansted: St. Croix's pint-size capital was laid out around a calm, reef-sheltered bay in 1733 and named in honor of the king of Denmark, Christian VI. Overlooking the waterfront in the **Christiansted National Historic Site,** spick-and-span **Fort Christiansvaern** looks like a child's toy carved out of yellow marzipan. It was built

between 1738 and 1749, and its battlements are still guarded by neatly blacked cannons, which have never been fired in anger; there are historical displays on the upper level.

Around the small park in front of the fort are the **Old Danish**

Along a covered stairway in St. Croix

Customs House dating from 1751; the 19th-century **Scale House,** where ship's cargos were inspected and weighed; the 1735 **Steeple Building,** a former Lutheran church housing a small museum; and the original **West**

Christiansted National Historic Site

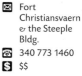 Fort Christiansvaern & the Steeple Bldg.

☎ 340 773 1460

$ $$

St. Croix Archaeology Museum

✉ 6 Company St.

☎ 340 692 2365

🕓 Open Sat. 10 a.m.–12 p.m.

www.stcroix archaeology.org

Indies & Guinea Company Warehouse, where slave auctions were once held in the courtyard. A short walk west down Company Street stands the 1832 Apothecary Hall, which has been restored to display pre-Columbian artifacts discovered on the island. The **St. Croix Archaeology Museum** traces human habitation on St. Croix dating back more than 5,000 years before the arrival of Columbus. Ax

Cruzan Rum Distillery

The Cruzan Rum Distillery (*Rte. 64, off Centerline Rd., tel 340 692 2280, www .cruzanrum.com, closed Sat. & Sun., $$*) is the largest commercial rum producer in the Virgin Islands and a popular side trip. Eight generations of the Nethropp family have perfected their rum-making skills on St. Croix, and although state-of-the-art prac- tices have crept into the modern produc- tion line, rum aficionados will be delighted to see that dark rums are still aged in the traditional charred oak barrels essential to their smooth, aromatic taste. Visits to the factory start with a video presentation and guided tour, followed by tastings of rums destined for tropical cocktails or enjoyed straight up over ice.

heads, pottery, beads, and tools are among the finds.

One block north on King Street is **Government House,** which occupies two fine 18th- century town houses converted into a residence for Peter von Scholten in the 1830s.

Between King Street and the bay is the **Kings Wharf open-air mall**—a pleasant place to shop or find a café table in the sun before taking a stroll up Strand Street, past boutiques and shops squir- reled away beneath picturesque, creeper-clad arcades.

Around St. Croix

St. Croix's history, from pre- Columbian to colonial, is on display in Frederiksted and at the **St. George Village Botani- cal Garden.** Snorkelers will want to head to Buck Island's reefs.

Buck Island Reef National Monument: Located 5 miles (8 km) off Christiansted (about an hour's sail), uninhabited Buck Island is renowned for its excellent reef snorkeling and diving. Here corals grow up to

30 feet (9 m) tall, and the reefs are home to a rich selection of marine life. On land visitors will find walking trails, sandy beaches, and picnic facilities.

Frederiksted: A 30-minute drive west of Christiansted, this sleepy small town is startled to life every year when the winter cruise ships arrive. Bloodred 1752 **Fort Frederik** *(closed Sat. & Sun.)* was named for King Frederik V. Governor von Scholten announced the (delayed) slave emancipation in the courtyard, and several rooms contain island

and colorful paintings is set amid the ruins of a 19th-century sugar plantation. The plantation was built on the site of a pre-Columbian Amerindian settlement dating back to around A.D. 100. The marked trail is lined with more than 1,500 native and exotic botanical species, and the site has a rain forest section as well as a cactus garden. Some of the plantation's ruins have been restored.

Whim Plantation Museum

St. Croix's Danish colonial past is on display at this restored

**Buck Island
Reef National
Monument**
 164 C2
☏ 340 773 1460
⑤ $$$$$ (includes transportation from Christiansted)
www.nps.gov/buis/

**St. George Village
Botanical Garden**
 164 B1
✉ Centerline Rd.
☏ 340 692 2874
⑤ $$$
www.sgvb.org

EXPERIENCE: Crystal Clear

Now here's a great idea: a totally see-through kayak. Father and son watersport fanatics, Craig and Bryce Scott of **Sea Thru Kayaks VI** *(tel 340 244 8696, www.seathrukayaksvi.com, $$$$$)*, have rustled up a fleet of sleek, totally transparent two-person kayaks molded from tough polycarbonate (the same material used for fighter jet canopies) for paddling expeditions around St. Croix's coastal lagoons and reefs. Setting off from the beach at Cane Bay for an

exploration of the coral-encrusted barrier reef, there's a chance of spotting sea turtles and dolphins, while among the mangrove nurseries of Altoona Lagoon, schools of juvenile fish dart beneath your feet and iguanas bask on the shore. The nighttime Creepy Crawly Critter Tour is a blast as kayaks equipped with lamps scoot above lionfish, lobsters, crab, and shrimp, or experience the magical glitter of bioluminescent organisms shimmering in the dark waters of Salt River.

---

history and cultural displays. The town's center is worth exploring for its pretty Victorian gingerbread houses and the trim row of arcaded waterfront buildings. North of town, a sandy beach extends beyond the fort to the old Sprat Hall Plantation.

St. George Village Botanical Garden: This 17-acre (6.8 ha) spread of lawned gardens

18th-century great house. The interior is kept remarkably cool by 3-foot-thick (90 cm) stone walls and an air moat. The rooms are furnished with antique mahogany pieces, including a splendid four-poster bed with typical pineapple carvings, the colonial symbol for hospitality. On the grounds are the remains of the old sugar mill. ■

**Whim Plantation
Museum**
 164 B1
✉ 52 Estate Whim, Frederiksted
☏ 340 772 0598
⊕ Closed Sun.
⑤ $$$
**www.stcroix
landmarks.com**

British Virgin Islands

Known locally as Nature's Little Secrets, these rugged small islands with amoebic outlines are scalloped into sheltered coves and bays. Once a haven for pirates and smugglers, the British Virgin Islands (BVI) now offer an escapist paradise for sailors and a surprising choice of luxurious resorts for vacationers. Part of the charm of the BVI, however, is to savor them as the islanders do—island-hopping by ferry, snorkeling, or having a quiet drink in a harborside bar.

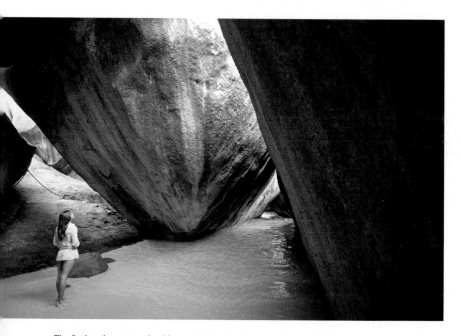

The Baths—the massive boulders on Virgin Gorda—tower above visitors.

Most of the islands and islets of the BVI group, from the verdant heights of Tortola and Virgin Gorda to the rocky jumble of Fallen Jerusalem, are arranged in two irregular lines flanking the 3-mile-wide (5 km) Sir Francis Drake Channel. Only 15 of the 60 or so volcanic outcrops are inhabited, including Anegada, the group's only coral island.

It took some time for the British to show a proper interest in their Virgin Island colonies and clear them of the piratical likes of Blackbeard, Henry Morgan (1635–1688), and Jost van Dyke (who has an island named after him). In the heyday of the 18th-century plantation era, settlers imported African slaves to plant and tend cotton and sugarcane on the challenging terrain, but their efforts were only moderately successful, and many planters sailed away, abandoning their slaves before emancipation in the 1830s. In order to survive, the freed slaves turned to small-scale farming. The BVI muddled along as part of the Leeward Islands federation of British colonies until independence. They toyed with the idea of political union with the USVI but opted to become a Crown Colony of Britain.

The BVI remain charmingly sleepy and friendlier than their better developed neighbors. But tourism and the financial services sector have brought increased prosperity, and a mini-construction boom is under way.

Tortola

Tortola was named for its turtle doves, which still outnumber the 23,000 inhabitants. It is the largest island in the BVI, measuring just 11 miles (18 km) east to west and 3 miles (5 km) north to south. To cross from the capital Road Town on the south coast to the beaches in the north, you have to tackle the central island ridge, where Mount Sage peaks at 1,716 feet (523 m), the highest point in the Virgin Islands archipelago.

Most visitors use Tortola as a springboard for yacht charters and visits to the outer islands. However, it is a relaxing place to stay for a few days, soak up the sun, hop aboard a couple of ferries, and generally unwind.

A handful of streets running parallel to the reclaimed waterfront, **Road Town** is the administrative and commercial center of the BVI. The harbor is usually a lively spot, with ferries coming and going and yachts checking in and out of the busy marinas, and there's a significant added bustle when a moderate-size cruise ship drops off passengers for an island tour and a bit of shopping.

Tortola
⚑ 151 D3

**J.R. O'Neal
Botanic Gardens**
🅰 167 C2
✉ Botanic Rd.
☎ 284 494 4557
🕐 Closed Sun.
💲 Donation

**Old Government
House Museum**
✉ Waterfront Dr.
☎ 284 494 4091
🕐 Closed Sun.
💲 $$

There is no need to allocate much sightseeing time to the town itself, although one very pleasant stop is the small **J.R. O'Neal Botanic Gardens.** A short walk from the town center, the lush palm-tree-shaded oasis of indigenous and exotic tropical plants is arranged around a water lily pond, orchid house, and pergola walk. Nearby, the **Old Government House Museum** offers tours of its formally furnished rooms and colorful BVI stamp collections laid out in the former governor's residence.

Another possible detour is the **Lower Estate Sugar Works Museum** (Station Ave., closed Sat. & Sun.), housed in a collection of wood-framed buildings dating from the 1780s. The Works have led a checkered career serving as a sugar factory, cotton gin, lime-juice press, courthouse, and dance hall in previous incarnations. Today, island history, culture, and crafts are represented by exhibits including Amerindian relics and articles salvaged from the wreck of the R.M.S. Rhone (see pp. 171–172).

Around the Island: Tortola's hotels and best beaches are strung out along the north coast. Starting in the west, secluded **Smuggler's Cove** is recommended for snorkeling and reached by a bumpy unpaved road from Long Bay. **Long Bay** itself is a mile-long (1.6 km) strip of blond sand backed by palm trees and a hotel. **Apple Bay** is the surfers' favorite and home to Bomba's Surfside Shack, a great beach

bar notorious for its full-moon parties. **Carrot Bay** has a couple of bars and a waterfront restaurant. Curving **Cane Garden Bay** is the island's best equipped beach, with windsurfing, waterskiing, and boating opportunities as well as beach bars, restaurants, and a few hotels. **Brewers Bay** is recommended for snorkeling when the sea is quiet; the sandy beaches at **Trunk Bay, Josiah's Bay, Lambert Long Bay,** and **Elizabeth Beach** are good for swimming. Attached to Tortola by a causeway is **Beef Island,** with fine beaches at **Trellis Bay** and **Long Bay.**

INSIDER TIP:

Soper's Hole on Tortola's West End is a delight. Wander about the marina on Frenchman's Cay, a strip of pastel-colored boutiques and cafés.

—OLIVIA STREN
National Geographic writer

In the center of Tortola is the 92-acre (37 ha) **Sage Mountain National Park,** which was established in 1964 to protect the remnants of the native forest that once covered the whole of Tortola. The park's **Rainforest Trail** features many typical rain forest plants, such as giant elephant ear vines, tree ferns, bromeliads, and philodendrons flourishing beneath an umbrella of

EXPERIENCE: Charter a Yacht

The Caribbean was surely created as a paradise for boaters. Its clear skies, calm blue seas, and arrestingly beautiful islands have seduced sailors since Columbus. Right at its heart lies Tortola, undisputed capital of Caribbean yachting, whose mountainous central spine is serendipitously positioned to form a wind barrier between the Atlantic and the Sir Francis Drake Channel.

This pint-size sailing center boasts the greatest concentration of bareboat charter vessels in the world (around 700 at the last count), yet it is still possible to set sail from Road Town or the West End, quickly lose the crowds, and discover your own private paradise amid the dozens of islands and islets scattered nearby. This exceptional wealth of anchorages and the ever changing scenery makes for an idyllic sailing holiday. The $64,000 question is whether to charter a crewed yacht or go it alone.

A team relaxes during the Mount Gay Rum yacht race.

Crewed Charters

Crewed charters offer all sorts of advantages, from complete relaxation and an itinerary tailored to your requirements to an experienced captain and a chef. The charter company will discuss your vacation needs in advance, including food preferences and the sort of activities (snorkeling, watersports, beaches) you have in mind. The type of vessel can be determined by the accommodation your party requires (number of cabins, bathrooms). Most crewed charters are multihulled (catamaran or trimaran) vessels, which provide more space and are particularly suited to families and groups. They are also more stable, and the smoother ride is worth considering if seasickness is a concern. You can treat your crewed vessel as a chauffeured limo, taking the helm occasionally, or select a charter that includes sailing instruction to prepare yourself to go it alone next time.

Bareboat Charters

If a bareboat charter appeals, the good news is that you don't have to be a seasoned navigator to captain your own boat. The charter company will check on previous boating experience (type of craft, conditions) and will give you a sail test. Less experienced sailors can opt to hire a captain for a couple of days to relearn the ropes before going solo. The plus side of bareboat chartering is independence and flexibility, as well as privacy. However, you need to consider provisioning (food, fuel, etc.), which is not included in charter rates except by prior arrangement.

Charter Operators

Dozens of yacht charter operations are based in Tortola alone. For an overview of what's available and what to consider before booking, two useful websites are run by the **Virgin Islands Charter Yacht League** (www.vicl.org) and **BVI Charter Yacht Society** (www.bvicrewedyachts.com). Some of the larger charter operators are **Bare Boats BVI** (www.bareboats bvi.com), **BVI Yacht Charters** (www .bviyachtcharters.com), **The Moorings** (www.moorings .com), and **Sunsail** (www.sun sail.com).

Sage Mountain National Park

🏔 167 B2

✉ Ridge Rd.

☎ 284 494 3904

💲 $$

Anegada

🏔 151 E5

100-foot-high (30 m) bulletwood trees and buttress-trunked ficus. The **Mahogany Forest Trail** leads off the main path up through white cedar, West Indian and broadleaf mahogany plantations.

Ferries for Jost van Dyke and the U.S. Virgin Islands depart from **Soper's Hole** harbor on Tortola's West End. Across the bay on Frenchman's Cay is the **Soper's Hole Marina,** which packs in private yachts and charter boats like sardines. On the dock, cute clapboard buildings house a few shops and restaurants.

More Places to Visit in the British Virgin Islands

Ferries and airplanes can take you around the smaller islands of the BVI, destinations for diving, hiking, and enjoying a drink on the beach.

Anegada: North of Virgin Gorda—and accessible via flights from Tortola—lies Anegada, the second largest of the BVI at 15 square miles (39 sq km). Its name means "the drowned one" in Spanish, as the island barely reaches 28 feet (8.5 m) above sea level. Anegada's main attraction is its offshore coral reefs, with their superb diving. The island has one small hotel with its own dive facilities, a couple of guesthouses, bar-restaurants, campgrounds, and food stores.

Cooper Island: Cooper Island's dinghy dock and bar-restaurant attract boaters sailing

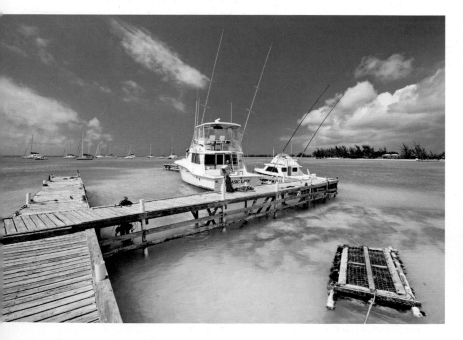

A marina on Anegada Island, the second largest of the British Virgin Islands

INSIDER TIP:

Sail your way across Drake Channel's emerald swells to Norman Isle, a deserted island and former pirate den.

—OLIVIA STREN
National Geographic writer

the Sir Francis Drake Channel Those who linger will find a good beach, dive shop, and the unpretentious Cooper Island Beach Club with cottages on Manchioneel Bay.

Jost van Dyke: A 4-mile (6.5 km) ferry hop across from Tortola's West End is the terminally laid-back island of Jost van Dyke, a popular day trip for beach lovers. The details are sketchy, but local legend claims van Dyke was a 17th-century Dutch pirate, one of many who rampaged around the islands at the time.

Jost van Dyke boasts several magnificent white sand beaches, although few visitors bother to venture beyond **Great Harbour,** where the ferry docks. Here there is a simple inn, a water-sports concession, and a couple of beach bars. **Foxy's,** at the east end of the beach, is the epicenter of one of the Caribbean's most excessive New Year's parties.

Norman Island: Uninhabited, save for a handful of goats, Norman Island is reputed to have been the setting for Robert Louis Stevenson's *Treasure Island.*

Snorkeling is good around **The Indians** (four jagged pinnacles accessible by yacht). Hungry explorers can refuel at the **Pirates Bight** *(tel 284 446 7827)* bar and grill on the beach, or the **Willy T** *(tel 284 496 8603),* a floating restaurant popular with the yachting crowd.

Peter Island: Just across the Sir Francis Drake Channel from Tortola is Peter Island, occupied by the exclusive **Peter Island Resort.** Even if you are not staying there, you can sample the luxury lifestyle on a day trip from Road Town by ferry.

Flamingo Restoration

At one time, many colonies of pink flamingos called Anegada home. But by the late 20th century, the flamingo population had been wiped out after humans rounded up and consumed the young birds.

Over the last 20 years the National Parks Trust of the Virgin Islands has pursued a campaign to restore the flamingos to Anegada. The trust introduced a few flamingos into the island's natural habitat, where the long-legged birds find a haven from storms and raise their offspring, born from a single egg. The new flamingos have begun forming their own colony, and over 200 flamingos now live on Anegada.

Salt Island: Salt Island's three salt ponds once supplied passing ships with their vital salt rations, and in an appropriate variation of the traditional peppercorn (nominal) rent system, the island still pays an annual tax of

Virgin Gorda

△ 151 E4

Christopher Columbus is to blame for Virgin Gorda's unflattering sobriquet, the "Fat Virgin." From the low and rock-strewn southern end, the island bulges up to a height of 1,359 feet (414 m) at **Gorda Peak** and is supposed to resemble a pregnant woman lying on her back. Most of Virgin Gorda's 2,500 inhabitants live in **The Valley** (often marked as **Spanish Town** on maps), a meandering collection

one bag of salt to the British monarch. While the minuscule local populace (two at a recent count) still harvests salt in the old-fashioned way, the island is chiefly known for the wreck of the RMS *Rhone,* one of the best wreck diving sites in the Caribbean. The British royal mail ship went down with 300 of its crew during a hurricane in 1867, and it lies in 30 to 80 feet (9–24 m) of water on the reefs south of the island. Other notable local dive sites are **Blonde Rock** and **Painted Walls** to the west.

INSIDER TIP:

The Baths on Virgin Gorda are a must-see—visitors should hike the Devil's Bay Trail, which winds under, around, and over huge granite boulders.

—LYNNE CAMPBELL
Owner, Carefree Yacht Charters

Virgin Gorda

of old West Indian houses and more modern concrete villas on the southwest coast. Ferry passengers from Tortola disembark here, and there is also a small airstrip.

To the south of town is the island's chief sightseeing attraction, **The Baths,** a bizarre jumble of monumental boulders piled along the shore. From the drop-off point (accessible by shared taxis from the dockside), a path leads 350 yards (320 m) downhill to the beach and the boulders. Turn left here and enter the caves for a ten-minute scramble up and down the giant rocks and across slapping, bubbling tidal pools to secluded **Devil's Beach,** which girdles an idyllic snorkeling spot.

Heading north from The Valley, the landscape becomes greener and more hilly. The road passes twin crescents of powdery white sand beach edging **Savannah Bay** on the west coast, and then it climbs toward **Gorda Peak National Park.** (There are hiking trails striking up to the mini-mountaintop signed from the roadside; the steep climb takes about 45 minutes round trip.)

The views from the mountain road are fantastic, stretching down the Sir Francis Drake Channel to the south and across the North Sound, a spectacular turquoise bay hemmed in by Mosquito and Prickly Pear Islands. When the road divides, the northern spur leads on to **Leverick Bay;** the other ends at **Gun Creek,** where small motorboats shuttle guests out to the Bitter End and Biras Creek resorts. ■

Two groups: one amid the northerly Leeward Islands and the other off the coast of Venezuela

Dutch Caribbean

You never know what you'll see during the colorful revelry of Carnival in Aruba.

Dutch Caribbean

More than 500 miles (800 km) separate the two very distinct groups of islands that make up the Dutch Caribbean (formerly the Netherlands Antilles). To the north are Sint Maarten, Sint Eustatius, and Saba, and to the south lie Aruba, Bonaire, and Curaçao (referred to as the ABCs). The northern group is known as the Dutch Windward Islands, although their closest neighbors are the British and former British Leeward Islands.

The confusing terms date from the days of sail, when they described an island's geographical location in relation to its home country's preferred outbound and inbound Caribbean trading routes. The ABCs, lying within plain view (on a clear day) of South America, are the Dutch Leewards. Although the Dutch are credited with introducing the sugar industry to the region, they didn't choose their possessions with an eye to sugar growing but as trading posts. Hence, they took control of arid, mountainous Sint Maarten, two tiny volcanic blips known as Sint Fustatius (shortened to Statia in local parlance) and Saba, and the ABCs, three low, wind-blasted, cactus-strewn islets close to South America and the Dutch colonies in Brazil. Before long the calculated gamble paid off, and the islands of Sint Eustatius and Curaçao boasted two of the richest mercantile ports during the 17th and 18th centuries.

Like other Caribbean islands, the Dutch possessions changed hands on several occasions. In an unusually pragmatic arrangement, the island of Sint Maarten/St.-Martin was divided between Dutch and French colonists in 1648. Dutch Sint Maarten and French St.-Martin continue to occupy the 37-square-mile (96 sq km) island, the smallest in the world shared by two sovereign states.

The Dutch secured the six Netherlands Antilles islands under the Treaty of Paris in 1816, but by then the sugar boom was over and by the mid-19th century the Caribbean trade had dried up. The discovery of oil in South America brought renewed prosperity to the ABCs in the 1920s, when North American and European oil companies built vast refineries on Aruba and Curaçao. The capital of Curaçao, Willemstad, became the administrative capital of the Netherlands Antilles and seat of the Staten (parliament), which was granted autonomy within the Kingdom of the Netherlands in 1954.

The collapse of the local oil industry in the mid-1980s was a time of major upheaval for the ABCs and forced the islands to rely on tourism. Aruba's festering resentment at Curaçao's domination in the Staten hardened into demands for independence, and the island was granted autonomy in 1986. When the Netherlands Antilles was dissolved in 2010, Sint Maarten and Curaçao devolved into constituent states within the Kingdom of the Netherlands (similar to Aruba). Bonaire, Saba, and Sint Eustatius chose to retain closer political ties and became "special municipalities."

NOT TO BE MISSED:

Aruba is now the tourism leader in the
Dutch Leewards. Its hotel-lined shores, casinos,
and busy cruise-ship terminal are the envy of
the Curaçaoans, whose tourist industry is taking
longer to develop. Quiet Bonaire has built up
a reputation as one of the world's top diving
destinations. Meanwhile, 500 miles (800 km)
to the north, tourism is also the mainstay of the
Dutch Windward Islands. Sint Maarten flourishes as a duty-free enclave in the old Dutch
West India Company tradition. Sint Eustatius
and Saba maintain a more low-key approach.
With few beaches, their rustic charm endears
them to visitors in search of peace and quiet. ■

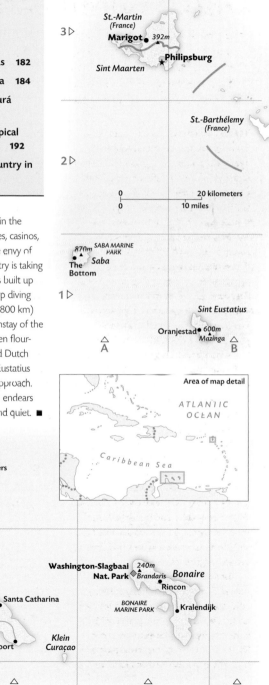

Sint Maarten/St.-Martin

Sint Maarten/St.-Martin, one of the smaller islands in the region at just 37 square miles (96 sq km), celebrated 350 years of dual nationality in 1998. The French occupy the slightly larger northern portion. Although there are no border controls between the two sides of the island, local people are proud of their separate identities. This is particularly noticeable in French St.-Martin, which cultivates a distinctive Gallic air.

Fort St. Louis overlooks Marigot's harbor on the French side of the island.

According to local legend, the division of the island was settled by a Frenchman and a Dutchman who set out to walk around the island in opposite directions, the former armed with a bottle of brandy, the latter with a bottle of gin. The Frenchman, refreshed by brandy, fared better and when the dividing line was drawn up, the French had secured a territory of 21 square miles (54 sq km), the Dutch only 16 square miles (41 sq km).

In spite of its diminutive proportions, Sint Maarten/St.-Martin attracts more than a million visitors a year. The Dutch capital of Philipsburg is the major gateway. This top Caribbean cruise-ship destination and duty-free port is well stocked with shopping bargains. The island is also famed for its beautiful beaches, which encircle the steep, scrub-covered hinterland. Most of the development is on the west coast between Philipsburg and the French capital, Marigot (St.-Martin), where hotels and time-share apartments jostle for space around the Simson Baai lagoon. You can travel between the two island capitals on minibuses.

INSIDER TIP:

The lolos—open air food stalls—of Grand Case [see p. 179] grill some of the best grub on the island. Expect communal picnic tables and lots of locals.

—CHARLES KULANDER
National Geographic Traveler
magazine writer

Philipsburg

Squeezed onto a narrow sandbar between Grand Bay and the landlocked expanses of Great Salt Pond, Philipsburg unfurls along four long, parallel streets linked by alleys known as *steeges.* The heart of town is **de Ruyterplein,** or Wathey Square, where day-trippers arrive by boat from the cruise ships anchored in the bay. At the top

of the square is the restored 19th-century **courthouse,** which has a carved pineapple topknot. To either side of the courthouse, bustling Front Street stretches off in a rich seam of duty-free shops, boutiques, and galleries. Follow the narrow steege down the right-hand side of the court-house to a street market offering bargains on T-shirts, Haitian carvings, and beachwear.

A ten minute walk east on Front Street will bring you to the **Guavaberry Emporium,** housed in a luridly painted gingerbread cottage on the sidewalk, dating from the 1830s. You can sample locally produced guavaberry liqueur (made from the fruit of *Eugenia floribunda,* not guavas).

A little farther up on the right, on an unnamed steege, is the **Sint Maarten Museum.** Laid out on

Philipsburg

 175 E3

Visitor Information

✉ Wathey Sq. cruise facility and Captain Hodge Wharf

☎ 721 542 2337

Sint Maarten Museum

✉ 7 Front St.

☎ 721 542 4917

🕐 Closed Sat. p.m. & Sun.

3▷

0 ————— 4 kilometers
0 ————— 2 miles

Saint-Martin (Fr.)

Anse Marcel   Pointe Nord
Bell Point   265m   Grandes Cayes
L'Espérance Airport
Grand Case ✈   Îlet Pinel   Île Tintamarre
Baie de Friar   Cul de Sac
Baie Orientale

Pointe d'Arago   **Fort St. Louis**   Rambaud   381m   Étang Chevrise   Caye Verte
Pointe du Bluff   Baie de la Potence   **Quartier du Colombier**   424m   Étang aux Poissons   **Ferme des Papillons**
Pointe aux Prunes   Baie Rouge   **Marigot**   Pic du Paradis   Baie de l'Embouchure
Baie aux Prunes   Terres Basses   Baie Nettlé   **Colombier**   **Loterie Farm**   **Quartier d'Orléans**
Pointe du Cannonier   Grand Étang   **Musée de Marigot**   392m   Flagstaff   Baie Lucas
Baie Longue   de Simson Baai   273m   **St. Peter**   Babit Point
Cupecoy Beach   340m   Cul de Sac   Lower Prince's Quarter
Mulletbaai   Princess Juliana Airport ✈   Sentry Hill   **Sint Maarten Park**
Maho Baai   Great Salt Pond   **Upper Prince's Quarter**   Guana Baai
Simsonbaai   Koolbaai   **Philipsburg** ★   Guana Bay Point
Simson Baai   Guana Key
Kool Baai   Groot Baai   Geneve Baai   Mal Aborder
Guana Key
Sint Maarten (Neth.)   Point Blanche   Hen and Chicken

2▷

1▷

△ A   △ B   △ C

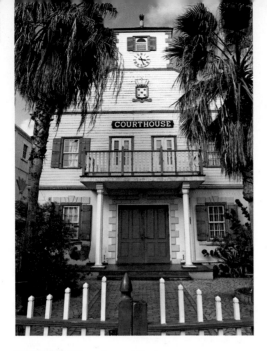

Philipsburg's 19th-century courthouse

Sint Maarten Park
- 177 C2
- Arch Rd. Madame Estate
- 721 543 2030
- $$

Marigot
- 177 B2

Visitor Information
- Rte. de Sandy Ground
- 0590 87 57 21

the second floor, the tiny museum is a mine of local information. Geological displays include a relief map illustrating how the island was once linked to neighboring St. Barthélmy (St. Barts) and Anguilla. Check out the colonial artifacts, old musket balls, and other relics salvaged from the 1801 wreck of the frigate H.M.S. *Proselyte,* as well as a nostalgic collection of antique ice-cream makers, flatirons, and photographs.

Beyond the museum the steege ends at the sandy bayfront, a short walk from **Bobby's Marina,** with its popular restaurants, daily ferries to Marigot, and boat trips to St. Barts and Saba. Minibuses depart for the French capital of Marigot from Back Street (one block behind Front Street).

Around Sint Maarten

The only sightseeing attraction on the Dutch side is the **Sint Maarten Park,** a family-friendly zoological garden on the far side of Great Salt Pond. Caribbean birds are displayed in walk-through aviaries, and there's a small but interesting selection of South American reptiles and mammals such as capybaras.

Beyond Philipsburg, Sint Maarten's chief lure is the beach. On the south side is **Simson Baai Beach,** which has good swimming and windsurfing, although it does lie in the flight path for Princess Juliana Airport. Head northwest along the coast for **Mulletbaai,** a tourist favorite with water-sports concessions. For something quieter, try **Cupecoy Beach,** which is backed by low cliffs; nude bathing is permitted at the northern end. Heading east from Philipsburg, just before the border with St.-Martin, a track leads right off the main road for lovely **Dawn Beach,** a good place to spend the day sunning, snorkeling and lunching at a local restaurant.

Further afield, a day trip to the ultra-chic neighboring island of St. Barts (see pp. 244–246) is a favorite pastime with visitors ready for a change of scene. A day-return boat service *(Tues.–Sat.)* makes the 45-minute crossing from the Pelican Marina in Philipsburg *(tel 721 544 2640),* or you can travel independently by water taxi.

Marigot

The appealing and unmistakably French capital of St.-Martin appears to have been plucked straight from the Côte d'Azur and grafted onto a Caribbean island. This is café-and-croissant country, where the sidewalk terraces blossom with bright umbrellas. The town center is laid out between the twin poles of the waterfront and the **Marina Port La Royale**. A craft market lines the waterfront, and the old warehouses along the boulevard de France have been converted into restaurants and cafés.

The ruins of 18th-century **Fort St. Louis** survey the scene from the heights above the harbor, where the frequent daily ferry service to Anguilla (*tel 264 497 2231*) and boat trips to St. Barts (*tel 0590 87 10 68*) depart from the pier.

A grid of shopping streets leads back to rue de Hollande and the minibus pick-up/drop-off points for Philipsburg and Grand Case. To the west are the yacht-filled slips of the marina, edged by a collection of cafés and boutiques selling souvenirs and French fashions.

The exemplary **Musée de Marigot** is well worth seeking out for its Amerindian section and exhibits detailing island history, geology, and marine life.

Around St.-Martin

The French side offers a further range of fine beaches (and topless bathing), starting with the alluring mile-long (1.6 km) expanse of **Baie Longue** on the southern tip of the Simson Baai lagoon peninsula. Around the corner is **Baie aux Prunes**, popular with surfers and snorkelers; **Baie Rouge**, where beachgoers can rent sun loungers and umbrellas or swim around the point to a secluded cove; and hotel-lined **Baie Nettlé**, which is good for water sports.

Social Butterflies

A couple of handy hints to get the best out of the Ferme des Papillons experience:

- **Arrive early when the doors open at 9 a.m. to watch the newly hatched butterflies take flight.**
- **Butterflies are attracted to bright colors, so wear yellow or pink if you want them to land on you.**
- **Citrus-based perfumes and the free tropical punch drink you receive on arrival will also bring the butterflies up close.**
- **Save your ticket: It's good for the duration of your vacation and can be used again.**

North of Marigot is **Grand Case**, its one pretty, sandy street lined with some of the island's best restaurants. Boats bob at anchor farther east in the harbor fronting **Anse Marcel**, which has safe swimming for children and water sports concessions. Off the east coast are glorious bayside beaches on the **Îlet Pinel**, accessible by ferry from Cul de Sac, and undeveloped **Île Tintamarre**. On the mainland is **Baie Orientale**, known for its sophisticated restaurants and shops.

Located in the lee of **Pic du Paradis**—at 1,390 feet (424 m) the island's highest peak—**Loterie Farm** is a secluded private forest reserve. Old mountainside slave trails have been restored for hikers; there's a zipwire and a great little café for refueling afterward. Another detour leads to the **Ferme des Papillons** (Butterfly Farm) at Baie de l'Embouchure. Hundreds of butterflies flutter about the gardens and miniature waterfalls inside a huge climate-controlled sphere. ∎

Musée de Marigot
- ✉ 7 rue Fichot
- ☎ 590 56 78 92
- $ $

Loterie Farm
- ◭ 177 B2
- ✉ Colombier
- ☎ 0590 87 86 16
- $ $

Ferme des Papillons
- ◭ 177 C2
- ✉ Rte. du Galion
- ☎ 0590 87 31 21
- $ $$

www.thebutterfly farm.com

Sint Eustatius

A sleepy Caribbean backwater some 35 miles (56 km) south of Sint Maarten, Sint Eustatius is the undeveloped Rip van Winkle of the Dutch Windwards, dozing quietly in the lee of its imposing volcanic cone, the Quill. Better known as Statia (pronounced STAY-sha), the island attracts a handful of curious visitors, day-trippers from Sint Maarten, and a motley crew of American and European expatriates who revel in the absence of chic resorts, shopping malls, discos, and other manifestations of mass tourism.

The Quill/Boven National Park became the Netherlands Antilles's first national park in 1998.

There are no decent beaches on Sint Eustatius, but therein lies the island's quirky charm. Instead, Statia's glittering past looms large from the history books, out of all proportion to its modest physical dimensions. The island is just 2 miles (3 km) wide and 5 miles (8 km) long from its hilly northern tip through the low central plain to the southern slopes of the Quill. The 3,000 islanders live in the capital, Oranjestad, on the central west coast.

Savvy traders from the Dutch West India Company set up shop in Oranjestad in 1636 and developed the port into such a phenomenally successful mercantile center and slave market that Statia was nicknamed the Golden Rock. Merchant vessels flying every conceivable national flag crowded the harbor, and as business expanded, land was reclaimed to build additional warehouses. On November 16, 1776, the cannon of Fort Oranje fired an 11-gun salute in reply to the merchant ship *Andrew Doria*, an American colonial brig flying the Stars and Stripes, and unwittingly Holland became the first nation to recognize the United

INSIDER TIP:

If heading out to hike the Quill, be sure to wear layers. The crater's volcanic interior can be steamy, especially in contrast with the cool of the mount's summit.

—LARRY PORGES
Editor, National Geographic Books

States of America. This act earned the tiny island the sobriquet "America's Childhood Friend." In 1781, in retaliation, a British naval expedition under Adm. George Brydges Rodney (1718–1792) descended on Statia, taking possession of all the ships and goods in the port.

Statia never recovered, and her beachless shores have hampered the tourist industry. Today, the island is quietly developing a reputation as the new Saba for attracting divers in search of pristine dive sites. With good walks around the Quill (Mount Mazinga) and incredibly friendly local people, the island makes an interesting offbeat escape for visitors with a no-frills, no-problem attitude.

Oranjestad

A small cliff divides the villagey island capital into two parts. Hurricanes and Admiral Rodney's handiwork have all but destroyed the Lower Town around the harbor, so everybody lives in the **Upper**

Town, perched on the clifftop guarded by 17th-century **Fort Oranje.** The Sint Eustatius Historical Foundation's **Simon Doncker Museum** is housed in a restored 18th-century brick home occupied by Rodney during his stay. Here pre-Columbian artifacts, blue glass trading beads used during the slave era,

A Jewish Heritage

In the 17th century, in an effort to improve the economies of their Caribbean holdings, the Dutch began offering grants to European Jews to encourage immigration to Sint Eustatius. Spanish, Portuguese, and Eastern European Jews accepted the offer, and Jewish communities grew and became an integral part of Statia's mercantile success for the next century. When the British attacked Statia in the 18th century (see this page), the Jews were expelled. As the ruins of Honen Dalim Synagogue attest, the island's Jewish community never recovered. Today, the synagogue is being rebuilt as a testament to the Jews' contributions to Sint Eustatius.

and porcelain from the Nanking cargo salvaged from the *South China Sea,* which foundered in 1752 en route to Statia, can be seen alongside rooms furnished in colonial style.

The town has several historic ruins, including the **Honen Dalim Synagogue,** the second oldest temple in the Western Hemisphere, dating from 1742. The building fell into disrepair after Rodney took the Jewish community's money and then deported the people.

Sint Eustatius

🅰 175 B1

Visitor Information

✉ Fort Oranjestraat

☎ 599 318 2433

www.statiatourism .com

Simon Doncker Museum

✉ Wilhelminaweg, Oranjestad

☎ 599 318 2288

🕐 Closed Sat. p.m. & Sun. p.m.

💲 $$

www.steustatius history.org

Around the Island

A trek up the Quill is a must during any visit to Sint Eustatius. Several routes go to the lip of the crater; the most direct follows a moderately steep path and takes about 45 minutes. Beneath the high point of **Mount Mazinga** (1,968 feet/ 600 m), the 550-foot-deep (168 m) crater is carpeted with lush vegetation. On the southwest coast are the ruins of **Fort de Windt,** which afford views across to St. Kitts. (Even though fortresses once ringed Sint Eustatius, the island still changed hands with monotonous regularity.)

Around to the southeast, the **Miriam C. Schmidt Botanical Garden** flourishes on the slopes of the Quill. Volunteers have created a series of tranquil areas showcasing native plant species and rarities, a local-style kitchen garden, a bird observation trail, and a Lookout Garden with magnificent views of St. Kitts across the channel, where migrating humpback whales may be seen in winter *(Jan.–March).*

Continuing on up the Quill's eastern flanks, the **Lynch Plantation Museum** *(tel 599 318 2338, by appt. only)* makes an intriguing detour. Here, the Berkel family's collections of period furnishings, tools, domestic utensils, and personal items offer a unique through-the-keyhole glimpse of life on Statia almost a century ago.

Beaches & Diving

Statia does have a couple of beaches, but with grayish volcanic sand. Close to the Lower Town is **Oranje Beach,** popular with locals, and **Crooks Castle** is farther south. Because of dangerous currents, swimming is not safe in the bays on the Atlantic coast. Statia's underwater landscape—even more dramatic than its textbook-perfect volcano—is protected by **St. Eustatius National Marine Park** *(www.statiapark.org).* There are 30-plus official sites ranging from coral reefs and canyons to the **Supermarket** wreck site, where rare flying fish occasionally put in an appearance. The site is composed of two shipwrecks around a section of reef. The easily accessible **City Wall** site, just outside the harbor, was the original sea wall for the old Lower Town warehouse district. ■

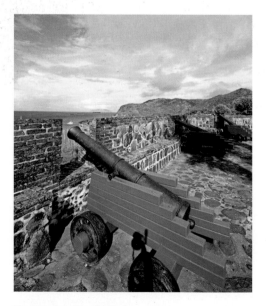

The view from Fort de Windt

Saba

From a distance, tiny Saba (pronounced SAY-ba) rises out of the sea like a witch's hat from its 5-square-mile (13 sq km) base. On closer inspection, the dramatic outline of Mount Scenery (2,909 feet/870 m) doesn't stand alone but among a supporting cast of lesser peaks and ridges that make up the impressively rugged, green interior. The cliffs that edge the island drop away beneath the waves into an underwater world no less fantastically sheer and rated one of the top dive destinations in the Caribbean.

The famous stairs leading down to Saba's Ladder Bay

Life on Saba moves at a sedate pace. The 1,500 Sabans live in attractive villages where little white cottages with uniform red roofs perch precariously one above the other on steep hillsides. The capital of the island is the town of The Bottom, but most travelers head up the twisting route known simply as The Road (see sidebar p. 185) to visit the steeply canted, upland village of Windwardside.

Columbus sighted Saba in 1493, but it took a shipwreck to land the first Europeans on the island more than a century later. Dutch colonists from Sint Eustatius founded the first permanent settlement in the 1640s. In 1665 the infamous Welsh pirate Henry Morgan (1635–1688) captured Saba and banished all non-English speakers during his short stay. Thereafter the almost impregnable island changed hands by treaty

Saba
🅰 175 A1
Visitor Information
✉ Windwardside, Saba
☎ 599 416 2231
www.sabatourism.com

Saba Museum

✉ Windwardside

🕐 Closed Sat. &
Sun.

💲 $

rather than invasion, supported a few small sugar plantations, and lived very quietly.

Around the Island

Saba's capital, The Bottom, lies in a sloping valley and probably takes its name from the Dutch word *botte* (bowl). Among the traditional clapboard homes are several small businesses, shops, and bars and the **Lieutenant-Governor's Residence,** an attractive old Saban house with balconies and gingerbread decoration.

To the south for about a mile (1.5 km), The Road wriggles steeply down to **Fort Bay,** the main port. A leg-trembling flight of 500-plus steps descends to the harbor on **Ladder Bay.** In pre-Road days this was the only route on and off the island, and everything from a box of nails to a tin bathtub had to be carried up on somebody's back.

Tucked into the lee of Mount Scenery, with fantastic views down to the coast, **Windwardside** clings tenaciously to the slopes, its neat cottages linked by a cat's cradle of narrow alleys. Housed in a 19th-century Dutch sea captain's cottage, the **Saba Museum** serves up a modest history of the island.

Although diving may be Saba's chief draw, hiking Mount Scenery

---

EXPERIENCE: Dive Saba Marine Park

Established in 1987 to protect Saba's pristine marine environment, the Saba Marine Park rings the small island. It is divided into commercial and recreational zones: Most of the dive sites are marked by permanent buoys off the west coast.

The astonishing diversity of the park's underwater landscapes is matched by vibrant marine life. Excellent visibility ranges upward from 125 feet (38 m) in winter. Varied, challenging diving is ensured by elkhorn forests, giant boulders encrusted with sponges, soft and hard corals, submerged pinnacles that attract big groupers, jacks, and rays, and walls dropping to depths of 1,000 feet (300 m)

within half a mile (800 m) of the shore. Green and hawksbill turtles feed in the protected waters.

The park is partially funded by the small fee paid for each dive. Further information about dives can be obtained from **Saba Marine Park**, Fort Bay Harbor *(The Bottom, tel 599 416 3295, www.sabapark .org/marine_park/)* or by contacting local dive operators such as **Saba Deep Dive** *(tel 599 416 3347 or U.S. 866 416 3347, www.sabadeep.com, $$$$$);* **Saba Divers** *(tel 599 416 2740, www.sabadivers.com, $$$$$);* and **Sea Saba Dive Center** *(tel 599 416 2246 or U.S. 800 883 7222, www.seasaba .com, $$$$$).*

A small cluster of homes on the mountain slope above Windwardside

is an excellent land-based diversion. The 1,064-step path to the summit passes through secondary rain forest to a gnarled and stunted world of elfin woodland carpeted with mosses and ferns and is frequently wreathed in mist. The tourist office and **Saba Trail Shop** *(tel 599 416 2630, www.sabapark .org/hiking_trails/trail_shop/)* in Windwardside have details of other trails and local guide services.

From Windwardside, The Road continues its serpentine way for just under a mile (1.5 km) to the settlement of **Hell's Gate** and on to the airport at Flat Point. From Flat Point, hike the steep crags down from the breathtaking heights of the forest to the tide pools below. In calm seas, the pools fill with still, crystal-clear water and ocean wildlife—sea urchins, kaleidoscopic-colored fish, and abundant sea flora. ■

The Road

A minor miracle of engineering and a monument to Saban stubbornness, The Road traverses Saba from Fort Bay in the southwest to Flat Point in the northeast. When the Sabans first investigated the possibility of a road to augment the old footpaths and donkey tracks in the 1930s, Dutch civil engineers said it couldn't be done. Josephus Hassell's response was to sign up for a correspondence course in civil engineering, and, utilizing his newly acquired knowledge, work began at Fort Bay in 1938. The Road reached The Bottom five years later, crept into Windwardside in 1951, and eventually arrived in Flat Point after carving a 19-mile (31 km) corkscrew passage across the island.

Curaçao

Curaçao has the greatest landmass of the Dutch Leewards. These lie amid the larger group of Caribbean islands known as the Lesser Antilles, running parallel to the northern coastline of Venezuela. The ethnic mix of the islanders is as beguiling as Curaçao's beaches and limpid blue waters, and it seems fitting that the island should also be known for its vividly colored liqueurs.

A colonial-era government building in Willemstad, Curaçao

Curaçao

⚑ 175 D1

Visitor Information

✉ Pietermaai 19, Willemstad

☎ 5999 434 8200

The chief Dutch possession in the Caribbean since the 17th century, Curaçao is the largest of the six Dutch Caribbean islands at 38 miles (61 km) by 9 miles (14.5 km). It lies only 35 miles (56 km) off the coast of Venezuela. Curaçao's rocky shoreline, with its cliffs and coves, is indented with fingernail slivers of white sand beach and lapped by staggeringly blue waters. Inland, giant cactuses straight out of a cowboy movie lord it over the rugged *cunucu,* a scrub-covered landscape that receives less than 23 inches (580 mm) of rain a year.

The Spanish landed on Curaçao in 1499 and dubbed it the Isla de los Gigantes (Island of Giants) for the tall, seafaring Caquetio people they encountered. The native population was soon shipped off to work in the gold mines of Hispaniola, and the ABCs were declared *islas inútiles* (useless islands). In 1634 the Dutch West India Company spotted the potential of Sint Annabaai, Curaçao's huge natural harbor, the largest in the region and seventh largest in the world. The company ejected a handful of Spanish settlers and set about fortifying the harbor entrance and constructing Willemstad within sturdy defensive walls.

Under the Dutch, Curaçao grew wealthy. A notable early governor of the island was Peter Stuyvesant (1592–1672), who lost his leg fighting the Spanish for possession of Sint Maarten in 1644 before sailing off to take up the governorship of Nieuw Amsterdam (New York). Willemstad's duty free port handled goods from sugar to gold bullion; it also developed into the Caribbean's busiest slave market. A few plantations were established on the island, but the struggle with the arid climate and infertile soil was a difficult one. Their legacy is a collection of pretty Dutch colonial *landhuizen* (plantation houses) in the rolling hinterland.

EXPERIENCE:
Taste Curaçao Cocktails

For some, the name Curaçao brings to mind the bottles of vivid blue, red, orange, and green liqueurs that lurk behind cocktail bars the world over. This is where they originate, courtesy of the bitter Laraha orange. The sun-dried peels of these inedible fruits, which were introduced by the Spanish, are distilled with water and sugar to form a clear liqueur that is then colored with flavorless additives. The **Senior Curaçao Liqueur Distillery** *(Mercuriusstraat, Salinja, tel 5999 461 3526, closed Sat. & Sun.)* welcomes visitors to its showroom in the 19th-century **Landhuis Chobolobo** in the eastern suburbs of Willemstad.

The Dutch didn't abolish slavery until 1863, and Curaçao idled along until 1918, when construction of the world's largest oil refinery refueled the island's prosperity. Workers poured in from around the Caribbean, the Americas, and beyond, creating a multiracial society. The present-day population of 145,000 is concentrated around Willemstad and the southwestern

Noordpunt

Westpunt • CHRISTOFFEL

372m ▲ **Landhuis Savonet**
Playu Mt. Sint Christoffel
Lagun NATIONAL
Lagun PARK   Playa Grandi

Boca
Santa Cruz
•Soto   •Barber

St. Martabaai

△
A   San Juanbaai

Landhuis Jan Kok
Sint Willibrordus•   **Landhuis Daniel**
                     Hato International
Kaap St. Marie Boca Airport
          St. Marie ✈

              **Landhuis
              Papaya** Suffisant
           Julianadorp Dorp **Landhuis**
                            Brievengat •Santa Catharina
                    Emmastad
           Piscaderabaai Schottegat •Santa Sint Jorisbaai
Curaçao Museum ★   Rosa
Willemstad ◆**Fortkerk**
              Museum Spaanse
△   **Curaçao Sea Aquarium**• Water
B   194m
              Caracasbaai ▲
                        Tafelberg
              Nieuwpoort•   Oostpunt•

◁3

◁2

◁1

0 _____ 10 kilometers
0 _____ 5 miles

△   △
C   D

Fortkerk Museum

🅰 187 C1

✉ Fort Amsterdam Gouvernement-splein

☎ 5999 461 1139

🕐 Closed Sat. & Sun.

💲 $

Mikvé Israël-Emanuel Synagogue & Jewish Museum

✉ Hanchi Snoa 29

☎ 5999 461 1633

🕐 Closed Sat. & Sun.

💲 $$

www.snoa.com

beaches. The northern part of the island contains Christoffel National Park (see p. 190). This area is very quiet, with just a few small hotels, restaurants, and dive shops on the shore backed by acres of green-gray cunucu backcountry.

Willemstad

A little pocket of the Caribbean that will be forever Amsterdam, Willemstad's **Handelskade** waterfront is charming. Dutch gables and terra-cotta roof tiles adorn buildings painted pastel pink and pistachio, with a dash of citrus yellow here and curlicue white stucco plaster-work there. Though modern excrescences now outnumber historic buildings, the effect is still startlingly attractive and a favorite photo opportunity for the scores of visitors who arrive by cruise ship to plunder the capital's duty-free stores and

explore its beautifully preserved streets. Willemstad is, not surprisingly, a UNESCO World Heritage site.

The city is divided by the Sint Annabaai channel, which leads into Schottegat Harbor. On the west side is the **Otrabanda quarter,** where the cruise ships dock; to the east Handelskade fronts the central **Punda district,** where the main shops and sights are found. One of the Punda's most popular attractions is the busy daily **Mercado Flotante** (Floating Market). Located around the corner from Handelskade, on the watery cul-de-sac of Waaigat, Venezuelan schooners line the **Sha Caprileskade** waterfront and goods spill out onto colorful market stalls arranged with fresh fruit and vegetables grown on the South American mainland.

A tour of historic Willemstad should begin on the waterfront along Handelskade at **Fort**

EXPERIENCE: Cracking Adventures

Getting out and about in the *cunucu* is a must, and several adventure tour operators offer hiking, mountain biking, and ATV experiences. If you want to explore Christoffel National Park, **Yellow Jeep Safaris** (tel 5999 462 6262, www.tourism-curacao.com, $$$$$) heads off the beaten track to explore the rugged north coast and the heart of the park with a stop at Brua Cave, a former refuge for escaped slaves. Guided mountain bike excursions are led by **WannaBike Curaçao** (tel 5999 527 3720, www.wannabike.com, $$$$$). Cyclists need to be reasonably fit; bikes, helmets, and water bottles are provided. Pilot your own ATV for a guided scramble

around the sights and into the backcountry with **Eric's ATV Adventures** (tel 5999 524 7418, www.curacao-atv.com, $$$$$). Or for something completely different, how about an ostrich safari? North of Willemstad, off the road to Santa Catarina, Curaçao's very own **Ostrich Farm** (Groot St. Joris, tel 5999 747 2777, www.ostrichfarm.net, $$$$) invites visitors to get up close and personal with African ostriches. After a guided driving tour, there are opportunities to weigh a giant ostrich egg, tuck into an ostrich burger at the Zambezi Restaurant, and even "ride" a full-grown ostrich for a memorable holiday snapshot.

Amsterdam. Government offices now occupy the former Dutch West India Company headquarters. There's free access to the courtyard and the 1769 fort church, which houses the small **Fortkerk Museum,** with its displays of antique silverware and maps. The church once doubled as a sail loft, and its rainwater cisterns were built of the tiny yellow and red bricks—used in many buildings around town—shipped from Holland as ballast.

Several years before Fortkerk was completed, Willemstad's Jewish community had begun to worship in the **Mikvé Israël-Emanuel Synagogue,** the oldest synagogue in continuous use in the Americas. Portuguese Jews arrived in Curaçao in the 1650s and founded the first synagogue in 1674; Mikvé Israël was dedicated in 1732. Located in the heart of the the Punda, the synagogue occupies an attractive courtyard complex alongside a museum displaying religious artifacts and memorabilia.

The old Jewish residential district of **Scharloo,** across Waaigat, is slowly being restored. In a reclaimed 18th-century waterfront mansion, the **Maritime Museum** displays collections of model ships, maps, and miniatures and offers ferry tours of the harbor. **Scharlooweg,** one block behind the waterfront, is lined with some of Willemstad's best preserved 18th- to 19th-century town houses.

The Otrabanda district is reached by the **Koningin Emmabrug** (Queen Emma Bridge) from Handelskade. The impressive swinging pontoon bridge was designed by U.S. consul Leonard B. Smith and installed in 1888. (A free ferry operates when the bridge is opened to allow ships through.) Otrabanda is home to the cruise-ship terminal and the **Riffort,** a 19th-century fort that guards one side of the harbor. Also here is the excellent **Museum Kurá Hulanda,** part of a beautifully restored complex of Dutch Colonial buildings, which

Maritime Museum

✉ Van der Brandhofstraat 7

☎ 5999 465 2327

🕓 Closed Sun. & Mon.

💲 $$$

Museum Kurá Hulanda

✉ Klipstraat 9

☎ 5999 434 7765

💲 $$

www.kurahulanda .com

Fresh produce for sale at the Punda's Mercado Flotante

houses one of the largest collections of African art and artifacts in the Caribbean. Exhibits range from art treasures of the West African empires to the re-created hold of a transatlantic slave ship.

One mile (1.5 km) north of the city center is the **Curaçao Museum,** located in a former seamen's hospital. The museum exhibits monumental colonial furniture, pre-Columbian relics, and works by local artists. ∎

Curaçao Museum

🗺 187 C1

✉ Van Leeuwenhoekstraat

☎ 5999 462 3873

🕓 Closed Sat.

Around Curaçao

A national park at the island's northern tip combines natural and colonial history in one hikable location. Fans of sea life can view it in tanks or from the beach at the Curaçao Sea Aquarium.

Christoffel National Park

 187 B3

✉ Savonet

☎ 5999 864 0363

💲 $$$

Curaçao Sea Aquarium

📍 187 C1

☎ Bapor Kibra, SE of Willemstad

☎ 5999 461 6666

💲 $$$$

**www.curacao-sea
aquarium.com**

Christoffel National Park

The 4,650-acre (1,880 ha) Christoffel National Park, in the north of the island, is composed of three former plantations on the slopes of **Mount Sint Christoffel** (1,220 feet/372 m), the highest point in the Dutch Leeward islands.

The park center, on the grounds of **Landhuis Savonet** plantation, has a small museum describing the island's geology, flora, and fauna, and it is the starting point for a network of trails that strike off into the cunucu or down to the wave-lashed cliffs at **Playa Grandi.** There are fascinating guided walks daily *(call for reservations)*, and special evening walks offer a chance to spot the rare Curaçaoan deer, a

subspecies of the North American white-tailed deer introduced to the island in pre-Columbian times. Guides can also be arranged for private hikes and bird-watching. Horseback riding and mountain bike rental are available from the Rancho Alfin concession *(tel 5999 864 0535)*.

Curaçao Sea Aquarium

A marine life showcase with family appeal, the Sea Aquarium offers outdoor lagoons for sea lions and sharks, tanks housing toothsome eels and tropical fish, and touch tanks. More unusual aspects are an underwater observatory anchored to the shore and the Animal Encounters program *(reservations required)*. The encounters take place in a natural reef pool, which is home to stingrays, sea turtles, jacks, tarpon, and sharks. After an introductory dive with a qualified instructor, participants can snorkel and scuba dive among the nondangerous residents on one side of the pool and hand-feed the segregated lemon and nurse sharks through holes in a Plexiglas wall.

Adjacent **Sea Aquarium Beach** is one of the island's best, providing access to the 12-mile-long (19 km) **Curaçao Underwater Park,** a magnet for snorkelers and divers. ■

Landhuizen

About 300 country estates had spread across the island's interior by the early 19th century. Most had a modest Dutch colonial *landhuis* (plantation house) for the owner's family. A handful have been restored, notably **Landhuis Brievengat, Landhuis Jan Kok,** and **Landhuis Knepa. Landhuis Papaya,** which is painted bloodred (the rarer of the two traditional Curaçaoan color schemes), and **Landhuis Daniel** are on the Westpunt road outside Willemstad. The latter has been transformed into a bar-restaurant and a simple hotel with a good restaurant *(information for all sites: tel 5999 434 8200)*.

Bonaire

Shaped like a distorted boomerang and lying 30 miles (48 km) east of Curaçao, Bonaire is a diver's paradise—and that's official, according to the legend adorning local car license plates. Along the sheltered leeward coast of the island and around the offshore islet of Klein (Little) Bonaire, more than 80 dive sites give access to some of the most spectacular and varied marine landscapes in the entire Caribbean.

Bonaire, a derivation of the Arawak word *bojnaj,* meaning "low country," was first noted by Italian explorer Amerigo Vespucci in 1499. When the Dutch wrested control of the island from Spain in 1634, they introduced slaves to harvest the salt pans in the flat southern portion of the island and raised cattle on the scrub-covered backcountry to supply the burgeoning colony of Curaçao.

Activity on the island stuttered to an almost complete halt with the abolition of slavery in 1863, but after a century's break, Bonaire's salt industry was revived in the 1960s. The decade also saw the first divers venturing to the out-of-the-way island, and Bonaire's special brand of low-key, dive-oriented tourism was born. Although the news about Bonaire's spectacular underwater world is well and truly out, and hotels are mushrooming, the island atmosphere is still quiet and definitely casual. Nondivers can find fantastic snorkeling from walk-in sites directly off the shore, as well as hiking, mountain biking, horseback riding, and bird-watching.

The modest capital of Bonaire is **Kralendijk** (Coral Dike), a small town of tidy yellow and gold Dutch Caribbean buildings,

Snorkeling in Bonaire

restaurants, and hotels facing the rounded outline of Klein Bonaire. For a slice of local history, take a stroll out to the **Museo Boneriano.** Assorted collections of archaeological finds, antiques, old photographs, and a wonderful shell collection are laid out in a handsomely restored 19th-century plantation house. From Kralendijk a road circles the southern portion of the island, passing the glittering white salt stacks awaiting shipment from the solar saltworks, which conceal flamingo nesting grounds at Pekelmeer. East of the capital there's an interesting detour to **Rooi Lamoenchi Kunuku Park** (*tel 599 717 8489, by appt. only, $$*). Call

Bonaire
⬛ 175 E1
Visitor Information
✉ Kaya Grandi 2, Kralendijk
☎ 599 717 8322 Fax 599 717 8408

Washington-Slagbaai National Park

- 🅜 175 E1
- ☎ 599 717 8444
- 🅢 Nature Tag $$

www.washington
parkbonaire.org

Bonaire Marine Park

- 🅜 175 E1
- ☎ 599/717-8444
- 🅢 Nature Tag $$ or dive fee $$$

www.bmp.org

NOTE: Bonaire's natural resources are partially supported by tariffs levied on park visitors. All snorkelers and swimmers are required to purchase a Nature Tag ($$), which is valid for a year and includes admission to land-based Washington-Slagbaai National Park. The divers' Nature Tag ($$$) is also valid for a year—both tags can be bought at dive shops and park offices.

ahead for a personal tour of this restored plantation homestead and gardens set amid aloe vera fields and cacti-strewn cunucu. There is also an old dam where water birds such as herons, egrets and duck congregate.

Northwest of Kralendijk is Bonaire's oldest settlement, the sleepy inland village of **Rincón,** on the road to the national park. A short distance away on the Atlantic coast, at Boca Onima, Caquetio Indians left their marks scribbled in red dye on cave walls.

To the north of Rincón, and covering the northwestern portion of the island, is **Washington-Slagbaai National Park.** This 13,500-acre (5,463 ha) tract of land occupying one-fifth of the island has operated as a wildlife preserve since the 1960s. It is crisscrossed by four-wheel-drive trails and hiking paths, one of which scales the high point of Mount Brandaris (784 feet/240 m). The park is home to most of Bonaire's 190 bird species, including parrots, hummingbirds, and a flamingo colony on the Gotomeer lagoon. Several snorkel

and dive sites lie off the leeward coast, such as **Boca Slagbaai** (Slaughter Bay), and **Playa Funchi.** The park's beaches are protected sea turtle nesting sites.

The island is surrounded by **Bonaire Marine Park,** a rigorously safeguarded conservation zone covering around 700 acres. Designated a marine preserve in 1971, the park rings the entire island and extends from the shore to the 200-foot-deep (60 m) contour through shallow, sloping terraces of fringe reefs to the drop-off. More than 80 species of corals have been identified, including elkhorn, staghorn, leaf, and brain corals, and the reefs are patrolled by a dazzling array of electric blue tangs, angelfish, parrot fish, grunts, and sea horses. All these delights are accessible to snorkelers, too. Simply locate one of the yellow stone dive markers and wade out. Top snorkeling sites include **Windsock Steep,** on the east coast near the airport; the beaches in **Washington-Slagbaai National Park;** and **Small Wall,** off the west coast and best accessed on a snorkel cruise. ∎

EXPERIENCE: A Fish-Eye View

Capturing holiday memories on camera is a great way to relive the high spots of your vacation, but it gets a little more complicated if the most memorable experiences (and mind-blowing vistas) occur underwater. Cue Tim Peters of **Fish-Eye Photo** *(Kaya Gobernador N. Debrot 77B, tel 599 717 2001, www .fisheyephoto.com, $$$$$),* a former studio photographer turned scuba instructor turned underwater photographer, who runs underwater photography courses in

the Bonaire Marine Park. Half- and one-day courses aimed at beginners, two- or three-day more advanced courses, and PADI digital underwater photographer (DUP) tuition combine the practicalities of underwater photography with camera skills and the opportunity to return home with truly spectacular souvenirs from the reef. Participants can bring their own cameras (SLR or digital), or borrow equipment for free during the course; camera rentals are available.

Aruba

Fifteen miles (24 km) as the pelican flies from the coast of Venezuela, with a population of 106,000, diminutive Aruba—20 by 6 miles (32 x 10 km)—was the first of the Dutch Caribbean islands to achieve Status Aparte from the Netherlands Antilles (1986) in the wake of the oil boom collapse. The islanders then turned wholeheartedly toward tourism, developing one of the Caribbean's hottest vacation destinations.

Dismissed as an *isla inútil* (useless island) by its Spanish discoverers, Aruba was eventually used for ranching and developed something of a reputation for horse breeding. In 1824 gold was discovered, prompting a small-scale gold rush, but the mining became unprofitable and ceased altogether in 1914. Remains of the old mines and smelting works can be seen around Balashi and Bushiribana. Aloe vera plantations sprouted in the early 1900s, but oil refineries built in the mid-1920s made the island's fortunes, caused a population explosion, and gave Aruba one of the highest standards of living in the Caribbean region.

Arubans still live comfortably. They are ruled by a 21-member democratic parliament presided over by the prime minister. The Kingdom of the Netherlands, which handles defense and foreign affairs, is represented by a governor. Aruba has its own legal system, currency, and an excellent education system, which gives foreign languages a high priority. Most people speak English and Spanish as well as Papiamento (see sidebar p. 196). The islanders' Amerindian heritage is reflected in their looks, though there are now

A fishing boat off the coast of Aruba

more than 40 nationalities bubbling in the Aruban melting pot.

Oranjestad

The island capital, Oranjestad was named in honor of the Dutch ruling family, the House of Orange. The town is a mixture of old Dutch Caribbean buildings and modern pastiches that house shops and busy malls. The oldest building on the island is **Fort Zoutman,** constructed on the waterfront in 1796. Now a short distance inland due to land reclamation, it still affords a good view over the yacht harbor. The Willem III Tower was added

Aruba
- 174 A2

Visitor Information
- L.G. Smith Blvd. 172, Eagle Beach
- 297 582 3777

Numismatic Museum

✉ Weststraat 7 (by Royal Plaza)

☎ 297 582 8831

🕐 Closed Fri. & Sat. p.m., all Sun.

Archaeological Museum

✉ Schlepstraat 42

☎ 297 582 8979

🕐 Closed Sat. & Sun.

Atlantis Submarines

✉ Renaissance Marina

☎ 297 583 6090

💲 $$$$$

www.atlantis submarines.com

to the fort in 1868, doubling as a lighthouse and the island's first public clock. The **Aruba Historical Museum's** modest collections of Spanish and Dutch Colonial artifacts are displayed here. Every Tuesday evening year-round, the Bon Bini Festival, an entertaining folkloric show featuring local crafts, food stalls, music, and dancing, takes place in the fort precincts.

Oranjestad has two more small museums. The **Numismatic Museum** boasts a collection of some 40,000 historic coins and banknotes from around the globe. The **Archaeological Museum** displays Amerindian tools, pottery, and 2,000-year-old skeletons unearthed from around the island.

Down on the waterfront, **Atlantis Submarines** offers a

popular mini-submarine excursion to the Bacadera Reef. There's a motorboat transfer to the dive site before boarding the window-lined sub for a trip 150 feet (46 m) beneath the waves for a fish-eye view of the *Mi Dushi I* shipwreck or the *Sonesta* airplane wreck. The dives are narrated, and identification charts are good guides. ■

Kudarebe
3▷ Arashi Beach
Malmok
Hadikurari
West Punt
Palm Beach
Alto Vista Chapel
Pos di Noord
Noord
Wariruri
Eagle Beach
Boca Mahos
Bushiribana
Paradera
Fort Zoutman
Casibari
Ayo
167m
Hooiberg
Santa Cruz
Arikok National Park
Oranjestad
Paardenbaai
2▷
Queen Beatrix Airport
Boton
188m Jamanota
Boca Prins
Dos Playa
Spaans Lagoen
Rincon
Savaneta
Sint Nicolaas
Boca Grandi
Commandeursbaai
Bachelors Beach
1▷
0   6 kilometers
0   3 miles
Rodgers Beach
Seroe Colorado
Baby Beach
Punta Basora
△   △   △
A   B   C

Around Aruba

Beaches at the north and south ends of Aruba provide plenty of sandy options for visitors. Desertlike scenery and ancient rock paintings mark the island's interior.

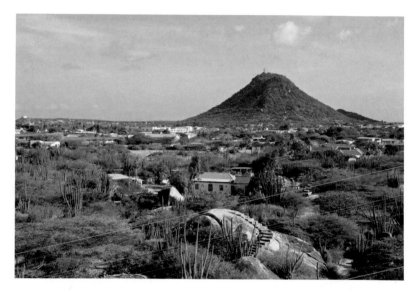

The Hooiberg Mountain dominates Aruba's landscape; its name translates to "haystack."

Aruba's Beaches

Northwest of Oranjestad, Aruba's twin tourist poles are the magnificent sandy sweeps of **Eagle Beach** (the "low-rise strip") and **Palm Beach** (the "high-rise strip"). Both are busy and hotel lined, with watersports concessions.

Two smaller, less crowded beaches lie to the north—**Malmok Beach** (a windsurfers' favorite) and **Arashi Beach.**

There's another clutch of beaches at the southeastern end of the island beyond Sint Nicolaas, Aruba's largest town. **Grapefield Beach** is a quiet spot, but the sea is rougher here and there are no facilities. **Baby Beach** is aptly named for its calm, shallow bay, and swimmers will enjoy **Roger's Beach** despite the presence of the refinery in the background. Around the tip of the island are the breezy strands of **Bachelors Beach** and **Boca Grandi,** while an adventurous 4x4 ride through Arikok National Park is rewarded by towering sand dunes, rocky cliffs, and thundering seas at **Boca Prins**, near the Fontein Cave.

Alto Vista Chapel

On the remote northwest coast, this tiny mustard-colored chapel was built on the site of an 18th-century Spanish chapel. It is a spectacular spot hedged by cacti and sea.

Aruba's Beaches
🅰 194 A3, B3, B1, C1

Alto Vista Chapel
🅰 194 B3

Arikok National Park

🏔 194 B2

☎ 297 5825 1234

Ayo Rock Formations

🏔 194 B2

The Hooiberg

🏔 194 B2

Arikok National Park

A short drive but seemingly light-years away from Aruba's urbanized west coast beach strip, this sprawling national park occupies around 20 percent of the island's interior and undeveloped east coast. Within its rugged confines, cactus-studded

INSIDER TIP:

Every Thursday night in Sint Nicolaas, in south Aruba, the colorful Carubbian Festival fills the streets with food and music.

—SJEIDY F. FELICIANO
Aruba Tourism Authority

hillsides, twisted *divi-divi* trees, great swords of aloe, limestone plateaus, sand dunes, and vast boulders illustrate Aruban nature in the raw. Some 20 miles (32 km) of walking trails wind across the dusty terrain to sites such as **Cunucu Arikok,** a century-old adobe farmhouse. Adventurous

hikers can explore several caves set in the eastern corner of the park, including the **Fontein Cave,** decorated with remarkable ancient rock paintings. Other trails scale the relative heights of Jamanota (615 feet/188 m), Aruba's highest point, and access the beaches on the east coast *(swimming not advisable).*

Ayo Rock Formations

Inland, around the village of Ayo, giant boulders litter the dusty cunucu, and there are Amerindian rock paintings in nearby caves. The incongruous smooth boulders, and those at Casibari, are a geological anomaly unrelated to the rest of the island's natural habitat.

The Hooiberg

Located at the center of the island, the Hooiberg (548 feet/167 m) is a local landmark. Steps lead to the hill's top, which does look a bit like its Dutch name suggests—a haystack. The view stretches across the island from coast to coast. ∎

Papiamento

The mother tongue of the Dutch Leewards, Papiamento (from the Spanish *papia* meaning "talk" or "babble") emerged from the pidgin speech of the early colonists and their African slaves. Dutch merchants, Portuguese Jews, Spanish missionaries, South American traders, and local Indians all added to the vocabulary. The language is now spoken throughout the region, with slight island variations (Aruban Papiamento is more Spanish sounding), and taught in schools.

Islanders will be hugely entertained if you try a few words.

Welcome	*Bon bini*
Good morning	*Bon dia*
Good afternoon	*Bon tardi*
Good evening	*Bon nochi*
How are you?	*Con ta bai?*
I am fine	*Mi ta bon*
Good-bye	*Aye*
Thank you very much	*Masha danki*
Beautiful	*Bunita*
Very good	*Hopi bon*

Between the Virgin Islands and the Windwards, six isles renowned for their laid-back charm

Leeward Islands

A sandy stretch of Friar's Bay, St. Kitts

Leeward Islands

The six English-speaking Leeward Islands head up the chain of the Lesser Antilles, mingling with the Dutch Windward Islands and the French possessions of St.-Martin and St.-Barthélemy (St. Barts). Antigua is the main gateway to this corner of the Caribbean, and it has been since the British established their chief Caribbean naval base here in the 18th century. Even now, the British influence lingers on throughout the region.

The main European influence on the Leeward Islands might be British, but indigenous Caribbean culture is here, too, in the exuberant local carnivals, reggae, rasta, and the studied art of relaxation. There are beaches galore, water sports, and hiking, plus accommodations ranging from family-friendly resorts to state-of-the-art spas to gorgeous plantation hotel retreats.

England's first successful Caribbean colony was St. Kitts, settled in 1623. Nevis followed in 1628, and a decade later Antigua and Montserrat were added to a growing portfolio of Caribbean possessions. At first, English and French settlers agreed to share St. Kitts, banding together to rid the island of inhospitable Carib people. Once the Carib were defeated, the good neighbors soon fell out. And so began the battle for control of the eastern Caribbean islands, which would continue into the 19th century and cause the demise of the sugar industry.

While Antigua was systematically stripped of its native forest to make way for sugar plantations—and settlers did their best to plant cane wherever the topography allowed on St. Kitts, Nevis, and Montserrat—barren, low-lying Anguilla became a nest of pirates and smugglers. Slaves brought to the island by prospective planters were soon turned loose to scratch a living from the thin, sandy soil; they developed a local reputation for carpentry and boat-building. This early self-reliance fostered the Anguillans' fiercely independent spirit, typified by the bizarre circumstances of the Anguillan "revolution" (actually a reactionary desire to remain British and avoid independence as a satellite of St. Kitts) in the late 1960s.

NOT TO BE MISSED:

Historic Nelson's Dockyard, Antigua **205–206**

Bird-watching at Barbuda's Frigate Bird Sanctuary **211**

Taking to the water at Shoal Bay, Anguilla **213**

The outlook from Brimstone Hill Fortress, St. Kitts **218–219**

The panoramic views of an active volcano at the Montserrat Volcano Observatory, Montserrat **226**

Slavery was abolished throughout the British Caribbean in 1834, although a term of forced "apprenticeship" legally bound former slaves to their masters for a further period of years. In the end European sugar beets undermined the Caribbean trade to emancipate the slaves for good in the late 1830s. The islands sank into an impoverished backwater status, administered under the presidency of the Leeward Islands until 1967, when associated statehood brought a degree of autonomy. The twin-island nation of Antigua and Barbuda achieved independence in 1981, followed by St. Kitts and Nevis in 1983. Anguilla and Montserrat elected to remain British Crown Colonies.

Sugar continued to be grown in Antigua until the 1970s and still provides a modest income for St. Kitts, but for more than a century the Leeward Islands' precarious economies had been almost entirely dependent on remittances—money sent by islanders working overseas. In the last 50 years tourism has gradually injected new life into the region, and the top beach islands of Antigua and Anguilla, in particular, have seen considerable hotel development.

Although the Leewards share a common background, each island enjoys its own identity. For the ultimate laid-back Caribbean beach vacation, it would be hard to beat Anguilla, which focuses all the attention on its fabulous white sand strands and super-luxurious resorts. Very quiet and relatively undiscovered, Barbuda boasts a selection of delectable and often deserted beaches, where the only crowds are propelled by fins and inhabit magical coral reefs.

Antigua is altogether a more lively choice. In addition to claiming a beach for every day of the year (a wild but forgivable exaggeration),

the island's historical sites make for interesting excursions, and friendly pubs provide live reggae and impromptu jump-ups at night. Lush St. Kitts and tiny Nevis combine colonial history with romantic plantation retreats and some fine upland hiking and riding country. Pint-size and once lush and lovely Montserrat suffered a major setback to its quietly developing nature-tourism industry when the Soufrière Volcano erupted in 1995. However, the enterprising islanders have reopened for business and now welcome volcano-watching visitors. ■

Area of map detail

ATLANTIC OCEAN

Caribbean Sea

Sombrero

Dog I.
Anguilla **The**
(U.K.) **Valley**
Wallblake Airport

St.-Martin (France)

Sint Maarten (Neth.)

St.-Barthélemy (France)

L e e w a r d   I s l a n d s

Saba (Neth.)

L e s s e r   A n t i l l e s

Sint Eustatius (Neth.)

1156m

ST. KITTS AND NEVIS

St. Kitts   **Basseterre**

Charlestown   Nevis

Codrington   Barbuda

ANTIGUA AND BARBUDA

St. John's

402m

Antigua

Redonda

0   60 kilometers
0   30 miles

Brades
Olveston   Montserrat (U.K.)

A   B   C   D

Antigua

At 108 square miles (280 sq km), Antigua (pronounced An-TEE-gah) is the largest of the Leeward Islands. Its irregular coastline, resembling a ragged Rorschach inkblot, incorporates hundreds of scalloped inlets and bays. The locals boast there are 365 beaches to choose from, many of them secluded coves backed by sea grape trees and accessible only by boat.

The harbor view from Antigua's Shirley Heights

Antigua
🅜 199 D2

Visitor Information

✉ Government Complex, Queen Elizabeth Hwy, St. John's

☎ 268 462 0480

www.antigua-barbuda.org

The interior of the island is rolling and dry. The lush carpet of sugarcane has disappeared and has been replaced by yellow-gray scrubland dotted with the shells of abandoned windmills. Small country villages provide brief bursts of color and greenery, painted wooden cottages and modern villas with flower gardens straggle along the roadside, and tethered

goats and cattle graze in the dust. Antigua's coastal heights are generally topped with the remains of British ramparts; the most interesting is Shirley Heights (see sidebar p. 204), in Nelson's Dockyard National Park, overlooking the confines of English Harbour.

The first human traces on Antigua date back to the Stone Age Ciboney people, who migrated

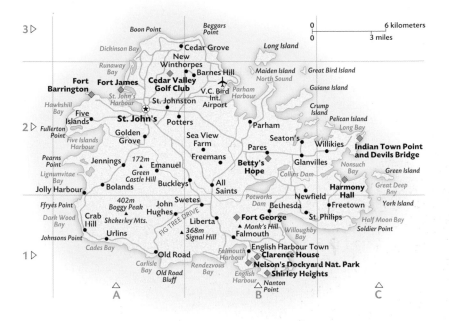

from South America to settle the island around 3000 B.C. Peaceable Arawak arrived on the scene about A.D. 100, and raiding parties of Windward Island Carib were moving up the island chain by the time Christopher Columbus sighted the island on his second voyage in 1493. He named it Santa Maria de la Antigua after a miraculous statue of the Virgin in Seville Cathedral. The Spanish and French showed little interest in the island, discouraged by its shortage of fresh water, but English colonists from St. Kitts established a base in 1632. Sugar was introduced in the 1650s, and by the height of the 18th-century plantation era, Antigua had more than 200 cane-crushing windmills, with African slaves forming 93 percent of the population.

Antigua's protected harbors (an important consideration in

the Caribbean hurricane belt) and strategic position at the apex of a rough triangle between the major-league sugar colonies of Barbados and Jamaica made the island a natural choice for Britain's chief naval and military base in the Lee-wards. Fortresses sprang up along the coast, with the main defenses concentrated in the south around English and Falmouth Harbours. The result was so formidable that Britain's enemies gave the whole island a wide berth.

After British emancipation of the slaves in 1834, Antigua's fate mirrored that of other colonial possessions. The dockyard was closed, most of the plantations failed, and the islanders slipped into an unremitting pattern of subsistence agriculture. They were consequently largely ignored by Britain.

Appalling working conditions

inspired the first organized labor movement in 1939. It gained strength during World War II, which heralded an influx of U.S. servicemen sent to man military bases on the island. The postwar Labour Party, under the leadership of Vere C. Bird, led Antigua and the sister island of Barbuda to self-governing associated statehood in 1967 and full independence in 1981.

Antigua and Barbuda's combined population numbers around 85,000, of which some 85 percent are of African descent. The capital of the twin-island nation is St. John's, a bustling port city and cruise-ship destination on the west coast, well worth a visit. Antigua has several diversions for the inquisitive traveler who would like to get off the beach and have a look around. Renting a car is

INSIDER TIP:

Save a Friday or Saturday morning to shop for artisan crafts and local foods at the farmer's market on Market Street on the southern edge of St. John's.

—LARRY PORGES
Editor, National Geographic Books

the best way to explore. Nelson's Dockyard National Park (see pp. 205–206) showcases the finest surviving Georgian naval complex in the world, while the history of the island's sugar industry is explained at the restored Betty's Hope Museum (see p. 208) in the center of the island.

A favorite out-of-the-way detour on the southeast coast is a

EXPERIENCE: Antigua Ecotours

For those interested in wandering off the beaten path, ecotourism provides a conservation-centered way to see Antigua untouched by tourist crowds. A variety of companies offer guided, educational tours that explore protected landscapes and ecosystems.

Local ecotour companies include **Antigua Nature Tours** (*Seaton's Village, tel 268 720 1761, www.antiguanaturetours .com, $$$$$*), located on the eastern shore of Antigua on Mercers Creek Bay. Start your day by discovering sanctuaries that provide a home to indigenous monkeys, parrots, brown pelicans, and assorted regional wildlife. From there, take a speedboat ride to the company's kayak dock where you will paddle among red mangrove-riddled inlets to the North

Sound Marine Park, a haven of Antiguan flora and fauna delights. After exploring the waterways, move on to Great Bird Island for snorkeling among brain coral and shoals of blue tang, sea cucumbers and upside-down jellyfish. Finish with a hike through coconut tree high-rises, stomping ground to an abundance of tropical birds, or settle in for a sun-soaked rest and a rum punch on the pink sands.

Other ecotour operators include **Adventure Antigua** (*Dickinson Bay, St. John's, tel 268 727 3261, www.adventure antigua.com, $$$$$*) run by former competitive kitesurfer Eli Fuller. For a round-island Jeep safari or a combination of safari and kayaking, contact **Tropical Adventures** (*Lower Redcliffe Street, St. John, tel 286 480 1225, www.tropicalad.com, $$$$$*).

trip to Harmony Hall (see p. 209), a charming old sugar mill complex housing an arts-and-crafts gallery and an excellent Italian restaurant.

Tourists are generally welcomed wherever they go, and for a surefire conversational gambit try cricket or sailing, the islanders' twin passions. To capture Antiguans at their most spontaneous, join the regattas and riotous partying that accompany the annual **Antigua Sailing Week** at the end of the December-to-April yachting season (see sidebar p. 207). For a more modest hint of the local atmosphere, the Sunday-afternoon jump-ups (impromptu dances) at Shirley Heights are entertaining rum-and-reggae-soaked affairs.

St. John's & Around

St. John's is an appealing West Indian town sloping gently back from the downtown waterfront in an orderly pattern of streets and narrow alleys, laid out in 1702. Old wooden buildings with drooping balconies cluster on the hill below the cathedral and its landmark silver cupolas. Charmingly time-worn, they appear anchored together for support by a web of telephone wires above the road.

The sidewalks of St. John's are always crowded. More often than not during the winter high season, armies of day-tripping cruise passengers pile ashore intent on plundering the duty-free stores in the modern **Heritage Quay** mall at the foot of the pier.

The compact waterfront district remains the focal point

The Cathedral of St. John the Divine opened its doors in 1847; it has withstood a massive earthquake and hurricanes.

of town. Next to Heritage Quay, there's a covered vendors' market full of souvenir stalls, and on its far side is **Redcliffe Quay,** a pretty shopping street lined with restored wood and stone town houses and warehouses now occupied by boutiques, galleries, and restaurants. The area behind the quay was once part of a large barracoon, or dockside slave-holding

Museum of Antigua & Barbuda

✉ Corner of Long & Market Sts., St. John's

☎ 268 462 1469

🕒 Closed Sun.

💲 Donation

www.antigua museum.org

compound, before emancipation.

It's a short walk up Long Street to the **Museum of Antigua & Barbuda,** housed in the neoclassical Old Court House, built in 1750 from stone quarried on Antigua's offshore islets. The fusty, old-fashioned layout conceals a remarkably informative introduction to the islands' history and geology. The archaeological finds are particularly interesting and include Stone Age Ciboney tools, an Arawak ax with a special hole

---

Exploring Shirley Heights

The military abandoned Shirley Heights in the 1850s, and since then many of its buildings have simply disappeared behind a screen of scrub. But signposts and footpaths still lead to an assortment of crumbling barracks and batteries, water cisterns, powder magazines, and the Military Cemetery, where the numerous victims of tropical fevers were laid to rest. The signal station at the highest point of the complex (490 feet/149 m) used flags to send messages to Fort George at Monk's Hill, above Falmouth, which were then relayed across a chain of hilltop signal stations to St. John's.

---

designed to allow tree spirits to escape, and a collection of *zemi,* small stone or carved bone objects that were believed to attract benevolent powers.

At the top of the hill is the **Cathedral of St. John the Divine,** flanked by its twin towers and presiding over the town center. Constructed on the site of a previous stone church demolished by an earthquake in 1843, the cathedral has a cool,

lofty interior clad in pitch pine to protect it against hurricane and earthquake damage. Take a little time to inspect the grand memorial plaques bedecked with coats-of-arms and flowery inscriptions. At the south gate of the tumble-down graveyard (a popular lunchtime picnic spot with local office workers) are the statues of St. John the Divine and St. John the Baptist, said to have been captured from an 18th-century French warship bound for Martinique.

The entrance to St. John's Harbour is overlooked by the ruins of two historic forts with good views. On the north side, reached by Fort Road, is **Fort James,** which was founded in 1706 shortly after the death of King James II. Continuing up the coast, there are a few hotels lining the beach at **Runaway Bay.** Just around a small headland is Antigua's most developed pocket of shoreline—**Dickenson Bay.** This is no Miami Beach high-rise strip but a mile-long (1.6 km) swath of fine, powdery white sand that turns the water a translucent opal. The beach is backed by just a handful of low-rise hotels set in landscaped gardens. A good spot for active beachgoers, Dickenson Bay has several water-sports concessions.

On the south side of St. John's Harbour is 17th-century **Fort Barrington,** one of Antigua's earliest (and most active) fortresses. The site was already fortified when it was named in honor of Admiral Barrington, who captured St. Lucia from the French in 1665, though most of the present defenses were

A relic of bygone days along the road through Nelson's Dockyard

constructed in 1779. From the ruins there are views across to the neighboring islands of St. Kitts and Nevis on a clear day.

Several of Antigua's best beaches are tucked into the bays and coves of the southwest coast. Out on the peninsula, near Fort Barrington, are **Deep Bay, Galley Bay,** and the assorted coves and hotel beaches of **Hawksbill Bay,** so named for the hawksbill turtle–shaped rock they overlook. The **Jolly Harbour** complex incorporates a busy marina, shops, and hotels, as well as a beach on Lignumvitae Bay. Farther south, **Dark Wood Bay** has a lovely strip of sand with a beach bar, and glorious views across to neighboring Montserrat. Busy at weekends, it is almost deserted on weekdays.

Nelson's Dockyard National Park

The national park covers 12 square miles (31 sq km) on the south coast around Falmouth Harbour, the original capital site of Antigua. A popular yachting center on its own sheltered bay, Falmouth is divided by a narrow isthmus from the virtually landlocked confines of English Harbour. English Harbour served as the British Royal Navy's eastern Caribbean headquarters during the 17th and 18th centuries.

Shirley Heights is the best place to begin a visit to the park. The sprawling 18th-century military complex was named for Gen. Sir Thomas Shirley, governor of the Leeward Islands between 1781 and 1791. It occupies a commanding position on the high ground above the dockyard, which is reached by a well-signed road from English Harbour. Make an initial stop at the **Dow Hill Interpretation Centre,** where a 15-minute multimedia presentation covers

Nelson's Dockyard National Park

🅰 201 B1

☎ 268 481 5021

💲 $$$

www.nationalparks antigua.com

Horatio Nelson

England's 18th-century naval hero spent a miserable posting in Antigua between 1784 and 1787. As captain of the 28-gun frigate H.M.S. *Boreas,* and head of the Squadron of the Leeward Islands, the youthful Nelson was dispatched to enforce the extremely unpopular Navigation Act, which banned planters and merchants from trading with the newly independent United States of America. At times his mission so incensed the islanders that he was afraid to put into shore and took refuge on Nevis, where he met and married the wealthy and well-connected young widow, Fanny Nisbet.

"Woefully pinched by mosquitoes," the miserable Nelson felt so ill when he left for England that he ordered a barrel of rum be taken on board to preserve his body for a home burial if he died during the voyage.

Boreas arrived in the Leeward Islands for a three-year tour of duty (see sidebar). The dockyard was decommissioned in 1889 and fell into disrepair until the 1960s, when it was restored, renamed, and opened to the public as a national park. It is a delightful place for a stroll, guided by a series of signs that identify the various stores and workshop buildings. You can take a guided tour from the entrance gate. Top sights include the **Admiral's Inn,** housed in a former pitch and tar

INSIDER TIP:

Try to time your visit to Shirley Heights with sunrise or sunset. The view is spectacular during those times of day.

—MATT PROPERT
National Geographic photographer

Antiguan history and culture from the Carib to cricket. The road continues to wind uphill, past the elegant stone colonnade of the officers' quarters, now open to the sky and studded with cactuses, until it reaches **Shirley Heights Lookout.** From here, eagle-eyed sentries could see all the way south across the water to the French island of Guadeloupe, giving the British plenty of advance warning in the event of an attack. The French were never foolhardy enough to attempt it.

Down at sea level is **Nelson's Dockyard,** which was considered a hardship posting and "an infernal hole" by its famous namesake, Admiral Lord Nelson (1758–1805). He was plain Captain Nelson in 1784, when he and his shipmates aboard HMS

store, with the coral rock pillars of a sail loft in the gardens. Note the rounded water cisterns flanking the brick walls of the charming **Copper & Lumber Store Hotel,** and visit the **Dockyard Museum,** laid out in the Admiral's House, the last house to be completed in the dockyard, in 1855. There's a short walk out to **Fort Berkeley,** the dockyard's first line of defense, built on a rocky spit of land in 1704. The path starts by the dinghy dock in the marina, and there are grand views back across the harbor basin to waterfront **Clarence House.** ∎

EXPERIENCE: A Passion for Sailing

"Sail fast, live slow," they say in Antigua, and there are many opportunities to do just that on this sail-obsessed island. Constant trade winds, sparkling seas, and a picture-perfect coastline dotted with dozens of secluded beaches and coves, many of which are only accessible by boat, make for terrific sailing whether the object is a relaxing day sail or deadly serious competitive racing.

Antigua's main sailing hubs are English Harbour and Falmouth Harbour on the south coast, and the Jolly Harbour Marina complex in the west. Day sail options with a barbecue lunch are readily available from the likes of **Treasure Island Cruises** *(tel 268 461 8875, www.treasure islandcruises.ag, $$$$$)*, and **Wadadli Cats** *(tel 268 462 4792, www.wadadlicats.com, $$$$$)*. Both operators offer a choice of snorkel trips to Cades Reef or family favorite Great Bird Island (popular with children). For a longer day's sailing, a circumnavigation of the island is a 60-mile

(96 km) round-trip with lunch and snorkel stops en route. **Tropical Adventures** *(tel 268 480 1225, www.tropicalad.com, $$$$$)* sails to Barbuda for the day; and **Miramar Sailing** *(tel 268 721 3456, www.miramar sailingschool.com, $$$$$)* offers training courses, private day sails, and charters.

With a little bit of experience you can go it alone. Yacht charter companies can supply vessels of all sizes, bareboat and crewed, by the day, week, or longer. Contact longtime Caribbean charter experts **Nicholson Yacht Charters** *(tel 268 460 1530 or U.S. 305 433 5533,*

www.nicholson-charters.com, $$$$$); or rent a dinghy from **Sunsail** *(tel 268 460 2615 or 800 327 2276, www.sunsail .com, $$$$$)*.

If all that relaxed cruising seems a bit tame, then consider **Antigua Sailing Week** *(www.sailingweek .com)*, a five-day celebration of international world-class yachting held at the end of April. In this week, more than 100 vessels ranging from 32-foot (10 m) family cruisers to 100-foot (30 m) state-of-the-art racing machines battle it out for a place at the prize-giving ceremony in historic Nelson's Dockyard.

A sailing crew catches the Caribbean wind.

Around Antigua

The eastern half of Antigua contains a number of interesting destinations for a day trip or longer. The ruins of old sugar plantations, where slavery built prosperity for a few, still stand in a few locations, while the Atlantic surf breaks on the islands's northeastern point.

One of the two windmills on the Betty's Hope sugarcane plantation still functions today.

Betty's Hope Museum

 201 B2

✉ Southeast of Pares

☎ 268 462 1469

🕒 Closed Sun. & Mon.

www.antigua museums.org/ bettyshope.htm

Fig Tree Drive

🅰 201 A1

✉ St. Mary's Parish

Betty's Hope Museum

Antigua's pioneer plantation, Betty's Hope was established during the 1650s. In 1668 it passed into the hands of the Codrington family of Barbados, who introduced sugar production to the island. For 250 years Betty's Hope was one of the island's most prosperous estates. Today, acacia bushes and tamarind trees have swallowed up the former canefields, but one of two windmills has been carefully restored. Refitted with wooden sails and cane-crushing machinery, it is the only working sugar mill in the Caribbean.

Inside the small **visitor center** are exhibits explaining sugar processing and the work of the slave gangs; Betty's Hope employed about 310 West African slaves. There are also maps and drawings relating to the history of the plantation, as well as a detailed scale model of the now demolished great house, complete with smartly dressed white settlers strolling in the great house gardens. In reality, most plantation owners preferred to live in Europe and leave their overseas estates in the hands of managers.

Fig Tree Drive

A rare pocket of lush natural vegetation in the southwest of the island, Fig Tree Drive runs 5 miles (8 km) from the inland village of Swetes down to Old Road, on the coast at Carlisle Bay. For a birds-eye view of the treetops, check out the **Antigua Rainforest Canopy Tour** (tel 268 562 6363, www.antigua rainforest.com). The exhilarating combination of bridges, trails, and ziplines provides a roller-coaster forest ride. To the west is **Boggy Peak** (1,319 feet/402 m), Antigua's highest point, rising above the Shekerley Mountains.

INSIDER TIP:

Rendezvous Bay's beach, on the south coast just west of Falmouth Harbour, is the most beautiful and unspoiled in Antigua.

—FEONA BAILEY
Manager, Catamaran Hotel, Falmouth

Fort George

An easy hiking expedition for history buffs, Fort George perches on the modest heights of Monk's Hill, behind Falmouth Harbour. To reach the fort, turn off the main road at the village of **Liberta** (one of the first settlements founded by freed slaves) in the direction of Table Hill Gordon. The mile-long (1.5 km) marked track is on the right, navigable by four-wheel-drive vehicles or on foot. The fort, which dates from 1689, was intended as a stronghold for livestock, women, and children if Falmouth was attacked. Sections

of the high defensive walls, powder magazines, and cannon emplacements have survived around the 8-acre (3 ha) site.

Harmony Hall

A delightful spot on the east coast, Harmony Hall is well worth a detour. The former great house of the Brown's Bay Mill sugar estate has been transformed into a gallery of Caribbean arts and crafts and a six-room B&B inn. The old windmill houses a bar overlooking Nonsuch Bay, and there is a restaurant serving lunch and afternoon tea. Call ahead, and they will even pack up a picnic and arrange a boat trip to a local beach from the dinghy dock. Visitors can also use the pool. A short drive (3 miles/5 km) southeast of Harmony Hall, beyond Freetown, is the alluring curve of **Half Moon Bay,** which is popular with swimmers, sun bathers, and bodysurfers.

Indian Town Point & Devils Bridge

Way out at the northeast tip of the island, a side road leads off 1 mile (1.6 km) to Indian Town Point and the site of Devils Bridge. On a blustery day the Atlantic surf crashes against the coastline, where it has hollowed out a natural limestone archway and blasts through blowholes in the rock. Archaeologists have made several excavations in the Indian Town Point area, which was declared a national park in the 1950s. A short drive to the north is sandy **Long Bay.** ■

Fort George
- 201 B1
- ✉ Monk's Hill, near Liberta

Harmony Hall
- 201 C2
- ✉ Brown's Bay (north of Freetown)
- ☎ 268 460 4120,
- 🕒 Closed May– Oct.
- **www.harmonyhall antigua.com**

Indian Town Point & Devils Bridge
- 201 C2
- ✉ East of Willikies

Barbuda

A 28-mile (45 km) puddle-jumper flight from Antigua, Barbuda bakes quietly in the sun and takes things very, very easy. The 14-by-8-mile (22.5 by 13 km) coral atoll is almost two-thirds the size of its more developed, upbeat sister, Antigua, but there are just 1,500 islanders, who live mainly by fishing, farming, and hunting.

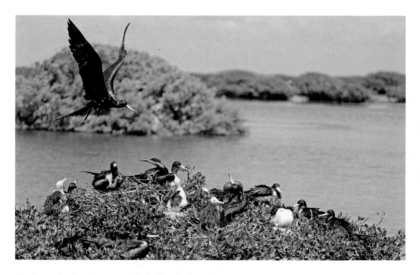

The frigatebird is the national bird of Barbuda and Antigua.

Barbuda

  199 D3

Visitor Information

✉ Codrington, Barbuda

☎ 268 562 7066

www.antigua-barbuda.org

Barbuda's top attractions are mind-blowing, pinkish-white sand beaches and superb snorkeling. Any visit comes with a caveat: Accommodations are limited to a brace of small luxury beach hotel retreats and a number of simple local-style guest houses in Codrington. You may want to consider a day trip.

Barbuda's only settlement is **Codrington,** a handful of streets leading back from the saltwater lagoon. Both were named for Christopher Codrington, a 17th-century governor-general of the Leeward Islands who leased the whole island from the British crown in 1691. (It remained in the family's hands until 1872.) Poor soil and an annual rainfall of only about 38 inches (965 mm) meant sugar cultivation was impossible on Barbuda, but Codrington introduced deer, wild boar, and guinea fowl for hunting, raised cattle, and grew provisions to supply his five Antiguan estates.

Barbuda is almost completely ringed by breathtaking beaches. One magnificent 14-mile (22.5 km) stretch starts at the southerly tip of **Cocoa Point** and sweeps up the west coast, past the landmark 18th-century **Martello Tower** to **Palmetto Point,** where it takes a sharp turn around the headland and continues on up the outer arm of **Codrington Lagoon.**

In the south, there's excellent snorkeling around **Gravenor Bay** and the 2-mile-long (3 km) **Palaster Reef,** a protected marine reserve off Cocoa Point. Goat Reef, in the north, is renowned for its wreck diving. As yet, Barbuda has no organized dive operation, so divers will need to bring all their equipment. Local fishing boats are available for charter.

Make it a point to take a boat trip out into the mangrove-lined **Frigate Bird Sanctuary** at the north end of Codrington Lagoon. *(Authorized bird-watching trips can be arranged through the National Park office, tel 268 460 0217. Visits are also included in day tours from Antigua.)* This is the largest nesting colony of magnificent frigatebirds in the world, with an estimated 2,500 pairs. The glossy black birds have an 8-foot (2.5 m) wingspan and can soar at altitudes of up to 2,000 feet (600 m). During the mating season (Aug.–Nov.), male birds try to attract a female by puffing out their scarlet neck pouches like a huge balloon, trembling their outstretched wings,

and emitting a strange drumming sound. Their ungainly, pure white young are born in winter (Dec.–Feb.). More than 400 other bird species have been identified in the lagoon area.

East of Codrington, **Dark Cave** and **Darby Sink Cave** harbor rare blind shrimp and surprising touches of greenery. ∎

Redonda

An uninhabited volcanic rock 30 miles (48 km) southwest of Antigua, Redonda is the third territory of Antigua and Barbuda. It has a rather bizarre recent history. In the mid-19th century, some enterprising souls recognized there was money to be made from Redonda's guano deposits.

Thousands of tons of bird droppings were shipped off the island for use as fertilizer. Subsequently, Britain annexed

Redonda to its Leeward Island possessions. But an Irishman from Montserrat proclaimed himself King of Redonda, and the title has since passed to a succession of colorful (nonresident) literary types who have generously created Redondan peers out of any famous people who attract their attention, from Welsh writer and poet Dylan Thomas to British film actress Diana Dors.

Anguilla

Long before a wealth of superb sandy beaches was considered an attraction, Spanish explorers took one look at the flat, desiccated, and most northerly of the Leeward Islands, christened it Anguilla, meaning "eel," and sailed on in search of richer, greener, and more promising territories. However, only 16 miles (25 km) long and 3 miles (5 km) wide at its broadest point, present-day Anguilla's fortunes are founded on its 33 dazzling white beaches with sand so fine and deep that you have to wade rather than walk along them.

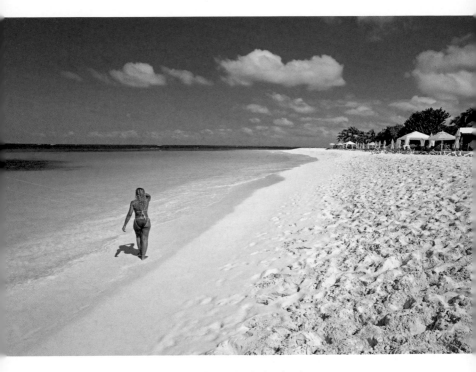

A quiet moment on Shoal Bay, one of Anguilla's liveliest beaches

Anguilla
🅰 199 B3
Visitor Information
✉ The Valley Anguilla
☎ 264 497 2759
🕐 Closed Sat. & Sun.

http://ivisitanguilla.com/

Forget rain forest hikes, historic forts, casinos, and duty-free shopping (although commercialized Sint Maarten/St.-Martin is only a 20-minute ferry ride away), and prepare to get horizontal. Anguilla has been neatly summed up in a one-line T-shirt slogan: "Life's a beach, and then you dine."

And you can dine spectacularly well on Anguilla. The island may be lacking somewhat in the general interest department, but it does boast a selection of the Caribbean's most luxurious spas and architecturally striking hotels, with dining opportunities to match, several on the shore in earshot of gently lapping waves.

This alluring combination draws an impressively star-studded A-list crowd.

To work up an appetite, wind-assisted water sports are available, and Anguilla boasts six marine parks, nine wreck dives, and terrific snorkeling. Most of the larger hotels have tennis courts and fitness centers, and the Greg Norman–designed CuisinArt Golf Course is a spectacular oceanfront affair. Rental bikes (available from hotels) are a great way to explore.

INSIDER TIP:

Rum lovers should be sure to try one of the several varieties of the local Anguillan tipple— Pyrat rum, a blend of elixirs fused with up to nine aged and flavored spirits.

– JENNIFER ALLARD
National Geographic contributor

The Valley

Exploring Anguilla takes a day, but most visitors enjoy a change of scene, even if it's just swapping one beach for another. In the middle of the island is The Valley, the capital and administrative center. The settlement has no real focus, but there are some attractive shingled and shuttered traditional houses in jaunty poster-paint colors.

Set back from the main street is the **Anguilla National Museum** (*closed Sat. & Sun., donations*), which

---

EXPERIENCE:
H Is for Heritage

To encourage visitors to explore the island, the Anguilla tourist office produces a self-guided tour map, which is also available from hotel reception desks. Called "H Is for Heritage," it describes some ten historic and interesting sites dotted around the island. For a more in-depth understanding of local history and culture, join an Anguilla Culture Tour run by **Anguilla Access** (*tel 264 772 9827, www.anguilla access.com, $$$$$*), which proudly claims that no two tours are the same. There are twice-daily departures (with hotel pickups) and the route might include visits to an island broom-maker, caves decorated with ancient Arawak petroglyphs, local boat-builders, and a Rastafarian community, ending up at a beach bar for a barbecue.

---

presents changing exhibits on local themes, and is home to the **Anguilla National Trust.** The trust (*tel 264 497 5297*) organizes tours that include visits to Amerindian sites, bird-watching spots, and hawksbill turtle nesting grounds in summer. Near the airport is the 1787 **Wallblake House,** an annex of the museum and the island's only surviving plantation house, complete with its old stable block and bakery (*tours Mon., Wed., Fri. 10–2; $$*).

Around the Island

Northeast of The Valley lies **Shoal Bay,** the island's liveliest beach, a broad belt of ankle-deep sand with a handful of beach bars, hotels, and water-sports concessions renting out snorkeling gear, windsurfing equipment, and dinghies.

St. Gerard's Church fronts Wallblake House, the island's only surviving plantation house.

Five miles (8 km) farther east by road, opposite the fishing village of Island Harbour, is **Gorgeous Scilly Cay,** a tiny offshore islet with a palm-thatched restaurant and good snorkeling. If it's too far to swim, wave for the water taxi.

In the southeast corner of the island, seek out the **Heritage Collection** (East End at Pond Ground, tel 264 497 4092, closed Sun.), a fascinating privately owned museum. The bulk of the exhibits are devoted to the revolution (see sidebar), with a detailed account of the proceedings and some entertaining photographs. There are also pieces of Amerindian pottery decorated with pelican heads, and antique kitchen implements made out of coral.

You'll find other attractions to the west of The Valley. The island's deep-water port is located on the north coast at **Sandy Ground,** balanced on a curved spit of sand dividing the old salt pans from the ocean. The old salt factory is now a restaurant, and a ferry provides regular service to **Sandy Island,** another offshore beach and snorkeling spot. Continuing west, several hotels and good restaurants are gathered in the **Mead's Bay** and **Barnes Bay** area.

On the south coast, the futuristic apartments of Covecastles preside over **Lower Shoal Bay;** the Cap Juluca resort fronts **Maunday's Bay;** and Anguilla's longest beach, **Rendezvous Bay,** stretches out in a curving ribbon of dunes facing St.-Martin. ∎

"The Eel That Squealed"

Laid-back Anguilla seems the last place on Earth to harbor revolutionary tendencies, but in the late 1960s it became the first British colony to stage a successful revolution *against* independence. In 1967, faced with the prospect of an unwanted union with St. Kitts and Nevis, the Anguillans rounded up and deported a detachment of Kittitian policemen, rolled an antique cannon onto the beach, and appealed to Britain for continued colonial status. Embarrassingly out of touch, the British government dispatched armed paratroopers to reestablish order two years later. They were greeted by cheering Anguillans waving Union Jacks and singing "God Save the Queen." The fiasco was dubbed Britain's Bay of Piglets. For an entertaining account of the whole saga, pick up a copy of Donald E. Westlake's *Under an English Heaven*, available on the island.

St. Kitts

The twin-island nation of St. Kitts and Nevis lies near the northern tip of a 500-mile-long (800 km) arc of volcanic peaks that stretches from Saba to Grenada along a curving submarine fault between the Atlantic Ocean and the Caribbean Sea. St. Kitts is the larger of the two islands at 68 square miles (176 sq km), with three distinct mountain ranges squeezed into its lush, green tadpole-shaped body. A spine of dry, rugged hills forms the tail, which trails southeast toward Nevis.

Honoring a former island estate owner, Basseterre's Berkeley Monument includes a clock and drinking fountain.

St. Kitts's main resort area, Frigate Bay, lies at the top of the tail section, close to the bustling island capital of Basseterre (see p. 217). The island's best beaches flank the isthmus as it reaches south to The Narrows, the channel dividing St. Kitts from neighboring Nevis. To the north, the green-clad lower slopes of the ranges rise to a peak at Mount Liamuiga (3,792 feet/1,156 m), and a single perimeter road hugs the coast, linking quiet rural villages.

The Amerindian name for St. Kitts was Liamuiga (meaning fertile land), but when Christopher Columbus sailed by in 1493, he named it St. Christopher after his own patron saint and the patron saint of travelers. Just over a century later, British colonists, led by Sir Thomas Warner (1575–1649), settled on St. Kitts and set about cultivating tobacco. Having defeated the resident Carib population at Bloody Point in 1626, they ousted French colonists from the southern portion of

St. Kitts

🗺 199 B2

Visitor Information

✉ Pelican Mall, Bay Rd., Basseterre

☎ 869 465 2620

🕐 Closed Sat.–Sun.

www.stkittstourism .kn

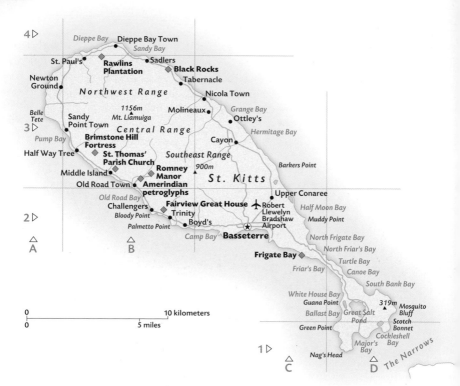

4 ▷

Dieppe Bay   Dieppe Bay Town
Sandy Bay
St. Paul's   •Sadlers
Rawlins   Black Rocks
Plantation   Tabernacle
Newton
Ground•   Northwest Range   Nicola Town
    Molineaux•   Grange Bay
Belle   1156m   Ottley's
Tete   Sandy   Mt. Liamuiga   Central Range   Hermitage Bay
Point Town
Pump Bay   Brimstone Hill   Cayon
    Fortress   Southeast Range
Half Way Tree•   St. Thomas'   900m   Barkers Point
    Parish Church
Middle Island•   Romney   St. Kitts
    Manor
Old Road Town•   Amerindian
    petroglyphs   Upper Conaree
Old Road Bay   Fairview Great House ✈Robert   Half Moon Bay
Challengers•   Trinity   Llewelyn
Bloody Point   •Boyd's   Bradshaw   Muddy Point
Palmetto Point   Camp Bay   Airport
    Basseterre   North Frigate Bay

2 ▷   Frigate Bay ◇   North Friar's Bay
        Turtle Bay
    Friar's Bay   Canoe Bay
△   South Bank Bay
A   △
    B   White House Bay
        Guana Point   319m Mosquito
0   Ballast Bay Great Salt   Bluff
0   10 kilometers   Pond   Scotch
    5 miles   Green Point   Bonnet
            Cockleshell
        Major's   Bay
        Bay
1 ▷   Nag's Head   The Narrows
        △   △
        C   D

the island, around Basseterre, and adopted St. Christopher as a base for colonizing the other Leeward Islands and Tortola in the Virgin Islands. The island's Spanish name was Anglicized and shortened, and St. Kitts became known as the Mother Colony of the West Indies.

Naturally, the French refused to give up easily. The island and neighboring Nevis were important sugar producers, and St. Kitts, or parts of it, changed hands regularly despite the vast fortress built by the British at Brimstone Hill (see pp. 218–219), grandly but inaccurately touted as the Gibraltar of the West Indies. Britain finally secured sovereignty of the islands under the Treaty of Versailles in 1783. When the sugar bubble burst half a century later, the

high-living plantocracy quit the islands in droves, and St. Kitts and Nevis shared the same dismal fate as other Caribbean sugar islands, largely ignored and left to fend for themselves by their uninterested colonial masters.

As Britain prepared to divest itself of its Leeward Island territories in the 1960s, plans were drawn up for a new tri-island state comprising St. Kitts, Nevis, and Anguilla. The Anguillans reacted immediately, staging a mini-revolution to avoid certain domination by larger and more populous St. Kitts (see sidebar p. 214). Despite similar reservations, Nevis entered into the state of St. Kitts and Nevis but inserted an escape clause in the constitution that would allow the smaller island to secede should the majority of Nevisians decide they would prefer to go it alone.

While local politicians sharpen their rhetoric in the Assembly of St. Kitts and Nevis, island life moseys gently on. Almost two-thirds of St. Kitts's population of 35,500 lives in and around Basseterre, with its boisterous street life and markets, restaurants tucked away in pretty stone courtyards, and harborfront cruise-ship pier. Beyond the town and the beach, rain forest hikes are popular. It takes a full day to hike the round-trip up to Mount Liamuiga's crater lip, but local guide companies offer several other less strenuous options, as well as Jeep safaris to ruined plantation houses and sugar mills.

Basseterre

Originally settled by the French, as its name implies, Basseterre (low ground) skirts a broad bay at the foot of the Southeast Range. The British moved their capital here from Old Road in 1727, but most of the attractive skirt-and-blouse buildings (so-called for their stone ground floors and wooden uppers) postdate the major fire of 1867.

The heart of town is arranged around the twin poles of **The Circus**—where the traffic makes its way around a fancy Victorian clock tower, public seating area and meeting place—and **Independence Square.** The grassy square (a former slave market) has a gaudily painted fountain, a few palms, and a single poinciana, the national tree, which sports brilliant red blooms in summer. On the east side of the square the Roman Catholic church dates from 1670 but has been reconstructed several times. Behind a row of metal railings on the south side of the square stands the handsome **Old Georgian House,** looking as though it has been transplanted from a centuries-old market town in the English Cotswolds.

Monkey Business

The French legacy of St. Kitts extends beyond a couple of place-names, such as Basseterre and the quiet former sugar port of Dieppe Bay. The poinciana tree, with its flamboyant red blooms, is named after the first French governor of the island, Philippe de Poincy. The French also introduced green vervet monkeys, which were kept as pets. An estimated 50,000 descendants of the original monkeys are now living in colonies in the mountains. They feed off insects, berries, and fruit, and during summer (when food in the forest is more limited) they make forays to pillage small-scale farms on the edge of villages, where they are considered pests.

The Basseterre waterfront is undergoing a major face-lift. An ambitious new marina, shopping area, and commercial development is taking shape around the **Port Zante** cruise-ship pier. Meanwhile, the Old Treasury Building has been restored to house assorted island artifacts gathered in the **National Museum.** Follow Bay Road west, past fishing boats and old warehouse buildings, for ferry services to Nevis, which depart from behind the bus station.

National Museum

 Bay Rd., Basseterre

☎ 869 465 5584

🕐 Closed Mon. p.m., Sat. p.m., & Sun.

Romney Manor

🗺 216 B3

✉ Old Road Town

☎ 869 465 6253

🕐 Closed Sat. p.m. & Sun.

Brimstone Hill Fortress & the North

A circumnavigation of northern St. Kitts makes a good day trip, with several historic sites, excellent scenery, and a choice of plantation house lunch stops along the way. You can hop aboard the **St. Kitts Scenic Railway** (tel 869 465 7263,

---

EXPERIENCE: Go Ape

Beat the island's green vervet monkeys at their own game with a rain forest **Sky Safari** at the Wingfield Estate, Old Road Village (tel 869 466 4259, www.skysafari stkitts.com, $$$$$). After a familiarization session on the trainer zipline, the sky's the limit for four further rides. The Boss, a 1,350-foot-long (411 m), 250-foot-high (76 m) flight through the forest canopy, skims over the Valley of the Giants, named for the mighty trees flourishing beneath. Back on terra firma, there are guided walks and the ruins of the former estate sugar plantation to explore.

---

www.stkittsscenicrailway.com) and follow the old sugar train route, or rent a car and take the coast road northwest from Basseterre out along the Caribbean shore.

First stop, some 3 miles (2 km) beyond the capital, is **Fairview Great House** (tel 869 465 3141, www.nirvanafairview.com), the historic former French military commander's residence with glorious views across to Nevis. The 300-year-old property has been recently restored with a handsome dining room furnished with a huge mahogany dining table, hurricane lamps, and elegant antique silver tableware. The separate kitchen building has its old volcanic stone and brick oven, and there are 2 acres (0.8 ha) of landscaped gardens to enjoy as well as a pleasant restaurant. The gift shop in the cellar sells Fairview's own homemade chutneys and jams.

South (0.25 mile/0.4 km) of the village of Challengers is **Bloody Point**, the scene of the last pitched battle between St. Kitts's European settlers and Carib Indians. At **Old Road Town**, the first permanent British settlement and island capital for a century, **Amerindian petroglyphs** are carved into a boulder on the side road leading up to **Romney Manor.** Badly damaged by fire, the partially rebuilt 17th-century manor houses the textile workshops of Caribelle Batik.

At Middle Island the tomb of Sir Thomas Warner lies in the overgrown graveyard of **St. Thomas' Parish Church.** Beyond the village the hulking volcanic outcrop of **Brimstone Hill** looms ahead enjoying commanding views across to the Dutch Windward Islands of Sint Eustatius and Saba.

A UNESCO World Heritage site, the colossal **Brimstone Hill Fortress National Park** covers a 37-acre (15 ha) site 800 feet (240 m) above the coast. Built from blackened volcanic stone beginning in 1690, the Gibraltar of the West Indies was considered impregnable until 8,000 French troops laid siege to it in 1782. It took a month of constant bombardment to destroy every building and breach the 7-foot-thick (2 m) walls, forcing the 1,000-strong garrison of defenders to surrender. The British regained control in 1794 and rebuilt the fortifications, crowned by **Fort George Citadel,** which is once again bristling with cannons.

As the main road rounds the north end of the island, it runs through the village of St. Paul's and past a bumpy track leading up to the lovely **Rawlins Plantation.**

Continuing down the east coast, make a stop at **Black Rocks,** jagged volcanic formations created by lava from Mount Liamuiga.

Frigate Bay & the South

Just south of Basseterre lies **Frigate Bay,** St. Kitts's hotel enclave, with an 18-hole golf course and beaches on both sides of the isthmus. The broad, sandy beach on the more sheltered (southern) Caribbean coast is the island's busiest. It has a beach bar and several restaurants. On the Atlantic side of the peninsula

the water is rougher, but there's good bodysurfing and the swimming is safe. Swimming isn't recommended at **North Friar's Bay,** however, which has dangerous currents, but its opposite number, **South Friar's Bay,** is lovely, sandwiched between palm trees and glassy calm water.

A 10-mile (15 km) highway roller-coasters down to the southern tip of the island, rounding the old salt ponds where several species of wading birds can be spotted and egrets balance on the backs of cattle by the roadside.

Facing Nevis across The Narrows are the small, undeveloped beaches on **Major's Bay** and **Banana Bay.** Busier **Cockleshell Bay** and **Turtle Bay** each boast a lively bar-restaurant, snorkeling off the beach, and water sports, including sailing, diving, and sailboard and kayak rental. ∎

Brimstone Hill Fortress

🅰 216 B3
✉ Brimstone Hill
☎ 869 465 2609
💲 $$$

www.brimstone hillfortress.org

The Brimstone Hill Fortress once had walls that were 7 feet (2 m) thick.

Nevis

Divided from St. Kitts by a 2-mile-wide (3 km) channel known as The Narrows, Nevis rears up precipitously to an imposing volcanic cone. Columbus named the island Nuestra Señora de las Nieves (Our Lady of the Snows) in a rather fanciful allusion to the almost permanently cloud-capped heights of Nevis Peak (3,232 feet/985 m); his poetic name was later mangled by British settlers to less romantic but more serviceable Nevis (pronounced NEE-viss).

Nevis Peak is nearly always shrouded in clouds.

Nevis
- 199 B2

Visitor Information
- Main St., Charlestown
- 869 469 7550

www.nevisisland.com

Colonists established a toehold on the island in 1627, and by the mid-18th century the planters of Nevis were so prosperous and fashionable that the pint-size island was hailed as the Queen of the Caribees, renowned for its grand plantation houses, fabulous parties, and the spa in Charlestown's Bath Hotel. Nevis was not immune to the French raiding parties that targeted St. Kitts, and it suffered several attacks that destroyed buildings and crops. African slaves captured from the famed and highly profitable slave market on Nevis were regarded as an additional prize and were shipped away to work the cane fields of Guadeloupe and Martinique. A century and a half after the abolition of slavery, Nevis accepted independence from Britain as part of the Federation of St. Kitts and Nevis.

The smaller (36 square miles/93 sq km) and quieter partner in the two-island coalition, Nevis retains vestiges of its rich colonial past in a clutch of gracious plantation house hotels and the sturdy stone buildings of the

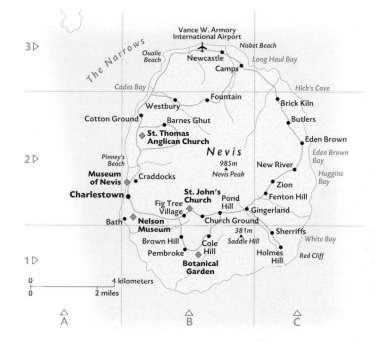

3 ▷

The Narrows

Oualie Beach

Newcastle

Vance W. Armory International Airport

Nisbet Beach

Long Haul Bay

Camps

Cades Bay

Hick's Cove

Fountain

Westbury

Brick Kiln

Cotton Ground

Barnes Ghut

Butlers

St. Thomas Anglican Church

Eden Brown

2 ▷

Nevis

Pinney's Beach

985m
Nevis Peak

New River

Eden Brown Bay

Museum of Nevis

Craddocks

Huggins Bay

Charlestown

Zion

St. John's Church

Pond Hill

Fenton Hill

Fig Tree Village

Gingerland

Bath

Nelson Museum

Church Ground

Brown Hill

Cole Hill

381m
Saddle Hill

Sherriffs

White Bay

Pembroke

Holmes Hill

Red Cliff

1 ▷

Botanical Garden

0 ___ 4 kilometers

0 ___ 2 miles

△ A   △ B   △ C

INSIDER TIP:

Try delaying your inevitable recognition as a tourist by pronouncing the island's name correctly: It's NEE-viss, not NEH-vis.

—LARRY PORGES
Editor, National Geographic Books

main settlement, Charlestown.

In recent years the Nevisian economy, boosted by offshore tax status, has outstripped that of St. Kitts, and traditional interisland rivalries have been further exacerbated by what the Nevisians feel is undue Kittitian interference in their affairs. The question of secession has been openly discussed in the assembly.

The 10,000 Nevisians are among the most hospitable hosts in the Caribbean region, and the island's unhurried pace and gentle charm are soothing antidotes to world-weariness. Tourism Nevis-style is relatively upscale but determinedly low key. Nevis has no casinos or air-conditioned malls, not even a major historical site, although Lord Nelson got married on the island, with a future king of England in attendance. Instead, guests at most of the plantation hotels have to journey to the beaches on the Caribbean (west) coast, work up an appetite horseback riding or hiking in the rain forest, and make a round-island tour that takes all of half a day.

Charlestown

Located two-thirds of the way down the Caribbean west coast,

Museum of Nevis

- 221 B2
- Low St., Charlestown
- ☎ 869 469 5786
- Closed Sat. p.m. & Sun.
- $ $$

Charlestown is the capital of Nevis and the liveliest spot on the island. Founded around 1660 and named in honor of King Charles II in 1671, the town straggles along the main round-island road to its hub, a grassy triangle that doubles as a meeting place and minibus depot a short walk from the pier. Traditional two-story stone and wood colonial buildings with balconies and gingerbread trim

whose image graces the ten-dollar bill (see sidebar opposite). The one-room museum's modest collections cover a broad spectrum of island history and culture, from Amerindian pottery shards to independence.

An early European visitor to Nevis was Capt. John Smith and a party of 144 Englishmen. They spent six days on Nevis in 1607 en route to found the colony at Jamestown, Virginia. The

Net casting at Pinney's Beach

Nelson Museum

- 221 B2
- Bath Rd., Charlestown
- ☎ 869 469 5786
- Closed Sat. p.m. & Sun.
- $ $$

line the street, and a selection of shops, cafés, and small businesses has moved into the alleys leading down to the rejuvenated waterfront, where ferries from St. Kitts unload passengers and provisions onto the dock.

At the north end of Main Street is the **Museum of Nevis,** housed in Alexander Hamilton House, birthplace of the American statesman (1757–1804)

group were revived by a dip in the hot spring that would later feature as the centerpiece of the 18th-century **Bath Hotel** at the southern end of town. Today the hotel buildings are being restored and visitors can once again take a dip in the steaming waters.

Just up from the hotel is the **Nelson Museum,** which examines the life and times of the great English naval hero. Horatio Nelson

Pinney's Beach has that great, rustic Caribbean island feel. And the views from the beach up to Nevis Peak are some of the best on the island.

—MATT PROPERT
National Geographic photographer

married local girl Fanny Nisbet at the Montpelier Estate in 1787, during an uncomfortable posting to Antigua (see p. 206). Exhibits include a plate from the wedding feast, a portion of the Union Jack flag under which Nelson stood when he was fatally wounded at the Battle of Trafalgar in 1805, and items from the mountain of memorabilia commissioned to commemorate his death.

Around the Island

Just north of Charlestown, parallel to the coast road, is **Pinney's Beach,** which unfurls in a 4-mile (6.5 km) reel of golden sand backed by palm trees. Along the way you'll pass **St. Thomas Anglican Church,** sitting on a small rise with views along the coast and across to St. Kitts. Founded in 1643, it is believed to be the oldest congregation on the island.

Farther north is **Oualie Beach,** which has good snorkeling and water sports. Beyond the airport is the **Newcastle Pottery,** set in a small roadside workshop, where simple handmade bowls, candle-holders, and jugs are fashioned from local red clay. As the road circles around to the rougher Atlantic coast, there is more reef snorkeling off the white coral sands of **Nisbet Beach.**

Four of Nevis's five plantation house hotels nestle beneath **Nevis Peak,** overlooking the south coast between Gingerland and Fig Tree Village. A glorious **Botanical Garden** has been established on the grounds of Montpelier Estate. The 8-acre (3 ha) site is ideal for a gentle stroll and offers plenty to interest the plant lover, from the fragrant rose and vine gardens to a rain forest conservatory, lily pools, and shady orchid terraces. Nelson's and Fanny Nisbet's marriage at Montpelier Estate is recorded in a copy of the register on display at **St. John's Church** in Fig Tree, on the road back to Charlestown. ∎

Botanical Garden
- 🅰 221 B1
- ✉ Montpelier Estate, St. John's Parish
- ☎ 869 469 3509
- 🕐 Closed Sun.
- 💲 $$$

Alexander Hamilton

Born on Nevis on January 11, 1757, Alexander Hamilton served as aide-de-camp to Gen. George Washington during the American Revolution. He was nicknamed "the Little Lion" on account of his relatively diminutive stature (5 feet 7 inches/170 cm) and ferocious temper, which, it was said, turned his blue eyes to black when he was angry. Hamilton trained as a lawyer, and Washington appointed him the first secretary of the treasury. He died in a duel with Vice President Aaron Burr (1756–1836), his political rival, in 1804.

Montserrat

The most southerly outpost of the Leeward Island group, Montserrat was long regarded as a haven of tranquility. A real slice of the old Caribbean with a smattering of beaches and hotels, it has a lush, mountainous interior that invites exploration. The island's peaceful idyll was shattered by the devastating eruption of the Soufrière volcano in 1995.

Montserrat's Tar River Valley before it was devastated by the Soufrière volcano in the 1990s

Montserrat

🅰 199 C1

Visitor Information

✉ Montserrat Tourist Board, 7 Farara Plaza, Brades

☎ 664 491 2230

www.visit montserrat.com

Montserrat is part of the volcanic Windward Island chain poised on the rim of the Atlantic and Caribbean tectonic plates. It was named by Columbus for the famous Montserrat Abbey near Barcelona, Spain, and settled in the 17th century by Irish Catholics seeking refuge from Protestant persecution on St. Kitts. This Irish connection earned Montserrat its nickname, "the Emerald Isle." Today the islanders celebrate St. Patrick's Day as a national holiday (see sidebar p. 226), in addition to the Queen's birthday in recognition of the island's status as a British Overseas Territory.

Apart from the occasional high-profile visitor, such as Stevie Wonder or Sir Paul McCartney recording at Sir George Martin's renowned Air Studios, life was a gentle round of fishing, farming, and a little low-key tourism until Montserrat's quiet repose was shaken by ominous grumblings from the volcano in the summer of 1995. All the major Windwards have an active volcano, usually called a *soufrière* from the French for sulfur. These tend to bubble along harmlessly, producing hot springs and boiling mud pools (notably on Dominica and St. Lucia), but as the tectonic plates ground together far beneath Montserrat, magma escaped from the earth's core and the *soufrière* erupted, raining ash, rocks, and lava over the southern portion of the island. The area was evacuated to a safe zone established in the northern third of the territory. Increased volcanic activity in 1997 saw the abandoned capital, **Plymouth,** destroyed and the island's population diminished from 10,000 to 4,000, with many former residents unable to return. At the present time volcanologists are unable to predict an end to the *soufrière's* intermittent activities.

This has not stopped the optimistic and engagingly friendly Montserratians from reinventing their island as a tourist destination with a difference. Forget your classic Caribbean beach holiday and visit Montserrat for a right-up-close volcano-watching experience, which might feature spectacular dome-collapses, massive ash clouds, and glowing nighttime lava flows. The extraordinary, postapocalyptic landscape of the Exclusion Zone has become a surprising tourist draw, viewed from lookout

INSIDER TIP:

The domino games outside Montserrat's rum shops provide an entertaining window into the island's colorful local culture.

—CAROLINE HICKEY
Editor, National Geographic Books

points in the surrounding hills and boat tours along the coast. Plymouth has even been touted as a "modern-day Pompeii." An unexpected benefit of the 2-mile (3 km) marine exclusion zone around the island has been the creation of an underwater reserve replete with pristine dive sites, abundant marine life, and some new and spectacular submarine landscaping formed by pyroclastic flow from the volcano.

After more than a decade, Montserrat's new capital is being developed at **Little Bay,** on the northwest coast just beyond Brades, temporary home of local government. In Olveston, the **Montserrat National Trust** *(tel*

EXPERIENCE: Day Trips to the Emerald Isle

All transportation services to Montserrat depart from neighboring Antigua *(for flights and ferry information, see Travelwise p. 343)*. Tour operators on both islands offer day-trip tours with volcano viewing, lunch, and maybe a beach or snorkeling opportunity. For details contact **Carib World Travel**, Antigua *(tel 268 480 2999, www.carib-world.com, $$$$$)*; **Jenny's Tours**, Antigua *(tel 268 722 8188, www.jennytours. webs.com, $$$$$)*; or **RTT Travel & Tours,**

Montserrat *(tel 664 491 4788, wwwrtttravel andtours.com, $$$$$)*. For an unforgettable sailing experience, Antigua-based **Ondeck Ocean Racing** *(tel 268 562 6696, www .ondeck oceanracing.com, $$$$$)* takes you on an eight- to nine-hour round-trip voyage aboard a sleek Farr 65 ocean-racing yacht out of Falmouth Harbour. The day trip leaves time for only an hour on Montserrat, so an overnight stop is recommended. Tailor-made island tours can be arranged.

Zone when conditions permit.

Not to be missed is a visit to the **Montserrat Volcano Observatory** *(tel 664 491 5647, www.mvo .ms, closed Fri.–Sun., $$$),* housed in a striking state-of-the-art facility with panoramic views of its objective. The MVO monitors the Soufrière Hills site constantly, posting real-time webcam images on its website. At the Interpretation Centre, visitors are treated to a documentary film of the eruption, interactive displays, and exhibits. Other excellent vantage points for volcano-watching are **Garibaldi Hill** (where the MVO sites its webcam) with sweeping views over Plymouth; and the purpose-built **Jack Boy Hill** viewing platform with a telescope, picnic area, and short trail.

In the middle of the island, the **Centre Hills** are beguiling hiking country. The luxuriant rain forest is rich in tropical bird and plant life and home to the Montserrat oriole, rare forest thrushes, hummingbirds, tree frogs, and the half-snake, half-lizard galliwasp. The terrain can be quite challenging, especially after heavy rain, and hikers are advised to take a guide *(contact the Montserrat National Trust, above).* The **Blackwood Allen Trail** is a favorite expedition, as is the hike up through banana plantations to **The Cot,** a former summer cottage 1,000 feet (304 m) above sea level.

Montserrat has just one white sand beach, **Rendezvous Bay,** accessible by boat from Little Bay. The rest are volcanic silver-gray, and those on the west coast, such as **Woodlands, Lime Kiln Bay,** and tiny **Bunkam Bay** are among the best and safest for swimming. ■

The Soufrière volcano is still active. The chance to spot ash clouds or glowing lava is now part of the island's draw.

664 491 3086, www.montserrat nationaltrust.ms) is an excellent source of information. The trust headquarters hosts changing exhibits illustrating different facets of island life from history and culture to wildlife. It is also the place to pick up hiking maps and arrange island tours, bird-watching trips, guides for expeditions into the hills, and visits to the Exclusion

Irish Heritage

Montserrat's affinity with distant Ireland is stamped into every visiting passport in the shape of a shamrock. The national flag features the legendary Irish figure of Erin with her harp alongside the British Union Jack, and the national dish, goat water, is supposed to be based on a traditional Irish stew. St. Patrick's Day in Montserrat is in reality St. Patrick's Week, celebrated on and around March 17, and it is a double celebration for it also marks a slave uprising on the island in 1768. Islanders let their hair down with an explosion of live music, feasting, dancing, masquerade processions, and special events. Be sure to wear something green!

The vibrant Creole culture of Guadeloupe and Martinique and the sybaritic, European chic of St.-Barthélemy

French Antilles

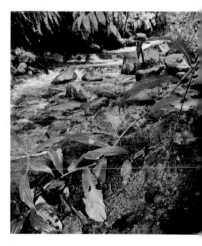

The Pitons du Carbet rain forest

French Antilles

At the heart of the French Caribbean are two of the largest islands in the Lesser Antilles (after Trinidad), Guadeloupe and Martinique, exuding a zesty Creole atmosphere that permeates every aspect of daily life. Some 150 miles (240 km) away, among the Dutch islands and former British colonies of the Leewards, the smaller French territory of St.-Barthélemy (St. Barts) sticks to the lifestyle of la métropole, as mainland France is known.

The first French colony in the Caribbean was founded on St. Kitts in 1624, the year after an English settlement was established on the island. A decade later, ambitious French colonists expanded their horizons and bravely tackled the Cannibal Isles, gaining a foothold on both Guadeloupe and Martinique between 1635 and 1636. The introduction of sugar cultivation in the latter part of the 17th century heralded *l'age d'or blanc* (the age of white gold) and the expansion of French influence down the eastern Caribbean chain and north to St. Domingue (present-day Haiti). As slave ships unloaded their human cargo to work the vast tracts of sugarcane, sizable fortunes flowed into the planters' coffers, and the town of St.-Pierre on Martinique developed into one of the most prosperous and fashionable cities in the West Indies.

Things did not always run smoothly, of course. Britain challenged France's authority at every turn and by a combination of treaties and brute force occupied virtually every French Caribbean territory during the 18th century. France did her best to return the compliment.

Ironically, the supporters of the *ancien régime* of Martinique actually called the enemy in to assist when the French Revolution decreed the abolition of slavery. The British ruled the island for 20 years without liberating the slaves. Napoleon (whose wife came from a family of Martiniquan planters) reintroduced slavery in 1802, causing widespread chaos and slave rebellions in Haiti and Guadeloupe. The law was not repealed until 1848, when the plantations turned to East Indian indentured laborers to replace the freed slaves.

Unlike the British islands, which were gently but firmly urged down the road to independence in the 20th century, France has bound her Caribbean territories more closely. Guadeloupe and Martinique have been integrated into the republic's political mainstream as semiautonomous overseas *régions*. The islanders have the same rights as their mainland counterparts and elect representatives to the Assemblée Nationale in Paris, vote in French elections, and enjoy the benefits of substantial government subsidies that have elevated local standards of living way above average for the region.

Dramatic volcanic eruptions raised Guadeloupe and Martinique from the seabed, and both islands boast beautiful mountain ranges choked with rain forest greenery and encircled by cane

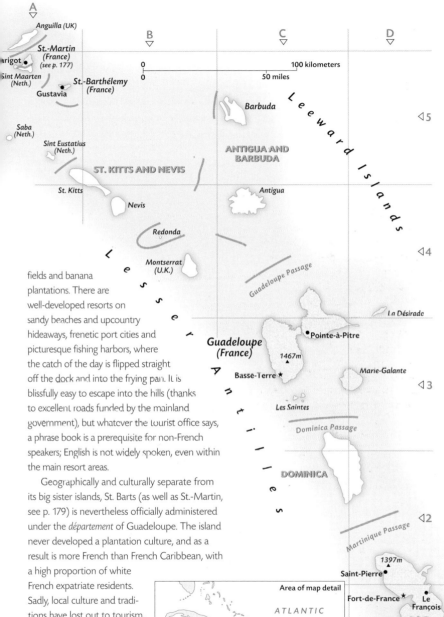

fields and banana plantations. There are well-developed resorts on sandy beaches and upcountry hideaways, frenetic port cities and picturesque fishing harbors, where the catch of the day is flipped straight off the dock and into the frying pan. It is blissfully easy to escape into the hills (thanks to excellent roads funded by the mainland government), but whatever the tourist office says, a phrase book is a prerequisite for non-French speakers; English is not widely spoken, even within the main resort areas.

Geographically and culturally separate from its big sister islands, St. Barts (as well as St.-Martin, see p. 179) is nevertheless officially administered under the *département* of Guadeloupe. The island never developed a plantation culture, and as a result is more French than French Caribbean, with a high proportion of white French expatriate residents. Sadly, local culture and traditions have lost out to tourism, albeit an upscale and sophisticated model, but excellent food, great beaches, and the prospect of fun in the sun with a French accent definitely have their charms. ■

Guadeloupe

Shaped like a butterfly with mismatched wings, Guadeloupe is in fact two islands crowded together by seismic upheavals and linked by a bridge over the Rivière Salée (Salt River). The western wing is Basse-Terre, marked by verdant and volcanic peaks, and the eastern is Grande-Terre, a rolling, dry limestone plateau fringed by beaches. Making up the Guadeloupean archipelago are the islands of La Désirade, Marie-Galante, and the eight tiny islets of Les Saintes.

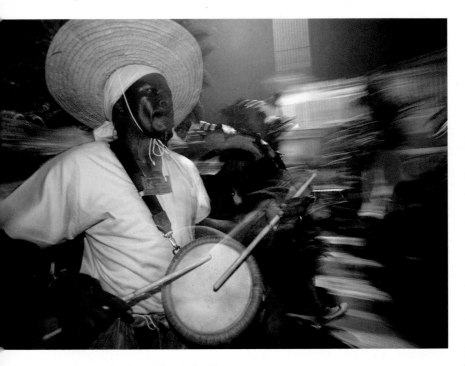

Drums provide a Carnival beat in Guadeloupe.

Guadeloupe

🅰 229 C3

Visitor Information

✉ 5 Square de la Banque, Pointe-à-Pitre

☎ 0590 82 09 30

www.lesilesde guadeloupe.com

Perhaps inspired by the dozens of streams and waterfalls that tumble down Basse-Terre's rain-forested flanks, the Carib people called the island Karukera (Island of Beautiful Waters). Christopher Columbus sailed past in 1493 and rechristened it Santa Maria de Guadalupe de Extremadura in honor of a famous Spanish monastery. A century and a half later the

French colonized Guadeloupe with indentured settlers who worked for three years to pay off their sea passage. Unaccustomed to tropical conditions, they farmed with limited success until a four-year British occupation (1759–1763) turned the plantations around. The slow start meant Guadeloupe was administered from more successful Martinique and was forced to trade through the commercial port of St.-Pierre on Martinique, whose merchants paid artificially low prices for Guadeloupean sugar. As news of the French Revolution traveled across the Atlantic in 1789, it found the unhappy Guadeloupeans ripe for change.

Guadeloupe's settlers embraced the revolutionary regime with enthusiasm. Bands of armed *patriotes* (supporters of the revolution) overthrew the planters and installed a revolutionary government led by Victor Hugues (1770–1826). They erected the mandatory guillotine in Pointe-à-Pitre, where more than 300 enemies of the revolution lost their

heads. The slaves were freed in 1794, but their freedom was short-lived. The old regime regained control, and slavery was bloodily reestablished; many former slaves preferred death to submission. The British came and went a couple more times before France secured the colony for

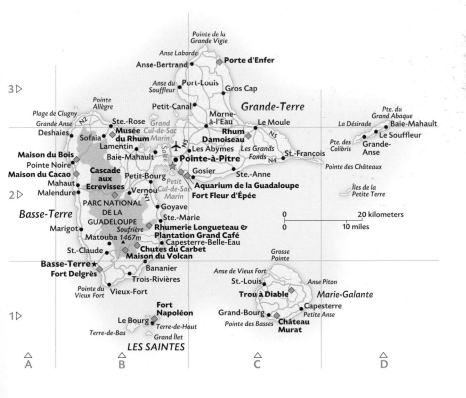

You'll be in for a real treat if you can time your visit with Gosier's spring Carnival. It seems the whole island descends on the little village for the wild festivities.

—MATT PROPERT
National Geographic photographer

good in 1815. The Guadeloupeans' independent cast of mind remains a force to be reckoned with today. There are occasional calls for independence from *la métropole,* but French cash is a powerful incentive to remain under the old colonial umbrella, particularly in view of the massive grants made available to help the island rebuild in the wake of hurricane damage.

Guadeloupe encompasses 530 square miles (1,372 sq km) and has a population of about 420,000. The contrasting island wings possess two equally diverse main cities. On the southwest coast of Basse-Terre is Basse-Terre town (see pp. 238–239), the modest administrative capital tucked in the lee of the volcano La Soufrière. A circlet of small towns and villages, linked by a round-island road, ring the coast of Guadeloupe's west wing. Only one route, La Traversée, scales the central mountain range, clambering up into the Parc National de la Guadeloupe (see sidebar p. 239), a magnificent

The beach town of Gosier is named after the brown pelican common in the Caribbean.

natural preserve with some of the best—and most challenging—hiking in the Caribbean.

In the southwest corner of Grande-Terre is Guadeloupe's biggest and busiest city—the sprawling commercial center and cruise-ship port of Pointe-à-Pitre (see below). No great beauty, it has a frenetic pace at odds with the usual leisurely Caribbean tempo, but it's fun to explore the local markets, and ferries for the offshore islands leave from the waterfront. Dotted east along the coast from Pointe-à-Pitre are the seaside resort towns of Gosier, Ste.-Anne, and St.-François. Gosier is the most developed, with a wall of large, modern hotels fronting the shore and packed beaches. Ste.-Anne and St.-François have retained more of their local character. Here it is sometimes possible to catch a game of *boules* in progress on one of the dusty, tree-shaded squares before dining out stylishly *à la française* at an excellent (although not inexpensive) fish restaurant along the promenade.

Pointe-à-Pitre

A teeming metropolis of 80,000 souls, Pointe-à-Pitre lies on a sheltered bay at the southern end of the Rivière Salée. Although the city dates from the 17th century, hurricanes, earthquakes, and fires have taken their toll, and modern concrete structures outnumber the few remaining colonial buildings.

With the sunlight blotted out by tall, thin buildings, downtown Pointe-à-Pitre is a maelstrom of traffic and pedestrians fighting for space on the narrow streets. At times it appears that there are more cars on the sidewalk than pedestrians, and jaywalking is obligatory. (Avoid driving in the downtown area at all costs.)

The focus of the old town is **La Darse,** the bustling waterfront area, with its ferry dock and jumble of street vendors' stalls selling anything from T-shirts and wood carvings to fresh produce and piping hot *accras*. Behind the dockside hubbub is **Place de la Victoire,** with its fringe of old colonial houses, their balconies full of flowers. A handful of sidewalk cafés provides a restful view of the city's green heart, planted with palm, mango, and African tulip trees.

Plunge into the grid of busy side streets west of the gardens

Pointe-à-Pitre
231 B2

EXPERIENCE:
Say It Like a Local

The French-speaking Caribbean islands offer some cultural challenges. In Guadeloupe, for instance, only large tourist spots offer assistance in English—French and its sister tongue, Creole, rule all residents' interactions. On the other hand, these differences give you the opportunity to immerse yourself in another idiom. If speaking like a local inspires you, try taking a French class during your stay on the island. Language classes are offered by **CESA Languages Abroad** in Ste.-Anne *(tel 44 1209 211 800, www.cesalanguages.com/learn-french-in-guadeloupe, $$$$).* Located near the beach, the school also offers surfing lessons to sports-minded students.

Musée Schoelcher

 24 rue Peynier

☎ 0590 82 08 04

⏱ Closed Sat. & Sun.

$ $

www.netgua.com.fr/museeSchoelcher

to the Cathédrale St.-Pierre et St.-Paul, Place Gourbeyre. Nicknamed *la cathédrale de fer* (iron cathedral) for its elaborate ironwork, the building was constructed in the early 19th century and has some fine stained glass.

Rue Frébault, the city's main shopping street, is lined with boutiques and stores full of French fashions and European imports. On the corner of Frébault and rue Peynier is the **Marché Couvert** (Covered Market), providing a boisterous slice of island life. Its maze of stalls is piled high with fruits and vegetables, bags of ground spices, and bunches of vanilla pods presided over by garrulous female vendors who giggle and haggle in a machine-gun patter of incomprehensible Creole.

West along rue Peynier is the **Musée Schoelcher,** devoted to the life and times of 19th-century

abolitionist Victor Schoelcher (1804–1893), a leading light in the French antislavery movement. When emancipation finally reached the French Caribbean in 1848, Schoelcher was elected a deputy of Guadeloupe. The museum occupies a pretty pink town house with wrought-iron decorations and a double staircase leading up to the entrance. Exhibits range from plantation-era

Creole Costume

Brightly checkered madras cotton is a ubiquitous feature of Guadaloupe, Martinique, and the French-speaking Windward Islands, which include Dominica and St. Lucia. Souvenir shops are piled high with madras table linen, costumed dollies, and, of course, traditional Creole costumes perfect for the dressing-up box back home.

Madras cotton was introduced to the islands by indentured laborers from the Indian subcontinent in the late 1800s. Colorful and cheap, it was enthusiastically adopted by former slaves whose drab clothing had been limited to cast-off canvas and even rough grain sacks. Renowned for their Gallic style, women fashioned the simple cotton fabric into elaborate robes

worn to celebrate feast days and holidays.

The five-piece costume consists of a white blouse trimmed with lace and ribbons, a madras skirt worn over flouncy petticoats, and a foulard scarf thrown over the shoulder and secured in the waistband, all topped by a silk headscarf. The scarf is a work of art in itself with a variable number of points *(bouts),* which signal the wearer's intentions:

Tête à un bout (one point)—my heart is for the taking

Tête à deux bouts (two points)—my heart is taken

Tête à trois bouts (three points)—my heart is spoken for, but . . .

The Renaissance Theater in Pointe-à-Pitre

artifacts and Schoelcher's campaigning pamphlets to African carved ivories, model ships, and other curios. The statue in front of the building depicts the revolutionary leader Victor Hugues.

Around Grande-Terre

Though Grande-Terre's southern beaches act as a magnet for tourists, most of the island is undeveloped, a rural backwater where rolling limestone hills, known as Les Grands Fonds, shelter a smattering of small farming hamlets, and the sugarcane harvest is still transported to the mill by ox-drawn carts.

Between Pointe-à-Pitre and Gosier is **Bas-du-Fort's** busy marina, the largest in the Caribbean. It's a good place to stop off and sample the nautical atmosphere from a sunny café or to dine out in one of the many restaurants. Next to the marina is the **Aquarium de la Guadeloupe**. A showcase for tropical fish, it also has a mangrove section and a huge shark tank with a walk-through Plexiglas tunnel.

On a headland above Bas-du-Fort are the 18th-century coral rock ruins of **Fort Fleur d'Epée,** laid out on a hilltop site shaded by flamboyant red-flowering trees.

Across Grande Baie is the seaside town of **Gosier,** Guadeloupe's chief resort, taking its name from the brown pelican, a familiar sight throughout the Caribbean. The old town has been swamped by an avalanche of hotels, restaurants, cafés, and discos spilling downhill to the shore and stretching for miles along the narrow sandy beaches. Hotels and concessions are well equipped for water sports, and small boats make the short voyage out to the tiny offshore pimple of **Îlet du Gosier,** where there's a lighthouse

Aquarium de la Guadeloupe
🅜 231 B2
✉ Place Créole-Marina
☎ 0590 90 92 38
💲 $$$

www.aquariumde
guadeloupe.com

Fort Fleur d'Epée
🅜 231 B2
☎ 0590 90 94 61

Gosier
🅜 231 C2

Club Med

✉ Quart Caravelle, Ste.-Anne

☎ 0590 86 33 06

www.clubmed.us

and another public beach (clothing optional).

Midway along the coast is **Ste.-Anne,** where long, sandy Caravelle beach offers water-sport activities and a Club Med resort to the west of town. Nearby is **Ste.-Anne Plage,** a lovely strip of fine white sand on a turquoise bay. It can get crowded, but plus points

INSIDER TIP:

Club Med at Ste.-Anne's Caravelle beach offers day passes to nonguests for the use of its beach and water-sports equipment, as well as lunch and drinks.

—JENNIFER ALLARD
National Geographic contributor

for families include shady trees, a row of café-restaurants across the street, and carts selling hot, sweet crêpes and ice cream.

St.-François has a salty tang, with fishermen constructing traditional hexagonal fish traps on the waterfront. The closest beach is **Plage des Raisins Clair,** but to the east of town is a 7-mile (11 km) road, lined with beaches along the southern shore. **Plage Tarare,** on the north side, is a nudist haunt. At the tip of the headland is **Pointe des Châteaux,** with its own small beach cove where surfers ride the powerful Atlantic waves that have hollowed caves from the soft limestone. A rocky path scales the cliffs to an orientation table with blustery views to the out islands and peaks of Basse-Terre.

From St.-François, Rte. N5 runs north to **Le Moule,** once the capital of Guadeloupe. On a back road

Beachgoers in the calm surf near Ste.-Anne

EXPERIENCE: Cruise Nature Preserved

On the west coast of Grande-Terre you'll find the **Réserve Naturelle du Grand Cul-de-Sac Marin,** *(www.guadeloupe-parc national.fr/?Le-Grand-Cul-de-Sac-Marin),* an annex of the Parc National de la Guadeloupe (see p. 239). Its 9,000-acre (3,600 ha) territory encompasses mangrove swamps, mud flats, wetland prairies, coastal forest, and an adjacent marine preserve renowned for its rich and rare biodiversity. Researchers at the park study estuaries, coral reefs,

river fauna, mangrove ecosystems, and more. The foreshore is a prime feeding ground for both saltwater and freshwater waterfowl and wading birds, such as egrets, terns, and kingfishers.

For a closer look at the preserve, its birds, and marine life, two-hour long mangrove cruises aboard the catamaran King Papyrus depart twice weekly from the **Marina de Pointe-à-Pitre** *(tel 0590 90 92 98, www.kingpapyrus.com, $$$$$).*

---

west of town is **Rhum Damoiseau** *(open for visits),* the only rum distillery on Grande-Terre.

A country road continues up to the northern tip of the island, past a viewpoint at **Porte d'Enfer** (Gate of Hell), before reaching **Pointe de la Grande Vigie** (Grand Lookout), where French sentries once scanned the horizon for signs of British activity on Antigua.

Beach stops on the west coast include **Anse Laborde** (just north of Anse-Bertrand) and **Anse du Souffleur** (at Port-Louis). In the center of the island is **Morne-à-l'Eau,** famous for its classic French Caribbean cemetery.

Around Southern Basse-Terre

Viewed from the sunny beaches of Grande-Terre, the towering, luxuriantly green bulk of neighboring Basse-Terre appears to brood like some giant leviathan beneath a blanket of clouds. About two-thirds of the island is the unspoiled Parc National de la Guadeloupe (see sidebar p.

239) with *traces* (walking trails) ranging from short, muddy scrabbles to waterfall beauty spots to serious long-distance hikes across the ridgeline or up to the Soufrière volcano. A fast modern road (Rte. N1) whisks you down the east coast from Pointe-à-Pitre to the capital of Basse-Terre in less than an hour, although there are several minor detours en route.

Inland from Petit-Bourg, the botanic gardens at **Domaine de Valombreuse** are laid out in the foothills. There are more than 1,000 species of plants, trails, bird life, and a children's play area. Just south of **Ste.-Marie,** a small coastal town where Christopher Columbus is thought to have encountered his first Carib in 1493, there are signs off the main road to the **Rhumerie Longueteau** distillery and Plantation Grand Café, a banana plantation. Cane fields surround the modern Longueteau estate house and its tiny, old-fashioned steam mill. Informal tours operate year-round, but the mill is only working (and

Rhum Damoiseau
- 231 C2
- Rte. D101, on the road from Le Moule to Les Abymes
- 0590 23 55 55

Basse-Terre
- 231 B1

Visitor Information
- Maison du Port, off blvd. du Général de Gaulle
- 0590 81 24 83

Domaine de Valombreuse
- 231 B2
- Cabout
- 0590 95 50 50
- $$

Rhumerie Longueteau
- 231 B2
- 0590 86 07 91
- Closed Sat. p.m. & Sun.; Dec.– April open Sun. a.m.

interesting) during the January-to-July harvest season. After the visit, you can sample straight rums and potent homemade rums spiked with tropical fruits.

Just up the road is the **Plantation Grand Café,** which

a peaceful 45-minute trek into the rain forest beneath giant mahogany, gommier, and bois rouge trees. Although the path continues on to the two upper falls, the most popular access point is another side road about a mile (1.6 km)

One of the many beautiful waterfalls on Basse-Terre

Plantation Grand Café

🗺 231 B2
☎ 0590 86 33 06
🕐 Closed Sat. & Sun.
💲 $$

celebrates the not-so-humble banana. A banana garden displays varieties from around the world—little plump pink velutinas from India and crocodile's fingers from Indonesia, among others. The 30-minute tours rattle around the plantation in open-sided trucks.

On the southern edge of the town of Capesterre-Belle-Eau a side road leads up to the trailhead for the third and least spectacular of the **Chutes du Carbet,** a series of three waterfalls in the national park fed by the Rivière Grand Carbe, which originates on La Soufrière. The third fall is a mere 65 feet (20 m) high, but it's

farther along Rte. N1, which takes a scenic route up to a parking area and collection of roadside barbecue stalls. It's a 20-minute uphill hike to the popular 360-foot-high (110 m) second fall. It takes two hours to reach the 410-foot-high (125 m) top fall and three hours to get up to la Soufrière.

Basse-Terre Town

At the southern tip of the island is Basse-Terre town, which offers little to detain the dedicated sightseer, although it has a bustling provincial charm. Across the street from its French-style, palm-lined seafront esplanade, stalls display succulent fruits and vegetables. A tight grid of shopping streets squeezes in between the Hôtel de Ville and the gray stone Catholic cathedral. To the south, **Fort Delgrès** stands guard over the harbor and houses a small history museum as well as the **Maison du Volcan,** with displays charting the origins of volcanoes and the history of La Soufrière. Behind the city center residential suburbs spread up the hillsides to St.-Claude, where a few old Creole houses cling to the slopes. Well worth a stop here is the tantalizing **La Bonifièrie,** a restored coffee mill with a gourmet chocolate factory and excellent on-site café.

Above St.-Claude, Rte. D11 strikes on up through the encroaching rain forest, narrowing as it climbs toward **Savane à**

Mulets, 1,000 feet (305 m) below the volcano's summit. From here the round-trip hike to the summit takes around two and a half hours along a well-marked trail past lava flows and boulders. The climb is generally accompanied by a steady drizzle and cool winds, so bring appropriate clothing. At the summit, not one crater but a chain of reeking, sulfur-spewing pits are staggered along the fault line.

To complete a tour of southern Basse-Terre, the slow west coast road (Rte. N2) parallels the shore, through Vieux-Habitants, where the **Musée du Café** (tel 0509 98 54 96) delves into the history of coffee on a working plantation, to **Mahaut.** Here, the Route de la Traversée (see pp. 240–241) crosses back to the east coast for Pointe-à-Pitre. If you're in a hurry, however, it's quicker to return along the east coast. ■

Fort Delgrès
🗺 231 B1
☎ 0590 81 37 48

Parc National de la Guadeloupe

A UNESCO-designated biosphere reserve covering 74,000 acres (30,000 ha) of central southern Basse-Terre, the national park cloaks the cloud-shrouded bulk of La Soufrière (4,813 feet/1,467 m), rising to the highest point in the Lesser Antilles.

Venturing into the virgin, green heart of the park, where La Soufrière's flanks course with rivers and waterfalls, is not recommended for the fainthearted. Conditions are frequently wet, muddy, and chilly, so hikers should come prepared with rain gear and sturdy boots.

Dozens of trails crisscross the mountainsides, ranging from a gentle stroll from a parking lot on the Route de la Traversée (see pp. 240–241) to extended

treks that require a considerable degree of fitness, the correct equipment, and an experienced guide. The main access points to the park's trail network are along the Route de la Traversée and to the south around La Soufrière.

The park headquarters at **Habitation Beausoleil** (Montéran 97120, St.-Claude, tel 0590 80 86 00, www.guadeloupe-parcnational.fr) is an excellent source of information, providing trail guides graded by difficulty. Guided hikes and rain forest experiences such as canyoning can be arranged through **Vert Intense** (tel 0590 99 34 73, www.vert-intense.com, $$$$$) and **Les Heures Saines** (tel 0590 98 86 63, www.heures-saines.gp, $$$$$).

A Drive Around Northern Basse-Terre

This clockwise circuit of northern Basse-Terre begins with a spectacular rain forest drive along the Route de la Traversée before looping around the top half of the island. You can experience a variety of suggested diversions along the way, from a glass-bottom boat trip to museums of cocoa, wood, and rum.

From **Pointe-à-Pitre ❶** (see p. 233), follow signs for Basse-Terre west across the Rivière Salée and south on the fast Rte. N1 to the exit for La Traversée (Rte. D23). The cross-island road skims west through the cane fields before ascending into the rain forest, where it enters the Parc National de la Guadeloupe (see sidebar p. 239).

Just inside the park boundary is the pretty **Cascade aux Écrevisses** (Crayfish Falls) ❷

a popular picnic spot at the foot of a scenic waterfall edged by dripping mosses and creepers. Beneath the forest canopy it's hard to resist scrambling around on the boulders that litter the stream like giant stepping-stones.

Just over a mile (1.6 km) on is the **Maison de la Forêt,** which provides an excellent introduction to the 74,000-acre (29,950 ha) park with exhibits covering geology, flora, and fauna (unfortunately only in French). Hiking maps are available giving details of the well-maintained, 190-mile (306 km) trail

NOT TO BE MISSED:

Maison de la Forêt • Col des
Mamelles • Musée du Rhum

network within the park, and there are several round-trip walks from the maison.

One of the park's more challenging hikes is the **Trace des Crêtes,** which follows the mountain ridge above the west coast and crosses La Traversée at the **Col des Mamelles** ❸ (1,922 feet/586 m), a mountain pass between twin volcanic peaks. This is the highest point on the road, with fantastic views of the park on a clear day, although the vista is frequently obscured by cloud and rain (the annual rainfall here is about 250 inches/6,350 mm).

After the hairpin descent to the coast at **Mahaut,** there's an optional short (3 miles/5 km) detour south to **Plage de Malendure** ❹, where glassbottom boat trips depart for the marine preserve surrounding the tiny Îlet de Pigeon. The **Reserve du Commandant Cousteau** honors one of its early champions, oceanographer Jacques Cousteau (1910–1997), who helped introduce a fishing ban and named Pigeon Island one

of the world's top ten dive sites (some considerable time ago). The coral reef site is rather crowded with divers and pleasure boats these days, but the visibility on a clear day (averaging 100 feet/30 m) ensures there's always something interesting to see.

One and a half miles (2.5 km) north of Mahaut on Rte. N2 is the Maison du Cacao ❺ *(tel 0590 98 25 23),* which delves into the history, cultivation, and manufacture of cocoa, introduced to Guadeloupe by Arawak Indians. Blocks of 100 percent natural cocoa are on sale.

It's worth stopping at **Maison du Bois** *(tel 0590 98 16 90),* a few minutes' drive up the coast. The House of Wood has built up an impressive collection of antique wooden tools and utensils. Among the coffee grinders, cassava-root crushers, and hand whisks are displays depicting boatbuilding and furniture-making.

The drive continues past the attractive fishing village of **Deshaies** ❻, with its pretty Jardin Botanique *(tel 0590 28 43 02, $$$)* and the broad bay at Grande Anse, graced by one of Guadeloupe's finest beaches. The 2 mile-long (3 km) sweep of rosy gold sand is backed by palm trees, and there's a choice of snack bars and Creole style café-restaurants serving traditional seafood specials and salads if it's time for a lunch break.

The road (Rte. N2) rounds the tip of the island and continues on to **Ste.-Rose;** follow signs for the **Musée du Rhum** ❼ *(tel 0590 28 70 04, closed Sun.)* at nearby Bellevue. Exhaustive signboards and displays examine every last detail of three centuries of rum-making in the Caribbean, and the museum contains such antique artifacts as an enormous cane juice vat hewn out of a single tree trunk. The interesting insect gallery displays some 5,000 butterflies, beetles, and bugs from around the world. After watching a short film (some showings in English), take a tour of the adjacent Distillerie Reimonenq.

Back on the main road (Rte. N2), it's a swift run back to Pointe-à-Pitre.

- ⓜ See also area map p. 231
- ► Pointe-à-Pitre
- 🕐 A full day with stops
- ↔ 58 miles/88 km
- ► Pointe-à-Pitre

The Guadeloupean Archipelago

The Guadeloupean archipelago forms a graceful southerly arc separating Guadeloupe from Dominica. These small islands compliment the busier pace of Guadeloupe with tranquil backdrops of humble fishing villages and rolling sugarcane farms guarded by windmills.

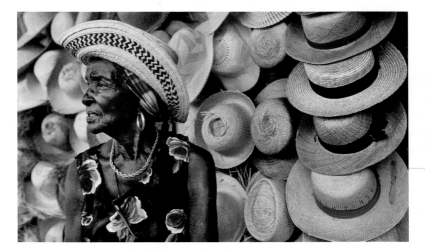

A hat seller displays (and wears) her goods in Grand-Bourg on Marie-Galante.

La Désirade
🄼 231 D2

Marie-Galante
🄼 231 C1

Les Saintes
🄼 231 B1

La Désirade

An arid, flat-topped table mountain 6 miles (10 km) off Pointe des Châteaux (the eastern tip of Guadeloupe), La Désirade signalled the end of a long Atlantic crossing for Columbus, hence "The Desired One." Only 8 miles (13 km) long and one mile (1.6 km) wide, the island has a population of 1,700 who lead a simple life farming or fishing. The main settlement is **Grande-Anse,** on the sheltered southern shore; farther up the coast, past the golden sands of Grande-Anse and **Le Souffleur,** you can see the ruins of an old leper colony at **Baie-Mahault.**

Daily ferry services (*Le Colibri, tel 0590 21 23 73*) depart from St.-François in Guadeloupe (one hour); you can also take scheduled flights (15 minutes). Car, scooter, and bicycle rentals are available through Jo Scooters (*tel 0590 20 07 41*). There are a few basic lodgings on the island, and locals offer B&Bs.

Marie-Galante

Twenty miles (32 km) south of Grande-Terre is the flat limestone island of Marie-Galante, settled in 1648. Old windmills dot the sugarcane fields, still harvested for the island's famous rums.

Grand-Bourg (*visitor information, tel 0590 97 56 51, www.ot -mariegalante.com*) is Marie-Galante's main settlement. South of town is the 18th-century **Château**

Murat *(tel 0590 97 94 41)* plantation house, which has a windmill
and a museum. Along the bottom
of the island there is good swimming at **Petite Anse,** and water
sports at **Pointe de la Feuillère,**
near Capesterre. Inland, a maze
of country lanes burrows through
tunnels of sugarcane; several rum
distilleries offer tours and tast-
ings. Another tourist stop is the
Trou à Diable (Devil's Hole), an
underground cavern that requires
a flashlight and sturdy footwear
to explore.

Fine beaches run the length
of the northwest coast between
Vieux Fort and the fishing village
of **St.-Louis.** Daily ferry services
*(Express des Iles, tel 0825 35 90 00,
www.express-des-iles.com or Brudey
0590 90 04 48, www.brudey-freres
.fr)* to Grand-Bourg and St.-
Louis leave from Pointe-à-Pitre
(one hour); scheduled flights are
available (15 minutes). Cars and
scooters are rented from Auto
Moto *(St.-Louis, tel 0590 97 19 42,
www.automoto-location.com).* For
hotel information contact the
tourist office *(tel 0590 97 56 51).*

Les Saintes

Only two of these tiny, volcanic
islets 7 miles (11 km) south
of Basse-Terre are inhabited.
The quieter and less visited is
Terre-de-Bas, a sleepy former
plantation island with a couple
of good beaches, one hotel, and
rooms to rent. **Terre-de-Haut,**
on the other hand, greets the
daily invasion of day-trippers
with the welcoming restaurants
and boutiques of **Le Bourg.** A
fishing port, Le Bourg is set on

The Battle of the Saints

One of the most famous naval battles of
the 18th century, the Battle of the Saints
was the decisive factor in determining
British supremacy in the Caribbean. In
the spring of 1782, the French fleet was in
Martinique, readying itself for an invasion
of Jamaica calculated to destroy British
credibility in the region. The preparations
were being monitored by Adm. George
Rodney (1718–1792) of the Royal Navy
from his base on Pigeon Island, St. Lucia.
On April 7, under Adm. François de Grasse,
33 French ships of the line set sail; Rodney
gave chase, meeting the French off Les
Saintes on the morning of April 12. In a
surprise maneuver, which owed more to
the weather than design, Rodney broke
the French line in not one but three places
and carried the day. The tactic was later
employed by Admiral Nelson at Trafalgar.

a magnificent bay sheltered by
the **Îlet à Cabrit** (Goat Island).
Nowhere on the island is more
than a 30-minute walk from Le
Bourg, although it's a stiff uphill
climb to **Fort Napoléon** *(tel 0690
61 01 51, closed p.m.).* The fortress
houses a museum of local history,
with a section devoted to the
Battle of the Saints (see above).

Terre-de-Haut's best beach is the
Plage Pont Pierre, in the east. Two
quieter beaches are **Petite Anse
Pain de Sucre,** west of Le Bourg,
and **Anse du Figuier,** on the south
coast (clothing optional). Daily ferry
services *(Express des Iles, tel 0825 35
90 00, or Brudey 0590 90 04 48,)* run
to Terre-de-Haut and Terre-de-Bas
from Pointe-à-Pitre (one hour) and
Trois-Rivières (30 minutes). There
are also daily sailings between Le
Bourg and Terre-de-Bas, and flights
from Guadeloupe. ■

St.-Barthélemy

Known as Manhattan-sur-Mer to the cognoscenti, St.-Barthélemy is the epitome of French Caribbean chic and arguably the most exclusive and expensive speck of volcanic rock in the region, give or take a private island or two. This is the winter playground of the super-rich and super-casual, where the shops overflow with Chanel and champagne, but dressing for dinner is frowned upon.

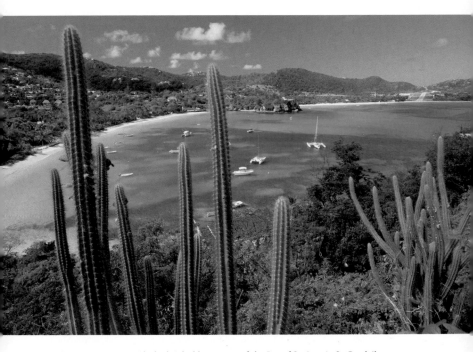

Cactuses contrast with the bright blue waters of the Bay of St.-Jean in St. Barthélemy.

St.-Barthélemy

229 A5

Visitor Information

Quai du Général de Gaulle, Gustavia

0590 27 87 2

www.saintbarth
-tourisme.com

One of the first things to strike visitors to St. Barts (or Saint-Barth in French) is the paucity of black faces; almost all 6,000 permanent inhabitants are white, affluent, and of French descent. French culture defines every detail, from the humble baguette to the rarefied heights of gourmet cuisine, from designer labels to traditional *calèche* bonnets, the old-fashioned women's hats (now rarely seen except on holidays) that recall St. Barts's colonists from Normandy and Brittany.

St. Barts was not born with a silver spoon in its mouth. The 8-square-mile (21 sq km) island was named San Bartolomé for Columbus's brother and colonized by 60 French settlers from St. Kitts in 1648. The first colony was wiped out by a Carib raiding party, but the strategic position of St. Barts amid the English

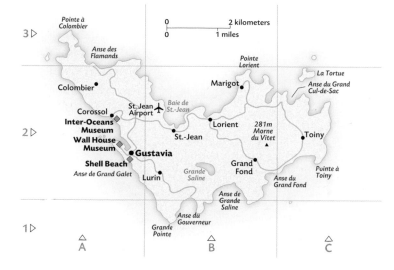

Leeward Island colonies prompted a second attempt by Protestant Huguenots in 1674. While other islands planted cotton and cane, St. Barts's stock in trade was piracy. Buccaneers frequently took refuge in its convenient coves.

In 1784 French King Louis XVI exchanged St. Barts for trading rights in the Baltic, and the island became Swedish for a century. The Swedes declared their sole Caribbean possession a free port, and for a while it profited handsomely, trading with the newly independent United States. When business tailed off, the island was sold back to France in 1878, and subsided into obscurity until quietly emerging as a stylish jet-set hideaway in the 1980s.

Gustavia

Postcard-pretty Gustavia was named in honor of the Swedish King Gustav III and hems in three sides of its sheltered harbor, guarded by four hilltop forts. During the height of the winter season, splendiferous gin palaces line the docks, berthed sleek cheek-by-elegant-jowl, and the boutiques, jewelers, and terrace cafés of the tiny town center are packed with serious shoppers and gawking day-trippers from Sint Maarten. The pointy-roofed Swedish belfry is a local landmark. On the western side of the harbor is the **Wall House Museum,** which provides a quick roundup of local history and customs in a former waterfront warehouse. Its collections include Amerindian votive objects, colonial documents, fish traps, and the stiff-sided calèche bonnets, also known as *quichenottes* (or kissme-not) and once regarded as the best defense against amorous

Wall House Museum

✉ La Pointe
☎ 0590 29 71 55
🕐 Closed Sun.
💲 $

Inter-Oceans Museum

- ✉ Corossol
- ☎ 0590 27 62 97
- 🕐 Closed Mon.
- 💲 $$

Le Sélect

- ✉ rue du Centenaire
- ☎ 0590 27 86 87

Englishmen and Swedes. The closest beach is **Shell Beach,** a ten-minute walk south of town at **Anse de Grand Galet.**

St. Barts peaks at less than 1,000 feet (300 m), but its tightly packed folds of perpendicular green hills make it seem much taller, while lovingly cultivated gardens create an impression of tropical lushness. The 18 small villages dotted about the island are linked by narrow roads that crawl doggedly up into the hills and then plummet back to the coast. At the bottom of a particularly vertiginous descent north of Gustavia is the charming fishing village of **Corossol.** Turn left at the waterfront for the **Inter-Oceans Museum,** an intriguing seashell collection said to be the second largest in the world.

On the north coast is St. Barts's chief tourist hub, **St.-Jean,** where a small group of hotels, restaurants, and shops have sprung

INSIDER TIP:

In Gustavia, check out Le Sélect, the hangout that inspired Jimmy Buffet's song "Cheeseburger in Paradise," and where fancy dress equals bare feet.

—BARBARA A. NOE
Editor, National Geographic Books

up along the roadside facing a glorious bay and busy beach.

A road circles the east end of the island, past the beach at Anse du Grand Cul-de-Sac and around **Morne du Vitet** (938 feet/ 281 m). The two best beaches are on the south coast: **Anse de Grande Saline,** reached via St.-Jean, and **Anse du Gouverneur,** south of Lurin. Both are undeveloped, with deep white sand and terrific views of distant Saba, Sint Eustatius, and St. Kitts. ∎

Racing Stripes

Yachting is not just a sport in St. Barts, it's a passion driven by the constant trade winds and sensational scenery, which create ideal conditions for spirited nautical challenges. The island's sporting calendar is jam-packed with regattas and races attracting every conceivable craft, from multimillion-dollar super-yachts to old-fashioned wooden boats lovingly crafted in local yards.

The Caribbean racing season opens in November with the prestigious St. Barth CataCup. One of the region's top sailing events, it attracts a world-class field of racing catamarans to the Baie de St.-Jean. New Year's is an excuse for a waterborne around-the-island parade featuring multicolored sails and upscale holiday visitors. Hundreds of craft big and small gather for the Bucket Regatta in March to enjoy three days of friendly races and onshore partying. The season draws to a close in April, but not before the weeklong Les Voiles de Saint-Barth. A recent addition to the racing calendar, Les Voiles (the sails) has gotten off to a flying start, earning a place among the top five Caribbean sailing events. Staged over six days, it pitches maxi yachts, racing yachts, and multihulls against each other over a series of stunning courses laid out around the offshore islands.

Martinique

Martinique is one of the most beautiful of all the Caribbean islands. The Amerindians called it Madinina, the Island of Flowers, and Martinique is still celebrated for its glorious gardens and rampant rain forest, as well as its lovely women, fine beaches, and distinctive Creole culture. Measuring 50 miles (80 km) long and 22 miles (35.5 km) wide, it is flanked by the Windward Islands of Dominica to the north and St. Lucia to the south.

Martinique's colorful Carnival culture on display during a celebration in the town of Grand Anse

Northern Martinique is tall and explosively green, swathed in dense rain forest that swoops down from the heights of Mont Pelée, the island's only active volcano, through the lesser but still impressive peaks of the Pitons du Carbet to a fringe of banana plantations clinging to the lower slopes. The central plain, stretching east from Fort-de-France, the island's capital on the west coast, is Martinique's sugarcane belt. The south of the island is characterized by the dry, hilly folds of the *mornes,* which back a scattered collection of beaches and small coastal resorts.

Columbus may have spotted Martinica, as he called it, on his second voyage, but he definitely stopped off here on his fourth expedition in 1502. He waxed lyrical about the beauty of the island and the Carib women

Martinique

🅰 229 D1

Visitor Information

✉ 76 rue Lazarre Carnot

☎ 0596 60 27 73

www.tourismefdf .com

who greeted his arrival with cries of "Madinina." It is uncertain whether Martinica is a corruption of Madinina or maybe a homage to St. Martin. The Carib were still in possession of the island when French settlers first came ashore near Le Carbet on the west coast in 1635. After a quarter of a century of violent skirmishes, a treaty ceded the Atlantic-facing east coast to the Carib, but before long the French had the whole island to themselves and proceeded to carpet it with sugarcane.

Martinique's administrative capital was established at Fort Royal (present-day Fort-de-France) in 1681, but the real focus of the island was St.-Pierre, a gracious harbor city at the foot of Mont Pelée, which became the hub of French trade and culture in the region. The British captured the island in 1762 but returned it a year later (along with Guadeloupe) in exchange for Dominica, Grenada, St. Vincent, and Tobago, plus French territories in Senegal and North America. The extent of

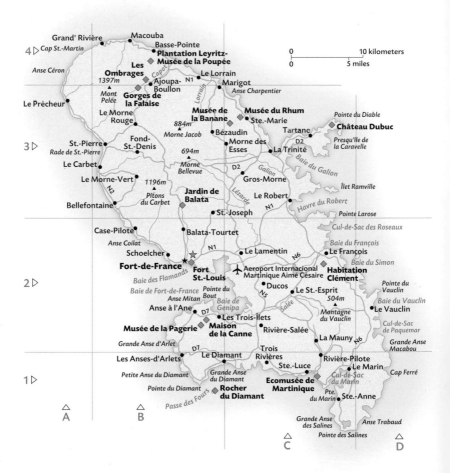

Crowning Glory

Some 4,350 miles (7,000 km) separates Martinique from the French capital, yet this far-flung territory was not without influence in royal circles. Only a few years after the colony was founded, young Françoise d'Aubigné left her father's home in Le Prêcheur in northern Martinique and sailed to find fortune in France. As Madame de Maintenon, she caught the eye of Louis XIV, and they were secretly married in 1684.

More than a century later, two young cousins were out for a stroll when they encountered a local fortune-teller. She read their palms and pronounced to the first, "You will be an empress," and to the second, "and you will be more than an empress." The cousins were Marie-Rose Joséphine Tascher de la Pagerie (see p. 254), who later married Napoleon Bonaparte to become Empress Josephine. Her companion, Aimée Dubuc de Rivery, was supposedly captured by Barbary pirates, sold as a slave in Algiers, and eventually gifted to the Ottoman sultan in Constantinople. Here she is said to have risen through the ranks of the harem to become the sultan's favorite wife and queen mother to his son and successor, Mahmud II.

the French concessions reflected the importance they attached to their Caribbean possessions. In 1793 the French Revolution arrived in Martinique, and initially the republicans carried the day. But within a year the planters had restored the old regime, with the help of the British.

Although relatively stable, Martinique witnessed several slave uprisings before the abolition of slavery in 1848 and the subsequent decline in wealth and importance of the sugar economy. Yet the most devastating day in the island's history occurred 54 years later, on May 8, 1902, when Mont Pelée erupted, destroying the city of St.-Pierre and killing all but one of its 30,000 inhabitants.

While life has returned to St.- Pierre in a small way, it remains a shadow of its former self. In contrast, Fort-de-France has boomed. A big and bustling port city with more than 100,000 inhabitants, the capital is gobbling up the wooded hillsides behind the Baie des Flamands and spreading eastward to the industrial quarter of Le Lamentin and the airport. Facing the city from across the broad mouth of the Baie de Fort-de-France are the well-developed hotel strip of Pointe du Bout and quieter Anse à l'Ane. The island's other two leading resort areas are the yachting center of Le Marin and Ste.-Anne, found down on the southeast peninsula close to Grande Anse des Salines, Martinique's best beach.

The Atlantic shore is rough and rocky, with another peninsula, the Presqu' île de la Caravelle, about halfway up the coast, home to a few small hotels, sugar mill ruins, and a nature reserve.

The rain forest luxuriance of the north is dominated by the cloud-capped bulk of simmering Mont Pelée. It's not a particularly interesting volcano to climb, but there are several pretty walks out (continued on p. 252)

Slavery

Sugar and slavery, twin bastions of the West Indian colonial era, arrived in the New World with Columbus. Spanish conquistadores created the first Caribbean slaves when they put Amerindians to work on the plantations of Hispaniola (in the present-day Dominican Republic). It took less than 20 years to decimate the population through disease and ill-treatment, prompting the Spanish to import African slaves to Hispaniola as early as 1511.

An engraving of slaves in the midst of preparing mandioca flour in the Antilles

The Triangular Trade

Portuguese merchants introduced the first African slaves to Europe in the 1450s as exotic ornaments for the court. Domestic slavery of captured enemies was accepted practice among the tribes of the West African coast, and local traders were keen to exchange slaves for European manufactured goods such as textiles, glass, and weapons. The colonization of South America added a new dimension to this modest two-way traffic, bringing a steady trickle of African slaves across the Atlantic during the 16th century.

At first the British and French West Indian colonies relied on European laborers, but a combination of unaccustomed heat and tropical diseases killed as many as three out of four white settlers within two years of their arrival. When the sugar boom in the mid-1700s unleashed an urgent requirement for plentiful, cheap labor better prepared for the climate and backbreaking plantation work, the "triangular trade" was born. Ships from Europe headed to Africa where manufactured goods paid for African slaves. The slaves then embarked on the infamous Middle Passage to the New World, where the living cargo was exchanged for raw materials such as sugar, tobacco, cotton, and rum bound for Europe.

The Middle Passage

For the terrified slaves destined for the New World, their ordeal often began months ahead of transportation. Slavers selected their cargo from the vast barracoons (slave forts) that dotted the West African coast from Cape Verde to the Bight of Biafra, journeying from port to port until their vessels were filled to capacity. In preparation for the five- to eight-week voyage, food and water were taken on board and the cargo holds were subdivided into "slave decks," wooden shelves often no more than 2.5 feet (0.75 m) apart, where the slaves were packed in lying flat, the males shackled together left leg to right leg and wrist to wrist. Sickness, disease, and despair were rampant on the slave ships: One in eight slaves died on the Middle Passage. The survivors were oiled up to make them look healthier and auctioned off to the highest bidder in the slave markets of Curaçao, Nevis, Martinique, and Sint Eustatius, or on the wharf where the ship came into land.

It has been estimated that more than four million African slaves survived the journey to the West Indian colonies. British slave traders alone imported 2.5 million live slaves between 1690–1807, and the French added at least another million. By the 1750s, black slaves already represented 90 percent of the population on sugar-growing islands, though the proportion was much lower in the Bahamas, Cayman Islands, and Netherlands Antilles where plantations were impractical. The dramatic imbalance between black and white meant the planters lived in constant fear of slave rebellions and ruled their private fiefdoms with rods of iron. Ferocious slave drivers, armed with whips, disciplined the slave gangs in the fields and savage penalties were meted out for acts of disobedience or theft.

Rebellion & Emancipation

Despite the planters' best efforts to suppress their workforce, there were slave rebellions throughout the colonies in the 18th century. Most lasted no more than a couple of weeks or months before being ruthlessly crushed, though a successful revolt in the French colony of St. Domingue led to the creation of the black Republic of Haiti in 1804. In the 1780s, European intellectuals who had long opposed slavery on moral grounds were joined by churchmen, and the combined pressure of forceful pamphleteering campaigns and sermons caused widespread antislavery sentiment. The British outlawed the slave trade to their colonies in 1808, and decreed the abolition of slavery in 1834. Sweden (1846), France and Denmark (1848), and Holland (1863) followed suit, while the Spanish held out until 1873 in Puerto Rico.

Working Patterns

West Indian planters devised two basic work regimes, the harshest of which was the "gang system" preferred on sugar estates. Slaves were divided into groups according to their strength, with the strongest first gang allocated the hardest manual tasks. Youths and old people in the second gang undertook lighter work, and the children in the third gang weeded and tidied. The gangs worked 10 to 12 hours a day, six days a week, and up to 18 hours during the harvest. The more liberal "task system" adopted on smaller farms and by slaves working as skilled craftsmen involved specific tasks that had to be completed in a given time. Slaves were then free to work their vegetable plots or undertake other jobs.

Fort-de-France

🅰 248 B2

**www.tourismefdf
.com**

of the village of Ajoupa-Bouillon and a memorable drive north through the Pitons du Carbet from Fort-de-France (see pp. 256–257). Although distances are modest and the roads good, leave plenty of time to explore, and allow at least three or four days for a really good look around.

Take a Ferry

Public ferries make a neat way to cross between Fort-de-France and beach resorts across the bay. Frequent, inexpensive ferry services are operated by Vedettes Madinina *(tel 0596 63 06 46, www.vedettes madinina.com, $$)* **from the downtown waterfront near Fort St.-Louis to Les Trois-Îlets, Pointe du Bout, Anse Mitan, and Anse à l'Ane. Ferries operate from around 6 a.m. until about 6 or 7 p.m. (reduced services on weekends and holidays) to Pointe du Bout; the crossing takes 20 minutes.**

**Musée
Départemental
d'Archéologie et
de Préhistoire**

✉ 9 rue de la
Liberté

☎ 0596 71 57 05

🕐 Closed Mon.
a.m., Sat. p.m. &
Sun.

💲 $

**Bibliothèque
Schoelcher**

✉ Corner of rue de
la Liberté & rue
Perrinon

☎ 0596 70 26 67

🕐 Closed Mon.
a.m., Sat. p.m. &
Sun.

Fort-de-France

A vibrant and attractive city, Fort-de-France enjoys a splendid position on the Caribbean coast, set against a backdrop of dark green hills. Its compact heart is inviting and easy to explore on foot, with a busy shopping district and narrow streets of flat-fronted buildings adorned with elaborate ironwork balconies.

The original settlement grew up around Fort St.-Louis, founded by the French in 1639. The sturdy fortress has been considerably extended and sits on a headland jutting out into the water, where it guards the **Baie des Flamands**

waterfront to the west and the yacht harbor to the east. There is always plenty of activity down on the wharf, where cruise-ship passengers arrive, ferries depart for the beaches across the **Baie de Fort-de-France** (see sidebar), and kids dive off the piers just for fun.

Across the street from the wharf is a colorful craft and souvenir market, which lays out its wares on the edge of **La Savane.** These 12-acre (4.5 ha) gardens are shaded by magnificent royal palms, and it's a pleasant place to take a stroll and admire the flowers or sit on a park bench and watch the world go by. Overlooking the gardens from rue de la Liberté is the **Musée Départemental d'Archéologie et de Préhistoire,** where you can find displays of pottery and other Amerindian artifacts, as well as exhibits on slavery and colonial life illustrated with the help of period furnishings, crafts, and clothing.

Continue along the west side of the gardens to the fabulously eccentric **Bibliothèque Schoelcher,** a library named in honor of the great French abolitionist Victor Schoelcher and housed in an exotic Byzantine–Romanesque Art Nouveau structure designed for the 1889 Paris Exhibition. When the show was over, the building was taken to pieces, shipped to Martinique, and reconstructed. Opposite the library is a headless statue of the Empress Joséphine (1763–1814). Once the pride of her Martiniquais compatriots, the empress was removed from her position at the center of La

INSIDER TIP:

Fort-de-France has a lively and colorful downtown area. Be sure to try a warm *pain au chocolat* at one of the Parisian-style cafés.

—MATT PROPERT
National Geographic photographer

Savane, and beheaded in 1991, after a guidebook revealed her role in encouraging Napoleon to reintroduce slavery in 1802.

For further insights into Martiniquan customs and traditions, take a detour to the **Musée Régional d'Histoire et d'Ethnographie,** housed in a pretty 19th-century Creole villa

and handsomely furnished in bourgeois period style.

Across the street from the library is rue Victor Sévère, which marks the top end of the main shopping district, bounded by rue de la Liberté, rue Victor Hugo, and rue de la République. The **Préfecture** is the first of several imposing colonial government buildings along this handsome street. Among the fashionable boutiques, patisseries, and stores chock-full of French luxury goods at the heart of the grid is the **Cathédrale de St.-Louis,** which stands on rue Victor Schoelcher. The brown-and-cream painted building, with its clock tower, steeple, and fancy ironwork, was erected on the foundations of six former churches in 1878. ∎

Musée Régional d'Histoire et d'Ethnographie

- ✉ 10 blvd. Général-de-Gaulle
- ☎ 0596 72 81 87
- 🕐 Closed Tue. a.m., Sat. p.m. & Sun.
- 💲 $$

The Bibliothèque Schoelcher was shipped from France to Martinique after the 1889 Paris Exhibition.

Around Southern Martinique

Visible across the bay from Fort-de-France, Martinique's most developed tourist enclave is the promontory of Pointe du Bout and the adjacent beach at Anse Mitan. This vacation center has a lively concentration of hotels, restaurants, beaches, and water-sports concessions frequented by day-tripping cruise passengers who hop across from the city by ferry.

A sea view near the town of Les Trois-Îlets

Les Trois-Îlets

△ 248 B2

Visitor Information

✉ Place Gabriel Hayot

☎ 0596 68 47 63

www.trois-ilets.com

Musée de la Pagerie

△ 248 B2

✉ Les Trois-Îlets

☎ 0596 68 38 34

🕐 Closed Mon.

💲 $$

Neighboring **Les Trois-Îlets** is an attractive little seaside village. A Saturday market is held on the square in front of the church where Napoleon's future empress was christened Marie-Rose Joséphine Tascher de la Pagerie in the summer of 1763. Just outside the village is the former family estate, now the home of the **Musée de la Pagerie,** which is laid out in a simple stone cottage among the ruins of the sugar mill. It houses collections of domestic utensils, period prints, and a few personal possessions of the empress, including letters from the emperor.

On the main road (Rte. D7) east of the village is the informative **Maison de la Canne,** occupying another restored old sugar mill. Exhibits cover the history of the early plantations and the slave trade amid a welter of antique paraphernalia, models, and bilingual signboards.

Heading counterclockwise around the coast from Les Trois-Îlets, you reach the narrow sandy beach at **Anse à l'Ane** and its popular beach bars. The lovely village of **Les Anses-d'Arlets** has several dark sand beaches nearby, including the tiny black sand strip of **Petit Anse du Diamant,** where dozens of traditional fishing boats painted orange, turquoise, and green ride the gentle swell in the bay. Around the headland there's a fine view of the **Rocher du Diamant,** an offshore islet shaped like a giant brioche with a slice carved out of it. In 1804 British troops from St. Lucia captured the rock to harass French shipping. It was "commissioned" into the British navy, armed with cannon, and nicknamed HMS *Diamond Rock.* The British garrison held out for 18 months, hoisting provisions ashore from visiting ships until a concerted French bombardment forced the occupiers to withdraw.

East of Ste.-Luce, across the Rivière-Pilote, is the **Ecomusée de Martinique,** providing a detailed and fascinating account of island history. Note, however, that the signs are all in French (although there's talk of providing English subtitles in the future). The excellent sections on Amerindian society and culture are accompanied by artifacts, models, and a list of common words derived from Amerindian languages, such as alligator, barbecue, and tobacco.

Continuing eastward, visit the yachting center of **Le Marin** at the foot of a deep, sheltered bay behind its packed marina. On the waterfront you can choose from a clutch of seafood restaurants serving up the catch of the day, accompanied by the creak of rigging in the breeze. Around the bay is the **Pointe du Marin** headland, with its crescent of sandy beach fringed by palms; a hillside Calvary dominates the approach to the pretty resort

town of **Ste.-Anne.** South of Ste.-Anne, the road passes the dry, sunbaked peninsula and salt ponds to **Grande Anse des Salines,** a refreshingly undeveloped curve of blond sand. Palms, sea grape trees, and Australian pines provide a shady retreat, and there are snack wagons, vendors selling fresh pineapple, and a restaurant.

From Le Marin, Rte. N6 cuts across to the east coast town of **Le François.** In the rolling countryside just south of town is the old **Habitation Clément** sugar estate, which opens its doors to the public. Rum hasn't been distilled here since 1988, but the fully equipped distillery is on display, as are the *chais* (storehouses) where up to 1,400 barrels of Rhum Clément mature in oak imported from

INSIDER TIP:

While on Martinique, try the local specialty dish, *matoutou des crabes,* a jambalaya-like blend of local land crab, regional vegetables, and island spices.

—GALEN SMITH
Illustrations specialist, National Geographic Books

France. The highlight of the visit is the lovely 19th-century **plantation house.** In the dining room, carved colonial furniture is enhanced by oil lamps and antique silver. Upstairs, see the embroidered coverlets on the four-poster beds. ■

Maison de la Canne
- 248 B2
- ✉ Les Trois-Îlets
- ☎ 0596 68 32 04
- ⏰ Closed Mon.
- 💲 $

Ecomusée de Martinique
- 248 C1
- ✉ Anse Figuier
- ☎ 0596 62 79 14
- ⏰ Closed Mon.
- 💲 $

Habitation Clément
- 248 C2
- ✉ Le François (2 miles/ 3 km from St.-François Rte. D18)
- ☎ 0596 54 75 51
- 💲 $$
- www.habitation-clement.fr

A Drive Through the Pitons du Carbet to St.-Pierre

The first leg of this tour follows the historic inland trail to St.-Pierre, La Route de la Trace, carved through the highlands in the 17th century. Martinique's tropical profusion is on display in the Jardin de Balata and in the untamed rain forest, while the grim but compelling story of St.-Pierre unfurls among century-old ruins.

From **Fort-de-France's ❶** (see p. 252) inner city ring road, boulevard Général-de-Gaulle, Rte. N3 follows the Rivière Madame north (toward Le Morne Rouge) and then climbs into the hillside suburbs. Stop off at the church of **Sacré Coeur ❷** for a tremendous view over the capital. The domed "Montmartre Martiniquais" was erected in 1923 as a memorial to the dead of World War I.

The air is noticeably cooler as the road winds on up to the **Jardin de Balata ❸** *(Rte. de Balata, tel 0596 64 48 73)*, a gorgeous tropical garden laid out around a Creole home some 1,475 feet (450 m) above the coast. Meandering paths trail through flaming red-and-pink torch ginger, orchids, and spice bushes gathered in the shade cast by palms, and flamboyant trees. The road begins to twist and turn in earnest as it passes through the Pitons (peaks) flanked by soft banks of ferns and huge rain forest trees dangling twisted lianas.

NOT TO BE MISSED:

Jardin de Balata • St.-Pierre • Musée Gauguin

At the town of **Deux Choux** take Rte. D1 8 miles (13 km) west to **St.-Pierre ❹** and the Caribbean coast, passing through the banana plantations. (See sidebar for a possible detour.) Overlooking a handsome bay in the shadow of Mont Pelée, St.-Pierre was once a thriving colonial city renowned for the wealth of its merchants and the elegance of its buildings. In the spring of 1902, after centuries of inactivity, Mont Pelée rumbled. After a belated warning on May 7, only a thousand Pierrotins packed their bags and headed for Fort-de-France. A little before 8 a.m. on May 8, Mont Pelée erupted, sending a giant cloud of burning ash and poisonous gases into the sky. The pyroclastic flow, reaching temperatures of over 3,700°F (2,040°C), swept down over the town and caused the sea to boil.

St.-Pierre's present-day population of 6,000 lives among the gaunt ruins of the eruption. The **Cyparis Express** tourist train *(place des Ruines du Figuier, tel 0596 55 50 92)*, named for the only survivor, makes a narrated (in French) circuit, or visitors can roam freely around the shell of the old theater, inspect the cell where Cyparis was sheltered, and visit the cathedral rebuilt behind its surviving facade. The **Musée Vulcanologique** *(rue Victor Hugo, tel 0596 78 15 16)* displays photographs of the old city, melted glass bottles, and other curios.

St.-Pierre on Film

An interesting detour is a visit to the **Maison Regionale des Volcans** *(tel 0596 52 45 45, closed Sat. p.m., Sun. p.m. & Mon. a.m.)* in Le Morne Rouge. As well as information (in French) on volcanism, this small museum on the main street shows a 45-minute video compiled from footage of St.-Pierre before and after the 1902 eruption (English version on request). The black-and-white images illustrate the grandeur of the former "Paris of the Antilles" and the aftermath of the cataclysmic eruption.

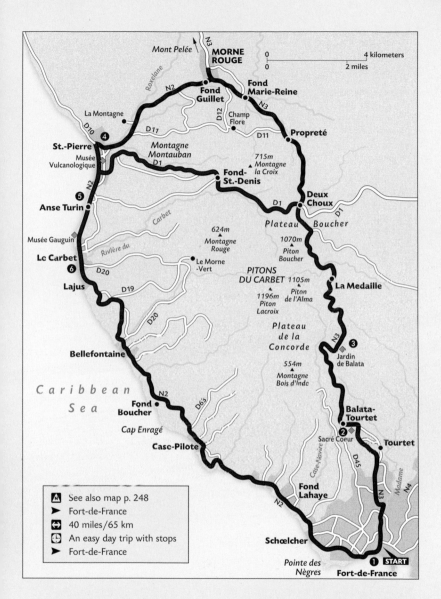

Take the Rte. N2 coast road a couple of miles (3 km) south of St.-Pierre to **Anse Turin** ❺, which once played host to Paul Gauguin (1848–1903). The French painter spent five months living by the beach in 1887 as he searched for a tropical isle where he could live like a "noble savage." Several of his letters and reproductions of his paintings are housed in the

Musée Gauguin (*Anse Turin, tel 0596 78 22 66, $*), which also exhibits local artwork.

Rte. N2 hugs the coast back to Fort-de-France, passing the village of **Le Carbet** ❻, where the founder of St.-Pierre, Pierre Belain d'Esnambuc, landed with a hundred Norman colonists to claim Martinique for France in 1635.

The North & Northeast

The verdant northern and northeastern regions of Martinique provide luxuriant rain forest scenery and glimpses into the island's agricultural mainstays: sugar, rum, and bananas.

Ajoupa-Bouillon
- 248 B4
- ✉ Immeuble Boulon, Quartier Racine
- ☎ 0596 53 32 87

Caravelle Peninsula
- 248 C3

Ajoupa-Bouillon

This self-proclaimed *ville florale* displays its roadside banks of wild begonias, massed crotons, and shrimp plants with pride. Ajoupa is also home to **Les Ombrages** *(tel 0596 53 31 90, $$)*, a lush botanical garden clambering up a rain forest ravine, and the village is the starting point for walks to the **Gorges de la Falaise** *(tel 0596 52 55 09)*. The 30-minute trail starts just west of town and leads through the rain forest to a swimming hole fed by a waterfall.

Plantation Leyritz–Maison de la Poupée

Plantation Leyritz is an attractive hotel-restaurant converted from an old sugar estate and a popular lunch stop on the tour bus trail. It has a small museum of figurines *(poupées)* in historical costume fashioned out of leaves and other plant matter.

Plantation Leyritz–Maison de la Poupée
- 248 B4
- ✉ Le Lorrain (Rte. D21 from Basse-Pointe)
- ☎ 0596 53 78 50
- $ $$

Ste.-Marie
- 248 C3

Caravelle Peninsula

From the main road follow signs for **Tartane** (Rte. D2), a small resort on the north coast of this wooded peninsula. At the end of the road a section of rough track leads to the ruins of 17th-century **Château Dubuc** *(tel 0596 64 42 59, $$)*, which crown a rise overlooking a protected bay and the foundations of an old sugar mill. A quirky little museum houses old belt buckles, broken bottles, and clay pipe stems unearthed around the estate. From the parking lot, footpaths strike off into a natural reserve and to the cliffs and coves lining the shore.

Ste.-Marie

Two of Martinique's most conspicuous products are showcased in museums just west and north of the town: rum and bananas. The **Musée de la Banane** *(Rte. de Bézaudin, tel 0596 76 27 09, $$$)* sits at the heart of a working banana plantation. Check out the history of the banana and amazing banana trivia (Germans devour more than 33 pounds/15 kg of bananas per person per year). Stroll along the banana walk and visit the packing houses on weekdays.

The **Musée du Rhum** *(tel 0596 69 30 02, closed Sat. & Sun., www.fondsaintjacques.com)* also believes in transporting visitors to the business end of its operations with guided tours of the Distillerie Saint-James during the sugar cane harvest (March–June). The museum with its collections of antique tools and memorabilia is located in the old plantation house, and there is also a 20-minute tourist train ride *($$)* out into the surrounding cane fields and banana plantations. ■

The lofty and richly forested islands of Dominica, St. Lucia, St. Vincent, and Grenada

Windward Islands

Nutmeg is a major agricultural product of Grenada.

Windward Islands

The majestic quartet of Windward Islands tapers off toward the tail end of the Lesser Antilles, rising sheer from the Atlantic surf on one side and the gentle wavelets of the Caribbean Sea on the other. The islands are the mere tips of a volcanic mountain range that has sprouted where the Atlantic and Caribbean tectonic plates collide. Three of the four main Windward Islands have an active *soufrière*, a sulfurous volcanic vent liable to erupt every hundred years or so (Grenada, the exception, has bubbling hot springs).

Tall enough to create their own microclimates by trapping the winds off the Atlantic and converting them to rain clouds, the Windwards are fantastically fertile. Islanders grow bananas, coconuts, and spices for export, and farmers have their work cut out for them trying to keep the encroaching sea of green at bay.

Today Dominica, St. Lucia, St. Vincent (with its chain of islands known as the Grenadines), and Grenada are independent nations, but their long association dates back to the days of sail when they fell to the windward side of the

English colonial trading routes between Europe and the Caribbean. Later the term was adopted by the 19th-century British administrators who governed the islands as a group distinct from British colonies in the Leeward Islands.

The earliest inhabitants of the Windward Islands were Arawak Indians, farmers and fishermen whose peaceful reign ended abruptly with the arrival of warlike Carib people (also known as Kalinago in Dominica today) about A.D. 1000. Spanish explorers gave the "Cannibal Isles" a wide berth, and they became the focus of Carib resistance in the region until the mid-17th century, when the sugar trade spurred French and English colonists into action. Initially the two most topographically challenging islands, Dominica and St. Vincent, were left to the Carib, who were joined by escaped African slaves. But a century later, white settlers had forced Dominica's few remaining Carib into exile on the Atlantic coast; on St. Vincent mixed-race Carib took refuge in the hills and continued a dogged resistance until the early 19th century.

Throughout the plantation era, Europe's conflicts were mirrored in the Caribbean arena, where Britain and France squabbled over the Windwards incessantly and won, lost, and regained territories with bewildering frequency. The islands inherited a confused legacy of French and English place-names, as well as the French-influenced Creole patois that is still widely spoken in Dominica and St. Lucia, although the islands have been officially English speaking for 200 years. When slavery was abolished in 1834, former slaves turned to the land and carved small-scale farms out of the rich soil. The islands slid into an agricultural backwater administered by a British governor based in Grenada. Several attempts to federate the British Caribbean territories came to nothing, and eventually the individual Windward Islands were granted self-government in the 1960s and full independence in the late 1970s. They are now members of the British Commonwealth.

Part of the Windward Islands' appeal is the coexistence of tourism and traditional island life. This is particularly true on Dominica, where vast tracts of primal rain forest and uplands remain in pristine condition, and fishing and farming still underpin the local economy. Also unspoiled and underappreciated, St. Vincent is another rain forest wilderness and tropical market garden but is generally consigned to the role of stepping-stone for yachtsmen heading for the Grenadines.

The Grenadines are a yachting paradise, an alluring chain of minuscule islands with great beaches, some uninhabited, some harboring exclusive resorts. Others, such as pretty Bequia, fall somewhere between the two. To the south is charming Grenada. Easygoing and friendly, the Spice Island is overloaded with natural beauties and ringed by sandy beaches, spice plantations, and pretty villages. St. Lucia is the most developed of the Windwards, but even here it's easy to escape the resort beaches of the northwest and take a trip to the mountains, where villages nestle amid tropical flowers and vegetable plots on the edge of the forest. ■

Dominica

Dominica (pronounced Dom-in-EE-ka) was known to the Carib as Wai'tukubuli ("tall is her body"). From a 29-by-16-mile (47 by 26 km) base, the soaring interior peaks at Morne Diablotin (4,747 feet/1,447 m) within 5 miles (8 km) of the coast, and the jagged mountains of the central north-south spine average more than 3,000 feet (900 m). Dominica is home to one of the world's last untouched rain forests, 300-plus rivers, and almost as many waterfalls.

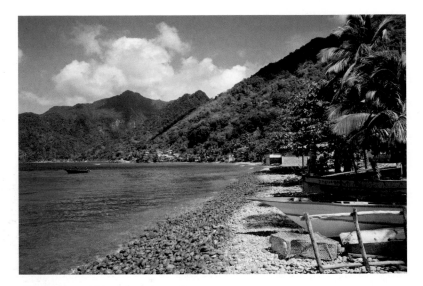

Boats line up near the fishing village of Scotts Head in Dominica.

Dominica

⛰ 261 B6

Visitor Information

✉ Discover Dominica Authority, first floor, Financial Centre, Roseau

☎ 767 448 2045

www.discover dominica.com

The population of about 72,000 is 98 percent black, mainly Roman Catholic, and most people still struggle to make a living from the land. Despite its undoubted beauty, Dominica is one of the Caribbean's least developed islands. Farming and fishing, augmented by traditional crafts, sustain one of the world's last surviving Carib, or Kalinago, communities, living on the Carib Territory in the northeast. With few beaches (and those that exist tend toward narrow strips of gray volcanic sand), tourism is still in

its infancy here. Dominica offers fairly low-key accommodations, and facilities are mostly modest and unsophisticated, though several delightful rustic retreats have sprung up in stunning (albeit remote) locations. On the plus side, Dominica is a rare Caribbean eco-haven for adventurous travelers keen to hike, dive, and explore without the usual tourist distractions. An exciting new development is the 125-mile (200 km) Wai'tukubuli National Trail, the first long-distance hiking route of its kind in the region, which traverses the island from end to end in 14 stages.

Dominica lies between the French islands of Guadeloupe and Martinique. (It is not to be confused with the Dominican Republic in the Greater Antilles, see pp. 97–124.) Christopher Columbus sailed around Wai'tukubuli's northern tip on his second voyage to the New World in November 1493. It was a Sunday, so he christened his find Dominica and noted in his logbook that the island was "remarkable for the beauty of its mountains . . . and must be seen to be believed." French colonists laid claim to Dominica in the 1750s but ceded it to Britain under the Treaty of Paris in 1763. Despite a century of French raids, slave rebellions, and isolated attacks by bands of marauding Maroons (escaped slaves who hid in the near-impenetrable mountains), the British remained more or less in control. From the mid-19th century Dominica was administered with the Leeward Islands until 1939, when it was transferred to the Windward Islands. Independence arrived in 1978, and two years later the Dominicans elected the Caribbean's first female prime minister, Dame Eugenia Charles.

The capital of the island, Roseau (see p. 264), is a small weather-beaten town and cruise-ship stopover with around 20,000 inhabitants. It lies at the mouth of the Roseau River on the south-west coast. Inland along the river are Trafalgar Falls (see p. 265), one of Dominica's most popular

tourist attractions. The nearby village of Laudat is the main drop-off point for hikes in the Morne Trois Pitons National Park (see p. 266). South of Roseau there are several hotels and dive outfits on the water at Castle Comfort, and a narrow road hugs the shore to the southern tip of the island, home to the spectacular Scotts Head/Soufrière Bay Marine Park (see p. 269).

Dominica's second largest settlement is Portsmouth. Above the coast, endangered sisserou

Dominica Museum

- ✉ Dame Eugenia Charles Blvd., Roseau
- ☎ 767 448 8932
- 🕐 Closed Sat. p.m. & Sun. in the low season
- 💲 $$

and jaco parrots are protected in the **Morne Diablotin National Park** on the slopes of Morne Diablotin, and a road crosses over to the Atlantic coast, past good swimming beaches at **Hampstead Estate** and **Hodges Bay.** There are a couple of beach bars and restaurants at **Calibishe** and coconut plantations around Melville Hall Airport. South of Melville Hall the Transinsular Road carves a splendid route to Roseau through the Central Forest Reserve and the pretty mountain village of Bells. The drive takes 90 minutes and affords grand views of cloudy peaks and the rain forest. Remaining on the windward side, the coastal road runs through Carib Territory, passing roadside stalls selling basketwork, to Castle Bruce and an alternative route back to the capital via the waterfall at Emerald Pool (see p. 267).

Jean Rhys (1894–1979)

Writer Jean Rhys was born in Roseau in 1894; her mother's family were white Creole planters. Rhys traveled to Europe at age 16 and drew on her own experiences as a chorus girl, artist's model, and poet's wife for her first collection of short stories, *The Left Bank* (1927), which explores the role of women on the edge of bohemian society. After a checkered literary career, she returned to her Caribbean roots for *Wide Sargasso Sea* (1966). It recounts the imagined history of the first Mrs. Rochester, a Creole heiress who became the mad wife of Charlotte Brontë's novel *Jane Eyre.* Set in Jamaica and Dominica in the early 1800s, the atmospheric novel describes the decadence of a Caribbean lifestyle on the verge of extinction.

Roseau & the Roseau Valley

Dominica's capital, which moved to Roseau (pronounced row-so) from Portsmouth in the late 18th century, is laid out in a neat grid between the banks of the Roseau River and Fort Young. Roseau has a certain dilapidated charm, with its motley collection of sturdy stone colonial buildings. Several historic gingerbread houses are being restored and the rundown bayfront has been smartened up with a couple of new developments. The town center is easy to explore on foot, and there are several small galleries, cafés, and craft shops around Cork Street.

Roseau's most animated corner is the local **produce market,** which spills out from the shade of its tin roof and onto the sidewalk at the river end of the waterfront.

The hub of colonial Roseau was the Old Market Place on **Dawbiney Square,** off King George V Street. Slave auctions were once held in the small cobbled, tree-shaded plaza, now annexed by a café and souvenir stalls. On one side of the square, facing the waterfront and downtown cruise-ship berth, is the **Dominica Museum,** which provides an interesting overview of island history and culture. Among the exhibits are Carib tools and a thatched *carbet* (hut), a section on Dominican writers, including Jean Rhys (see sidebar this page), and a series of fascinating 18th-century prints by Agostino Brunias, an Italian-born artist employed by Dominica's first British governor, Sir William Young.

INSIDER TIP:

Bring a bathing suit when visiting Trafalgar Falls—there are numerous pristine hot springs at the base of the falls on the left.

—BARBARA A. NOE
Editor, National Geographic Books

Sir William's name lives on at **Fort Young,** a short walk away along the seafront. Now a hotel, the fort was constructed of blackened volcanic stone in 1775. It retains few reminders of its military heyday, except for a couple of fancy brass cannons and workmanlike snipers' embrasures in the walls of the dining room.

Opposite the fort is the **Anglican Church,** which contains memorial tablets eulogizing 19th-century British colonial officials, and stained-glass windows behind the altar. The **Roman Catholic Cathedral,** on Turkey Lane, is in rather better shape, built of dark river rocks between 1800 and 1916. To the east are the green expanses of the **Botanical Gardens** *(map 263 B2; off King George V St.),* stretching over a 40-acre (16 ha) former cane field on the lower slopes of Morne Bruce. Teams play cricket in the large grassy park, and an aviary houses indigenous sisserou and jaco parrots. Among the botanical exhibits are flowering cannonball trees with their strange waxy blooms, teaks, flamboyants, and cassia trees. The Forestry, Wildlife and Parks Division Offices *(tel*

767 266 3817) are a good source for information on hiking in the national parks, passes, maps, and experienced guides.

Trafalgar Falls lie about 5 miles (8 km) east of town at the head of the Roseau Valley. *(Map 263 B2; take King George V St. out of central Roseau, in the direction of Laudat, and follow signs.)* Carving an imposing cleft deep into the green buttress of the Morne Trois Pitons

One of the major cascades at Trafalgar Falls

highlands, the valley walls swoosh up to either side of the road. The bumpy track runs out near the **Papillote Wilderness Retreat** *(map 263 B2; tel 767 448 2287),* a delightful small hotel and restaurant set in pretty gardens, where guides offer their services. From here it's a steep 10- to 15-minute hike to the twin waterfalls, known as "mother" and "father." The father fall on the left is warm, while the mother is cold, and they plummet down the 200-foot (60 m) cliff face in a roar of tumbling water and spray to a pool below.

Morne Trois Pitons National Park

🗺 263 B2

✉ Forestry Division, Roseau

☎ 767 448 2401 ext. 3431

💲 National Park passes: one site pass ($); day pass ($$); one week pass ($$$)

Below the viewing platform are paths leading to swimming areas.

Morne Trois Pitons National Park

Most of Dominica's best known natural attractions are found in the 17,000-acre (6,880 ha) national park, a UNESCO World Heritage site, stretching south of Morne Trois Pitons (4,550 feet/1,387 m). Sprinkled with mountain lakes, hissing volcanic fumaroles, sulfur springs, and an annual rainfall of almost 300 inches (7,600 mm), this is superb (if rather damp) upland hiking country. Together with Morne Diablotin National Park (see opposite), the central highlands showcase the many different faces of the rain forest, from the grandeur of 100-foot-tall (30 m) secondary forest to stunted, high-altitude elfin woodlands, and a treasury of island plant life

that includes some 74 species of orchids and 22 kinds of fern.

Dominican wildlife is fairly difficult to spot, but there are occasional sightings of agoutis, iguanas, and five non-venomous snakes, including elusive boa constrictors. More than 170 bird species have been identified.

The easiest starting point for explorations in the park is the village of **Laudat,** east of Roseau. For a soft adventure into the rain forest canopy, the **Rain Forest Aerial Tram** *(tel 767 448 8775, www.rainforestaerialtram.com)* skims the treetops over gorges and waterfalls, with commentary from a guide. Within the national park, **Freshwater Lake,** 2,500 feet (760 m) above sea level, is accessible by car, and **Boeri Lake,** cupped in a volcanic crater, is an attractive 40-minute walk farther on.

The park's best known and most challenging hike is the trail

Hanging out in Roseau, Dominica, at the end of a school day

to **Boiling Lake,** a 200-foot-wide (60 m) flooded volcanic fumerole that bubbles and steams at 180° to 200°F (82–93°C). It's best to engage a qualified guide before undertaking the strenuous seven- to eight-hour round-trip trek. Local guides wait at the trailhead, or you can hire one through a reputable guide company. En route to Boiling Lake, the trail crosses the **Valley of Desolation,** a suitably hellish landscape cluttered with huge boulders, where the fumes from sulfur springs and pools of bubbling gray mud have killed off all but the hardiest plants.

At the western edge of the park are the **Middleham Trails** (3 hours round-trip), which strike out from Cochrane or Laudat for the dramatic 500-foot-high (150 m) **Middleham Falls** via the **Stinking Hole bat caves.**

A challenging four- to five-hour round-trip trail from Pont Cassé tackles **Morne Trois Pitons** itself, climbing into the eerily quiet world of elfin forest frosted with lichens and wrapped in mosses and mist.

A few miles farther east, outside the park and just off the Castle Bruce road, is **Emerald Pool.** The small swimming hole is fed by a waterfall and set in a fern-flanked rain forest grotto beneath lianas and elephant ears.

Morne Diablotin National Park & Northern Forest Reserve

Larger than the neighboring Morne Trois Pitons National Park, this 22,000-acre (8,900 ha) forested preserve (*map 263 B3;*

EXPERIENCE: Community Tourism

Eleven small communities scattered around the island offer a warm welcome and unique insight into Dominican life through **Community Tourism Dominica** *(tel 767 266 3005, www.communitytourism .dm),* a grassroots initiative. Take to the hills with **Bellevue Organic Farmers** and learn about growing spices and medicinal herbs, or sign up for a day of garden tours, flower arranging, and Creole cooking in Eggleston, the "flower basket of Dominica." Other entertaining and unusual day tour options include kayaking and tubing on the **Layou River** *($$$$$);* paddling your own canoe down mangrove waterways as featured in Pirates of the Caribbean; and an eccentric, 100 percent natural spa experience in the steaming mud pools and mineral springs of **Wotten Waven.**

---

tel 767 448 2733) on the slopes of Morne Diablotin is a refuge for Dominica's two endemic parrot species: sisserou and jaco. The green-and-brown sisserou is the national bird and the rarer of the two. Captive breeding programs have helped swell numbers in the wild to approximately 300. There are about a thousand of the more colorful jaco, or red-necked parrots.

A road from Dublanc, south of Portsmouth, clambers up to the park entrance at Syndicate Estate. At this former citrus and banana plantation, 1,800 feet (550 m) above sea level, a short trail provides good bird-watching opportunities. The best way to see the birds is on a tour.

A guide is also recommended for a strenuous six- to seven-hour

Carib Territory

🅐 263 C3

round-trip ascent of **Morne Diablotin.**

Around Dominica

Dominica's Carib Territory provides a rare glimpse into pre-colonial culture, while birders and divers will enjoy parks at either end of the island.

Carib Territory: Established in 1903, the 3,700-acre (1,500 ha) Carib Territory encompasses eight small villages along the Atlantic coast between Atkinson and Castle Bruce. Some 2,200 Kalinago (formerly Carib) people live in the territory, descendants of Amerindian migrants who paddled their dugout canoes across from the Amazon Basin.

Modern Carib have abandoned traditional thatched huts in favor of more comfortable wooden Creole homes balanced on stilts overlooking the sea. Basket-weaving is a local specialty on display at roadside stalls alongside model boats and other wood carvings. At the **St. Marie of the Caribs Catholic Church,** Salybia, there is an altar carved in the shape of a dugout canoe.

A few ancient ceremonies and traditions such as boatbuilding survive, and there's an opportunity to see traditional dancing, crafts, and practices in action during a 45-minute guided tour of **Kalinago Barana Autê** (Carib Cultural Village by the Sea) on the Atlantic coast near Salybia *(tel 767 445 7979, www.kalinagobaranaaute .com, $$$).* Farther down the coast, south of Sineku, a petrified natural lava flow called the **Escalier Tête de Chien** (Snake's Staircase) tumbles down the cliffs to the sea.

Portsmouth & Cabrits National Park: Portsmouth,

EXPERIENCE: Whale-Watching

Though Dominica's dive credentials are now well established, a lesser-known fact is that the island is the only country in the world where whales can be spotted year-round; around 90 percent of whale-watching trips make a successful sighting. Twenty-two recorded species of cetaceans are found in Dominican waters, but the prize is a clear view of a sperm whale. These marine leviathans come to breed and calve in the deep, sheltered bays off the west coast during winter (Nov.–March), when there is also a good chance of sighting humpback, pilot, pygmy, and false killer whales. Acrobatic bottlenose, spinner, and spotted dolphins provide plenty of entertainment while visitors scan the horizon for the whales' telltale water spouts.

During summer (late March–Oct.), the Dominican wildlife nursery moves ashore to the beaches, where huge female leatherback turtles lumber out of the water to lay their eggs.

Nighttime turtle excursions can be arranged through the **Dominica Sea Turtle Conservation Organization** *(sea turtle hotline: tel 767 616 8684, $$).* Whale-watching expeditions with **Anchorage Hotel, Whale Watch & Dive Centre** *(tel 767 448 2638, www.anchorage hotel.dm, $$$$$),* and **Dive Dominica** *(tel 767 448 2188, www.divedominica.com, $$$$$)* depart from Castle Comfort.

the island capital until malarial mosquitoes in the nearby swamps sent the British scurrying down to Roseau, is a scruffy little town of 5,000 souls set on the yachtsman's haven Prince Rupert Bay.

On the southern edge of town take a boat trip on the **Indian River.** You can paddle upstream through a tunnel of swamp ferns, bwa mang trees, and anthuriums. Herons and egrets stalk the shallows.

Just over a mile (1.5 km) north is **Cabrits National Park** (map 263 A4; tel 767 448 2401), occupying the forested peninsula at the top of the bay and extending into wetlands areas and a marine preserve totaling over 1,300 acres (900 ha). In 1765 the British founded **Fort Shirley** to defend the harbor. Its remains, linked by footpaths, litter the hillside. Some of the old volcanic stone and redbrick buildings have been overtaken by jungle, but several others have been partially restored, and the former **Powder Magazine** houses a small museum.

Black sand beaches fringe Prince Rupert Bay, with several hotels and a dive shop at **Picard Beach.** The best snorkeling and coral reef and wall diving sites are located in **Douglas Bay,** north of Cabrits Peninsula.

Scotts Head & the South

A half-hour drive from Roseau around the curve of Soufrière Bay, the narrow finger of Scotts Head Peninsula juts out from the Caribbean coast at the southern tip of the island. From

A makeshift fish market in the village of Soufrière

the ruins of **Fort Cashacrou,** the view stretches off to the French island of Martinique 20 miles (32 km) to the south and back up the Dominican coast to the mountains.

Beneath the waters of the bay is a submerged volcanic caldera a mile (1.6 km) across and almost 1,000 feet (300 m) deep, forming the centerpiece of the **Scotts Head/ Soufrière Bay Marine Park** (map 263 B1), Dominica's top dive site. Around the crater rim lava pinnacles and reef sites are frequented by a kaleidoscope of marine species. Corals and forests of sponges stud the walls of dramatic drop-offs. One site with particular appeal for snorkelers is **Champagne,** which lives up to its name in a cloud of tiny bubbles released from a volcanic vent in the seabed.

The fishing village of **Soufrière** takes its name from the hot sulfur springs reached by a winding road up into the hills. You can also reach the springs from the Tête Morne road above Berekua, on the shore at Grand Bay. ■

St. Lucia

Lavishly bestowed with dense green rain forest, landmark peaks rising sheer from the sea, golden beaches, rare parrots, and a profusion of vivid tropical flowers, St. Lucia is a first-rank Caribbean beauty. The 27-by-14-mile (43 by 23 km) island is shaped like a pear and lies between Martinique to the north and St. Vincent in the south.

St. Lucia (pronounced LOO-sha) is the most developed and populous of the Windward Islands. Nevertheless, the entire central portion of the island is mountainous forest ringed by rolling acres of banana plantations, sugarcane, and coconut groves. Small fishing villages dot the coast, mountain hamlets cling perilously to absurdly verdant valleys, and most telltale signs of tourist development have been tucked neatly into the northwestern corner of the island above the capital, Castries (see pp. 272–273), home to more than a third of St. Lucia's 170,000 inhabitants.

Christopher Columbus may have set foot on St. Lucia on his fourth voyage to the New World in 1502, but the island's earliest recorded European resident was one François Le Clerc, a 16th-century French pirate who established a base on Pigeon Island and attacked passing Spanish galleons. Also known as Jambe de Bois for his wooden leg, Le Clerc appears to have survived the attentions of the island's resident Carib people, who had already dispatched two attempted British settlements before the French finally established a colonial toehold in 1651.

St. Lucia was one of the most hotly contested plantation islands in the eastern Caribbean, nicknamed "the Fair Helen of the West Indies" for all the ships launched in the battle for her favors. Strategically placed next to the flourishing French sugar

The town of Soufrière is dwarfed by the famous Pitons ("peaks") that tower above it.

colony of Martinique and just as cultivable, the colony represented a considerable prize and changed hands 14 times, shuttling between her French founders and British usurpers. The British finally gained the upper hand after a fierce battle culminating on the slopes of Morne Fortune (see pp. 273–274) above Castries in 1796, although French revolutionaries continued a guerrilla war from hideouts in the mountains for some time afterward. St. Lucia was secured by

Britain under the Treaty of Paris in 1814. The island, which became independent in 1979, remains part of the British Commonwealth.

Despite a century and a half of British occupation, St. Lucia displays her Gallic heritage at every turn. French place-names are

St. Lucia

⚑ 263 B4

Visitor Information

✉ Top Floor
Sureline Bldg.,
Vide Bouteille,
Castries

☎ 758 452 4094

www.stlucianow.org

more common than English, and the local patois is based on Creole. Creole cooking, Creole architecture with its fancy gingerbread trimmings, and a lingering fondness for the checkered madras fabrics, more usually seen on the French islands, conspire to make St. Lucia stand out from her Windward Island neighbors. St. Lucians are spontaneous and party loving. The island's summertime Carnival is a riot of costumes, music, and food. The Friday-night jump-up street

and houses are made safe by magical wreaths of thorny acacia and special herbs.

Although St. Lucia's traditional tourist heartland is the northwest, around the popular yachting center of Rodney Bay, most of the island's attractions are found south of Castries along the Caribbean coast and in the rain forest highlands. There has also been a recent flurry of luxury hotel developments, and a number of elegant spa resorts have opened their doors around Marigot, Soufrière, and even on the previously uncharted Atlantic coast.

Near the town of Soufrière are the Pitons ("peaks"), St. Lucia's most famous landmarks, which are depicted on the national flag. A brace of lofty volcanic plugs, they soar dramatically from the shore, upstaging the island's tallest peak, Mount Gimie (3,118 feet/950 m) a few miles inland. Close by are a marine park, a "drive-in" volcano, the gardens at Diamond, working cocoa plantations, and the rain forest. The Soufrière district itself makes a good base for exploring, hiking, diving, or enjoying the low-key atmosphere.

Views of the Pitons

Heading south from Castries, drivers have their work cut out on the stretch of serpentine road that drops briefly to sea level at Canaries, a small fishing community, before carving a path up through the rain forest and emerging above Soufrière. This is one of the best views of the Pitons, with the Petit Piton (2,461 feet/ 743 m) in the foreground and the Gros Piton (2,619 feet/ 798 m) 1.5 miles (2.5 km) behind.

Castries

⚑ 271 B4

Visitor Information

✉ La Place
Carenage &
booth at Pointe
Seraphine

☎ 758 452 7577

party at Gros Islet (see p. 274) is an institution which has inspired Anse la Raye's Friday seafood cookout and Dennery's Saturday-night Fish Fiesta, enjoyed by locals and visitors alike. Musical events are scheduled throughout the year, including a world-class summer jazz festival, and any number of fêtes, sailing regattas, and impromptu jump-ups.

African traditions also maintain a hold on the local imagination. Although the majority of the population is Roman Catholic (a French legacy), St. Lucia has a rich folkloric culture. Evil spirits are banished by the beating of drums,

Castries

St. Lucia's unremarkable capital lies at the foot of a sheltered inlet encircled by steep, forested hills. Castries was founded in the 1760s and named for the French Minister of the Marine, the Maréchal de Castries, who would have appreciated the well-protected natural harbor.

EXPERIENCE: Join a Heritage Tour

Stepping off the beaten track isn't always easy in the Caribbean, but a great way to dig beneath the surface of St. Lucia is to take a Heritage Tour with the **Heritage Tourism Association of St. Lucia** (HERITAS; tel 758 458-1454, www .heritagetoursstlucia.org, $$$$$). With 22 members in small communities and attractions dotted around the island, the selection of half- and full-day tours offers plenty of variety and local interest.

Active visitors can enjoy horseback-riding excursions, turtle-watching, and hiking. For a gentler introduction to local life and landscapes, take a tour to the glorious **Mamiku Gardens** (see p. 277) above the Atlantic coast. Or head up to beautiful **Anthony's Farm** for the Lushan Country Life tour, which invites guests to explore forest and garden trails while learning about traditional beekeeping skills and ways of preparing herbal medicines. Be sure to sample the delicious fresh farm produce and taste coconut jelly straight from the shell, ripe mangoes, and golden apples.

Foodies interested in local cuisine might also enjoy an evening outing to Anse la Raye's **Fish Friday** for a barbecued seafood extravaganza.

But the city has a bad habit of burning down, and most of its uninspiring concrete architecture dates from the last conflagration, in 1948. St. Lucia is a regular feature on cruise-ship itineraries, and as the giant liners enter the harbor, they pass the old French battery at Vigie (Lookout) Point before berthing at the modern Pointe Seraphine cruise complex or right up against the downtown waterfront.

Set back from the waterfront is **Jeremie Street,** a bustle of market stalls, traffic, and pedestrians. T-shirt sellers and souvenir stalls perch on the dockside. Across the street the old covered market building has been hijacked by wood carvings, basketware, and beach bag vendors, while the produce market has been relegated to a concrete monstrosity with orange pyramid-shaped roofs. This is still the place to find a healthy dash of local color among the piles of citrus fruits and bananas, squashlike christophene, yams, gingerroots, and hot peppers.

A couple of blocks inland, past the Parliament and Court House on Laborie Street, lies the 19th-century **Cathedral of the Immaculate Conception.** The interior is painted from floor to ceiling with murals depicting biblical figures, African clerics, and pineapple motifs (the traditional Caribbean symbol for hospitality). Next to the cathedral is **Derek Walcott Square,** which honors the St. Lucian poet and playwright who won the Nobel Prize for Literature in 1992. There's a massive samaan tree on the square and a few old-style West Indian buildings around the edge.

Running south from the city center, Government House Road labors up Morne Fortune (pronounced For-TU-nay), past the governor-general's residence, and on to the **Morne Fortune Historic Area** at the top of the

In the waterfront village of Gros Islet

Pigeon Island National Park

🄰 271 B5
✉ Pigeon Point
☎ 758 452 5005
💲 $$

hill. In 1796, British soldiers of the 27th Inniskilling Regiment spent two days fighting their way to the summit of the morne, forcing the French to surrender. Their bravery is commemorated by the Inniskilling Memorial on the grounds of **Fort Charlotte**, where old military buildings have been restored and transformed into a college.

Rodney Bay & the North

From Castries the main road north swings alongside the local airport, which is edged by 2-mile-long (3 km) **Vigie Beach**, and on past the Gablewoods Mall and Choc Bay hotel enclave to Rodney Bay, St. Lucia's busiest resort area. On the southern side of the bay, hotels line the soft white sands of **Reduit Beach.** At the head of the beach a narrow channel gives access to the yacht harbor and Rodney Bay Marina. This bustling Caribbean sailing center is bordered to the north by the waterfront village of **Gros Islet,** home to the famous Friday-night jump-up.

The north shore of Rodney Bay curves around to **Pigeon Island,** the gros islet (big island) that gave the neighboring village its name. The former pirate lair of notorious Capitaine Jambe de Bois is now the **Pigeon Island National Park,** linked to the mainland by a sandy causeway. In 1778 Adm. George Rodney of the British Royal Navy set up a naval base in Gros Islet Bay (later renamed in his honor) and established a lookout post on the island. According to one story, the sentries on hilltop Fort Rodney used

---

EXPERIENCE: Rain Forest Lite

If you'd like to experience the rain forest but haven't brought your hiking boots, **Rain Forest Adventures St. Lucia** *(east of Rodney Bay at Babonneau, tel 866 759 8720, www.rainforestadventures.com, $$$$$)* can hoist you up into the canopy either for a gentle two-hour circuit on the aerial tramway or a zipline tour. Naturalist guides comment on the forest and its wildlife as the tramway's open gondolas travel through the treetops. Hiking trails and birding tours are also available.

carrier pigeons to report sightings of passing vessels and developments on the French island of Martinique, clearly visible 20 miles (32 km) to the north. (A more prosaic explanation attributes the name to the quantities of red-necked pigeons that congregated here before the native forest was stripped away.) The ruins of Fort Rodney still afford spectacular views north to Martinique, and south down the serried peaks of St. Lucia's mountainous interior to the Pitons. A botanical trail meanders around the 40-acre (16 ha) island, and there are several old military ruins, such as barracks, powder magazines, and a sunken musket redoubt, to explore.

The restored 1824 Officers' Quarters contain an interpretive center with exhibits tracing Admiral Rodney's famous victory at the Battle of the Saints in 1782 (see sidebar p. 243). Look for the tavern under the arches of the cellars and bring beach towels for a swim.

To the east of Rodney Bay, the exclusive **Cap Estate** residential quarter occupies the hilly northern tip of the island. There are several stunning private houses, a golf course, and a lovely restaurant in the estate's original 250-year-old great house.

South to Soufrière

There are two ways to explore the sights of southern St. Lucia, and visitors staying in the north of the island should reckon on a full day to visit the Soufrière area sights with a stop for lunch. A hassle-free option is to take a

Rain Forest Birds

Of the 43 or so bird species that inhabit the St. Lucian rain forest, 33 are endemic, such as the rare white-breasted thrasher, St. Lucia oriole, St. Lucia wren, and the endangered St. Lucian parrot. Conservation measures established in the 1970s brought this last species back from the edge of extinction. Known as the jacquot locally, the 16- to 18-inch-tall (40 to 45 cm) parrot is one of the most colorful inhabitants of the rain forest. It has a green back, blue head, red throat patch, and flashes of yellow and red under its wings.

A good way to find the parrots is to look for a stand of towering santinay trees, where they like to nest and feed on the small pink fruits. Their raucous screech is another telltale sign.

day sail from Castries or Rodney Bay, which includes a land tour of the attractions around Soufrière. On the other hand, you can rent a car and tackle the beautiful switchback road down the Caribbean coast, with the option of continuing right around the island on a tour from the capital.

The road south to Soufrière starts from Morne Fortune, south of Castries, and swoops downhill into the banana plantations and cane fields of the Cul de Sac Valley. Across the ridge at the end of the valley, there is a turn on the right to **Marigot Bay,** an idyllic little hurricane hole surrounded by steep wooded hills, where Rex Harrison talked to the animals during the filming of Doctor Dolittle in 1967.

The bay has been transformed from a sleepy yachting backwater into the setting for one of St. Lucia's newer and most luxurious hotel and villa resorts, with an upscale marina village complete with shopping and dining opportunities. A regular miniature ferry shuttles across the mouth of the bay to the beach opposite.

A short run farther south is **Anse la Raye** (Skate Bay, named after the fish once caught here), a picturesque West Indian fishing village. Its narrow streets are lined with sun-bleached wooden cottages, and down on the waterfront you'll see a few fishing boats hollowed out of gommier trees. On Friday evenings, the village comes alive as crowds gather for the fish feast (from 6:30 p.m.).

Framed by Morne Gimie and the Pitons, and ranged along sheltered Soufrière Bay, **Soufrière** was St. Lucia's first capital, founded by the French in 1746. The thriving 18th-century port was transformed into a hotbed of revolutionary zeal during the French Revolution and renamed La Convention. A guillotine was erected on the central market square. Soufrière's fortunes waned when the British chose Castries as their new capital, and the town subsided into a gentle decline, relying on its fishing fleet to keep afloat.

Today, Elizabeth Square remains the focal point of town, though the only threat it poses these days comes from overenthusiastic street traders. There are a few surviving traditional Creole houses with gingerbread trim and the market building has been brightened up with colorful friezes. Cruise liners disgorge their passengers onto the wharf for a flying visit to the south of the island. Chief among the sightseeing stops are the Soufrière Estate, home to the Diamond Botanical Gardens; and the pungent sulfur springs fed by the town's namesake Soufrière volcano (see opposite). ∎

EXPERIENCE: Hiking the Slopes

A number of trails carve their way through St. Lucia's 19,000-acre (7,700 ha) **National Rain Forest.** From the lush lower slopes, some hikes strike up into areas of cloud forest and elfin woodland with fabulous views and bird-spotting opportunities. Permission to hike in the rain forest must be obtained from the Forest and Lands Department *(tel 758 450 2078),* which provides information and guides.

Their short guided walking tour through the **Barre de l'Isle Forest Reserve** makes a good introduction to St. Lucia's unspoiled hinterland. Accessed from the Castries-Dennery road, the reserve spans the island's spine, affording peerless sea views over both coasts. A more challenging option is the **Edmund Forest Reserve** above Soufrière or the vertiginous scramble up the Pitons.

On the Atlantic coast, the **Frégate Island Nature Reserve,** near Praslin, is maintained by the St. Lucia National Trust *(reservations tel 758 453 7656, www .slunatrust.org).* A clifftop trail overlooks a brace of offshore islands where soaring frigate birds, known as *scisseux* (scissors) for their distinctive tail feathers, descend to their nesting grounds from May to July (binoculars an advantage). The National Trust also arranges excursions to the southerly **Maria Islands Nature Reserve,** home to lizards, seabirds, and the kuowes, a rare harmless snake.

Around Soufrière

A drive around to St. Lucia's Atlantic coast brings you to several charming nature reserves, with fine views and bird-watching. At La Soufrière's crater, an olfactory experience awaits.

To the Atlantic Coast

Not far beyond Soufrière, the round-island route exchanges its border of lush green forest for open countryside. At Choiseul Bay, the village lines a crescent of sand where fishing boats unload at the waterfront market.

The town of **Vieux Fort** crouches at the neck of the Moule à Chique, St. Lucia's most southerly point, facing St. Vincent in the distance. Off the east coast is the

INSIDER TIP:

For awesome ocean views, visit the lighthouse at Moule à Chique on the tip of St. Lucia's south coast at Vieux Fort.

—NICK PINNOCK
Owner, Ti-Kaye Village Resort & Spa, St. Lucia

Maria Islands Nature Reserve (see sidebar opposite), harboring seabirds and several endemic wildlife species. On the outskirts of Vieux Fort, the **Mankote Mangrove Swamp** is a rewarding bird-watching area with several short trails and a viewing tower.

The relatively swift return route to Castries passes the hamlet of Micoud, the **Mamiku Gardens,** near Praslin *(tel 758 455 3729)* with their lovely woodland trails and

ocean views, and an observation point overlooking the **Frégate Island Nature Reserve** (see sidebar opposite). At the banana town of Dennery, the road heads inland, crossing the Barre de l'Isle Ridge on its journey back to the island capital.

Diamond Botanical Gardens, Mineral Baths & Waterfalls

Set in the hills above Soufrière, these lovely botanical gardens display a glorious profusion of tropical plants and trees crowding narrow pathways. The mineral baths were built for French troops on the orders of Louis XVI.

La Soufrière Sulphur Springs

Because you can drive to within a few yards of La Soufrière's sinister and smelly volcanic vent, this attraction has been billed as "the world's only drive-in volcano." At the heart of the 7-acre (3 ha) crater, pools of boiling mud belch in the chalky moonscape.

Fond Doux Estate

One of St. Lucia's oldest estates, Fond Doux was once in the thick of the fighting between French revolutionaries and the British. This plantation's handsome 19th-century estate house offers a B&B, lunch, and trails through areas of cocoa, coconuts, coffee, cinnamon, and nutmeg. ∎

Diamond Botanical Gardens, Mineral Baths & Waterfalls
🔺 271 A2
✉ E of Soufrière
💲 $$

La Soufrière Sulphur Springs
🔺 271 A2
✉ SE of Soufrière
💲 $

Fond Doux Estate
🔺 271 A2
✉ S of Soufrière
☎ 758 459 7545
www.fonddoux
estate.com

St. Vincent & the Grenadines

St. Vincent heads up the chain of the Grenadine Islands like an emerald green kite with a 75-mile-long (120 km) tail trailing down toward Grenada. At 18 by 11 miles (29 by 18 km), it's the smallest and probably the least discovered of the Windward Islands, with a slumbering volcano and a nearly impenetrable jungle heart where generations of Carib once hid out and kept the Europeans at bay for more than two centuries.

A secluded beach on Bequia in the Grenadines

St. Vincent

🅰 261 B3

Visitor Information

✉ Cruise Ship Terminal, Kingstown

☎ 784 457 1502

www.svgtourism .com

St. Vincent

St. Vincent is still relatively overlooked today, outshone by the golden beaches and yachting havens of the Grenadines (see pp. 285–287) and the more widely publicized attractions of St. Lucia and Barbados. But while St. Vincent is no classic Caribbean idyll, all palm-fringed sands and rum punches (although the latter can be found), it does offer a quiet backwater charm, a miraculously undeveloped hinterland, and several hotels with discreet appeal for less hidebound travelers.

Successive waves of Ciboney, Arawak, and Carib settlers paddled their way from South America to Hairoun, as they called St. Vincent before Europeans added it to the New World map. But the island's rugged terrain and the prospect of ending up at the sharp end of a Carib barbecue curtailed further

INSIDER TIP:

If you like scuba diving and photographing tiny, weird looking marine critters, St. Vincent and the Grenadines is your place. A macro lens is a must.

—BILL TEWES
Professional diver/photographer

investigation, and St. Vincent became a refuge for Carib people forced from other islands. They were joined by escaped African slaves, some the survivors of shipwrecks off the coast, while others set sail on rafts from Barbados and were blown to St. Vincent by the westerly trade winds. Mixed Afro-Carib/Black Carib soon outnumbered the original Yellow Carib and started to take their lands. In retaliation the Yellow Carib allowed the French to establish a small colony in 1719. The Black Carib took to the hills to continue their resistance, surviving the First Carib War, initiated by a British invasion in 1763—a Caribbean extension of Britain's and France's long-running European conflicts.

The French snatched the island back with embarrassing ease in 1779. When the challengers sailed in for the attack, the entire British garrison was away working the governor's plantation in the north of the island, and no one could locate the key to the gun battery. With the British reinstated by the Treaty of Versailles in 1783, the French switched allegiance to the Black Carib and backed the

uprising that became known as the Second Carib War, or Brigands' War, lasting from 1795 to 1797. British plantations and settlements were torched and planters fed through the cane-crushing gear of their own sugar mills until the army regained control. The surviving 5,000 Black Carib were deported to British Honduras (present-day Belize). The last Yellow Carib retreated to the far north of St. Vincent, where their descendants still live today. The wars over, St. Vincent settled down to a quiet agrarian existence, growing a little sugar, Sea Island cotton, and arrowroot. The

Kingstown

🅰 279 B1

Visitor Information

☎ 784 457 1502

island was granted independence from Britain in 1979, and it remains a member of the British Commonwealth.

Agriculture is still a mainstay of St. Vincent's economy, and the island is rampantly fertile. There's no escaping the evidence, from the stranglehold of its creeper-clad rain forest peaks to the vegetable plots and tropical fruit orchards clinging to steep-sided valleys. Jagged mountains rip the underbellies of lowering gray rain clouds, so it always appears to be raining somewhere on the island. Regular dustings of volcanic fertilizer from La Soufrière, one of the Caribbean's most active volcanoes, further enrich the crumbling red earth. They say you could plant a pencil here, and it would take root.

The capital of St. Vincent and the Grenadines is Kingstown on the south coast of St. Vincent, a 20-minute drive from the main tourist enclave at Villa. A busy working port, Kingstown is a transportation hub for the Grenadines

and is served by regular ferries and small island-hopper aircraft. It's also a good place to begin any exploration of the island. Look to the west coast for quiet volcanic sand beaches and secluded coves accessible only by boat. Yachting is a major attraction, and day sails can be combined with diving and snorkeling. Hikers can plan some great days out around La Soufrière and the Buccament River Valley, where the beautiful and rare St. Vincent parrot makes its home.

Kingstown: Hemmed in by a crown of steep, wooded ridges, the capital of St. Vincent and the Grenadines hugs the mile-long (1.5 km) curve of Kingstown Bay and pushes back up the hillside. Down on the waterfront there's a lively bustle of cargo ships, ferries, and fishing boats, and the new cruise-ship and yachting complex sits smartly at the eastern end of the harbor. Behind the docks is Kingstown's pocket-size downtown district,

Critter Capital of the World

Some tourist destinations might cringe at the moniker "Critter Capital of the World," but for St. Vincent it's a ringing endorsement that the island's spectacular coral reefs are in terrific shape, and they are justly proud of the accolade. *Scuba Diving* magazine voted St. Vincent the "world's #1 small animal destination" with a perfect score of 100 for its extraordinary wealth of teensy marine critters. You need sharp eyes to spot the southern teardrop crab—no bigger than a penny—pea crabs, snapping shrimp, anemone shrimp, delicate sea stars, baby sea horses, expertly

camouflaged sea slugs, and shy octopuses. There are darting, agile beauties like the neon pink and orange fairy basslet, pug-ugly spotted scorpion fish, and pop-eyed frog fish.

The best critter dive sites are usually close to the leeward shore, where the dense volcanic granite sand settles quickly when disturbed, so visibility is excellent. Keen photographers should arm themselves with a macro lens and seek out local critter expert and photographer Bill Tewes of **Dive St. Vincent** *(tel 784 457 4928, www.divestvincent.com, $$$$$).*

St. Vincent is covered in greenery; it's said even a pencil could take root here.

which still has a few bumpy, old-fashioned cobbled streets and rows of arcaded shops sheltering the sidewalk from the sun and occasional cloudburst.

Heading west on Halifax Street, take a detour down Hillsboro Street (by the Cenotaph) to investigate the **produce market.** The busiest days are Friday and Saturday, when farmers venture into town from all around the island. On the opposite side of Halifax Street, iron railings fence in the imposing gray stone **Law Courts,** where the St. Vincent Parliament meets. Pastel-painted **St. George's Anglican Cathedral,** founded in 1820, is just a little farther on. The interior of the church has an unusual stained-glass window depicting a red-robed angel. Supposedly commissioned by Queen Victoria to celebrate the birth of her first grandson, it was destined for St.

Paul's Cathedral in London. But the monarch preferred her angels white, so the homeless window was presented to St. George's by the dean of St. Paul's. Among the many memorial plaques set in the walls of the cathedral, one commemorates Maj. Alexander Leith, a British war hero, who killed the Carib leader Chatoyer in a fencing duel on Dorsetshire Hill in 1795.

Across the way from the cathedral is Kingstown's most bizarre architectural monument, the 19th-century **St. Mary's Roman Catholic Church.** A riot of conflicting styles with a playful assortment of turrets, towers, pinnacles, and twisted barley-sugar columns, it was designed by a Belgian priest who drew his inspiration from pictures of famous European cathedrals.

Visitors with an interest in island history should make a stop at the **SVG National Trust** *(Old*

SVG National Trust

🅰 279 B1

Fort Charlotte
- ✉ 10 min. drive W of Kingstown

Botanical Gardens
- ▲ 279 B1
- ✉ Off Leeward Hwy.
- ☎ 784 457 1003
- 💲 $$ for a guide

Carnegie Public Library, Heritage Square, tel 784 451 2921, closed Sat. & Sun.), where a small but fascinating collection of Amerindian artifacts is displayed on the ground floor.

On top of Berkshire Hill, at the western end of town, stands **Fort Charlotte,** which affords magnificent views down the Grenadines from its aerie 600 feet (180 m) above the bay.

Named for George III's queen, the sprawling fortress was constructed in 1806 but never fired a shot in anger. A pictorial history of "St. Vincent and the Carib Wars" by William Linzee Prescott adorns the former cells.

Kingstown's pride and joy are the **Botanical Gardens,** set in the hills above the town center. The gardens, founded in 1763, are the oldest of their kind in the Western Hemisphere. They were intended as a research and breeding station for useful tropical plants, run as a distant adjunct of Kew Gardens in London. Their most famous success story concerns the breadfruit tree, introduced from the South Pacific to provide cheap, nutritious food for slaves working on the Caribbean plantations. Capt. William Bligh (1754–1817) set sail with the first consignment of saplings from Tahiti aboard HMS *Bounty* in 1787, but the small matter of a mutiny delayed his arrival until 1793. At first the slaves refused to touch the bland, alien fruit, but now the breadfruit's starchy flesh is a staple vegetable dish.

Guides loiter near the entrance waiting to conduct tours, and their services certainly liven up a visit. They know all the good stories, such as how the traveler's palm tree automatically aligns itself east-west and contains a reservoir of water for the lost and thirsty adventurer.

There's no need to search for the aviary; the piercing screech of the St. Vincent parrot is guide enough. Predominantly yellow-gold with a glorious lilac head,

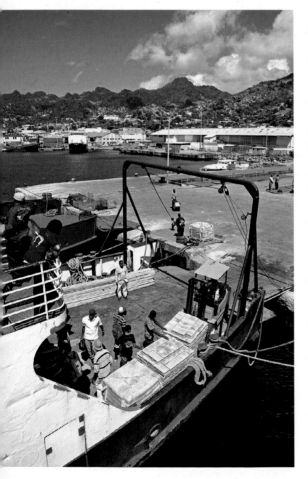

The bustling harbor at Kingstown in St. Vincent

EXPERIENCE: Local Knowledge

You can undertake short walks such as the Vermont Nature Trails easily without a guide, but local knowledge adds greatly to the rain forest experience, and guides are recommended for volcano hikes. If you plan to tackle La Soufrière, the **Kings-town tourist office** (tel 784 457 1502) can assist, or contact experienced local ecotour operators Clint and Millie Hazell of **HazECO Tours** (tel 784 457 8634), who offer a wide range of hiking, sightseeing, and historical tours. Trevor "Sailor" Bailey

at **Sailor's Wilderness Tours** (tel 784 457 1721, www.sailorswildernesstours.com, $$$$$) also offers hiking and mountain biking trips. Wear sturdy boots, pack insect repellent, and be prepared for rain.

The deceptively named **Sam's Taxi Tours** (tel 784 456 4338, $$$$$) can drive you around, but the company also provides hiking guides, nature walks, and an excursion to Bequia.

For details on boat trips to the Falls of Baleine, see Sports & Activities, p. 399.

---

these parrots are part of a captive breeding program.

Villa & the East Coast: Most visitors will embark on their explorations from hotels in the small town of Villa, southeast along the coast from Kings-town. It makes an ideal starting point for touring the east coast of St. Vincent, along with its adjacent—and highly produc-tive—agricultural lands.

Facing Villa's narrow sand beaches is the **Young Island resort,** which you can reach by water taxi from the waterfront. According to legend, the island was a gift from a Carib chief to Sir William Young, a British governor of St. Vincent who had presented the local leader with a horse. Behind Young Island are the ruins of **Fort Duvernette,** hugging another rocky islet. A staircase carved into the cliff leads to the 200-foot (60 m) summit, from which there are fine views.

North of Villa via the Vigie Highway, a panoramic

vista extends over Kingstown to the Grenadines and inland to the misty mountains from a lookout point on the knife-edge ridge of **Ayri Hill.** The road continues to the fertile Marriaqua (or Mesopo-tamia) Valley, where much of the island's fresh produce is grown. A side road leads up to the gorgeous **Montreal Estate Gardens,** set in a circlet of cloudy peaks scoured by waterfalls. Giant orchids and tulip trees shade tropical flowers on terraces built of river rocks.

The Yambou River flows down from the village of Mesopotamia, past rocks carved with Arawak petroglyphs, and through the Yambou Gorge toward the Atlantic coast. Here the Windward Highway wriggles along the shore to Georgetown, through banana and coconut plantations, and continues around to the north of the island, dominated by the impressive bulk of La Soufrière volcano (4,048 feet/1,234 m).

At **Rabacca Dry River,** just north of Georgetown, a four-wheel-drive track strikes up to

Villa & Young Island Resort

Ⓜ 279 B1

Montreal Estate Gardens

Ⓜ 279 B2

✉ N of Mesopotamia

☎ 784 458 1198

🕐 Closed Sept.– Nov. & Sat. Sun.

💲 $$

the trailhead for the 3.5-mile (5.5 km) four-hour round-trip hike up the east side of La Soufrière. It's a rewarding walk to the mile-wide (1.5 km) crater rim and back. A more challenging route sets out from Chateaubelair on the Caribbean side, and the two can be combined if you're in the mood for a really strenuous expedition (see sidebar p. 283).

Palm Island & Petit St. Vincent

The Grenadine Islands make idyllic miniature resorts. In addition to Young Island, off the south coast of St. Vincent, there are two more pint-size hideaways in the southern Grenadines. A mile off Union Island is Palm Island *(www.palmislandresort grenadines.com)***, which changed its name from Prune Island after owners John and Mary Caldwell planted coconut palms in their laid-back resort. Three miles farther south is Petit St. Vincent (better known as PSV; map 285 B2, www.petitstvincent.com), another paradise for sailors.**

The West Coast & Falls of Baleine: The Leeward Highway clambers north out of Kingstown and begins a roller-coaster journey past a series of small fishing villages to the beaches around Barrouallie and Richmond. Beyond these coastal attractions are a series of diverting stops, ranging from archaeological artifacts to exotic wildlife and scenery on a grand scale.

About 5 miles (8 km) from Kingstown, as the highway runs through the Buccament River Valley, a side road leads to the **Vermont Nature Trails.** The connecting trails are well marked and easy to follow, making a 2-mile (3 km) rain forest loop between the 1,000- to 2,000-foot (300 to 600 m) levels of Grand Bonhomme Mountain in the 10,870-acre (4,440 ha) **St. Vincent Parrot Reserve** *(map 279 B2)*. One path follows the Dalaway River, which supplies 45 percent of St. Vincent's drinking water, and heads on through an area of Caribbean pine trees dripping with epiphytes. It continues into the rain forest proper, where giant buttressed santinay trees are a favorite parrot habitat.

Between 500 and 700 parrots live in colonies spread about the preserve. It's usually easiest to spot them in the late afternoon at the **Parrot Lookout,** perched on the edge of a wooded valley. Also keep an eye out for the brilliantly colored hooded tanagers found only on St. Vincent and Grenada, several species of hummingbirds, and broad-winged and black hawks.

Back on the highway, at **Layou,** 1,300-year-old Arawak petroglyphs adorn a 20-foot (6 m) rock. *(The site is on private land, so call the Kingstown Tourist Office, tel 784 457 1502, in advance, or ask for permission to visit the site.)*

Peter's Hope Bay and **Keartons Beach,** lying on either side of the fishing village of Barrouallie, are good spots for a dip in the Caribbean Sea, and scenes from the movie *Pirates of the Caribbean* were filmed in lovely **Wallilabou Bay.** There's another beach near

Richmond at the end of the highway. A popular excursion from here is the 45-minute hike to **Trinity Falls** *(map 279 B3)*, which you can reach from a trail several miles north of town. The lovely rain forest walk emerges at a swimming hole fed by the waterfall.

At the north end of the island, accessible only by boat, are the **Falls of Baleine,** tumbling down from La Soufrière in a 60-foot (18 m) cascade to a rock pool. A day sail trip to the falls makes a great day out with beautiful views along the coast, lunch, a spot of snorkeling, and the opportunity to take a dip in the pool beneath the cascade.

The Grenadines

An irregular chain of 30-plus tiny islands and cays interspersed with a host of lesser sandbars and reefs, the Grenadines trail off from St. Vincent for about 75 miles (120 km) toward Grenada and the Grenadian Grenadine islands of Carriacou and Petit Martinique (see pp. 295–296).

Fewer than a quarter of the islands are inhabited (part of their charm for yachtsmen), and while some welcome no-frills sailors and divers, others have been transformed into tiny oases of barefoot luxury.

It's not essential to be a yachtsman to see the Grenadines by boat. The *M/V Barracuda* mail boat *(tel 784 455 9835)* sails from St. Vincent to Bequia and Canouan, Mayreau, and Union Islands on Mondays and Thursdays,

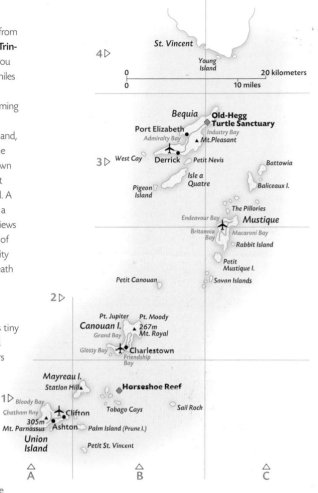

returning Tuesdays and Fridays, and a round-trip minus Bequia on Saturday. The *M/V Gem Star (tel 784 526 1158)* makes a down-island run Tuesdays and Fridays, returning the following day. The St. Vincent–Bequia crossing is made several times a day by the *M/V Admiral I* and *II (tel 784 458 3348),* and the *Bequia Express (tel 784 458 3539)*. A speedier, though pricier, option for services

The Grenadines
🅰 261 B2

Visitor Information

✉ Cruise Ship Terminal, Kingstown, St. Vincent

☎ 784 457 1502

www.svgtourism.com

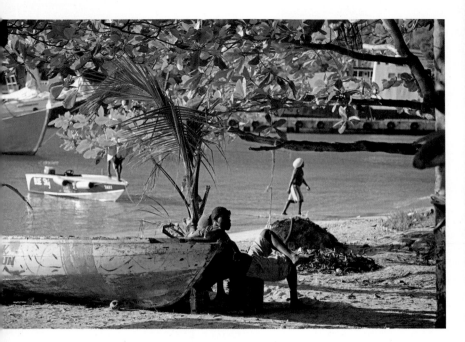

A boat taxi driver waits for a fare at Port Elizabeth on Bequia.

throughout the Grenadines is the new Jaden Sun Fast Ferry *(tel 784 451 2192, http://jadeninc.com).*

Bequia: An hour's ferry ride from St. Vincent is Bequia (BECK-way; *map 285 B3),* the largest of the St. Vincent Grenadines at 6 square miles (15 sq km). The quaint settlement of Port Elizabeth *(tel 784 458 3286, www.bequiatourism .com)* fringes Admiralty Bay, where the ferry docks within a stone's throw of shops and restaurants overlooked by the 18th-century Hamilton Battery. Water taxis shuttle around the bay to the palm-backed sands of Princess Margaret Beach and Lower Bay.

You can tour the island on foot or by taxi, or rent a scooter for a trip up to **Mount Pleasant,** with its view south to the tip of Grenada. Down on the windward side there's safe swimming and snorkeling at **Industry Bay,** and it's worth continuing along the shore to the **Old Hegg Turtle Sanctuary** *(tel 784 458 3245)* at the end of the track that leads to Park Beach.

Canouan Island: Midway down the Grenadines, dry and hilly Canouan Island (pronounced CAN-oo-ahn; *map 285 B2)* has beautiful sandy beaches around the port settlement of **Charlestown** in the curve of Grand Bay. A popular yachting center, the island also harbors the ultra-luxurious Canouan Resort *(tel 784 458 8000, www .canouan.com).*

Mayreau Island: Two fabulous beaches flank the 1.5-square-mile (4 sq. km) scrubby island of Mayreau (pronounced MY-row; *map 285 B1*). It's a steep climb from the makeshift dock to the village on **Station Hill** (population fewer than 200). A couple of bar-restaurants cater to yachtsmen, and there are rooms to rent and a low-key resort on **Salt Whistle Bay.**

Tobago Cays: The five low-lying, uninhabited islands of Tobago Cays *(map 285 B1)* lie east of Mayreau in shimmering turquoise waters protected by the gentle curve of **Horseshoe Reef.** For snorkelers, these are the crown jewels of the Grena-dines, set in shallow lagoons where you can feast your eyes on the dazzling tropical fish nursery beneath and swim with giant turtles, feel sugar-soft sand between your toes, and generally live the dream. It's no wonder the location scouts for the *Pirates of the Carib-bean* franchise chose to shoot here, though the movies' star, Johnny Depp, was ferried back to St. Vincent's Young Island resort to sleep. The **Tobago Cays National Marine Park** is accessible only by boat, but it's a popular spot and there are usually several day-sail boats and visiting yachts at anchor.

Mustique: The ultra-chic Caribbean hideaway of Mustique *(map 285 C2)* offers money-is-no-object

accommodations in 60 or so private villas, a 20-room hotel, and an upscale boutique hotel *(www.mustique-island.com).*

Yachts gather in **Britannia Bay,** and day-trippers are permit-ted ashore (no ferry service) to sample the gleaming white sands of **Macaroni Bay** or enjoy a drink at Basil's Bar. There are good walks around the 1,350-acre (546 ha) island and more swimming and snorkeling at secluded **Gallicaux Bay** and the hotel beach at **Endeavour Bay.**

INSIDER TIP:

Salt Whistle Bay is great for people-watching. Popular with yachters, it presents an endless parade of worldly travelers.

—JENNIFER ALLARD
National Geographic contributor

Union Island: While not the most alluring Grenadine, Union *(map 285 A1)* is certainly visually arresting, with a range of peaks culminating in Mount Parnassus (999 feet/305 m), the island chain's highest point. It's a busy transportation hub, with a lively yacht harbor and a couple of hotels at **Clifton,** the main town *(tel 784 485 8082, www.unionisland.com).*

The best beaches are **Chatham Bay** on the west coast and **Bloody Bay** to the north, both accessible only on foot or by boat. ∎

Grenada

Typically green and mountainous, Grenada is the southernmost Windward Island, only 100 miles (150 km) or so from the coast of South America. Its smaller sister islands, Carriacou and Petite Martinique, are part of the Grenadines chain, which stretches north to St. Vincent. Grenada is wrapped in rain forest and sprinkled with sandy beaches. Visitors can hike and dive, swim in waterfalls, stock up on spices from stalls run by pipe-chewing old biddies, and generally relax on one of the friendliest small islands (21 by 12 miles/34 by 19 km) in the region.

The port of St. George's was named for England's King George III.

Grenada

🗺 261 A1

Visitor Information

✉ S side of the Carenage (Burns Point), St. George's

☎ 473 440 2001 or 473 440 2279

www.grenada grenadines.com

Christened Concepción by Columbus in 1498, Grenada (pronounced gren-AY-dah) was renamed by Spanish sailors homesick for the hills of southern Spain. French settlers from Martinique purchased the island from indigenous Carib for a handful of beads and tools in 1650, but the peace was short-lived and the last Carib are said to have jumped to their deaths from the cliffs at La Morne des Sauteurs (Leapers' Hill) in 1651 (see p. 294). The French and English fought for control of the plantation island until it was ceded to Britain in 1783. During the French Revolution, Grenada was the scene of a bloody slave revolt led by Julien Fédon, a French planter, from his isolated coffee and cocoa estate at Belvidere. Arms were smuggled in from Guadeloupe, and the rebels overran most of the island, slaughtering British settlers, including the governor, during the 15-month insurrection. When the British finally regained control in June 1796, Fédon disappeared and the plantations were in ruins.

Grenada was rescued from the doldrums by the introduction of nutmeg in the 1830s. Popular legend has it that a doctor from the East Indies arrived with a couple of nutmeg trees in his baggage and jazzed up the local rum punch with a dusting of grated nutmeg. Grenada's nutmeg

industry took off in the 1850s, and other spices were introduced. Thus the West Indies finally achieved a spice island by default, 400 years after Columbus had set out to find one.

Grenada took full independence from Britain in 1974, but freed from colonial restraints, the new regime became increasingly despotic. In March 1979 the opposition staged a bloodless coup led by Maurice Bishop, who initiated

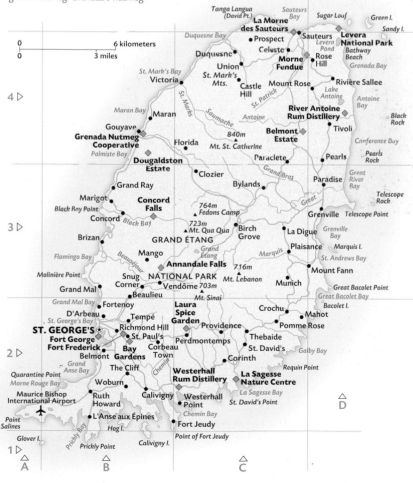

a program of socialist reforms that revitalized the economy, but soon he began to look equally repressive. Democratic elections were not called, and in October 1983 Bishop was ousted by a faction of his own party and executed in Fort

up and running. Today, despite the absence of tall trees and the roofless Parliament building, it is hard to see anything but improvements.

The Grenadians are easygoing and welcoming hosts. There is much to see and do, and the island

Grenadian Spices

Grenada is an olfactory banquet of spices, redolent with the pungent tang of nutmeg, cloves, and sweet woody cinnamon. Nutmeg is the island's most important spice and easy to find by the roadside and in the hills. The nutmeg tree *(Myristica fragrans)* produces an apricot-like yellow fruit that splits when ripe to reveal a brown shell covered with a waxy red web of mace. The fruit is used to make preserves, the mace is processed

as a separate spice, the inedible shell is recycled as a path-building material, and the inner kernel is the spice used in cooking and pharmaceuticals.

Like the nutmeg tree, cinnamon trees were imported from the East Indies. The bark is used as a food flavoring. Allspice *(Pimenta officinale)* originated in Jamaica. As its name implies, it tastes like nutmeg, cinnamon, and cloves all rolled into the one tiny unripe fruit.

George. Four days later, a joint U.S.-eastern Caribbean "friendly invasion" restored order. (A couple of decades on, Bishop's reputation has been posthumously rehabilitated and Grenada's international airport bears his name.)

Putting the episode behind them, the Grenadians set about building up a low-key but very successful tourist infrastructure with a range of hotels concentrated in the south of the island, good roads and communications, and the national pride and joy, a cricket stadium. On September 7, 2004, disaster struck when Grenada met the full force of Hurricane Ivan, which caused almost a billion U.S. dollars of damage.

The islanders began to rebuild immediately. Within a year almost 80 percent of the island was back

enjoys a high percentage of repeat visitors. Sweet-smelling nutmeg and cocoa estates beckon, as do St. George's craft shops and galleries. There are secluded beaches, nature trails, beautiful gardens, and captivating dive sites including a slightly spooky underwater sculpture park peopled by 55 life-size figures standing sentry on the Molinière Reef.

St. George's

There's no better introduction to Grenada than sailing into St. George's Harbour. It is one of the most picturesque ports in the Caribbean, nestled within the steep-sided walls of an extinct volcanic crater and guarded by a battery of old fortresses. St. George's was founded by the French but renamed in honor of

England's King George III, and there are numerous examples of Georgian colonial architecture among the church steeples and neat rows of red-roofed homes that cling to the precipitous hillsides like contour lines.

A sharp ridge divides St. George's into two parts, which are linked by a Victorian tunnel bored through the rock in 1895. On the harbor side the horseshoe-shaped **Carenage** hugs the waterfront, edged by shops and restaurants. It is named for the wharves where ships were once careened (tipped on their sides to have their hulls cleaned), now a bustle of cargo boats and ferries, fishing sloops from nearby Carriacou, and huge visiting cruise liners.

In the shadow of the ridge is the **Grenada National Museum,** housed in former French barracks dating from 1704. Island history and culture are explored in an assortment of Amerindian finds, colonial knickknacks, and a detailed, well-balanced account of the 1983 intervention.

Close to the museum is the 350-foot-long (107 m) **Sendall Tunnel,** which burrows beneath the ridge to the seafront **Esplanade** on the bay side of St. George's. Protecting the town from the headland at the harbor mouth is **Fort George,** which now serves as the police headquarters. It is open to the public, and there are great views over town from the 18th-century battlements.

A block back from the minibus depot on the bayfront is the **market square,** a hive of activity best visited on a Saturday morning. Women in headscarves and bright cotton dresses preside over an edible carpet of fresh fruit, vegetables, and spices spread out on the sidewalk as they banter with customers from the shady recesses of large, striped umbrellas.

A strenuous climb up Market Hill leads to **Church Street,** where several of St. George's finest Georgian buildings once perched on the hillside. Hurricane Ivan caused considerable damage to historic **York House,** seat of the Grenadian Parliament and Supreme Court, and also to **St. George's Anglican Church,** constructed in 1825. Both

INSIDER TIP:

If you head out very early to the underwater sculpture park at Molinère Reef, the sun illuminates all the bright colors of the corals and sponges on the statues' faces.

—JASON DECAIRES TAYLOR
Underwater sculptor and photographer

are undergoing major reconstruction and it is uncertain when they will reopen. Market Hill continues up to a busy junction orchestrated by a white-gloved traffic officer. Lucas Street heads past **Government House,** the governor-general's official residence guarded by pith-helmeted sentries, to tumble-down **Fort Matthew** and the rather better-preserved remains of **Fort Frederick.**

Grenada National Museum

 Monckton St. (off Long St.)

📞 473 440 3725

🕐 Closed Sat. p.m. & Sun.

💲 $

Fort George

✉ Church St.

Grand Anse & the South Coast

Lying just over 2 miles (3 km) south of St. George's is Grand Anse, Grenada's main tourist enclave. A clutch of low-rise hotels lines the 2-mile (3 km) stretch of white sand beach facing the Caribbean Sea. The swimming is safe, and water-sports concessions rent wind-surfers, dinghies, and kayaks. Waterskiing and parasailing are also available, and dive operators arrange trips to the reef sites off Molinière Point just north of St. George's, the Kick 'Em Jenny submarine volcano, and the scuttled wreck of the cruise ship *Bianca C.*

West of Grand Anse, en route to the very tip of the island at Point Salines, is **Morne Rouge Beach,** set in a quiet cove. There are sandy crescents at **Dr. Grooms Beach, Magazine Beach,** and the deliciously named **Pink Gin Beach,** which nestles beneath a fashionable spa hotel. Tucked into the rocks at the end of **Tamarind Beach** is a great bar-restaurant with kayak rentals and snorkel-ing. On the southern shore of the peninsula a handful of hotels, apartments, and homes inhabit the secluded coves of **Prickly Bay** and the narrow strip of sand beach at **L'Anse aux Épines.**

As the main road heads east from St. George's and the beaches, it swiftly runs into the countryside and cane fields grow-ing at the foot of steep, forested hills. The **Bay Gardens,** set in the hills, make an interesting detour with more than 5,000 species of tropical plants. You could also drop in at **Laura Herb & Spice Garden,** on the road to Windsor Castle, where top-quality herbs and spices are grown and pack-aged for export. At **Westerhall**

The New Black Gold

For centuries many of the Caribbean islands' upcountry estates, planted on rich, volcanic soil, have cultivated small quantities of coffee for domestic consumption. (The exception being Jamaica, whose fine, flavorsome Blue Mountain coffee beans are exported around the world.) Recently on the Windward Islands, chocolate has emerged as a niche crop. Chocoholic visitors to Grenada can get a taste of heaven at the **Belmont Estate** *(tel 473 442 9524, closed Sat.),* a 400-year-old plantation in the St. Patrick's district 20 miles (32 km) north of St. George's. The beans cultivated here are known as Trinitario, developed in Trinidad, with a low yield but sensational taste.

Estate tours follow the cocoa-making process from the orchard to the drying rack. There is a small museum, and the Creole lunch buffet served in the planta-tion house is not to be missed.

At this stage the beans are ready for transportation to the nearby **Grenada Chocolate Company,** Hermitage *(tel 473 442 0050, closed Sat. & Sun., www.grenada chocolate.com)* an engagingly eccentric but highly successful operation founded by Mott Green in 1999. Here, the beans are roasted, ground, mixed and molded into rich, dark chocolate bars, or packaged as cocoa powder. The company's award-winning wares are sold around the island and exported overseas.

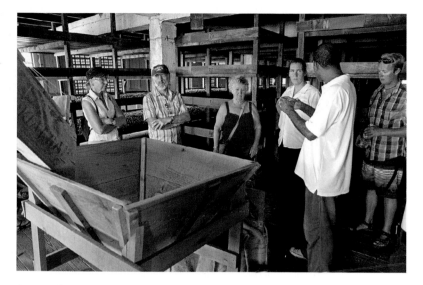

A tour guide explains old-fashioned nutmeg processing—Grenada is one of the world's top producers of the spice.

Rum Distillery, they will probably provide an impromptu factory tour on weekdays. A few pieces of antique plantation machinery can still be seen, and there is a small museum of local memorabilia, distilling equipment, and oddities including a World War I Maxim machine gun.

Midway along the south coast, look for signs to **La Sagesse Nature Centre.** Follow the bumpy track to the beach, past a carefully tended checkerboard of vegetable gardens. The nature center is rather less official than it sounds. In reality it is a charming guesthouse and alfresco restaurant arranged around a little pink plantation house on a lovely beach.

Around Northern & Central Grenada

A clockwise circuit of northern Grenada, returning to St. George's via the central highlands, reveals a landscape of rich diversity from sea-level mangrove swamps to rain forest mountains, and scenes from island life in spice plantations, a nutmeg factory, and charming Creole villages.

Heading north of St. George's, the main road hugs the twisting coastline, edged by cliffs and the Caribbean Sea. At Concord, follow signs for **Concord Falls** inland up into the hills through spice plantations and cocoa walks (cocoa tree groves) to the lowest of the three falls. It's an energetic 30-minute climb to the second fall and one and a half hours to the upper fall; both have swimming holes. The hike (4.5 hours) may be continued all the way to Grand Étang (see sidebar p. 294).

Back on the main road just south of the fishing village of

Bay Gardens
🅐 289 B2
✉ Morne Delice, St. Paul's
☎ 473 435 4544

Laura Herb & Spice Garden
🅐 289 C2
✉ Perdmontemps, St. David's
☎ 473 443 2604
🕐 Closed Sat. & Sun.
💲 $

Grenada Nutmeg Cooperative

Ⓐ 289 B4

✉ Gouyave

🕐 Closed Sat. &
    Sun.

Ⓢ $

Grand Étang National Park Center

Ⓐ 289 C3

✉ Grand Étang

☎ 473 440 6160

Ⓢ $

Gouyave, look for the **Dou-galdston Estate** on the right. In a sweet-smelling clapboard barn learn how nutmeg and other spices are still processed in the old-fashioned way. In Gouyave (French for "guava"), you'll find the **Grenada Nutmeg Cooperative** processing station, which welcomes visitors interested in sniffing around its processing plant, stuffed full with sacks of nutmeg kernels.

Beyond Gouyave the round-island road circles the St. Mark's Mountains and **Mount St. Catherine** (2,757 feet/840 m), Grenada's highest peak. The

---

Hiking in Grand Étang National Park

Grenada's best hiking opportunities lie within this national park in the central highlands. The **Mount Qua Qua Trail** is a moderately energetic, three-hour round-trip from the park center through elfin woodlands to the rocky summit of Mount Qua Qua. For a more challenging hike, take the **Concord Trail,** which continues from Mount Qua Qua for another three hours to Concord Falls.

Other popular hiking destinations include **Honeymoon Falls** and **Seven Sisters Waterfalls,** both of which are best tackled with a guide. Contact **Henry's Safari Tours** (tel 473 444 5313, www.henry safari.com, $$$$$) or **Telfor Bedeau** (tel 473 442 6200, $$$$$), who has been hiking Grenada's rain forest for half a century.

---

clifftop known as **La Morne des Sauteurs** (Leapers' Hill), on the north coast, is where in 1651 the island's last Carib threw themselves to their deaths (see p. 288). A handful of Amerindian exhibits

mark the spot. South of Sauteurs is **Morne Fendue,** a plantation house B&B, which makes a great lunch stop (reservations necessary, tel 473 442 9330).

On the virgin northeast coast is **Levera National Park** (map 289 D4), with its mangrove swamp and fine stretch of golden sand where leatherback turtles come ashore to lay their eggs in summer (April–June). The swimming is safer, however, at nearby **Bathway Beach.** Bird-watching is good around **Levera Pond,** a wildfowl breeding and feeding ground where scarlet ibis are occasionally spotted. Nearby is the Rivière Sallee Boiling Spring, which provides Grenada's token volcanic activity.

The main road runs inland above the Atlantic coast, through the pretty country villages of Mt. Rose, Tivoli, and Paradise. From **Grenville,** Grenada's second-largest town, the cross-island road climbs into the rain forest and **Grand Étang** (Big Pond) **National Park.** Natural history displays at the park center detail local geology, flora, and fauna, and a 15-minute nature trail offers views off to the coast and a chance of spotting Mona monkeys, introduced from Africa more than 300 years ago. Across the road a path leads to **Grand Étang,** a crater lake encircled by a 90-minute hike. The trailhead for longer hikes to Mount Qua Qua and Concord Falls is a short distance west of the park center.

On the road back to St. George's, **Annandale Falls** is a popular beauty spot with a swimming hole fed by the 30-foot (9 m) cascade. ■

Carriacou

The largest Grenadine island is a laid-back destination where visitors can get a close-up view of the craft of boatbuilding, appreciate imaginative local art, or simply enjoy the fine snorkeling and secluded white sand beaches.

A Carriacouan tends to his goats.

Some 23 miles (37 km) north of Grenada (a three-hour ferry ride or 90 minutes by power catamaran), Carriacou (pronounced CARRI-ah-COO) is the largest of the Grenadines (8 by 5 miles/ 13 by 8 km), with a population of about 7,000.

The island is hilly and dry, largely undeveloped, and fringed by white sand. It takes its name from the Carib word for "land of reefs," and there's good snorkeling and diving offshore. Carriacou was once planted with cotton and sugar, but when the plantations died out in the 19th century, the islanders turned to fishing,

INSIDER TIP:

During school vacations, you may come across makeshift roadside boatbuilding schools offered to youngsters by the Ministry of Culture.

—LARRY PORGES
Editor, National Geographic Books

boatbuilding, and smuggling.

Hillsborough, the tiny capital, is built on a curving bay. Close by are several waterfront restaurants and the small **Carriacou Museum**

Carriacou
🗺 261 B2
Visitor Information
✉ Main St., Hillsborough
☎ 473 443 7948
www.carriacou petitemartinique .com

Petite Martinique

The diminutive island of Petite Martinique is a volcanic cone lying 2.5 miles (4 km) off the northeast coast of Carriacou. Ferries from Hillsborough make the 20-minute crossing a couple of times daily during the week, less frequently on weekends.

Petite (pronounced PETT-y) Martinique is pretty much a closed community of 900 or so islanders who live in and around the sole settlement of Paradise. Most make their living from fishing and boatbuilding, and tourist facilities are limited to a small guesthouse or two. There are some fine beaches on the leeward side and excellent snorkeling, but apart from a taxi tour along the 2-mile-long (3 km) main road, there is little else to do unless you visit during the surprisingly energetic pre-Lenten Carnival.

(Paterson St., closed Sat. & Sun.). Its collections of Amerindian and colonial relics are laid out in a former cotton ginnery. There is also a collection of charming naïve-style paintings by local artist Canute Calliste (1914–2005). Mainly painted in acrylic on hardboard, Calliste's lively and often humorous island subjects—boatbuilders, Carnival goers, fishing boats, and his trademark mermaids—became highly collectible overseas. International renown failed to change this true island character, who continued to live in the wooden shack he built himself in L'Esterre and play the fiddle right up until his death at the ripe old age of 91.

Just north of town, beyond Bogles, the **KIDO Foundation** *(tel 473 443 7936, www.kido-projects .org)* runs a wildlife rescue project. Passers-by are welcome to drop in and see rescued sea turtles, injured birds, and reptiles being nursed back to health before they are returned to the wild. During the March to October sea turtle nesting season, observers can join the nightly beach patrols overseeing the safety of female leatherback turtles and their precious eggs.

Further up the west coast, **Anse la Roche** has a pretty and secluded beach. Over on the east coast, the village of **Windward** is a good place to watch the local boatbuilders in action, working the white island-grown cedar wood

South of Hillsborough, **Paradise Beach** boasts a lovely sweep of white sand with a beach bar facing a palm-shaded island.

Farther afield on the southwest shore is **Tyrrel Bay,** a popular yacht anchorage with a modest restaurant row. ∎

A cottage in the coastal village of Windward. The island of Petite Martinique rises offshore.

Exquisite beaches, sophisticated lodgings, and a wealth of things
to see and do in the Gateway to the West Indies

Barbados

A palm-studded beach at Bathsheba
in Barbados

North Point
Animal Flower Bay
Archer's Bay
Animal Flower Cave
The Spout

6 ▷

Crab Hill
Hope
Stroud Bay
Greenidge
Archers
Norse's Bay
Spring Hall
ST. LUCY
Harrison Point
Greshie Bay
Bromefield
Trents
Nesfield
Maycock's Bay
Babbs
Bentham's
Fryer's Well Point
Fustic
Fryer's Well Bay

Ladder Bay
River Bay
Antilles Flat
Pie Corner
Cuckold Point
Rock Hall
The Landlock
Cave Hill
Paul's Point
Pico Teneriffe

Castle
Boscobelle
The Choyce
Diamond Corner
Mount Gay Rum Distillery
St. Nicholas Abbey

5 ▷

ST. PETER
Smitons Bay
Rose Hill
Mile and a Quarter
Six Men's Bay
Barbados Wildlife Reserve
Morgan Lewis Sugar Mill
Green Pond
Shorey
Walkers Beach

Heywoods Beach
Farley Hill National Park
Grenade Hall Signal Station & Forest
Litchfield
Speightstown
Indian Ground
Belleplaine
Long Pond

Godings Bay
Black Bess
Walkers
167m
Lakes Beach

2A

4 ▷

Mullins Bay
Gibbes Bay
Rock Dundo
ST. ANDREW
Scotland
P
l
a
t
i
n
u
m

Lower Carlton
Upper Carlton
ST. JAMES
Mose Bottom
Hill Crest
Three Ro...
Bathsheba

Weston
Endeavour
340m Mt. Hillaby
Joe's River
Andromeda Botanic Garde...

Alleynes Bay
The Garden
326m Mt. Misery
Flower Forest
ST. JOSEPH
Hothersal
Hackleton's Cliff

Porters
Greenwich
Chapman
Coffee Gully
Venture
Clifton H...

Folkestone Underwater Park
Portvale Sugar Factory
Welchman Hall Gully
Clifton Hall
Sma... Hop...

St. James' Church
Rock Hall
Harrison's Cave
Parris Hill

Holetown
Arch Hall
ST. THOMAS
Hopewell
3B
Four Cross Roads

Sunset Crest
Sandy Lane Bay
Sandy Lane Golf Course
Proutes
Prerogative

3 ▷

C
o
a
s
t
Paynes Bay
Holders Hill
Belair
Gun Hill Signal Station
Greens

Thorpe
Halls
Jackson
Cane Wood
Hillbury
Ellerton
Drax Hall

Husbands
Clermont
Friendship
2A
3
Francia Plantation House
Walkers Terrace
Melverton

Prospect
Batts Rock Bay
Valley
ST. GEORGE
Brerete...

Fresh Water Bay
Spring Garden
Tyrol Cot Heritage Village
Salters
4
Dash Valley
Skeenes Hill
Packe...

Mount Gay Rum Visitors Centre
Grazettes
Black Rock
ST. MICHAEL
Bank Hall
Rouen
Mapp Hill
Edey

2 ▷

Bridgetown Harbour
Ivy
Upton
St. Davids
6
Sea...

Bridgetown Synagogue
BRIDGETOWN
Highgate
CHRIST CHURCH
Newton
Providence
Pil... R...

△ A
△ B
★
Carlisle Bay
Barbados Museum
Clapham
Warners
Kendal Hill
Lodge Road
Chan... La...

Garrison Savannah
Worthing
Hastings
Rockley Beach
Maxwell Coast
Inch...
Marle...

St. Lawrence
Dover
Graeme Hall Swamp
Oistins
Goodland
Silver Sands
Wo...

Oistins Bay
Enterprise
Ananial... Point

1 ▷

South Point
△ C
△ Bow Bells Reef
△ D

0 ——— 6 kilometers
3 miles

Area of map detail

ATLANTIC OCEAN

Caribbean Sea

Barbados

Barbados lies 100 miles (160 km) east of the Windward Islands, surrounded by the Atlantic Ocean. Unlike its volcanic neighbors, the island is an undulating limestone massif. Its coral rock underpinnings are responsible for the famous Platinum Coast beaches, the island's upscale tourist heartland. The more informal (and affordable) side of Barbados is the south coast resort area, with a string of equally appealing destinations.

The British ruled Barbados for 340 uninterrupted years before independence and left an indelible, slightly formal imprint on this former sugar colony. There's considerable pride in the Barbados Parliament and more than a touch of Little England in the local passion for cricket, the ritual of afternoon tea, and the practice of dressing for dinner in some quarters.

Barbados takes its name from the huge, native bearded fig tree, also known as a banyan, which drops a curtain of aerial roots to the ground. Portuguese explorers called them *barbados* (bearded ones). Although Amerindian settlers discovered the island almost 4,000 years ago, it was uninhabited when English colonists landed near the site of Holetown on the west coast in 1627. Dutch settlers played a significant part in developing the early plantations, and they introduced sugarcane from Brazil in 1637. As the colony prospered, indentured laborers were shipped out from Britain, but they struggled with the climate, and soon African slaves were brought in to swell the plantation workforce. With the abolition of slavery in 1834, the sugar industry lurched

Congor Rocks
Congor Bay
astle
Conset Bay
Coach Hill
Conset Point
Codrington College
Bell Point
Palmers
JOHN
Bayfield
Ragged Point
Massiah Street
Thicket
Marley Vale
Deebles Point
The Chair
Kitridge Bay
Kitridge Point
ottage ale
Merricks
Church
Palmetto Bay
Bottom Bay
ST. PHILIP
Robinsons
Cave Bay
ezer Sunbury Plantation House
Sam Lord's Castle
Long Bay
Six Cross Roads
Shark's Hole
m Factory & eritage Park
Blades
The Crane
dbourne atricks
Mangrove
Crane Bay
Cobbler's Rock
Foul Bay
Walronds
St. Martins
Salt Cave Point
Cobbler's Reef
rantley Adams ternational irport
arlowe Point
E   F

from virtual failure to moderate success, and Barbados eventually achieved independence from Britain.

The colonial heart of the island is Bridgetown, together with the old British military headquarters just south of the city at Garrison Savannah. Barbados is a gift for history buffs, who will have a field day perusing handsome examples of traditional Georgian architecture and visiting historic Holetown (the original British settlement), restored plantation houses, and picturesque sugar mill ruins.

Beyond the sprawling capital city, and the resort areas to either side, Barbados's

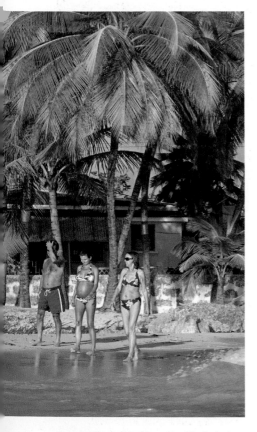

A typical day in Worthing, one of Barbados's resort towns

INSIDER TIP:

When blacks weren't allowed to play in the white-only tennis clubs of the 1930s, they came up with their own street game: road tennis. Bajans play it across the island on Sunday afternoons.

—CHARLES KULANDER
National Geographic Traveler *magazine writer*

landscape is remarkably rural. The island is divided into 11 parishes (Christchurch and 10 more named after saints), which are frequently given as an address rather than the name of the nearest village. Sugarcane fields and pockets of woodland roll back from the leeward coast, and dozens of tiny (and spectacularly unsigned) country roads burrow into the interior. Renting a car is a great way to explore, but it's very easy to get lost, so leave plenty of time, relax, and enjoy the mystery tour. For less intrepid travelers, ground operators offer all manner of sightseeing excursions, or you can arrange a taxi tour with a clued-up local driver.

To the northeast, Mount Hillaby (1,089 feet/340 m) is the highest point on the island, and the 1,000-foot (300 m) crest of Hackleton's Cliff is poised dramatically over the Atlantic on the windward coast. This exhilarating, surf-dashed shore is in complete contrast to the silky, smooth resort beaches, and it is where the Bajans come to relax. The atmosphere is low-key with little sign of development, though visitors looking for peace and quiet will find several small guesthouses and B&Bs. The damper climate on this side of the island has encouraged the creation of several sensational gardens clinging to the hillsides perched above the ocean.

Because of its height, Mount Hillaby provides one of the best scenic lookouts in Barbados, especially to the east, west, and north coasts of the island. ■

Bridgetown

Bridgetown, the island's energetic capital city, is an important Caribbean business center and home to about 100,000 residents. The heart of the city lies on the Careenage, a narrow inner harbor at the mouth of Constitution River, where an English expedition discovered an Amerindian bridge in 1625. A handful of waterfront cafés makes the Careenage a pleasant place to take a break and watch the world go by.

Bustling Careenage, complete with waterfront cafés, in Bridgetown

On the north bank of the inlet is **National Heroes Square,** the old colonial heart of the city. Here the mellow complex of coral rock public buildings contains the House of Assembly, the seat of the Barbados Parliament where the island's legislators meet. Although the buildings only date from the 19th century, the historic assembly was first established in 1639.

Crop Over—Carnival Bajan-Style

The Bajan summer Carnival dates back to the late 1700s, when Barbados was the world's largest sugar producer and the island celebrated a successful harvest. Today, preparations begin far in advance with magnificent costumes sewn (constructed in some cases), dance routines practiced, and calypso acts honed over months leading up to the event *(check schedules on websites such as www.barbados cropoverfestival.com or www.crop overbarbados. com).* **For a taste of the joie de vivre** year-round, try the dinner show **Bajan Roots & Rhythms** at The Plantation Theatre, St. Lawrence *(tel 246 621 5048, www.plantationtheatre.com, $$$$$).*

George Washington Slept Here!

A dilapidated 18th-century plantation home on Garrison Savannah, formerly known as Bush Hill House, **George Washington House** *(tel 246 228 5461, closed Sun., $$$)* has undergone a remarkable restoration since it was discovered that future U.S. president George Washington stayed here in his teens. The house was rented out to George and his half-brother Lawrence for a two-month stay in 1751. Lawrence, who suffered from tuberculosis, was searching for a cure in the tropics, and the trip was the only time young George ever left his native shores. The plantation house kitchens and reception rooms have been furnished in period style, while a museum of Bajan memorabilia and artifacts occupies the upper story.

Bridgetown
🅐 298 B2

Visitor Information
✉ Bridgetown Harbour
☎ 246 427 2623
🕐 Closed Sat. & Sun.

www.visitbarbados .org

Bridgetown Synagogue
✉ Magazine Lane
🕐 Closed Sat. & Sun.
💲 $

A short walk east on St. Michael's Row leads you to **St. Michael's Cathedral,** which has been rebuilt several times (most recently in 1831) on the site of the original church, founded in 1625. George Washington (1732–1799) is said to have worshiped in one of its former incarnations in 1751, during his only trip outside what is now the United States. Washington was just age 19 when he sailed into Carlisle Bay on November 3. At that time Bridgetown was the biggest city in the English-speaking world outside Britain. George and his brother, Lawrence, stayed at Bush Hill House in Garrison Savannah (see sidebar this page), which has been restored by the Barbados National Trust.

West of National Heroes is **Broad Street,** the city's main shopping and business district.

Among modern offices and department stores are a number of fine old colonial buildings dressed up with fancy ironwork balconies. A few blocks away, off Magazine Lane, is the ice-cream pink-and-white **Bridgetown Synagogue.** The first synagogue on the island was established by Jewish immigrants from Brazil and consecrated in 1654. Bridgetown's prosperous Jewish community acted as financial agents and export brokers for the fledgling colony, and it grew considerably in the mid-17th century, when the

INSIDER TIP:

At sunrise on Pebbles Beach (just north of the Hilton) on race days, grooms from the nearby Garrison Savannah racetrack bathe their horses in the ocean.

—MATT PROPERT
National Geographic photographer

British islands offered freedom of religious practices under the direction of Oliver Cromwell (1599–1658). Largely destroyed by a hurricane in 1831, the present synagogue was reconsecrated in 1833, but many tombs in the cemetery date back much further.

From the city center the Princess Alice Highway heads west to **Bridgetown Harbour** and the cruise-ship complex.

To the south, across the

Careenage (so named because ships were once tipped onto their sides here-—careeened—to have their hulls cleaned) on the Chamberlain Bridge, Bay Street follows the curve of Carlisle Bay into the **Bayville** district, where a few pretty 19th-century town houses with gingerbread trimmings have survived on quiet back streets shaded by palm and mango trees.

A mile (1.5 km) south of Bridgetown is **Garrison Savannah,** once a British parade ground. The enclosure now doubles as a jogging track and a small racecourse where the Barbados Turf Club hosts weekend races *(tel 246 426 3980, www.barbadosturfclub.org)*. Nearby are several 19th-century buildings, including the distinctive **Main Guard** (also known as the Savannah Club), the former barracks and crumbling ramparts of 17th-century **Fort Charles,** and **St. Anne's Fort,** founded in 1704 but never completed.

Bridgetown on a typical bright sunny day

Barbados Museum

The old military prison houses the excellent Barbados Museum. A circuit of the exhibits begins with an overview of the island's natural history and early Amerindian inhabitants accompanied by archaeological finds and copious background notes.

In the plantation-era section, the Aall Gallery displays rare antique maps, including a second edition of Richard Ligon's original map of Barbados, published in 1657. It shows the island still partially covered in native forest, with plantations blocked neatly along the leeward coast and wild

boars rampaging about the interior. Prisoners once broke stones in the museum's lower courtyard and lived in cells around the leafy upper courtyard, now occupied by a series of rooms furnished in 19th-century style.

The Chancellor Gallery has a small selection of military memorabilia, and a fascinating collection of 17th- and 18th-century engravings is a highlight in the Cunard Gallery. Island views and studies of plantation great houses compete for attention with portraits of fashionable planters, dandies, dancers, and Rachel Pringle, Barbados's most famous 18th-century madame. ■

Barbados Museum

🅼 298 C2
✉ St. Anne's Garrison, St. Michael
☎ 246 427 0201
🕐 Closed Sun. a.m.
💲 $$

www.barbmuse .org.bb

Sugar

At the height of the 17th- to 18th-century sugar era, Barbados was one of the most powerful islands in the Caribbean. For two centuries sugar was the backbone of the West Indies, the "white gold" that lined the planters' coffers, shaped the foreign policy of distant European countries, and instigated the largest forced transportation of human beings in history.

Sugarcane stalks can grow to a height of 20 feet (6 m) and can make for an arduous harvest.

Sugar Arrives in the New World

The Spanish conquest of the New World in the 16th century was fueled by South and Central American gold and precious gems. Lacking the mineral wealth of the mainland, the success of the West Indian colonies founded in the early 17th century depended on finding a profitable crop that could not be grown in Europe, yet one that would survive the vagaries of transatlantic transportation. Cotton, indigo, and coffee were early contenders, but tobacco proved the most profitable option until new plantations in Virginia flooded the market with better quality tobacco, leaving the Caribbean settlers searching for an alternative.

Sugarcane was among a selection of experimental crops brought to the Spanish colony of Hispaniola by Christopher Columbus in 1493. Although the cane flourished, it was more than a century before Dutch planters from Brazil introduced sugarcane and their vital expertise to Barbados in the 1630s. By this time the new fashion for coffee and chocolate drinking in Europe provided a burgeoning home market, and the success of the first sugar crops ignited a planting frenzy that carpeted Barbados with cane by the 1650s.

Cultivation & Processing

Compared with tobacco, which could be grown profitably on small holdings, sugar required larger plantations and extensive capital outlay for buildings and processing equipment. The labor force on the islands was also insufficient, so slaves were imported from West Africa to work the cane fields.

To prepare the land for sugar cultivation, the planter's first task was to clear native vegetation and divide his estate into large fields arranged around the central mill and processing facility. A crop grown from cane tops planted in well-prepared earth could be harvested after 18 months; but the Dutch introduced *ratooning*, a less expensive and faster method of propagation using shoots grown on cane roots left in the ground after the previous harvest and ripe for harvesting within a year.

Slaves cut the crop by hand—brutally hot, backbreaking labor—during the dry season (Jan.–May) and carried it to the mill, which could be powered by wind, water, animal, or slave labor. Here the cane was crushed by rollers, the *bagasse* (trash) removed for fuel, and the cane juice diverted into a series of copper boiling pans. Lime water was added to assist clarification, and as the boiling syrup progressed through pans of ever decreasing size and increased temperature, it was skimmed to remove impurities. From the final pan, liquid sugar was poured into wooden cooling troughs where it separated into *muscovado* sugar crystals and molasses. The molasses was then drained off and distilled to make rum, and the semi-refined sugar was packed into hogsheads (large wooden barrels) to await shipment overseas.

INSIDER TIP:

Descendents of Irish and English "Redlegs"—white slaves who worked the sugar plantations—still live off the land in the hills of eastern Barbados.

—LARRY PORGES
Editor, National Geographic Books

Boom & Bust

At the beginning of the 18th century, the lucrative spoils of the booming Caribbean sugar trade were shared between Britain and France, and trade was at the core of a century of bitter rivalry between the two countries. Peace treaties inevitably involved the transfer of colonial powers to the victors.

Peace with France in 1814 brought Britain a handful of former French West Indian colonies and a glut of sugar accompanied by a dramatic reduction in profits. Across the Channel, the French turned to sugar beets, grown in Europe as a vegetable since Roman times, and a far cheaper and easier way of producing sugar since the discovery of a viable method of sugar extraction in 1812. The widespread cultivation of sugar beets in Europe, coupled with the emancipation of the slave workforce, spelled the end of the sugar industry in the smaller West Indian colonies in the 1840s. Only the big producers such as Barbados, Jamaica, and Trinidad survived by importing indentured labor from overseas.

The Origins of Sugar

The recorded history of sugar begins in India, though how sugarcane reached the subcontinent from its probable origins in Polynesia is unknown. Discovered by Persian invaders circa 510 B.C., sugarcane and the secret of "honey without bees" traveled to the Middle East. A few centuries later, the ancient Greeks and Romans prized it as a luxury and a medicine, and during the Middle Ages small quantities of sugarcane were cultivated around the Mediterranean region. It was still regarded as a rare and expensive alternative to honey when crusaders returning from Syria introduced the "new spice" to England in 1099.

Plantation Houses & Gardens

The colonial heritage of Barbados comes alive in its wonderful plantation houses and lush tropical gardens. Plantation owners built gracious residences to reflect their exalted social standing. In doing so, they achieved a refinement that matched that of the sugar that underpinned their wealth, while lush gardens reinforced the notion of living in an island paradise.

The Sunbury Plantation House was built in the 1660s.

Sunbury Plantation House

🅐 299 E2

✉ St. Philip

☎ 246 423 6270

💲 $$

www.barbados greathouse.com

The Southern Heartland

The rolling countryside of southern Barbados cuts a swath eastward from Bridgetown and north of Grantley Adams Airport. The atmosphere here is redolent of two Barbadian mainstays: sugar-processing and rum. Set back from the coast amid the undulating green carpet of cane fields that provided its wealth for centuries, the 350-year-old **Sunbury Plantation House** was a private home until the 1980s. This historic great house still retains charmingly homey touches such as fresh-cut flowers and potted plants dotted among the traditional Barbadian mahogany furniture and collections of antique china, glass, and silver. The bedrooms upstairs are open for inspection, with Victorian clothes laid out on capacious four-poster beds. The old yam cellar has been turned into a carriage museum and repository

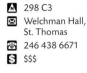

of old-fashioned agricultural and domestic implements. The Court-yard Restaurant in the garden serves lunch and afternoon tea. If the idea of a hurricane-lamp-lit dinner in the main house appeals, call and make a reservation for the five-course Plantation Dinner.

A short distance to the west, Drax Hall is one of the oldest houses in the region, dating from the mid-17th century. It is occasionally opened to the public under the Barbados National Trust's Open House Programme (see sidebar this page).

Highland Sites

The central highlands of Barbados lie just to the east of the Platinum Coast. The terrain here was too hilly for large-scale plantations, so the landscape feels more unspoiled.

The first garden you come to is **Welchman Hall Gully,** located about 5 miles (8 km) due east from Holetown along the west coast. Originally laid out as a botanical walk in the 1860s, this fabulously lush mile-long (1.5 km) wooded gorge was created by the collapse of a limestone chamber in part of the Harrison's Cave underground cavern network (see p. 311). Around the fantastical pinnacles and limestone rock formations, more than 200 species of exotic plants and flowers flourish in the cool shade of giant forest trees and stands of bamboo. Ferns and trailing lianas adds to the jungle-like atmosphere, and you might hear vervet monkeys crashing about in the treetops in the early morning or late afternoon.

Another haven of exuberant tropical plant life, the 50-acre (20 ha) **Flower Forest** lies just 2 miles (3 km) northeast of Welchman Hall Gully. It occupies a commanding position in the Scotland district with views across a ruffle of hills to the wide blue Atlantic. In the woodlands, steep paths zigzag down through a forest of gingers, lobster claw heliconias, Chinese hat plants, and red hot cattails to a grassy lookout. A leisurely inspection of the orchid collection provides a welcome break on the trek back.

Barbados Open House

Barbados's rich architectural history runs the gamut of styles from Jacobean gems and imposing contemporary mansions to wooden chattel houses. Most of these architectural treasures remain in private hands. The popular annual Open House Programme (Jan.–Apr.) encourages owners to open their homes for a few hours once a year. In recent times, access has been given to the prime minister's official residence, as well as to a couple of stunning modern residences in exclusive Sandy Lane. Contact the **Barbados National Trust** (Wildey House, Wildey, St. Michael, tel 246 426 2421, or www .thebarbadosnationaltrust.com, $$$$$).

If orchids are your thing, then don't miss **Orchid World,** near Gun Hill. More than 20,000 orchids are gathered here in a dazzling display. Paths traverse the 6.5-acre (2.6 ha) landscaped gardens and there are five orchid houses to explore.

The views from Gun Hill Signal Station (see p. 311) nearby

Welchman Hall Gully
- 298 C3
- Welchman Hall, St. Thomas
- 246 438 6671
- $$$

Flower Forest
- 298 C4
- St. Joseph
- 246 433 8152
- $$$

Orchid World
- 298 D3
- Groves, St. George
- 246 433 0306
- $$$ (discounted joint ticket with Flower Forest)

**Andromeda
Botanic Gardens**
- 298 D4
- Bathsheba,
  St. Joseph
- 246 433 9261
- $$$

**St. Nicholas
Abbey**
- 298 C5
- Cherry Tree Hill,
  St. Peter
- 246 422 8725
- Closed Sat.
- $$$

reach all the way to the coast. Just down the hill, the handsome early 20th-century great house, Francia Plantation, is now a private school.

Northeast Coast

The rolling uplands of the interior end abruptly in a series of dramatic coastal cliffs in the east. Although relatively unpopulated, the northeast coast of Barbados has a pair of memorable sites.

The first is **Andromeda Botanic Gardens,** lying some 4 miles (6.5 km) east of Flower Forest. World-renowned for a fabulous collection of indigenous and exotic tropical flowers, these lovely gardens cling to the cliffs above the Atlantic coast like their namesake heroine in Greek mythology. The 6-acre (2.5 ha) gardens were established privately by Mrs. Iris Bannochie in 1954 and arranged in outdoor "rooms," where orchids, heliconias, hibiscus, and clouds of bougainvillea abound alongside fragrant bowers,

water-lily ponds, and shady corners planted with ferns and striking ornamental foliage.

A shore road runs northward along the rocky eastern coast of Barbados, where there are few settlements but extensive beaches. About 9 miles (14.5 km) north from Andromeda Botanic Gardens is **St. Nicholas Abbey.** A rare example of Jacobean architecture in the Caribbean, the "abbey" rejoices in a splendid gabled facade dating from around 1650–1660, although the building never had any religious connections. Recently, the property has undergone an impeccable restoration. The elegant, panelled reception rooms have been filled with antique furnishings, Wedgwood china, and exquisite glassware.

Guests are free to wander in the beautiful gardens, discover an avenue of 250-year-old mahogany trees, and explore leafy gullies. The estate is once more producing fine rum and a steam mill operates several times a week during the reaping season (Feb.–May). ∎

Flowers bloom at the Andromeda Botanic Gardens.

South Coast

Around the southwest tip of Barbados from Garrison Savannah (see p. 303), the main coastal highway runs into Christchurch parish and the island's busiest resort area.

Between Hastings and Worthing on the south coast

Hastings, Worthing, and **Dover** back the best of the lovely south coast beaches, while **St. Lawrence Gap** is a veritable restaurant row with the best nightlife on the island. By day the action moves to water sports on the beach. A little known escape from the crowds at Worthing, the **Graeme Hall Bird Sanctuary** has a swamp boardwalk lookout on the island's largest expanse of inland water.

Beyond **Oistins,** a fishing center with a popular Friday-night fish fry, is lively **Silver Sands Beach,** a favorite with wind-surfers. Farther east you'll find secluded beach coves at Foul Bay, Crane Bay, and Long Bay, over-looked by **Sam Lord's Castle,** an 1820s mansion turned hotel.

The interior of the south coast also has its share of attractions, including the unashamedly touristy **Heritage Park & Foursquare Rum Distillery** at Six Cross Roads. The south coast runs out at Ragged Point, where the rocks beneath the East Point Lighthouse are lashed by the Atlantic. ■

Heritage Park & Foursquare Rum Distillery

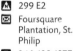 299 E2

✉ Foursquare Plantation, St. Philip

☎ 246 420 1977

Rum Punch

On the French islands the blending and aging of rums is a serious business, and the top producers even date their premium products to create vintages like wines. Rum punch was the planters' favorite tipple and was once a good way of transforming some of the rougher local brews into a palatable drink. The traditional recipe for rum punch calls for one measure of sour (lemon or lime), two of sweet (cane juice), three of strong (rum), and four of weak (water).

Around Barbados

There's no excuse for boredom on Barbados, where dozens of fascinating sites, natural and historical, are scattered about the island. From local architecture at Tyrol Cot Heritage Village, to the legacy of sugar and rum, to agoutis and anemones, it's all within a short drive.

The 700-foot-high (213 m) perch of Gun Hill Signal Station

Animal Flower Cave

🄰 298 B6
✉ St. Lucy
☎ 246 439 8797
💲 $$

Barbados Wildlife Reserve & Grenade Hall Signal Station & Forest

🄰 298 C5
✉ Farley Hill, St. Peter
☎ 246 422 8826
💲 $$$

Codrington College

🄰 299 E3
✉ St. John
☎ 246 423 1140
💲 $

Animal Flower Cave

At the northern tip of the island, dozens of multicolored sea anemones flower in the rock pools of this subterranean cave hollowed out of the cliffs by wave action. Visitors can swim around with a guide, watch the "animal flowers" waving their tiny tentacles, and take a dip in one of the larger pools.

Barbados Wildlife Reserve & Grenade Hall Signal Station & Forest

The first of three attractions conveniently grouped in the same location, the Barbados Wildlife Reserve is a miniature animal kingdom set in a 4-acre (1.5 ha) pocket of mahogany forest. Vervet monkeys, shy Brocket deer, porcupines, and agoutis (tropical

rodents) wander freely in the woodlands and provide real wildlife spotting opportunities that delight children. The reserve has an iguana sanctuary decorated with orchids, a walk-through aviary, and a secure caiman pool, as well as a caged python.

Across the parking lot is the Grenade Hall Signal Station, one of half a dozen lookout towers constructed in the early 1800s to keep a watch on slaves working on the plantations. Sentries used semaphores to relay news of disturbances or approaching ships at sea.

Nature trails in the adjacent Grenade Hall Forest offer a glimpse of how Barbados would have appeared to the first settlers. Native trees such as the whitewood, poison tree, and silk cotton tree are marked along the route.

Nearby, **Farley Hill Park** is a favorite picnic spot on the grounds of a ruined plantation house with an arboretum.

Codrington College

A magnificent avenue of slender cabbage palms flanks the driveway leading to the imposing facade of this Anglican theological college. The college was founded in 1743 and financed by a bequest from Christopher Codrington (1668–1710), a one-time governor general of the

Leeward Islands whose family was among the earliest settlers on Barbados. Access to the college buildings is limited, but visitors can view the outside of the Principal's Lodge (the original 17th-century estate house where Codrington was brought up), stroll around the gardens that lead down to Consett Bay, and take a turn around the pretty water-lily pond. Codrington Woods offers a short nature trail through mature woodland, where native silk cotton trees, ironwood and whitewood, and mahogany flourish.

Gun Hill Signal Station

A strategic position 700 feet (213 m) above sea level gives this 1818 signal station unparalleled views across the island and off to the Atlantic. The site was first used as a lookout in 1697 and later became a convalescent station on account of the comfortably cool breezes. At the foot of the hill is the white-washed Military Lion, carved from a single piece of rock by a convalescent British officer.

Harrison's Cave

The island's top sightseeing attraction is a miniature trolley ride around a subterranean cave carved out of the coral limestone by underground rivers. Passengers don hard hats and set off on a nearly mile-long (1.5 km) ride through a series of spooky, theatrically lit caverns festooned with dripping stalactites, rimstones, flowstones, and a spiky forest of stalagmites. The

speleothems (cave formations) take approximately a hundred years to grow a single cubic inch of solid calcite, but eventually the stalactites and stalagmites can join up to create impressive pillars. There is an underground lake fed by a 40-foot (12 m) cascade. The cave lies at one end of the Welchman Hall Gully botanic walk (see p. 307).

EXPERIENCE: Submarine Views

Scuba diving is one way of seeing marine life up close, but if you don't want to get your hair wet, take the **Atlantis Submarine** tour *(tel 246 436 8929, www .barbados.atlantissubmarines.com, $$$$$).* There's a short boat ride from the dock to the dive site, where the 48-passenger minisub awaits. The submarine excursion lasts around 45 minutes and reaches depths of around 150 feet (46 m) with clear views of a coral reef and a shipwreck site. Nighttime dives are also available.

Morgan Lewis Sugar Mill

Hundreds of sugar-grinding mills once dotted the Barbadian landscape, and their crumbling ruins are a common sight along the tiny roads of the sugarcane belt today.

The 250-year-old Morgan Lewis Mill was the last old-style mill to close when it ceased operations in 1944. Placed on the List of 100 Most Endangered Sites in the World by the World Monuments Fund (1996), its weathered stone cone is the largest surviving windmill in the Caribbean. All its working parts are intact, and the

Gun Hill Signal Station

- 298 C3
- Gun Hill, St. George
- 246 429 1358
- Closed Sun.
- $$

Harrison's Cave

- 298 C3
- Welchman Hall, St. Thomas
- 246 438 6640
- $$$$

Morgan Lewis Sugar Mill

- 298 C5
- Cherry Tree Hill, St. Andrew
- 246 422 7429
- $$

Mount Gay Rum Visitors Centre

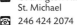 298 B2

✉ Spring Garden Hwy., Bridgetown

☎ 246 425 8757

🕐 Tours every 30 min. (closed Sat. & Sun.)

💲 $$

www.mountgay.com

Portvale Sugar Factory

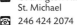 298 B4

✉ St. James

☎ 246 425 1941

🕐 Closed Sun.

💲 Museum $$, including factory tour $$$

old sails and wooden parts have been repaired with South American hardwoods. Climb up to the sail compartment for panoramic views of the surrounding Scotland district.

Mount Gay Rum Visitors Centre

Rum is synonymous with Barbados and has been produced on the island since the 1640s. The Mount Gay distillery is in the north of the island at St. Lucy, but here at the visitor center near Bridgetown Harbour (*Brandons, St. Michael*) the aging, blending, and bottling processes are on display, followed by tastings at the end of the tour.

Brightly painted shops in Holetown's Chattel Village

Tyrol Cot Heritage Village

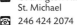 298 C2

✉ Codrington Hill, St. Michael

☎ 246 424 2074

🕐 Closed Sat. & Sun.

💲 $$$

Platinum Coast

The focus of the famed Platinum Coast is **Holetown** (*map 298 B3; 7 miles/11 km N of Bridgetown on Rte. 1*), where English settlers first disembarked in 1627 and established a small village they called Jamestown after King James I. The original name (it was changed to Holetown after a tidal hole close to the beach) is still

preserved in the little coral rock church of St. James', founded in 1629. Many of the island's most elegant hotels and private houses are located here. **Paynes Bay** is a particularly lively section of the beach, with beach bars and water-sports concessions.

Just north of Holetown there's snorkeling in the **Folkestone Underwater Park** (*map 298 B4, tel 246 422 2314*) as well as an aquarium and marine museum. Farther north along the coast is another busy beach strip at **Heyward's Bay,** north of Speightstown.

Portvale Sugar Factory

The sugar factory produces about 14,500 tons of sugar a year. The spring harvest season (Feb.–May) is the best time to visit, when tours plunge into the sweet and steamy atmosphere of the factory floor.

The informative **Sir Frank Hutson Sugar Machinery Museum,** adjacent to the factory, traces the history of the industry.

Tyrol Cot Heritage Village

A single-story stone house painted a jaunty white and orange, Tyrol Cot, built in 1854, was the home of former prime minister Sir Grantley Adams (1898–1971). It is furnished with many family pieces, handcrafted mahogany furniture, paintings, and photographs.

In the gardens the Heritage Village illustrates how the local architectural style developed from a basic slave hut to its gingerbread-trimmed descendants. The cottages now house artisans' workshops, and craft work is on sale. ■

Twin islands with different paces: the rhythms of steel pan and calypso on Trinidad, and the more relaxed beats on Tobago

Trinidad & Tobago

A boy fishes with a hand line off the north coast of Tobago.

Trinidad

A twin-island nation at the southern extent of the Lesser Antilles, Trinidad and Tobago make an odd couple. Boisterous, multicultural Trinidad is the larger of the two and home to the capital, Port of Spain. At 50 by 38 miles (80 by 61 km), it's also the largest of the eastern Caribbean islands, a chunk of South America severed from the Venezuelan coast. Trinidad's industrialized economy has shunned tourism until recently. Tobago, a more typical West Indian escapist haven, offers one of the warmest welcomes in the region.

The Iere (Land of Hummingbirds) of the Arawak was rechristened Trinidad (Trinity) by Christopher Columbus, who sighted three peaks in the southeast of the island on his third voyage to the New World in 1498. Although the island was claimed for Spain, its Amerindian inhabitants kept settlers at bay until 1592, when the Spanish established a toehold, grew a little tobacco, and kept watch over their treasure fleets.

French planters introduced sugar and cocoa plantations in the 18th century, but Britain snatched the island in 1797, taking possession of neighboring Tobago in 1814.

Trinidad's plantations foundered after emancipation in 1838, but the island found the solution by bringing in East Indian indentured laborers. Many stayed after their five-year term, and their descendants now number 40 percent of the island's unusually diverse population of about 1.3 million. Another 40 percent of Trinidadians can trace their roots back to Africa, while the remaining 20 percent are of European, Chinese, Middle Eastern, and South American extraction.

World War II brought Americans to 225 bases around the island. At about this time the first stirrings of steel-pan music were heard in the "panyards" of Port of Spain, as musical Trinidadians recycled old oil drums as musical instruments.

Trinidad and Tobago gained independence from Britain in 1962 and became a republic within the Commonwealth in 1976. Trinidad's oil wealth insulated the island from the tourism development that swept through other islands in the 1960s and '70s, but the 1980s oil slump changed attitudes. Trinidad's tourist industry is still rudimentary (beach hotels are a novelty), but ecotourism is the island's trump card. ■

NOT TO BE MISSED:

The all-out festivities of Carnival in Trinidad **317**

The mating dance of the manakin at Asa Wright Nature Centre, Trinidad **321**

Turtle-watching at Grande Rivière & Matelot Beach, Trinidad **324**

Rain forest hikes in Tobago Forest Reserve **329**

Diving (and limin') in Charlotteville, Tobago **330**

Port of Spain

Trinidad's frenetic capital city, Port of Spain, reflects the island's multicultural heritage. Its teeming streets overflow with shoppers and market stalls, while pompous British colonial architecture rubs shoulders with Muslim mosques, West Indian gingerbread houses, and modern concrete office buildings.

A busy shopping street in Port of Spain. The city is more than 200 years old.

Port of Spain

🅰 314 C4

Visitor Information

✉ Trinidad & Tobago Tourism Development Company, Maritime Centre, 29 Tenth Ave., or booth at Piarco Airport

☎ 868 638 7962

www.gotrinidad andtobago.com

Port of Spain's main downtown thoroughfare is **Frederick Street,** which links Brian Lara Promenade (named for a famous Trinidadian cricket player) with the grassy expanse of Queen's Park Savannah. The southern end of Frederick Street resembles an Eastern bazaar, with its Indian fabric shops spilling out onto the sidewalk.

Midway up the street is **Woodford Square,** a small park bisected by paths where locals meet to "lime" (hang out and chat) on benches under the trees. The entire west side is flanked by the imposing bulk of the **Red House,** seat of the Trinidad and Tobago Parliament. On the south side is the mellow stone **Trinity Cathedral,** dating from the early 19th century. It's worth a visit for its soaring wooden ceiling and patchwork of stained glass (entrance on Queen Street).

A 15-minute walk north on Frederick Street takes you to the **National Museum & Art Gallery.** There's an interesting section on the famous Carnival, complete with sequined-and-plumed costumes, elaborate masks, and a photo montage of Carnival kings and queens. Among the art on display, look for works by Michel

INSIDER TIP:

Port of Spain currently has issues with crime. Be sure to keep cameras, jewelry, and other signs of wealth secure and well out of sight.

—MATT PROPERT
National Geographic photographer

Jean Cazabon, as well as Jackie Hinkson's colorful depictions of Port of Spain in the 1940s.

Frederick Street ends at **Queen's Park Savannah,** a large open space with a circumference of 2.5 miles (4 km) proudly hailed by Trinidadians as the "largest traffic circle in the world." The Savannah plays a central role in the Carnival festivities and doubles as a sports field during the rest of the year. At one time Trinidad's premier racecourse was located in the park.

On the northwest side are seven grand old colonial mansions built in various styles around 1900. They have been nicknamed the **Magnificent Seven,** although several are now looking tired.

To the north is **Emperor Valley Zoo** (*Queen's Park Savannah, tel 868 622 3530, $*), which showcases various South American mammals from capybaras and tapirs to the giant Brazilian otter. Here you can find deer, agoutis, and tree porcupines from Trinidad's forests, and aviaries for wetland birds.

Next door to the zoo are the **Botanical Gardens** (*Queen's Park Savannah*), laid out in the 1820s

by Sir Ralph Woodford. Although many of the magnificent tropical trees are carefully numbered, there are no names. At the far side of the gardens stands the President's House, a sturdy, L-shaped British colonial affair.

Southwest of the Savannah is the **Woodbrook district,** noted for its attractive gingerbread houses; there are also several good restaurants in the area.

Farther west is the **Western Main Road** in the St. James district. It's known as "the city that never sleeps," thanks to its lively nightlife, bars, ice-cream parlors, and street vendors selling *rotis* (Indian-style bread pockets stuffed with chicken, meat, or vegetables). ■

National Museum & Art Gallery

✉ 117 Frederick St.
☎ 868 623 5941
🕐 Closed Sun. a.m. & Mon.

Carnival

Trinidad's famous Carnival originated in the late 18th century with French Roman Catholic settlers, who marked the approach of Lent with elaborate feasts and parties or masquerades (which, shortened to "mas," is the traditional Trinidadian word for Carnival). The buildup to Carnival begins in the New Year with calypso and panorama (steel band) competitions around the island. The main event kicks off in Port of Spain the Friday before Lent. For calypsonians, the big night is Dimanche Gras (Sunday), while the main parade, J'Ouvert, hits the streets at 4 a.m. on Monday (it's not called "daybreak" or *j'ouvert* for nothing!) Carnival culminates on Shrove Tuesday as the Parade of Bands gathers on Queen's Park Savannah. Anyone can join in Carnival (or "play mas"), whether it's just dancing in the street or signing up with a mas camp and renting a fabulous Carnival costume. The tourist office carries details and a countdown to Carnival on its website (*www.gotrinidadandtobago.com*).

Cricket in the Caribbean

Cricket occupies a unique position in the Caribbean region. In many countries, particularly former British colonies such as Jamaica, Barbados, Antigua, and Trinidad, the sport is followed with a passion that verges on the religious. But, more importantly, it is one of the very few successful cooperative endeavors in a region where most other attempts at integration have failed.

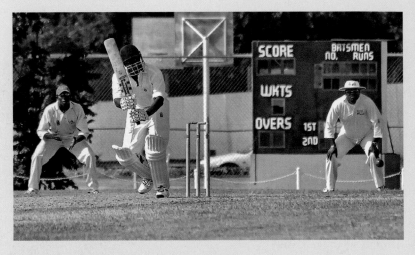

A cricket batsman plays a shot during a match in Barbados.

19th-Century Origins

The story of the development of West Indian cricket is a fascinating one, and it says much about the importance of the sport in the region that one of the best accounts of its development, *A History of West Indian Cricket* (1988) should have been written by no less a person than Michael Manley, former prime minister of Jamaica.

When cricket was introduced by the British, it was mostly played by army officers and plantation owners, but in the sweltering heat they preferred to bat rather than bowl (pitch), and it was the slaves and sons of slaves who were drafted in to bowl for them. After emancipation a network of cricket clubs sprang up, and it soon became clear that the descendants of the former slaves were incredibly good at cricket.

The first English team toured the West Indies in 1895, and in 1897 the first All–West Indies team was picked to play against another visiting English team. The first tour of England by a West Indies team took place in 1900, but the great turning point came in the 1920s, when the West Indies were granted Test status—that is, the right to compete on the international cricket circuit.

The West Indian team soon gained a reputation for stylish and exuberant playing, bringing a free-flowing athleticism and sense of humor to the game and earning them the nickname of the "calypso cricketers."

During the 1930s West Indian cricket was dominated by the presence of George Headley, judged to be the greatest West Indian batsman ever and globally among the six best of all time. He has a unique place in Caribbean history in that he personified black excellence in a white-dominated sport, a symbol of self-worth for the adoring crowds. During the postwar years the game was dominated by three Barbados players—Frank Worrell, Everton Weekes, and Clive Walcott. They were followed by one of the great West Indian stars of all time, the legendary Garfield (Gary) Sobers. The Sobers era, from 1960 to 1974, witnessed the highest level attained by the West Indies up to that date, during which they played 67 tests, of which they won 21, lost 16, drew 29, and tied 1.

The Golden Age & Later Challenges

The golden age of West Indies cricket, however, was yet to come. This was the decade, from 1976 to 1986, when they dominated the cricketing world. Out of 17 test matches they won 15, drew 1, and lost 1—a remarkable record of victories in any sport. They achieved a level of preeminence that was so great that opposing sides were almost beaten before the game began, so formidable was their reputation.

Since then the West Indies team has struggled to find its footing in a cricketing world dominated by a resurgent England and the southern hemisphere nations.

Commentators believe that this malaise will pass, and that the region will continue to produce great cricketers such as Vivian Richards (from Antigua), Clive Lloyd (Guyana), and more recently Brian Lara, who comes from Trinidad. But others worry that the ascent of alternative sports will eclipse Caribbean cricket. Soccer, basketball, and track and field are becoming increasingly popular among the younger generations. Baseball has long been the national sport of Cuba, the Dominican Republic, and Puerto Rico, with many Dominicans and Puerto Ricans playing major league baseball—and earning big money—in the United States.

Nonetheless, the local fans were out in force for the 2007 World Cup, hosted by cricketing nations across the region. On many Caribbean islands an impromptu game of cricket will spring up anywhere that the youngsters can find a few sticks to act as stumps and a tennis ball to practice with, be it on the beach or the back streets. The aspirations and hopes of generations have become embedded in a game that symbolizes a rare sense of unity among Caribbean peoples.

EXPERIENCE: Catch a Match

Whether you are a diehard cricket fan or just along for the Caribbean-flavored fun of the sport, catching a match is easy. Most Caribbean islands have a sports complex that puts on seasonal games at reasonable prices year-round.

In Trinidad, the **Queen's Park Oval** (94 Tragarete Road, Port of Spain, tel 868 622 3787, www.qpcc.com) is one of the many official venues of the West Indies team, as well as of district and regional lineups. The same is true of the locally dubbed "mecca of cricket," Barbados's **Kensington Oval** in Bridgetown (Fontabelle, tel 246 274 1200,

http://kensingtonoval.org), where you can also attend women's and youth tournaments. The **Antigua Recreation Ground** in St. John's, Antigua (Factory Road, tel 268 462 9090), hosts local, regional, and international matches and offers a scenic atmosphere that satisfies both sports enthusiasts and tag-along tourists.

For an insider's tour of the history of the game as it has developed in the islands, visit the **West Indies Cricket Heritage Museum** at the Grenada National Stadium (Queen's Park, St. George's, tel 473 437 2007, http://grenada stadium.com, $).

Around the North

Trinidad's flora, fauna, and waterfront life can be viewed via a scenic looping drive around the northern third of the island. Bird-watchers in particular will find much to enjoy at the Asa Wright Nature Centre and at the Caroni Bird Sanctuary, home to spectacular scarlet ibis. History buffs can explore Trinidad's contributions to World War II in Chaguaramas.

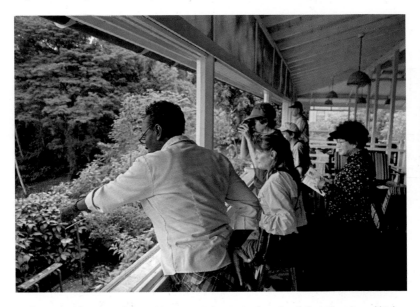

At the Asa Wright Nature Centre, visitors can see hundreds of species of plants, insects, and birds.

The mountains of the Northern Range stretch right across the north of Trinidad, dividing the coast from the central plain. This is where you'll find the island's two highest peaks, **El Cerro del Aripo** (3,083 feet/940 m) and **El Tucuche** (3,075 feet/936 m). The range is cloaked in a lush tangle of rain forest that is home to many of Trinidad's 430 bird species, 630 species of butterflies, and 2,300 varieties of flowering plants. Two roads cross the mountains: the **Saddle Road,** which links Port of Spain and the beach at Maracas Bay; and the **Blanchisseuse Road** from Arima, which can also be accessed from Lopinot. The roads form the basis of a good circular day tour out of Port of Spain, heading counterclockwise to Arima, then up to the Asa Wright Nature Centre, north to Blanchisseuse, and along the coast to Maracas before returning over the Saddle Road.

West from Port of Spain is the **Chaguaramas Peninsula** (*map 314 C4*), Port of Spain's busy weekend playground on the Gulf of Paria. The beaches are not particularly enticing, though there's a man-made sandy strand at **Chagville**, and **Macqueripe Beach** on the north coast has been spruced up with hiking and biking trails. More appealing is a boat trip out to the holiday islands off the tip of the peninsula, colonized by vacation homes and a popular stop-off with sailors.

Asa Wright Nature Centre

A visit here provides an unmissable opportunity to sample Trinidad's myriad and colorful birdlife and plant life; more than 170 species of birds have been recorded in the Arima Valley, where the nature center sits at a comfortable 1,200 feet (365 m) above sea level, hemmed in by the rain forest.

A series of trails explores the 200-acre (80 ha) estate, and guided walks provide a window on the rain forest, where leaf cutter ants share the paths and blue morpho butterflies flutter past like elegant turquoise magic carpets. The mating dance of the white-bearded manakin makes an entertaining sideshow, accompanied by what sounds like a salvo of Chinese firecrackers as the male birds snap their wings with a loud popping noise. For a comfortable seat overlooking the main event, settle down on the veranda at the lodge to watch hummingbirds, honeycreepers, tanagers, and trogons drop in to snack on sugar water or fresh fruits.

Guests staying a minimum of three nights at the center qualify for a visit to the world's most accessible colony of oilbirds. Known as guacharos ("one who wails" in Amerindian), these cave-dwelling birds feed their young on oily fruits such as palm, camphor, and laurels. Guacharos were prized for their fat, which was used for cooking and fueling oil lamps. They are now a protected species.

Bring sensible footwear as the trails can be muddy and slippery, as well as a bathing suit for a dip in the swimming hole, and adequate supplies of mosquito repellent.

Caroni Bird Sanctuary

This 40-acre (16 ha) wetlands preserve in the Caroni Swamp is renowned for the evening flight of the scarlet ibis returning to

**Asa Wright
Nature Centre**
🗺 314 D4
✉ Arima Valley
☎ 868 667 5162
🕐 Guided tours daily, by reservation only, 10:30 a.m. & 1:30 p.m.
💲 $$$
www.asawright.org

**Caroni Bird
Sanctuary**
🗺 314 C4
✉ Uriah Butler Hwy.
💲 $$$

G.I. Memories

A 20-minute drive west of the Port of Spain, the **Chaguaramas Military History & Aviation Museum** (*Western Main Road, Chaguaramas, tel 868 634 4391, closed Sun., $*) is sure to appeal to military history enthusiasts. Leave plenty of time to ramble around the extensive collections of military hardware and memorabilia, much of which relates to the U.S. forces stationed here during World War II. There are also displays devoted to conflicts dating back to the native Amerindians and Spanish conquistadors, and Trinidad's short-lived coup by Muslim extremists in 1990.

mangrove roosts just before sunset. Flat-bottom boat tours leave from the dock (follow the signs from the highway) at about 4:30 p.m., puttering through tree-lined waterways to the heart of the swamp. Along the way you can spot caimans, four-eyed

Lopinot Complex

A twisting scenic route leads up into the Northern Range, passing through small villages with burgeoning gardens and flapping Hindu prayer flags, to the settlement of Lopinot, founded by French cocoa planter Charles Joseph, Comte de Lopinot, in 1806. The count's simple wooden estate house contains a one-room museum surrounded by magnificent saaman trees, and there's a cocoa barn and old slave quarters.

Lopinot is one of the main centers of *parang*, the Spanish-based traditional music of Christmas in Trinidad. Introduced from Venezuela, parang is played on tiny, four-stringed *cuatro* guitars.

Lopinot Complex

🅰 314 D4

✉ Lopinot Valley

fish, mangrove roots festooned with oysters, maybe even a silky anteater, and 186 species of birds from the not-so-common common potoo, a nocturnal bird that is devilishly difficult to spot, to the egrets, herons, and scampering willets feeding on the mudbanks among a lunatic orchestra of fiddler crabs sawing away with their outsize pincers.

About 10,000 scarlet ibis inhabit the sanctuary, nesting between March and September. Ibis chicks don't achieve their brilliant red-orange adult plumage for two to three years. Scarlet ibis are now protected from hunters, who once prized the feathers for Carnival costumes.

About half an hour before sunset the ibis begin to knife through the sky, iridescent red darts congregating in the dark mangrove greenery until it blazes like a Christmas tree caught in the last rays of the sun.

Maracas Bay & the Northwest Coast

Protected by steep wooded headlands and a stately border of palm trees, Maracas Bay (*map 314 D4*) is Trinidad's most

INSIDER TIP:

Just east of Maracas Bay is Blanchisseuse, a small fishing village where the days revolve around the tides and the fish. Seeing locals living their daily routine provides real insight into West Indian culture.

—JENNIFER ALLARD
National Geographic contributor

popular beach and attracts the crowds on weekends. This is the place to sample traditional shark-and-bake, a fish sandwich served with hot pepper–and–tamarind sauce, served up from palm-thatched vendors' stalls.

Five miles (8 km) east of Maracas there's another curve of fine white sand at **Las Cuevas**, which takes its name from the caves (*cuevas* in Spanish) along the shore. Vacation homes dot the coast road from there to the fishing village of **Blanchisseuse.** Neighboring **Damier Beach** is a favorite destination for windsurfers.

Northeast Coast

The rugged and windswept northeast coast lies well off the beaten track but richly rewards any visitor who ventures up here. Take the Toco Main Road north up the island's eastern shore, passing the safe swim-

an escapist break. In season (March–Aug.), with a permit, you can watch turtles nesting on the beach (see sidebar p. 324).

Gasparee Caves

A group of five small islands lies off the tip of the Chaguaramas Peninsula, colonized by holiday homes. A 15-minute boat ride from the mainland, **Gasparee Grande Island**

A secluded beach near the fishing village of Blanchisseuse

ming beach at **Salybia;** bodysurfers prefer to congregate at **Balandra Bay.** At Toco, make a right to the **Point Galera Lighthouse** for stupendous, blustery views across to neighboring Tobago from Trinidad's most easterly point.

The laid-back fishing village of **Grande Rivière,** on the north shore, has a few low-key hotels, guesthouses, and restaurants for

is renowned for its caves. It's also a popular picnic spot, and you can ramble around its old military fortifications. Inexpensive water taxis depart from several marinas along Western Main Road (20 minutes from Port of Spain). Permission to visit the caves must be obtained from the Chaguaramas Development Authority *(tel 868 634 4227).* ■

Around the East & South

A journey around Trinidad's eastern and southern coasts takes you to a number of good beaches and wildlife viewing sites, including the fine Pointe-à-Pierre Wildfowl Trust. In the southwest, the vast reservoir of bitumen known as Pitch Lake is an inky curiosity.

The Eastern Main Road from the town of Arima cuts across to Trinidad's Atlantic coast and a long palm-fringed sandy shore stretching down to the southeast tip of the island at Galeota Point. There are good beaches at **Manzanilla Bay** (named for the green, poisonous machineel trees behind the beach), **Cocos Bay,** and **Mayaro Bay.**

Inland is the 3,840-acre (1,554 ha) **Nariva Swamp,** home to a fantastic variety of wildlife. To visit the Nariva's **Bush Bush Wildlife Sanctuary,** get a permit from the Wildlife Section of the Ministry of Agriculture *(tel 868 622 5114)* or approach an accredited tour operator (see sidebar opposite).

On the west coast, just north of Trinidad's second largest city and oil center San Fernando, is the **Pointe-à-Pierre Wildfowl Trust** *(map 314 C2; call ahead, tel 868 628 4145, $).* Somewhat bizarrely located in the shadow of a vast (and rather smelly) refinery, the trust's wetlands and forest trails provide remarkable bird-watching opportunities.

Pitch Lake

Around Otaheite Bay from San Fernando is the Pitch Lake at La Brea *(map 314 C2),* one of Trinidad's most famous (but least exciting) sights. Probably the world's largest natural bitumen reservoir, the 100-acre (40 ha) "lake" looks like a massive parking lot, although predatory guides aim to liven up a visit with a fund of anecdotes (fix a fee in advance). The gloopy black tar was used to caulk the hulls of conquistadores' galleons and to pave the streets of Paris and London, as well as Port of Spain, where it was also employed as fuel for 19th-century streetlamps until residents complained about the fumes. A small museum *(tel 868 651 1232)* outlines the lake's history. ∎

Turtle Watch

Endangered leatherback turtles lay their eggs on the beaches of eastern and northern Trinidad during the March-to-August breeding season. To see them, take the Toco Main Road, found beyond Arima and Valencia, which reaches the turtle beaches at Matura Bay and then rounds the tip of the island to the beautiful, undeveloped north coast beaches at Grande Rivière and Matelot. (It is about a two-hour drive from Port of Spain to Toco.) The turtle beaches are strictly monitored and permits are required from the Forestry Department *(tel 868 668 2518),* which issues a limited number per day. Local guides can be arranged through **Nature Seekers,** Matura *(tel 868 668-7337, www.natureseekers.org, donations),* and the **Nature Tour Guides Association,** Grande Rivière *(tel 868 670 4257).*

EXPERIENCE: Birding in Trinidad

The first thrill was a green honeycreeper, followed by a ravenous flock of pushy little banana-quits. A jaunty red cap and flash of yellow breast announced the fleeting visit of a ruby topaz hummingbird, to be replaced by a common or garden (for the Asa Wright Centre) mot mot. Breakfast time at the bird tables, 1,200 foot (365 m) up in the Arima Valley, is a smorgasbord of tropical fruit for the star attractions and the dawn of another magical day in the rain forest for assorted onlookers gathered on the veranda, binoculars and birding guides at the ready.

The Arawak didn't call Trinidad "The Land of the Hummingbird" for nothing. Sixteen different species of these tiny jewel-like creatures flit through the island's woodlands and gardens. In total some 433 different bird species flourish in and around Trinidad's notably diverse natural habitats, which range from rain forest and littoral woodland to mudflats and mangrove swamplands. Many more visit regularly as both Trinidad and Tobago lie at a migratory crossing point.

Birding Sites

A former cocoa and coffee estate high in the lush Northern Range, the **Asa Wright Nature Centre** (see p. 321) is legendary in tropical bird-watching circles. The New York Zoological Society established a research station here in 1949, and enthusiasts continue to be dazzled by the forest's birdlife.

A few miles west along the Northern Range as the toucan flies, **Pax Guest House, Tunapuna** (tel 868 662 4084, www.paxguest house.com) is another popular pilgrimage with birders. Set in the tranquil grounds, Pax makes an excellent base for woodland hikes, and the gardens attract trogons, tanagers, and the tufted coquette, a glorious little hummingbird the size of a large moth and the third smallest bird in the world.

Less than an hour's drive from Port of Spain, **Caroni Swamp**'s (see pp. 321–322) dense tangle of mangrove waterways is navigable only by boat. The rich, silty waters, fed by drift from the Orinoco Delta in Venezuela, support numerous waterfowl and wading birds, while pride of place goes to Trinidad's national bird, the scarlet ibis. The ideal time to visit is late afternoon, when the ibis return to roost. Make boat trip reservations with Caroni expert Winston Nanan of **Nanan's Eco Tours** (tel 868 645 1305, www .nananecotours.com, $$).

Farther south down the west coast, 120 bird species have been recorded at the **Pointe-à-Pierre Wildfowl Trust** (see opposite). Its lakes are popular with whistling ducks, cormorants, and gallinules, amongst others. The Ramsar-accredited **Nariva Swamp,** on the Atlantic coast, is Trinidad's largest freshwater wetlands area, interspersed with littoral forest, mangroves, and flooded marshlands. **Limeland Tours**

A male green honeycreeper in Trinidad's Northern Range

(tel 868 668 1356, www .limeland-tours.com, $$$$$) leads kayak expeditions into the swamp, where caiman and manatees may be seen and hawks, kites, and osprey wheel overhead. On higher ground, the **Bush Bush Wildlife Sanctuary** is a haven for red-bellied macaws, Amazonian parrots, manakins, and cascaras, as well as red howler monkeys and anacondas.

Wherever you go bird-watching in Trinidad, mosquito repellent and binoculars are essential, while a copy of Richard ffrench's illustrated *A Guide to the Birds of Trinidad and Tobago* is an excellent investment.

Tobago

Trinidad's little sister island, Tobago, also broke away from South America (several million years ago in this case), but in look and feel it's more similar to the Windward Islands in the north. Just over 20 miles (32 km) from the hustle and bustle of Trinidad, Tobago is a mountainous green oasis of charm and calm, where the Trinidadians come to relax and the Tobagonians take pride in their easygoing hospitality and unspoiled natural surroundings.

Playing reggae in the village of Charlotteville

It's probable that Christopher Columbus sighted Tobago when he discovered Trinidad in 1498. He called it Bellaforma ("beautiful form"), although the original Amerindian name (derived from the word for "tobacco") has stuck. The Dutch, English, and French all laid claim to the island, which changed hands more than 20 times and developed into one of the richest sugar islands in the region. Secured by the British in 1814 and administered with the Windward Island group, Tobago found that its fortunes waned after emancipation in the 1830s. It was declared bankrupt in 1888 and appended to neighboring Trinidad. After a century as an impoverished rural backwater, Tobago now has a small but flourishing tourist industry, concentrated on the northwest coast

The cooperative tradition of "Len' Hand" is alive and well on Tobago. If you see villagers hauling nets to the beach, go ahead and lend a hand.

—CHARLES KULANDER
National Geographic Traveler
magazine writer

between ANR Robinson International Airport and Plymouth.

For a mere strip of an island at 20 by 5.5 miles (32 x 9 km), Tobago packs a punch. A central spine of mountains rises in the east and falls sharply through the rain forest to the broad bays of the southern windward coast and sheltered north shore. Here at the eastern end of the island, wooden *pirogues* from the villages of Speyside and Charlotteville ferry scuba enthusiasts out to Tobago's famous coral reefs. Enriched by nutrients swept along on the Guyana Current from Venezuela's Orinoco River, the reef sites boast 44 species of coral, including the world's biggest brain coral (12 feet by 16 feet/3.5 m x 5 m), a colony of giant manta rays, and occasional visitations by black-tipped, hammerhead and huge plankton-eating whale sharks. The western end of the island is flat and covered in coconut palms, with stunning white sand beaches created by offshore reefs. ■

Around the Island

Tobago is an ideal island to explore if you don't want to feel pressured to pack too much into a single excursion. The island's compact size ensures that no single trip is too long, and the laid-back atmosphere encourages you to linger along the way, pausing to admire the view, stop for a swim, or chat with local fishermen mending their nets on the shore.

Scarborough

The majority of the 54,000 Tobagonians (most of African descent) live in the island's west end and in the pint-size capital

One of Crown Point settlement's beautiful beaches

of Scarborough *(map 327 B1; visitor information, Doretta's Court, 5126 Mt. Marie, tel 868 639 2125, www.gotrinidadand tobago.com)* on the south coast.

This unpretentious town climbs steeply from Rockly Bay into a circlet of hills overlooked by **Fort George.** The Lower Town is a melee of fish sellers and noisy market stalls. Take a break from the town's hustle and bustle in the charming **Botanic Gardens** *(Greenside St.),* once part of a sugar estate, where the grassy slopes are planted with poinciana and poui trees, spreading Indian almonds, a mango grove, and a huge silk cotton tree near the gazebo.

Scarborough's few remaining colonial buildings are found in the Upper Town. On the way up to Fort George, look for **Gun Bridge,** with its black metal railings made out of old rifle barrels. The fort dates from the 1780s and affords a commanding view along the southeastern coast. The **Tobago Museum** *(84 Fort St., tel 868 639 3970, closed Sat. & Sun.)* is next door. It has a marvelous collection of Amerindian finds including tools, religious objects, and pottery adorned with animal motifs.

INSIDER TIP:

If you're heading to Charlotteville on the northern coast, be sure to take the walk over the headland to Pirate's Bay, one of the most scenic and secluded beaches on the island.

—HEATHER BRADY
National Geographic contributor

Crown Point

The Crown Point settlement occupies the western tip of Tobago, with the airport and a handful of hotels and guesthouses set on Store Bay. Behind the scrap of beach, where fishing boats are drawn up on the sand, is a clutch of stands selling crafts and souvenirs. There are bars and snack shops. On Sandy Point you will find the low coral rock battlements of 18th-century **Fort Milford,** which now contain a small garden facing Pigeon Point, a classic Caribbean beach bordered by leaning palms. Offshore is **Buccoo Reef,** Tobago's most visited underwater attraction, although it has suffered somewhat from the glass-bottom boat crowds.

Around the Northern Coast

Beach hotels are scattered along the road to **Plymouth** *(map 327 B2),* where the ruins of Fort James are still guarded by antique cannons. The drive through the hills behind the coast to **Parlatuvier** is charming, and you'll find fine secluded beaches down dirt tracks at King Peter's Bay, Englishman's Bay, and Bloody Bay before the road cuts up into the rain forest (see sidebar) and down to the Atlantic coast at **Roxborough.**

Just short of Roxborough, a side road leads to **Argyle Waterfall**

EXPERIENCE: Hiking in the Tobago Forest Reserve

Tobago's eastern highlands are cloaked in fabulously unspoiled rain forest. The **Main Ridge Forest Reserve** was established back in 1764 in order to protect a tract of native forest from rapacious sugar planters. It is the Western Hemisphere's oldest legally protected forest, so perhaps with this degree of preservation it is not surprising that there are very few established trails that can be followed without a guide.

An exception is the 2-mile (3 km) **Gilpin Trace,** which loops off the Roxburgh-Parlatuvier cross-island road.

If you park at the trailhead, the Trace loops off the road down to The Hut and it's a simple hike back up.

Otherwise you can hike into the heart of the reserve with an experienced guide from **Harris' Jungle Tours** *(tel 868 639 0513, www.harris-jungle-tours.com, $$$$$),* or Peter Cox of **Tobago Nature Tours** *(tel 868 751 5822, www.tobagonaturetours .com, $$$$$).* Cox also offers night safaris in the rain forest, when armadillos, opossums, bats, owls, and other beasties that go bump, screech, and howl in the night come out.

Overlooking Man O' War Bay on Tobago's northern coast

(map 327 C2). From the parking area in an old cocoa plantation, it's a shady 15-minute walk upriver to the falls, which bounce down a series of ledges on the cliff face to a swimming hole.

Tobago Homage

A Tobago resident since 1979, German-born sculptor Luise Kimme draws much of her inspiration directly from the island and its people. Her life-size Tobagonian figures are carved from whole tree trunks or cast in bronze, and she has created the **Kimme Museum** *(tel 868 639 0257, open Sun. 10 a.m. –2 p.m. or by appt., $)* to display her work in the hills above the Mount Irvine Hotel. As well as her sculpture, Kimme's murals decorate The Castle, a fanciful terra-cotta and white stucco home-studio (which bears more than a passing resemblance to a Hindu temple). You can see more of her work in the Church of Transfiguration at Black Rock.

Speyside and Charlotteville flank the northeastern end of Tobago. Speyside borders Tyrrel's Bay along the Atlantic coast, overlooking the islets of Little Tobago *(map 327 D2)* and Goat Island. **Little Tobago** is a seabird sanctuary and a breeding ground for frigatebirds, boobies, and tropic birds. Boat trips run from the jetty, where dive operators and glass-bottom boats depart with visitors for the offshore reefs.

Charlotteville, on the Caribbean side, is a sleepy little fishing village and dive center on the broad expanse of **Man O'War Bay.** Here, old wooden houses nestle beneath giant breadfruit trees, and the stone seawall is shaded by sea grape trees.

A 15-minute walk to the east of the village takes you to **Pirate's Bay,** a good beach. ■

Travelwise

Scooting around Bridgetown, Barbados

TRAVELWISE

GENERAL INFORMATION

Airlines

Although price is a factor in your choice of airline, check also on the number of stops (flights to smaller islands often include one stop at a hub destination) and frequency of flights. No-frills airlines usually have a limited number of flights.
Major airlines: American Airlines, tel 800/433-7300, www.aa.com; JetBlue, tel 800/538-2583, www.jetblue.com; United Airlines, tel 800/538-2929, www.united.com; US Airways, tel 800/428-4322, www.usairways.com
Smaller airlines: American Eagle, tel 800/433-7300, www.aa.com; Air Sunshine, tel 800/327-8900, www.airsunshine.com; Caribbean Airlines, tel 800/920-4225, www.caribbean-airlines.com; LIAT, tel 888/844-5428 or 268/480-5601, www.liatairline.com; Spirit Air, 800/772-7117, www.spiritair.com; and Winair, tel 866/466-0410, www.fly-winair.com.

Climate

Temperatures average 77°–86°F (25°–30°C) year-round. Northeasterly trade winds are fairly constant and provide some respite from the heat and humidity. The higher the latitude, the cooler the temperature, especially from November to January. May to October is the wettest period, and the hurricane season is July to October. The Weather Channel Connection gives up-to-date forecasts, tel 900/932-8437, www.weather.com.

Driving

Driving regulations vary, so consult the Getting Around section for each island. As a rule, current and former British dependencies drive on the left-hand side; French and Dutch on the right. Some islands require you to have a temporary visitor license (or local license). These are generally available from rental companies, or contact the local police station or tourist office. The state of main roads is good, although local roads can be poor. Take a road map with you.

Electricity

On most islands 110 and 120 volts AC supply is used, and outlets are identical to those in the United States. On the French and Dutch islands, and those with a British background, you may need an adapter for U.S. appliances. When making a reservation, ask your hotel which voltage is used. Most hotels have adapters.

Festivals & Events

These are listed by island in this section. Contact local tourist offices and websites for more detailed festival information.

Insurance

A comprehensive travel insurance policy is a useful precaution and will include cancellation, interruption, default, trip delay, and full medical coverage.

Time Zones

Most islands are on Atlantic Standard Time (AST), which is Eastern Standard Time (EST) plus one hour (GMT -4). AST is not affected by daylight saving time (DST). Jamaica and the Cayman Islands are on EST with no daylight saving, and the Turks and Caicos Islands are on EST with daylight saving.

Tipping

Rules for tipping vary, so check your bill for a service charge. If no service charge is included in the bill, leave a tip of 10 to 15 percent, depending on service. Tipping can be an important source of income.

Travelers with Disabilities

The Caribbean travel industry is becoming more aware of the needs of travelers with disabilities, but the region can prove quite a challenging destination for those with mobility problems. One area where compliance with ADA (Americans with Disabilities Act) regulations is vastly improved is the cruise sector, with wheelchair accessible cabins and facilities for assisted embarkation/disembarkation. The U.S. Virgin Islands and Puerto Rico are also good destinations. When making reservations, ask specific questions concerning your needs and give airlines plenty of advance warning. Better still, consult a specialist agency such as Connie George Travel Associates (tel 610/532-0989 or 888/532-0989, www.cgta.com).

 JAMAICA

PLANNING YOUR TRIP

Arrival/Departure

Visitors heading for Montego Bay, Ocho Rios, Negril, and other resorts on the north coast arrive at Sangster International Airport, 2 miles (3 km) east of Montego Bay. For Kingston and Port Antonio, use Norman Manley International Airport, 13 miles (21 km) from Kingston. Small aircraft can access the new Ian Fleming International Airport at Ocho Rios.

Air Jamaica, tel 800/523-5585, www.airjamaica.com, as well as American Airlines, JetBlue, Northwest, US Airways, and Air Canada provide service from gateways such as New York, Boston, Chicago, Miami, Atlanta, Baltimore, and Toronto. Numerous charter airlines also fly from the United States and Canada. Regional services are provided by Cayman Airways, and Caribbean Airlines. There are also small domestic airstrips in Negril, Port Antonio, and Tinson Pen (near the center of Kingston). They are served by Jamaica Air shuttle, tel 876/906-9026, www.jamaicaairshuttle.com.

Departure tax is: J$100 (approx. US$27).

Entry Requirements
A valid passport is required, along with onward or return ticket.

Festivals & Events
January Accompong Maroon Festival; Jamaica Jazz and Blues Festival (Montego Bay)
February Bob Marley Week
March–April Carnival celebrations in Kingston, Montego Bay, and Ocho Rios
May Calabash International Literary Festival
June Ocho Rios International Jazz Festival
July Reggae Sumfest (Montego Bay), Portland Jerk Festival
October International Marlin Tournament (Port Antonio)

National holidays include New Year's Day (Jan. 1), Ash Wednesday, Good Friday, Easter Monday, Labor Day (4th Mon. in May), Emancipation Day (Aug. 1), Independence Day (Aug. 6), National Heroes Day (3rd Mon. in Oct.), Christmas Day, and Boxing Day (Dec. 26).

GETTING AROUND
Car Rental
Major companies include Avis, tel 876/952-0762, www.avis.com; Budget, tel 876/924-8762, www.budget.com; Island Car Rentals, tel 876/926-8012, www.islandcarrentals.com; and Thrifty, tel 876/952-1126, www.thrifty.com. To rent a car you must be 25 years old with a valid driver's license and major credit card. Driving is on the left.

Although major roads are generally good, you may encounter stray goats, dogs, chickens, erratic cyclists, pedestrians—and potholes. At intersections, traffic coming from the right has priority, but don't rely on this. Always use your horn when passing, in case the driver in front suddenly swerves to avoid a pothole. There are few good signs, and you can rely on only major towns and resorts being shown. In towns, watch out for No Entry signs, which are often below hood level.

Public Transportation
Local bus timetables are erratic, and the buses are overcrowded. Minibuses travel on many of the same routes and may be slightly quicker, but are equally overcrowded. Fares are inexpensive. Buses or minibuses can be flagged down along the roadside.

Taxis are widely available and most are unmetered: Agree on a fare before setting off (ask at your hotel for advice). Licensed taxis display red PPV (Public Passenger Vehicle) plates; avoid unlicensed cabs. Route taxis (or shared taxis) ply set routes around large towns or between popular destinations. The Jamaican Union of Travellers Association (JUTA) operates a fleet of tourist buses and taxis, and are often contracted for ground transfers.

PRACTICAL ADVICE
Emergencies
Ambulance or fire: tel 110.
Police: tel 119.

Telephones
The area code is 876.

Tourist Information
Kingston: 64 Knutsford Blvd., tel 876/929-9200 or 800/233-4582 (U.S.), fax 876/929-9375, www.visitjamaica.com.

U.S. & Canada Offices
Florida: 5201 Blue Lagoon Drive, Suite 670, Miami, FL 33126, tel 305/665-0557 or 800/233-4582, fax 305/666-7239.
Toronto: 303 Eglinton Ave. East, Suite 200, Toronto, ON M4P IL3, tel 416/482-7850 or 800-465-2624, fax 416/482-1730.

■ CAYMAN ISLANDS

PLANNING YOUR TRIP
Arrival/Departure
The Owen Roberts International Airport on Grand Cayman is the main point of entry, with direct flights every day from Miami. The national flag carrier is Cayman Airways, which has direct flights from Miami, Tampa, Fort Lauderdale, Chicago, Boston, Houston, Havana (Cuba), and Kingston and Montego Bay (Jamaica).

Other carriers include American Airlines, Delta, Northwest, and US Airways, with departures from Atlanta, Charlotte, Chicago, Detroit, Philadelphia, New York, Miami and Tampa. Continental flies out of Newark. Air Canada has a nonstop service from Toronto.

Cayman Airways Express provides daily small aircraft services to the sister islands of Cayman Brac and Little Cayman. Charter operator Island Air, tel 345/949-5252;

www.islandaircayman.com, also provides flights to both islands from Grand Cayman.

Entry Requirements
All visitors including U.S. citizens require a valid passport and onward or return ticket.

Festivals & Events
January Taste of Cayman Food & Wine Festival; Cayman Cookout (Ritz Carlton Hotel)
April Cayman Batabano Carnival
November Pirates Week
December Jazz Fest

National holidays include New Year's Day (Jan. 1), Ash Wednesday (Feb. or March), Good Friday, Easter Monday (March or April), Discovery Day (mid-May), the Queen's Birthday (mid-June), Constitution Day (1st Mon. in July), Christmas Day, and Boxing Day (Dec. 26).

GETTING AROUND
Car Rental
Rental companies (or the police station) will issue a temporary driving permit (US$7.50) on production of a valid driver's license. Reputable companies include Avis, tel 345/949-2468, www.avis cayman.com; Budget Rent-A-Car, tel 345/949-5605, www.budget cayman.com; Coconut Car Rentals, tel 1-800/941-4562, www .coconutcarrentals.com; Dollar Rent-A-Car, tel 345/949-4790, www.dollarrac.com; Thrifty Car Rental, tel 345/949-0064, www .cayman.com.ky/com/thrifty.

Driving is on the left. Speed limits of between 20 and 50 mph (30 and 80 kph) are strictly enforced. Seat belts are required. Avoid driving into George Town during rush hours.

On Little Cayman, hotels provide free bicycles for guests, and this is just about all you need

to explore the western end of the island. Rental cars are available from McLaughlin Rentals, tel 345/948-1000, in Blossom Village if you want to reach the more remote beaches on the eastern end of the island. Hotels also offer a drop-off/pickup service to Point of Sands.

On Cayman Brac, Brac Rent-A-Car, tel 345/948-1515, has cars and Jeeps; B & S Motor Ventures, tel 345/948-1646, www.bandsmv .com, supplies cars, Jeeps, scooters, and bicycles.

Public Transportation
Grand Cayman: Minibus services operate from a terminal by the Public Library in downtown George Town. Routes include a service to Seven Mile Beach. Taxis are available from the airport, all resorts, and the taxi stand by the cruise-ship dock in George Town.

Little Cayman and Cayman Brac have no bus services, but taxis are available for transfers or sightseeing tours.

PRACTICAL ADVICE
Emergencies
Grand Cayman
Police, fire, ambulance: tel 911. Royal Cayman Islands Police: tel 345/949-4222. George Town Hospital: tel 345/949-8600.
Little Cayman
Police: tel 345/926-0639. Clinic: tel 345/948-0072.
Cayman Brac
Emergency: tel 911. Hospital: tel 345/948-2225.

Telephones
The area code is 345.

Tourist Information
Cayman Islands Department of Tourism, Regatta Office Park, Windward 3, West Bay Road, P.O. Box 67 GT, George Town, Grand Cayman, tel 345/949-0623,

fax 345/949-4053, www.cayman islands.ky

U.S. & Canada Offices
New York: Empire State Building, 350 Fifth Avenue, Suite 1801, New York, NY 10118, tel 212/889-9009 or 1-877/4CAY-MAN, fax 212/889-9125.
Toronto: 1200 Bay Street, Suite 1101, Toronto, ON M5R 2A5, tel 416/485-1550 or 1-800/263-5805, fax 416/485-0832.
.

■ TURKS & CAICOS

PLANNING YOUR TRIP
Arrival/Departure
There are international airports on Providenciales, Grand Turk, and South Caicos. Providenciales is the main international gateway, served by daily flights from Miami by American Airlines. There are also scheduled services from Atlanta, Boston, Charlotte, New York, Philadelphia, and Toronto, and regular services to Jamaica, Haiti, the Dominican Republic, and the Bahamas. Inter-island services are provided by Air Turks & Caicos, tel 649/946-4999, www .airturksandcaicos.com.

Departure tax is US$40 (included in cost of international tickets).

Entry Requirements
Visitors require a valid passport and onward or return ticket.

Festivals & Events
January Junkaroo Jump-up (Jan. 1, most islands)
May Big South Regatta Festival (last weekend; in South Caicos)
June Heineken Game Fishing Tournament (Grand Turk)
July Summer Festival (Providenciales)

November Turks & Caicos Conch Festival (Providenciales)

National holidays include New Year's Day (Jan. 1), Good Friday, Easter Monday, Commonwealth Day (spring), National Heroes Day (end of May), Queen's Birthday (mid-June), Emancipation Day (1st Mon. in Aug.), National Youth Day (late Sept.), Columbus Day (October), International Human Rights Day (Oct. 25), Christmas Day, and Boxing Day (Dec. 26).

GETTING AROUND
Car Rental
Rental agencies on Providenciales include Avis, tel 649/946-4705; Budget, tel 649/946-4079; and Tropical Auto Rental, tel 649/946-5300. Foreign driver's licenses are valid; driving is on the left-hand side of the road.

Public Transportation
Taxis are widely available and they can also be hired for island tours (agree on the price beforehand). A daily ferry service operates between Providenciales and North Caicos; contact Caribbean Cruisin', Walkin Marina, Leeward, Providenciales, tel 649/946-5406. There is also a ferry from Grand Turk to Salt Cay twice a week; contact Salt Cay Ferry, tel 649/946-6909.

PRACTICAL ADVICE
Emergencies
Call either 999 or 911.

Telephones
The area code is 649.

Tourist Information
Grand Turk: Turks & Caicos Islands Tourist Board, Front St., Grand Turk, tel 649/946-2321, fax 649/946-2733, www.turks andcaicostourism.com.

Providenciales: Stubbs Diamond Plaza, tel 649/946-4970, fax 649/941-5494.

U.S. & Canada Offices
Philadelphia: 5 Applewood Dr., HC1 Box B8, Swiftwater, PA 18370, tel 800/241-0824, fax 646/375-8830.
Toronto: 81 Rumsey Road, Toronto, ON M4G 1P1, tel 416/642-9771 or 866/413-8875, fax 416/642-9774.

■ DOMINICAN REPUBLIC

PLANNING YOUR TRIP
Arrival/Departure
The main international gateway is Las Américas International Airport, 18 miles (29 km) to the east of Santo Domingo, which receives frequent scheduled services from North America. American Airlines, American Eagle, Continental, Delta, and US Airways are among the many airlines offering flights either direct to the Dominican Republic or one-stop services via Miami or San Juan, Puerto Rico. In addition to Santo Domingo, there are international airports at Barahona (María Montez), Puerto Plata (Gregorio Luperón), Punta Cana, La Romana/Casa de Campo, Samaná, and Santiago. Domestic flights are operated by Air Santo Domingo, tel 809/683-8006; www.airsantodomingo.com, and Caribair, tel 809/826-4441; www .caribair.com.do.
Departure tax is US$20.

Entry Requirements
Visitors require a full valid passport and a tourist card (US$10). Tourist cards can be purchased on arrival (US$, cash only, valid for 30 days), and the receipt

must be kept safely and shown on departure.

Festivals & Events
January The festival of the patron saint of the Dominican people, Our Lady of Altagracia, is celebrated with all-night vigils, family visits, and singing and dancing.
July Merengue Festival (Santo Domingo)
November Jazz Festival (Cabarete)

National holidays include New Year's Day, Epiphany (Jan. 6), the birthday of Juan P. Duarte (Jan. 26), Independence Day (Feb. 27), Good Friday, Labor Day (May 1), Restoration Day (Aug. 16), Columbus Day (Oct. 12), and Christmas Day.
Each town also celebrates its own saint's day with a *fiesta patronal*.

GETTING AROUND
Car Rental
Santo Domingo offices: Avis, tel 809/535-7191; Budget, tel 809/566-6666; Dollar, tel 809/221-7368; National-Alamo, tel 809/562-1444. Valid driver's license or international driver's license required, as well as a credit card. Driving is on the right; speed limits are 50–62 mph (80–100 kph) on highways, 25 mph (40 kph) in cities, unless otherwise indicated.

Public Transportation
Taxis are available in all tourist areas, at hotels, and at the airports. They are generally cream-colored and marked Taxi Turístico. Look for taxi tariff information boards and always agree on a price before setting off.
The country has a widespread network of public buses, with the better ones featuring air-conditioning and onboard snacks and videos on long-distance routes;

it is advisable to reserve seats in advance. On lesser routes, privately operated minibuses known as *guaguas* operate between towns and villages, stopping to pick up or drop off passengers frequently.

PRACTICAL ADVICE
Emergencies
Police, fire, ambulance: tel 911. Tourism Police, tel 809/686-8639, or toll-free on island, tel 809/200-3500.

Telephones
The area code is 809.

Tourist Information
Santo Domingo: Ministry of Tourism, Ave. Luperón, cnr. Cayetano Germose, tel 809/537-6169, fax 809/682-3806, www .godominicanrepublic.com.

U.S. & Canada Offices
Chicago: 561 W. Diversey Bldg., Suite 202, Chicago, IL 60614, tel 773/529-1336 or 888-303-1336, fax 773/529-1338.
Miami: 848 Brickell Ave., Suite 747, Miami, FL 33131, tel 305/358-2899 or 888/358-9594, fax 305/358-4185.
New York: 136 E. 57th St., Suite 805, New York, NY 10022, tel 212/588-1012 or 888/374-6361, fax 212/588-1015.
Montréal: 2080 rue Crescent, Montréal, QC H3G 2B8, tel 514/499-1918 or 800-563-1611, fax 514/499-1393.
Toronto: 26 Wellington St. East, Suite 201, Toronto, ON M5E 1S2, tel 416/361-2126 or 888/494-5050, fax 416/361-2130.

■ PUERTO RICO

PLANNING YOUR TRIP
Arrival/Departure

The main gateway is San Juan's Luis Muñoz Marín International Airport. Most U.S. airlines offer direct flights to Puerto Rico from gateway cities across North America. The dominant carriers are American Airlines, with nonstop flights from Miami, Los Angeles, Chicago, Dallas, New York, and Boston; and JetBlue from Boston, Fort Lauderdale, New York, and Tampa. Other regular scheduled services depart from Atlanta, Charlotte, Philadelphia, and Washington, D.C. There are frequent short-hop services to destinations throughout the region with local carriers including American Eagle and LIAT. Many shorter flights, including services to the islands of Vieques and Culebra, depart from Ribas Dominicci Airport in San Juan's Isla Grande district, which is more centrally located than the international airport.

Entry Requirements
Currently there is no requirement for U.S. citizens to present a passport on re-entry to the mainland United States from Puerto Rico. However, check updated travel news on www.travel.state.gov/travel. Other visitors will need to present a valid passport, visa, and onward or return ticket in compliance with standard U.S. immigration procedures on arrival in Puerto Rico.

Festivals & Events
March/April Pre-Lenten Carnival parties, parades, and music throughout the island. Ponce hosts one of the most colorful celebrations.
April Saborea Food & Wine Festival, Escambrón Beach, San Juan
May Heineken Jazz Festival
June Celebrations of St. John the Baptist (June 23)
December The Christmas season

starts early in Dec. and lasts through Three Kings Day (Jan. 6).

National holidays include all U.S. holidays as well as nine local holidays honoring local leaders or events of the island's history.

GETTING AROUND
Car Rental
Avis, tel 787/253-5927, 800/331-1212; Budget, tel 787/791-0600, 800/527-0700; and Dollar, tel 787/253-7074. Local rental companies are usually a better value; try Charlie Car Rental, tel 787/728-2418; Vias, tel 787/791-4120; or Target, tel 787/728-1447, 800/934-6457.

Public Transportation
All taxis are metered, except when they are chartered for long-distance rides. In San Juan, *taxis turísticos* (white, with a logo on the door) operate with fixed rates between the airport, ports, and tourist areas. City buses are a good way to get around San Juan.
There are no scheduled bus services between cities, although you can catch shared taxis (known as *publicos*, they have yellow number plates with the letters P or PD at the end) that run to most parts of the island.

PRACTICAL ADVICE
Emergencies
Police, fire, and ambulance: tel 911. Medical emergencies: tel 787/754-2550. Tourist Zone Police (Condado): tel 787/343-2020.

Telephones
The area code is 787.

Tourist Information
San Juan: Ochoa Building, 550 Calle Tanca, Old San Juan, tel 787/721-2400 or 800/866-7827,

fax 787/722-5208; Luis Muñoz Marín Airport, tel 787/791-1014; www.seepuertorico.com.

U.S. Office
New York: Puerto Rico Tourism Company, 135 W. 50th St., 22nd floor, New York, NY 10020, tel 212/586-6262, fax 212/586-1212.

■ VIRGIN ISLANDS

U.S. VIRGIN ISLANDS

Entry Requirements
U.S. citizens do not require a passport to visit the USVI, but will need to provide proof of identity and a photo ID upon departure.

Telephones
The area code is 340.

National Holidays
These include New Year's Day (Jan. 1), Martin Luther King Jr. Day (3rd Mon. in Jan.), President's Day (3rd Mon. in Feb.), Transfer Day (March 31), Good Friday, Easter Monday, USVI Emancipation Day (July 3), Independence Day (July 4), Labor Day (1st Mon. in Sept.), Columbus Day (2nd Mon. in Oct.), Thanksgiving Day (4th Thurs. in Nov.), Christmas Day, and Boxing Day (Dec. 26).

ST. CROIX

PLANNING YOUR TRIP
Arrival/Departure
Nonstop flights to St. Croix are available through American Airlines (from Miami) and Delta (from Atlanta). There are regular connecting services daily via Puerto Rico (see p. 336), and St. Thomas (see below) with American Eagle. Seaborne Airlines, tel

340/773-6442 or 888/359-8687, www.seaborneairlines.com, has frequent daily services between St. Croix and St. Thomas, as does Cape Air, tel 508/771-6944 or 866/227-3247, www.capeair.net, with services between St. Thomas, St. Croix, and Puerto Rico.

Festivals & Events
December–January The month-long Crucian Christmas Festival culminates in the Three Kings Day parade (Jan. 6).
May St. Croix Ironman
July Emancipation Day celebrations
September Grand Crucian Quadrille. For a glimpse of the island's heritage catch a performance by Crucian quadrille dancers.

GETTING AROUND
Car Rental
Avis, tel 340/778-9355; Budget Rent a Car, tel 888/264-8894, www.budgetstcroix.com; Judi of Croix, tel 340/773-2123 or 877/903-2123, www.judiofcroix.com; and Olympic Rent-a-Car Ace, tel 340/718-3000 or 888/878-4227, www.olympicstcroix.com all arrange airport and hotel pickups and delivery. U.S. driver's licenses are valid on the island; driving is on the left in St. Croix.

Public Transportation
It costs just a dollar to take the bus from Christiansted to Frederiksted (every 40 minutes 5:30 a.m.–9:30 p.m; hourly on Sundays). Taxis are readily available at the airport and hotels or from taxi stands on King Street and at Market Square in Christiansted, or by Fort Frederik in Frederiksted. Taxis are not metered, but are instead regulated by an official tariff carried by drivers. Check the fare in advance. Taxi vans offer cut-price

transfers from the airport to island hotels.

PRACTICAL ADVICE
Emergencies
Police, fire, and ambulance: tel 911. Governor Juan F. Lewis Hospital & Medical Center, tel 340/778-6311, has a 24-hour emergency room. Hotels have access to a 24-hour duty doctor, and the Department of Tourism Helpline is tel 340/772-0357.

Tourist Information
Christiansted: P.O. Box 4538, 1105 Kings Street, Christiansted, VI 00820, tel 340/773-1404, fax 340/712-8101, www.visitusvi.com.

U.S. Offices
New York: 999-32 Montauk Hwy, Ste. 406, Shirley, NY 11967, tel 212/502-5300 or 888/273-4741, fax 212/332-2223.
Miami: 2655 South LeJeune Rd., Suite 907, Coral Gables, FL 33134, tel 305/442-7200, fax 305/445-9044.

ST. THOMAS & ST. JOHN

PLANNING YOUR TRIP
Arrival/Departure
The major U.S. airlines provide daily direct flights to St. Thomas, and there are connections from numerous U.S. cities via Puerto Rico on American Airlines. St. John does not have an airport, but it is a short ferry ride from St. Thomas. Regular services depart from St. Thomas, either from Charlotte Amalie (45 minutes) or Red Hook (20 minutes), throughout the day. The Westin and Caneel Bay hotels provide a private boat service for guests.

Festivals & Events
March St. John Blues Festival

March–April International Rolex Regatta (fourth weekend, St. Thomas), including long-distance Pillsbury Sound race
April Virgin Islands Carnival (St. Thomas)
June St. John Festival (month-long event)
August Open/Atlantic Blue Marlin Tournament

GETTING AROUND
Car Rental
Avis, tel 340/774-1468 and Budget, tel 340/776-5774. Local operators, including Dependable, tel 340/774-2253 or 800/522-3076, www.dependablecar.com, on St. Thomas, and St. John Car Rental, tel/fax 340/776-6103, www.stjohncarrental.com, on St. John, can offer more competitive rates. U.S. driver's licenses are valid on the islands, but unlike the U.S., mainland driving is on the left.

Public Transportation
There is a local bus service on St. Thomas. On St. John, a regular bus shuttles between the ferry dock at Cruz Bay and Coral Bay on the east coast throughout the day. Taxis are readily available from St. Thomas's Airport and St. John's Cruz Bay ferry dock, as well as from hotels and taxi stands in tourist areas. They are not metered, but regulated by an official tariff carried by drivers. Check the fare in advance. Taxi vans offer cut-price transfers from the St. Thomas Airport to hotels around the island.

PRACTICAL ADVICE
Emergencies
Police, fire, and ambulance: tel 911. Roy Schneider Hospital, tel 340/776-8311, has a 24-hour emergency room. There are clinics in St. John, but medical emergencies will be transferred to St. Thomas. Hotels have access to a 24-hour duty doctor.

Tourist Information
Charlotte Amalie: U.S. Virgin Island Department of Tourism, P.O. Box 6400, St. Thomas, USVI 00804, tel 340/774-8784, fax 340/774-4390, www.visitusvi.com

U.S. Offices
See St. Croix, p. 337.

BRITISH VIRGIN ISLANDS

PLANNING YOUR TRIP
Arrival/Departure
There are no direct flights to the British Virgin Islands from North America, but American Eagle and several local airline companies, including Air Sunshine and LIAT, offer frequent short-hop services to Tortola from Puerto Rico, and from St. Thomas, USVI. Onward flights to Virgin Gorda or Anegada are by private charter only. With the exception of Anegada, the main BVIs are linked to each other, and St. Thomas and St. John in the USVI, by regular, inexpensive ferry services. Ferry services from Tortola to Anegada depart three times a week from Road Town.

Departure tax is US$20 for air travelers, or US$5 for those leaving by sea.

Entry Requirements
Visitors are required to produce a valid passport, together with a return or onward ticket. A passport may not be necessary for U.S. citizens on day trips from the USVI, but check current U.S. re-entry requirements before departure.

Festivals & Events
April–May BVI Spring Regatta, a weeklong festival of sailing,

races, and parties based on Nanny Cay, Tortola
May BVI Music Fest Local and international musicians gather on the beach at Cane Garden Bay, Tortola.
June–July HIHO windsurfing championships and regatta
August BVI Festival (Tortola, 1st Mon., Tues., and Wed.)
December Foxy's famous New Year's Party (Jost van Dyke's Great Harbour, Dec. 31)

National holidays include New Year's Day, Commonwealth Day (2nd Mon. in March), Good Friday, Easter Monday, Whit Monday (May), Queen's Birthday (2nd Mon. in June), Territory Day (July 1), St. Ursula's Day (Oct. 21), Prince Charles's Birthday (Nov. 14), Christmas Day, Boxing Day (Dec. 26).

GETTING AROUND
Car Rental
On Tortola, Avis, tel 284/494-3322, www.avis.com; Dollar, tel 284/494-6093, www.dollar.com; and Hertz, tel 284/495-4405, www.hertz.com, offer rental cars and 4WD vehicles.

On Virgin Gorda, contact L & S Jeep Rental, tel 284/495-5297, www.landsjeeprentals.com, or Mahogany, tel 284/495-5469, http://mahogany.nfshost.com.

On Anegada, try Anegada Reef Hotel, tel 284/495-8002, www.anegadareef.com, or DW Jeep Rentals, tel 284/495-9677. Visitors are required to purchase a temporary license (US$10) in addition to a valid foreign driver's permit. Roads can be rough, and 4WD vehicles are preferable for negotiating bumpy tracks to the beach. Driving is on the left.

Public Transportation
On Tortola, an irregular bus service operates out of Road Town to destinations along the south coast, but

taxis are a more reliable alternative. There are taxi stands at the airport and at ferry terminals.

There are frequent ferry services daily from Tortola to Virgin Gorda, Jost van Dyke, and the U.S. Virgin Islands of St. John and St. Thomas. Ferries also link Tortola and Anegada, and Virgin Gorda with St. Thomas/St. John several times a week.

PRACTICAL ADVICE
Emergencies
Police, fire, and ambulance: tel 999 or 911. Peebles Hospital: Road Town, Tortola, tel 284/494-3497. Hotels can assist with locating a duty doctor. Serious medical emergencies are airlifted to St. Thomas, USVI, or San Juan, Puerto Rico.

Telephones
The area code is 284.

Tourist Information
Tortola: BVI Tourist Board, Akara Bldg., 2nd floor, DeCastro Street, Road Town, tel 284/494-3134, fax 284/494-3866, www .bvitourism.com. There is also a bureau in the Virgin Gorda Yacht Harbour, tel 284/495-5181, fax 284/495-6517.

U.S. Office
New York: BVI Tourist Board, 1 West 34th Street, Suite 302, New York, NY 10001, tel 563-3117 or 800/835-8530, fax 212/563-2263.

■ DUTCH CARIBBEAN

Entry Requirements
For all islands in the group, U.S. citizens are required to produce a valid passport, together with a return or onward ticket. On the Dutch/French island of Sint Maarten/St.-Martin, there are no passport controls between the two halves of the island.

National Holidays
These include New Year's Day, Good Friday, Easter Monday, Queen's Birthday (April 30), Labor Day (May 1), Ascension Day (May), Christmas Day, and Boxing Day (Dec. 26). St.-Martin only: Whit Monday and All Saints Day (Nov. 1).

ARUBA

PLANNING YOUR TRIP
Arrival/Departure
Aruba's Queen Beatrix International Airport is served by direct daily flights from Miami with American Airlines, and from Atlanta with Delta. Other scheduled services include JetBlue from Boston and New York; United Airlines flies from Chicago; US Airways from Charlotte and Philadelphia. There are charter flights from many other U.S. cities.

Festivals & Events
January New Year celebrations
January–February Carnival Monday (early Jan.)
June Windsurfing Festival
October Aruba Music Festival
December Sint Nicolaas's (Santa Claus) Birthday (Dec. 5)

GETTING AROUND
Car Rental
Avis, tel 297/585-0041, www.avis .com; Budget, tel 297/582-8600, www.budget.com; Econo Car Rental, tel 877/461-9913; and Value Car Rental, tel 297/586-4188, www.valuearuba.com, have offices at the airport and other useful tourist locations. Foreign driver's licenses held for a minimum of two years are valid on Aruba; driving is on the right.

Public Transportation
Aruba has an inexpensive and reliable bus service that links the hotel areas with Oranjestad, the airport, and San Nicolas; private minibus services offer greater flexibility. Taxis are easy to find at the airport or hotel, or call the Oranjestad depot, tel 297/582-2116.

PRACTICAL ADVICE
Emergencies
All emergencies: tel 911. Police: tel 911. Hospital: tel 297/587-4300. All hotels have a doctor on-call 24 hours.

Telephones
The country code is 297.

Tourist Information
On the island, contact the Aruba Tourism Authority, L.G. Smith Blvd., 8, Eagle Beach, tel 297/582-3777, fax 297/583-4702, www.aruba .com.

U.S. Office
New Jersey: Aruba Tourism Authority, 100 Plaza Drive, Secaucus, NJ 07094, tel 201/558-1110 or 800/TO-ARUBA, fax 201/558-4768.

BONAIRE

PLANNING YOUR TRIP
Arrival/Departure
There are a number of one-stop flights from U.S. gateway cities to Bonaire's Flamingo Airport (via Puerto Rico, Aruba, Curaçao, and Montego Bay, Jamaica). Continental Airlines makes direct flights once a week from Newark and Houston, Delta flies weekly from Atlanta and New York, and local carrier Insel Air, tel 5999/737-0444, www .fly-inselair.com, offers scheduled services to Miami. Direct flights into Curaçao and Aruba connect

with local carriers Dutch Antilles Express, www.flydae.com, Insel Air, and Divi-Divi, www.flydivi .com.

Departure tax is US$35 (or US$5.75 to Aruba or Curaçao).

Festivals & Events
February Carnival
April Rincon Day
September Bonaire Day (Sept. 6)
October Annual Sailing Regatta

GETTING AROUND
Car Rental
Avis, tel 599/717-5795, www .avis.com; Budget, tel 599/717-4700, www.budget.com; and Hertz, tel 599/717-7221, www .hertz.com, all have offices at the airport. Local operators include Caribe Car Rental, tel 599/717-6711, and Island Rentals, tel 599/717-2100, www.islandrentals bonaire.com.

Foreign driver's licenses are valid. Driving is on the right.

Public Transportation
Taxis are available at the airport and can be booked through hotels, or call Taxi Despatch, tel 599/717-8100. Rates are fixed.

PRACTICAL ADVICE
Emergencies
Ambulance, tel 717-8900. Police and fire: tel 717-8000. St. Francis Hospital in Kralendijk, tel 599/717-8900, has a decompression chamber.

Telephones
The country code is 599.

Tourist Information
Bonaire: Kaya Grandi 2, Kralendijk, tel 599/717-8322, fax 599/717-8408, www.tourism bonaire.com.

U.S. Office
New York: Tourism Corporation Bonaire, c/o Adams Unlimited, 80 Broad Street, Suite 3202, New York, NY 10004, tel 800/ BONAIRE, fax 212/956-5913.

CURAÇAO

PLANNING YOUR TRIP
Arrival/Departure
Hato International Airport receives daily direct flights from Miami with American Airlines and Curaçao-based Insel Air, tel 5999/737-0444, www.fly-inselair .com, which also offers a weekly service from Charlotte. There are regular interisland shuttles from Aruba, and Dutch Caribbean Express links Curaçao with Kingston, Jamaica, and Sint Maarten. Air Jamaica flies via Montego Bay, and there are regular services from Aruba.

Departure tax is US$32.50 for international flights, or US$8 for trips within the Netherlands Antilles.

Festivals & Events
February/March Carnival
March Springtime fishing tournaments
April Celebration of the Queen's Birthday (April 30); Sailing Regatta
July Flag Day (July 2)
August Salsa Festival
October Jazz Festival

GETTING AROUND
Car Rental
Avis, tel 5999/961-4700, www .avis.com; Budget, tel 5999/868-3466, www.budget.com; National, tel 5999/869-4433, www.national.com; and Thrifty, tel 5999/461-3089, www.thrifty .com. Foreign driver's licenses are valid and driving is on the right.

Public Transportation
Inexpensive public buses cover main routes around the island from Willemstad. Taxi tariffs are fixed.

PRACTICAL ADVICE
Emergencies
Police and fire: tel 911. Ambulance: tel 912. St. Elisabeth Hospital, Willemstad, tel 5999/462-4900. Emergencies: tel 910.

Telephones
The country code is 599.

Tourist Information
Willemstad: Curaçao Tourist Board, P.O. Box 3266, Pietermaai 19, tel 5999/434-8200, fax 5999/461-5017, www.curacao.com.

U.S. Office
Newark: One Gateway Center, Ste. 2600, NJ 07102, tel 973/353-6200 or 800/328-7222.

SABA

PLANNING YOUR TRIP
Arrival/Departure
No direct flights from the United States, but Winair, tel 599/545-4237 or 800/634-4907, www.fly-winair.com, makes the 15-minute hop from Sint Maarten to J.E. Yrausquin Airport several times a day. High-speed ferries run from Sint Maarten with Saba-based Dawn II, tel 5999/416-2299, www.sabatransport.com, Tue., Thurs., Sat.; and Sint Maarten–based *The Edge*, tel 599/544-2640, www.stmaarten-activities .com, Wed.–Sun., between Pelican Marina in Philipsburg and Saba's Fort Bay. Crossings take 75–90 minutes.

Departure tax is US$20 for flights connecting with a same-day international service; or US$6 for flights within the Dutch Windward Islands.

Festivals & Events
April Celebration of the Queen's Birthday (April 30)
July–August Carnival
December Saba Day Festivities (1st weekend Dec.)

GETTING AROUND
Car Rental
The island has just one car rental operator: Caja's Car Rental, The Bottom, tel 599/416-2388 or cell 522-7755, fax 599/416-3513.

Public Transportation
Taxis are available at the airport or can be booked through hotels.

PRACTICAL ADVICE
Emergencies
Police: tel 599/416-3237. Medical Centre, The Bottom: tel 599/416-3288. Medical emergencies are generally flown to Sint Maarten.

Telephones
The country code is 599.

Tourist Information
Windwardside: Saba Tourist Office, P.O. Box 527, tel 599/416-2231, fax 599/416-2350, www .sabatourism.com.

SINT EUSTATIUS

PLANNING YOUR TRIP
Arrival/Departure
There are no direct flights from the U.S., but Winair operates several daily island-hopper services into F. D. Roosevelt Airport from Sint Maarten; the flight takes 20 minutes. There are also connections to St. Kitts.

Departure tax is US$12 for flights connecting with a same-day international service; or

US$5.65 for journeys including a stopover in the Dutch Caribbean.

Festivals & Events
April Celebration of the Queen's Birthday (April 30)
July Carnival
October Antillean Day (Oct. 21)
November Statia/America Day (Nov. 16)

GETTING AROUND
Car Rental
Browns, tel 599/318-2266, and Reddy Car Rental, tel 599/318-5564, are a couple of the dozen or so local rental operators. Foreign licenses are valid in Statia; driving is on the right.

Public Transportation
With no buses on Statia, most visitors tend to walk or cycle. Taxis are available at the airport and can be ordered at hotels.

PRACTICAL ADVICE
Emergencies
Police: tel 911. Fire: tel 912. Ambulance: tel 913. Queen Beatrix Medical Center, tel 599/318-2211. Medical emergencies are generally flown to Sint Maarten.

Telephones
The area code is 599.

Tourist Information
Oranjestad: Sint Eustatius Tourism Development Foundation, Fort Oranje, 3 Fort Oranjestraat, tel/fax 599/318-2433, www .statiatourism.com

SINT MAARTEN/ ST.-MARTIN

PLANNING YOUR TRIP
Arrival/Departure
Princess Juliana Airport in Sint Maarten is the main island

gateway. American Airlines flies direct from New York and Miami and provides connections from other North American cities via Puerto Rico. Continental, Delta, JetBlue, United Airlines, and US Airways all offer services originating in the United States.

The island is a transportation hub for regional carriers Caribbean Airlines, LIAT, and Winair, providing air links to the Leeward Islands, Saba, Statia, St Barts, Tortola (BVI), and Puerto Rico. Insel Air, www.fly-insel air.com, flies to the ABCs; while Air Antilles Express, www.airantilles.com and Air Caraïbes, www.aircaraibes .com serve the French Antilles and St. Lucia with smaller planes departing from St.-Martin's L'Espérance-Grand-Case regional airport.

Departure tax is US$30 for international flights or US$10 for trips within the Dutch Caribbean.

Festivals & Events
January Epiphany (Jan. 6, St.-Martin)
February/March Carnival (St.-Martin)
March Heineken Regatta
April Queen's Birthday celebrations (Sint Maarten, April 30), Carnival (Sint Maarten)
June June Fest cultural events
July Bastille Day (St.-Martin, July 14); Schoelcher Day, marked with boat races in Grand Case (St.-Martin, July 21)
November Discovery Day (Nov. 11)

GETTING AROUND
Car Rental
Avis, tel 721/545-2847, www.avis .com; Budget, tel 721/545-4030, www.budget.com; and Hertz, tel 721/545-4541, www.hertz.com, operate out of Princess Juliana Airport with local offices in St.-Martin. Foreign driver's licenses are valid on the island, and driving is on the right.

Public Transportation

Frequent and inexpensive mini-bus services shuttle between Philipsburg and Marigot with connections to Grand Case. Taxis are plentiful (rates are fixed in US$).

PRACTICAL ADVICE

Emergencies

Sint Maarten Emergencies: 911. Ambulance: 912. Doctors on call: 5111. Hospital: 721/543-1111. **St.-Martin** Police: tel 17. Fire: tel 18. S.A.M.U. (medical emergences): 15. Hospital: 590/52 25 52.

Telephones

The country code for French St.-Martin is 590; while Sint Maarten is a member of the North American Numbering Plan with an assigned area code of 721. To call from the Dutch side to the French side of the island is an international call. To call St.-Martin from the U.S., dial the international access code (011) + the country and area codes (590 590) + the local number; to call Sint Maarten from the U.S. dial area code 721 + the local number. For calls within Sint Maarten, dial the seven-digit local number; for calls from the Dutch to the French side, dial 011+ 590 590 + the 6-digit local number. For calls within St.-Martin, dial the 10-digit number beginning 0590 for landlines or 0690 for cells; for calls from the French side to the Dutch side, dial 001 + 721 + the local number.

Tourist Information

Sint Maarten
Philipsburg: W.G. Buncamper Rd. 33, tel 721/542-2337, fax 721/542-2734, www.vacation stmaarten.com. Information kiosk by the Philipsburg pier.

St.-Martin
Marigot: Office de Tourisme de St.-Martin, Route de Sandy Ground, Marigot, 97150 St.-Martin, tel 0590/87 57 21, fax 0590/87 56 43, www .iledesaintmartin.org.

U.S. Office
New York: Atout France, 825 3rd Ave. 29th Floor, New York, NY 10022-7519, tel 514/288-1904, fax 212/838-7855, www .stmartinisland.org.

■ LEEWARD ISLANDS

Entry Requirements

For all islands in the group, U.S. citizens are required to produce a valid passport, together with a return or onward ticket.

National Holidays

Holidays common to all islands include New Year's Day (Jan. 1), Good Friday, Easter Monday, Labour Day (1st Mon. in May), Christmas Day, and Boxing Day (Dec. 26).

ANGUILLA

PLANNING YOUR TRIP

Arrival/Departure

There are no direct flights from the United States to Anguilla's Clayton Lloyd International Airport. Anguilla Air Express, www .anguillaairexpress.com, operates daily services from Puerto Rico (see p. 336), and there are regular connections from neighboring Sint Maarten/St.-Martin and Antigua.

A frequent (every 45 minutes from 7:30 a.m.–6:15 p.m.) and inexpensive 20-minute ferry service operates between Blowing Point, Anguilla, and Marigot, the capital of French St.-Martin, tel 264/497-2231.

Departure tax is US$20 at the airport, or US$5 for the ferry crossing to St.-Martin.

Festivals & Events

March Moonsplash Music Festival
April Festival Del Mar
May Anguilla Day
June Celebration of the Queen's Birthday
August Carnival
November Tranquility Jazz Festival

National holidays include Anguilla Day (May 30), Whit Monday, and Constitution Day (Aug. 6).

GETTING AROUND

Car Rental

Apex/Avis, tel 264/497-2642, www.avis.com; Island Car Rentals, tel 264/497-2723, www.island car.ai; Thrifty, tel 264/497-2656, www.thrifty.com; and Triple K/ Hertz, tel 264/497-5934, www .hertz.com. Visitors must purchase a temporary license (US$20) in addition to presenting a valid overseas permit. Driving is on the left.

Public Transportation

There is limited public bus service on Anguilla. Taxis are available at the airport, tel 264/497-5054, and ferry dock, tel 264/497-6089, or arranged through the hotel.

PRACTICAL ADVICE

Emergencies

All emergencies: tel 911. Police: tel 264/497-2333. Princess Alexandra Hospital, Stoney Ground: tel 264/497-2551. Serious medical cases are airlifted to Puerto Rico.

Telephones

The area code is 264.

Tourist information

The Valley: Anguilla Tourist Board, Coronation Ave., tel

264/497-2759 or 800/553-4939, fax 264/497-2710, www.ivisit anguilla.com.

U.S. & Canada Offices
New York: 264 Central Ave., White Plains, NY 10606, tel 914/287-2400 or 877/4-ANGUILLA, fax 914/287-2404.
Ontario: SRM Marketing, 20-225 Dundas St. East, Ste. 411, Waterdown, ON L0R 2H6, tel 905/689-7697 or 866/348-7447, fax 905/689-1026.

ANTIGUA & BARBUDA

PLANNING YOUR TRIP
Arrival/Departure
Several carriers serve Antigua's V. C. Bird International Airport direct from the United States, including American Airlines out of New York and Miami, Delta from Atlanta, and US Airways from Charlotte. Antigua is also the hub for local carrier LIAT, www.liat.com, which together with Caribbean Airlines, www.col.com, and SVG Air, www.svgair.com, offers frequent connections to other islands.

Barbuda is served daily by SVG Air, tel 268/562-7181, from Antigua (ten minutes flight time); and the Barbuda Express ferry, tel 268/560-7989, www.antiguaferries.com, 90-minute power catamaran service.

Departure tax from Antigua is US$25; there is no tax payable for trips between Antigua and Barbuda, but passports are required for identification.

Festivals & Events
April Antigua Sailing Week; Antigua & Barbuda International Kite Festival
July Carnival

National holidays include Good Friday, Easter Monday, Labor Day (1st Mon. in May), and Independence Day (Nov. 1).

GETTING AROUND
Car Rental
Avis, tel 268/462-2840, www.avis.com; Dollar Rent-A-Car, tel 268/462-0362, www.dollarantigua.com; and Hertz, tel 268/462-4114, www.hertz.com, are found at Antigua's airport and other locations around the island. Visitors have to purchase a temporary driver's permit (US$20) in addition to presenting a valid overseas license.

On Barbuda there are no rental cars, but trips around the island can be arranged through Barbuda Shorelines Tours (www.visit-barbuda.com) and Crystal Bay Tours (268/561-5558).

Public Transportation
Antigua has an irregular daytime bus service geared to commuters heading into St. John's from around the island. Buses leave only when they are full; fares are inexpensive.

Taxis, bookable from the hotel, are not metered, but government fixed rates apply. Agree on the fee in advance. Check out fares or book a taxi online at www.antiguanice.com. There is no public transportation on Barbuda.

PRACTICAL ADVICE
Emergencies
Police Headquarters in St. John's: tel 268/462-0125. Mount St. John Medical Centre: Queen Elizabeth Hwy., St. John's, tel 268/462-0251. Serious cases are airlifted to Puerto Rico or Miami. Most hotels are served by a 24-hour duty doctor.

Telephones
The area code for Antigua and Barbuda is 268.

Tourist Information
St. John's: Antigua and Barbuda Department of Tourism, Government Bldg., Queen Elizabeth Hwy., tel 268/462-0480, fax 268/462-2483, www.antigua-barbuda.com.

U.S. & Canada Offices
Miami: 25 S.E. 2nd Ave., Suite 300, Miami, FL 33131, tel 305/381-6762, fax 305/381-7908.
Toronto: 60 St. Claire Ave. East, Ste. 304, Toronto ON M4T 1N5, tel 416/961-3085, fax 416/961-7218.

MONTSERRAT

PLANNING YOUR TRIP
Arrival/Departure
Access to Montserrat is via the neighboring island of Antigua. There are regular short-hop flights into Gerald's Airport with Winair (www.fly-winair.com) and Fly Montserrat (www.flymontserrat.com). Ferry services are also available; check schedules with the Montserrat Tourist Board (tel 664/491-2230 or www.visitmontserrat.com). See also Day Trips to the Emerald Isle, p. 225.

Departure tax is EC$55 (approx. US$21).

Festivals & Events
March St Patrick's Week celebrations. See Irish Heritage, p. 226
July Calabash Festival
December–New Year's Day Carnival

GETTING AROUND
Car Rental
Jefferson Car Rental, Palm Loop (tel 664/491-2126), Montserrat Enterprises, Brades (tel

664/491-2431), and Neville Bradshaw Agencies, St. Peters (tel 664/491-5270) all rent out cars and Jeeps. There are two coastal roads, which end short of the Exclusion Zone; be sure to respect the marked boundaries of the Zone. Visitors require a local driver's license (approx. US$20) available from Police Headquarters in Brades.

Public Transportation

Taxis and minibuses have green license plates starting with an "H". They can be hailed anywhere (there are no fixed routes). Taxis are unmetered and rates are fixed. Most drivers make knowledgeable guides and offer set fees for tours depending on duration.

PRACTICAL ADVICE
Emergencies

Police: tel 999. Fire: tel 911. Operator assistance: tel 411. Minor emergencies can be dealt with at the Glendon Hospital, St. John's: tel 664/491-2552; air ambulance services fly to Antigua.

Telephones

The country code is 664.

Tourist Information

Brades: Montserrat Tourist Board, #7 Farara Plaza, Buildings B&C, tel 664/491-2230, fax 664/491-7430, www.visitmont serrat.com.

ST. KITTS & NEVIS

PLANNING YOUR TRIP
Arrival/Departure

American Airlines offers daily direct flights from Miami, and flies twice weekly from New York, to St. Kitts's Robert L. Bradshaw International Airport. Delta flies direct from Atlanta, and US Airways from Charlotte. There is easy access to both islands via regional gateways including Puerto Rico with American Eagle; Antigua with LIAT (www.liat.com); and Nevis is linked to Sint Maarten with Winair (www.fly-winair.com). Regular flights also link St. Kitts and Newcastle Airport, Nevis. Ferries run several times a day between island capitals Basseterre and Charlestown (crossings take 45 minutes).

Departure tax is US$22 from St. Kitts; US$20.50 from Nevis.

Festivals & Events

June St. Kitts Music Festival
August Culturama, around Emancipation Day (1st Mon. in Aug. Nevis)
September Heritage Festival on Independence Day (St. Kitts and Nevis, Sept. 19)
December–January National Carnival kicks off on Dec. 26 and lasts into the New Year (St. Kitts).

National holidays include Whit Monday, the Queen's Birthday (2nd Sat. in June), and National Heroes Day (Sept. 16).

GETTING AROUND
Car Rental

Car and Jeep rentals are available through Avis, www.avis. com: St. Kitts, tel 869/465-6507; and local operator Thrifty/TDC Rentals: St. Kitts, tel 869/465-2991; Nevis, tel 869/469-5430. TDC also offers an exchange rental arrangement between St. Kitts and Nevis (minimum three days). Visitors must obtain a temporary driver's permit (US$24) in addition to presenting a valid foreign license. Driving is on the left.

Public Transportation

Inexpensive minibus services leave the ferry dock in Basseterre, and from Main Street Charlestown when they are full or the driver is ready. Taxis are readily available and fares are fixed by the government.

PRACTICAL ADVICE
Emergencies

Police: tel 911. Fire: tel 333 St. Kitts; or 469-3444 Nevis. For medical problems, hotels can call for a doctor. The Joseph N. France Hospital in Basseterre, tel 869/465-2551, and Alexandra Hospital in Nevis, tel 869/469-5473, treat minor casualties. Serious medical emergencies are sent to Puerto Rico.

Telephones

The area code is 869.

Tourist Information

St. Kitts: St. Kitts Tourism Authority, Pelican Mall, Bay Rd., Basseterre, tel 869/465-4040, fax 869/465-8794, www.stkitts tourism.kn.
Nevis: Nevis Tourism Authority, Main St., Charlestown, tel 869/469-7550, fax 869/469-7551, www.nevisisland.com.

St. Kitts U.S. & Canada Offices
New York: 414 E. 75th St., Ste. 5, NY 10021, tel 212/535-1234 or 800/582-6208, fax 212/734-6511.
Washington: 3216 New Mexico Ave. NW, DC 20016-2745, tel 202/364-8123 or 877/533-1555, fax 202/364-8126.
Toronto: 133 Richmond St. West, Ste. 311, ON M5H 2L3, tel 416/368-3934 or 888/395-4887, fax 416/368-3934.

Nevis Telephone Inquiries:
U.S.: tel 407/287-5204
Canada: tel 403/770-6697

■ FRENCH ANTILLES

National Holidays

Holidays common to all islands include New Year's Day (Jan. 1), Shrove Tuesday, Ash Wednesday, Good Friday, Easter Monday, Labor Day (May 1), Victory Day 1945 (May 8), Ascension Day (May), Abolition of Slavery Day (May 22), Whit Monday, Bastille Day (July 14), Feast of the Assumption (Aug. 15), All Saints Day (Nov. 1), All Souls Day (Nov. 2), and Christmas Day.

GUADELOUPE

PLANNING YOUR TRIP

Arrival/Departure

Air France operates direct services to Guadeloupe from Miami and Air Canada provides nonstop service from Montreal; while American Airlines flies daily from Puerto Rico (see p. 336). Pôle Caraïbes Airport lies just east of Pointe-à-Pitre, convenient for Gosier and other Grande-Terre coastal resorts. There are also regular services from regional transportation hubs such as Antigua (see p. 343) and Sint Maarten/ St.-Martin (see p. 341) with LIAT, www.liat.com, and Air Antilles Express, www.air antilles.com, as well as short-hop flights to the islands of the Guadeloupean archipelago.

Inexpensive daily ferry services link Guadeloupe with Martinique (3 hours 45 minutes), and the islands of the archipelago. Ferries to Dominica and St. Lucia operate several times a week. For schedule information, contact L'Express des Îles, tel 0825/35 90 00, www .express-des-iles.com. Crossings can be rough; travelers might prefer a short plane ride.

Entry Requirements

Visitors will need to produce a passport and a return or onward ticket. Check visa requirements.

Festivals & Events

January Carnival preparations begin early in the New Year and culminate in a giant three-day event running up to Ash Wednesday.

July Creole Arts Festival (Ste.-Anne)

August The Fête des Cuisinières, a gastronomic showcase

GETTING AROUND

Car Rental

Avis, tel 0590/82 33 47, www.avis .com; Budget, tel 0590/90 26 37, www.budget.com; Europcar, tel 0590/82 59 51, www.europcar. com, are among the rental agencies. Scooter rentals are also widely available. Overseas driver's licenses are valid for 20 days in Guadeloupe; driving is on the right.

Public Transportation

Public buses serve most destinations around the island and operate from early morning until around 6–7 p.m. There is a useful service along the south coast of Grande-Terre to Pointe-à-Pitre with drop-off and pickup points near the ferry terminal on La Darse. Carry small change for the fare. To stop the bus, shout "arrêt" or press a buzzer.

Taxi rates are fixed; agree on the price in advance.

PRACTICAL ADVICE

Emergencies

Police: tel 17. Fire: tel 18. Ambulance: tel 15 or SAMU 0590/89 11 00. There are hospitals in all major towns, and duty doctors can be summoned by hotels.

Telephones

The country code is 590. Guadeloupean local telephone numbers have ten digits. Landline numbers begin 0590; cell phones begin 0690. To make calls within Guadeloupe and to the other French Caribbean islands, dial the full ten digits. To call Guadeloupe from the U.S., dial 011 590 590 plus the remaining six-digit number. To call the U.S. from Guadeloupe, dial 00 1 followed by the area code and telephone number. Calls made from phone boxes require a prepaid *télécarte*.

Tourist Information

Pointe-à-Pitre: Comité du Tourisme des Îles de Guadeloupe, 5 Square de la Banque, 97166, tel 0590/82 09 30, fax 0590/ 83 89 22, www.lesilesde guadeloupe.com.

U.S. Office

New York: Atout France, 825 3rd Ave. 29th Floor, New York, NY 10022-7519, tel 212/838-6887, fax 212/838-7855, www .franceguide.com.

ST.-BARTHÉLEMY

PLANNING YOUR TRIP

Arrival/Departure

St. Barts's Gustave III Airport can only take small STOL (Short Take-Off and Landing) aircraft, so the easiest access to St. Barts is from Sint Maarten (see p. 341), which is well served by direct flights from North America, and only a ten-minute hop away. St. Barth Commuter, www.stbarth commuter.com, Air Caraïbes, www .aircaraibes.com, and Winair, www .fly-winair.com, offer frequent daily services from Sint Maarten/ St.-Martin, and there are Winair connections to many other destinations in the Eastern Caribbean.

Air Caraïbes also operates services to Guadeloupe (45 minutes).

Express ferries make the sea crossing daily from Sint Maarten/ (45 minutes)/St. Martin (75 minutes). For services from Philipsburg, contact The Edge, tel 721/544-2640, www.stmaarten-activities.com, or Great Bay Express, tel 721/542-0032, www.greatbayferry.com; from Marigot contact Babou One, tel 0590/29 81 25 www.westindiesferry.com, or Voyager, tel 0590/87 10 68, www.voy12.com. Voyager also has departures from Oyster Pond. The trip can be quite rough, however fine the weather. Catamaran trips are slower but smoother.

Entry Requirements

Visitors will need to produce a passport and a return or onward ticket. Check visa requirements.

There is a departure tax payable of €4.50 (US$6).

Festivals & Events

January Festival de Musique
March–May Sailing regatta season
April Festival du Cinéma Caraïbe
July Deep Sea Fishing Tournament
December New Year's Eve Regatta

GETTING AROUND
Car Rental

Avis, tel 0590/27 71 43; Budget, tel 0590/27 66 30; and Hertz, tel 0590/27 71 14. Motorbikes and scooters can be rented through Barth'loc, tel 0590/27 52 81, and Chez Béranger, tel 0590/27 89 00, among others. Foreign driver's licenses are valid; driving is on the right. The gas station at St. Jean is closed Sun., and also Tues. p.m. in low season (April–Nov.); the only other gas station is at Lorient and closes Thurs. p.m., Sat. p.m., and all day Sun.

Public Transportation

There is no public bus service on the island. Taxis are available from the airport, and the taxi stand on Quai du Général de Gaulle in Gustavia, tel 0590/27 66 31. There is a flat rate for rides up to five minutes, and it goes up every three minutes thereafter.

PRACTICAL ADVICE
Emergencies

Police: tel 17. Ambulance and fire: tel 18. The Hôpital de Bruyn in Gustavia, tel 0590/27 60 35, can handle most casualties and hotels can help locate the duty doctor. Serious medical emergencies are taken to Sint Maarten or Puerto Rico.

Telephones

The country code is 590. When making a local call or calling from another French Antillean island, dial 0590 and the six-digit number. When calling from the U.S., dial 011 590 590 and the remaining six-digit number.

Tourist Information

Gustavia: Office du Tourisme, Quai du Général de Gaulle, 97133, tel 0590/27 87 27, fax 0590/27 74 47, www.saintbarth-tourisme.com.

U.S. Office

See Guadeloupe, p. 245.

MARTINIQUE

PLANNING YOUR TRIP
Arrival/Departure

Air France flies daily direct from Miami to Martinique's Aimé Césaire Airport, at Lamentin, outside Fort-de-France. There are direct flights from Montreal with Air Canada, and interisland services with American Eagle from Puerto Rico, providing connections to a wide variety of U.S. gateways.

Local carriers serve other regional transportation hubs such as Antigua (see p. 343), Barbados (see p. 350), and Sint Maarten (see p. 341).

Inexpensive ferry services link Martinique to Guadeloupe (3 hours 45 minutes); to Dominica (1 hour 45 minutes); and St. Lucia (1 hour 20 minutes). For schedule information, contact the Fort-de-France interisland ferry terminal, tel 0596/59 00 00. Crossings can be rough, so travelers might prefer a short-hop plane ride.

Entry Requirements

Visitors will need to produce a passport and a return or onward ticket. Check visa requirements.

No departure tax.

Festivals & Events

January Pre-Carnival activities kick off in January and climax on Ash Wednesday.
April Martinique Food Show
July Fort-de-France Cultural Festival
August La Yole Rond (round-island boat race)
December Winter Music Festival

GETTING AROUND
Car Rental

Avis, tel 0596/42 11 00, www.avis.com; Budget, tel 0596/42 04 04, www.budget.com; Europcar, tel 0596/42 42 42; and Jumbo Car, tel 0596/42 22 22. Overseas driver's licenses are valid for 20 days and driving is on the right.

Public Transportation

Public buses from Fort-de-France operate from early morning until around 7 p.m. They stop at designated bus stops; to get off shout "arrêt." Ferries from Fort-de-France serve a number of local beaches and Ste.-Anne. Taxi rates are fixed; agree on the price in advance.

PRACTICAL ADVICE
Emergencies
Police: tel 17. Fire: tel 18. Medical emergencies and ambulance: tel 15 or SOS Médècins (24-hour doctor service), tel 0596/63 33 33. There are well-equipped hospitals and local clinics. Hotels or the tourist office can assist with locating an English-speaking doctor.

Telephones
The country code is 596. Martiniquais telephone numbers have ten digits beginning 0596, or 0696 for cell phones. When making a local call or calling from another French Antillean island, dial 0596 and the six-digit number. When calling from the U.S., dial 011 596 596 and the number. To the U.S., dial 001, followed by the area code and number.

Tourist Information
Fort-de-France: Comité Martiniquais du Tourisme, Beaupré, Pointe de Jaham, 97233 Schoelcher, tel 0596/61 61 77, fax 0596/61 22 72, www.martinique tourisme.com.

U.S. & Canada Offices
New York: CMT USA, 825 3rd Ave. 29th Floor, New York, NY 10022-7519, tel 212/838-6887, fax 212/838-7855, www .martinique.org.
Montréal: CMT Canada, 4000 rue Saint Amboise, Ste. 265, Québec H4C 2C7, tel 514/844-8566 or 800/361-9099, fax 514/844-8901.

■ WINDWARD ISLANDS

National Holidays
Holidays for the group include New Year's Day, Good Friday, Easter Monday, Whit Monday, Labor Day (1st Mon. in May) May Day,

Dominica (May 1), Christmas Day, and Boxing Day (Dec. 26).

DOMINICA

PLANNING YOUR TRIP
Arrival/Departure
There are no direct flights to Dominica from the U.S. mainland, but American Eagle has a daily service from Puerto Rico (see p. 336) to Dominica's Melville Hall Airport in the north of the island (1 hour 20 minutes from Roseau). Local carrier LIAT, www.liat.com, provides services from regional transportation hubs including Antigua (see p. 343), Barbados (see p. 350), Sint Maarten (see p. 341), and the French Antilles. Some smaller planes use Canefield Airport, just outside Roseau.
Dominica can also be reached by high-speed ferries from Guadeloupe (1 hour 45 minutes), Martinique (1 hour 30 minutes), and St. Lucia (3 hours 20 minutes), contact L'Express des Îles in Roseau, tel 767/448-2181, www .express-des-iles.com. The crossing can be rough.

Entry Requirements
U.S. visitors require a passport and a return or onward ticket.
Departure tax is US$23.

Festivals & Events
February–March Carnival (Mon. & Tues. before Lent)
July Dive Fest
October World Creole Music Festival
November Independence Day (Nov. 3)

Other holidays include 1st Mon. in Aug. and Community Day of Service (Nov. 4).

GETTING AROUND
Car Rental
Bonus, tel 767/448-2650; Garraway, tel 767/448-2891; Island Car Rentals, tel 767/255-6844; and Valley Rent-A-Car, tel 767/448-3233. Drivers will need a temporary visitor's permit (US$ 12) in addition to their valid overseas license. Driving is on the left.

Public Transportation
Irregular but frequent minibus services cover all the major island destinations from Roseau. Taxis are readily available from the airports and Roseau by day, or make an arrangement with your hotel. Reserve a taxi in advance for evening excursions. Government rates apply.

PRACTICAL ADVICE
Emergencies
Police, fire, and emergencies: tel 999. Princess Margaret Hospital in Roseau, tel 767/448-2231, and Portsmouth Hospital, tel 767/445-5237, are the main medical facilities. Serious medical emergencies are dispatched to Puerto Rico. Hotels can assist in locating a duty doctor.

Telephones
The area code is 767.

Tourist Information
Roseau: Discover Dominica Authority, Financial Centre Bldg., P.O. Box 293, Commonwealth of Dominica, tel 767/448-2045. **U.S. & Canada Inquiries:** tel 866/522-4057.

GRENADA, CARRIACOU & PETIT MARTINIQUE

PLANNING YOUR TRIP
Arrival/Departure
Grenada's Maurice Bishop

International Airport receives direct flights from New York with Delta, from Miami with American Airlines, and from Miami, New York, Orlando, and Toronto with Caribbean Airlines. There are also regular American Eagle services from Puerto Rico connecting to numerous North American departure points. Otherwise, regional carrier LIAT, www.liat .com, provides connections from island gateways such as Antigua (see p. 343), Barbados (see p. 350), St. Lucia and Trinidad (see p. 350).

Lauriston Airport on Carriacou is served by daily island-hopper flights from Grenada with SVG Air, www.svgair.com. The islands are also connected by a weekday round-trip ferry service with Osprey Lines, tel 473/440-8126, www.ospreylines.com, which operates a reduced service at weekends.

Petite Martinique can be reached by water taxi from Windward, on the northeast coast of Carriacou.

Entry Requirements
Visitors will be required to produce a passport together with a return or onward ticket.

Departure tax from Grenada is US$20.

Festivals & Events
February–March Carriacou Carnival (held before beginning of Lent); week-long St. Patrick's Day celebration (Sauteurs, Grenada) **June** Fisherman's Birthday in Gouyave (end June) **July–August** Carriacou Regatta; Grenada Carnival (St. George's) **December** Carriacou Parang Festival

National holidays include Independence Day (Feb. 7), Corpus Christi (June), Emancipation Day (1st Mon. & Tues. in Aug.), and Thanksgiving Day (Oct. 25).

GETTING AROUND
Car Rental
Archie Auto Rentals, tel 473/ 439-0086, www.archierentals .com; and David's Car Rental, tel 473/444-3399, www.davidscars .com, operate in Grenada. For rentals in Carriacou, contact Barba's Jeep Rentals, tel 473/443-7454, or Sunkey's Auto Rentals, tel 473/443-8382. Drivers will require a temporary local driver's permit (US$12) plus a valid overseas license. Driving is on the left.

Public Transportation
Private minibuses (dollar buses) cover virtually every corner of Grenada and Carriacou on an unscheduled though frequent basis from early morning until early evening. Visitors can flag them down and be squeezed in by the "put-man" who also collects the money. Rap hard on the roof to get off.

Taxis are available from the airport and main taxi stand on the Careenage in St. George's, by the ferry dock in Hillsborough, or make arrangements with your hotel. Always agree the price in advance.

For interisland ferry information, see Arrival/Departure.

PRACTICAL ADVICE
Emergencies
Police and fire: tel 911. Ambulance, St. George's: tel 473/440-2113. St. George's Hospital in Grenada, tel 473/440-2050, can cope with most sicknesses, though serious medical emergencies may be transferred to Puerto Rico. Hotels can contact the duty doctor. On Carriacou, contact Princess Royal Hospital, tel 473/443-7400; or the ambulance, tel 774.

Telephones
The area code for Grenada, Carriacou, and Petite Martinique is 473.

Tourist Information
Grenada: Grenada Board of Tourism, P.O. Box 293, St. George's, tel 473/440-2279, fax 473/440-6637, www.grenadagrenadines.com. **Carriacou:** Main St., Hillsborough, tel 473/443-7948.

U.S. & Canada Offices
Lake Worth: P.O. Box 1668, FL 33460, tel 561/588-8176 or 800/927-9554, fax 561/558-7267. **Toronto:** 439 University Ave., Ste 920, ON M5G 1Y8, tel 416/595-1339, fax 416/595-8278.

ST. LUCIA

PLANNING YOUR TRIP
Arrival/Departure
Hewanorra Airport on the island's south is St. Lucia's chief gateway for international jet flights, served by direct flights from the United States with American Airlines from Miami, JetBlue from New York, Delta from Atlanta, and US Airways from Philadelphia and Charlotte. It is a 90-minute transfer to hotels in the north of the island. George Charles Airport at Vigie/Castries can accept only smaller planes, including American Eagle's daily services from Puerto Rico, and frequent LIAT services from local transportation hubs such as Antigua (see p. 343) and Barbados (see p. 349).

High-speed ferry services link St. Lucia with Martinique (1 hour 20 minutes). For information, contact Cox & Co., Castries, tel 758/452-2211, agents for Express des Îles, www.express-des-iles.com.

Entry Requirements
Visitors are required to produce a passport and return or onward ticket.

Festivals & Events

May St. Lucia Jazz Festival (Pigeon Island & Castries)
July Carnival
September–October St. Lucia Billfishing Tournament (all welcome); Jounen Kweyol Entenasyonnal (International Creole Day)
November–December Atlantic Rally for Cruisers (Rodney Bay Marina)

National holidays include Independence Day (Feb. 22), Corpus Christi (June), Emancipation Day (1st Mon. in Aug.), Thanksgiving Day (Oct. 4), and National Day (Dec. 13).

GETTING AROUND
Car Rental

Avis, tel 758/452-2700, www
.avisstlucia.com; Budget, tel
758/452-8673, www.budget
stlucia.com; Hertz, tel 758/ 452-
0679; and West Coast Jeeps,
tel 758/459-5457, www
.westcoastjeeps.com. A temporary visitor's permit (US$20) is required plus a valid overseas license. Driving is on the left.

Public Transportation

Frequent and inexpensive minibus services run between Castries, Rodney Bay, and the north until about 11 p.m. (later on Fri. for visitors to the Gros Islet jump-up party). Less frequent services to Soufrière and the south depart from Bridge St.

Taxi rates are fixed by the government; always agree on the fare in advance.

PRACTICAL ADVICE
Emergencies

Police, fire, and ambulance: tel 911. St. Lucia's main hospitals are the Victoria Hospital in Castries, tel 758/452-2421, and St. Jude's

in Vieux Fort, tel 758/454-6041. All hotels have a resident or on-call doctor.

Telephones

The area code is 758.

Tourist Information

Castries: St. Lucia Tourist Board, Sureline Building, Vide Bouteille, P.O. Box 221, Castries, tel 758/452-4094, fax 758/453-1121, www.stlucia.org.

U.S. & Canada Offices

New York: St. Lucia Tourist Board, 800 2nd Ave., Ste. 910, NY 10017, tel 212/867-2950 or 800/456-3984, fax 212/697-4993.
Toronto: 65 Overlea Blvd., Ste. 250, ON M4H 1P1, tel 416/362-4242 or 800/869-0377.

ST. VINCENT
& THE GRENADINES

PLANNING YOUR TRIP
Arrival/Departure

There are no direct flights to St. Vincent and the Grenadines from the U.S. mainland. There are easy connections from the neighboring islands of Barbados, Grenada, and St. Lucia, as well as Puerto Rico, Martinique, and Trinidad. Local carriers include LIAT, ww.liat.com, and SVG Air, www.svgair.com. St. Vincent's E.T. Joshua Airport, outside the capital city of Kingstown, is a transportation hub for the Grenadine islands, with onward flights to Bequia, Canouan, Mustique, and Union Island. The islands can also be reached by scheduled boat services originating from Kingstown.

Entry Requirements

Visitors will be required to produce a passport and a return or onward ticket.

Departure tax is US$15.

Festivals & Events

March–April Bequia Easter Regatta
June–July Carnival or Vincy Mas (Kingstown, St. Vincent)
December Nine Mornings marks the nine-day run-up to Christmas with arts and crafts, parades, carol singers, and night-time jump-ups.

National holidays include St. Vincent and the Grenadines Day (Jan. 22), Caricom Day (July 5), Emancipation Day (Aug. 2), and Independence Day (Oct. 27).

GETTING AROUND
Car Rental

On St. Vincent, Avis, tel 784/456-6861, www.avis.com, has an office at the airport while Ben's Auto Rental, tel 784/456-2907; David's Auto Clinic, tel 784/457-1116, and Rent and Drive, tel 784/457-5601, www.rentanddrivesvg.com, will pick up from the airport. A temporary driving permit costs around US$25. You can find rental cars on the Grenadines, too. Driving is on the left.

Public Transportation

Private minibuses (known as dollar buses) ply the south coast route between Kingstown and Villa/Calliaqua throughout the day, less frequently in the evening. To hail a bus anywhere along the route, point down at the road; to get off, rap on the roof or shout "driver, stop" over the music. There are services to Layou and the west coast from the waterfront depot in Kingstown. Taxis are available from the airport, downtown Kingstown, and through hotels. Fares are fixed by the government.

PRACTICAL ADVICE
Emergencies

Police, fire, coast guard: tel 911.
Police HQ: tel 784/457-1211.

Kingstown General Hospital, A&E: tel 784/456-1955; inquiries, tel 784/456-1185. Medical emergencies can be airlifted to Barbados or Puerto Rico. Hotels will contact a duty doctor.

Telephones
The area code for St. Vincent and the Grenadines is 784.

Tourist Information
Kingstown: St. Vincent and the Grenadines Tourism Authority, P.O. Box 834, NIS Bldg., Upper Bay Street, tel 784/456-6222, fax 784/485-6020, www.discoversvg .com.

U.S. & Canada Offices
New York: 801 2nd Ave., 21st Floor, New York, NY 10017, tel 212/687-4981 or 800/729-1726, fax 212/949-5946.
Toronto: 333 Wilson Ave., Ste. 601, ON M3H 1T2, tel 416/630-9292 or 866/421-4452, fax 416/630-9291.

■ BARBADOS
PLANNING YOUR TRIP
Arrival/Departure
Barbados has good air connections with North America. American Airlines flies direct from New York, Dallas/Fort Worth, and Miami to Grantley Adams International Airport; American also provides daily services from Puerto Rico. US Airways has flights from Charlotte; Caribbean Airlines flies from Miami, New York, and Toronto. LIAT, www .liat.com, and other local airlines provide a network of inter-Caribbean links with the Leeward and Windward Islands, the French Antilles, Sint Maarten, and Trinidad and Tobago.

Entry Requirements
U.S. visitors require a passport or proof of citizenship and photo ID, plus a return or onward ticket.

Festivals & Events
January Barbados Jazz Festival
February Holetown Festival, week-long celebration of the first settlers
July–August Crop Over Festival, the Bajan Carnival.

National holidays include New Year's Day, Good Friday, Easter Monday, Labor Day (May 1), Whit Monday, Emancipation Day (July 31), U.N. Day (Oct. 6), Christmas Day, and Boxing Day (Dec. 26).

GETTING AROUND
Car Rental
Local operators include Coconut Cars, tel 246/437-0297, www .coconutcars.com; Courtesy Rent-A-Car, tel 246/431-4160, www .courtesycars.com; Stoutes Car Rental, tel 246/416-4456, www .stoutescar.com; and Top Class, tel 246/228-7368, www.topclass rentals.com. In addition to a valid overseas license, drivers must purchase a temporary visitor's driving license (US$5). Driving is on the left.

Public Transportation
Regular and inexpensive public bus and minibuses serve the coastal regions and Bridgetown from early morning until around midnight. Taxis are not metered, so agree on a price in advance.

PRACTICAL ADVICE
Emergencies
Police: tel 211. Fire: tel 311. Ambulance: tel 511. Queen Elizabeth Hospital, Bridgetown North: tel 246/436-5446. Hotels can contact a duty doctor.

Telephones
The area code is 246.

Tourist Information
Bridgetown: Barbados Tourism Authority, P.O. Box 242, Harbour Rd., tel 246/427-2623, fax 246/426-4080, www.barbados.org.

U.S. & Canada Offices
New York: Barbados Tourism Authority, 820 2nd Ave., 5th floor, New York, NY 10017, tel 212/986-6516 or 800/221-9831, fax 212/573-9850.
Toronto: 105 Adelaide St. West, Ste. 1010, ON M5H 1P9, tel 416/214-9880 or 800/268-9122, fax 416/214-9882.

■ TRINIDAD & TOBAGO
PLANNING YOUR TRIP
Arrival/Departure
There are direct flights to Trinidad's Piarco Airport, 30 miles east of Port of Spain, with American Airlines from Miami; Caribbean Airlines, www.caribbean-airlines .com, from Miami, New York, and Toronto; and with Continental from Houston. LIAT, www.liat .com, also offers connections from Antigua, Barbados, Grenada, and St. Lucia. Caribbean Airlines offers a weekly service between New York and Tobago's ANR Robinson International Airport (formerly Crown Point), but most visitors fly to the neighboring islands for connections with LIAT, or fly to Trinidad and hop to Tobago on the frequent Caribbean Airlines airbridge service (25 minutes) between the two islands.
Ferry services also provide an inexpensive but slow sea bridge between the islands. Contact the Port Authority of Trinidad & Tobago, www.patnt.com.
Departure tax is TT $100

(US$16), which must be paid in local currency.

Festivals & Events
January–March Preparations for the famous Trinidad Carnival
March Phagwa (Hindu New Year)
June Muslim Hosay, a three-day event tied to the Islamic calendar
July Tobago Heritage Festival
August Steelband Week (Trinidad)
September Tobago Festival
October–November Divali (Hindu Festival of Light)

National holidays include New Year's Day, Good Friday, Easter Monday, Labour Day (June 19), Emancipation Day (Aug. 1), Independence Day (Aug. 31), Christmas Day, and Boxing Day (Dec. 26).

GETTING AROUND
Car Rental
Rental cars can be picked up from Trinidad's Piarco Airport from Auto Rentals, tel 868/669-227; Budget, tel 868/669-1635, www.budget.com; and Econo Car Rentals, tel 868/669-1119, www.econocarrentalstt.com. All three companies have offices on Tobago: Auto Rentals, tel 868/639-0644; Budget, 868/631-8456; and Econo Cars, tel 868/660-8728.

U.S. and Canadian driver's licenses are valid on the islands. Driving is on the left. Gas stations are sparse, so fill up before leaving.

Public Transportation
Inexpensive public buses cover most destinations on Trinidad from the main depot at South Quay in Port of Spain. Tickets have to be purchased in advance.

Private minibuses, known as maxi-taxis, are faster. The maxis are color coded by destination: yellow stripes for Port of Spain area; red for the east; green for the south. Taxis are readily available from the airport (fixed fares to Port of Spain and other popular destinations).

Tobago has public and private bus systems. Public buses depart from Gardenside Road, Scarborough, for Crown Point and other destinations. Maxi-taxis (minibuses with a blue stripe) are often a better option and can be flagged down along any roadside.

Taxis wait at the airport and some of the busier hotels. There are fixed rates from the airport to hotels.

PRACTICAL ADVICE
Emergencies
Police: tel 999. Fire and ambulance: tel 990. Port of Spain General Hospital: tel 868/623-2951. In Tobago, minor casualties are handled by Scarborough Hospital, tel 868/639-2551. Emergencies may be airlifted to Trinidad.

Telephones
The area code for Trinidad and Tobago is 868.

Tourist Information
Port of Spain: Trinidad and Tobago Tourism Development Company, Level 1, Maritime Centre, 29 10th Ave., Barataria, tel 868/675-7034, fax 868/638-7962, www.gotrinidadandtobago.com.

U.S. Office
Coral Gables: Cheryl Andrews Marketing, 331 Almeria Ave., FL 33134, tel 305/444-4033, fax 305/447-0415.

Hotels & Restaurants

Accommodations in the Caribbean are generally very expensive, although cheaper options are available. Prices drop dramatically in low season, but you will be taking more chances with the weather. All-inclusive resorts can offer good value, although it can be too easy to stay in the resort and not explore the islands.

Rewarding dining experiences can range from jerk chicken to top-class French cuisine. Restaurants are informal and seating arrangements and closing times are flexible. Call ahead to check.

Hotels and restaurants in this section have been organized by region, then price, then in alphabetical order.

■ JAMAICA

KINGSTON & THE BLUE MOUNTAINS

SOMETHING SPECIAL

🏨 STRAWBERRY HILL

🍴 Perched 3,000 feet (900 m) above Kingston in the Blue Mountains with fabulous views over the city, Strawberry Hill is an award-winning property owned by the exemplary Island Outpost hotel group. The pretty colonial-style villas have private verandas, kitchens, hand-crafted plantation furniture, four-poster mahogany beds with mosquito nets, and louvered windows. The hotel also features a spa, multimedia center, and an excellent restaurant renowned for its "new Jamaican" cuisine and superb Sunday brunch.

$$$$$
IRISH TOWN
TEL 876/944-8400 OR
800/688-7678
FAX 876/944-8408
www.islandoutpost.com
🛈 12 villas 🏊 🆚 All major cards

🏨 HILTON KINGSTON

$$$–$$$$
77 KNUTSFORD BOULEVARD
TEL 876/926-5430
FAX 876/929-7439
www.hilton.com
Centrally located in New

Kingston, this landmark hotel is set on over 7 acres (2.8 ha) of tropical gardens and has an Olympic-size pool, health club and tennis courts, business center, gaming room, and a range of bars and restaurants.
🛈 290, 13 suites 🆚 🆚 🏊 🆚
🆚 All major cards

🏨 LIME TREE FARM

$$–$$$
TOWER HILL, MAVIS BANK
TEL 876/881-8788
www.limetreefarm.com
You don't have to move farther than the veranda to go bird-watching at this delightful Blue Mountain hideaway on a working coffee farm. Spacious cottages with fabulous views, wonderfully hospitable staff, delicious locally grown food (full board inclusive), and nature walks and hikes.
🛈 3 🅿

🍴 NORMA'S ON THE TERRACE

$$$
DEVON HOUSE
TEL 876/968-5488
One of Kingston's top restaurants. Sophisticated setting and creative menu inspired by Jamaican ingredients, with an international flavor. Excellent desserts.
🆚 All major cards

🍴 GLORIA'S RENDEZVOUS

$$

PRICES

HOTELS
An indication of the cost of a double room in the high season is given by **$** signs.

$$$$$	Over $400
$$$$	$300–$400
$$$	$200–$300
$$	$100–$200
$	Under $100

RESTAURANTS
An indication of the cost of a three-course meal without drinks is given by **$** signs.

$$$$$	Over $80
$$$$	$50–$80
$$$	$35–$50
$$	$20–$35
$	Under $20

5 QUEEN STREET, PORT ROYAL
TEL 876/967-8066
Sidewalk dining at its most basic, but don't miss out on scrumptious fresh seafood specials including jerk lobster and garlic shrimp washed down with chilled Red Stripe.
🆚 No credit cards

MANDEVILLE

🍴 BLOOMFIELD GREAT HOUSE

$$
8 PERTH ROAD
TEL 876/962-7130
A breezy veranda on the hillside with views over the palm tops, friendly service, and well-rounded menu of Jamaican classics and European staples. Spicy seafood, filet mignon, or hearty roasted oxtail are recommended.
🆚 All major cards

MONTEGO BAY

🏨 ROUND HILL HOTEL & VILLAS

$$$$$
P.O. BOX 64, MONTEGO BAY
TEL 876/956-7050 OR
800/972-2159
FAX 876/956-7505
www.roundhilljamaica.com
One of Jamaica's finest
traditional resorts, perched on
a promontory 10 miles (16 km)
west of Mo'Bay. Timeless style;
impeccable service. The villas all
have kitchens and housekeep-
ers to prepare your breakfast,
and many have pools.
📋 36 plus 27 villas 🏊 🏋
💳 All major cards

🏨 HALF MOON GOLF, TENNIS & BEACH CLUB
$$$$–$$$$$
TEL 877/956-7628 OR 888/830-5974
FAX 876/953-2731
www.halfmoon.rockresorts.com
Seven miles (12 km) east of
Mo'Bay, this huge colonial-style
resort is set on over 400 acres
(162 ha) and offers a range
of rooms, suites, and villas.
Activities include an 18-hole
golf course, tennis, horseback
riding, and water sports.
📋 197 plus 33 villas 🆒 🏊
🏋 💳 All major cards

🏨 EL GRECO ALL SUITES RESORT
$$
11 QUEEN'S DRIVE
TEL 876/940-6116, U.S. 888/354-7326, CANADA 800/397-7326
FAX 876/940-6115
www.elgrecojamaica.com
A handy central option for
families and friends an elevator-
ride away from Doctor's Cave
Beach (free daily pass). One-
and two-bedroom suites on
the hillside with kitchen and
private balcony. Restaurant;
tennis; shop.
📋 93 🅿 🍴 🆒 🏊 💳

🍴 THE NATIVE
$$–$$$

29 GLOUCESTER AVENUE
TEL 876/979-2769
Just the spot to sample Jamai-
can specialties in the heart
of touristy Mo'Bay. Share a
boonoonoonoos platter to sample
staples such as jerk chicken, salt
fish, and ackee. Tasty vegetarian
options, delicious coconut-
crusted fish, and the shady
terrace setting is a bonus.
💳 All major cards

🍴 PORK PIT
$
27 GLOUCESTER AVENUE
TEL 876/940-3008
The local jerk stop on the Hip
Strip. Be warned, the full, fiery,
high-octane Jamaican recipe
is served up here with no
concessions to delicate tourist
tastebuds. Delicious nonethe-
less and a bargain. Sidewalk
tables and take out.

NEGRIL

SOMETHING SPECIAL

🏨 THE CAVES
Set above the honeycomb
cliffs of Negril's West End, this
beautiful property features
hand-crafted thatched and
wood cottages nestled in
tropical gardens. A series of
steps lead down to sundecks
and hidden grottos at sea level.
All rooms have CD players and
king- or queen-size beds, and
there's an Aveda spa treatment
center.
$$$$$
LIGHTHOUSE ROAD, WEST END
TEL 876/957-0270 OR 800/688-7678
FAX 876/957-4930
www.islandoutpost.com
📋 12 cottages 🏊 💳 All major
cards

🏨 TENSING PEN
$$–$$$
P.O. BOX 3013
LIGHTHOUSE ROAD
TEL 876/957-0387
FAX 876/957-0161

www.tensingpen.com
A collection of stylish, indi-
vidually designed bamboo and
wood cottages set in lovely
cliff-top gardens. A superb
West End retreat.
💳 All major cards

🏨 ROCKHOUSE HOTEL
$$
LIGHTHOUSE ROAD
TEL 876/957-4373
FAX 876/957-0557
www.rockhousehotel.com
The resort's thatched-roof,
octagonal beehive huts overlook Pristine Cove on West
End's foreshore. Connected by
wooden walkways, the huts
have four-poster beds and
ceiling fans. There is a stunning
pool on the shore.
📋 28 🆒 🏊

🍴 LE VENDÔME
$$$$
CHARELA INN, NEGRIL BEACH
TEL 876/957-4648
Pretty and deservedly popular
terraced dining room serving
light pizza/pasta/salad type
lunches. In the evening the
culinary bar is set higher with
an à la carte and five-course
gourmet menu of French
cuisine with a Jamaican twist.
Live entertainment.
💳 All major cards

🍴 NORMA'S
$$–$$$
SEA SPLASH HOTEL, NORMAN
MANLEY BLVD.
TEL 876/957-4041
Don't let the modest setting
fool you, leading Jamaican
chef Norma Shirley cooks up
a storm delivering an often
surprising and always delicious
take on traditional local fare.
💳 All major cards

🍴 RICK'S CAFÉ
$$
WEST END ROAD
TEL 876/957-4335
A Negril institution, with

🆒 Air-conditioning 🏊 Indoor pool 🏊 Outdoor pool 🏋 Health club 💳 Credit cards

a lively terrace restaurant. Specialties include seafood pasta dishes, broiled lobster, and enticing desserts.
🅢 All major cards

OCHO RIOS/ORACABESSA

SOMETHING SPECIAL

🏨 GOLDENEYE
This makeover of Bond author Ian Fleming's holiday home is a masterpiece. Luxurious, discreet, and casually chic, GoldenEye's villas and beach cottages combine the best of local (jalousies and outdoor bathrooms) and contemporary design. Fabulous food, private beaches, water sports, kids' stuff, and activities from riding to deep-sea fishing by arrangement.
$$$$$
ORACABESSA
TEL 876/975-3354 OR 800/688-7678
FAX 876/975-3620
www.goldeneyehotel.com
🛈 4 villas, 11 cottages, 6 suites
🅢 🏊 🅢 All major cards

🏨 HIBISCUS LODGE
$$–$$$
87 MAIN STREET
TEL 876/974-2676
FAX 876/974-1874
www.hibiscusjamaica.com
Small, friendly hotel set in pretty gardens on the cliff side with pool and tennis courts. Pleasant rooms.
🛈 26 🅢 🅢 🏊 🅢 All major cards

🍴 EVITA'S
$$–$$$
EDEN BOWER ROAD
TEL 876/974-2333
Set on the hillside above town, this cheerful Italian-owned restaurant serves authentic homemade pasta (albeit with a Jamaican twist), salads, soups, and a wide range of desserts in an elegant setting overlooking the bay.
🅢 All major cards

🍴 SCOTCHIES TOO
$
NORTH COAST HIGHWAY., DRAX HALL
TEL 876/794-9457
A ten-minute drive west of Ochi, this outpost of the original Scotchies in Mo'Bay is worth finding. Succulent jerk chicken threaded on bamboo skewers, sides of sweet dumpling-like festival and roast breadfruit, lashings of house hot sauce, cold beers, and tables in tin-roofed gazebos dotted about the garden.
🅢 MC, V

PORT ANTONIO

🏨 MOCKING BIRD HILL
$$$–$$$$
SAN SAN
TEL 876/993-7267
FAX 876/993-7133
www.hotelmockingbirdhill.com
Charming and comfortable little eco-resort in the hills above San San. The light, airy rooms feature bamboo furniture, ocean-view balconies, and works by the artist-owner.
🛈 10 🏊 🅢 All major cards

🍴 NORMA'S AT THE MARINA
$$
ERROL FLYNN MARINA
TEL 876/993-9510
Norma Shirley brings her culinary skills to bear at this waterfront spot in the new marina. Drink in the views and enjoy smoked marlin, devilled crab, or grilled shrimp with mango salsa.
🕒 Closed Sun. 🅢 MC, V

🍴 BLUE LAGOON
$–$$
FAIRY HILL
TEL 876/993-8491
This famous waterfront bar has a spectacular setting on the Blue Lagoon itself and serves top-quality jerk chicken, pork, and fish, as well as crayfish and pizzas. A beautiful spot for either lunch or dinner. Live music weekends.
🅢 All major cards

SOUTH COAST

🏨 JAKE'S
$$
TREASURE BEACH, CALABASH BAY, ST. ELIZABETH
TEL 876/965-0635
FAX 876/965-0552
www.islandoutpost.com
Funny collection of rooms and cottages designed in a mix of Jamaican, Mexican, and Catalan styles. Cooled by sea breezes and ceiling fans, the cottages have private outdoor showers, no phones or television. Spa; buzzy bar; excellent restaurant.
🛈 14 cottages 🏊 🅢 All major cards

🍴 JACK SPRATT
$$
CALABASH BAY, TREASURE BEACH
TEL 876/965-3583
Colorful tin-roofed diner with a woodsy interior and shady terrace tables right on the beach. Blackboard menu featuring pizzas (lobster a specialty) and seafood served with disks of delicious fried bammy (cassava bread soaked in coconut milk). Live music.
🅢 All major cards

◼ CAYMAN ISLANDS

CAYMAN BRAC

🏨 BRAC REEF RESORT
$$
WEST END
TEL 345/948-1323 OR 800/594-0843
FAX 345/948-1207
www.bracreef.com
Relaxing and friendly property on the white sand shore. All rooms feature balcony or patio.

🏨 Hotel 🍴 Restaurant 🛈 No. of guest rooms 🔲 No. of seats 🅿 Parking 🕒 Closed

The hotel has a good beach and a full-service dive shop, tennis, and spa.

🏨 40 🅢 🌊 🍴 🅒 All major cards

🏨 CAYMAN BREAKERS
$$
EAST END
TEL/FAX 345/948-1463
www.caymancondosonline.com
A row of ice-cream pink, low-rise condos stretched along the sandy beach below the bluff offering comfortable two bed/two bath units with fully equipped kitchens.

🏨 18 🅟 🅢 🌊 🅒 MC, V

🏨 WALTON'S MANGO MANOR
$
STAKE BAY
TEL/FAX 345/948-0518
www.waltonsmangomanor.com
Quaint B&B in an old house with beach access, and fruit trees and parrots in the garden. Seven spotlessly clean rooms and a two-bed villa ($$).

🏨 8 🅢 🅢 🅒 All major cards

GRAND CAYMAN

🏨 CARIBBEAN CLUB
$$$$$
871 WEST BAY ROAD, SEVEN MILE BEACH
TEL 345/623-4500 OR 800/941-1126
FAX 345/946-9954
www.caribclub.com
Über-luxurious boutique condominium hotel comprising 37 three-bedroom, three-bathroom beachfront suites and villas. Each spacious apartment is fitted with the latest technology. Infinity pool; nanny service; concierge.

🏨 37 🅟 🅢 🅢 🌊 🅒 All major cards

🏨 WESTIN CASUARINA RESORT & SPA

$$$$–$$$$$
WEST BAY ROAD,
SEVEN MILE BEACH
TEL 345/945-3800 OR 800/WESTIN-1
FAX 345/949-5825
www.westincasuarina.net
One of the smarter resorts along Seven Mile Beach and a great choice for families. Kid programs (4–12); water sports; diving. Round-the-clock room service and swim-up pool bar.

🏨 347 🅢 🅢 🌊 🅒 All major cards

SOMETHING SPECIAL

🏨 RITZ-CARLTON GRAND CAYMAN
This fabulous beachfront behemoth has set a new gold standard for luxury in the region. Facilities include a La Prairie Spa, a Nick Bollettieri tennis school, Greg Norman–designed golf course, gourmet cuisine.

$$$–$$$$$
SEVEN MILE BEACH
TEL 345/815-6851
FAX 345/815-6855
www.ritzcarlton.com

🏨 365 🅟 🅢 🌊 🅒 All major cards

🏨 COLBALT COAST
$$$–$$$$
18-A SEA FAN DRIVE, WEST BAY
TEL 345/946-5656 OR 888/946-5656
FAX 345/946-5657
www.cobaltcoast.com
Designed in the style of a Caribbean great house, this comfortable and welcoming hotel is well away from the bustle of Seven Mile Beach and has a 120-foot (37 m) jetty with access to great shore diving.

🏨 18 🅢 🅒 All major cards

🏨 THE REEF RESORT
$$–$$$
EAST END, P.O. BOX 30865 SMB

TEL 345/947-3100 OR 888/232-0541
FAX 345/947-9920
www.thereef.com.ky
Good value beachfront resort, 20 miles (32 km) from George Town at the quieter east end of the island. Generous condo-sized suites ideal for families. Close to first-rate diving and snorkeling.

🏨 152 🅢 🅢 🅢 🌊 🅒 All major cards

🏨 TURTLE NEST INN
$$–$$$
BODDEN TOWN
TEL 345/947-8665
FAX 345/947-6379
www.turtlenestinn.net
Spacious and attractive one-bedroom apartments in a friendly and intimate seaside inn 10 miles (16 km) from George Town. Patios/verandas with barbecues; good snorkeling off a quiet sandy beach.

🏨 26 🅢 🌊 🅒 All major cards

🏨 SUNSET HOUSE
$–$$
S. CHURCH STREET, GEORGE TOWN
TEL 345/949-7111 OR 800/854-4767
FAX 345/949-7101
www.sunsethouse.com
A popular choice for dedicated divers, Sunset has a fully equipped dive school, underwater photo tuition, and good shore diving. Deluxe rooms have ocean views.

🏨 54 🅢 🌊 🅒 All major cards

🍴 LIGHTHOUSE RESTAURANT
$$$
BREAKERS, EAST END
TEL 345/947-2047
A Cayman landmark for the last 30 years. Very popular and romantic with a nautical theme and terrace overlooking the seashore. Caribbean-Italian specialties include pasta, fish,

---

🅢 Air-conditioning 🅢 Indoor pool 🌊 Outdoor pool 🅒 Health club 🅒 Credit cards

and mixed seafood grills.
⬚ All major cards

🍴 CRACKED CONCH BY THE SEA
$–$$$
WEST BAY
TEL 345/945-5217
A long-standing institution, serving distinctly upscale Caribbean cuisine: signature conch chowder, jerk-seasoned tuna. Caribbean Sunday brunch. Patio dining and mellow tiki bar overlooking the ironshore.
⬚ All major cards

🍴 CIMBOCO
$$
MARQUEE PLAZA, SEVEN MILE BEACH
TEL 345/947-2782
Jaunty island-style Caribbean café with an open kitchen and wood-burning oven. Home-baked breads and pizzas, pasta salads, jerk grills, and posher nosh such as banana leaf roasted snapper followed by epic homemade desserts. Great weekend brunches.
⬚ All major cards

LITTLE CAYMAN

🏨🍴 PIRATES POINT RESORT
$–$$$
PRESTON BAY
TEL 345/948-1010
FAX 345/948-1011
www.piratespointresort.com
Perennial favorite with simple but charming bungalows set on a small beach. Gladys Howard's cuisine is legendary (non-residents book in advance). Fully equipped dive operation run by experienced staff.
ⓘ 11 ⬚ ⬚ ⬚ ⬚ All major cards

🏨 LITTLE CAYMAN BEACH RESORT
$$
BLOSSOM VILLAGE
TEL 345/948-1033 OR

800/327-3835
FAX 345/948-0124
www.littlecayman.com
Modern resort with good facilities set out around a small pool with funky underwater lighting. Tennis, spa, water sports, and dive center.
ⓘ 40 ⬚ ⬚ ⬚ ⬚ All major cards

🏨 SOUTHERN CROSS CLUB
$$
SOUTH HOLE SOUND
TEL 345/948-1099 OR
800/899-2582
FAX 345/948-1098
www.southerncrossclub.com
Luxurious chalets spaced out across a white sandy beach; excellent food and service; sportfishing, kayaks, and dive center.
ⓘ 12 chalets ⬚ ⬚ ⬚ All major cards

🍴 HUNGRY IGUANA
$$
SOUTH HOLE SOUND
TEL 345/948-0007
Next door to the airport at Paradise Villas, the restaurant is a popular meeting place with ocean views. Local and international cuisine.
⬚ All major cards

■ TURKS & CAICOS

GRAND TURK

🏨 ISLAND HOUSE
$$–$$$
COCKBURN TOWN
TEL 649/946-1519
FAX 649/946-2646
www.islandhouse.tc
A few minutes outside of town, overlooking North Creek, this newly refurbished complex features spacious and well-equipped suites.
ⓘ 8 ⬚ ⬚ ⬚ All major cards

🏨 OSPREY BEACH HOTEL
$$
DUKE STREET, COCKBURN TOWN
TEL 649/946-2666
FAX 649/946-2817
www.ospreybeachhotel.com
Attractive beachfront rooms/suites with cool, crisp decor and patio/balcony; some four-posters (atrium rooms face inner courtyard). Bar, restaurant, scuba packages.
ⓘ 27 ⬚ ⬚ All major cards

🏨 SALT RAKER INN
$–$$
DUKE STREET, COCKBURN TOWN
TEL 649/946-2260
FAX 649/946-2263
www.hotelsaltraker.com
Dating from the 1840s, this charming old inn (once a Bermudian shipwright's home) has a hospitable atmosphere and lovely shady garden.
ⓘ 13 ⬚ ⬚ All major cards

🍴 BIRDCAGE RESTAURANT
$$–$$$
OSPREY BEACH HOTEL
DUKE STREET, COCKBURN TOWN
TEL 649/946-2666
Salads and fish sandwiches for lunch; classic steaks and seafood for dinner, but the real key to its success is the twice-weekly barbecue nights (Wed. and Sun.). Great atmosphere, live music.
⬚ MC, V

🍴 THE SAND BAR
$$
DUKE STREET, COCKBURN TOWN
TEL 649/946-1111
Popular hangout for sundowners with locals and visitors. Tasty, no-nonsense menu of fish sandwiches, cracked conch, quesadillas, and burgers served on the deck overlooking the beach.
⬚ MC, V

🏨 Hotel 🍴 Restaurant ⓘ No. of guest rooms 🪑 No. of seats 🅿 Parking 🕒 Closed

MIDDLE CAICOS

🏨 BLUE HORIZON RESORT
$$–$$$
CONCH BAR
TEL 649/946-6141
FAX 649/946-6139
www.bhresort.com
Unpretentious beachfront
cottages and villas sporting
bright blue tin roofs. Kitchens,
screened porches, bicycles
available. Spectacular views, but
quite remote.
ⓘ 7 🏧 All major cards

NORTH CAICOS

🏨 CAICOS BEACH CONDOMINIUMS
$$–$$$$
DRAKE COURT, WHITBY
TEL 649/241-4778 OR U.S.
786/338-9264
FAX 649/946-7339
www.caicosbeachcondos.com
Set in tranquil tropical gardens
on the beachfront, rooms and
one-, two- and three-bedroom
suites with kitchens and living
areas decorated with island
prints. Families welcome.
ⓘ 10 🅿 🏊 🏧 All major cards

🏨 PELICAN BEACH HOTEL
$–$$
WHITBY
TEL 649/946-7112
FAX 649/946-7139
www.pelicanbeach.tc
This was the first locally owned
hotel on the island and has a
friendly, laid-back atmosphere.
Very quiet; no phones. Rooms
are showing their age but
charming nonetheless.
ⓘ 14 🆑 🏧 All major cards

PROVIDENCIALES

🏨 GANSEVOORT TURKS + CAICOS
$$$$
LOWER BIGHT ROAD, GRACE BAY
TEL 649/941-7555
FAX 309/210-9091

www.gansevoortturksand
caicos.com
One of the latest upscale
arrivals on Grace Bay, this
fabulous new boutique resort
is on every "hot hotel" list.
Sleek urban chic married to a
cool cream and blue palette,
infinity pool, luxurious spa,
and modern bistro-bar.
ⓘ 91 (incl. 4 penthouse
suites) 🅿 🆑 🏊 🎽 🏧 All
major cards

🏨 GRACE BAY CLUB & VILLAS
$$$$
GRACE BAY ROAD
TEL 649/946-5050 or
800/946-5757
FAX 649/946-5758
www.gracebayclub.com
Intimate, all-suites hotel
with excellent resort facilities
featuring stylishly equipped
ocean-facing accommodations
with kitchens and terraces
(no children under 12 in
hotel). Families can opt for the
stunning new villa complex
equipped with health club,
spa, and kids' club.
ⓘ 59 suites 🏊 🎽 🏧 All
major cards

🏨 SIBONNÉ BEACH HOTEL
$$
GRACE BAY
TEL 649/946-5547
or 888/570-2861
FAX 649/946-5770
www.sibonne.com
Small, casual, and bang on the
beach, Sibonné is the oldest
property on the bay, but one
of the friendliest. Good value
courtyard and attractive
ocean-view rooms (plus airy
one-bedroom apartment); bar
and veranda dining; close to
diving and amenities.
ⓘ 30 🆑 🏊 🏧

🍽 O'SOLEIL
$$$$$
THE SOMERSET, PRINCESS DRIVE,
GRACE BAY

TEL 649/946-5900
Sleek white minimalist decor
lit by crystal chandeliers and
a sophisticated menu packed
with creative fusion cuisine:
a caesar salad served with
plantain croutons; jerk salmon
with polenta; Australian rack
of lamb spiked with harissa.
Reservations advised.
🏧 All major cards

SOMETHING SPECIAL

🍽 ANACAONA
A serious contender for the
island's finest dining experi-
ence, this gourmet restaurant
has a romantic setting on the
beachfront beneath a circular
thatched roof. The Caribbean/
Mediterranean-inspired cuisine
is light and assured and features
fresh island seafood. Dress code
elegant, no children under 12.
Reservations essential.
$$$$
GRACE BAY CLUB
TEL 649/946-5050
🏧 All major cards

🍽 CAICOS CAFÉ
$$$
GRACE BAY ROAD, GRACE BAY
TEL 649/946-5278
Pretty West Indian cottage
with a shady terrace ideal for
a romantic evening. Perfectly
grilled steaks, lobster and
shrimp from the barbecue,
French-Mediterranean specialties, and an impressive wine list.
🕐 Closed Sun.

🍽 DA BUGALOO'S CONCH SHACK
$–$$
BLUE HILLS BEACH
TEL 649/946-8877
The best fresh conch in the
islands. Conch every which
way from spiced to salad via
cracked and fritters, plus chilled
rum punch in an eye-catching
beachside shack.
🏧 No credit cards

🆑 Air-conditioning 🏊 Indoor pool 🏊 Outdoor pool 🎽 Health club 🏧 Credit cards

SALT CAY

🍴 PORTER'S ISLAND THYME
$$
TEL 649/946-6977
www.islandthyme.tc
Start the day with homemade cinnamon-dusted dough-nuts; snap up a zesty chicken sandwich for lunch; and head back for cocktails and delicious Caribbean-Asian fusion cuisine at dinnertime. Fun island hangout with accommodations in oceanfront cottages.
🔲 MC, V

■ DOMINICAN REPUBLIC

CENTRAL HIGHLANDS

🏨 RANCHO BAIGUATE
$–$$
JARABACOA
TEL 809/574-6890 OR U.S./CANADA 646/727-7783
www.ranchobaiguate.com
The country's only dedicated adventure sports center, set on extensive grounds bordered by the Baiguate and Jimenoa Rivers just outside Jarabacoa. Activities include trekking, mountain biking, quad-biking, canyoning, paragliding, rafting, plus expeditions to Pico Duarte. The center has a large pool, restaurant, and bar. Accommodations (including dorms) are clean and simple, and will appeal to those seeking peace and quiet.
🛏 27 🏊 🔲 All major cards

NORTH COAST

CABARETE

🏨 NATURA CABAÑAS
$$
PLAYA PERLA MARINA
TEL/FAX 809/571-1507
www.naturacabana.com
Eco-sensitive, upscale Robinson Crusoe thatched-roof cabañas

and rustic stone bungalows shaded by palms and almond trees on the beachfront just outside Cabarete. Take a yoga class, relax with a spa therapy. Family-run and kid-friendly; healthy eating.
🛏 11 🏊 🔲 All major cards

🏨 WINDSURF RESORT
$$
TEL 809/571-0718
FAX 809/571-0710
www.windsurfcabarete.com
A useful budget option in this busy international resort area. Spic-and-span apartments (some with air-conditioning) in a modern complex with on-site restaurant.
🛏 60 🏊 🔲 All major cards

PUERTO PLATA

🏨 CASA COLONIAL BEACH & SPA
$$$–$$$$$
PUERTO PLATA
TEL 809/320-3232 or 866/376-7831
FAX 809/320-3131
www.casacolonialhotel.com
A delectable boutique hotel, impeccably tasteful from the rooftop infinity pool to the wine cellar via spacious suites with Roman tubs in the bathroom, Asian-Mediterranean cuisine, and a Bagua spa.
🛏 50 🅿 🔄 🏊 🔲 All major cards

🏨 BLUE BAY VILLAS DORADAS
$$$
CALLE PRINCIPAL 538, PLAYA DORADA, PUERTO PLATA
TEL 809/320-3000 or 877/305-8229
FAX 809/320-4790
www.bluebayresorts.com
Relaxing adults-only all-inclusive with a great beachfront location adjacent to the Playa Dorada golf course. Simple, stylish rooms;

PRICES

HOTELS
An indication of the cost of a double room in the high season is given by **$** signs.

$$$$$	Over $400
$$$$	$300–$400
$$$	$200–$300
$$	$100–$200
$	Under $100

RESTAURANTS
An indication of the cost of a three-course meal without drinks is given by **$** signs.

$$$$$	Over $80
$$$$	$50–$80
$$$	$35–$50
$$	$20–$35
$	Under $20

---

attractive and well-maintained grounds; excellent food and service; plus tennis, spa and entertainment.
🛏 245 🅿 🔄 🏊 🔲 All major cards

🏨 VH VICTORIA RESORT GOLF & BEACH
$$$
PLAYA DORADA, PUERTO PLATA
TEL 809/320-1200
FAX 809/320-4862
www.vhhr.com
Smaller all-inclusive property focusing on golf and honey-moon packages. Comfortable rooms with balcony or terrace (most have fairway views); beach club with water sports; fine dining and pizzeria; cigar bar.
🛏 190 🅿 🔄 🏊 🔲 All major cards

SOSÚA

🏨 PIERGIORGIO PALACE
🍴 HOTEL
$$–$$$

CALLE LA PUNTILLA 1,
EL BATEY
TEL 809/571-2626
FAX 809/571-2786
www.piergiorgiopalacehotel
.com
Terrific location on the Sosúa
cliff tops with views out to the
Atlantic. Romantic Victorian
decor and ocean-facing rooms
with billowing curved balconies.
Also two-bedroom penthouses
with kitchens and private terraces. No beach, but motorized
water sports and scuba diving
off the rocks. Italian restaurant
and an excellent pizzeria with
wood-fired oven.
🛏 51 rooms/suites
🅿 🌊 🅰 All major cards

PENINSULA DE SAMANÁ

🏨 VILLA SERENA
$$
LAS GALERAS
TEL 809/538-0000
FAX 809/538-0009
www.villaserena.com
Pretty colonial-style villa hotel
set in tropical gardens by the
beach. Spacious rooms with
generous verandas and sea
views, some four-posters.
Conservatory restaurant; spa
treatments; yoga; excursions
by arrangement; free kayaks
and bikes.
🛏 21 🅿 🅰 🌊 🅰 All major
cards

🍴 MI CORAZON
$$$–$$$$
CALLE DUARTE 7, LAS TERRENAS
TEL 809/240-5329
Traditional town house on the
main street with an upstairs
dining room arranged around
a galleried courtyard open to
the stars. Great *mojitos* from
the bar, ambitious interna-
tional cuisine with local and
Oriental touches, patisseries
from the street level bakery.
⏰ Closed L, and Oct.; Mon.
Nov.–April; Sun.–Mon.
May–Sept.

SANTIAGO

🍴 PEZ DORADO
$
CALLE DEL SOL 43
PARQUE COLÓN
TEL 809/582-2518
Fish and Asian cuisine are the
staples of this long-standing
and well-regarded restaurant in
the center of the city.

SANTO DOMINGO

🏨 SOFITEL NICOLAS OVANDO
$$$–$$$$$
CALLE LAS DAMAS
TEL 809/685-9955
FAX 809/686-6590
www.sofitel.com
A luxurious landmark hotel
carved out of a historic
16th-century residence in the
heart of the Colonial City. The
elegant conversion is a chic
modern take on colonial style
with high ceilings, exposed
stonework, and spacious
bedrooms featuring minimalist
four-posters and rattan furniture. Fine dining; cigar club.
🛏 104 🅿 🅰 🌊 🅰 🎾 🅰 All
major cards

🏨 RENAISSANCE JARAGUA HOTEL & CASINO
$$–$$$$$
AVE. GEORGE WASHINGTON 367
TEL 809/221-2222
FAX 809/686-0528
www.renaissancehotels.com
On the Malecón, this well-
managed hotel has a gym,
tennis facilities, a free-form
swimming pool, meetings facili-
ties, and four restaurants.
🛏 300 🅰 🅰 🌊 🎾 🅰 All
major cards

🏨 HOTEL DOÑA ELVIRA
$
PADRE BILLINI 207, COLONIAL
CITY
TEL 809/221-7415

FAX 809/221-7369
www.dona-elvira.com
Behind a discreet street
entrance, this lovingly restored,
beamed and tiled 16th-century
colonial mansion B&B is a
haven. Simple rooms, comfy
beds, charming pool patio.
🛏 15 🅰 🅰 All major cards

🍴 MESÓN DE BARI
$$$$
EUGENIA MARIA DE HOSTOS 302,
COLONIAL CITY
TEL 809/687-4091
Reservations are advisable for
this memorable artist's haunt.
Top notch *cochina criolla* from
mouth-watering crab empana-
das to superb grilled chicken.
Extraordinary artwork on every
wall, family-friendly, and great
service.
🅰 All major cards

🍴 VESUVIO TIRADENTES
$$$$
AVE. TIRADENTES 17
TEL 809/562-6060
Considered to be one of
the city's top restaurants, the
Vesuvio specializes in gourmet
international and Caribbean
dishes, and homemade pasta.
🅰 All major cards

🍴 CANTÁBRICO
$$$
AVE. INDEPENDENCIA 54
TEL 809/687-5101
Informal Spanish restaurant
with a wood-panel dining room
well-known for its paella and
seafood as well as Segovian
suckling pig.
🅰 All major cards

🍴 MESÓN DE LA CAVA
$$$
AVE. MIRADOR DEL SUR 1
TEL 809/533-2818
Funky restaurant, set in
a natural cave 50 feet (15 m)
below ground and reached
via a spiral staircase. Renowned
for its steaks and seafood. Live

music and dancing in the evening.

🏵 All major cards

🍴 SCHEHEREZADE
$$–$$$
AVE. ROBERTO PASTORIZA 226,
ENSANCHE NACHO
TEL 809/227-2323
Located in a lavish Moorish-style building, this atmospheric restaurant specializes in Mediterranean and Middle Eastern food, plus fish and seafood.

🏵 All major cards

🍴 EL CONUCO
$–$$
CALLE CASIMIRO DE MOYA 152
TEL 809/686-0129
Highly atmospheric restaurant with a country theme. The food is excellent, and at lunchtime there is a popular buffet. When the waiters and waitresses are finished serving they perform a song-and-dance routine.

🏵 All major cards

SOUTHEAST COAST

🏨 CASA DE CAMPO
$$$$$
LA ROMANA
TEL 809/523-3333 OR
1-800/877-3643
FAX 809/523-8548
www.casadecampo.com
The only hotel complex in the region with its own international airport (daily American Airlines services from the U.S.), Casa de Campo claims to be the Caribbean's most complete resort. Accommodations comprise luxury villas and spacious rooms. Its four golf courses are world famous, and it also features a shooting center, polo stables, its own beach and marina, dive shop, 20 restaurants, and 13 tennis courts.

🛏 265 plus 150 villas
🈳 🛥 🍸 🏵 All major cards

🏨 IBEROSTAR BÁVARO
$$$
PLAYA BÁVARO, HIGÜEY
TEL 809/221-6500
FAX 809/688-6186
www.iberostar.com
Spacious and comfortable all-inclusive resort on a good stretch of Punta Cana's beach. Diving, golf, water sports.

🛏 596 🈳 🈵 🛥 🏵 All major cards

🏨 PUNTACANA RESORT & CLUB
$$–$$$$$
PUNTA CANA, HIGÜEY
TEL 809/959-2262 OR
888/442-2262
www.puntacana.com
Attractive suites and two- and three-bedroom beach or garden casita cottages well spread out over a 105-acre (42 ha) site. Excellent facilities include tennis, diving, water sports, and horseback riding.

🛏 240 🈳 🈵 🛥 🏵 All major cards

■ PUERTO RICO

CENTRAL HIGHLANDS

🏨 CASA GRANDE
🍴 MOUNTAIN RETREAT
$
RTE. 612, KM 0.3, UTUADO
TEL 787/894-3939
FAX 787/894-3900
www.hotelcasagrande.com
Set high up in the mountains of the Cordillera Central, with stunning views across an unspoiled valley, this peaceful, small hotel has simple rooms equipped with balcony and hammock. Once a coffee plantation, the house is surrounded by tropical gardens, and there are several hiking trails in the surrounding hills. It also has its own restaurant.

🛏 20 🛥 🏵 All major cards

CULEBRA

🏨 CLUB SEABOURNE
🍴 $$–$$$
RTE. 252, PLAYA SARDINAS II
TEL 787/742-3169
www.clubseabourne.com
Charming boutique hotel with simple but chic rooms and villas tucked into a tree-shaded hillside above Fulladoza Bay. Wooden floors, pastel colors, and natural fabrics. Private dock; water sports; and a good Nuevo Latino restaurant on the screened porch.

🛏 12 🅿 🛥 🏨 🈵 🏵 All major cards

DORADO

🏨 EMBASSY SUITES HOTEL DORADO DEL MAR
$$–$$$$
201 DORADO DEL MAR BLVD.
TEL 787/796-6125 OR
800/362-2779
FAX 787/796-6145
www.embassysuitesdorado.com
An all-suites hotel fronting Dorado Beach 25 miles from San Juan, this is a good location and excellent family option. Water sports, tennis, spa, shopping, restaurants with ocean views, and a highly rated golf course.

🛏 251 🅿 🛥 🍸 🏵 All major cards

FAJARDO

🏨 WALDORF ASTORIA EL CONQUISTADOR RESORT & GOLDEN DOOR SPA
$$$$$
AVE. EL CONQUISTADOR
TEL 787/863-1000 OR
888/543-1282
FAX 787/863-6500
www.elconresort.com
This enormous complex occu-

🏨 Hotel 🍴 Restaurant 🛏 No. of guest rooms 🈳 No. of seats 🅿 Parking 🕐 Closed pies a commanding position above the point where the Atlantic and Caribbean meet. Fabulous ocean views and lush landscaping; bright, spacious rooms with a splash of crisp color; also Las Casitas, one, two, and three bedroom villas. There is no beach, but the hotel boasts it's own offshore island, with regular shuttle service from the on-site marina. There is a water park with speed slides and a lazy river, tennis, horseback riding, and the 18-hole Arthur Hills championship golf course. The resort has more than 20 restaurants.

ℹ️ 910 🔌 ❄️ 🏊 🏋️ 💳 All major cards

GUANICA

🏨 COPAMARINA BEACH RESORT
$$$–$$$$
KM 6.5, RTE. 333, CANA GORDA
TEL 787/821-0505 OR
800/468-4553
FAX 787/821-0070
www.copamarina.com
On 20 acres (8 ha) of lawned gardens at the water's edge, this resort offers a full range of facilities including water sports, diving, tennis, mountain biking, and ecotours in the neighboring Guánica Biosphere Reserve. The hotel has two pools, two restaurants, a spa, and a fitness center. The comfortable rooms are decorated in bright tropical colors and equipped with all amenities.

ℹ️ 106 ❄️ 🏊 🏋️ 💳 All major cards

PONCE

🏨 HOLIDAY INN & EL TROPICAL CASINO
$$
PLAYA PONCE
TEL 787/844-1200
or 800/465-4329

FAX 787/841-8683
www.holidayinn.com/ponce
Efficiently managed and pleasant hotel just outside of Ponce, with views of the city and the ocean from its hilltop position. The comfortable rooms all have balconies and cable TV. The casino and nightclub are popular with locals on the weekends.

ℹ️ 116 ❄️ 🏊 🏋️ 💳 All major cards

🍴 PITO'S SEAFOOD
$$$
LAS CUCHARAS
TEL 787/841-4977
With a large terrace overlooking the ocean just outside Ponce, Pito's is a great place for a long, indulgent lunch. Specialties include plantain stuffed with shrimp and lobster, stuffed clams, grilled mahimahi, and red snapper in Creole sauce.
💳 All major cards

RINCÓN

SOMETHING SPECIAL

🏨 HORNED DORSET PRIMAVERA
Undoubtedly the island's most chic and exclusive hotel, this hacienda-style resort is impeccably run and caters to a discerning clientele seeking absolute tranquility and relaxation—there are no TVs or radios. The rooms, furnished in antiques, are immaculate. Set on its own beach, the hotel has won numerous awards. It is also a member of the prestigious Relais & Châteaux group, with two restaurants, including the gourmet Restaurant Aaron (see below).
$$$$$
KM 3, ROAD 429
TEL 787/823-4030 OR
800/633-1857
FAX 787/823-5580
www.horneddorset.com
ℹ️ 52 ❄️ 🏊 💳 All major cards

🍴 RESTAURANT AARON
$$$$$
KM 3, ROAD 429
TEL 787/823-4030
One of the island's top restaurants outside of the capital, Restaurant Aaron's sophisticated setting and imaginative cuisine have won it many admirers. The repertoire includes dishes such as shrimp and fennel bisque, grilled tuna with mango salad, and grilled marlin with fresh herbs and lemon.
🕐 Closed L & Mon.–Wed. off-season 💳 All major cards

RIO GRANDE

🏨 WYNDHAM RIO MAR BEACH RESORT & SPA
$$$–$$$$$
6000 RIO MAR BLVD.
TEL 787/888-6000 OR
887/636-0636
FAX 787/888-6320
www.wyndhamriomar.com
Well-run property on its own beach, handy for El Yunque National Park. The hotel's impressive range of facilities includes spa and fitness center, a tennis center, restaurants, casino, shops, a full range of water sports, and swimming pools. The 481-acre complex also includes two world-class golf courses (the River Course and the Ocean Course).
ℹ️ 600, 72 suites, 59 villas
❄️ 🏊 🏋️ 💳 All major cards

🍴 PALIO AT THE WYNDHAM RIO MAR
$$$$
6000 RIO MAR BLVD.
TEL 787/888-6000
The resort's top restaurant offers a wonderfully tempting array of dishes styled with Italian flair. Specialties include fish baked in a banana leaf, with tomatoes, fresh peppers, and onions.
💳 All major cards

SAN JUAN

🏨 HOTEL EL CONVENTO
$$$$–$$$$$
100 CALLE CRISTO,
OLD SAN JUAN
TEL 787/723-9020 OR
800/468-2779
FAX 787/723-9944
www.elconvento.com
This small, deluxe hotel occupies the top floors of a historic building (once a convent) in the heart of the old town; the inner courtyard features cafés, restaurants, galleries, and shops. All rooms have views over San Juan and the sea. Access to beach club at sister hotel on Isla Verde.
🛏 54 rooms, 4 suites 🔽 🅢
🖼 🆃 🆂 All major cards

🏨 GALLERY INN
$$–$$$$
NORZAGARAY 204,
OLD SAN JUAN
TEL 787/722-1808 OR
866/572-2783
FAX 787/977-3929
www.thegalleryinn.com
Charming and idiosyncratic hostelry in an old rambling building, with great views over the venerable colonial city.
🛏 13 rooms, 10 suites
🅢 🆂 All major cards

🍴 CASA LOLA
$$$$
1006 ASHFORD AVE., CONDADO
TEL 787/725-9195
A new look and a new location for a Condado stalwart, Casa Lola specializes in local Puerto Rican cuisine. Most people start with the excellent assorted fritters (pumpkin, white yam and cheese, plantain, chicken, and corn) followed by classic grills such as pork, chicken, beef, or swordfish.
🆂 All major cards

🍴 PIKAYO
$$$$

CONRAD CONDADO PLAZA HOTEL, 999 ASHFORD AVE., CONDADO
TEL 787/721-6194
Chef Wilo Benet is an established star in the island's culinary world, and his restaurant is one of the most celebrated in the city. His imaginative take on criolla cuisine and perfectionist attitude ensure a steady stream of repeat customers to this stylish, contemporary restaurant.
🕒 Closed L 🆂 All major cards

🍴 PAMELA'S CARIBBEAN CUISINE
$$$
NUMERO UNO GUESTHOUSE,
CALLE SANTA ANA 1,
OCEAN PARK
TEL 787/726-5010
On the beach with indoor and outdoor dining, Pamela's has a relaxed atmosphere with first-class service that matches the culinary creations emerging from chef Esteban Torres's kitchen. Fresh seafood is the mainstay, accompanied by an extensive wine list and some delectable desserts.
🆂 All major cards

🍴 DRAGONFLY
$–$$
364 FORTALEZA STREET
TEL 787/977-3886
In the heart of the hip SOFO (South Fortaleza) sector of Old San Juan, Dragonfly is a popular eaterie with a difference, offering Latin-Asian cuisine dishes such as pork and amarillo dumplings and Peking duck nachos.
🕒 Closed L & Sun. 🆂 All major cards

🍴 LA BOMBONERA
$
CALLE SAN FRANCISCO 259, OLD SAN JUAN
TEL 787/722-0658
A local landmark, this café-

bakery is a great spot for breakfast or a pit stop on a walking tour of the old town (closes at 8 p.m.). Huge sandwiches, fabulous pastries, choice of traditional hot dishes.
🆂 No credit cards

VIEQUES

🏨 W RETREAT & SPA
🍴 $$$$$
RTE. 200, KM 3.2
TEL 787/741-4100 OR 877/946-8357
www.wvieques.com
Fabulous beachfront retreat long on style (think Sean Connery–era Bond with a contemporary twist) and mood with stunning pools, palm trees, fire pits, and tree swing seats. Two private beaches, spa, tennis, and Latino-Caribbean inspired menus from Alain Ducasse at miX On The Beach restaurant.
🛏 138 🍴 🅟 🅢 🖼 🆃 🆂 All major cards

🍴 CARAMBOLA
$$$
INN ON THE BLUE HORIZON,
RTE. 996, ESPERANZA
TEL 787/741-3318
Pretty island-style dining room extending onto a terrace under the stars. A good mix of local seafood (ceviche, grills) alongside house-smoked pork ribs and delicious chicken *pinchos* flavored with tamarind and cilantro.
🆂 All major cards

■ VIRGIN ISLANDS

U.S. VIRGIN ISLANDS

ST. CROIX

🏨 BUCCANEER HOTEL
$$$$–$$$$$
GALLOWS BAY
TEL 340/712-2100 OR
800/255-3881
FAX 340-712-2104
www.thebucaneer.com

🏨 Hotel 🍴 Restaurant 🛏 No. of guest rooms 🍴 No. of seats 🅟 Parking 🕒 Closed

Luxurious family-run resort with secluded beaches, water sports, golf, tennis, kids' club, and eco-packages. Spacious accommodations (all with private balconies) in the attractive hilltop main building or nearer the beach, also family villas and deluxe suites.

🛈 138 P ☷ ☀ 🏊 🏋 🗖 All major cards

🏨 RENAISSANCE ST. CROIX CARAMBOLA BEACH RESORT & SPA
$$$
KINGSHILL
TEL 340/778-3800 OR
888/236-2427
FAX 340/718-1682
www.carambolabeach.com
Elegant former Rockresort spread across 28 beachfront acres (12 ha) with a Trent Jones–designed golf course and excellent sports facilities. Generous suite-style rooms with screened porches and fully equipped kitchenettes.

🛈 151 P ☀ 🏊 🏋 🗖 All major cards

🏨 HIBISCUS BEACH RESORT
$$$
4131 LA GRANDE PRINCESSE
TEL 340/718-4042 OR
800/442-0121
FAX 340/718-7668
www.hibiscusbeachresort.com
Small, relaxing resort arranged in two-story blocks with gingerbread decoration near a lovely beach 2 miles (3 km) west of Christiansted. Well-equipped rooms all with balcony or patio.

🛈 38 P ☀ 🏊 🗖 All major cards

🏨 WAVES AT CANE BAY
$$
CANE BAY
TEL 340/718-1815 OR
800/545-0603
FAX 340/718-4945
www.canebaystcroix.com

Airy and comfortable studios and a villa on the waterfront a couple of minutes' walk from the beach. Low-key and friendly; good snorkeling and diving; on-site dive shop.

🛈 11 studios, 1 villa P ☀ Some rooms 🏊 🗖 All major cards

🏕 MT. VICTORY CAMP
$
CREQUE DAM ROAD
P.O. BOX 696
FREDERIKSTED
TEL 340/772-1651 OR
866/772-1651
FAX 340/772-1651
www.mtvictorycamp.com
Small, friendly eco-camp in a valley enfolded in the green hills west of Frederiksted. Three tented platforms and two two-story bungalows (sleeping up to six) are fashioned from local hardwoods. All have kitchenette, linen, cold water. Hot water bathhouse. Campsites available.

🛈 5 units P 🗖 No credit cards

🍴 BLUE MOON
$$$
17 STRAND STREET,
FREDERIKSTED
TEL 340/772-2222
Bistro cum jazz spot (live music Fri. night and Sun. brunch) facing the waterfront with a garden patio and eclectic menu—Cajun shrimp, Luna Pie (cheese and vegetable phyllo pastry parcel), and hot, hot, hot Creole chicken.

🕐 Closed Mon. 🗖 All major cards

🍴 LE ST. TROPEZ
$$$
67 KING STREET, FREDERIKSTED
TEL 340/772-3000
French restaurant in an old gingerbread house opening onto a leafy courtyard. Salade Niçoise and croque monsieur at lunch; homemade pâtés, frog's legs, and

lobster for dinner.

🕐 Closed Sun. & L Sat.
🗖 All major cards

🍴 TUTTO BENE
$$$
BOARDWALK BUILDING, HOSPITAL STREET, CHRISTIANSTED
TEL 340/773-5229
Italian bistro serving great food with great atmosphere. Drop in for a chicken pesto sandwich at lunchtime, have an evening drink at the bar, or settle in for hearty seafood and impeccable pasta dishes. Reservations recommended.

🗖 All major cards

🍴 KENDRICKS
$$–$$$
21–32 COMPANY STREET,
CHRISTIANSTED
TEL 340/773-9199
Take your place among the locals dining at this popular downtown eatery. The menu is eclectic; the chef's signature dish is roast pecan-encrusted loin of pork.

🕐 Closed L & Sun.–Mon.

🍴 RUM RUNNERS
$$–$$$
HOTEL CARAVELLE,
BOARDWALK,
CHRISTIANSTED
TEL 340/773-6585
Location, location, location is a clue to Rum Runners' success. This local favorite enjoys a wonderful harborfront position in the center of town and serves up a pretty good burger, too. Ribs, steaks, pick-your-own lobster salad.

🗖 All major cards

🍴 OFF THE WALL
$–$$
NORTH SHORE (RTE. 80)
TEL 340/778-4771
An all-day beach bar and restaurant that can offer anything from eggs Benedict for breakfast to spectacular

---

☀ Air-conditioning   🏊 Indoor pool   🏊 Outdoor pool   🏋 Health club   🗖 Credit cards sunsets and a hammock for a postprandial nap. Burgers, pizzas, nachos, and seafood, plus jazz on weekends.

⬧ All major cards

ST. JOHN

SOMETHING SPECIAL

🏨 CANEEL BAY RESORT
Classic Laurance Rockefeller–built luxury resort on a stunning 170-acre (68 ha) peninsula site with seven beaches. Rooms in two-story blocks or stone-walled cottages strung along the shore (no phone, TV, or air-conditioning); tennis, water sports, children's activities.

$$$$$

CANEEL BAY
TEL 340/776-6111 OR
888/ROSEWOOD
FAX 340/693-8280
www.caneelbay.com

ⓘ 166 🅿 🏖 🍴 ⬧ All major cards

🏨 GALLOWS POINT SUITE RESORT
$$$$–$$$$$

CRUZ BAY
TEL 340/776-6434 OR
800/323-7339
FAX 340/776-6520
www.gallowspointresort.com
Very comfortable rental suites (individually decorated) in two-story units amid gardens, five minutes' walk from Cruz Bay town. Swimming and snorkeling from the shore.

ⓘ 52 🅿 🍴 🏖 ⬧ All major cards

🏨 MAHO BAY CAMPS
$–$$

MAHO BAY
TEL 340/715-0501 OR
800/392-9004
FAX 340/776-6504
www.maho.org
Screened tent-style cottages grafted onto the steep forested hillside above Maho Bay in the national park. Communal bathhouses, basic cooking facilities, and eco-conscious ethos. Also more luxurious solar-powered Harmony Studios constructed from recycled materials.

ⓘ 114 🅿 ⬧ All major cards

🍴 ASOLARE
$$$$

NORTH SHORE ROAD
TEL 340/779-4747
Gorgeous views overlooking Cruz Bay and St. Thomas, and a dynamic fusion of Asian and Pacific Rim cuisine make this one of St. John's hottest dining experiences. There are a few classical French dishes among the Thai beef salads and specialty seafood dishes. Reservations advised.

🕐 Closed L ⬧ All major cards

🍴 FISH TRAP
$$$

RAINTREE COURT, CRUZ BAY
TEL 340/693-9994
Locals recommend this casual alfresco restaurant for its fresh fish specialties, grilled steaks, pasta dishes, and diet-breaking homemade desserts.

🕐 Closed L & Mon. ⬧ All major cards

🍴 SWEET PLANTAINS
$$$

16118 LITTLE PLANTATION, CORAL BAY
TEL 340/777-4653
Tasty Caribbean/Creole cooking and rum samplers served up in a colorful little dining room opening on to a courtyard by the waterfront. Meaty Cuban-style *ropa vieja* stews, great seafood, not-to-be-missed curry nights, and rich desserts.

⬧ All major cards

🍴 MORGAN'S MANGO
$$

CRUZ BAY
TEL 340/693-8141

PRICES

HOTELS
An indication of the cost of a double room in the high season is given by **$** signs.

$$$$$	Over $400
$$$$	$300–$400
$$$	$200–$300
$$	$100–$200
$	Under $100

RESTAURANTS
An indication of the cost of a three-course meal without drinks is given by **$** signs.

$$$$$	Over $80
$$$$	$50–$80
$$$	$35–$50
$$	$20–$35
$	Under $20

Lively dinner spot and bar with a lamp-lit wooden deck opposite the national park dock. International influences range from the Caribbean and South America to Asia; also a long cocktail menu and live music on Thursdays.

🕐 Closed L ⬧ All major cards

ST. THOMAS

🏨 RITZ-CARLTON
$$$$$

6900 GREAT BAY
TEL 340/775-3333 OR
800/241-3333
FAX 340/775-4444
www.ritzcarlton.com
Sybaritic luxury in elegant faux-Italianate surroundings with gardens and tinkling fountains. All the balconied rooms have sea views. Excellent facilities include fine dining, tennis, boat trips, water sports, and a beach.

ⓘ 228 🅿 🍴 🏖 🍴 ⬧ All major cards

🏨 Hotel 🍴 Restaurant ⓘ No. of guest rooms 🪑 No. of seats 🅿 Parking 🕐 Closed

BOLONGO BAY BEACH RESORT

$$$$

7150 BOLONGO BAY

TEL 340/775-1800 OR

800/524-4746

www.bolongobay.com

Lively family-run beach resort property offering extensive water sports facilities, tennis, beach volleyball, and basketball courts.

🛈 65 P 🕃 🌊 🎽 🕃 All major cards

SECRET HARBOUR BEACH RESORT

$$$–$$$$

6280 ESTATE NAZARETH

TEL 340/775-6550 OR

800/524-2250

FAX 340/775-1501

www.secretharbourvi.com

Spacious studios and one- and two-bedroom housekeeping condos with tropical decor. Palm-lined beach, water sports center, tennis.

🛈 64 P 🕃 🌊 🕃 All major cards

POINT PLEASANT RESORT

$$$

ESTATE SMITH BAY

TEL 340/775-7200 OR

800/524-2300

FAX 340/7789-4009

www.antillesresorts.com

Spacious suites in a series of red-roofed villas spread across the hillside (kitchens, cable, balconies). Snorkeling from the beach; dive packages; tennis; trails through 15 acres (6 ha) of tropical greenery.

🛈 128 suites P 🕃 🌊 🕃 All major cards

HOTEL 1829

$$–$$$

30–31 KONGENSGADE,

CHARLOTTE AMALIE

TEL 340/776-1829 OR

800/524-2002

www.hotel1829.com

A national historic site, the atmospheric inn is furnished with antiques, painted tiles, and Tiffany glass. The rooms vary in size (the best are in the original building). Splendid bar; tiny courtyard pool.

🛈 14 🌊 🕃 All major cards

🍽 OLD STONE FARM HOUSE

$$$$$

MAHOGANY RUN GOLF COURSE

TEL 340/777-6277

Fine dining amid the 200-year-old brick arches of a former sugar estate building. Sample a light garden vegetable strudel, Caribbean crab cakes, flash grilled tuna, or pan-seared potato-crusted pork loin with Calvados brandy sauce.

🕑 Closed L & Mon. 🕃 All major cards

🍽 AGAVÉ TERRACE

$$$–$$$$

POINT PLEASANT RESORT

ESTATE SMITH BAY

TEL 340/775-4142

Head out to the East End for this excellent seafood restaurant with stunning views across to St. John. Lobster is a specialty, also pasta dishes and steak. Live entertainment nightly.

🕑 Closed L 🕃 All major cards

🍽 GRANDE CRU

$$$–$$$$

YACHT HAVEN GRANDE

TEL 340/774-7263

Grande Cru's veranda sits right over the water in this mega-yacht marina. Excellent burgers, club sandwiches, tapas, and chacuterie platters are among the lunchtime offerings. Chef's pasta and cracked pepper shrimp recommended in the evenings; long wine list.

🕃 All major cards

🍽 CUZZIN'S CARIBBEAN RESTAURANT & BAR

$$

7 BACK STREET,

CHARLOTTE AMALIE

TEL 340/777-4711

Delicious local cooking in an attractive downtown brick dining room decorated with Carnival props and local art. Mutton stew, curried chicken, shrimp creole, and a host of tasty local side dishes.

🕑 Closed Sun. & D Tues. 🕃 All major cards

🍽 DUFFY'S LOVE SHACK

$–$$

RED HOOK PLAZA,

EAST END

TEL 340/779-2080

It's loud, it's fun—that applies to the decor, the waitstaff, the music, and the outrageous cocktails. Classic burgers and wings, plus coconut-smoked New York Strip and tamarind-honey ribs.

🕃 No credit cards

BRITISH VIRGIN ISLANDS

ANEGADA

ANEGADA REEF HOTEL

$$–$$$

SETTING POINT

TEL 284/495-8002

FAX 284/495-9362

www.anegadareef.com

Total peace and quiet in simple but charming rooms (ocean-front or garden); rates include three meals a day. Fishing and diving from the hotel boat; Jeep rentals.

🛈 20 P 🕃 🕃 All major cards

TORTOLA

FRENCHMANS HOTEL

$$$$–$$$$$

FRENCHMANS CAY, WEST END

TEL 284/494-8811

www.frenchmansbvi.com

Tropical hideaway on a secluded peninsula near Soper's Hole Marina. Attractive one- and two-bedroom cottages set on a hillside above

---

🕃 Air-conditioning 🌊 Indoor pool 🌊 Outdoor pool 🎽 Health club 🕃 Credit cards the beach. Gorgeous views from swing seats on the veranda; tennis, kayaks, and snorkel gear. Good food in the clubhouse (breakfast included).

🛈 9 cottages 🅿 🛎 🏊 🆑 All major cards

🏨 LONG BAY RESORT
$$$$–$$$$$
LONG BAY
TEL 284/495-4252 OR
866/237-3491
FAX 284/495-4677
www.longbay.com
Very comfortable and well-equipped rooms, studios, and one- to three-bedroom villas on the hillside, and waterfront cabanas on the beach. All boast generous decks. Pool rooms (recommended for families); tennis; water sports.

🛈 155 🅿 🛎 🏊 🆑 All major cards

🏨 SUGAR MILL HOTEL
🍴 $$$–$$$$$
APPLE BAY
TEL 284/495-4355
FAX 284/495-4696
www.sugarmillhotel.com
Quiet hideaway attached to a notable restaurant. There are comfortable modern rooms and family suites, a two-bedroom villa, and two simple rooms in a wooden cottage set in rampant garden foliage.

🛈 23 🅿 🛎 Some rooms 🏊 🆑 All major cards

🍴 BRANDYWINE BAY
$$$$
BRANDYWINE BAY
TEL 284/495-2301
Tortola's most elegant dining room with a terrace overlooking the Sir Francis Drake Channel. Florentine specialties grilled over charcoal, homemade pasta and sauces with fresh garden herbs, plenty of Italian wines, and superb attention to detail.

🕒 Closed L, Mon. 🆑 All major cards

🍴 THE DOVE
$$$$
67 MAIN STREET, ROAD TOWN
TEL 284/494-0313
You have to fight the locals for a table at this traditional West Indian gingerbread house. Small, creative menu of French/Asian-inspired dishes (dainty dumplings, softshell crab, Thai curries) and perfectly cooked steaks; sublime homemade sorbets, chocolate soufflé. Upstairs, the more affordable BarFly serves cocktails and tapas with a side order of jazz.

🕒 Closed L, Sun.–Mon. 🆑 All major cards

SOMETHING SPECIAL

🍴 MRS. SCATLIFFE'S
Reservations are a must for Mrs. Una Scatliffe's West Indian restaurant, which she operates out of her own home. The veranda serves as the dining room, and the four-course set dinner menu features traditional soups, home-baked bread, pot roasts, and fruit and vegetables from the garden.

$$$
CARROT BAY
TEL 284/495-4556
🆑 All major cards

🍴 SUGAR MILL
$$$
APPLE BAY
TEL 284/495-4355
Lovely evening setting in the former boiling house of an old sugar mill; lunch is served in the bar. Cookbook writers Jinx and Jefferson Morgan offer a small but delicious daily menu: Caribbean sweet potato soup with gingered shrimp, tropical game hen with orange curry butter, and fresh garden vegetables.

🆑 All major cards

🍴 QUITO'S GAZEBO
$–$$

CANE GARDEN BAY
TEL 284/495-4837
Bar/restaurant with a covered deck overhanging the beach. Burgers and sandwiches, fettuccine Alfredo, or grilled kingfish followed by homemade brownies or pecan pie. Quito himself leads the live music on Fri. and Sat. nights.

🆑 All major cards

VIRGIN GORDA

🏨 BITTER END YACHT CLUB
$$$$$
NORTH SOUND
TEL 284/494-2745 OR
800/872-2392
FAX 284/494-4756
www.beyc.com
Friendly yacht-club ambience, excellent sailing school, and a selection of kayaks, windsurfers, dinghies, and yachts. Hillside villas (good for families) or romantic thatched huts on stilts with wooden decks.

🛈 85 🛎 🏊 🆑 All major cards

🏨 LITTLE DIX BAY
$$$$$
LITTLE DIX BAY
TEL 284/495-5555 or
888/767-3966
FAX 284/495-5661
www.littledixbay.com
Sister to Caneel Bay on St. John (USVI), casually elegant Little Dix bears the inimitable Rockefeller stamp. Hexagonal and stilted rooms catch the breeze, though a/c (and phone) is an option here. Hiking, tennis, water sports, boat trips, children's program.

🛈 98, plus 4 villas 🅿 🏊 🍽 🆑 All major cards

🏨 LEVERICK BAY HOTEL
$$
LEVERICK BAY
TEL 284/495-7421 OR
800/848-7081
FAX 284/495-7367

www.leverickbay.com
Brightly painted villas with sea views and amazingly affordable rates for hotel rooms and one- and two-bedroom suites with kitchen. Tennis, spa, water sports, and dive shop.
🛈 18 P 🅢 🏖 🅢 All major cards

🍴 THE RESTAURANT AT LEVERICK BAY
$$–$$$$
LEVERICK BAY MARINA
TEL 284/495-7154
Located at the top end of the island, the beach bar makes a useful lunchtime pit stop serving salads, burgers, and pasta. In the evening, the upstairs terrace offers more sophisticated dining with lovely views over North Sound and a classic menu of steak, seafood, and rack of lamb.
🅢 All major cards

🍴 TOP OF THE BATHS
$$
THE BATHS
TEL 284/495-5497
A terrific position above The Baths augments the all-day menu with views over the Sir Francis Drake Channel. Salads, sandwiches, and burgers at lunch; dinner entrées might include filet mignon and fresh lobster.
🅢 All major cards

■ DUTCH CARIBBEAN

ARUBA

🏨 HYATT REGENCY RESORT & CASINO
$$$$–$$$$$
J.E. IRAUSQUIN BLVD. 85
PALM BEACH
TEL 297/586-1234 or
800/554-9288
FAX 297/586-1682
www.aruba.hyatt.com
Luxurious resort complex on

12 acres (5 ha) of beachfront. Attractive, well-equipped rooms and suites; spectacular pool area, tennis, golf, water sports, and Camp Hyatt offering kids' activities.
🛈 357 P 🅢 🏖 🅢 🍽 🅢 All major cards

🏨 PLAYA LINDA BEACH RESORT
$$$–$$$$
J.E. IRAUSQUIN BLVD. 87
PALM BEACH
TEL 297/586-1000 OR
800/992-2015
FAX 297/586-3479
www.playalinda.com
Fully equipped one- and two-bedroom condos and three-bedroom town houses in a smart beachfront development. Tennis, water sports, shopping, and kids' programs.
🛈 213 P 🅢 🏖 🅢 🍽 🅢 All major cards

🏨 AMSTERDAM MANOR BEACH RESORT
$$
J.E. IRAUSQUIN BLVD. 252
EAGLE BEACH
TEL 297/527-1100 OR
800/969-2310
FAX 297/527-1112
www.amsterdammanor.com
Pretty Dutch colonial-style all-suite resort. Studios and two-bedroom apartments with kitchens and sea views across from the beach. On-site mini market; water sports nearby.
🛈 72 P 🅢 🏖 🅢 All major cards

🍴 PAPIAMENTO
$$$$
WASHINGTON 61
NOORD
TEL 297/586-4544
Utterly charming family restaurant set in the gardens of a 150-year-old manor house. The Ellis parents occupy the front of the house, while the

children cook award-winning seafood, steaks, and special healthy and vegetarian dishes.
🕐 Closed L & Mon. 🅢 All major cards

🍴 CUBA'S COOKIN'
$$$
RENAISSANCE MARKETPLACE,
L.G. SMITH BLVD. 30,
ORANJESTAD
TEL 297/588-0627
Cocktails, live music, Cuban art, and a menu of classic Cuban and Nuevo Latino favorites served up in a lovingly re-created 1960s Havana-style bar-restaurant. Generous Cuban sandwiches at lunchtime; try succulent roast pork, fried chicken, or Cuban steaks for dinner.
🕐 Closed Sun. 🅢 All major cards

🍴 DRIFTWOOD
$$$
KLIPSTRAAT 12, ORANJESTAD
TEL 297/583-2515
Rugged, woodsy dining room with a seafood menu, much of it sourced by the owner's fishing charter business. Great fish soup, catch of the day, lobster, garlic shrimp, and homemade pan bati (cornbread) to sop up the juices.
🕐 Closed Tues. 🅢 All major cards

🍴 GASPARITO
$$$
GASPARITO 3, NOORD
TEL 297/586-7044
Combination restaurant and Aruban art gallery specializing in local cuisine and international dishes. Try barracuda-stuffed ravioli, shrimp in coconut milk and brandy, or a typical stoba (stew).
🕐 Closed L & Sun. 🅢 All major cards

🅢 Air-conditioning 🏊 Indoor pool 🏖 Outdoor pool 🍽 Health club 🅢 Credit cards

BONAIRE

🏨 HARBOUR VILLAGE BEACH CLUB
$$$$–$$$$$
KAYA GOB. N. DEBROT 73
TEL 599/717-7500 OR
800/424-0004
FAX 599/717-7507
www.harbourvillage.com
Bonaire's top hotel boasts a palm-fringed beach and attractive rooms or housekeeping condos in Mediterranean-style villas. Also tennis, diving, a full-service marina, and shopping.
🛏 40 🅿 🅂 🌊 🚫 All major cards

🏨 CAPTAIN DON'S HABITAT
$$$
KAYA GOB. N. DEBROT 103
TEL 599/717-8290 OR
800/327-6709
FAX 599/717-8240
www.habitatbonaire.com
Captain Don's is Bonaire's dive supremo, and his Habitat offers casual, comfortable suites, villas, and two-bedroom cottages, plus diving, water sports, and a minuscule beach.
🛏 93 🅿 🅂 🌊 🚫 All major cards

🏨 SAND DOLLAR CONDOMINIUM RESORT
$$–$$$
KAYA GOB. N. DEBROT 79
TEL 599/717-8738 OR
800/288-4773
FAX 599/717-8760
www.divesanddollar.com
Studio, one-, two-, and three-bedroom individually furnished apartments with full kitchens and balconies overlooking the waterfront. Top-rated dive operation, tennis, grocery store, and wide-ranging activities programs.
🛏 68 🅿 🅂 🌊 🚫 All major cards

🏨 DIVI FLAMINGO BEACH RESORT
$$
J. A. ABRAHAM BLVD. 40
TEL 599/717-8285 OR
800/367-3484
FAX 599/717-8238
www.diviflamingo.com
Low-rise hotel and a clutch of brightly painted studio suites set in waterfront gardens. A friendly atmosphere, tennis, a casino, and entertainment. Dive programs include special facilities for the disabled.
🛏 129 🅿 🅂 🌊 🚫 All major cards

🍴 LA GUERNICA
$$$
KAYA BONAIRE 4C, KRALENDIJK
TEL 599/717-5022
Fine boardwalk location overlooking the harbor with a terrace and distinctly laid-back dining room with a tapas menu. Also good seafood, some Japanese dishes.
🚫 All major cards

🍴 PATAGONIA ARGENTINEAN STEAKHOUSE
$$$
HARBOUR VILLAGE MARINA, KRALENDIJK
TEL 599/717-7725
Lively grill in the harborfront lighthouse. Gargantuan portions—the mixed grill could comfortably feed a small family on steak, ribs, chicken, pork loin, sausages, and seafood.
🕐 Closed L Sun. & Mon.
🚫 All major cards

🍴 RICHARD'S WATERFRONT
$$$
J.A. ABRAHAM BLVD. 60
TEL 599/717-5263
Romantic waterfront setting and a relaxed welcome from Bostonian owner, Richard Beaty.

Daily blackboard menus feature plenty of fresh local seafood, filet mignon, and signature chicken Benito with chopped spinach and Dutch cheese.
🕐 Closed L & Mon. 🚫 All major cards

🍴 MONA LISA BAR & RESTAURANT
$$–$$$
KAYA GRANDI 15, KRALENDIJK
TEL 599/717-8718
This popular off-waterfront bar-diner serves excellent French-Dutch-international fare. Memorable tuna sashimi, beautifully cooked catch of the day, and classics from steak to schnitzel. Good wine list; open late.
🕐 Closed L & Sat-Sun 🚫 All major cards

CURAÇAO

🏨 CURAÇAO MARRIOTT BEACH RESORT & EMERALD CASINO
$$$$
PISCADERA BAAI
TEL 5999/736-8800 OR
800/223-6388
FAX 5999/462-7502
www.curacaomarriott.com
Elegant and very upscale resort with a contemporary colonial-style motif. Very comfortable accommodations with balcony or terrace set in landscaped gardens. Excellent water sports facilities and dive shop, tennis, kids' program, full casino.
🛏 247 🅿 🅂 🌊 🍽 🚫 All major cards

🏨 LODGE KURÁ HULANDA & BEACH CLUB
$$$–$$$$$
WESTPUNT
TEL 5999/839-3600 or
877/264-3106
FAX 5999/839-3601
www.kurahulanda.com

🏨 Hotel 🍴 Restaurant 🛏 No. of guest rooms 🪑 No. of seats 🅿 Parking 🕐 Closed

Gorgeous upscale beach hotel retreat featuring spacious rooms/suites, tropical chic decor, a range of water sports, an on-site dive shop, tennis, spa, and fine dining.

🛈 74 🅿 ❄ 🏊 🍸 ❖ All major cards

🏨 AVILA BEACH HOTEL
$$$–$$$$
PENSTRAAT 130–134, WILLEMSTAD
TEL 5999/461-4377 OR 800/747-8162
FAX 5999/461-1493
www.avilahotel.com
The heart of this waterfront complex is a charming historic hotel ($$), now flanked by tasteful modern wings. The newest, the Octagon Wing, boasts a spa and pool.

🛈 165 🅿 ❄ 🏊 🍸 ❖ All major cards

🏨 ALL WEST APART-MENTS & DIVING
$
BANDA ABAO, WESTPUNT
TEL 5999/461-2310
FAX 5999/461-2315
www.allwestcuracao.com
Simple, bright, and attractive studios and apartments (sleep four) with kitchenettes, balconies/terraces, and sea views. Quiet location; dive packages and PADI courses.

🛈 7 🅿 ❖ All major cards

SOMETHING SPECIAL

🍴 BISTRO LE CLOCHARD
Cozy dining room in the former fortress jail with a waterfront terrace. Delectable Swiss-French cuisine includes fondues, beef and shrimp cooked on a heated stone slab brought to the table, and rich chocolate desserts.
$$$$$
RIFFORT, WILLEMSTAD
TEL 5999/462-5666
❖ All major cards

🍴 ASTROLAB
$$$–$$$$
KURÁ HULANDA, LANGESTRAAT 8, OTROBANDA, WILLEMSTAD
TEL 5999/434-7700
One of several restaurant options in this attractive hotel/museum complex, Astrolab's beautifully lit courtyard setting amid sculpture and greenery is perfect for a romantic dinner. Enjoy signature fish and beef dishes, intelligent wine pairing suggestions, and spot-on service.
🕐 Closed L, Sun.–Mon.
❖ All major cards

🍴 JAANCHIE'S
$$–$$$
WESTPUNT 15
TEL 5999/864-0126
Great spot for a lazy lunch. Outdoor tables shaded by greenery. Seafood and local dishes such as goat stew, or iguana for the adventurous.
🕐 Closed D ❖ All major cards

🍴 LANDHUIS DANIEL
$$
WEG NAAR WESTPUNT
TEL 5999/864-8400
Great setting on the shady, breeze-cooled veranda of a historic plantation house hotel set back from the sea. The imaginative menu is full of unusual ideas. Authentic Dutch pancakes, seasonal local game dishes, French-Italian-Mediterranean influences with a Caribbean twist.
❖ All major cards

SABA

🏨 JULIANA'S
$$–$$$
WINDWARDSIDE
TEL 599/416-2269 OR 866/783-3319
FAX 599/416-2389
www.julianas-hotel.com
A cute and cozy small hotel set in gardens bursting with

colorful tropical plants. There are studio-style rooms with balconies, and three adorable one- or two-bedroom Saban cottages, all simply but comfortably decorated.
🛈 12 🅿 🏊 ❖ All major cards

🏨 SHEARWATER RESORT
$$–$$$
BOOBY HILL
TEL 599/416-2498
FAX 599/416-2482
www.shearwater-resort.com
A small, upscale retreat with a fabulous setting 2,000 feet (610 m) above sea level in the hills south of Windwardside. Accommodations in the main building and bright, spacious bungalows with ocean views from private balconies. Good restaurant; tennis. No children under 14.
🛈 7 🅿 🏊 ❖ All major cards

🍴 SCOUT'S PLACE
$$$
WINDWARDSIDE
TEL 599/416-2740
A country inn with rooms and a local institution just above the village. The lively bar is a popular hangout, and the veranda restaurant serves plenty of fresh seafood and local dishes.
❖ All major cards

🍴 BRIGADOON
$$
WINDWARDSIDE
TEL 599/416-2380
The dining area is hemmed in by trellises, and the menu is long on seafood. Try the local bouillabaisse-style fish soup, Creole shrimp, or fresh lobster.
🕐 Closed L ❖ All major cards

SINT EUSTATIUS

🏨 OLD GIN HOUSE
$$–$$$
ORANJE BAAI
TEL 599/318-2319 or

800/634-4907
FAX 599/318-2135
www.oldginhouse.com
This historic inn is one of
the island's most appealing
addresses. Colonial-style rooms
with tiled floors and dark
wood furnishings overlook a
pool. Good restaurant; also
a grill and four ocean-facing
rooms over the road.
🛈 18 🅿 🔃 ⛱ 🐾 All major
cards

🍽 BLUE BEAD BAR & RESTAURANT
$$–$$$
GALLOWS BAY
TEL 599/318-2873
Popular with locals and visitors, this is the place to settle
in for sunset drinks and a bar
snack. Fresh catch of the day,
coconut shrimp, and other
seafood specials, plus good
pizzas, pasta, and burgers.
🕐 Closed Tues. 🐾 All major
cards

SINT MAARTEN

🏨 DIVI LITTLE BAY BEACH RESORT
$$$
LITTLE BAY,
PHILIPSBURG
TEL 721/542-2333 OR
800/367-3484
FAX 721/542-4336
www.divilittlebay.com
An appealing jumble of red
roofs, whitewashed buildings,
and palm trees balanced on a
narrow peninsula just outside
Philipsburg. Good value rooms
and suites in cool pastel shades
with wooden latticework.
Water sports, tennis, diving,
spa, and children's programs.
🛈 265 🅿 🔃 ⛱ 📺 🐾 All
major cards

🏨 MARY'S BOON BEACH PLANTATION
$$–$$$
SIMSON BAAI 117

TEL 721/545-7000 or
877/260-7483
FAX 721/545-3403
www.marysboon.com
Relaxed, friendly inn on a
3-mile (5 km) stretch of white
sand beach close to shops and
restaurants. Colorful studios
and suites with Indonesian
furnishings. Charming staff.
Restaurant; honor bar.
🛈 32 🅿 ⛱ 🐾 All major cards

🏨 PASANGGRAHAN ROYAL GUESTHOUSE
$$
FRONT ST. 19, PHILIPSBURG
TEL 721/542-3588
FAX 721/542-2885
www.pasanroyalinn.com
Bayfront, 19th-century former
governor's residence where
Queen Wilhelmina once
stayed. The old-fashioned
charm extends to afternoon
tea. Town center location, but
quiet, stylishly refurbished
rooms with colonial-style
furnishings, and balconies.
🛈 30 🔃 🐾 All major cards

🍽 ANTOINE'S
$$$–$$$$
119 FRONT ST., PHILIPSBURG
TEL 721/542-2964
Pretty blue-and-white terrace
dining room with a view across
the bay. Classical French menu
featuring chilled vichyssoise,
scallops Nantaise, veal Dijon-
naise, plus a few Italian pasta
and Creole dishes.
🐾 All major cards

🍽 THE GREENHOUSE
$$$
BOBBY'S MARINA,
PHILIPSBURG
TEL 721/542-2941
A restaurant, bar, and nightclub
rolled into one, this island
institution has been packing
them in since 1986. Happy
hour is a 150-minute marathon
complete with reduced price
appetizers. The official menu

PRICES
HOTELS
An indication of the cost of
a double room in the high
season is given by **$** signs.

$$$$$	Over $400
$$$$	$300–$400
$$$	$200–$300
$$	$100–$200
$	Under $100

RESTAURANTS
An indication of the cost of
a three-course meal without
drinks is given by **$** signs.

$$$$$	Over $80
$$$$	$50–$80
$$$	$35–$50
$$	$20–$35
$	Under $20

offers steak, ribs, lobster, and
fresh Caribbean fish.
🐾 All major cards

🍽 ZEE BEST
$
PLAZA DEL LAGO, SIMSON BAAI
TEL 721/544-2477
Certainly zee best breakfast
you can find in Simpson Bay.
Divine flaky almond croissants,
apple turnovers, Danish
pastries. Generously stuffed
baguettes, chicken salad wraps,
and Zee pizzas for lunch.
🐾 No credit cards

ST.-MARTIN

SOMETHING SPECIAL

🏨 LA SAMANNA
🍽 Gorgeous super-luxurious
enclave with a Moorish-Medi-
terranean theme set in tropical
gardens above the beach.
Elegant accommodations in
rooms, suites, and villas. Gourmet restaurant, superb service,
tennis, and water sports.
$$$$$

BAIE LONGUE
TEL 0590/87 64 00 or
800/957-6128
FAX 590/87 87 86
www.lasamanna.com
🛈 82 🅿 🔂 🏊 🏋 🔑 All
major cards

🏨 LE PETIT HOTEL
$$$$–$$$$$
BLVD. DE GRAND CASE 248,
GRAND CASE
TEL 590/29 09 65
FAX 590/87 09 19
www.lepetithotel.com
Intimate and romantic
boutique hotel in a stucco villa
right on the beachfront restaurant row. Spacious studios and
suites with a sleek, contemporary look, dark wood Balinese
furnishings, and ocean-facing
balconies. Helpful staff.
🛈 10 🅿 🔂 🔑 All major
cards

🏨 CAPTAIN OLIVER'S
$$$$
OYSTER POND
TEL 590/87 40 26
FAX 590/87 40 84
www.captainolivers.com
Comfortable efficiency
bungalows decorated in pastel
shades and set on landscaped
grounds beside a lagoon. The
complex includes a marina,
dive shop, and bar frequented
by yachting types. Water taxi
service to Dawn Beach.
🛈 50 🅿 🔂 🏊 🔑 All major
cards

🍴 LE PRESSOIR
$$$$$
BLVD. DE GRAND CASE 30,
GRAND CASE
TEL 590/87 76 62
A local institution set in a
pretty 19th-century Creole
cottage across the street from
its namesake antique salt press.
Seriously good seafood such
as lobster ravioli (there's a
dedicated lobster menu), and
Dover sole with a warm hint

of turmeric. Fine wines and
smiling service.
🕒 Closed L 🔑 All major cards

🍴 LE TASTEVIN
$$$$$
BLVD. DE GRAND CASE 86,
GRAND CASE
TEL 590/87 55 45
Delicious French Caribbean
fusion fare and attentive service in a casual/elegant setting
overlooking the beach. Begin
with prawns with mint and
ginger; entrées might include
duck breast smoked in Chinese
tea or Moroccan-style lamb;
memorable crème brulée.
Reservations advised.
🔑 All major cards

🍴 BISTRO NU
$$–$$$
ALLÉE DE L'ANCIENNE GEÔLE,
MARIGOT
TEL 590/87 97 09
Cozy dining room tucked away
in an alley off rue de Hollande.
Generous traditional brasserie-style cuisine (snails, steak
frites) and very popular.
🕒 Closed L, Sun. 🔑 MC, V

🍴 CLAUDE MINI-CLUB
$$–$$$
BLVD. DE FRANCE 49,
MARIGOT
TEL 590/87 50 69
Lovely views of Marigot harbor
and bright-checked madras
cotton providing a splash of
traditional color to go with the
Creole/French menu specialties. Plenty of seafood and
great value barbecue buffets
on Wed. and Sat. nights.
🕒 Closed Sun. p.m. 🔑 All
major cards

◼ LEEWARD ISLANDS

ANGUILLA

🏨 CAP JULUCA
$$$$$

MAUNDAY'S BAY
TEL 264/497-6666 OR
888/852-5822
FAX 264/497-6617
www.capjuluca.com
Gorgeous Moorish-style oasis
set on a curving white sand
beach surrounded by lush
gardens. Huge rooms decorated
in restful beige and white,
monumental double tubs in
the suites, a tented restaurant,
babysitting, and top-notch
sports facilities.
🛈 79 rooms/suites, 6 pool villas
🅿 🔂 🏊 🏋 🔑 All major cards

🏨 CUISINART GOLF
🍴 RESORT & SPA
$$$$$
RENDEZVOUS BAY
TEL 264/498-2000 OR
800/943-3210
www.cuisinartresort.com
Dazzling white beachfront
accommodations trimmed with
blue echo sand and sky. Light
and spacious rooms, lovely
villas, and a raft of activities:
water-sports, tennis, gym, Greg
Norman-designed 18-hole golf
course, and spa. A hydroponic
farm supplies the restaurants
with fresh vegetables and salad
leaves.
🛈 93, 6 villas 🅿 🔂 🏊
🏋 🔑 All major cards

🏨 ANGUILLA GREAT HOUSE
$$$
RENDEZVOUS BAY
TEL 264/497-6061 OR
800/583-9247
FAX 264/497-6019
www.anguillagreathouse.com
Friendly, unpretentious spot
on a fabulous beach. Simple,
spacious gingerbread cottages
with tin roofs, shutters, and
mahogany furnishings. Beach
bar and restaurant.
🛈 31 🅿 🔂 Some 🏊 🔑 All
major cards

🔂 Air-conditioning 🏊 Indoor pool 🏊 Outdoor pool 🏋 Health club 🔑 Credit cards

🍴 BLANCHARD'S

$$$$$

MEAD'S BAY

TEL 264/497-6100

Candlelit tropical elegance on Mead's Bay. Melinda Blanchard's cuisine incorporates New American and Asian flavors with specialties such as lemon-glazed lobster dumplings and Japanese-inspired tuna fillet. Award-winning wine list. Reservations advised.

🕐 Closed L & Sun. 💳 All major cards

🍴 MANGO'S SEASIDE GRILL

$$$$

BARNES BAY

TEL 264/497-6479

Casual beachfront setting with a canvas awning over the wooden deck. Homemade bread, "famous" Barnes Bay lobster cakes, sesame-crusted snapper fillet marinated in soy, mouthwatering cakes and pies, and an extensive wine list.

🕐 Closed L & Tues. 💳 All major cards

🍴 TASTY'S

$$–$$$

SOUTH HILL

TEL 264/497-2737

Malliouhana-trained chef Dale Carty's upscale diner combines great island cuisine with a distinctly funky paint job. Traditional Johnny cakes for breakfast, knockout lobster salad for lunch, and delicious dinners.

🕐 Closed Thur. 💳 All major cards

🍴 JACQUIE'S RIPPLES

$$

SANDY GROUND

TEL 264/497-3380

A cozy indoor dining room and tables on the veranda (reserve ahead). The broad-ranging menu features grilled fish, Thai salads, pasta, crispy coconut chicken, and the like. The bar gets buzzy in the evening.

💳 All major cards

ANTIGUA

🏨 CURTAIN BLUFF

🍴 $$$$$

MORRIS BAY

TEL 268/462-8400 or 888/289-9898

FAX 268/462-8409

www.curtainbluff.com

Antigua's most famous and elegant hotel perched on a steep bluff winding down to the beach. Excellent all-inclusive sports facilities and gourmet dining on the terrace or casual on the beach.

🛏 72 P ⚓ 🏐 💳 All major cards

🏨 HAWKSBILL BY REX RESORTS

$$$$

FIVE ISLANDS

TEL 268/462-0301

FAX 268/462-1515

www.rexresorts.com

Bright and comfy rooms and cottage-style accommodations strung out along the shore (access to four beaches including one "clothing optional"). Deluxe club cottages for romantics; beach cottages with connecting doors for families. Water sports, tennis, kids' activities.

🛏 111 P 🚭 ⚓ 💳 All major cards

🏨 CATAMARAN HOTEL

$$–$$$

FALMOUTH HARBOUR

TEL 268/460-1036

FAX 268/460-1339

www.catamaran-antigua.com

Friendly, intimate, and right on the bayfront, the plantation-style "Cat Club" really does feel clubby. Helpful staff can organize activities or lend you a dinghy to pop across to English Harbour. Spic-and-span rooms with views, some with broad verandas and kitchenettes. Family-friendly.

🛏 14 rooms/suites

P 🚭 ⚓ 💳

🏨 SIBONEY BEACH CLUB

$$–$$$

DICKENSON BAY

TEL 268/462-0806 OR 800/533-0234

FAX 268/462-3356

www.siboneybeachclub.com

Delightful small property at the quiet end of Antigua's busiest beach. Twelve one-bedroom suites with kitchenettes and balconies overlooking tropical gardens. The restaurant is a big plus (see Coconut Grove, below). Water sports nearby.

🛏 12 P 🚭 ⚓ 💳 All major cards

🏨 ADMIRAL'S INN

$$

ENGLISH HARBOUR

TEL 268/460-1027

FAX 268/460-1534

www.admiralsantigua.com

Charming historic inn and waterfront garden in Nelson's Dockyard. Simple rooms with antique furnishings in both the main building and an annex (rather dark).

🛏 14 P 🚭 Some 💳 All major cards

🍴 COCONUT GROVE

$$$$

SIBONEY BEACH CLUB, DICKENSON BAY

TEL 268/462-1538

Romantic lantern-lit beach-front setting with smoochy music. Offerings include fresh swordfish and salmon carpaccio, seared mahimahi with Antiguan herbs, and Jamaican jerk chicken with banana-guava marmalade. Good wine and brandy list.

💳 All major cards

🍴 LA BUSSOLA

$$$–$$$$

RUNAWAY BEACH

🏨 Hotel   🍴 Restaurant   🛏 No. of guest rooms   🍴 No. of seats   P Parking   🕐 Closed

TEL 268/562-1545

Persevere down the bumpy track for a warm Mediterranean welcome and excellent Italian cuisine on the bay. Classic dishes with a modern twist from fresh pasta to scene-stealing lobster; the beachfront setting is delightful.

⏰ Closed Tues. 🚫 All major cards

🍴 RUSSELL'S
$$$
FORT JAMES
TEL 268/462-5479

Fabulous views over St. John's Harbour are reason enough to seek out this welcoming spot. Sunsets are a specialty, and a predominantly seafood menu includes steamed cockles in white wine, conch fritters, and grilled lobster. Traditional Antiguan lunch buffet on Sat.; Jazz on Sun.

⏰ Closed Sun. L 🚫 MC, V

🍴 PAPA ZOUK
$$–$$$
HILDA DAVIS DRIVE, GAMBLES
TEL 268/464-6044

Take a taxi to this eccentric little Creole-style bar-restaurant in a residential quarter north of St. John's. The blackboard sign reads "fish 'n' rum" and that's exactly what you get: More than 200 rums behind the bar, and the seafood specials (bouillabaisse, grilled snapper, lobster, shrimp) are simple and perfectly cooked.

⏰ Closed Sun. 🚫 No credit cards

🍴 BIG BANANA PIZZAS IN PARADISE
$$
REDCLIFFE QUAY, ST. JOHN'S
TEL 268/480-6985

A handy refueling stop in an old brick warehouse in the shopping district. Pizzas, sub sandwiches, salads, espressos, capuccinos, and cold drinks.

⏰ Closed Sun. 🚫 All major cards

🍴 CATHERINE'S CAFÉ
$$
ENGLISH HARBOUR
TEL 268/460-5050

Cracking little dockside café with marina views and a French-inspired menu served with authentic Gallic flair. Lunchtime crêpes, quiches, salads; moules marinières for dinner.

⏰ Closed D Sat.–Mon., Tues., Thur. 🚫 MC, V

BARBUDA

🏨 LIGHTHOUSE BAY RESORT
$$$$$
LOW BAY (ACCESS BY BOAT ONLY)
TEL 268/562-1481 OR
U.S. 888/214-8552
www.lighthousebayresort.com

Decorating a narrow strand of pink and white sand beach caught between the Codrington Lagoon and the Caribbean Sea, this escapist retreat promises barefoot luxury. High-ceilinged, woodsy suites with marble bathrooms, in-room wi-fi, and espresso machines. Beachfront dining; spa services; activities include tennis, kayaking, diving, and fishing.

🛏 9 ❄ 🏊 🚫 All major cards

MONTSERRAT

🏨 OLVESTON HOUSE
🍴 $$–$$$
OLVESTON
TEL 664/491-5210
www.olvestonhouse.com

Once occupied by Beatles producer Sir George Martin, this attractive guesthouse boasts a pool with views, spacious and comfy rooms, and a broad wraparound veranda for lolling in the shade. The popular restaurant serves fine Anglo-Caribbean cuisine.

🛏 6 ❄ Some 🅿 🚫 MC, V

🏨 GINGERBREAD HILL
$
ST. PETER'S
TEL 664/491-5812
www.volcano-island.com

Up in the hills with superlative views to the ocean, this little eco-retreat run by the hands-on Lea family is a find. Simple self-catering accommodations set in lush gardens and citrus orchards; car rental, mountain bikes, diving packages, volcano tours.

🛏 6 rooms/cottages 🅿 🚫 All major cards

🍴 TINA'S
$–$$
MAIN ROAD, BRADES
TEL 664/491-3538

Friendly local dining room in a traditional building with tables out on the veranda. Tuck into a lobster burger, chicken or fish curry, lunchtime sandwiches and salads, and don't miss the coconut cream pie.

⏰ Closed Sun. 🚫 No credit cards

ST. KITTS

At time of press, the hotel scene in St. Kitts is in an unusual state of flux. Two classic plantation house hotels, the Golden Lemon (www.goldenlemon.com) and the Rawlins Plantation (www.rawlinsplantation.com) are between owners; and several new, upscale properties on the southern peninsula slated for 2012 are yet to open. Currently, the island's premier beachfront property is the huge, and somewhat impersonal, St. Kitts Marriott Resort & Casino (www.marriott.com).

🏨 OTTLEY'S PLANTATION INN
$$$–$$$$$
OTTLEY'S
TEL 869/465-7234 OR
800/772-3039
FAX 869/465-4760
www.ottleys.com

Splendid 18th-century plantation great house set in gardens surrounded by cane fields. Huge, pretty rooms in the main house with its antique furnishings and breezy verandas, plus two- or three-bedroom cottages on the grounds. Shuttle to the beach.

ⓘ 23 Ⓟ Ⓢ ⛱ 🏊 All major cards

🏨 **TIMOTHY BEACH RESORT**
$$–$$$
FRIGATE BAY
TEL 869/465-8597
FAX 869/466-7085
www.timothybeach.com
The only property on the Caribbean beachfront in Frigate Bay. Good value accommodations, all with balconies or patios. Versatile layout, excellent for groups/families. On-site restaurant; shops and tennis nearby.

ⓘ 60 Ⓟ Ⓢ ⛱ 🏊 All major cards

🏨 **ROCK HAVEN BED & BREAKFAST**
$$
FRIGATE BAY
TEL 869/465-5573
FAX 869/466-6130
E-MAIL judith4jc@hot mail.com
Book early to secure one of the two rooms in this friendly B&B perched above Frigate Bay: Word of Judith Blake's warm Kittitian hospitality has spread far and wide. Airport pick up, dining and sightseeing advice, and mighty breakfasts.

ⓘ 2 🏊 MC, V

🍴 **THE BEACH HOUSE**
$$$$
CHRISTOPHE HARBOR, TURTLE BEACH
TEL 869/469-5299
Beachfront chic with lovely views of Nevis, billowing cotton drapes, hurricane lamps,

and a deft Mediterranean/Caribbean-inspired menu with plenty of seafood and good steaks. Excellent wine cellar.
🕐 Closed L, Sun.–Mon. 🏊 All major cards

🍴 **FISHERMAN'S WHARF**
$$$
FORTLANDS, BASSETERRE
TEL 869/465-2754
Something of an island institution with sweeping views of the harbor from a big wooden deck. Steak and seafood cooked on an open charcoal grill, good and spicy jerk chicken, lobster, excellent chowder. Live music on weekends.
🏊 All major cards

🍴 **BALLAHOO**
$$
THE CIRCUS, BASSETERRE
TEL 869/465-4197
Popular downtown meeting place. Tuna melt subs, sandwiches, and burgers for lunch, hot chili shrimp, mahimahi steaks with basil-mustard butter, and vegetarian options in the evening.
🕐 Closed Sun. 🏊 All major cards

🍴 **STONEWALLS**
$–$$
5 PRINCES ST., BASSETERRE
TEL 869/465-5248
An exuberant tropical garden greets visitors to this friendly bar-restaurant set in a stone-walled courtyard. The constantly changing menu runs the gamut from mega-spicy jerk pork to pasta or roast beef and Yorkshire pudding.
🕐 Closed L, Sun. 🏊 All major cards

NEVIS

🏨 **FOUR SEASONS RESORT**
$$$$$
PINNEY'S BEACH
TEL 869/469-1111 OR

800/819-5053
FAX 869/469-1040
www.fourseasons.com
Terrific position on Nevis's main beach for this luxurious property. Large rooms and suites with oversize baths and private patios by the waterfront or golf course. Sports packages, excellent children's facilities, polished service.

ⓘ 237 Ⓟ Ⓢ ⛱ 🏐 🏊 All major cards

🏨 **MONTPELIER**
🍴 **PLANTATION INN**
$$$$$
FIG TREE
TEL 869/469-3462
FAX 869/469-2932
www.montpeliernevis.com
Glorious old stone plantation house on a former sugar estate. Airy, elegant rooms in cottages set in the 10-acre (4 ha) landscaped grounds. Meals served in the main building English country house–style. Tennis, beach shuttle.

ⓘ 17 Ⓟ ⛱ 🏊 All major cards

SOMETHING SPECIAL

🏨 **HERMITAGE**
Enchanting plantation inn with rooms in gingerbread cottages dotted about the flower-filled gardens of the oldest wooden house in the Caribbean (circa 1680–1740). Romantic four-posters, hammocks on the veranda, horseback riding, peace and quiet.
$$$$–$$$$$
GINGERLAND
TEL 869/469-3477 OR
800/682-4025
FAX 869/469-2481
www.hermitagenevis.com
ⓘ 15 Ⓟ ⛱ 🏊 All major cards

🏨 **OUALIE BEACH HOTEL**
$$$
OUALIE BEACH
TEL 869/469-9735 OR
800/682-5431

house or superb cottages.

[i] 9 [P] [S] [≈] [S] All major cards

LA TOUBANA
$$$

STE.-ANNE, GRANDE-TERRE
TEL 590/88 25 78
FAX 590/88 38 90
www.toubana.com

Lovely sea views and quaint one- and two-bedroom cottages (*toubanas*) with kitchenettes on the hill leading down to a small beach cove with water sports. Tennis; some evening entertainment.

[i] 32 [P] [≈] [S] All major cards

AUBERGE LES PETITS SAINTS AUX ANARCADIERS
$$–$$$

TERRE-DE-HAUT, LES SAINTES
TEL 590/99 50 99
FAX 590/99 54 51
www.petitssaints.com

Pretty Creole home overflowing with antiques and collectibles. Ten comfortable rooms five minutes from the town center; good restaurant.

[i] 11 [S] All major cards

HÔTEL-RÉSIDENCE CANELLA BEACH
$$–$$$

POINTE DE LA VERDURE, GOSIER, GRANDE-TERRE
TEL 590/90 44 00
FAX 590/90 44 44
www.canellabeach.fr

Well-equipped studios and duplex apartments on a beachfront property in Gosier's resort area. This is a good option for families, with a children's pool and range of water-sports activities.

[i] 143 units [P] [S] [≈] [S] All major cards

LE VERGER DE STE.-ANNE
$

FAX 869/469-9176
www.oualiebeach.com

Small and informal beachfront property with well-priced rooms and studios in wooden cottages; screened porches overlook the beach. Diving and windsurfing packages; mountain bikes.

[i] 32 [P] [S] [S] All major cards

MISS JUNE'S
$$$$$

JONES BAY
TEL 869/469-5330

A local institution, Miss June Meister cooks a grand Caribbean-Asian-European buffet in her home about three times a week (reservations essential). Guests meet for cocktails at 7:30 before being unleashed on two dozen gourmet dishes.

[◷] Call ahead for schedule
[S] All major cards

DOUBLE DEUCE
$$$

PINNEY'S BEACH
TEL 869/469-2222

Classic beach bar-restaurant with a difference: chef Mark Roberts knows his seafood. Expect perfectly barbequed catch of the day, grilled lobster, garlicky jumbo shrimp, fish soup with tania fritters, juicy steaks, and ice cold beers. Karaoke Thursday night.

[◷] Closed Mon. [⊗] No credit cards

■ FRENCH ANTILLES

GUADELOUPE

LE JARDIN MALANGA
$$$–$$$$

LES TROIS RIVIÈRES, BASSE-TERRE
TEL 590/92 67 57
FAX 590/92 67 58
www.jardinmalanga.com

Fabulous hillside setting with views of the Îles des Saintes from the deck of this low-key hideaway. Minimalist chic rooms in 1920s plantation

5 LOT. MARGUERITE
STE.-ANNE, GRANDE-TERRE
TEL 590/88 27 56
FAX 590/88 21 45
www.guadeloupe-hebergement.com

Six delightful Creole cottages dotted around the gardens. Verandas with sea views, fully equipped kitchenettes, rattan furnishings, and inside and outside showers. A genuinely warm welcome from Danièle Vic, who can arrange rental cars, organize itineraries, and serve a mean ti-punch!

[i] 6 [P] [S] [S] All major cards

LA VIEILLE TOUR
$$$$

AUBERGE DE LA VIEILLE TOUR
GOSIER, GRANDE-TERRE
TEL 590/84 23 23

Elegant hotel dining room with sea views (reserve a window seat) and a classic French-Creole menu. Crayfish tartare, fresh fish with lobster butter, and magnificent desserts.

[◷] Closed L [S] All major cards

LA PORTE DES INDES
$$$–$$$$

DEVARIEUX, SAINT-FRANÇOIS, GRANDE-TERRE
TEL 590/21 30 87

Connoisseurs of Indian cuisine cannot praise this delightful *temple de la gastronomie* highly enough. A statue of the elephant god Ganesh presides over the dining pavilion and a classic and creative Indian menu. Excellent wine list.

[◷] Closed Sun. D–Mon. [S] V

IGUANE CAFÉ
$$$

RTE. DE LA POINTE DES CHÂTEAUX, ST-FRANÇOIS
GRANDE-TERRE
TEL 590/88 61 37

Chic-rustique eaterie on the beach road serving a creative menu strong on local ingredients. Marble of foie gras and lobster with dark rum and

---

shellfish aspic, crispy saffron conch and christophine gratin, five-spice fish.

🕐 Closed Tues., and L except Sun. 🐚 All major cards

🍴 LES TORTUES
$$
ANSE DUCHÉ, BOUILLANTE, BASSE-TERRE
TEL 0590/98 82 83
You could almost hook your own lunch from the Turtles' big wooden deck hanging over the bay, but local fishermen will do that for you. Creole seafood dishes, such as bar-becued conch or crayfish, and the catch of the day.
🐚 All major cards

🍴 LE TOULOULOU
$$
PETITE-ANSE, CAPESTERRE-MARIE-GALANTE
TEL 0590/97 32 63
Right on the beach, this island institution serves fresh-off-the-boat seafood and excellent ti-punch, as well as local spe-cialty *bébélé*, an offal stew. Live music, an after-dinner disco, and also a couple of simple beach bungalows.
🕐 Closed Sun. D–Mon.
🐚 MC, V

MARTINIQUE

🏨 CAP EST LAGOON
🍴 RESORT & SPA
$$$$$
LE FRANÇOIS
TEL 0596/54 80 80 OR
800/735-2478
FAX 0596/54 96 00
www.capest.com
A sense of Zen-like calm pervades this quiet, upscale beach resort set on the edge of a lagoon among palms and sea grape trees on the east coast. Vibrant Creole colors juxtaposed with Asian-style simplicity, luxurious suites, a gorgeous pool and gardens, excellent cuisine as befits a

Relais & Châteaux property.
🛏 50 P 🅿 🏊 📺 🐚 All major cards

🏨 DOMAINE ST. AUBIN
🍴 $$$
PETITE RIVIÈRE SALÉE, LA TRINITÉ
TEL 0596/69 34 77
FAX 0596/69 41 14
www.ledomainesaint aubin.com
Wonderful views and charming hosts put this rather remote restored plantation hotel on the map. Set in rolling hillside gardens, the fanciful Louisiana-style house has been furnished with antiques. Joelle Rosemain's French-Caribbean cooking is a treat.
🛏 36 P 🅿 🏊 MC, V

🏨 HOTEL BAKOUA
$$$
POINTE DU BOUT, TROIS ILETS
TEL 0596/66 02 02
FAX 0596/66 00 41
www.mgallery.com
Attractive and well-equipped resort set on a bluff above a private beach. Comfortably appointed rooms with views. Tennis, water sports, helpful tour desk, golf nearby.
🛏 138 P 🅿 🏊 🐚 All major cards

🏨 FRÉGATE BLEUE
$$
LE FRANÇOIS
TEL 0596/54 54 66
FAX 0596/54 78 48
www.fregatebleue.com
A peaceful little Relais du Silence with rooms, suites, and a cute Creole cottage set on an inland hill with sea views. Simple antique furnishings with a splash of Creole color; kitchenettes and balconies; breakfast by the pool; dinner on request.
🛏 10 P 🅿 🏊 MC, V

🍴 FLEUR DE SEL
$$$$
27 AVE. DE L'IMPÉRATRICE JOSÉ-

PHINE, BOURG DE TROIS-ILETS
TEL 0596/68 42 11
Fine French dining in a hand-some brick town house with a leafy terrace. Cappuccino of cepes and scallops with black truffle foam, gently spiced lamb tagine, and classic magret de canard.
🕐 Closed L and Sun. 🐚 MC, V

🍴 LA TABLE DE MAMY NOUNOU
$$$–$$$$
HOTEL LA CARAVELLE, TARTANE
TEL 0596/58 07 32
Picturesque hotel-restaurant clinging to a wooded hillside with breezy verandas and views. Innovative Creole-influenced cuisine such as the seafood platter with cider and cinnamon cream sauce and delectable iced soufflés. Dinner reservations essential.
🕐 Closed Tues. 🐚 MC, V

🍴 LE ZANZIBAR
$$$
11 BLVD. ALLÉGRE, LE MARIN
TEL 0596/74 08 46

Restaurant and lounge bar with an eclectic Creole-Moroccan vibe and lovely views over the bay and marina. The cooking is similarly worldly, tuna tartare, chicken tagine, and even *moules frites* (mussels and fries); fine Belgian beers.

🕐 Closed Sun. p.m. 🕎 MC, V

🍴 LE TOULOULOU
$$–$$$
POINTE MARIN, SAINTE-ANNE
TEL 0596/76 73 27
Great beachfront spot for an authentic French-Creole dining experience. Generous *plateaux de fruits de mer* (seafood platters) piled with lobster, clams, and shrimp, classic *tarte aux pommes* to finish.

🕐 Closed Sun. p.m. & Mon. p.m.

🍴 AU POISSON D'OR
$$
ANSE MITAN, TROIS ILETS
TEL 0596/66 01 80
Popular Creole restaurant on the Pointe du Bout road. Lots of bamboo, greenery, and waitresses in traditional costume. Specialties include lime-marinated conch, spicy shark, and grilled lobster Creole.

🕐 Closed Sun. p.m.–Mon. 🕎 All major cards

ST.-BARTHÉLEMY

🏨 EDEN ROCK
🍴 $$$$$
ST. JEAN
TEL 0590/29 79 99 OR
U.S./CAN. 855/333-6762
FAX 0590/27 88 37
www.edenrockhotel.com
St. Barts's first hotel has been stylishly rebuilt. The new buildings seem to grow organically from a rocky promontory above the beach. Cool classic suites featuring natural wood or colorful silks, romantic boudoirs, and delectable cottages. Good restaurants.

🛏 36 P 🕎 ⛱ 🕎 🕎 All major cards

🏨 LE TOINY
$$$$$
ANSE DE TOINY
TEL 0590/27 88 88 OR
800/680-0832
FAX 0590/27 89 30
www.letoiny.com
Superbly elegant and secluded Relais & Châteaux property, with a dozen spacious and beautifully decorated cottages boasting private pools, kitchenettes, and fitness equipment. Excellent restaurant (see Le Gaïac, below).

🛏 15 P 🕎 ⛱ 🕎 All major cards

🏨 NORMANDIE HOTEL
$$
ROUTE DE SALINE, LORIENT
TEL 0590/27 61 99
FAX 0590/27 98 83
www.normandiehotelstbarts.com
Small, friendly B&B hotel a two-minute walk from the beach, restaurants, and shops. Lots of stylish contemporary glass block and a nautical nod to the 1930s Art Deco liner, the SS *Normandie*. In-room fridge and wi-fi; plunge pool in the tiny tropical garden.

🛏 8 P 🕎 ⛱ 🕎 All major cards

🍴 LE GAÏAC
$$$$$
LE TOINY, ANSE DE TOINY
TEL 0590/27 88 88
Small and chic with sea views, Le Gaïac delivers top-notch French-Caribbean cuisine. Beetroot and raspberry gazpacho, king crab curry with green apple foam, conch ravioli. Reservations recommended.

🕐 Closed Mon., Sept.–Oct. 🕎 All major cards

🍴 EDDY'S
$$$$
RUE DU CENTENAIRE, GUSTAVIA
TEL 0590/27 54 17
Balinese teak, bamboo, and an explosion of greenery lend a Southeast Asian note to the decor, further reflected in the French-Caribbean-Asian menu. Fashionable spot for shrimp green curry, Creole colombo, and grilled fish.

🕐 Closed L & Sun. 🕎 All major cards

🍴 LE SÉLECT
$
RUE DE LA FRANCE, GUSTAVIA
TEL 0590/27 86 87
Hip downtown bar with bustling garden patio and pumping reggae, zouk, and live music in the old brick ware-house at night. Cheeseburgers and cocktails are the highlights.

🕎 All major cards

■ WINDWARD ISLANDS

CARRIACOU

🏨 GREEN ROOF INN
$–$$
HILLSBOROUGH
TEL/FAX 473/443-6399
www.greenroofinn.com
This unpretentious little Scandinavian-owned guesthouse is an absolute charmer. Clean pastel shades and white linen in the guest rooms and a romantic white clapboard cottage hideaway with its own kitchenette. Fabulous views, beach access, friendly bar, and veranda restaurant.

🛏 5 rooms, 1 cottage
P 🕎 MC, V

DOMINICA

🏨 FORT YOUNG
$$–$$$
ROSEAU
TEL 767/448-5000 or
U.S. 855/223-9519
FAX 767/448-5006
www.fortyounghotel.com
Attractive rooms and spacious suites built around a pool deck nestled in the remains of a historic seafront fortress, plus

a smart new ocean view block down on the water. Good location, in-house tour desk.

[i] 73 [P] [S] [≈] [S] All major cards

🏨 ANCHORAGE HOTEL & DIVE CENTRE
$$
CASTLE COMFORT
TEL 767/448-2638 OR
U.S. 888/790-5264
FAX 767/440-2639
www.anchoragehotel.com
Small block of modern units with a splash of Creole color and balconies overlooking the sea just south of Roseau. This is a great base for activities, with a PADI dive center and hiking trips, a squash court, plus helpful and friendly staff.

[i] 32 [S] [≈] [S] All major cards

🏨 PICARD BEACH COTTAGE RESORT
$$
PICARD BEACH, PORTSMOUTH
TEL 767/445-5131 OR
U.S. 888/790-5264
FAX 767/445-5599
www.picardbeach
cottages.com
Simple rooms in quiet Creole cottages on one of Dominica's better black sand beaches. Private verandas and kitchenettes; lovely gardens on an old coconut plantation.

[i] 18 [P] [S] Some [≈] [S] All major cards

SOMETHING SPECIAL

🏨 ZANDOLI INN
🍴 A lovely little country inn balanced on cliffs 80 feet (24 m) above the ocean in the island's south. Fabulous views, delightful gardens with a plunge pool, and pretty guest rooms decked out in soothing blues and greens. Good food (and company) in the restaurant. Walking trails nearby. No children under 12.
$$

ROCHE CASSÉE-STOWE
TEL 767/446-3161
FAX 767/446-3344
www.zandoli.com
[i] 5 [P] [≈] [S] MC, V

🍴 LE BISTRO
$$$
19 CASTLE STREET, ROSEAU
TEL 767/440-8117
Classically trained chef Vincent Binet unleashes his talent on locally sourced ingredients at this charming candlelit dining room in a restored colonial building. Fresh watermelon salad, velvety shrimp curry, rib-eye steak with butter sauce, French cheeses.
[🕐] Closed L, Sat.–Sun. [S] MC, V

🍴 PAPILLOTE WILDERNESS RETREAT
$$$
TRAFALGAR VALLEY
TEL 767/448-2287
Neat rain forest inn (8 simple rooms) with tables on a leafy terrace hemmed in by greenery. The unpretentious menu is packed with favorite Caribbean staples, seasonal fruits, and vegetables. Reservations recommended for dinner.
[S] All major cards

🍴 WATERFRONT
$$$
FORT YOUNG HOTEL, ROSEAU
TEL 767/448-5000
The island's smartest restaurant overlooks Roseau Bay from its wraparound veranda. Baked crab with parmesan, grilled tuna in a creamy watercress sauce, conch Creole served with ground provisions, and fresh garden vegetables.
[S] All major cards

🍴 COCORICO CAFÉ
$–$$
BAYFRONT (AT KENNEDY AVE.), ROSEAU
TEL 767/449-8686

A French café set in a jauntily painted Creole house, and a great spot in front of the ferry terminal to hang out and watch the world go by. Croissants for breakfast, homemade cake with morning coffee, and delicious filled baguettes, salads, crêpes, and spicy jerk chicken for lunch.
[🕐] Closed D, Sun. (except when a cruise ship is in) [S] MC, V

GRENADA

🏨 SPICE ISLAND BEACH RESORT
$$$$$
GRAND ANSE
TEL 473/444-4258 OR
U.S. 727/786-1258
FAX 473/444-4807
www.spicebeachresort.com
Elegant, family-run beachfront all-inclusive that combines Grenadian hospitality with impeccable service. Classical-contemporary decor in spacious suites (some have private pools and exercise facilities). Tennis and nonmotorized water sports.

[i] 66 [P] [S] [≈] [TV] [S] All major cards

🏨 CALABASH HOTEL & VILLAS
$$$$
L'ANSE AUX EPINES
TEL 473/444-4334 OR
U.S. 201/244-7723
FAX 473/444-5050
www.calabashhotel.com
Tranquil and charming beachfront hotel with comfortable suites (some with small private pools) arranged in an arc of two-story garden cottages. Caring service includes breakfast prepared in your suite. Tennis and nonmotorized water sports; good food. An exclusive development of architect-designed villas lies to the west.

[i] 30 rooms, 5 villas [P] [S] [≈] [TV] [S] All major cards

🏨 LA SOURCE
$$$–$$$$

🏨 Hotel 🍴 Restaurant [i] No. of guest rooms 🛏 No. of seats [P] Parking 🕐 Closed

PINK GIN BEACH
TEL 473/444-2556 or
888/527-0044
FAX 473/444-2561
www.lasourceresort.com
This luxurious, all-inclusive spa
property offers a raft of treatments, yoga, pilates, tennis,
water sports, and more. Stylish
accommodations with marble
floors and mahogany beds.
⚐ 100 🅿 ⚐ ⚐ ⚐ ⚐ All
major cards

⬚ FLAMBOYANT
$$–$$$
GRAND ANSE
TEL 473/444-4247 OR
U.S. 866/978-8013
FAX 473/444-1234
www.flamboyant.com
A steep (but mercifully short)
hike up from the beach, great
views across to St. George's,
and a selection of comfy
rooms, self-catering one- or
two-bedroom suites and
studios, all with balconies.
⚐ 67 🅿 ⚐ Some
⚐ ⚐ ⚐ All major cards

⬚ LA SAGESSE
NATURE CENTRE
$$–$$$
LA SAGESSE, ST. DAVID'S
TEL/FAX 473/444-6458
www.lasagesse.com
An off-the-beaten-track
beach hideaway with
simple, spacious rooms in
a 1920s estate house, an
oceanfront annex (including a
suite and two duplexes), and
two rooms in a cottage. Ceiling
fans, verandas, good food.
⚐ 12 🅿 ⚐ MC, V

⬚ RHODES RESTAURANT
$$$$
CALABASH HOTEL, L'ANSE AUX
EPINES, GRENADA
TEL 473/444-4334
This elegant and pretty terrace
dining room is a Caribbean
outpost for acclaimed British
chef Gary Rhodes. The season-
ally inspired menu features

local produce from jerk chicken
with sweet paw-paw salad to
Grenadian fish stew. Reservations recommended.
⚐ Closed L ⚐ All major cards

⬚ COCONUT BEACH
RESTAURANT
$$$
GRAND ANSE
TEL 473/444-4644
Dine on the sand or inside the
old wooden house. French
Creole specialties such as conch
curry, lobster, or catch of the
day in a variety of sauces.
⚐ Closed Tues. ⚐ All major
cards

⬚ AQUARIUM BEACH
CLUB & RESTAURANT
$$
TAMARIND BEACH
POINT SALINES
TEL 473/444-1410
Woodsy, open-air beach restaurant. Well-prepared world
food from satay or pumpkin
and ginger soup to snapper
with a coriander-herb crust, callaloo canneloni, New Zealand
lamb, and U.S. steaks. Sunday
barbecues.
⚐ All major cards

⬚ MORNE FENDUE
$
NEAR SAUTEURS, ST. PATRICK'S
DISTRICT
TEL 473/442-9330
This small plantation home is
renowned for its West Indian
lunch buffet. A groaning table
of local fish, meat, rice 'n' peas,
and vegetable dishes including
pepperpot stew.
⚐ Closed D ⚐ All major cards

⬚ THE NUTMEG
$
THE CARENAGE, ST. GEORGE'S
TEL 473/440-2539
Casual local meeting place
with harbor views, a lively bar,
and a simple menu of soups,
sandwiches, roti, and fruit or

rum punches with a generous
sprinkling of nutmeg.
⚐ Closed B & L Sun. ⚐ All
major cards

ST. LUCIA

⬚ ANSE CHASTANET RE-
SORT
$$$$$
SOUFRIÈRE
TEL 758/459-7000 OR
800/223-1108
FAX 758/459-7700
www.ansechastanet.com
Set in a steep-sided beach
cove down a bumpy track,
this delightful small spa resort
is wonderfully relaxing and a
good dive center. Lovely rooms
in octagonal gazebos with
wraparound balconies, hillside
or beachside suites, great views,
tennis, attentive service.
⚐ 49 🅿 ⚐ All major cards

⬚ TI KAYE VILLAGE
⬚ **$$$–$$$$**
ANSE COCHON
TEL 758/456-8101
FAX 758/456-8105
www.tikayc.com
Grafted onto a wooded bluff
above the beach between Castries and Soufrière, charming
cottages and duplexes (great for
families) in landscaped grounds.
Hammocks on the balcony,
net-draped beds, some private
plunge pools. Super restaurant,
beach bar-grill, diving.
⚐ 33 ⚐ ⚐ ⚐ ⚐ All major
cards

⬚ MARIGOT BEACH CLUB
& DIVE RESORT
$$–$$$
MARIGOT BAY
TEL 758/451-4974
FAX 758/451-4973
www.marigotbeachclub.com
Delightful waterfront property
which will appeal to independent travelers. Studios and
two- and three-bedroom villas
above Marigot Bay. Tiny beach,

water sports, dive shop, sailing packages.

ⓘ 25 🅿 🏊 🛝 🅰 All major cards

🏨 HARMONY SUITES
$$

RODNEY BAY
TEL 758/452-8756 OR
U.S. 888/790-5264
FAX 758/452-8677
www.harmonysuites.com

Small and friendly complex on the water minutes from Reduit Beach. Well-equipped standard suites and deluxe units, some kitchenettes. On-site bistro, and The Edge (see below).

ⓘ 30 🅿 🍴 🏊 🅰 All major cards

🍴 THE EDGE
$$$$–$$$$$

HARMONY SUITES, RODNEY BAY VILLAGE
TEL 758/451-4745

Smart, creative Eurobbean (European-Caribbean fusion) cuisine from award-winning chef Bobo Bergström. Stunning presentation and delicate flavors, from the sushi bar to entrées such as rosemary-scented and rum-glazed lobster. Torch-lit, waterfront veranda; attentive service.

🅰 All major cards

SOMETHING SPECIAL

🍴 RAINFOREST HIDEAWAY

Imagine a rustic-chic water-front dock set with tables, a champagne bar among the mangroves, and gentle jazz. The fusion dinner menu combines Caribbean and Asian flavors (ravioli stuffed with ginger and coconut crab); lighter and simpler lunches.

$$$$–$$$$$

MARIGOT BAY
TEL 758/451-4485

🕐 Closed L & Tues. 🅰 All major cards

🍴 JACQUES' WATER-FRONT DINING
$$$–$$$$

RODNEY BAY MARINA
TEL 758/458-1900

In a pretty new marina location, French patron-chef Jacky Rioux serves up fish and seafood including favorites such as octopus and conch in a curried coconut sauce. Excellent Sunday brunch.

🅰 All major cards

🍴 HUMMINGBIRD
$$

HUMMINGBIRD BEACH RESORT, SOUFRIÈRE
TEL 758/459-7232

Delightful garden restaurant with views of the Pitons and a reputation for Creole cuisine. The signature seafood dish is dorado with local herbs, salads and sandwiches are available at lunchtime, and the vegetables are homegrown.

🅰 All major cards

🍴 THE LIME
$$

RODNEY BAY
TEL 758/452-0761

A longstanding favorite with visitors and locals alike. Tables inside and out, and a menu that opens with breakfast and fills out to include Caribbean and international dishes from steaks and seafood to Jamaican jerk.

🅰 All major cards

ST. VINCENT & THE GRENADINES

BEQUIA

🏨 FIREFLY PLANTATION
$$$$–$$$$$

SPRING BAY
TEL 784/458-3414
FAX 784/457-3305
www.fireflybequia.com

Idyllic rural retreat on a working plantation in the hills above Spring Bay. Romantic

rooms with stone floors and gauzy drapes on four-posters; views over citrus orchards and coconut groves to the sea; hammocks, tennis, plantation tours; pavilion dining room on the site of the 18th-century great house.

ⓘ 4 rooms, 1 cottage

🅿 🏊 🅰

🏨 BEQUIA BEACH HOTEL
🍴 $$$–$$$$$

FRIENDSHIP BEACH
TEL 784/458-1600
FAX 784/458-1700
www.bequiabeach.com

Delectable new upscale resort on one of Bequia's prettiest beaches. Breezy, gingerbread-trimmed, contemporary/colonial-style suites and villas. Lovely gardens, spa, fine dining, charming staff.

ⓘ 41 rooms/suites/villas 🅿
🍴 🏊 🛝 🅰

🍴 GINGERBREAD
$–$$

PORT ELIZABETH
TEL 784/458-3800

Three dining options in one: The daytime Gingerbread Café does a great line in coffees, juices, and homemade cakes. Fresh seafood kebabs and chicken end up on the Gingerbread BBQ at lunch. Or there is the Gingerbread Restaurant, with bay views from the veranda and a lunch menu of pasta, salads, omelets. Callalloo and shrimp soup and curries in the evening.

🅰 All major cards

CANOUAN

🏨 CANOUAN RESORT & GRENADINES ESTATE VILLAS
$$$$$

TEL 784/458-8000
FAX 784/458-8885
www.canouan.com

Peerless luxury resort set amphitheater-style around a

pristine bay. Huge and elegant accommodations in single- and double-story villas, every amenity from personal golf carts and Fazio-designed golf course to kids' clubs and a luxurious spa.

🛈 156 ❄ ⛱ 🏋 💳 All major cards

MUSTIQUE

🏨 MUSTIQUE VILLA RENTALS
$$$$$
TEL 784/488-8000
FAX 784/488-9000
www.mustique-island.com
There are about 70-plus two- to nine-bedroom villa rentals on the island. All come with cook and maid. Meals can be taken at the 17-room Cotton House Hotel, and facilities on the island include horseback riding, tennis, and diving.

🛈 74 villas 💳 All major cards

ST. VINCENT

🏨 YOUNG ISLAND
$$$–$$$$$
OPPOSITE VILLA
TEL 784/458-4826 or
U.S 800/223-1108
FAX 784/457-4567
www.youngisland.com
A private island resort with pretty wood and stone cottages enfolded in tropical greenery. Patios and sea views, some small swimming pools. Tennis, water sports, yachting excursions, spa treatments.

🛈 30 ⓟ ⛱ 💳 All major cards

🏨 GRAND VIEW BEACH HOTEL
$$
VILLA POINT
TEL 784/458-4811
FAX 784/457-4174
www.grandviewhotel.com
Suitably grand views and very comfortable rooms in a turn-of-the-20th-century plantation

house with a bright and airy modern wing on a cliff top promontory. Steps down to the beach, tennis, squash; friendly and helpful staff.

🛈 19 ⓟ ❄ ⛱ 🏋 💳 All major cards

🍴 FRENCH VERANDAH RESTAURANT
$$$$
MARINERS HOTEL,
VILLA BEACH
TEL 784/457-4000
Charming hotel-restaurant on the waterfront facing the twinkly lights of Young Island at night. The menu is long on fish and seafood, some local flavors such as *calaloo* and conch soup and stuffed crab backs, and indubitably French garlic snails and steak frites. Good French wines.

💳 All major cards

🍴 LIME 'N' PUB
$$
VILLA
TEL 784/458-4227
Jolly pub with a terrace, dining room, and bar decorated with fishing nets and colored lights. Huge choice of British-style pub grub, sandwiches, and burgers, plus a more formal dinner menu offering plenty of seafood.

💳 All major cards

■ BARBADOS

🏨 COBBLERS COVE
🍴 $$$$$
SPEIGHTSTOWN, ST. PETER
TEL 246/422-2291 OR U.S./
CANADA 800/890-6060
FAX 246/422-1460
www.cobblerscove.com
Small and elegant all-suite hotel. Lovely accommodations with balcony or terrace overlooking the tropical gardens, plus two fabulous luxury suites. Tennis, water sports, notable restaurant.

🛈 40 ⓟ ❄ ⛱ 💳 All major cards

🏨 CORAL REEF CLUB
$$$$$
PORTERS, ST. JAMES
TEL 246/422-2372 OR
U.S. 800/223-1108
FAX 246/422-1776
www.coralreefbarbados.com
Gracious family-owned operation with a faithful clientele. Accommodations in thoughtfully appointed garden cottages and more luxurious suites. Lovely grounds, tennis, water sports, good food.

🛈 88 ⓟ ❄ ⛱ 💳 All major cards

🏨 ALMOND BEACH VILLAGE
$$$$
HEYWOODS, ST. PETER
TEL 246/422-4900 OR
U.S. 800/425-6663
FAX 246/422-0617
www.almondresorts.com
Large and attractive all-inclusive property on a fine beach. Wide range of accommodations and facilities ranging from golf, water sports, tennis, and squash to children's programs.

🛈 403 ⓟ ❄ ⛱ 🏋 💳 All major cards

🏨 BOUGAINVILLEA BEACH RESORT
$$$–$$$$
MAXWELL, CHRIST CHURCH
TEL 246/418-0990 OR
U.S./CANADA 800/495-2524
FAX 246/428-2524
www.bougainvillearesort.com
Very spacious and comfortable studios and one- or two-bedroom suites with kitchenettes and waterfront balconies or terraces. Dining, tennis, and water sports are all available.

🛈 138 ⓟ ❄ ⛱ 🏋 💳 All major cards

🏨 SEA U GUEST HOUSE
$$$

TENT BAY, BATHSHEBA, ST. JOSEPH
TEL 246/433-9450
FAX 246/433-9210
www.seaubarbados.com
Delightful B&B in a clapboard
Bajan inn above the Atlantic
coast. Romantic rooms/suites
with louvred shutters, polished
wooden floors, mahogany
or bamboo beds. Amazing
homemade breads for breakfast;
dinner in the gazebo restaurant.
🛈 9 🅿 Some 🔣 🔣 MC, V

🏨 PEACH AND QUIET
$$
INCH MARLOW,
CHRIST CHURCH
TEL 246/428-5682
FAX 246/428-2467
www.peachandquiet.com
This really is a peachy little
spot. An affordable oceanfront
all-suites guesthouse with charm-
ing Brit owners, a restaurant,
and peace and quiet virtually
guaranteed (no kids under
12). All suites have balcony/ter-
race. Snorkeling; hiking.
🛈 22 🅿 🔣 🔣 MC, V

🍴 THE CLIFF
$$$$$
DERRICKS, ST. JAMES
TEL 246/432-1922
A brace of theatrically lit
terraces carved into the lime-
stone sea cliffs and clientele
poised to sample some of the
finest cuisine in the region.
Combinations such as lightly
char-grilled tuna with coriander
cream sauce; impressive wines.
Reservations.
🕐 Closed L 🔣 All major cards

🍴 DAPHNE'S
$$$$$
PAYNE'S BAY, ST. JAMES
TEL 264/432-2731
A Caribbean outpost for one
of London's exclusive restau-
rants. Flaming torches in the
courtyard, beachside dining,
and stylish modern Italian
cuisine that's both delicious
and beautifully presented.

Reservations advised.
🔣 All major cards

🍴 PISCES
$$$
ST. LAWRENCE GAP,
CHRIST CHURCH
TEL 246/435-6564
Split-level dining room with
trellises, clambering plants,
and terra-cotta lanterns on the
water's edge. Seafood specialties include shrimp and tomato
stuffed snapper in a parsley-
lime sauce or pasta and chicken
dishes. Delicious desserts.
🕐 Closed L 🔣 All major cards

🍴 RAGAMUFFINS
$$$
1ST ST., HOLETOWN,
ST. JAMES
TEL 246/432-1295
Jaunty green and blue chattel
house with a lively bar and
cozy-casual atmosphere. West
Indian curries, blackened
shrimp, grilled kingfish, T-bone
steaks, and vegetarian options.
🕐 Closed L 🔣 All major cards

🍴 ATLANTIS HOTEL
$$
BATHSHEBA, ST. JOSEPH
TEL 246/433-9445
The panoramic clifftop terrace
and dining room make this a
popular lunch stop on round-
island tours. Wednesday's set
price West Indian buffet lunch
is a veritable feast and Sunday
brunch (reservations) an island
institution.
🕐 Closed D Sun. 🔣 All major
cards

■ TRINIDAD & TOBAGO

TRINIDAD

🏨 TRINIDAD HILTON
$$$
LADY YOUNG RD.,
PORT OF SPAIN

PRICES

HOTELS
An indication of the cost of
a double room in the high
season is given by $ signs.
$$$$$	Over $400
$$$$	$300–$400
$$$	$200–$300
$$	$100–$200
$	Under $100

RESTAURANTS
An indication of the cost of
a three-course meal without
drinks is given by $ signs.
$$$$$	Over $80
$$$$	$50–$80
$$$	$35–$50
$$	$20–$35
$	Under $20

TEL 868/624-3211
FAX 868/624-4485
www.hiltoncaribbean.com/
trinidad
A reliable option on Queen's
Park Savannah, the Hilton
combines polished service and
good facilities. Well-appointed
rooms, tennis, and entertainment.
🛈 412 🅿 🔣 🔣 🔣 🔣 All
major cards

🏨 ASA WRIGHT NATURE CENTRE & LODGE
$$
ARIMA
TEL 868/667-4655 OR
U.S./CANADA 800/426-7781
FAX 868/667-4540
www.asawright.org
Simple lodgings at the famous
rain forest nature center.
Rooms with screened verandas
in garden cottages, a two-bed
cottage, or two large, airy
rooms in the main building. All
meals included; field trips extra.
🛈 25 🅿 🔣 All major cards

🏨 MT. PLAISIR ESTATE
🍴 $$
GRANDE RIVIÈRE
TEL 818/670-1868
FAX 868/670-1015
www.mtplaisir.com
Remote, no-frills beach getaway with a rain forest backdrop and sea views. Rooms furnished by local craftsmen (sleep 4 to 6); turtle-watching and eco excursions; restaurant serves local dishes including lobster, fruit and vegetables from the estate and homemade bread.
🛈 13 💠 All major cards

🍴 APSARA
$$$–$$$$
LEVEL 1, 13 QUEEN'S PARK EAST, BELMONT,
PORT OF SPAIN
TEL 868/623-7959
A handsomely renovated colonial house is the setting for impeccably authentic Northern Indian food (not the Trinidadian version) in stagy Indian surroundings. Sample specialities from the tandoori ovens including locally caught lobster tails.
🕐 Closed Sat. L, Sun. 💠 All major cards

🍴 TIKI VILLAGE
$$$
KAPOK HOTEL (8TH FLOOR)
16–18 COTTON HILL,
PORT OF SPAIN
TEL 868/622-5765
The great Trinidadian culinary melting pot continues with this popular Chinese and Polynesian restaurant perched above Queen's Park Savannah with views over the city lights at night. Lunchtime dim sum buffet, and dinner specialties include walnut-shrimp firepot.
💠 All major cards

🍴 VENI MANGÉ
$–$$
67A ARIAPITA AVE.,
WOODBROOK, PORT OF SPAIN

TEL 868/624-4597
Funky lunch spot run by local talk show hostess Allyson Hennessy and her sister Roses. Nouvelle Caribbean dining adds up to great soups, creative seafood, and vegetarian options such as black-eyed pea croquettes.
🕐 Closed D Mon., Tues., Thur. & Sat.–Sun. all day 💠 All major cards

TOBAGO

🏨 COCO REEF RESORT
$$$$
COCONUT BAY
TEL 868/639-8571
FAX 868/639-8574
www.cocoreef.com
Contemporary plantation-style with a grand foyer opening onto a man-made beachfront lagoon. Rooms, suites, and villas with terra-cotta tiles and white wicker furnishings. Tennis, water sports, spa, golf nearby. Walking distance to shops and restaurants.
🛈 135 🅿 ❄ 🏊 🏋 💠 All major cards

SOMETHING SPECIAL

🏨 FOOTPRINTS ECO
🍴 RESORT
Hammocks and solar jacuzzis for latter-day Robinson Crusoes. Rooms, suites, and villas built of teak and recycled hardwoods, thatched, and perched on stilts like tree houses. Spa, hiking, snorkeling, organic produce in the restaurant.
$$–$$$
CULLODEN BAY
TEL 868/660-0118
FAX 868/660-0416
www.footprints-resort.com
🛈 15 🅿 ❄ 🏊 💠 All major cards

🏨 KARIWAK VILLAGE
$$
CROWN POINT

TEL 868/639-8442
FAX 868/639-8441
www.kariwak.com
A "holistic haven and hotel," Kariwak nurtures guests with yoga, relaxation sessions, massage, and healthy food (see below). Accommodations in garden rooms or pool cabanas a ten-minute walk from the beach. Daily shuttle to Pigeon Point.
🛈 24 🅿 ❄ 🏊 💠 All major cards

🍴 LA TARTARUGA
$$$$
BUCCOO BAY ROAD,
BUCCOO
TEL 868/639-0940
Italian specialties include homemade pasta, pizzas, authentic antipasto, fish and rock lobsters, and scrumptious desserts served inside or on the terrace. Over 200 Italian wines in the cellar.
🕐 Closed Sun. 💠 All major cards

🍴 KARIWAK VILLAGE
$$
KARIWAK VILLAGE,
CROWN POINT
TEL 868/639-8442
Alfresco dining in a nest of palm-thatched tiki huts. Flavorful homecooking from seafood soup with cumin and basil to scrumptious nutmeg ice cream. Buffet and band Friday and Saturday.
💠 All major cards

🍴 CIAO CAFÉ
$
20 BURNETT STREET,
SCARBOROUGH
TEL 868/639-3001
A handy Italian café and gelateria in downtown Scarborough. Enjoy a break with a real cappuccino or espresso and a slice of cheesecake, or choose from 20 different flavors of ice cream. More substantial offerings include lasagne al forno and freshly made pizzas.
🕐 Closed Sun. L 💠 No credit cards

Shopping

If your idea of the perfect vacation is not complete without a spot of shopping, the Caribbean is for you. With a few exceptions, the islands provide visitors with a wealth of stores featuring local crafts, jewelry, colorful, lightweight clothing, and the region's famous spices, coffee, and rum.

■ JAMAICA

Jamaica offers something for everyone, from hand-rolled cigars to elaborate wood carvings or duty-free goods. The roadside stalls and crafts markets' bestsellers are wood carvings, T-shirts, hammocks, shell craft, straw hats, bamboo items, and alabaster sculptures.

Almost every town has a market, usually with some craft items. However, for the widest range of straw goods, hats, and similar items, the best place to go is **Market Street** in Montego Bay, Negril's **Rutland Point** market, or the **Craft Market** in Kingston (Ocean Boulevard, Mon.–Sat.). Bargaining over the price (or "haggling") is the norm—never pay the first asking price. Avoid items made using "tortoiseshell" (from the endangered hawksbill turtle), black coral, or crocodile skins: Importing these into the United States is illegal.

Another great buy is reggae music: There are good music outlets in most towns and resorts, although the best are in Kingston and the **Island Village** complex in Ocho Rios. Island Village also has some good boutiques, but for a more upscale shopping experience, try **Half Moon Village** and the **Shoppes at Rose Hall.**

Essential oils and bodycare products also make excellent souvenirs. Local spices are always a good buy, particularly food seasonings such as the spicy Pickapeppa sauces or "jerk" sauces, and guava jelly. Blue Mountain coffee (or the less expensive High Mountain type), either pre-ground or as beans, is another good and easily transported souvenir. Premium Jamaican rums

are also widely available, as is the superb locally made Tia Maria coffee liqueur.

Duty-free or "in bond" shops carry items such as silverware, crystal, china, watches, jewelry, linens, and perfumes. Savings can be made, but check the purchase price at home before leaving. All goods must be paid for in U.S. currency; you will need your travel documents (airline/cruise ticket and identification). Alcohol and tobacco purchases are delivered to airports/cruise-ship piers before you leave. Last-minute buys and souvenirs are also available at the well-stocked duty-free shopping area in Sangster International Airport.

■ CAYMAN ISLANDS

On duty-free Grand Cayman, discounts of between 20 and 50 percent on U.S. prices are promised, particularly on items such as linens, leather goods, designer clothes, crystal, porcelain, perfumes, watches, and camera equipment. Most shops are in George Town, but several malls have sprung up on the West Bay Road, including the **West Shore Centre, Galleria Plaza, Coconut Place, The Strand,** and **The Falls.** The latest development is **Camana Bay,** an upscale shopping, dining, and entertainment destination with the island's only cinema, live music, and children's activities. In George Town itself, the **Anchorage Shopping Centre, Landmark,** and **Kirk Freeport Plaza** are some of the main outlets. (To avoid the cruise-ship crowds, go on Fridays and Saturdays.)

Local arts and crafts are worth

seeking out in galleries such as **Pure Art** (S. Church St., tel 345/949-9133) and **Cayman Craft Market** (Hog Sty Bay, tel 345/949-0049). Sea-salvaged coins from Spanish or Dutch treasure ships can be bought at **Mitzi's Fine Jewelry** (Bay Harbour Centre, tel 345/945-5014), and similar numismatic items are also available at **24 K-Mon Jewelers** (several locations including The Falls, tel 345/949-1499). For an unusual underwater souvenir, take home a stunning print by world famous underwater photographer Cathy Church (Sunset House Hotel, S. Church St., tel 345/949-7415).

The islands' biggest-selling export item is rum cake. Made from a recipe reputedly over 100 years old, this cake features as its chief ingredient five-year-old Tortuga Gold rum. Buy it at any one of the many outlets of the **Tortuga Rum Company,** which can be found in the island's major shopping centers.

■ TURKS & CAICOS ISLANDS

If you are planning to go shopping in TCI, then head for the gateway island of Providenciales. Most of the shops here are in small malls along the Leeward Highway, such as **Ports of Call, Arch Plaza, Central Square, Market Place, Salt Mills Plaza,** and Grace Bay's **Regent Village.**

With no sales tax on the islands, you can buy duty-free goods such as jewelry, watches, perfumes, crystal, cameras, cigars, and liquor. One of the island's best-known galleries, the **Bamboo Gallery** (Market Place), features paintings by local and Haitian artists, beaded jewelry, ceramics, and sculpture.

Other craft and art outlets include **Anna's Art Gallery & Studio** (Salt Mills) and **Greensleeves** (Central Sq.). **Flavours of the Turks & Caicos Islands,** Regent Village, is a good source of Bambarra Rum, locally made teas, and seasonings. Handmade crafts, such as woven baskets from the Middle Caicos Cooperative, are on sale from National Trust shops on Providenciales and Grand Turk.

■ DOMINICAN REPUBLIC

Santo Domingo has several top-end malls including **Acrópolis, Plaza Central,** and the **Malécon Center.** The main shopping streets are **Calle Duarte** and pedestrianized **Calle El Conde.** Most major resorts have shops selling summer attire, T-shirts, and swimwear. Crafts can be found in the main markets in every town (the biggest is the **Mercado Modelo** on Ave. Esquina Santomé in Santo Domingo), with a wide range of ceramics, straw hats, wood carvings, and naïve Haitian art. Amber and blue larimar jewelry is also a popular buy. Local jewelers **Harrisons** are a reputable source with branches in most resorts. The Dominican Republic produces reasonably priced rum and cigars.

■ PUERTO RICO

Puerto Rico is not a duty-free island (sales tax is 5.5 percent), but there is no duty on items taken into the U.S., so you can find good prices on china, crystal, fashions, and crafts. All prices are in U.S. dollars. Old San Juan offers a variety of shops, especially for jewelry, leather, and clothes. Check out the factory outlet stores on Calle Cristo. There are also some fine art galleries.

Condado is known for its exclusive boutiques and fashion designer shops, which congregate around exclusive Avenida Ashford.

In the heart of the San Juan metropolitan area is **Plaza Las Américas,** the largest shopping center in the Caribbean, with over 300 stores.

Old San Juan has a number of souvenir and handicraft shops. For local arts and crafts buys, don't miss the excellent **Centro Nacional de Artes Populares y Artesanias** (Calle Cristo 253).

Popular gifts include *santos* (small carved saint figures), Carnival masks, and *mundillo*, handmade bobbin lace. Fine hammocks are still made here, and, of course, Puerto Rico is a major producer of rum and cigars.

■ VIRGIN ISLANDS

U.S. VIRGIN ISLANDS

ST. CROIX

Downtown **Christiansted** offers the best shopping on the island, centered on Strand, King, and Company Streets, and King's Alley Walk. The Walk offers boutiques and galleries, craft stalls selling coconut shell carvings, and jewelry stores, where the turquoise-colored gemstone larimar (found exclusively in the Caribbean) has been incorporated in pendants, rings, and bracelets. Cruzan Hook bracelets are a popular souvenir re-created by jeweller Sonya Hough, (**Sonya's,** 1 Company St.). You wear the hook facing your heart if it is taken, away from the heart if you are available.

The shops of **Frederiksted's** main shopping area are clustered near the cruise-ship pier, and offers a selection of specialty shops and art galleries displaying works by local artists.

You can watch artists work in the **St. Croix LEAP** woodwork

studio (Mahogany Rd. Rte. 76), north of Frederiksted, and buy carvings on island hardwoods. The **Whim Museum** gift shop has a good range of local crafts, condiments, books, and maps.

ST. JOHN

Shopping on St. John is low-key. There are a few small boutiques and jewelers in **Wharfside Village,** close to the ferry dock. For more of a selection, head to **Mongoose Junction** (North Shore Rd.)—an open-air complex in the local plantation house style. **R. & I. Patton Goldsmithing** sell Rudy and Irene's island-inspired designs in 14- to 18-carat gold and sterling silver, as well as authenticated antique Spanish coins set in rings and pendants.

Big Planet Adventurer Outfitters can outfit hikers and offers colorful swimwear and resortwear. **Fabric Mill** specializes in table and bed linens, batik, and fabulous hand-painted cotton T-shirts and sweaters by local designer Sloop Jones, who has a shop in the East End (off Rte. 10).

ST. THOMAS

U.S. visitors can take advantage of a $1,600 duty-free allowance on returning home, and families can pool their allowances for larger purchases. Any items actually made in the USVI do not count toward the duty-free exemption. Popular buys are fine crystal and china, electronics, jewelry, and perfume, sold in large stores on Dronningens Gade/Main Street and the Havensight Mall. Stores are generally open Monday to Saturday 9 a.m. to 5 p.m. If a cruise ship calls on a Sunday, some stores will open for at least part of the day.

In Charlotte Amalie, a slew of boutiques is tucked in the narrow alleys leading down to the Waterfront, where the eye-catching boutique **Local Color** does a fun line in pretty Jams World uncrushable sundresses as well as other cotton prints, straw hats, handpainted T-shirts, and silver jewelry.

For great Caribbean crafts and souvenirs, check out the **Native Arts and Crafts Cooperative,** bottom of Tolbod Gade, piled high with locally produced items including wood carvings, costume dolls, and Taste of Paradise sauces and jellies. At the **Caribbean Marketplace** in Havensight Mall, duty-free stores sell jewelry, cameras and electronics, liquor, and tobacco.

Outside Charlotte Amalie, **Tillett Gardens** is an artisans' enclave with galleries, craft studios, a restaurant, and tame iguanas basking in the shade.

BRITISH VIRGIN ISLANDS

TORTOLA

Road Town's top souvenir stop has to be the **Sunny Caribbee Spice Co.** on Main Street (also at Soper's Hole). This is condiment city, piled high with exotic fruit teas and liqueurs, preserves made from guava, papaya, and passionfruit, tamarind chutney, jerk seasonings, and even love potions and hangover cures for the adventurous. The art gallery next door showcases Caribbean paintings, affordable prints, Haitian voodoo flags, and pottery.

You can purchase Pusser's rum and yachting-style casualwear at **Pusser's Company Store;** or take a stroll while searching for T-shirts and other small souvenirs at the colorful pastel-painted stalls behind the waterfront.

In the West End, assorted boutiques and souvenir outlets at the **Soper's Hole Marina** provide retail therapy.

■ DUTCH CARIBBEAN

ARUBA

Bargain hunters will find most of the big stores in **Oranjestad's Ports of Call Marketplace, Renaissance Marketplace & Mall, Royal Plaza,** and along the main street, **Caya G.F. Betico Croes.** China, linens, electronic goods, perfumes, and designer clothes are all good buys. At Palm Beach, the new upscale **Paseo Herencia** mall is a magnet for style-conscious shoppers.

Jewelry is a popular buy, and **Gandelmen Jewelers** outlets around town stock precious and semiprecious jewelry items, designer watches, Montblanc pens, Baccarat crystal, china, and leather accessories.

For arts and crafts, check out **Art & Tradition Handicrafts** (Caya G.F. Betico Croes 30 and Royal Plaza Mall). Also, the **Bonbini Festival** at Fort Zoutman every Tuesday evening.

CURAÇAO

Willemstad offers good deals on perfume, jewelry, china, cameras, and electronic goods. The major stores and boutiques are crowded into the Punda district around Breedestraat. On the Otrabanda side, close to the cruise terminal, **Kas Di Alma Blou** (the Blue House) is a popular stop with art lovers. A small and well-stocked gallery, it showcases local artwork, photographs, and a few antique maps and prints.

Out in the countryside, several *landhuisen,* including **Landhuis Jan Kok, Landhuis Groot Santa Martha,** and **Landhuis Bloemhof,** house arts and crafts galleries.

SABA

Mary Gertrude Johnson introduced the art of drawn threadwork, or Saban lace, to the island in the 1870s, and intricately embroidered linen tableware is sold in several **Windwardside** craft shops. Another local specialty is Saba Spice, a 75.5-proof rum flavored with cinnamon, cloves, nutmeg, orange peel, and brown sugar. For local artworks, look in at potter Judy Stewart's **Peanut Gallery,** Lambee Plaza, for ceramics, wood carvings and colorful paintings.

SINT MAARTEN/ ST.- MARTIN

Both Dutch and French sides of the island offer duty-free shopping and deals worth 15 to 30 percent on U.S. prices for perfumes, electronic goods, jewelry, china, crystal, linens, and fashions.

Philipsburg's **Front Street** shopping district boasts the widest array of goods. It is worth noting that the U.S. dollar prices on the Dutch side are likely to offer better savings than the euro deals on the French side.

For locally made souvenirs, check out the open-air **Philipsburg Market Place,** on Back Street. Also the boutiques, stores, and sidewalk cafés on Old Street.

Marigot is the island's fashion capital, with plenty of temptations to be found on rue de la République and on rue de la Liberté. The small mall in the smart **Marina Royale** is brimful with boutiques selling designer labels, and the fashion-conscious can take their pick from racks of elegant apparel from the high priests of the fashion scene. Around the dock, **Gingerbread Mahogany** is one of the best Haitian art galleries in the Caribbean.

Down by the waterfront in the West Indies Mall, there is an outpost of **Hédiard,** the famous Parisian delicatessen, well stocked with foie gras, fine wines, caviar, and confits.

◼ LEEWARD ISLANDS

ANGUILLA

Black-belt shopaholics may suffer withdrawal symptoms on Anguilla. However, it does offer a couple of interesting arts and crafts outlets. The **Savannah Gallery** in The Valley specializes in Haitian paintings, tin carvings, fabulous sequined voodoo flags, and works by local photographers.

On Main Road West, look for **Cheddie's Carving Studio,** where Cheddie Richardson exhibits his driftwood sculptures and limited edition bronzes. Also Fabiana Liburd's **Why Knot** boutique selling lovely lightweight and versatile cotton fashions.

ANTIGUA

Downtown **St. John's** is this island's chief shopping district. **Heritage Quay** is packed with duty-free stores selling jewelry, designer fashions, perfumes, and gifts. On **Redcliffe Quay,** there are boutiques stocked with colorful island fashions; Hans Smit sells his innovative and temptingly affordable jewelry at the **Goldsmitty;** and **The Pottery Studio** displays Sarah Fuller's 100 percent Antiguan pieces created from local clays.

Outside St. John's, **Harmony Hall** on the east coast is a great place to check out local arts and crafts. Also **Rhythm of Blue,** English Harbour, where potter Nancy Nicholson and scrimshaw artist Michael Strzalkowski showcase their work alongside other local and regional artists (gallery open Dec.–May; studio visits May–Nov.). In Nelson's Dockyard, **Things Local** offers works by Carl Henry, one of Antigua's finest wood sculptors, who selects Antiguan hard woods such as mahogany and almond for his carvings.

MONTSERRAT

Not surprisingly, volcano-related souvenirs are popular on Montserrat. Stunning photographs of Soufrière in its active phase sell at **Woolcock's Craft & Photo Gallery,** Brades; and look out for David Lea's DVD *The Price of Paradise* (Lea is the proprietor of Gingerbread Hill, p. 373), which charts the effect of the eruption on the island and its people. The **Oriole Gift Shop,** National Trust Building, Salem, is a good source of island handicrafts, and you can drop into the adjacent **Montserrat Philatelic Bureau** for unusual and beautiful stamps. Last-minute purchases can be made at the well-stocked **Jus Lookin** craft and rum shop at Gerald's Airport.

ST. KITTS

Cruise-ship visitors to St. Kitts are greeted by the **Port Zante** shopping complex at the foot of the gangplank, complete with all the usual duty-free jewelry and booze stores. Unique to the island, the **Caribelle Batik Factory** at Old Road Town is a favorite stop on the St. Kitts shopping trail; Caribelle's comfy, loose-fitting Hawaiian-style shirts, sundresses, and wraps are popular buys. **Island Hopper,** on The Circus in downtown Basseterre, stocks colorful beachwear and souvenirs.

Glass Island (4–5 Princes St.) is chock-full of fused-glass plates, picture frames, Christmas tree decorations, and colored-glass earrings with silver fittings.

NEVIS

Charlestown's restored waterfront district boasts a few small boutiques and souvenir outlets, as does the Cotton Ginnery building nearby, where **The Craft House** stocks a range of hand-crafted local pottery, coconut and shell jewelry, and leather sandals. **Island Hopper,** on Main Street, carries Caribelle Batik's bright, casual clothing from St. Kitts.

Stamp collectors can capture a little local color at the **Nevis Philatelic Bureau,** in Lower Happy Hill Alley between the ferry berth and Main Street.

East of Charlestown, **Bocane Ceramics,** Stoney Grove, is Cheryl Liburd's pottery studio and shop. As well as colorful platters and bowls depicting traditional island scenes of clapboard cottages, exotic flowers, and jolly fish, she paints pretty tiles and mosaic signs.

◼ FRENCH ANTILLES

GUADELOUPE

Shopping is not a high priority in Guadeloupe, though French luxury goods at mainland prices can be tempting. Some **Pointe-à-Pitre** stores offer an extra 20 percent discount on purchases made with a credit card or traveler's checks.

The capital's main shopping streets are **rue Frébault, rue Schoelcher,** and **rue de Noziers,** and there are small, upscale boutiques in the **Centre St.-John Perse** mall by the cruise-ship terminal.

Rum is available from supermarkets, the airport duty-free, or the **Musée du Rhum** in Bellevue. Gosier, Ste.-Anne, and St.-François all have handicrafts shops and stalls specializing in Caribbean arts and crafts, and souvenirs such as costume dolls dressed in bright Madras cotton.

MARTINIQUE

Fort-de-France is the style capital of the French Antilles, offering French luxury goods from designer fashions and perfumes to china and glass at prices lower than in mainland France. Some stores give an additional 20 percent discount for luxury purchases made with certain credit cards (always ask).

The best selection of boutiques is found along **rue Victor Hugo** and the grid of streets between **rue de la République** and **rue de la Liberté.** Jewelers on rue Lamartine and rue Isambert are an excellent hunting ground for Baccarat crystal, Limoges porcelain, and jewelry including the *chaîne forçat*, a gold "slave chain" necklace that puts the finishing touch to traditional Creole costume. Madras cotton traditional costumes and frilly white shirts are sold at market stalls in most towns.

Beyond the capital, the bustling resort of Les Trois-Ilets is a good spot for art galleries and boutiques selling fashions and beachwear. Or stop by **Domaine Château Gaillard,** rte. des Trois-Ilets, which combines crafts studios with the island's biggest plant nursery and an on-site restaurant.

Martiniquan rum is among the Caribbean's finest, and the island's basketware, pottery, shell art, and patchwork are displayed in souvenir stores and galleries.

ST.- BARTHÉLEMY

St. Barts's duty-free status is a good excuse to indulge in some seriously upscale retail therapy. Cartier, Gucci, and Hermès all maintain outposts in **Gustavia,** alongside duty-free emporiums such as **Carat,** on rue de la République. The upscale mall **Le Carré d'Or,** quai de la République, is a favorite shopping destination. French perfumes and cosmetics,

jewelry, watches, and crystal are all popular buys.

Wine buffs can check out the impressive vintage selection at **Cellier du Gouverneur,** quai de la République.

For the best French and Italian designer fashions, try **Stéphane & Bernard** at Gallerie Gréaux. **Villa Créole** mall in St. Jean has more boutiques, and **La Boutique Made in St.-Barth** carries souvenir T-shirts, paintings, and handcrafted works of art produced on the island.

■ WINDWARD ISLANDS

DOMINICA

The island's Carib craftsmen are famous for their basketware made from l'arouma reeds. The intricate designs are fashioned in a combination of natural, brown, and black, and can be bought from roadside stalls in **Carib Territory,** or from one of Roseau's many crafts shops. The **Talipot Gallery** (cnr. Victoria and High St.) features works by several local artists and arranges regular exhibitions in a historic building with a super courtyard veranda restaurant. Another good gallery and source of local handicrafts is **Butterfly Boutique** at Papillote Wilderness Retreat.

There is a **Craft Market,** behind the Dominican Museum, which combines local crafts with a raft of souvenirs, and **Louis Desiré Wood Carvings,** Old Market, showcases one of the island's most accomplished artists. Dominican products to look out for include the island's 100 percent Arabica coffee, Café Sisserou, bay rum and colognes from Dominica Essential Oils & Spices, and Bello's pepper sauces, fruit syrups, and marmalades.

GRENADA

Spices are a great buy on Grenada. Mixed baskets of nutmeg, cinnamon, cloves, and bay rum leaves make great gifts for cooks, or as souvenir potpourri.

The **Carenage** boasts several small galleries and craft shops. Check out **Yellow Poui Art Galleries** (Cross St.) for local art, photography, crafts, and antique map prints. In the **Art Fabrik** boutique you can see the batik process in the courtyard factory (9 Young St.) opposite **Tikal,** another crafts store.

Convenient for the southern beach hotels, **Grand Anse Shopping Centre** has a good selection of gift shops and galleries selling Caribbean arts and crafts, and boutiques stocking island fashions. There is a local spice market, too, located between the main road and the beach.

ST. LUCIA

The waterfront **Castries craft market,** and the vendors' market across the street, offer T-shirts, hand-woven straw goods, local pottery, and wood carvings.

For a more upscale shopping experience, the attractive open-air mall on the cruise-ship pier at **Pointe Seraphine** presides over a selection of duty-free stores, boutiques, and galleries, as does the larger **La Place Carenage** on the opposite side of the harbor.

Just outside Castries, at La Toc on the slopes of Morne Fortune, **Bagshaw Studios** has a factory shop. This local cottage industry specializes in colorful hand-printed clothing, good-quality T-shirts, and a range of pretty table linens adorned with parrots and tropical hibiscus and poinsettia flowers.

Farther up Morne Fortune, **Eudovic's Studio & Gallery** showcases works by master wood-carver

Victor Eudovic and artists including his son Jallim. Eudovic Senior's stunning abstract pieces are displayed alongside more affordable souvenir items such as African-style masks and pineapple-shaped wall decorations symbolizing Caribbean hospitality. Purchases can be shipped home.

In the north of the island, boutiques, gift stores, and mini-marts can be found at **Gablewoods Mall,** Choc Bay, and the **J.Q. Charles Rodney Bay Mall.**

ST. VINCENT & THE GRENADINES

There is duty-free shopping at the new cruise berth in **Kingstown,** as well as boutiques and souvenir outlets offering a selection of Caribbean crafts, spices, and gift ideas.

On Bequia, **Noah's Arkade** at the Frangipani Hotel, Port Elizabeth, stocks a good range of island arts, crafts, and souvenir items. Bequia's boat-building heritage is celebrated in miniature at **Sargeant Brothers Model Boats,** Front Street. **The Oasis Art Gallery** displays original works and giclée prints of colorful hummingbirds, mermaids, and ships at anchor in the bay by gallery curator L.D. Lucy, as well as her husband Prop's model boats-that-sail. Regular exhibitions showcase the talents of other local artists.

Farther afield, artist **Julie Savage Lea** has her studio at Belmont (for appt. tel 784/455-4677); also check out the **Spring Pottery & Art Gallery,** in an old sugar mill at Spring.

■ BARBADOS

Bridgetown is a duty-free port offering savings of up to 30 to 50 percent off European and U.S. retail prices. The best of the tax-free action is on Broad Street, where the **Cave Shepherd** and

Harrisons department stores, and the **DaCostas Mall** offer the widest selection of jewelry and watches, cameras, electronic goods, china, crystal, perfumes, and cosmetics. To make a duty-free purchase, take the immigration slip issued on arrival in Barbados; most stores will deliver to the airport or hotel.

For Caribbean crafts and island fashions, check out the **Pelican Craft Centre,** near Bridgetown Harbour, and colorful **Chattel Village** shopping complexes in Holetown and St. Lawrence Gap. Holetown also boasts the **West Coast Mall,** while Speightstown has a duo of art galleries— **Mango's** and the **Gallery of Caribbean Art.**

A terrific range of decorative island pottery is on sale at **Earthworks,** Edgehill Heights, St. Thomas, where you can also watch the assortment of bowls, platters, mugs, and jugs being made and painted.

On the south coast, shoppers head for **Hastings Plaza** and the **Quayside Centre** in Rockley.

The **Best of Barbados** boutiques around the island are a good source of quality local crafts and gifts.

■ TRINIDAD & TOBAGO

The lower end of **Frederick Street** in Port of Spain resembles a hectic international bazaar. Indian sari shops and boutiques spill out onto the sidewalk, street vendors hawk jewelry, leather goods, and the latest calypso, soca, and chutney CDs.

For a more upscale shopping experience, take a trip to the **Ellerslie Court shopping center** in Maraval, and the **Market Shoppes,** with its boutiques, galleries, and craft shops attached to the Normandie Hotel (Nook Ave., St. Ann).

Tobago is somewhat limited on mainstream shopping, but there is no shortage of arts and crafts. The small shopping village at **Store Bay** offers a colorful array of batik and tie-dye beachwear, T-shirts, straw hats, bead jewelry, pottery, and other crafts. Check out local galleries and studios as you tour the island.

Sports & Activities

One of the best regions in the world for outdoor activities, the Caribbean offers superb diving, snorkeling, boating, and fishing in its turquoise waters, as well as golfing and rain forest hiking.

■ JAMAICA

Adventure & Sightseeing Tours

Jamaica's leading provider of soft adventures with outposts in Montego Bay/Negril (tel 876/953-5619) and Ocho Rios/Falmouth (tel 876/972-2506), **Chukka Caribbean Adventures** (tel 876/953-6699 or U.S. 877/424-8552, www.chukkacaribbean .com) has activities ranging from rain forest ziplining to visiting the Bob Marley Centre.

Boating

Day sails are available through a number of operators including **Dreamer Catamaran Cruises** (tel 876/979-0102, www.dreamer catamarans.com).

Diving & Water Sports

The best diving is off the north coast, on the edge of the Cayman Trench. PADI-certified **Scuba Jamaica, Montego Bay** (tel 876/381-1113, www.scuba-jamaica.com) offers a full range of dive services and will pick up from destinations along the coast to Ocho Rios. In Negril, **Sun Divers Watersports**, Travellers Beach Resort (tel 876/474-7002, www .sundiversnegril.com) combines dive services with water sports including kayaking, parasailing, and snorkeling.

Golf

Golfers flock to the north coast resort areas for the pick of Jamaica's dozen or so courses, many of which occupy spectacular sites. West of Montego Bay is the stunning championship course at the **Tryall Club,** Sandy Bay (tel

876/956-5681, www.tryallclub .com); to the east, the White Witch course at the **Ritz-Carlton Golf & Spa Resort,** Rose Hall (tel 876/518-0174, www.ritzcarlton .com). Golfers of all abilities can benefit from the on-site golf academies at the Trent-Jones Sr.–designed championship course **Golf at Half Moon,** Montego Bay (tel 876/953-2560, www .halfmoon.rockresorts.com); and **SuperClubs Golf Club** at Runaway Bay, Breezes Runaway Bay (tel 876/973-7319, www.breezes.com).

Horseback Tours

Riding excursions can be arranged through Chukka (above) and **Prospect Plantation,** just outside Ocho Rios (tel 876/994-1058, www.prospectplantationtours .com). The **Half Moon Equestrian Centre** in Montego Bay (tel 876/953-2286, www.horseback ridingjamaica.com) offers beach rides and swimming with horses.

Sportfishing

Full- and half-day sportfishing charters are available from marinas along the north coast and from Port Antonio, or contact **Glistening Waters Marina,** Falmouth (tel 876/954-3229, www .glisteningwaters.com).

■ CAYMAN ISLANDS

Boat Trips

For non-divers who want to experience the wonders of the deep off Grand Cayman, the 48-passenger **Atlantis Submarine,** S. Church Street, George Town (tel 345/949-770, www.caymanislandssubma rines.com) is the solution. **Cayman Kayaks** offers a brace of excellent tours, including the amazing

nighttime Bio Bay tour on a secret lagoon where bioluminescence blooms (tel 345/746-3249, www .caymankayaks.com).

Diving

The Cayman Islands' superb dive sites are matched by well-equipped dive operators offering everything from snorkeling and basic tuition to highly sophisticated technical training.

Cayman Brac: **Indepth Watersports,** South Side (tel 345/948-8037 or 866/476-2195, www .indepthwatersports.com); **Reef Divers,** West End (tel 345/948-1642, www.bracreef.com).

Grand Cayman: **DiveTech,** Cobalt Coast Resort, Sea Fan Drive (tel 345/946-5658 or 888/946-5656, www.divetech .com); **Ocean Frontiers,** 346 Austin Connelly Drive, East End (tel 345/947-7500 or 800/348-6096, www.oceanfrontiers.com).

Little Cayman: **Reef Divers,** Little Cayman Reef Beach Resort (tel 345/948-1033 or 800/327-3835, www.littlecayman.com); **Southern Cross Club** (tel 345/948-1099 or 800/899-2582, www.Southern CrossClub.com).

Hiking

On Grand Cayman, there are regular guided tours of the National Trust's **Mastic Trail,** a 2-mile (3 km) woodland hike through old-growth forest (tel 345/949-0121, www.nationaltrust.org.ky). Guided hikes are also offered by butterfly and plant expert **Ann Stafford** (www.caymANNature .ky). On the sister islands, **Nature Cayman** (tel 345/948-2222, www.itsyourstoexplore.com) provides free tours and information.

Sportfishing

Visitors seek out the Caymans for deep-water game fish as well as for tarpon, bonefish, and reef fishing expeditions. The **Cayman Islands Angling Club** (tel 345/945-3131, www.fish cayman.com) is a useful source of information and hosts an annual International Fishing Tournament (May). Full and half-day fishing trips are available from charter boat operators such as **Bayside Watersports,** Morgan's Harbor (Grand Cayman, tel 345/949-3200, www.baysidewatersports .com); and **Captain Ron Ebanks,** Fly Fish Grand Cayman, Coconut Place, West Bay Road, Grand Cayman (tel 345/946-0214, www .flyfishgrandcayman.com).

■ TURKS & CAICOS ISLANDS

Adventure Tours

See Heart of the Islands, p. 91.

Diving & Snorkeling

The TCI offers world-class diving opportunities in the archipelago's calm, crystal clear waters. Recommended dive operators include:

Grand Turk: **Blue Water Divers** (tel 649/946-2432, www.grand turkscuba.com); **Oasis Divers** (tel 649/946-1128 or 800/892-3995, www.oasisdivers.com).

Providenciales: **Big Blue Unlimited** (tel 649/946-5034 or 649/231-6455, www .bigblueunlimited.com); **Dive Provo** (tel 649/946-5040 or 800/234-7768, www.diveprovo .com); **Provo Turtle Divers** (tel 649/946-4232 or 800/833-1341, www.provoturtledivers.com).

Golf

Fringed with palm trees and studded with lakes, the **Provo Golf & Country Club** (Grace Bay, tel 649/946-5991 or U.S./ Can. 877/218-9124, www.provo

golfclub.com) is an 18-hole championship course.

■ DOMINICAN REPUBLIC

Adventure Tours & Hiking

Whether you want to hike, bike, horseback ride, or try your hand at white-water rafting, the island's two leading adventure tour operators should be able to help. Contact **Iguana Mama,** Cabarete (tel 809/571-0908 or U.S. 800/849-4720, www .iguanamama.com); and **Rancho Baiguate,** Jarabacoa (tel 809/574-6890 or U.S./Can. 646/727-7783, www.rancho baiguate.com).

Diving

Every major resort area has dive operators, including: **Dressel Divers,** Iberostar, Punta Cana (tel 809/221-6500, www.dressel divers.com); **Las Terrenas Divers,** Playa Bonita (tel 809/889-2422, www.lt-divers.com); **Neptuno Dive Center,** Juan Dolio (tel 809/526-2005, www.neptuno dive.com); **North Coast Aqua-sports,** Sosúa (tel 809/571-1028, www.northerncoastdiving.com).

Golf

The Dominican Republic boasts around 40 championship courses, mostly concentrated in the eastern Coconut Coast region. Try **Cocotal Golf & Country Club,** Playa Bavaró, Punta Cana (tel 809/687-4653, www.cocotalgolf .com); also the stunning ocean-front Corales and La Cana courses at **Puntacana Resort & Club** (tel 809/959-4653 or 1-888/442-2262, www.puntacana.com.). On the north coast, the **Playa Dorada Resort,** Puerto Plata (tel 809/320-3472, www.playa doradagolf.com) is recommended. Southeast of Santo

Domingo, **Casa de Campo** (tel 809/523-6898 or 1-800/877-3643, www.casadecampo.co.do) boasts three world-class courses designed by Pete Dye.

Sportfishing

Dozens of charter boats offering deep-sea fishing excursions occupy marinas along the east coast. Half- and full-day trips can be arranged through the Aquatic Center at **PUNTACANA Resort,** Punta Cana (tel 809/959-2262, www.puntacana.com); also with the **Casa de Campo Marina,** La Romana (tel 809/523-8648, www.casadecampo.com.do).

Water Sports

Cabarete is one of the world's top windsurfing and kiteboarding destinations. Well-equipped operators offering equipment rentals and tuition include **Cabarete Windsports Club** (tel 809/571-0784, www.cabarete windsportsclub.com); **Carib Wind Center** (tel 809/571-0604, www .caribwind.com); **Kitexcite** (tel 809/962-4556, www.kitexcite .com); and **Laurel Eastman Kiteboarding** (tel 809/571-0564, www.laureleastman.com).

■ PUERTO RICO

Adventure Tours & Hiking

Puerto Rico's mountainous rain forest is a playground for adrenaline junkies. The **Toro Verde Nature Adventure Park,** Orocovis (tel 787/867-7020, www.tororoverdepr.com) offers rock climbing, a mountain bike trail, and ziplines. For hiking, rappelling, and waterfall climbing, contact **Nature Adventure Tours** (tel 787/706-0695, www.acampapr .com); or **Rocaliza** (tel 787/268-0101, www.rocaliza.com).

Diving

Puerto Rico's south coast has fantastic wall diving from La Parguera and Guánica in the southwest. Off the east coast, the idyllic islands of Vieques and Culebra are fringed with coral reefs, while the calm seas, mini walls, and caverns around the mainland dive center of Fajardo create the perfect conditions for beginners. Contact local operators **Culebra Divers** (tel 787/742-0803, www .culebradivers.com); **Island Scuba**, Guánica (tel 787/309-6556, www.sanjuandiver.com); or **Sea Ventures Dive Center**, Fajardo (tel 800/739-3483, www.divepuerto rico.com).

Golf

Puerto Rico has some 20 fine golf courses to choose from, including Robert Trent Jones Sr.'s magnificent oceanside creations, slated to reopen as part of the **Ritz Carlton Reserve Dorado Beach** in 2012. Meanwhile, Trent Jones Jr.'s beautiful and environmentally friendly 2008 course at **Bahía Beach Golf Club**, Río Grande (tel 787/809-8920, www.bahiabeachpuertorico .com) has won an Audubon award; local golfing hero Chi Chi Rodríguez designed the **Dorado del Mar Golf Course**, Embassy Suites, Dorado (tel 787/796-3070, www .doradodelmargc.com); and there are two stunning courses at the **Wyndham Río Mar Golf Club**, Río Grande (tel 787/888-7060, www.wyndhamriomar.com) poised between the ocean and El Yunque. The **Arthur Hills Golf Course** at the Waldorf Astoria El Conquistador, Fajardo (tel 787/863-6784, www.elconresort.com) is literally breathtaking with its 200-foot elevation changes.

Sportfishing

Charter fishing boats are available year-round from harbors in San Juan, Fajardo, Humacao, and Mayagüez. The best fishing is from October to early March, when game fish are in season. However, the aptly-named "Blue Marlin Alley" off the north coast sees plenty of migrating fish in summer. Half-day, full-day (or longer) charters from **Bill Wraps Fishing Charters P.R.**, Fajardo (tel 787/364-4216, www.billwraps fishingpr.com); and, just east of San Juan, **Caribbean Outfitters**, Carolina (tel 787/396-8346, www.fishinginpuertorico.com).

■ VIRGIN ISLANDS

U.S. VIRGIN ISLANDS

ST. CROIX
Boating

Plenty of local operators offer day trips to Buck Island with lunch and snorkeling. Day and half-day boat trips with **Caribbean Sea Adventures** (tel 340/773-2628, www.caribbeanseaadventures .com) depart from the Christiansted waterfront; or sail off with Captain Dee of **Bilinda Charters** (tel 340/514-2270, www.sailbilinda.com).

Diving & Snorkeling

Sites appealing to divers of all skill levels include the Cane Bay Wall, a short wade from Cane Bay beach and home turf for the **Cane Bay Dive Shop** (tel 340/718-9913 or 800/338-3843, www.canebayscuba.com); while the **Anchor Dive Center** (tel 340/778-1522 or 800/532-3483, www.anchordivestcroix.com) is based at Salt River, another top site.

Golf

Fine golf courses include the elegant Trent Jones Sr. course at the **Carambola Golf Club** (tel 340/778-5638, www.golfvi.com); and the scenic 18-hole course at the **Buccaneer Hotel** (tel 340/712-2144, www.thebuccaneer .com).

Horseback Riding

Just north of Frederiksted, beach rides and nature tours in the hills surrounding the Sprat Hall Plantation with **Paul and Jill's Equestrian Stables**, Creque Dam Rainforest Road/Rte. 58 (tel 340/772-2880, www.paulandjills.com).

Island Tours

Explore the island on a minibus tour with **St. Croix Safari Tours** (tel 340/773-6700, www.gotostcroix .com/safaritours).

ST. JOHN
Boating

Hop aboard the *Fantasy* (tel 340/775-5652, www.daysailfantasy .com) for a day of swimming, snorkeling, and exploring the beaches of the National Park; or take a little beach catamaran and a guide from **Sail Safaris** (tel 340/626-8181 or 866/820-6906, www.sailsafaris.net) to the neighboring islands.

Diving & Snorkeling

Snorkeling off St. John is as easy as wading off the beach (see sidebar "Get Scuba Certified," p. 158). Divers will need transportation to the best sites, which lie a little farther offshore and in the BVIs. Recommended local operators include **Cruz Bay Watersports** (tel 340/776-6234, www.divestjohn .com), and **Low Key Watersports** (tel 340/693-8999 or 800/835-7718, www.divelowkey.com).

Horseback Riding

Scenic 60- or 90-minute rides in the hills above the East End with views from **Carolina Corral** (tel 340/693-5778, www.carolinacorral.vi).

Kayaking

St. John's scalloped coastline is perfectly suited to kayaking expeditions. Guided coastal tours and rentals from **Arawak Expeditions**, Cruz Bay (tel 340/693-8312, www.arawakexped.com).

ST. THOMAS
Boating

See Island-Hopping Excursions, p. 153, for details of day sails to neighboring islands. Another option is a powerboat rental from **Nauti Nymph** (tel 340/775-5066, www.nautinymph.com).

Diving

Calm seas, excellent visibility, and superb reef and wreck diving make for a great dive break in the islands. Look for hotel dive packages. Independent operators include **Coki Beach Dive Club** (tel 340/775-4220, www.coki dive.com), and **Red Hook Dive Center** (tel 340/777-3483, www .redhookdivecenter.com).

Golf

Fabulous views across the BVI from the north shore and a challenging 18-hole Fazio-designed course draw golfers to **Mahogany Run Golf Course**, Mahogany Run Road (tel 340/777-6250 or 800/253-7103; book tee times at www.mahoganyrungolf.com).

Sportfishing

St. Thomas lies about 20 miles (32 km) below the North Drop, famed for blue marlin fishing in the prime June through September season. Several outfits operate out of American Yacht Harbor at Red Hook. Contact **Marlin Prince** (tel 340/693-5929, www.marlinprince.com); or **Reel Therapy Sportfishing**, Compass Point Marina (tel 340/715-0472, www.reel-therapy.com).

BRITISH VIRGIN ISLANDS
Boating

Excursions from Tortola to Virgin Gorda or Norman Island, with lunch and snorkeling, can be booked through the schooner *White Squall II* (tel 284/541-2222, www.whitesquall2.com); catamaran *Aristocat* (tel 284/499-1249, www.aristocatcharters.com); or **Voyage Yacht Charters** (tel 284/494-0740, www.daysailbvi .com).

Diving & Snorkeling

Superb diving and snorkeling opportunities abound in the Sir Francis Drake Channel. The BVI's top dive sites include the wreck of RMS *Rhone* off Salt Island, while snorkelers shouldn't miss The Baths on Virgin Gorda. Recommended local operators include **Blue Water Divers** (tel 284/494-2847, www.bluewater diversbvi.com); **BVI Scuba Co.** (tel 284/540-2222, www.bviscubaco .com); **Sail Caribbean Divers** (tel 284/495-1675, www.sailcarib beandivers.com); and **Jost van Dyke Scuba** (tel 284/495-0271, www.Jostvandykescuba.com).

Windsurfing & Water Sports

Trellis Bay is Tortola's windsurfing center. Making the best of the BVI's steady 15-knot trade winds, **Boardsailing BVI Watersports** (tel 284/495-2447, www .windsurfing.vi) rents out boards (tuition available) and other water sports toys including kayaks. On Virgin Gorda, **Leverick Bay Watersports** (tel 284/495-7376, www.watersportsbvi.com) rents dinghies, powerboats, snorkeling and water-skiing gear.

■ DUTCH CARIBBEAN

ARUBA
Diving & Snorkeling

Prime sites are found amid the calm waters of the protected western and southern coasts, and the 400-foot-long wreck of the *Antilla* is one of the largest in the Caribbean. Trips, refresher tuition, and PADI certification courses are available through operators including **Native Divers Aruba** (tel 297/586-4763, www.native divers.com), and **Red Sail Sports** (tel 297/586-1603 or U.S. 305/454-2538, www .redsailaruba.com).

Golf

Aruba's best golfing is the scenic Trent Jones Jr.–designed **Tierra del Sol**, Tierra del Sol Resort (tel 297/586-0978 or 866/978-5158, www.tierradelsol.com).

Guided Tours

Offering a range of excursions encompassing minibus tours, day sails, dive trips, horseback riding, and Jeep safaris, **De Palm Tours** (tel 297/582-4400, www .depalm.com) is Aruba's leading tour operator. ATV tours can be arranged through **Rancho Daimari** (see Horseback Riding, below).

Horseback Riding

Horseback trails are a great way to explore the rugged *cunucu* backcountry. Saddle up with **Rancho Daimari** (tel 297/586-6284, www.arubaranchodaimari .com), or **Rancho Notorious** (tel 297/586-0508, www.rancho notorious.com).

Hiking

Hiking on Aruba means a trip to the Arikok National Park (see

p. 196). Check schedules for ranger-led tours, or contact Jos Winterman of **Makuaku Hiking Tours** (tel 297/593-9873, www .makuaku-hiking-aruba.com). The best times to trek are early morning or late afternoon.

Sportfishing

Mahi Mahi, Seaport Marina, Oranjestad (tel 297/587-0538, www.aruba-mahimahi.com) has a small, well-equipped fleet; or let one-stop water sports operator **Red Sail Sports,** Oranjestad (tel 297/586-1603 or U.S. 305/454-2538, www.redsailaruba.com) make the arrangements.

Water Sports

Palm Beach is Aruba's water sports capital, where concessions offer a host of motorized and nonmotorized water activities. Windsurfing and kitesurfing are available through **Aruba Active Vacations,** Hadikurai Beach (tel 297/586-0989, www.aruba-active-vacations.com), and **Vela Aruba,** Palm Beach (tel 297/586-9000 or U.S. 800/223-5443, www.velawindsurf.com).

BONAIRE

Diving & Snorkeling

Without doubt one of the world's most magnificent reef diving destinations, Bonaire is equipped to satisfy snorkelers and divers of all skill levels. Hotel/dive packages are available through such established operators as **Buddy Dive Resort** (tel 599/717-5080 or U.S./Can. 866/462-8339, www .buddydive.com), and **Captain Don's Dive Center** (tel 599/717-8290 or U.S./Can. 800/327-6709, www.habitatbonaire.com). Or contact **Bonaire Dive & Adventure** (tel 599/717-2227, www.bonairediveandadventure .com), who also arrange kayaking and mountain biking, as well as an

excellent five-day Island Explorer package based around activities and tours of your choice.

Horseback Riding

Explore the island's back roads on horseback with the **Riding Academy Club,** Kunuku Warahama Ranch (tel 599/560-7949, www .horsebackridingbonaire.com). The route passes the Pekelmeer flamingo habitat and ends with a horse-and-rider swim at Lac Bay.

Windsurfing & Kayaking

Breezy Bonaire is a great place to learn to windsurf; contact **Jibe City** (tel 599/717-5233, www .jibecity.com), which also rents kayaks. Coastal kayaking tours can be arranged through the **Mangrove Info Center,** Kaminda Lac (tel 599/780-5353, www .mangrovecenter.com), and **Bonaire Dive & Adventure** (see Diving & Snorkeling, above).

CURAÇAO

Adventure Tours & Hiking

See Cracking Adventures, p. 188.

Boating & Sportfishing

Half- or full-day snorkel and dive trips, sunset cruises, and deep-sea fishing charters can be booked with **Bounty Adventures** (tel 5999/767-9998, www.bounty adventures.com). The handsome 120-foot (37 m) 1931 sailing ship *Insulinde* (tel 5999/560-1340, www.insulinde.com) departs on afternoon snorkel and swim sails from the historic Willemstad waterfront, and makes occasional weekend trips to Bonaire and longer cruises to the San Blas islands off Panama.

Diving & Snorkeling

The best dive and snorkel sites lie off the protected leeward coast. Conveniently located right

on Seaquarium Beach, **Ocean Encounters,** Lions Dive & Beach Resort (tel 5999/461-8131, www .oceanencounters.com) is a one-stop dive shop offering dive trips to sites around the island, courses ranging from PADI certification to underwater photography, and a raft of water-sports activities.

SABA

Diving & Snorkeling

See Dive Saba Marine Park, p. 184.

Hiking

For information about trails, guided walks and hiking Mount Scenery, drop in at the **Saba Trail Shop,** Windwardside (tel 599/416-2630).

SINT EUSTATIUS

Diving, Snorkeling & Hiking

The island's dive operations are centered on Gallows Bay. General information and divers' marine tags can be obtained from the **Statia National Parks Office,** Bay Road, Lower Town (tel 599/318-2884, www.statiapark.org), which also supplies details of hiking trails. Statia's three dive shops are found on Bay Road: contact **Dive Statia** (tel 599/318-2435, www .divestatia.com); **Golden Rock Dive Center** (tel 599/318-2964, www.goldenrockdive.com); and **Scubaqua** (tel 599/318-5450, www.scubaqua.com).

SINT MAARTEN/ST.-MARTIN

Bicycling & Kayaking

The island is not renowned for its sporting facilities, but on the Dutch side, **TriSport,** Simpson Bay (tel 721/545-4384, www.tri sportsxm.com) arranges mountain bike and ocean kayak tours and bike and kayak rentals.

Boating & Sportfishing

Visiting the neighboring islands of St. Barts and Anguilla is a favorite pursuit either by ferry or on day-sail vessels. **Bluebeard Charters,** Simpson Bay (tel 721/587-5935, www.bluebeard charters.com) visits Shoal Bay, Anguilla, and Prickly Pear Island aboard its 60-foot (18 m) catamaran; or circumnavigate the island with **Eagle Tours,** Philipsburg (tel 721/542-3323, www.sailingsxm.com). Sportfishing trips can be arranged with **Rudy's Deep Sea Fishing,** Simpson Bay (tel 721/545-2177, www.rudys deepseafishing.com).

Diving & Snorkeling

Several dive shops in Simpson Bay, Sint Maarten, provide instruction and equipment rental, including **Dive Safaris,** La Palapa Marina (tel 721/545-3213, www.divest maarten.com). On the French side, **Baie Orientale** has a marine reserve as well as water sports Dive and snorkel trips can be arranged here through the PADI-registered **Neptune Dive Centre,** Plage d'Orient (tel 690/50 98 51, www.neptune-dive.com).

Horseback Riding

Nature trails, beach rides, and children's pony rides on Sint Maarten from **Seaside Nature Park,** Cay Bay (tel 721/544-5255, www .luckystables.com); on St.-Martin, contact **Bayside Riding Club** (rue de le Galion, tel 590/87 36 65).

◼ LEEWARD ISLANDS

ANGUILLA

Bicycling

Flat-as-a-pancake Anguilla provides some great off-road tracks in the undeveloped East End. A number of hotels and villas provide bikes free to guests; rentals are available from **Exotic Plus** (tel 264/497-8803) and **Premier**

Mountain Bike (tel 264/235-8931) in The Valley.

Diving & Snorkeling

Calm and exceptionally clear conditions, reefs, wreck dives, and abundant marine life tick all the boxes for divers and snorkelers at every level. Contact **Anguillian Divers,** Meads Bay (tel 264/497-4750, www.anguilliandiver.com), and **Shoal Bay Scuba,** Shoal Bay (tel 264/235-8438, www.shoal baysuba.com).

Golf

The 18-hole course at the **CuisinArt Golf Club** (tel 264/498-5602, www.cuisinartresort.com) combines magnificent views with eco-friendly credentials and course design from Greg Norman.

Horseback Riding

Riders of all abilities are welcome at **El Rancho del Blues,** Blowing Point Road (tel 264/497-6164), and **Seaside Stables,** Cove Bay (tel 264/497-3667, www.seaside-stables-anguilla.com).

Sportfishing

The go-to guy for sportfishing off Anguilla is Garfield Richardson of **Garfield's Sea Tours** (tel 264/497-2956, www.gotcha-garfields-sea-tours-anguilla.com).

ANTIGUA & BARBUDA

Boating
See A Passion for Sailing, p. 207.

Diving & Snorkeling

Antigua's best reef sites are off the sheltered south and west coasts. Dive operators around English Harbour include **Dockyard Divers** (tel 268/460-1178, www.dockyard-divers.com) and **Sea Wolf Diving School** (tel 268/783-3466, www.seawolf

divingschool.com). On the west coast, contact **Indigo Divers,** Jolly Harbour (tel 268/562-3483, www.indigo-divers.com). For snorkeling trips to Cades Reef, Green Island, and Bird Island, contact **Treasure Island Cruises** (tel 268/461-8675, www.treasure islandcruises.ag).

Eco- & Island Tours

A half-day eco-experience with **Paddles,** Seaton's Village (tel 268/463-1944, www .antiguapaddles.com) includes kayaking through mangrove-lined waterways, bird-watching, and snorkeling in the North Sound Marine Park. Or launch into a full day of eco discovery with **Adventure Antigua** (tel 268/727-3261, www.adventureantigua.com). For a round-island Jeep safari or a combination of safari and kayaking, contact **Tropical Adventures** (tel 268/480-1225, www.tropical ad.com), who can also whisk you off on a day trip to Barbuda.

Golf

Antigua's top golfing spot is the 18-hole championship course at the **Jolly Harbour Golf Club** (tel 268/562-6951 ext. 608, www .jollyharbourantigua.com). Northeast of St. John's, there's another 18-hole course at the **Cedar Valley Golf Club** (tel 268/462-0161, www.cedarvalleygolf.ag).

Horseback Riding

Take a gentle hack up into the hills above English Harbour and down to the beach for a swim with **Spring Hill Riding Club,** Falmouth (tel 268/773-3139, www .springhillridingclub.com).

Sportfishing

Head out to Antigua's Atlantic fishing grounds with **Nightwing Charters** (tel 268/464-4665, www.fishantigua.com) and

Overdraft (tel 268/464-4954, www.antiguafishing.com). Fly-fishing for bonefish is also possible.

Turtle-Watching

During the sea turtle nesting season (March–Nov.), female hawksbill, green, leatherback, and loggerhead turtles come ashore at night to lay their eggs on Antigua's beaches. Contact the **Environmental Awareness Group** (tel 268/462-6236) for turtle-watching.

MONTSERRAT

Diving, Snorkeling, & Kayaking

Montserrat's superb diving is one of the Caribbean's best-kept secrets. The **Green Monkey Dive Shop** (tel 664/491-2628, www .divemontserrat.com), and **Scuba Montserrat** (tel 664/491-7807, www.scubamontserrat.com) both offer dive and snorkel trips, customized packages and tuition, as well as extras like kayaking, beach picnics, and deep-sea fishing.

Hiking & Bird-Watching

The **Montserrat Tourist Board** (tel 664/491-2230, www .visitmontserrat.com), and the **National Trust** (tel 664/491-3086) can advise on routes and trail guide services, or contact nature guide **James "Scriber" Daley** (tel 664/492-2943).

ST. KITTS & NEVIS

Boating & Snorkeling

The **Reggae Beach Bar & Grille,** Cockleshell Bay (tel 869/762-5050, www.reggaebeachbar .com) is the home of the **St. Kitts Sailing School,** which rents out ocean kayaks and snorkel equipment, and can arrange private day-sail charters and deep-sea fishing. **Leeward Island Charters** (tel 869/465-7474,

www.stkittsleewardislandchar ters.com), and **Blue Water Safaris** (tel 869/466-4933, www .bluewatersafaris.com) can also arrange cruises and snorkel trips.

Diving

Though not a major-league dive destination, St. Kitts has plenty to entertain novice and more experienced divers. Local PADI-certified operators include **Dive St. Kitts** (tel 869/465-1189, www.divest kitts.com), and **Pro-Divers** (tel 869/466-3483, www .prodiversstkitts.com). On Nevis, Oualie Beach is home to high-tech, PADI five-star outfit **Scuba Safaris** (tel 869/469-9518, www .scubanevis.com).

Golf

Sandwiched between the Atlantic Ocean and the Caribbean Sea, the 18-hole course at the **Royal St. Kitts Golf Club** (tel 869/466-2700 or 866/STK-GOLF, www .royalstkittsgolfclub.com) provides challenges and views. On Nevis, there is an excellent 18-hole course at the **Four Seasons** (tel 869/469-1111, www.four seasons.com).

Hiking, Safari, & Heritage Tours

Lush rain forest hikes on St. Kitts and more strenuous treks up through areas of cloud forest to Mt. Liamuiga's crater rim can be arranged through knowledgeable guide outfit **Greg's Safaris** (tel 869/465-4121, www.gregsafaris .com). Greg's Off-the-Beaten-Track 4x4 safaris visit plantations and sugar mill ruins. Nevisian history is uncovered on eco-rambles with Lynnell Liburd of **Sunrise Tours** (tel 869/469-2758, www.nevisnaturetours .com), whose varied excursions include rain forest hikes, village walks, and bird-watching. Michael

Herbert of **Heb's Nature Tours** (tel 869/469-3512) leads treks to Nevis Peak.

Mountain Biking

For top-of-the-range bike rentals and tours from former windsurfing champ Winston Crooke, contact **Wheel World/Windsurfing Nevis** (tel 869/469-9682, www .bikenevis.com).

■ FRENCH ANTILLES

GUADELOUPE

Boating & Whale-Watching

Guadeloupe is a major sailing center and base for yacht charter operators **Sunsail** (tel 0590/90 92 02, www.sunsail.com). For day sails from St.-François (Grande-Terre) to Marie-Galante, Les Saintes, and La Désirade in the Guadeloupean archipelago, contact **Paradoxe Croisières,** Marina St.-François (tel 0590/88 41 73, www.im-caraibes.com), or **Tip Top Cruises** (tel 0590/84 66 36, www.tip-top-one.com). Whale-watching cruises can be arranged in winter (Dec.–March) through **Les Heures Saines,** Plage de Malendure, Basse-Terre (tel 0590/98 86 63, www.heures-saines.gp).

Diving

The Cousteau Underwater Reserve surrounding Pigeon Island is the island's best dive destination, but also its busiest. Experienced operators **Les Heures Saines** (tel 0590/98 86 63, www.heures-saines.gp) are based at Bouillante and offer a variety of dive options including night dives. **Plaisir Plongée Karu-kera** (tel 0590/98 82 43, www .plaisir-plongee-karukera.com) despatches several dive boats a day to Pigeon Island.

Hiking

See Parc National de la Guadeloupe, p. 239.

Mountain Biking

Adventure tour specialists **Vert Intense** (tel 0590/98 86 63, www.vert-intense.com) offers guided mountain bike excursions into the National Park (reservations essential), or contact the **Association Guadeloupeen de VTT** (tel 0590/82 82 67). Grande-Terre offers gentler cycling. Bike and scooter rentals are widely available; details of tour operators from local tourist offices.

Sportfishing

For day trips off the west coast of Basse-Terre, contact **Michel Pêche au Gros,** Bouillante (tel 0590/99 19 18, www.michelpecheaugros.com).

ST.-BARTHÉLEMY

Boating

Conveniently encircled by protected harbors, St. Barts is a sailing Mecca. The Gustavia tourist office on the marina can advise on day-sail options and schedules, or check out two dockside operations: **Jicky Marine Service** (tel 0590/27 70 34, www.st-barths.com/jicky-marine-service) and **Ocean Must** (tel 0590/27 62 25, www.oceanmust.com), which offer a range of water activities.

Tours

Taxi tours are available from the dock in Gustavia; or inquire at the tourist office for details of their own minibus tour itineraries.

MARTINIQUE

Boating

Boating excursions from Pointe du Bout north to St.-Pierre, or down the coast for a view of Diamond Rock, a buffet lunch, and a spot of snorkeling are a popular option with **Kata Mambo** (tel 0596/66 11 83). Or head further afield to St. Lucia with **Passion** (tel 0596/66 03 39, www.catamaranpassion.com).

Diving & Snorkeling

Martinique's best reef sites are off the south coast; there's also good snorkeling off the beach at Anses d'Arlet. Contact **Acqua Sud,** Le Diamant (tel 0596/76 51 01, www.acquasud.com), and **Crazy Frog,** Anses d'Arlet (tel 0596/48 32 17, http://crazy.frog.free.fr/us/welcome). In the north of the island, **Papa d'Lo** (tel 0696/92 07 39, www.papadlo.net) is based in St.-Pierre, where the eruption of Mont Pelée in 1902 created a unique wreck dive site.

Golf

The l'Impératrice Joséphine course at the **Golf Country Club de la Martinique,** Les Trois-Ilets (tel 0596/68 32 81) is a glorious Trent Jones Sr.–designed 18-hole, 71-par challenge on the bayfront.

Hiking

There are 31 marked trails totaling around 100 miles (161 km) of hiking paths around the island. Information is available from the offices of the **Parc Naturel Régional de la Martinique,** 9 blvd. Général de Gaulle, Fort-de-France (tel 0596/73 19 30), or contact the **Bureau de la Randonée et du Canyoning** (tel 0596/55 04 79, www.bureaurando-martinique.com).

Horseback Riding

Ride through a plantation estate with **Ranch de Trenelle,** Rivière Salée (tel 0596/48 07 20), or head inland and circle back to the beach with **Black Horse Ranch,** Les Trois-Ilets (tel 0596/68 37 80). Hacks with **Ranch des Caps,** Le Marin (tel 0596/74 70 65, www.ranchdescapes.com, closed Mon.) take you to the beach.

Mountain Biking

Cyclists looking to team up with a group for tours (full- and half-day options), can contact **VT Tilt,** Les Trois-Ilets (tel 0596/66 01 01).

Water Sports

Hotels and concessions provide water sports facilities on main tourist beaches. For windsurfing and kiteboarding, contact **Alizé Fun,** Ste.-Anne (tel 0596/74 71 58, www.alizefun.com); experienced windsurfers will find more challenging conditions on the Atlantic side, where the **Bliss École de Surf de Martinique,** Tartane (tel 0596/58 00 96, www.surf-martinique.com), offers rentals and tuition.

■ WINDWARD ISLANDS

DOMINICA

Diving & Snorkeling

A top ten entry on any list of the world's best dive destinations, Dominica has two main dive areas, both off the sheltered west coast. The must-do site is the southern Soufrière Scott's Head Marine Reserve, ranged around a submarine crater. Snorkelers can also get their fill of exotic marine life at the Reserve's Champagne Reef. Contact **Anchorage Whale Watch & Dive Centre** (tel 767/448-2638 or U.S. 888/790-5264, www.anchoragehotel.dm), and **Dive Dominica** (tel 767/448-2188, www.divedominica.com), both based at Castle Comfort. To the north, there are some fine dive sites in the Cabrits Marine Park and midway down the coast at Mero; contact **Cabrits Dive,** Portsmouth (tel 767/445-3010, www.cabritsdive.com).

Hiking & Tours

Intrepid hikers are spoiled for choice in Dominica's mountainous and densely forested interior. For longer treks a local guide is strongly recommended. Completed in 2011, the **Wai'tukubuli National Trail** is the jewel in the crown of Dominican hiking: A 115-mile (185 km) transisland hiking path, it is divided into 14 sections that can be hiked in part or in total (alow at least a week). Guides can be arranged in Roseau through the **Forestry Department,** Botanical Gardens (tel 767/266-3817), and the tourist office, **Discover Dominica,** Valley Road (tel 767/448-2045, www .discoverdominica.com).

Part of the **Anchorage Whale Watch & Dive Centre** (see Diving p. 397), **Dominica Tours** (www .experience-dominica.com) offers a raft of island and heritage tours, hiking, birding, and whale-watching excursions. Or contact **Ken's Hinterland Adventure Tours** (tel 767/448-1660 or U.S. 866/880-0508, www.khatts tours.com).

Whale-Watching

See Whale-Watching, p. 268.

GRENADA & CARRIACOU

Boating

Grenada is a hub for yacht charters and boat trips. Round-island excursions, snorkeling, and sunset cruises are available from **Carib Cats** (tel 473/444-3222), **First Impressions** (tel 473/440-3678, www.catamaranchartering.com), and **Shadowfax** (tel 473/443-2535, www.bananaboattours grenada.com). One of the region's leading yacht charter brokers, **Horizon Yacht Charters** (tel 473/439-1000 or U.S. 866/463-7245, www.horizonyachtcharters .com), supplies crewed and

bareboat charters, and teaches ASA sailing courses.

Diving & Snorkeling

Grenada's 50 dive sites line the protected Caribbean coast, with the best underwater scenery found in the southwest Marine Protected Area. Carriacou, which translates as "land of reefs," also has some superb diving and snorkeling. In Grenada, contact **Aquanauts** (tel 473/444-1126, www.aquanautsgrenada.com), **Dive Grenada** (tel 473/444-1092, www.divegrenada.com), and **Eco Dive** (tel 473/444-7777, www.ecodiveandtrek.com). On Carriacou, contact **Arawak Divers** (tel 473/443-6906, www .arawak.de), **Carriacou Silver Diving** (tel 473/443-7882, www .scubamax.com), and **Lumba Dive** (tel 473/443-8566, www .lumbadive.com).

Hiking

See Hiking in Grand Étang National Park, p. 294.

Sportfishing

Grenada's sportfishing fraternity heads out into the Atlantic in search of marlin and sailfish, as well as dorado, tuna, and wahoo. Contact **First Impressions** (tel 473/440-3678, www.catamaran chartering.com), and **True Blue Sportfishing** (tel 473/444-2048, www.yesaye.com).

Tours

Sightseeing tours, rain forest hikes, day sails, and fishing trips can all be arranged through **Henry's Safari Tours** (tel 473/444-5313, www.spiceisle.com/safari), or there's Jeep tours, mountain biking, and river tubing with aptly named **Adventure Tours** (tel 473/444-5337, www .adventuregrenada.com).

Whale-Watching

Day-sail operators **First Impressions** (tel 473/440-3678, www .catamaranchartering.com) also offer dolphin- and whale-watching excursions throughout the year. Winter (Dec.–April) is high season for whale sightings.

ST. LUCIA

Boating

Picture-perfect St. Lucia is a glorious backdrop for a day sail, and one of the most picturesque ways to travel from Castries down the coast to Soufrière is aboard the tall ship *Brig Unicorn* (tel 758/452-9842). **Sea Spray Cruises** (tel 758/452-8644 or U.S. 321/220-9423, www .seaspraycruises.com) run catamaran trips with sightseeing shore excursions included, and sunset cruises are popular. Sea Spray also operates a replica pirate ship, *Liana's Ransom,* for fun-packed family days out. Based in Soufrière, **Mystic Man Tours** (tel 758/459-7783, www .mysticmantours.com) offers a full range of day and evening sails, whale-watching, sportfishing, and snorkeling excursions.

Plenty of crewed and bareboat charter operations work out of the busy Rodney Bay and Marigot Bay marinas. One of the largest and most experienced is **The Moorings,** Marigot Bay (tel 758/451-4357 or U.S. 888/952-8420, www.moor ings.com).

Diving & Snorkeling

St. Lucia's underwater scenery is every bit as impressive as its terrestrial landscape. Snorkelers can access the reefs straight off the beach at Anse Chastanet, where **Scuba St. Lucia** (tel 758/459-7755 or 888/GOLUCIA, www .scubastlucia.com) offers tuition, beach and boat dives, and snorkel excursions in Soufrière Marine

Park. For dive adventures off the northwest coast and snorkeling around Pigeon Island, **Scuba Steve's Diving**, Rodney Bay Marina (tel 758/452-9086, www .scubastevesdiving.com), promises a range of marine life.

Golf

So far, St. Lucia has just one 18-hole golf course, the **St. Lucia Golf & Country Club**, Rodney Bay (tel 758/450-8523, www .stluciagolf.com), set in the private Cap Estate on the northern tip of the island. There's also an attractive 9-hole course at the **Sandals La Toc Golf Resort & Spa,** Castries (tel 758/452-3081, www.sandals.com).

Hiking

See Hiking the Slopes, p. 276.

Horseback Riding

Mosey through rolling farmland to Pigeon Island National Park on a trail ride with **Trim's National Riding Academy**, Gros Islet (tel 758/450-8273, www.trims ridingstlucia.com).

Sportfishing

Full- and half-day charters on well-equipped craft depart from the Vigie Marina in Castries. Contact **Captain Mike's** (tel 758/452-7044, www.captmikes .com), a third-generation family operation; and **Hackshaw's Boat Charters** (tel 758/453-0553, www.hackshaws.com).

ST. VINCENT & THE GRENADINES

Boating

The must-do day sail on St. Vincent is a trip around the northern tip of the island to the Falls of Baleine. Boat trips to the falls, and down the Grenadines to Tobago Cays and Mustique, are offered by Bequia-based **Caribbean Schooner Cruises** (tel 784/495-0886, www.friendshiprose.com) and **Fantasea Tours** (tel 784/457-4477, www.fantaseatours.com). **Sea Breeze Nature Tours** (tel 784/458-4969, www.seabreeze naturetours.com) pioneered whale- and dolphin-watching off the island.

The Grenadine islands are a magnet for sailors and there are numerous operations offering crewed and bareboat charters. Family-run **Barefoot Yacht Charters** (tel 784/456-9526, www.barefootyachts.com) also operates a sailing school; while **Sunsail** (tel 784/458-4308, www.sunsail.com) offers flotilla holidays for less confident (or more gregarious) yachtsmen as well as individual charters. Charter brokers **The Moorings** (tel 784/482-0653 or U.S. 888/952-8420, www.moor ings.com) has one of its five Caribbean bases on Canouan, allowing for one-way charters to St. Lucia, St.-Martin, or even the BVI.

Diving & Snorkeling

For an expert introduction to local marine life, you can't beat an outing with dive master Bill Tewes of **Dive St. Vincent** (tel 784/457-4928, www.divest vincent.com). **Indigo Dive** (tel 784/493-9494, www.indigodive .com) also offers lessons, cruises, and snorkel tours. Some of the best snorkeling around the island is found at Chateaubelair and Buccament Bay, or take a day sail (see Boating above) to reach less accessible sites.

For diving and snorkeling in Bequia, contact **Dive Bequia** (tel 784/458-3504, www.bequiadive .com). Farther down the islands **Canouan Dive Center,** Canouan (tel 784/528-8030 or U.S. 917/796-1100, www.canouandivecenter .com), and **Grenadines Dive,** Union Island (tel 784/458-8138, www .grenadinesdive.com), also run dive and snorkel trips to Tobago Cays.

Golf

The pint-size Grenadine Island of Canouan is a somewhat unlikely location for the glorious **Grenadines Estate Golf Club** (tel 784/458-8000, www.canouan .com), a challenging, 18-hole Jim Fazio creation carved into the undulating shoreline.

Hiking & Tours

See Local Knowledge, p. 283.

■ BARBADOS

Boating

A number of day-sail vessels ply the west coast offering excursions with lunch, a snorkel stop, and a sea turtle encounter. For daily departures from Bridgetown, contact **Cool Runnings** (tel 246/436-0911, www.cool run ningsbarbados.com), **El Tigre** (tel 246/417-7245, www .eltigrecruises.com), and **Tiami Catamarans** (tel 246/430-0900, www.tallshipscruises.com). Call ahead to make reservations, and check schedules for sunset cruises.

Diving & Snorkeling

Along the west coast from Maycocks Bay down through the Platinum Coast to Carlisle Bay, south of Bridgetown, the sea is calm and visibility is excellent. Well-established dive operations offering single dives, packages, and PADI-certification courses include **Barbados Blue**, Carlisle Bay, St. Michael (tel 246/434-5764, www.divebarbadosblue .com); **High Tide Watersports,** Holetown, St. James (tel 246/432-0931 or 800/970-0016, www.divehightide.com); and **The Dive Shop Ltd.,** Carlisle Bay, St. Michael (tel 246/426-9947 or

U.S. 888/898-3483, www
.divebds.com).

Golf

Barbados' most prestigious
pay-as-you-play course is
Country Club course at **Sandy
Lane,** Paynes Bay, St. James (tel
246/444-2500, www.sandylane
.com/golf). Sandy Lane's intimate
and attractive par-36 **Old Nine**
course is also open to visitors.
Two exceptional guest-only
courses in St. James are the
Apes Hill Club (tel 246/432-
4500, www.apeshillclub.com),
and the **Royal Westmoreland**
(tel 246/422-4653, www.royal
westmoreland.com). On the
south coast, the **Barbados Golf
Club,** Durants, Christ Church (tel
246/428-8463, www.barbados
golfclub.com) welcomes visitors.
The popular and very sociable
Rockley Golf Club, Rockley,
Christ Church (tel 246/435-7873,
www.rockleygolfclub.com) has a
surprisingly challenging nine-hole
parkland course.

Sportfishing

Half- and full-day boat charters
from Bridgetown's Careenage
provide a choice of coastal and
deep-sea fishing expeditions. The
high season for billfish is December through April. Contact **Blue
Marlin Barbados,** Durants,
Christ Church (tel 246/234-1688,
www.bluemarlinbarbados
.com), **Billfisher II,** Bridgetown
(tel 246/431-0741), and **Cannon Charters,** Bridgetown (tel
246/424-6107, www.fishing
barbados.com).

Tours

Adventureland 4x4 Tours (tel
246/418-3687, www.adventure
landbarbados.com), and **Island
Safari** (tel 246/429-5337, www
.islandsafari.bb) take in the sights
from clifftop lookouts to beaches.

They also offer powerboat excursions with snorkeling and turtle
encounters.

Walks

The **Barbados National Trust**
(tel 246/426-2421, www.trust
.funbarbados.com) organizes the
free Hike Barbados Sunday fun
walk program. The guided walks
depart at 6 a.m. and 3:30 p.m.
(call ahead for details).

Water Sports

Water sports facilities are widely
available from hotels and beach
concessions on the Caribbean
coast. Along the south coast,
breezy Silver Sands Beach is the
hub of the local windsurfing and
kiteboarding scene. Experienced
surfers come for the big Atlantic
swells that thunder onto the
east coast December through
April. **Barbados Surf Trips** (tel
246/262-1099, www.surf
barbados.com) offers tuition,
rentals, tips, and customized surfing packages.

■ TRINIDAD & TOBAGO

Diving & Snorkeling

Trinidad's proximity to the Orinoco Delta hampers submarine
visibility. Most divers head for
Tobago and its pristine reefs,
where visibility is excellent.
Snorkelers can just step off
the beach along the Caribbean
coast. For more experienced
divers, the excitement lies farther
north around Charlotteville and
Speyside, where the Japanese
Gardens and Aquarium off
Batteaux Bay are world-class
dives. Dive operators in Speyside
include **AquaMarine Dive** (tel
868/660-5445, www.aquamarine
dive.com) and **Tobago Dive
Experience** (tel 868/660-5445,
www.tobagodiveexperience.com).

For diving off the south coast,
contact **R & Sea Divers,** Crown
Point (tel 868/639-8120, www
.rseadivers.com).

Golf

Set in the smart residential suburbs of Port-of-Spain, Trinidad's
finest golfing is found at the **St.
Andrew's Golf Club,** Maraval
(tel 868/629-0066). On Tobago,
the **Mt. Irvine Golf Club**
(tel 868/639-8871, www
.mtirvine.com) has a lovely old
hillside course laid out around
the estate with views of the
Caribbean, and the more recent
PGA-designed **Tobago Plantations Golf & Country Club** (tel
868/631-0875) rolls down to the
mangrove-lined shore.

Guided Tours

Wildlife photographer Stephen
Broadbridge of **Caribbean Discovery Tours** (tel 868/624-7281,
www.caribbeandiscoverytours
.com) offers a wide range of
eco- and island discovery tours; or
contact **Kalloo's** (tel 868/622-
9073, www.kalloos.com) for taxi
tours, and trips to Caroni, Asa
Wright, and Tobago.
    On Tobago, **Peter Cox** (tel
868/751-5822, www.tobago
naturetours.com) also offers
sightseeing tours and visits to Scarborough market, or contact **Yes
Tourism** (tel 868/631-0286, www
.yes-tourism.com) for island tours
and side trips to Trinidad.

Turtle-Watching

For turtle-watching in Trinidad,
see Turtle Watch, p. 324. On
Tobago, contact **Peter Cox
Nature Tours** (tel 868/751-5822,
www.tobagonaturetours.com).

INDEX

ILLUSTRATIONS CREDITS

All photographs by Matt Propert, except:

Cover, Michael Grimm/Getty Images; 8, RoxyFer/Shutterstock; 20-21, Geography & Map Division, Library of Congress; 25, Pack-Shot/Shutterstock; 58, Bob Thomas/ iStockphoto.com; 59, Diana Halstead/Shutterstock.com; 69, Gina Hanf/iStockphoto. com; 76, Mike Sutton Brown/National Geographic My Shot; 78, Ocean Image Photography/Shutterstock; 79, Michael Stubblefield/iStockphoto.com; 83, Jeremy Edwards/iStockphoto.com; 86, Michael Melford/National Geographic Stock; 88, Steve Geer/iStockphoto.com; 90, Els van der Gun/iStockphoto.com; 93, Chris A. Crumley/Alamy; 95, Luan Tran/iStockphoto.com; 96, cbarnesphotography/ iStockphoto.com; 97-118 (all), Gilles Mingasson/Reportage by Getty Images; 120, Raul Touzon/National Geographic Stock; 121, Gilles Mingasson/Reportage by Getty Images; 123, Gilles Mingasson/Reportage by Getty Images; 136, Ramunas Bruzas/ National Geographic My Shot; 138, Victor Nieves/iStockphoto.com; 145, JHeini-mann/Alamy; 163, Paul Strawn/iStockphoto.com; 170, Diego Pagani/Cutcaster. com; 173, Fotografie K.J. Schraa/iStockphoto.com; 176, Alysta/Shutterstock; 178, Michael Mattner/iStockphoto.com; 180, Frans Lemmens/Alamy; 182, RJ Lerich/ Shutterstock; 186, Caramaria/Dreamstime.com; 189, Adrian Beesley/iStockphoto. com; 191, fotokik_dot_com/Shutterstock; 193, SlidePix/iStockphoto.com; 195, CarolineTolsma/Shutterstock; 208, Hemis/Alamy; 210, Temmuz Can Arsiray/iStock-photo.com; 212, Steve Geer/iStockphoto.com; 214, Steve Geer/iStockphoto.com; 224, Vincent J. Musi/ National Geographic Stock; 226, Michael Utech/iStockphoto. com; 238, Steve Geer/iStockphoto.com; 242, Hemis/Alamy; 244, Fred Friberg/ Getty Images; 250, After Francois-Hippolyte Lalaisse/Bridgeman Art Gallery/Getty Images; 295, Sigrid Estrada/Getty Images; 296, htomas/iStockphoto.com; 304, Steve Raymer/ National Geographic Stock; 308, Melissa Bouyounan/Shutterstock; 312, Danita Delimont/Getty Images; 318, MAT/Shutterstock.com.